connect to learning, connect to their futures.

McGraw Hill connect™ plus+ | BUSINESS STATISTICS

Integration of Excel Data Files

Learning to use Excel successfully is a staple in the business statistics environment. In Connect, Excel data file links are available in many of the problems. With a single click of the mouse, students can launch the problem's data file which opens directly in Excel. This gives students the freedom to focus on working the problem, rather than searching for data files or keying data manually into Excel. After they compute the solution in Excel, they simply return to Connect for feedback on their answer.

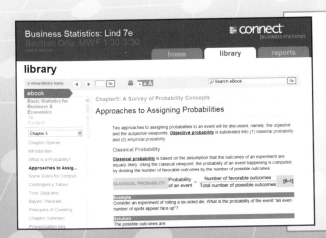

Connect Plus Business Statistics

Read the full textbook online with Connect Plus Business Statistics! Like Connect Business Statistics, Connect Plus Business Statistics provides students with all the benefits of Connect, with the added bonus of 24/7 online access to an eBook—an identical, online edition of the printed text to aid them in successfully completing their work, wherever and whenever they choose.

Try it, Use it, Love it

Instructors and students alike love Connect. Connect Business Statistics is a powerful and dynamic system that gives you and your students the freedom to work almost anywhere. Create assignments, give tests, check grades, and focus on teaching. Your students will be able to spend their time learning with feedback on their work all along the way. They will thank you for choosing Connect!

Contact your local McGraw-Hill/Irwin representative to learn more about Connect Business Statistics, or visit www.mcgrawhillconnect.com for more information.

ALEKS®

Basic Statistics for
Business & Economics

Seventh Edition

Douglas A. Lind
Coastal Carolina University and The University of Toledo

William G. Marchal
The University of Toledo

Samuel A. Wathen
Coastal Carolina University

McGraw-Hill
Irwin

McGraw-Hill Irwin

BASIC STATISTICS FOR BUSINESS & ECONOMICS
Published by McGraw-Hill/Irwin, a business unit of The McGraw-Hill Companies, Inc., 1221 Avenue of the Americas, New York, NY, 10020. Copyright © 2011, 2008, 2006, 2003, 2000, 1997, 1994 by The McGraw-Hill Companies, Inc. All rights reserved. No part of this publication may be reproduced or distributed in any form or by any means, or stored in a database or retrieval system, without the prior written consent of The McGraw-Hill Companies, Inc., including, but not limited to, in any network or other electronic storage or transmission, or broadcast for distance learning.

Some ancillaries, including electronic and print components, may not be available to customers outside the United States.

This book is printed on acid-free paper.

2 3 4 5 6 7 8 9 0 DOW/DOW 1 0 9 8 7 6 5 4 3 2 1 0

ISBN   978-0-07-340178-2 (student edition)
MHID   0-07-340178-1 (student edition)
ISBN   978-0-07-732690-6 (instructor's edition)
MHID   0-07-732690-3 (instructor's edition)

Vice president and editor-in-chief: *Brent Gordon*
Editorial director: *Stewart Mattson*
Publisher: *Tim Vertovec*
Executive editor: *Steve Schuetz*
Director of development: *Ann Torbert*
Senior development editor: *Wanda J. Zeman*
Vice president and director of marketing: *Robin J. Zwettler*
Marketing director: *Sankha Basu*
Vice president of editing, design and production: *Sesha Bolisetty*
Senior project manager: *Bruce Gin*
Senior production supervisor: *Debra R. Sylvester*
Lead designer: *Matthew Baldwin*
Senior photo research coordinator: *Lori Kramer*
Lead media project manager: *Brian Nacik*
Cover design: *Evan Modesto*
Cover Image: © *Getty Images*
Typeface: 9.5/11 *Helvetica Neue 55*
Compositor: *Aptara®, Inc.*
Printer: *R. R. Donnelley*

Library of Congress Cataloging-in-Publication Data

Lind, Douglas A.
    Basic statistics for business & economics / Douglas A. Lind, William G. Marchal, Samuel A. Wathen. — 7th ed.
        p. cm. — (The McGraw-Hill/Irwin series Operations and decision sciences)
    Includes index.
    ISBN-13: 978-0-07-340178-2 (student edition : alk. paper)
    ISBN-10: 0-07-340178-1 (student edition : alk. paper)
    ISBN-13: 978-0-07-732690-6 (instructor's edition : alk. paper)
    ISBN-10: 0-07-732690-3 (instructor's edition : alk. paper)
    1. Social sciences—Statistical methods. 2. Economics—Statistical methods. 3. Industrial management—Statistical methods. I. Marchal, William G. II. Wathen, Samuel Adam. III. Title. IV. Title: Basic statistics for business and economics.
HA29.L75 2011
519.5—dc22   2009044030

www.mhhe.com

The McGraw-Hill/Irwin Series
Operations and Decision Sciences

Business Statistics

Aczel and Sounderpandian
Complete Business Statistics
Seventh Edition

ALEKS Corporation
ALEKS for Business Statistics
First Edition

Alwan
Statistical Process Analysis
First Edition

Bowerman, O'Connell, and Murphree
Business Statistics in Practice
Sixth Edition

Bowerman, O'Connell,
Orris, and Murphree
Essentials of Business Statistics
Third Edition

Bryant and Smith
**Practical Data Analysis: Case
Studies in Business Statistics,
Volumes I, II, and III***

Cooper and Schindler
Business Research Methods
Tenth Edition

Doane, Mathieson, and Tracy
Visual Statistics
Second Edition, 2.0

Doane and Seward
**Applied Statistics in Business
and Economics**
Third Edition

Doane and Seward
**Essential Statistics in Business
and Economics**
Second Edition

Gitlow, Oppenheim, Oppenheim,
and Levine
Quality Management
Third Edition

Kutner, Nachtsheim, Neter and Li
Applied Linear Statistical Models
Fifth Edition

Kutner, Nachtsheim, and Neter
Applied Linear Regression Models
Fourth Edition

Lind, Marchal, and Wathen
**Basic Statistics for Business and
Economics**
Seventh Edition

Lind, Marchal, and Wathen
**Statistical Techniques in Business
and Economics**
Fourteenth Edition

Olson and Shi
**Introduction to Business
Data Mining**
First Edition

Orris
**Basic Statistics Using Excel
and MegaStat**
First Edition

Wilson, Keating, and John Galt
Solutions, Inc.
Business Forecasting
Sixth Edition

Zagorsky
Business Information
First Edition

Quantitative Methods and Management Science

Hillier and Hillier
**Introduction to Management
Science**
Third Edition

Stevenson and Ozgur
**Introduction to Management
Science with Spreadsheets**
First Edition

*Available only through McGraw-Hill's PRIMIS Online Assets Library.

iii

Over the years, we have received many compliments on this text and have been told it's a favorite among students. We accept that as the highest compliment and continue to work very hard to maintain that status.

The objective of *Basic Statistics for Business & Economics* is to provide students majoring in management, marketing, finance, accounting, economics, and other fields of business administration with an introductory survey of the many applications of descriptive and inferential statistics. While we focus on business applications, we also use many exercises and examples that are student oriented and do not require previous courses.

In this text we show beginning students every step needed to be successful in a basic statistics course. This step-by-step approach enhances performance, accelerates preparedness, and significantly improves motivation. Understanding the concepts, seeing and doing plenty of examples and exercises, and comprehending the application of statistical methods in business and economics are the focus of this book.

The first edition of *Statistical Techniques in Business & Economics* was published in 1967. The first edition of *Basic Statistics for Business & Economics* was published in 1994. At that time locating relevant business data was difficult. That has changed! Today locating data is not a problem. The number of items you purchase at the grocery store is automatically recorded at the checkout counter. Phone companies track the time of our calls, the length of calls, and the number of the person called. Credit card companies maintain information on the number, time and date, and amount of our purchases. Medical devices automatically monitor our heart rate, blood pressure, and temperature. A large amount of business information is recorded and reported almost instantly. CNN, *USA Today,* and MSNBC, for example, all have Web sites where you can track stock prices with a delay of less than 20 minutes.

Today, skills are needed to deal with a large volume of numerical information. First, we need to be critical consumers of information presented by others. Second, we need to be able to reduce large amounts of information into a concise and meaningful form to enable us to make effective interpretations, judgments, and decisions.

All students have calculators and most have either personal computers or access to personal computers in a campus lab. Statistical software, such as Microsoft Excel and MINITAB, is available on these computers. The commands necessary to achieve the software results are available in a special section at the end of each chapter. We use screen captures within the chapters, so the student becomes familiar with the nature of the software output. Because of the availability of computers and software it is no longer necessary to dwell on calculations. We have replaced many of the calculation examples with interpretative ones, to assist the student in understanding and interpreting the statistical results. In addition we now place more emphasis on the conceptual nature of the statistical topics. While making these changes, we still continue to present, as best we can, the key concepts, along with supporting examples.

What's New in This Seventh Edition?

We have made several changes to this edition that we think you and your students will find useful.

- New exercises and examples using Excel 2007 screenshots and the latest version of MINITAB. We have also increased the size and clarity of these screenshots.

- There are also new Excel 2007 software commands and updated MINITAB commands at the ends of chapters.
- At the end of each chapter, we have added a Practice Test. We think this will give the student an idea of what might appear on a test and how the test might be structured. Hopefully, this will reduce test anxiety. The test includes a section on vocabulary and a section of problems.
- We have carefully reviewed the Exercises within the chapters and those at the ends of the chapters and revised or replaced those that were outdated. You can still find and assign your favorites that have worked well, or you can introduce fresh examples.
- There is new content on nominal-level data and its properties in Chapter 1.
- There are many new photos throughout with updated exercises in the chapter openers.
- Much of the relevant data and statistics within the text and exercises have been updated.

Dedication

To Jane, my wife and best friend, and our sons, their wives, and our grandchildren: Mike and Sue (Steve and Courtney), Steve and Kathryn (Kennedy and Jake), and Mark and Sarah (Jared, Drew, and Nate).

Douglas A. Lind

To Thalika and the Oum family. Welcome to our family.

William G. Marchal

To my wonderful family: Isaac, Hannah, and Barb.

Samuel A. Wathen

Chapter Learning Objectives

Each chapter begins with learning objectives designed to provide focus for the chapter and motivate student learning. These objectives indicate what the student should be able to do after completing the chapter.

Chapter Opening Exercise

A representative exercise opens the chapter and shows how the chapter content can be applied to a real-world situation.

Describing Data:

Numerical Measures

Learning Objectives
When you have completed this chapter you will be able to:

LO1 Calculate the arithmetic mean, weighted mean, median, and mode.

LO2 Explain the characteristics, uses, advantages, and disadvantages of each measure of location.

LO3 Identify the position of the mean, median, and mode for both symmetric and skewed distributions.

LO4 Compute and interpret the range, mean deviation, variance, and standard deviation.

LO5 Understand the characteristics, uses, advantages, and disadvantages of each measure of dispersion.

LO6 Understand Chebyshev's theorem and the Empirical Rule as they relate to a set of observations.

U.S. housing prices reached their peak in July of 2006. Based on the data given in the table, showing the ratio of the prices reported in a recent month to the July 2006 figure, find the mean, median, and mode of these statistics. (Exercise 65, LO1)

Introduction to the Topic

Each chapter starts with a review of the important concepts of the previous chapter and provides a link to the material in the current chapter. This step-by-step approach increases comprehension by providing continuity across the concepts.

Introduction

The highly competitive automotive retailing business has changed significantly over the past decade, due in part to consolidation by large, publicly owned dealership groups. Traditionally, a local family owned and operated the community dealership, which might have included one or two manufacturers, like Buick and GMC Trucks or Chrysler and the popular Jeep line. Recently, however, skillfully managed and well-financed companies have been acquiring local dealerships across large regions of the country. As these groups acquire the local dealerships, they often bring standard selling practices, common software and hardware technology platforms, and management reporting techniques. The goal is to provide an improved buying experience for the consumer, while increasing the profitability of the larger dealership organization. In many cases, in addi-

Example/Solution

After important concepts are introduced, a solved example is given to provide a how-to illustration for students and to show a relevant business or economics-based application that helps answer the question, "What will I use this for?" All examples provide a realistic scenario or application and make the math size and scale reasonable for introductory students.

Example

The number of cappuccinos sold at the Starbucks location in the Orange County Airport between 4 and 7 p.m. for a sample of 5 days last year were 20, 40, 50, 60, and 80. In the LAX airport in Los Angeles, the number of cappuccinos sold at a Starbucks location between 4 and 7 p.m. for a sample of 5 days last year were 20, 49, 50, 51, and 80. Determine the mean, median, range, and mean deviation for each location. Compare the differences.

Solution

For the Orange County location the mean, median, and range are:

Mean	50 cappuccinos per day
Median	50 cappuccinos per day
Range	60 cappuccinos per day

The mean deviation is the mean of the absolute

Self-Reviews

Self-Reviews are interspersed throughout each chapter and closely patterned after the preceding Examples. They help students monitor their progress and provide immediate reinforcement for that particular technique.

Self-Review 3–2 Springers sold 95 Antonelli men's suits for the regular price of $400. For the spring sale the suits were reduced to $200 and 126 were sold. At the final clearance, the price was reduced to $100 and the remaining 79 suits were sold.
(a) What was the weighted mean price of an Antonelli suit?
(b) Springers paid $200 a suit for the 300 suits. Comment on the store's profit per suit if a salesperson receives a $25 commission for each one sold.

Engage Students and Promote Learning?

Statistics in Action

Statistics in Action articles are scattered throughout the text, usually about two per chapter. They provide unique and interesting applications and historical insights in the field of statistics.

Margin Notes

There are more than 300 concise notes in the margin. Each is aimed at reemphasizing the key concepts presented immediately adjacent to it.

Definitions

Definitions of new terms or terms unique to the study of statistics are set apart from the text and highlighted for easy reference and review.

Variance and Standard Deviation

Variance and standard deviation are based on squared deviations from the mean.

The **variance** and **standard deviation** are also based on the deviations from the mean. However, instead of using the absolute value of the deviations, the variance and the standard deviation square the deviations.

VARIANCE The arithmetic mean of the squared deviations from the mean.

The variance is nonnegative and is zero only if all observations are the same.

Formulas

Formulas that are used for the first time are boxed and numbered for reference. In addition, a formula card is bound into the back of the text, which lists these key formulas.

POPULATION VARIANCE
$$\sigma^2 = \frac{\Sigma(X - \mu)^2}{N}$$
[3–6]

Exercises

Exercises are included after sections within the chapter and at the end of the chapter. Section exercises cover the material studied in the section.

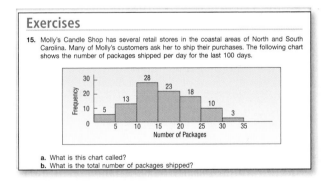

Exercises

15. Molly's Candle Shop has several retail stores in the coastal areas of North and South Carolina. Many of Molly's customers ask her to ship their purchases. The following chart shows the number of packages shipped per day for the last 100 days.

a. What is this chart called?
b. What is the total number of packages shipped?

Computer Output

The text includes many software examples, using Excel, MegaStat®, and MINITAB. Screen captures are highlighted with either a MINITAB or Excel logo in the margin.

BY CHAPTER

Chapter Summary

Each chapter contains a brief summary of the chapter material, including the vocabulary and the critical formulas.

> **Chapter Summary**
> I. A frequency table is a grouping of qualitative data into mutually exclusive classes showing the number of observations in each class.
> II. A relative frequency table shows the fraction of the number of frequencies in each class.
> III. A bar chart is a graphic representation of a frequency table.
> IV. A pie chart shows the proportion each distinct class represents of the total number of frequencies.
> V. A frequency distribution is a grouping of data into mutually exclusive classes showing the

Pronunciation Key

This tool lists the mathematical symbol, its meaning, and how to pronounce it. We believe this will help the student retain the meaning of the symbol and generally enhance course communications.

> **Pronunciation Key**
>
> | SYMBOL | MEANING | PRONUNCIATION |
> |--------|---------|---------------|
> | μ | Population mean | mu |
> | Σ | Operation of adding | sigma |
> | ΣX | Adding a group of values | sigma X |
> | $\bar{X}$ | Sample mean | X bar |

Chapter Exercises

Generally, the end of chapter exercises are the most challenging and integrate the chapter concepts. The answers and worked-out solutions for all odd-numbered exercises appear at the end of the text. For exercises with more than 20 observations, the data can be found on the Student CD and on the text's Web site. These files are in Excel and MINITAB formats.

> **Chapter Exercises**
> 23. Describe the similarities and differences of qualitative and quantitative variables. Be sure to include:
>   a. What level of measurement is required for each variable type?
>   b. Can both types be used to describe both samples and populations?

Data Set Exercises

The last several exercises at the end of each chapter are based on four large data sets. These data sets are printed in Appendix A in the text and are also on the text's Web site. These data sets present the students with real-world and more complex applications.

> **Data Set Exercises**
> 82. Refer to the Real Estate data, which reports information on homes sold in the Phoenix, Arizona, area during the last year.
>   a. Sort the data into a table that shows the number of homes that have a pool versus the number that don't have a pool in each of the five townships. If a home is selected at random, compute the following probabilities.
>   1. The home is in Township 1 or has a pool.
>   2. Given that it is in Township 3, that it has a pool.
>   3. Has a pool and is in Township 3.
>   b. Sort the data into a table that shows the number of homes that have a garage attached versus those that don't in each of the five townships. If a home is selected at random, compute the following probabilities:
>   1. The home has a garage attached.
>   2. Given that it is in Township 5, that it does not have a garage attached.
>   3. The home has a garage attached and is in Township 3.
>   4. Does not have a garage attached or is in Township 2.
> 83. Refer to the Baseball 2008 data, which reports information on the 30 Major League Baseball teams for the 2008 season. Set up a variable that divides the teams into two groups, those that had a winning season and those that did not. That is, create a variable to count the teams that won 81 games or more, and those that won 80 or less. Next create

Software Commands

Software examples using Excel, MegaStat®, and MINITAB are included throughout the text. But, the explanations of the computer input commands for each program are placed at the end of the chapter. This allows students to focus on the statistical techniques rather than on how to input data.

> **Software Commands**
> 1. The Excel commands to select a simple random sample on page 225 are:
>   a. Select the **Data** tab on the top of the menu. Then on the far right select **Data Analysis**, then **Sampling** and **OK**.
>   b. For **Input Range** insert *B1:B31*. Since the column is named, click the **Labels** box. Select **Random**, and enter the sample size for the **Number of Samples**, in this case 5. Click on **Output Range** and indicate the place in the spreadsheet you want the sample information. Note that your sample results will differ from those in the text. Also recall that Excel samples with replacement, so it is possible for a population value to appear more than once in the sample.

Reinforce Student Learning?

Answers to Self-Review

The worked-out solutions to the Self-Reviews are provided at the end of each chapter.

Practice Test

The Practice Test which appears at the end of each chapter is intended to give students an idea of content that might appear on a test and how the test might be structured. The Practice Test includes both objective questions and problems covering the material studied in the chapter.

Practice Test

Part I Objective

1. A listing of the possible outcomes of an experiment and the probability associated with each outcome is called a _____.
2. The essential difference between a discrete random variable and a discrete probability distribution is a discrete probability distribution includes the _____
3. In a discr
   to ____
4. The expe
5. How mar
6. Under wh
   mial expe
7. In a Poiss
8. The Poiss
   tion wher
9. Suppose
   we select
   fer undes
10. The mea
    1.70. Wh
    month?

Part II Problems

1. The IRS reports that 15 percent of the tax returns where the adjusted gross income is more than $1,000,000 will be subject to computer audit. For a particular year a CPA completed 16 returns where the adjusted gross income was more than $1,000,000.
   a. Which probability model does this situation follow?
   b. What is the probability exactly one of these returns is audited?
   c. What is the probability at least one of these returns is audited?
2. Under certain conditions, the IRS will compute the amount of refund due a taxpayer. Suppose the Cincinnati office of the IRS completes an average of three of this type of return per hour.
   a. Which probability model does this situation follow?
   b. What is the probability the IRS completes exactly three of this type of return in a particular hour?
   c. What is the probability the IRS does not complete any of this type of return in an hour?
   d. What is the probability the IRS completes at least one of these returns in a particular hour?
3. A CPA studied the number of exemptions claimed on tax returns. The data are summarized in the following table.

Exemptions	Percent
1	20
2	50
3	20
4	10

a. What is the mean number of exemptions claimed?
b. What is the variance of the number of exemptions claimed?

McGraw-Hill Connect™ Business Statistics

Less Managing. More Teaching. Greater Learning. McGraw-Hill *Connect Business Statistics* is an online assignment and assessment solution that connects students with the tools and resources they'll need to achieve success.

McGraw-Hill Connect Business Statistics helps prepare students for their future by enabling faster learning, more efficient studying, and higher retention of knowledge.

Features.
Connect Business Statistics offers a number of powerful tools and features to make managing assignments easier, so faculty can spend more time teaching. With *Connect Business Statistics,* students can engage with their coursework anytime and anywhere, making the learning process more accessible and efficient. *Connect Business Statistics* offers you the features described below.

Simple Assignment Management. With *Connect Business Statistics,* creating assignments is easier than ever, so you can spend more time teaching and less time managing. The assignment management function enables you to:

- Create and deliver assignments easily with selectable end-of-chapter questions and test bank items.
- Streamline lesson planning, student progress reporting, and assignment grading to make classroom management more efficient than ever.
- Go paperless with the eBook and on-line submission and grading of student assignments.

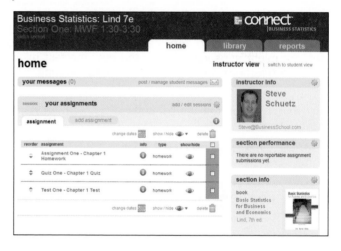

Smart Grading. When it comes to studying, time is precious. *Connect Business Statistics* helps students learn more efficiently by providing feedback and practice material when they need it, where they need it. When it comes to teaching, your time also is precious. The grading function enables you to:

- Have assignments scored automatically, giving students immediate feedback on their work and side-by-side comparisons with correct answers.
- Access and review each response; manually change grades or leave comments for students to review.
- Reinforce classroom concepts with practice tests and instant quizzes.

Integration of Excel Data Sets. A convenient feature is the inclusion of an Excel data file link in many problems using data sets in their calculation. This allows students to easily launch into Excel, work the problem, and return to *Connect* to key in the answer.

Instructor Library. The *Connect Business Statistics* Instructor Library is your repository for additional resources to improve student engagement in and out of class. You can select and use any asset that enhances your lecture. The *Connect Business Statistics* Instructor Library includes:

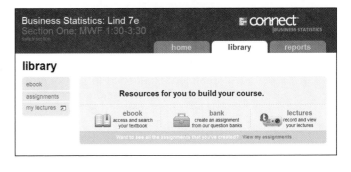

- eBook
- PowerPoint presentations
- Test Bank
- Solutions Manual
- Digital Image Library

Student Study Center. The *Connect Business Statistics* Student Study Center is the place for students to access additional resources. The Student Study Center:

- Offers students quick access to lectures, practice materials, eBooks, and more.
- Provides instant practice material and study questions, easily accessible on-the-go.

Student Progress Tracking. *Connect Business Statistics* keeps instructors informed about how each student, section, and class is performing, allowing for more productive use of lecture and office hours. The progress-tracking function enables you to:

- View scored work immediately and track individual or group performance with assignment and grade reports.
- Access an instant view of student or class performance relative to learning objectives.
- Collect data and generate reports required by many accreditation organizations, such as AACSB.

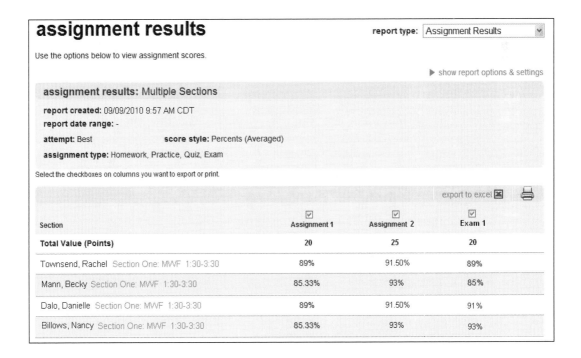

McGraw-Hill CONNECT™ PLUS BUSINESS STATISTICS

McGraw-Hill Connect Plus Business Statistics. McGraw-Hill reinvents the textbook learning experience for the modern student with *Connect Plus Business Statistics.* A seamless integration of an eBook and *Connect Business Statistics, Connect Plus Business Statistics* provides all of the *Connect Business Statistics* features plus the following:

- An integrated eBook, allowing for anytime, anywhere access to the textbook.
- Dynamic links between the problems or questions you assign to your students and the location in the eBook where that problem or question is covered.
- A powerful search function to pinpoint and connect key concepts in a snap.

In short, *Connect Business Statistics* offers you and your students powerful tools and features that optimize your time and energies, enabling you to focus on course content, teaching, and student learning. *Connect Business Statistics* also offers a wealth of content resources for both instructors and students. This state-of-the-art, thoroughly tested system supports you in preparing students for the world that awaits. For more information about *Connect,* go to www.mcgrawhillconnect.com or contact your local McGraw-Hill sales representative.

Tegrity Campus: Lectures 24/7

Tegrity Campus is a service that makes class time available 24/7 by automatically capturing every lecture in a searchable format for students to review when they study and complete assignments. With a simple one-click start-and-stop process, you capture all computer screens and corresponding audio. Students can replay any part of any class with easy-to-use browser-based viewing on a PC or Mac.

McGraw-Hill Tegrity Campus

Educators know that the more students can see, hear, and experience class resources, the better they learn. In fact, studies prove it. With *Tegrity Campus,* students quickly recall key moments by using *Tegrity Campus*'s unique search feature. This search helps students efficiently find what they need, when they need it, across an entire semester of class recordings. Help turn all your students' study time into learning moments immediately supported by your lecture.

To learn more about *Tegrity,* watch a 2-minute Flash demo at http://tegritycampus.mhhe.com.

Assurance-of-Learning Ready

Many educational institutions today are focused on the notion of *assurance of learning* an important element of some accreditation standards. *Basic Statistics for Business & Economics* is designed specifically to support your assurance-of-learning initiatives with a simple, yet powerful solution.

Each test bank question for *Basic Statistics for Business & Economics* maps to a specific chapter learning outcome/objective listed in the text. You can use our test bank software, EZ Test and EZ Test Online, or *Connect Business Statistics* to easily query for learning outcomes/objectives that directly relate to the learning objectives for your course. You can then use the reporting features of EZ Test to aggregate student results in similar fashion, making the collection and presentation of assurance of learning data simple and easy.

AACSB Statement

The McGraw-Hill Companies is a proud corporate member of AACSB International. Understanding the importance and value of AACSB accreditation, *Basic Statistics for Business & Economics* recognizes the curricula guidelines detailed in the AACSB standards for business accreditation by connecting selected questions in the text and the test bank to the six general knowledge and skill guidelines in the AACSB standards.

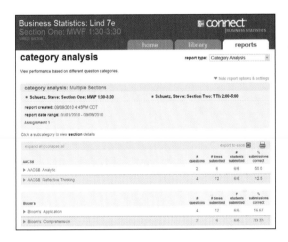

The statements contained in *Basic Statistics for Business & Economics* are provided only as a guide for the users of this textbook. The AACSB leaves content coverage and assessment within the purview of individual schools, the mission of the school, and the faculty. While *Basic Statistics for Business & Economics* and the teaching package make no claim of any specific AACSB qualification or evaluation, we have labeled selected questions within *Basic Statistics for Business & Economics* according to the six general knowledge and skills areas.

McGraw-Hill Customer Care Information

At McGraw-Hill, we understand that getting the most from new technology can be challenging. That's why our services don't stop after you purchase our products. You can e-mail our Product Specialists 24 hours a day to get product-training online. Or you can search our knowledge bank of Frequently Asked Questions on our support Web site. For Customer Support, call **800-331-5094**, e-mail hmsupport@mcgraw-hill.com, or visit www.mhhe.com/support. One of our Technical Support Analysts will be able to assist you in a timely fashion.

MegaStat® for Excel® (ISBN: 0077395131)

MegaStat® for Excel® by J. B. Orris of Butler University is a full-featured Excel add-in that is available with this text. The software performs statistical analyses within an Excel workbook. It does basic functions, such as descriptive statistics, frequency distributions, and probability calculations as well as hypothesis testing, ANOVA, and regression.

MegaStat output is carefully formatted and ease-of-use features include Auto Expand for quick data selection and Auto Label detect. Since *MegaStat* is easy to use, students can focus on learning statistics without being distracted by the software. *MegaStat* is always available from Excel's main menu. Selecting a menu item pops up a dialog box. *MegaStat* works with all recent versions of Excel including Excel 2007. Help files are built in and an introductory user's manual is also included.

MINITAB®/SPSS®/JMP®

MINITAB® Student Version 14, SPSS® Student Version 17.0, and JMP® Student Edition Version 8 are software tools that are available to help students solve the business statistics exercises in the text. Each is available in the student version and can be packaged with any McGraw-Hill business statistics text.

Instructor's Resources CD-ROM
(ISBN: 0077327004)

This resource allows instructors to conveniently access the Instructor's Solutions Manual, Test Bank in Word and EZ Test formats, Instructor PowerPoint slides, data files, and data sets.

Online Learning Center:
www.mhhe.com/lind7e

The Online Learning Center (OLC) provides the instructor with a complete Instructor's Manual in Word format, the complete Test Bank in both Word files and computerized EZ Test format, Instructor PowerPoint slides, text art files, an introduction to ALEKS®, an introduction to McGraw-Hill Connect Business Statistics™, access to the eBook, and more.

All test bank questions are available in an EZ Test electronic format. Included are a number of multiple-choice, true/false, and short-answer questions and problems. The answers to all questions are given, along with a rating of the level of difficulty, chapter goal the question tests, Bloom's taxonomy question type, and AACSB knowledge category.

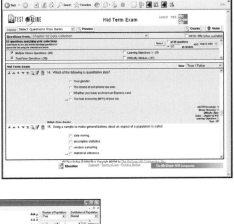

Visual Statistics
www.mhhe.com/lind7e

Visual Statistics 2.2 by Doane, Mathieson, and Tracy is a package of 21 software programs for teaching and learning statistics concepts. It is unique in that it allows students to learn the concepts through interactive experimentation and visualization. The software and worktext promote active learning through competency building exercises, individual and team projects, and built-in data bases. Over 400 data sets from business settings are included within the package as well as a worktext in electronic format. This software is available on the Online Learning Center (OLC) for Lind 7e.

WebCT/Blackboard/eCollege

All of the material in the Online Learning Center is also available in portable WebCT, Blackboard, or eCollege content "cartridges" provided free to adopters of this text.

www.blackboard.com

CourseSmart

CourseSmart is a new way to find and buy eTextbooks. CourseSmart has the largest selection of eTextbooks available anywhere, offering thousands of the most commonly adopted textbooks from a wide variety of higher-education publishers. Course Smart eTextbooks are available in one standard online reader with full text search, notes and highlighting, and e-mail tools for sharing notes between classmates. Visit www.CourseSmart.com for more information on ordering.

ALEKS®

ALEKS is an assessment and learning system that provides individualized instruction in Business Statistics. ALEKS delivers precise assessments of students' knowledge, guides them in the selection of appropriate new study material, and records their progress toward mastery of goals.

ALEKS interacts with students much as a skilled human tutor would, moving between explanation and practice as needed, correcting and analyzing errors, defining terms and changing topics on request. By accurately assessing their knowledge, ALEKS focuses precisely on what to learn next, helping students master the course content more quickly and easily.

Online Learning Center: www.mhhe.com/lind7e

The Online Learning Center (OLC) provides students with the following content:

- Quizzes
- PowerPoint
- Screencam tutorials (includes how to solve specific problems in the text.)

- Visual Statistics
- Data sets/files

The following resources are available through McGraw-Hill's Primis online: http://www.primisonline.com. Primis online allows you to build either a print or ebook supplement based on your course and students' needs.

Student Study Guide (ISBN: 0077398610)

This supplement helps students master the course content. It highlights the important ideas in the text and provides opportunities for students to review the worked-out solutions, review terms and concepts, and practice.

Basic Statistics Using Excel 2007 (ISBN: 0077398629)

This workbook introduces students to Excel and shows how to apply it to introductory statistics. This manual presumes no prior familiarity with Excel or statistics and provides step-by-step directions in a how-to style using Excel 2007 with text examples and problems.

Business Statistics Center (BSC): www.mhhe.com/bstat/ BSC
BUSINESS STATISTICS CENTER

The BSC contains links to statistical publications and resources, software downloads, learning aids, statistical Web sites and databases, and McGraw-Hill/Irwin product Web sites and online courses.

Acknowledgments

This edition of *Basic Statistics for Business and Economics* is the product of many people: students, colleagues, reviewers, and the staff at McGraw-Hill/Irwin. We thank them all. We wish to express our sincere gratitude to the survey and focus group participants, and the reviewers:

Reviewers

Robert F. Abbey, Jr.
Troy University

Ram Acharya
New Mexico State University

Larry Ammann
University of Texas—Dallas

Hope Baker
Kennesaw State University

Doug Barrett
University of North Alabama

Doris Bennett
Jacksonville State University

Nancy Burnett
University of Wisconsin—Oshkosh

Derek Burnett
Loras College

Susan Carter
Doane College

Juan Castro
LeTourneau University

Gary Cummings
Walsh College

Jeremy DalleTezze
Grove City College

Linda Dawson
University of Washington—Tacoma

Carol B. Diminnie
Angelo State University

Joe Easton
Pueblo Community College

Ronald Elkins
Central Washington University

Kathryn Ernstberger
Indiana University Southeast

Joseph Fuhr
Widener University

Kemit Grafton
Oklahoma State University—Oklahoma City

Mary Gray
American University

Don Gren
Salt Lake Community College

Frank T. Griggs
Grand Valley State University

M. Ryan Haley
University of Wisconsin—Oshkosh

Janice Harder
Motlow State Community College

Richard Herschel
Saint Joseph's University

Stacey Jones
Seattle University

Susan Lenker
Central Michigan University

Melody Kiang
California State University—Long Beach

Bharat R. Kolluri
University of Hartford

Carel Ligeon
Auburn University—Montgomery

Michael McLain
Hampton University

Stephen McMillion
Midlands Technical College

Kristen Monaco
California State University—Long Beach

Steve Montreal
Concordia University

Mihail Motzev
Walla Walla College

Alan W. Neebe
University of North Carolina

Joe Nowakowski
Muskingum College

Pin Ng
Northern Arizona University

John O'Neill
Siena College

Kevin Palmateer
Yakima Valley Community College

Kameliia Petrova
State University of New York—Plattsburgh

Darlene Riedemann
Eastern Illinois University

Samme Wallace-Ormiston
Otero Junior College

Yvonne Sandoval
Pima Community College, West

Bongsik Shin
San Diego State University

Teresa Speck
Saint Mary's University of Minnesota

Leonie Stone
State University of New York—Genneseo

Debbie Tesch
Xavier University

John W. Yarber, Jr.
Northeast Mississippi Community College

Survey and Focus Group Participants

Larry Ammann
University of Texas—Dallas

Scott Bailey
Troy University

Doug Barrett
University of North Alabama

Quidong Cao
Winthrop University

James Carden
University of Mississippi

Juan Castro
LeTourneau University

Joan Donahue
University of South Carolina

Chia-Shin Chung
Cleveland State University

Gary Cummings
Walsh College

Linda Dawson
University of Washington—Tacoma

Kathryn Ernstberger
Indiana University Southeast

Joseph Fuhr
Widener University

Alison Kelly Hawke
Suffolk University

Fred Hulme
Baylor University

L. Allison Jones-Farmer
Auburn University

John Landry
Metropolitan State College of Denver

Carel Ligeon
Auburn University—Montgomery

Ed Melnick
New York University

Carol Monroe
Baylor University

Khosrow Moshirvaziri
California State University—Long Beach

Maureen O'Brien
University of Minnesota—Duluth

J. Burdeane Orris
Butler University

Priya Rajagopalan
Purdue University

Mary Anne Rothermel
University of Akron

Paul Sen
University of North Florida

Murali Shanker
Kent State University

Debra Stiver
University of Nevada—Reno

Jesus Valencia
Slippery Rock University

Kathleen Whitcomb
University of South Carolina

Blake Whitten
University of Iowa

Bill Younkin
University of Miami

Xiaolong (Jonathan) Zhang
Georgia Southern University

Zhiwei (Henry) Zhu
University of Louisiana

Their suggestions and thorough reviews of the previous edition and the manuscript of this edition make this a better text.

Special thanks go to a number of people. Julia Norton of California State University–Hayward, Christopher Rogers of Miami Dade College and Carol Diminnie of Angelo State University reviewed the manuscript and page proofs, checking exercises for accuracy. Professor Kathleen Whitcomb of the University of South Carolina prepared the study guide. Dr. Samuel Wathen of Coastal Carolina University prepared the quizzes and the Test Bank. Professor René Ordonez of Southern Oregon University prepared the PowerPoint presentation and the screencam tutorials. Ms. Denise Heban and the authors prepared the Instructor's Manual.

We also wish to thank the staff at McGraw-Hill. This includes Steve Schuetz, Executive Editor; Wanda Zeman, Senior Development Editor; Bruce Gin, Senior Project Manager; and others we do not know personally, but who have made valuable contributions.

In addition we wish to personally acknowledge Richard T. Hercher, Jr., who served as our Sponsoring and Executive Editor for many editions of this book as well as *Statistical Techniques in Business and Economics.* His insight and efforts made our texts better for students and instructors. It was always a pleasure to work with him. We wish him continued success in his new position at McGraw-Hill.

Changes made in all chapters:
- Added a Practice Test at the end of each chapter to help students evaluate their understanding of the material and prepare for an examination.
- Changed Goals to Learning Objectives and identified the location in the chapter where the learning objective is first discussed.
- Revised the Major League Baseball data set to reflect the latest complete season, 2008.
- Revised the Real Estate data to ensure the outcomes are more realistic to the current economy.
- Updated Excel screens to use Excel 2007, Minitab 15, and the updated version of MegaStat.
- Added updates and clarifications throughout.

Chapter 1   What Is Statistics?
New chapter opening exercise on cell phone providers.

Census updates on U.S. household income, sales of Boeing aircraft, and *Forbes* data in "Statistics in Action" feature.

New content on why statistics is required for so many majors with new *USA Today* Snapshot on enrollments in online college courses.

New content on nominal-level data, its properties, and how it is a measurement consisting of counts; new supporting *USA Today* Snapshot on "What Workers Want."

Updated Excel 2007 and Minitab screens.

New chapter exercises 9 (exits along interstate highways), 10 (polling college students on cell phone providers), 11 (sales receipts at the Gap), and 12 (presidential election).

Chapter 2   Describing Data: Frequency Tables, Frequency Distributions, and Graphic Presentation
New data on Ohio State Lottery expenses for 2007, with new Excel 2007 screenshot.

New exercises 31 (use of iPods by college students), 32 (purchasing and selling stock), 33 (iTunes library), 34 (*Journal of Finance* on the internet), and 52 (families using the day care service at the Minneapolis YWCA).

Chapter 3   Describing Data: Numerical Measures
New opening exercise on U.S. housing prices.

New data on averages in the introduction: average TV sets, average earnings, average spending on a wedding.

Updated example on number of traffic citations in Beaufort County, South Carolina.

"Statistics in Action" update on highest batting average in Major League Baseball for 2008. It was Chipper Jones of the Atlanta Braves, with an average of .364.

Updated the unemployment rate in Alaska for 2008, Exercise 26.

New chapter exercises 63 (entertainment expenses of undergraduates), 64 (EPA air quality indexes), 65 (U.S. housing prices), and 66 (Kentucky Derby payoffs).

Chapter 4   Describing Data: Displaying and Exploring Data
New exercise 14 with 2009 salary data for New York Yankees.

Chapter 5   A Survey of Probability Concepts
New opening exercise on tourists in China.

New exercises 45 (probability of winning horse races), 53 (winning a tournament), and 54 (winning *Jeopardy*).

New probability exercises 79, 80, and 81.

New Excel 2007 software commands for determining permutations and combinations.

Chapter 6   Discrete Probability Distributions
New opening exercise on retail sales on Web sites.

New exercises 18 (cell phone use) and 24 (toll road transponder use).

Chapter 7   Continuous Probability Distributions
New chapter opener credit card exercise.

New Self-Review 7-4 involving Jose's Delivery Service.

New exercise 20 (viewers watching *American Idol*).

Several glossary updates and clarifications.

Chapter 8   Sampling Methods and the Central Limit Theorem
New exercises 21 (shapes of distributions) and 22 (random sampling on time spent playing sports).

Several revised exercises.

Updated software commands and screen for Excel 2007.

Chapter 9   Estimation and Confidence Intervals
Some updated exercises.

New exercises 58 (car fuel efficiency), 59 (iPhone), 65 (weight loss), and 66 (news poll).

Updated software commands and screens for Minitab.

Chapter 10   One-Sample Tests of Hypothesis
New opening exercise on Dole pineapple.

New exercises 58 (football) and 59 (lung cancer fatalities).

Updated Minitab Commands and screens.

Chapter 11   Two-Sample Tests of Hypothesis
New chapter opening exercise on a grape vineyard in Upstate New York.

Reference added to formula for calculating standard deviation.

New exercises 35 (testing computer products), 36 (participation in Nation Basketball Association), and 49 and 50 (winning the Indianapolis 500 race).

Chapter 12   Analysis of Variance
New exercises 29 (postal service) and 30 (junk email).

Added definition of *treatment*.

Chapter 13   Linear Regression and Correlation
New exercises 47 (median age of residents in large cities) and 48 (buying a fuel efficient used car).

Some revised exercises.

Chapter 14   Multiple Regression and Correlation Analysis
Small changes and clarifications throughout.

New exercises 17 (sizes of LCD televisions) and 18 (relationship between median income and median age in a portion of a state).

Chapter 15   Nonparametric Methods: Chi-Square Applications
New chapter opening exercise on viewers of each of the three major television networks.

New exercise 23 (digits and frequency in a California lottery) and 24 (numbers of employees visiting doctors).

Brief Contents

Contents

Chapter

7 Continuous Probability Distributions   194

Chapter

8 Sampling Methods and the Central Limit Theorem   221

Chapter

9 Estimation and Confidence Intervals   253

What Is Statistics?

A poll solicits a large number of college undergraduates for information on the following variables: the name of their cell phone provider, the number of minutes used last month, and their satisfaction with the service. What is the data scale for each of these three variables? (See Exercise 10 and LO5.)

Introduction

More than 100 years ago H. G. Wells, an English author and historian, suggested that one day quantitative reasoning will be as necessary for effective citizenship as the ability to read. He made no mention of business because the Industrial Revolution was just beginning. Mr. Wells could not have been more correct. While "business experience," some "thoughtful guesswork," and "intuition" are key attributes of successful managers, today's business problems tend to be too complex for this type of decision making alone.

One of the tools used to make decisions is statistics. Statistics is used not only by businesspeople; we all also apply statistical concepts in our lives. For example, to start the day you turn on the shower and let it run for a few moments. Then you put your hand in the shower to sample the temperature and decide to add more hot water or more cold water, or that the temperature is just right and to enter the shower. As a second example, suppose you are at Costco Wholesale and wish to buy a frozen pizza. One of the pizza makers has a stand, and they offer a small wedge of their pizza. After sampling the pizza, you decide whether to purchase the pizza or not. In both the shower and pizza examples, you make a decision and select a course of action based on a sample.

Businesses face similar situations. The Kellogg Company must ensure that the mean amount of Raisin Bran in the 25.5-gram box meets label specifications. To do so, it sets a "target" weight somewhat higher than the amount specified on the label. Each box is then weighed after it is filled. The weighing machine reports a distribution of the content weights for each hour as well as the number "kicked-out" for being under the label specification during the hour. The Quality Inspection Department also randomly selects samples from the production line and checks the quality of the product and the weight of the contents of the box. If the mean product weight differs significantly from the target weight or the percent of kick-outs is too large, the process is adjusted.

Alan Greenspan, former chairman of the Federal Reserve Board, knows and understands the importance of statistical tools and techniques to provide accurate and timely information to make public statements that have the power to move global stock markets and influence political thinking. Dr. Greenspan, speaking before a National Skills Summit, recently stated: "Workers must be equipped not simply with technical know-how, but also with the ability to create, analyze, and transform information and to interact effectively with others. That is, separate the facts from opinions, and then organize these facts in an appropriate manner and analyze the information."

As a student of business or economics, you will need basic knowledge and skills to organize, analyze, and transform data and to present the information. In this text, we will show you basic statistical techniques and methods that will develop your ability to make good personal and business decisions.

Why Study Statistics?

LO1 Understand why we study statistics.

If you look through your university catalog, you will find that statistics is required for many college programs. Why is this so? What are the differences in the statistics courses taught in the Engineering College, the Psychology or Sociology Departments in the Liberal Arts College, and the College of Business? The biggest difference is the examples used. The course content is basically the same. In the College of Business we are interested in such things as profits, hours worked, and wages. Psychologists are interested in test scores, and engineers are interested in how many units are manufactured on a particular machine. However, all three are interested in what is a typical value and how much variation there is in the data. There may also be a difference in the level of mathematics required. An engineering statistics course usually requires calculus. Statistics courses in colleges of business and education usually teach the course at a more applied level. You should be able to handle the mathematics in this text if you have completed high school algebra.

So why is statistics required in so many majors? The first reason is that numerical information is everywhere. Look in the newspapers *(USA Today),* news magazines *(Time, Newsweek, U.S. News and World Report),* business magazines *(BusinessWeek, Forbes),* or general interest magazines *(People),* women's magazines *(Ladies Home Journal* or *Elle),* or sports magazines *(Sports Illustrated, ESPN The Magazine),* and you will be bombarded with numerical information.

Examples of why we study statistics

Here are some examples:

- The national average weekly income rose 2.5 percent, from $598 in 2007 to $613 in 2008. Inflation increased just over 0.1 percent during the same period.
- In 2008 the average U.S. household had $10,728 in credit card debt.
- In 2006 Boeing, Inc., an aircraft manufacturer, ordered 1,057 aircraft, in 2007 they ordered 1,423, and in 2008 they ordered 669. The table below summarizes the information by year and aircraft type.

	Sales of Boeing Aircraft					
	Aircraft					
Year	737	747	767	777	787	Total
2006	738	72	10	77	160	1,057
2007	850	25	36	143	369	1,423
2008	488	4	29	54	94	669

You can view the sales for the most recent periods by going to the Boeing website at www.boeing.com and searching for "Orders and Deliveries."
- *USA Today* (www.usatoday.com) prints "Snapshots" that are the result of surveys conducted by various research organizations, foundations, and the federal government. The following chart summarizes the increase in college courses taken online.

USA TODAY Snapshot

05/02/2008-Updated 12:40 AMET

Enrollment in online college courses keeps climbing. Among the reasons: convenience for students with jobs and families to support.

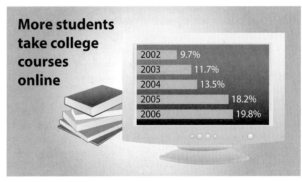

By David Stuckey and Keith Carter, USA Today
Source: National Association for College Admission Counseling

A second reason for taking a statistics course is that statistical techniques are used to make decisions that affect our daily lives. That is, they affect our personal welfare. Here are a few examples:

- Insurance companies use statistical analysis to set rates for home, automobile, life, and health insurance. Tables are available showing estimates that a 20-year-old female has 60.25 years of life remaining, an 87-year-old woman 4.56 years remaining, and a 50-year-old man 27.85 years remaining. Life insurance premiums are established based on these estimates of life expectancy.

- The Environmental Protection Agency is interested in the water quality of Lake Erie as well as other lakes. They periodically take water samples to establish the level of contamination and maintain the level of quality.
- Medical researchers study the cure rates for diseases using different drugs and different forms of treatment. For example, what is the effect of treating a certain type of knee injury surgically or with physical therapy? If you take an aspirin each day, does that reduce your risk of a heart attack?

A third reason for taking a statistics course is that the knowledge of statistical methods will help you understand how decisions are made and give you a better understanding of how they affect you.

No matter what line of work you select, you will find yourself faced with decisions where an understanding of data analysis is helpful. In order to make an informed decision, you will need to be able to:

1. Determine whether the existing information is adequate or additional information is required.
2. Gather additional information, if it is needed, in such a way that it does not provide misleading results.
3. Summarize the information in a useful and informative manner.
4. Analyze the available information.
5. Draw conclusions and make inferences while assessing the risk of an incorrect conclusion.

The statistical methods presented in the text will provide you with a framework for the decision-making process.

In summary, there are at least three reasons for studying statistics: (1) data are everywhere, (2) statistical techniques are used to make many decisions that affect our lives, and (3) no matter what your career, you will make professional decisions that involve data. An understanding of statistical methods will help you make these decisions more effectively.

What Is Meant by Statistics?

How do we define the word *statistics?* We encounter it frequently in our everyday language. It really has two meanings. In the more common usage, statistics refers to numerical information. Examples include the average starting salary of college graduates, the number of deaths due to alcoholism last year, the change in the Dow Jones Industrial Average from yesterday to today, and the number of home runs hit by the Chicago Cubs during the 2009 season. In these examples statistics are a value or a percentage. Other examples include:

- The typical automobile in the United States travels 11,099 miles per year, the typical bus 9,353 miles per year, and the typical truck 13,942 miles per year. In Canada the corresponding information is 10,371 miles for automobiles, 19,823 miles for buses, and 7,001 miles for trucks.
- The mean time waiting for technical support is 17 minutes.
- The mean length of the business cycle since 1945 is 61 months.

The above are all examples of **statistics.** A collection of numerical information is called **statistics** (plural).

We often present statistical information in a graphical form. A graph is often useful for capturing reader attention and to portray a large amount of information. For example, Chart 1–1 shows Frito-Lay volume and market share for the major snack and potato chip categories in supermarkets in the United States. It requires only a quick glance to discover there were nearly 800 million pounds of potato

Statistics in Action

We call your attention to a feature title—*Statistics in Action.* Read each one carefully to get an appreciation of the wide application of statistics in management, economics, nursing, law enforcement, sports, and other disciplines.

- In 2008, *Forbes* published a list of the richest Americans. William Gates, founder of Microsoft Corporation, is the richest. His net worth is estimated at $57.0 billion. (www.forbes.com)
- In 2008, the four largest American manufacturing companies, ranked by revenue, were ExxonMobil, Chevron, ConocoPhillips, and General Motors. (www.Industryweek.com)
- In the United States, a typical high school graduate earns $1.2 million in his or her lifetime, a typical college graduate with a bachelor's degree earns $2.1 million, and a typical college graduate with a master's degree earns $2.5 million. (usgovinfo.about.com/library/weekly/aa072602a.htm)

chips sold and that Frito-Lay sold 64 percent of that total. Also note that Frito-Lay has 82 percent of the corn chip market.

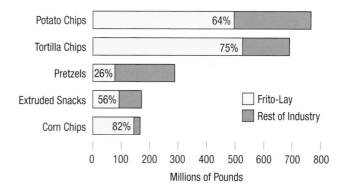

Potato Chips	64%
Tortilla Chips	75%
Pretzels	26%
Extruded Snacks	56%
Corn Chips	82%

☐ Frito-Lay
■ Rest of Industry

0 100 200 300 400 500 600 700 800
Millions of Pounds

CHART 1–1 Frito-Lay Volume and Share of Major Snack Chip Categories in U.S. Supermarkets

The subject of statistics, as we will explore it in this text, has a much broader meaning than just collecting and publishing numerical information. We define statistics as:

> **STATISTICS** The science of collecting, organizing, presenting, analyzing, and interpreting data to assist in making more effective decisions.

As the definition suggests, the first step in investigating a problem is to collect relevant data. They must be organized in some way and perhaps presented in a chart, such as Chart 1–1. Only after the data have been organized are we then able to analyze and interpret them. Here are some examples of the need for data collection.

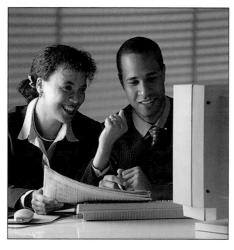

- Research analysts for JPMorgan Chase evaluate many facets of a particular stock before making a "buy" or "sell" recommendation. They collect the past sales data of the company and estimate future earnings. Other factors, such as the projected worldwide demand for the company's products, the strength of the competition, and the effect of the new union–management contract, are also considered before making a recommendation.
- The marketing department at Colgate-Palmolive Co., a manufacturer of soap products, has the responsibility of making recommendations regarding the potential profitability of a newly developed group of face soaps having fruit smells, such as grape, orange, and pineapple. Before making a final decision, the marketers will test it in several markets. That is, they may advertise and sell it in Topeka, Kansas, and Tampa, Florida. On the basis of test marketing in these two regions, Colgate-Palmolive will make a decision whether to market the soaps in the entire country.
- The United States government is concerned with the present condition of our economy and with predicting future economic trends. The government conducts a large number of surveys to determine consumer confidence and the outlook of managers regarding sales and production for the next 12 months. Indexes, such as the Consumer Price Index, are constructed each month to assess inflation. Information on department store sales, housing starts, money turnover, and industrial production are just a few of the hundreds of items used to form the basis of the projections. These projections are used by banks to decide their

prime lending rate and by the Federal Reserve Board to decide the level of control to place on the money supply.

- Managers must make decisions about the quality of their product or service. For example, customers call software companies for technical advice when they are not able to resolve an issue regarding the software. One measure of the quality of customer service is the time a customer must wait for a technical consultant to answer the call. A software company might set a target of one minute as the typical response time. The company would then collect and analyze data on the response time. Does the typical response time differ by day of the week or time of day? If the response times are increasing, managers might decide to increase the number of technical consultants at particular times of the day or week.

Types of Statistics

The study of statistics is usually divided into two categories: descriptive statistics and inferential statistics.

Descriptive Statistics

LO2 Explain what is meant by descriptive statistics and inferential statistics.

The definition of statistics given earlier referred to "organizing, presenting, analyzing . . . data." This facet of statistics is usually referred to as **descriptive statistics.**

> **DESCRIPTIVE STATISTICS** Methods of organizing, summarizing, and presenting data in an informative way.

For instance, the United States government reports the population of the United States was 179,323,000 in 1960; 203,302,000 in 1970; 226,542,000 in 1980; 248,709,000 in 1990, and 265,000,000 in 2000. This information is descriptive statistics. It is descriptive statistics if we calculate the percentage growth from one decade to the next. However, it would **not** be descriptive statistics if we used these to estimate the population of the United States in the year 2010 or the percentage growth from 2000 to 2010. Why? Because these statistics are not being used to summarize past populations but to estimate future populations. The following are some other examples of descriptive statistics.

- There are a total of 46,837 miles of interstate highways in the United States. The interstate system represents only 1 percent of the nation's total roads but carries more than 20 percent of the traffic. The longest is I-90, which stretches from Boston to Seattle, a distance of 3,099 miles. The shortest is I-878 in New York City, which is 0.70 of a mile in length. Alaska does not have any interstate highways, Texas has the most interstate miles at 3,232, and New York has the most interstate routes with 28.
- According to the *Bureau of Labor Statistics,* the average hourly earnings of production workers were $18.50 in March 2009. You can review the latest information on wages and productivity of American workers by going to the Bureau of Labor Statistics website at: http://www.bls.gov/home.htm and selecting Average Hourly Earnings.

Masses of unorganized data—such as the census of population, the weekly earnings of thousands of computer programmers, and the individual responses of 2,000 registered voters regarding their choice for president of the United States—are of little value as is. However, statistical techniques are available to organize this type of data into a meaningful form. Data can be organized into a **frequency distribution.** (This procedure is covered in Chapter 2.) Various **charts** may be used to describe data; several basic chart forms are also presented in Chapter 4.

Specific measures of central location, such as the mean, describe the central value of a group of numerical data. A number of statistical measures are used to describe how closely the data cluster about an average. These measures of central tendency and dispersion are discussed in Chapter 3.

Inferential Statistics

The second type of statistics is **inferential statistics**—also called **statistical inference.** Our main concern regarding inferential statistics is finding something about a population from a sample taken from that population. For example, a recent survey showed only 46 percent of high school seniors can solve problems involving fractions, decimals, and percentages; and only 77 percent of high school seniors correctly totaled the cost of salad, a burger, fries, and a cola on a restaurant menu. Since these are inferences about a population (all high school seniors) based on sample data, we refer to them as inferential statistics. You might think of inferential statistics as a "best guess" of a population value based on sample information.

> **INFERENTIAL STATISTICS** The methods used to estimate a property of a population on the basis of a sample.

Note the words *population* and *sample* in the definition of inferential statistics. We often make reference to the population living in the United States or the 1.31 billion population of China. However, in statistics the word *population* has a broader meaning. A **population** may consist of *individuals*—such as all the students enrolled at Utah State University, all the students in Accounting 201, or all the CEOs from the Fortune 500 companies. A population may also consist of *objects,* such as all the Cobra G/T tires produced at Cooper Tire and Rubber Company in the Findlay, Ohio, plant; the accounts receivable at the end of October for Lorrange Plastics, Inc.; or auto claims filed in the first quarter of 2008 at the Northeast Regional Office of State Farm Insurance. The *measurement* of interest might be the scores on the first examination of all students in Accounting 201, the tread wear of the Cooper Tires, the dollar amount of Lorrange Plastics's accounts receivable, or the amount of auto insurance claims at State Farm. Thus, a population in the statistical sense does not always refer to people.

> **POPULATION** The entire set of individuals or objects of interest or the measurements obtained from all individuals or objects of interest.

To infer something about a population, we usually take a **sample** from the population.

> **SAMPLE** A portion, or part, of the population of interest.

Reasons for sampling

Why take a sample instead of studying every member of the population? A sample of registered voters is necessary because of the prohibitive cost of contacting millions of voters before an election. Testing wheat for moisture content destroys the wheat, thus making a sample imperative. If the wine tasters tested all the wine, none would be available for sale. It would be physically impossible for a few marine biologists to capture and tag all the seals in the ocean. (These and other reasons for sampling are discussed in Chapter 8.)

As noted, using a sample to learn something about a population is done extensively in business, agriculture, politics, and government, as cited in the following examples:

- Television networks constantly monitor the popularity of their programs by hiring Nielsen and other organizations to sample the preferences of TV viewers.

For example, in a sample of 800 prime-time viewers, 320, or 40 percent, indicated they watched *CSI: Crime Scene Investigation* on CBS last week. These program ratings are used to set advertising rates or to cancel programs.

• Gamous and Associates, a public accounting firm, is conducting an audit of Pronto Printing Company. To begin, the accounting firm selects a random sample of 100 invoices and checks each invoice for accuracy. There is at least one error on five of the invoices; hence the accounting firm estimates that 5 percent of the population of invoices contain at least one error.

• A random sample of 1,260 marketing graduates from four-year schools showed their mean starting salary was $42,694. We therefore estimate the mean starting salary for all marketing graduates of four-year institutions to be $42,694.

The relationship between a sample and a population is portrayed below. For example, we wish to estimate the mean miles per gallon of SUVs. Six SUVs are selected from the population. The mean MPG of the six is used to estimate MPG for the population.

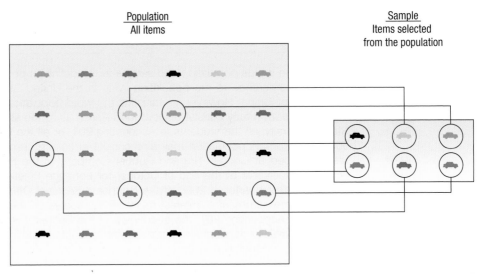

We strongly suggest you do the Self-Review exercise.

Following is a self-review problem. There are a number of them interspersed throughout each chapter. They test your comprehension of the preceding material. The answer and method of solution are given at the end of the chapter. You can find the answer to the following Self-Review on page 20. We recommend that you solve each one and then check your answer.

Self-Review 1–1

The answers are at the end of the chapter.
The Atlanta-based advertising firm, Brandon and Associates, asked a sample of 1,960 consumers to try a newly developed chicken dinner by Boston Market. Of the 1,960 sampled, 1,176 said they would purchase the dinner if it is marketed.
(a) What could Brandon and Associates report to Boston Market regarding acceptance of the chicken dinner in the population?
(b) Is this an example of descriptive statistics or inferential statistics? Explain.

Types of Variables

Qualitative variable

There are two basic types of variables: (1) qualitative and (2) quantitative (see Chart 1–2). When the characteristic being studied is categorical or nonnumeric, it is called a **qualitative variable** or an **attribute.** Examples of qualitative variables are gender, religious affiliation, Social Security number, telephone number, and eye color. When the data are qualitative, we are usually interested in how many or what percent fall in each category. For example, what percent of the population has blue eyes? How many Catholics and how many Protestants are there in the United States? What percent of the total number of cars sold last month were SUVs? Qualitative data are often summarized in charts and bar graphs (Chapter 2).

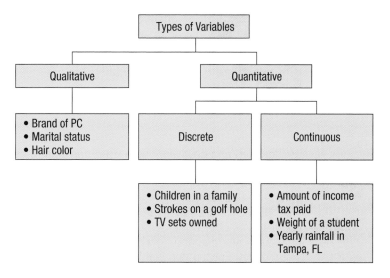

CHART 1–2 Summary of the Types of Variables

Quantitative variable

When the variable studied indicates how many or how much it is called a **quantitative variable.** Examples of quantitative variables are the balance in your checking account, the ages of company presidents, the life of an automobile battery (such as 42 months), and the number of children in a family.

LO4 Describe how a *discrete variable* is different from a *continuous variable.*

Quantitative variables are either discrete or continuous. **Discrete variables** can assume only certain values, and there are "gaps" between the values. Examples of discrete variables are the number of bedrooms in a house (1, 2, 3, 4, etc.), the number of cars arriving at Exit 25 on I-4 in Florida near Walt Disney World in an hour (326, 421, etc.), and the number of students in each section of a statistics course (25 in section A, 42 in section B, and 18 in section C). We count, for example, the number of cars arriving at Exit 25 on I-4, and we count the number of statistics students in each section. Notice that a home can have 3 or 4 bedrooms, but it cannot have 3.56 bedrooms. Thus, there is a "gap" between possible values. Typically, discrete variables result from counting.

Observations of a **continuous variable** can assume any value within a specific range. Examples of continuous variables are the air pressure in a tire and the weight of a shipment of tomatoes. Other examples are the amount of raisin bran in a box and the duration of flights from Orlando to San Diego. Grade point average (GPA) is a continuous variable. We could report the GPA of a particular student as 3.2576952. The usual practice is to round to 3 places—3.258. Typically, continuous variables result from measuring.

Levels of Measurement

LO5 Distinguish among the *nominal, ordinal, interval,* and *ratio* levels of measurement.

Data can be classified according to levels of measurement. The level of measurement of the data dictates the calculations that can be done to summarize and present the data. It will also determine the statistical tests that should be performed. For example, there are six colors of candies in a bag of M&M's. Suppose we assign brown a value of 1, yellow 2, blue 3, orange 4, green 5, and red 6. From a bag of candies, we add the assigned color values and divide by the number of candies and report that the mean color is 3.56. Does this mean that the average color is blue or orange? Of course not! As a second example, in a high school track meet there are eight competitors in the 400-meter run. We report the order of finish and that the mean finish is 4.5. What does the mean finish tell us? Nothing! In both of these instances, we have not properly used the level of measurement.

There are actually four levels of measurement: nominal, ordinal, interval, and ratio. The lowest, or the most primitive, measurement is the nominal level. The highest, or the level that gives us the most information about the observation, is the ratio level of measurement.

Nominal-Level Data

For the **nominal level** of measurement observations of a qualitative variable can only be classified and counted. There is no particular order to the labels. The classification of the six colors of M&M's milk chocolate candies is an example of the nominal level of measurement. We simply classify the candies by color. There is no natural order. That is, we could report the brown candies first, the orange first, or any of the colors first. Gender is another example of the nominal level of measurement. Suppose we count the number of students entering a football game with a student ID and report how many are men and how many are women. We could report either the men or the women first. For the nominal level the only measurement involved consists of counts. Sometimes, for better reader understanding, we convert these counts to percentages. The following "Snapshot" from *USA Today* shows the results from a survey of workers. The variable of interest is "Perks" and there are five possible outcomes: "More money," "Better healthcare," "Better retirement," "Work/family balance," and, we will assume, "Other." The outcome "Other" is not shown on the chart, but is necessary to make the percent of respondents total 100 percent. There is no natural order to the outcomes; we could have put "Better healthcare" first instead of "More money."

To process the data, such as the information regarding worker perks, or information on gender, employment by industry, or state of birth of a student, we often numerically code the information. That is, we assign students from Alabama a code of 1, Alaska a code of 2, Arizona as 3, and so on. Using this procedure, Wisconsin is coded 49 and Wyoming 50. This coding facilitates counting by a computer. However, because we have assigned numbers to the various categories, this does not give us license to manipulate the numbers. To explain, 1 + 2 does not equal 3; that is, Alabama + Alaska does *not* yield Arizona.

To summarize, the nominal level has the following properties:

1. The variable of interest is divided into categories or outcomes.
2. There is no natural order to the outcomes.

USA TODAY Snapshot

03/15/2007-updated 11:51 PM ET

Workers say they prefer higher salaries to any other perks.

By Anne R. Carey and Chad Palmer, USA Today
Source: hudson-index.com

Ordinal-Level Data

The next higher level of data is the **ordinal level.** Table 1–1 lists the student ratings of Professor James Brunner in an Introduction to Finance course. Each student in the class answered the question "Overall, how did you rate the instructor in this class?" The variable rating illustrates the use of the ordinal scale of measurement. One classification is "higher" or "better" than the next one. That is, "Superior" is better than "Good," "Good" is better than "Average," and so on. However, we are not able to distinguish the magnitude of the differences between groups. Is the difference between "Superior" and "Good" the same as the difference between "Poor" and "Inferior"? We cannot tell. If we substitute a 5 for "Superior" and a 4 for "Good," we can conclude that the rating of "Superior" is better than the rating of "Good," but we cannot add a ranking of "Superior" and a ranking of "Good," with the result being meaningful. Further we cannot conclude that a rating of "Good" (rating is 4) is necessarily twice as high as a "Poor" (rating is 2). We can only conclude that a rating of "Good" is better than a rating of "Poor." We cannot conclude how much better the rating is.

TABLE 1–1 Rating of a Finance Professor

Rating	Frequency
Superior	6
Good	28
Average	25
Poor	12
Inferior	3

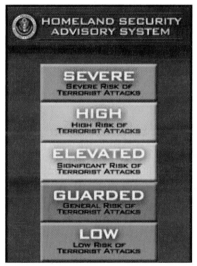

Another example of ordinal-level data is the Homeland Security Advisory System. The Department of Homeland Security publishes this information regarding the risk of terrorist activity to federal, state, and local authorities and to the American people. The five risk levels from lowest to highest, including a description and color codes, are shown to the left.

This is an example of the ordinal scale because we know the order or the ranks of the risk levels—that is, orange is higher than yellow—but the amount of the difference in risk is not necessarily the same. To put it another way, the difference in the risk level between yellow and orange is not necessarily the same as between green and blue.

In summary the properties of the ordinal level of data are:

1. Data classifications are represented by sets of labels or names (high, medium, low) that have relative values.
2. Because of the relative values, the data classified can be ranked or ordered.

Interval-Level Data

The **interval level** of measurement is the next highest level. It includes all the characteristics of the ordinal level, but, in addition, the difference between values is a constant size. An example of the interval level of measurement is temperature. Suppose the high temperatures on three consecutive winter days in Boston are 28, 31, and 20 degrees Fahrenheit. These temperatures can be easily ranked, but we can also determine the difference between temperatures. This is possible because 1 degree Fahrenheit represents a constant unit of measurement. Equal differences between two temperatures are the same, regardless of their position on the scale. That is, the difference between 10 degrees Fahrenheit and 15 degrees is 5, the difference between 50 and 55 degrees is also 5 degrees. It is also important to note that 0 is just a point on the scale. It does not represent the absence of the condition. Zero degrees Fahrenheit does not represent the absence of heat, just that it is cold! In fact 0 degrees Fahrenheit is about −18 degrees on the Celsius scale.

Another example of the interval scale of measurement is women's dress sizes. Listed below is information on several dimensions of a standard U.S. women's dress.

Size	Bust (in)	Waist (in)	Hips (in)
8	32	24	35
10	34	26	37
12	36	28	39
14	38	30	41
16	40	32	43
18	42	34	45
20	44	36	47
22	46	38	49
24	48	40	51
26	50	42	53
28	52	44	55

Why is the "size" scale an interval measurement? Observe as the size changes by 2 units (say from size 10 to size 12 or from size 24 to size 26) each of the measurements increases by 2 inches. To put it another way, the intervals are the same.

There is no natural zero point for dress size. A "size 0" dress does not have "zero" material. Instead it would have a 24-inch bust, 16-inch waist and 27-inch hips. Moreover, the ratios are not reasonable. If you divide a size 28 by a size 14, you do not get the same answer as dividing a size 20 by 10. Neither ratio is equal to two as the "size" number would suggest. In short, if the distances between the numbers make sense, but the ratios do not, then you have an interval scale of measurement.

The properties of the interval-level data are:

1. Data classifications are ordered according to the amount of the characteristic they possess.
2. Equal differences in the characteristic are represented by equal differences in the measurements.

Ratio-Level Data

Practically all quantitative data is recorded on the ratio level of measurement. The **ratio level** is the "highest" level of measurement. It has all the characteristics of the interval level, but in addition, the 0 point is meaningful and the ratio between two numbers is meaningful. Examples of the ratio scale of measurement include wages, units of production, weight, changes in stock prices, distance between branch offices, and height. Money is a good illustration. If you have zero dollars, then you have no money. Weight is another example. If the dial on the scale of a correctly calibrated device is at 0, then there is a complete absence of weight. The ratio of two numbers is also meaningful. If Jim earns $40,000 per year selling insurance and Rob earns $80,000 per year selling cars, then Rob earns twice as much as Jim.

Table 1–2 illustrates the use of the ratio scale of measurement. It shows the incomes of four father-and-son combinations.

TABLE 1–2 Father–Son Income Combinations

Name	Father	Son
Lahey	$80,000	$ 40,000
Nale	90,000	30,000
Rho	60,000	120,000
Steele	75,000	130,000

Observe that the senior Lahey earns twice as much as his son. In the Rho family the son makes twice as much as the father.

In summary, the properties of the ratio-level data are:

1. Data classifications are ordered according to the amount of the characteristics they possess.
2. Equal differences in the characteristic are represented by equal differences in the numbers assigned to the classifications.
3. The zero point is the absence of the characteristic and the ratio between two numbers is meaningful.

Chart 1–3 summarizes the major characteristics of the various levels of measurement.

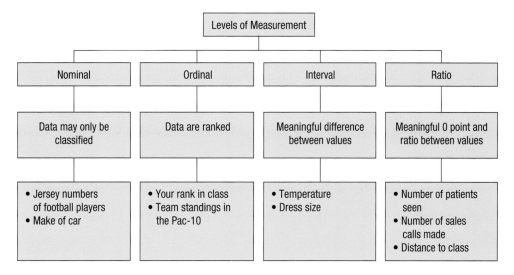

CHART 1–3 Summary of the Characteristics for Levels of Measurement

Self-Review 1–2

What is the level of measurement reflected by the following data?

(a) The age of each person in a sample of 50 adults who listen to one of the 1,230 talk radio stations in the United States is:

35	29	41	34	44	46	42	42	37	47
30	36	41	39	44	39	43	43	44	40
47	37	41	27	33	33	39	38	43	22
44	39	35	35	41	42	37	42	38	43
35	37	38	43	40	48	42	31	51	34

(b) In a survey of 200 luxury-car owners, 100 were from California, 50 from New York, 30 from Illinois, and 20 from Ohio.

Exercises

connect™

The answers to the odd-numbered exercises are at the end of the book.

1. What is the level of measurement for each of the following variables?
   a. Student IQ ratings.
   b. Distance students travel to class.
   c. The jersey numbers of a sorority soccer team.
   d. A classification of students by state of birth.

    e. A ranking of students as freshman, sophomore, junior, and senior.
    f. Number of hours students study per week.
2. What is the level of measurement for these items related to the newspaper business?
    a. The number of papers sold each Sunday during 2009.
    b. The departments, such as editorial, advertising, sports, etc.
    c. A summary of the number of papers sold by county.
    d. The number of years employed by the newspaper for each employee.
3. Look in the latest edition of *USA Today* or your local newspaper and find examples of each level of measurement. Write a brief memo summarizing your findings.
4. For each of the following, determine whether the group is a sample or a population.
    a. The participants in a study of a new cholesterol drug.
    b. The drivers who received a speeding ticket in Kansas City last month.
    c. Those on welfare in Cook County (Chicago), Illinois.
    d. The 30 stocks reported as a part of the Dow Jones Industrial Average.

Ethics and Statistics

Following the events of Enron, Tyco, HealthSouth, WorldCom, and other corporate disasters, business students need to understand that these events were based on the misrepresentation of business and financial data. In each case, people within each organization reported financial information to investors that indicated the companies were performing much better than the actual situation. When the true financial information was reported the companies were worth much less than advertised. The result was many investors lost all or nearly all of the money they put into these companies.

    The article "Statistics and Ethics: Some Advice for Young Statisticians," in *The American Statistician* 57, no. 1 (2003), offers guidance. The authors advise us to practice statistics with integrity and honesty, and urge us to "do the right thing" when collecting, organizing, summarizing, analyzing, and interpreting numerical information. The real contribution of statistics to society is a moral one. Financial analysts need to provide information that truly reflects a company's performance so as not to mislead individual investors. Information regarding product defects that may be harmful to people must be analyzed and reported with integrity and honesty. The authors of *The American Statistician* article further indicate that when we practice statistics, we need to maintain "an independent and principled point-of-view."

    As you progress through this text, we will highlight ethical issues in the collection, analysis, presentation, and interpretation of statistical information. We also hope that, as your learn about using statistics, you will become a more informed consumer of information. For example, you will question a report based on data that do not fairly represent the population, a report that does not include all relevant statistics, one that includes an incorrect choice of statistical measures, or a presentation that introduces the writer's bias in a deliberate attempt to mislead or misrepresent.

Computer Applications

Computers are now available to students at most colleges and universities. Spreadsheets, such as Microsoft Excel, and statistical software packages, such as MINITAB, are available in most computer labs. The Microsoft Excel package is bundled with many home computers. In this text we use both Excel and MINITAB for the applications. We also use an Excel add-in called MegaStat. This add-in gives Excel the capability to produce additional statistical reports.

    The following example shows the application of computers in statistical analysis. In Chapters 2, 3, and 4 we illustrate methods for summarizing and describing data. An example used in those chapters refers to the price reported in thousands of dollars of 80 vehicles sold last month at Whitner Autoplex. The following Excel output reveals, among other things, that (1) 80 vehicles were sold last month, (2) the mean (average) selling price was $23,218, and (3) the selling prices ranged from a minimum of $15,546 to a maximum of $35,925.

	A	B	C	D	E	F	G	H
	Price	Price($000)	Age	Type		*Price($000)*		
1								
2	23197	23.197	46	0				
3	23372	23.372	48	0		Mean	23.218	
4	20454	20.454	40	1		Standard Error	0.487	
5	23591	23.591	40	0		Median	22.831	
6	26651	26.651	46	1		Mode	20.642	
7	27453	27.453	37	1		Standard Deviation	4.354	
8	17266	17.266	32	1		Sample Variance	18.961	
9	18021	18.021	29	1		Kurtosis	0.543	
10	28683	28.683	38	1		Skewness	0.727	
11	30872	30.872	43	0		Range	20.379	
12	19587	19.587	32	0		Minimum	15.546	
13	23169	23.169	47	0		Maximum	35.925	
14	35851	35.851	56	0		Sum	1857.453	
15	19251	19.251	42	1		Count	80.000	
16	20047	20.047	28	1				

The following output is from the MINITAB system. It contains much of the same information.

Had we used a calculator to arrive at these measures and others needed to fully analyze the selling prices, hours of calculation would have been required. The likelihood of an error in arithmetic is high when a large number of values are concerned. On the other hand, statistical software packages and spreadsheets can provide accurate information in seconds.

At the option of your instructor, and depending on the software system available, we urge you to apply a computer package to the exercises in the **Data Set Exercises** section in each chapter. It will relieve you of the tedious calculations and allow you to concentrate on data analysis.

Chapter Summary

I. Statistics is the science of collecting, organizing, presenting, analyzing, and interpreting data to assist in making more effective decisions.

II. There are two types of statistics.
   A. Descriptive statistics are procedures used to organize and summarize data.
   B. Inferential statistics involve taking a sample from a population and making estimates about a population based on the sample results.
      1. A population is an entire set of individuals or objects of interest or the measurements obtained from all individuals or objects of interest.
      2. A sample is a part of the population.

III. There are two types of variables.
   A. A qualitative variable is categorical or nonnumeric.
      1. Usually we are interested in the number or percent of the observations in each category.
      2. Qualitative data are usually summarized in graphs and bar charts.
   B. There are two types of quantitative variables and they are usually reported numerically.
      1. Discrete variables can assume only certain values, and there are usually gaps between values.
      2. A continuous variable can assume any value within a specified range.

IV. There are four levels of measurement.
   A. With the nominal level, the data are sorted into categories with no particular order to the categories.
   B. The ordinal level of measurement presumes that one classification is ranked higher than another.
   C. The interval level of measurement has the ranking characteristic of the ordinal level of measurement plus the characteristic that the distance between values is a constant size.
   D. The ratio level of measurement has all the characteristics of the interval level, plus there is a 0 point and the ratio of two values is meaningful.

Chapter Exercises

connect™

5. Explain the difference between qualitative and quantitative variables. Give an example of qualitative and quantitative variables.

6. Explain the difference between a sample and a population.

7. Explain the difference between a discrete and a continuous variable. Give an example of each not included in the text.

8. For the following questions, would you collect information using a sample or a population? Why?
   a. Statistics 201 is a course taught at a university. Professor A. Verage has taught nearly 1,500 students in the course over the past 5 years. You would like to know the average grade for the course.
   b. As part of a research project, you need to report the average profitability of the number one corporation in the Fortune 500 for the past 10 years.
   c. You are looking forward to graduation and your first job as a salesperson for one of five large pharmaceutical corporations. Planning for your interviews, you will need to know about each company's mission, profitability, products, and markets.
   d. You are shopping for a new MP3 music player such as the Apple iPod. The manufacturers advertise the number of music tracks that can be stored in the memory. Usually, the advertisers assume relatively short, popular music to estimate the number of tracks that can be stored. You, however, like Broadway musical tunes and they are much longer. You would like to estimate how many Broadway tunes will fit on your MP3 player.

9. Exits along interstate highways were formerly numbered successively from the western or southern edge of a state. However, the Department of Transportation has recently changed most of them to agree with the numbers on the mile markers along the highway.

   a. What level of measurement were data on the consecutive exit numbers?
   b. What level of measurement are data on the milepost numbers?
   c. Discuss the advantages of the newer system.

10. A review solicits a large number of college undergraduates for information on the following variables: the name of their cell phone provider (AT&T, Verizon, and so on), the numbers of minutes used last month (200, 400, for example), and their satisfaction with the service (Terrible, Adequate, Excellent, and so forth.). What is the data scale for each of these three variables?

11. Assume you have records of the daily sales receipts from the Gap store at Ridgedale Mall. Describe a condition in which this information could be considered a sample. Illustrate a second situation in which is same data would be regarded as a population.

12. Utilize the concepts of sample and population to describe how a presidential election is unlike an "exit" poll of the electorate.

13. Place these variables in the following classification tables. For each table, summarize your observations and evaluate if the results are generally true. For example, salary is reported as a continuous quantitative variable. It is also a continuous ratio scaled variable.

   a. Salary
   b. Gender
   c. Sales volume of MP3 players
   d. Soft drink preference
   e. Temperature
   f. SAT scores
   g. Student rank in class
   h. Rating of a finance professor
   i. Number of home computers

	Discrete Variable	**Continuous Variable**
Qualitative		
Quantitative		a. Salary

	Discrete	**Continuous**
Nominal		
Ordinal		
Interval		
Ratio		a. Salary

14. Using data from such publications as the *Statistical Abstract of the United States, The World Almanac, Forbes,* or your local newspaper, give examples of the nominal, ordinal, interval, and ratio levels of measurement.

15. The Struthers Wells Corporation employs more than 10,000 white collar workers in its sales offices and manufacturing facilities in the United States, Europe, and Asia. A sample of 300 of these workers revealed 120 would accept a transfer to a location outside the United States. On the basis of these findings, write a brief memo to Ms. Wanda Carter, Vice President of Human Services, regarding all white collar workers in the firm and their willingness to relocate.

16. AVX Stereo Equipment, Inc., recently began a "no-hassles" return policy. A sample of 500 customers who had recently returned items showed 400 thought the policy was fair, 32 thought it took too long to complete the transaction, and the rest had no opinion. On the basis of this information, make an inference about customer reaction to the new policy.

17. The table below reports the number of cars and light-duty trucks sold by the six largest automakers in January 2006 and in 2007.

	Units	
Company	**2007**	**2006**
General Motors	244,614	293,302
Toyota	175,850	160,594
Chrysler	173,407	168,030
Ford Motor	165,668	204,528
Honda	100,790	98,428
Nissan	82,644	75,890

  a. Compare the total sales in the two months. What would you conclude? Has there been an increase or a decrease in sales?
  b. Compare the percent change in sales for the six companies. Has there been a change in the size of the market or did one company gain sales at the expense of another?

18. The following chart depicts the average amounts spent by consumers on holiday gifts.

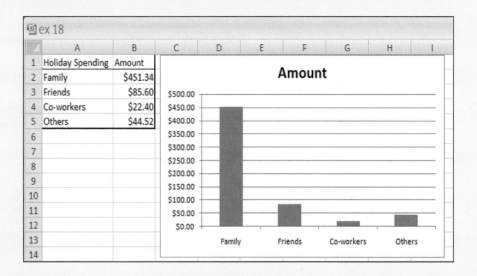

Write a brief report summarizing the amounts spent during the holidays. Be sure to include the total amount spent, and the percent spent by each group.

19. The following chart depicts the earnings in billions of dollars for ExxonMobil for the period 2003 to 2007. Write a brief report discussing earnings at ExxonMobil during the period.

Did earnings increase or decrease over the period? Provide evidence to support your answer.

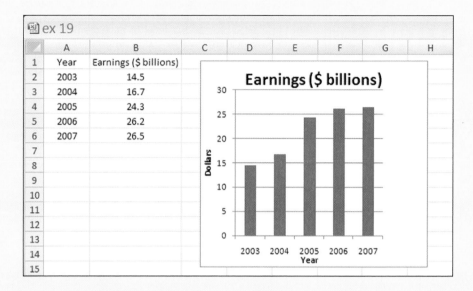

Data Set Exercises

20. Refer to the Real Estate data at the back of the text, which report information on homes sold in the Phoenix, Arizona, area last year. Consider the following variables: selling price, number of bedrooms, township, and distance from the center of the city.
   a. Which of the variables are qualitative and which are quantitative?
   b. Determine the level of measurement for each of the variables.
21. Refer to the Baseball 2008 data, which report information on the 30 Major League Baseball teams for the 2008 season. Consider the following variables: number of wins, team salary, season attendance, whether the team played its home games on a grass field or an artificial surface, and the number of home runs hit.
   a. Which of these variables are quantitative and which are qualitative?
   b. Determine the level of measurement for each of the variables.
22. Refer to the Wage data, which report information on annual wages for a sample of 100 workers. Also included are variables relating to industry, years of education, and gender for each worker.
   a. Which of the 12 variables are qualitative and which are quantitative?
   b. Determine the level of measurement for each variable.

Practice Test

There is a practice test at the end of each chapter. The tests are in two parts. The first part contains several objective questions, usually in a fill-in-the-blank format. The second part is problems. In most cases it should take 30 to 45 minutes to complete the test. The problems will require a calculator. Check your answers against those provided in the Answer Section in the back of the book.

Part I Objective

1. The science of collecting, organizing, presenting, analyzing, and interpreting data to assist in making more effective decisions is referred to as _____ .
2. Methods of organizing, summarizing, and presenting data in an enlightening way are called _____ .

3. The methods used to estimate a value of a population on the basis of a sample are called _____ .

4. A portion, or part, of the group of interest is referred to as a _____ .

5. The entire set of individuals or objects of interest or the measurements obtained from all individuals or objects of interest is known as a _____ .

6. With the _____ level of measurement, the data are sorted into categories with no particular order to the categories.

7. The _____ level of measurement has a significant zero point.

8. The _____ level of measurement presumes that one classification is ranked higher than another.

9. The _____ level of measurement has the characteristic that the distance between values is a constant size.

10. Is the number of bedrooms in a house a discrete or continuous variable? _____

11. The jersey numbers on baseball uniforms is an example of the _____ level of measurement.

12. What level of measurement is used when students are classified by eye color? _____

Part II Problems

1. Thirty million pounds of snack food were eaten during a recent Super Bowl. The chart below describes this information.

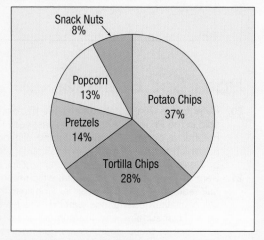

a. What is the name for this type of graph?

b. Estimate, in millions of pounds, the amount of potato chips eaten during the game.

c. Approximate the ratio of potato chips consumed to popcorn consumed (twice as much, half as much, three times as much, etc.).

d. What percent of the total consists of potato chips and tortilla chips?

2. There are 14 freshmen, 18 sophomores, 10 juniors' and 6 seniors in an introductory psychology class. Prepare a suitable graph to visually display this data.

Chapter 1   Answers to Self-Review

1–1 **a.** On the basis of the sample of 1,960 consumers, we estimate that, if it is marketed, 60 percent of all consumers will purchase the chicken dinner $(1,176/1,960) \times 100 = 60$ percent.

b. Inferential statistics, because a sample was used to draw a conclusion about how all consumers in the population would react if the chicken dinner were marketed.

1–2 **a.** Age is a ratio-scale variable. A 40-year-old is twice as old as someone 20 years old.

b. Nominal scale. We could arrange the states in any order.

Describing Data:

Frequency Tables, Frequency
Distributions, and Graphic Presentation

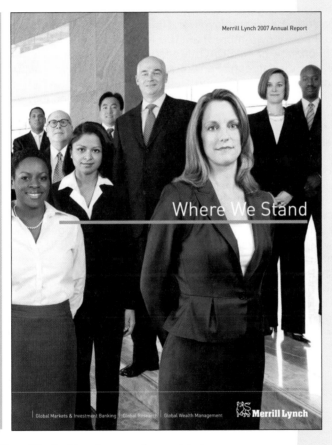

Merrill Lynch, a subsidiary of Bank of America, recently completed a
study of the amounts (in dollars) for a sample of online investment
portfolios. Seventy clients were a part of the study. Draw a histogram
depicting the amounts. (See Exercise 43 and LO4.)

Learning Objectives

When you have completed
this chapter you will be
able to:

LO1 Organize qualitative
data into a *frequency table*.

LO2 Present a frequency
table as a *bar chart* or a *pie
chart*.

LO3 Organize quantitative
data into a *frequency
distribution*.

LO4 Present a frequency
distribution for quantitative
data using *histograms, frequency polygons*, and *cumulative frequency polygons*.

Introduction

The highly competitive automotive retailing business has changed significantly over the past decade, due in part to consolidation by large, publicly owned deal-

ership groups. Traditionally, a local family owned and operated the community dealership, which might have included one or two manufacturers, like Buick and GMC Trucks or Chrysler and the popular Jeep line. Recently, however, skillfully managed and well-financed companies have been acquiring local dealerships across large regions of the country. As these groups acquire the local dealerships, they often bring standard selling practices, common software and hardware technology platforms, and management reporting techniques. The goal is to provide an improved buying experience for the consumer, while increasing the profitability of the larger dealership organization. In many cases, in addition to reaping the financial benefits of selling the dealership, the family is asked to continue running the dealership on a daily basis. Today, it is common for these megadealerships to employ over 10,000 people, generate several billion dollars in annual sales, own more than 100 franchises, and be traded on the New York Stock Exchange or NASDAQ. Megadealerships include AutoNation (ticker symbol AN and the largest), Penske Auto Group (PAG and second largest), Asbury Automotive Group (ABG), and Hendrick Auto Group (which is privately held).

The consolidation has not come without challenges. With the acquisition of dealerships across the country, AutoUSA, one of the new megadealerships, now sells the inexpensive Korean import brands Kia and Hyundai, the high-line BMW and Mercedes Benz sedans, and a full line of Ford and Chevrolet cars and trucks.

Ms. Kathryn Ball is a member of the senior management team at AutoUSA. She is responsible for tracking and analyzing vehicle selling prices for AutoUSA. Kathryn would like to summarize vehicle selling prices with charts and graphs that she could review monthly. From these tables and charts, she wants to know the typical selling price as well as the lowest and highest prices. She is also interested in describing the demographics of the buyers. What are their ages? How many vehicles do they own? Do they want to buy or lease the vehicle?

Whitner Autoplex, which is located in Raytown, Missouri, is one of the AutoUSA dealerships. Whitner Autoplex includes Chevrolet, GMC, and Buick franchises as well as a BMW store. General Motors is actively working with its dealer body to combine at one location several of its franchises, such as Chevrolet and Buick, or Cadillac. Combining franchises improves the floor traffic and a dealership has product offerings for all demographics. BMW, with its premium brand and image, wants to move away from calling its locations dealerships, instead calling them stores. Instead of offering a traditional automobile dealership experience, BMW wants to be more like Nordstrom, a U.S. retail store selling fine quality apparel. Like Nordstrom, BMW wants to offer customers superior service, great products, and a unique personalized shopping experience.

Excel

	A	B	C	D
1	Price	Price($000)	Age	Type
2	23197	23.197	46	0
3	23372	23.372	48	0
4	20454	20.454	40	1
5	23591	23.591	40	0
6	26651	26.651	46	1
7	27453	27.453	37	1
8	17266	17.266	32	1
9	18021	18.021	29	1
10	28683	28.683	38	1
11	30872	30.872	43	0
12	19587	19.587	32	0
13	23169	23.169	47	0
14	35851	35.851	56	0
15	19251	19.251	42	1

Whitner

Ms. Ball decided to collect data on three variables at Whitner Autoplex: selling price ($000), buyer's age, and car type (domestic, coded as 1, or foreign, coded as 0). A portion of the data set is shown in the adjacent output. The entire data set is available on the student CD (included with the book), at the McGraw-Hill website, and in Appendix A.4 at the end of the text.

Constructing a Frequency Table

LO1 Organize qualitative data into a frequency table.

Recall from Chapter 1 that techniques used to describe a set of data are called descriptive statistics. To put it another way, descriptive statistics organize data to show the general pattern of the data and where values tend to concentrate and to expose extreme or unusual data values. The first procedure we discuss to organize and summarize a set of data is a **frequency table.**

> **FREQUENCY TABLE** A grouping of qualitative data into mutually exclusive classes showing the number of observations in each class.

In Chapter 1, we distinguished between qualitative and quantitative variables. To review, a qualitative variable is categorical or nonnumeric, that is, it can only be classified into distinct categories. There is no particular order to these categories. Examples of qualitative data include political affiliation (Republican, Democrat, Independent), state of birth (Alabama, . . . , Wyoming), and method of payment for a purchase at Barnes and Noble (cash, check, or charge). On the other hand, quantitative variables are numerical in nature. Examples of quantitative data relating to college students include the price of their textbooks, their age, and hours they spend studying each week.

In the Whitner Autoplex data, Ms. Ball observed three variables for each vehicle sale: selling price, age of the buyer, and car type. Selling price and age are quantitative variables, but vehicle type is a qualitative measure with two values, domestic or foreign. Suppose that Ms. Ball wanted to summarize last month's sales using vehicle type.

To summarize this qualitative data, we classify the vehicles as either domestic (coded as 1) or foreign (coded as 0) and count the number in each class. We use vehicle type to develop a frequency table with two mutually exclusive (distinctive) classes. This means that a particular vehicle cannot belong to both classes. The vehicle is either domestic or foreign and can never be both domestic and foreign. This frequency table is shown in Table 2–1. The number of observations in each class is called the **class frequency.** So the class frequency for domestic vehicles sold is 50.

TABLE 2–1 Frequency Table for Vehicles Sold at Whitner Autoplex Last Month

Car Type	Number of Cars
Domestic	50
Foreign	30

Relative Class Frequencies

You can convert class frequencies to **relative class frequencies** to show the fraction of the total number of observations in each class. So, a relative frequency captures the relationship between a class total and the total number of observations. In the vehicle sales example, we may want to know the percent of total cars sold that were domestic or foreign.

To convert a frequency distribution to a *relative* frequency distribution, each of the class frequencies is divided by the total number of observations. For example, 0.625, found by 50 divided by 80, is the fraction of domestic vehicles sold last month. The relative frequency distribution is shown in Table 2–2.

TABLE 2–2 Relative Frequency Table of Vehicles Sold by Type at Whitner Autoplex Last Month

Vehicle Type	Number Sold	Relative Frequency
Domestic	50	0.625
Foreign	30	0.375
Total	80	1.000

Graphic Presentation of Qualitative Data

LO2 Present a frequency table as a bar chart or a pie chart.

The most common device to present a qualitative variable in graphic form is a **bar chart.** In most cases the horizontal axis shows the variable of interest and the vertical axis the amount, number, or fraction of each of the possible outcomes. A distinguishing characteristic of a bar chart is the distance or gap between the bars. That is, because the variable of interest is qualitative, the bars are not adjacent to each other. Thus, a bar chart graphically describes a frequency table using a series of uniformly wide rectangles, where the height of each rectangle is the class frequency.

> **BAR CHART** A graph in which the classes are reported on the horizontal axis and the class frequencies on the vertical axis. The class frequencies are proportional to the heights of the bars.

We use the Whitner Autoplex data as an example (Chart 2–1). The variable of interest is the vehicle type and the number of each type sold is the class frequency. We scale the vehicle type (domestic or foreign) on the horizontal axis and the number of each item on the vertical axis. The height of the bars, or rectangles, corresponds to the number of vehicles of each type sold. So for the number of foreign vehicles sold the height of the bar is 30. The order of foreign or domestic on the *X*-axis does not matter because the values of car type are qualitative.

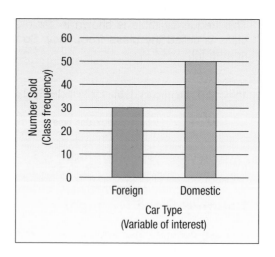

CHART 2–1 Vehicle Sold by Type Last Month at Whitner Autoplex

Another useful type of chart for depicting qualitative information is a **pie chart.**

> **PIE CHART** A chart that shows the proportion or percent that each class represents of the total number of frequencies.

We explain the details of constructing a pie chart using the information in Table 2–3, which shows a breakdown of the expenses for the Ohio State Lottery in 2007.

TABLE 2–3 Ohio State Lottery Expenses in 2007

Use of Sales	Amount ($ million)	Percent of Share
Prizes	1,311.1	65
Education	464.3	23
Bonuses	139.8	7
Expenses	109.8	5
Total	2,025.0	100

The first step to develop a pie chart is to record the percentages 0, 5, 10, 15, and so on evenly around the circumference of a circle (see Chart 2–2). To plot the 65 percent share awarded for prizes, draw a line from the center of the circle to 0 and another line from the center of the circle to 65 percent. The area in this "slice" represents the lottery proceeds that were awarded in prizes. Next, add the 65 percent of expenses awarded in prizes to the 23 percent payments to education; the result is 88 percent. Draw a line from the center of the circle to 88 percent, so the area between 65 percent and 88 percent depicts the payments made to education. Continuing, add the 7 percent for bonuses, which gives us a total of 95 percent. Draw a line from the center of the circle to 95, so the "slice" between 88 percent and 95 percent represents the payment of bonuses. The remainder, 5 percent, is for operating expenses.

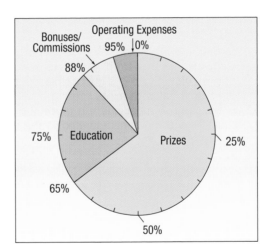

CHART 2–2 Pie Chart of Ohio Lottery Expenses in 2007

Because each slice of the pie represents the relative share of each component, we can easily compare them:

- The largest expense of the Ohio Lottery is for prizes.
- About one-fourth of the proceeds are transferred to education.
- Operating expenses account for only 5 percent of the proceeds.

The Excel system will develop a pie chart. See the following chart for the information in Table 2–3.

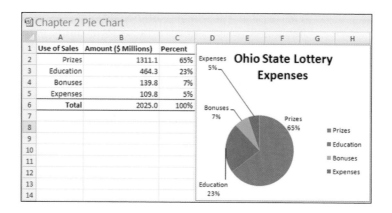

	A	B	C	D	E	F	G	H
	Chapter 2 Pie Chart							
1	Use of Sales	Amount ($ Millions)	Percent					
2	Prizes	1311.1	65%					
3	Education	464.3	23%					
4	Bonuses	139.8	7%					
5	Expenses	109.8	5%					
6	Total	2025.0	100%					

Ohio State Lottery Expenses

Example

SkiLodges.com is test marketing its new website and is interested in how easy its Web page design is to navigate. It randomly selected 200 regular Internet users and asked them to perform a search task on the Web page. Each person was asked to rate the relative ease of navigation as poor, good, excellent, or awesome. The results are shown in the following table:

Awesome	102
Excellent	58
Good	30
Poor	10

1. What type of measurement scale is used for ease of navigation?
2. Draw a bar chart for the survey results.
3. Draw a pie chart for the survey results.

Solution

The data are measured on an ordinal scale. That is, the scale is ranked in relative ease when moving from "poor" to "awesome." Also, the interval between each rating is unknown so it is impossible, for example, to conclude that a rating of good is twice the value of a poor rating.

We can use a bar chart to graph the data. The vertical scale shows the relative frequency and the horizontal shows the values of the ease of navigation scale.

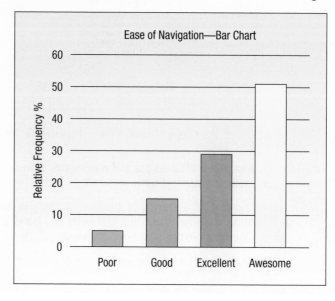

A pie chart can also be used to graph this data. The pie chart emphasizes the fact the more than half of the respondents rate the relative ease of using the website awesome.

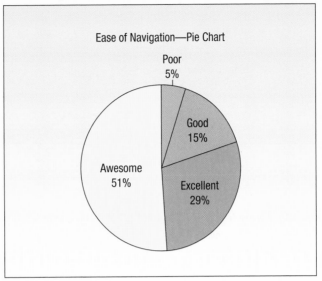

Ease of Navigation—Pie Chart

Poor 5%

Good 15%

Excellent 29%

Awesome 51%

Self-Review 2–1   *The answers are at the end of the chapter.*

DeCenzo Specialty Food and Beverage Company has been serving a cola drink with an additional flavoring, Cola-Plus, that is very popular among its customers. The company is interested in customer preferences for Cola-Plus versus Coca-Cola, Pepsi, and a lemon-lime beverage. They ask 100 randomly sampled customers to take a taste test and select the beverage they preferred most. The results are shown in the following table:

Beverage	Number
Cola-Plus	40
Coca-Cola	25
Pepsi	20
Lemon-Lime	15
Total	100

(a) Is the data qualitative or quantitative? Why?
(b) What is the table called? What does it show?
(c) Develop a bar chart to depict the information.
(d) Develop a pie chart using the relative frequencies.

Exercises

The answers to the odd-numbered exercises are at the end of the book.

1. Refer to your local paper, *USA Today,* or the Internet and find two examples of qualitative variables.
2. In a marketing study, 100 consumers were asked to select the best digital music player from the iPod, the iRiver, and the Magic Star MP3. To summarize the consumer responses with a frequency table, how many classes would the frequency table have?
3. A total of 1,000 residents in Minnesota were asked which season they preferred. The results were 100 liked winter best, 300 liked spring, 400 liked summer, and 200 liked fall. If the data were summarized in a frequency table, how many classes would be used? What would be the relative frequencies for each class?

4. Two thousand frequent Midwestern business travelers are asked which Midwest city they prefer: Indianapolis, Saint Louis, Chicago, or Milwaukee. The results were 100 liked Indianapolis best, 450 liked Saint Louis, 1,300 liked Chicago, and the remainder preferred Milwaukee. Develop a frequency table and a relative frequency table to summarize this information.

5. Wellstone, Inc., produces and markets replacement covers for cell phones in a variety of colors. The company would like to allocate its production plans to five different colors: bright white, metallic black, magnetic lime, tangerine orange, and fusion red. The company set up a kiosk in the Mall of America for several hours and asked randomly selected people which cover color was their favorite. The results follow:

Bright white	130
Metallic black	104
Magnetic lime	325
Tangerine orange	455
Fusion red	286

    a. What is the table called?
    b. Draw a bar chart for the table.
    c. Draw a pie chart.
    d. If Wellstone, Inc., plans to produce 1 million cell phone covers, how many of each color should it produce?

6. A small business consultant is investigating the performance of several companies. The fourth quarter sales for last year (in thousands of dollars) for the selected companies were:

Corporation	Fourth-Quarter Sales ($ thousands)
Hoden Building Products	$ 1,645.2
J & R Printing, Inc.	4,757.0
Long Bay Concrete Construction	8,913.0
Mancell Electric and Plumbing	627.1
Maxwell Heating and Air Conditioning	24,612.0
Mizelle Roofing & Sheet Metals	191.9

The consultant wants to include a chart in his report comparing the sales of the six companies. Use a bar chart to compare the fourth-quarter sales of these corporations and write a brief report summarizing the bar chart.

Constructing Frequency Distributions: Quantitative Data

In Chapter 1 and earlier in this chapter, we distinguished between qualitative and quantitative data. In the previous section using the Whitner Autoplex data, we summarized the qualitative variable, vehicle type, using a frequency table, a relative frequency table, a bar chart, and a pie chart.

LO3 Organize quantitative data into a frequency distribution.

The Whitner Autoplex data also includes two quantitative variables: selling price and age of the buyer. Suppose Ms. Ball wants to summarize last month's sales using selling price. We can describe selling price using a **frequency distribution.**

> **FREQUENCY DISTRIBUTION** A grouping of data into mutually exclusive classes showing the number of observations in each class.

How do we develop a frequency distribution? The first step is to tally the data into a table that shows the classes and the number of observations in each class. The steps in constructing a frequency distribution are best described by an example. Remember, our goal is to construct tables, charts, and graphs that will quickly reveal the concentration and shape of the data.

Example

We return to the situation where Ms. Kathryn Ball of AutoUSA wants tables, charts, and graphs to show the typical selling price on various dealer lots. Table 2–4 reports only the price of the 80 vehicles sold last month at Whitner Autoplex. What is the *typical* selling price? What is the *highest* selling price? What is the *lowest* selling price? Around what value do the selling prices tend to cluster?

TABLE 2–4 Prices of Vehicles Sold Last Month at Whitner Autoplex

Lowest

$23,197	$23,372	$20,454	$23,591	$26,651	$27,453	$17,266
18,021	28,683	30,872	19,587	23,169	35,851	19,251
20,047	24,285	24,324	24,609	28,670	15,546	15,935
19,873	25,251	25,277	28,034	24,533	27,443	19,889
20,004	17,357	20,155	19,688	23,657	26,613	20,895
20,203	23,765	25,783	26,661	32,277	20,642	21,981
24,052	25,799	15,794	18,263	35,925	17,399	17,968
20,356	21,442	21,722	19,331	22,817	19,766	20,633
20,962	22,845	26,285	27,896	29,076	32,492	18,890
21,740	22,374	24,571	25,449	28,337	20,642	23,613
24,220	30,655	22,442	17,891	20,818	26,237	20,445
21,556	21,639	24,296				

Highest

Solution

We refer to the unorganized information in Table 2–4 as **raw data** or **ungrouped data.** With a little searching, we can find the lowest selling price ($15,546) and the highest selling price ($35,925), but that is about all. It is difficult to determine a typical selling price. It is also difficult to visualize where the selling prices tend to cluster. The raw data are more easily interpreted if organized into a frequency distribution.

The steps for organizing data into a frequency distribution.

Step 1: Decide on the number of classes. The goal is to use just enough groupings or **classes** to reveal the shape of the distribution. Some judgment is needed here. Too many classes or too few classes might not reveal the basic shape of the data set. In the vehicle selling price example, three classes would not give much insight into the pattern of the data (see Table 2–5).

TABLE 2–5 An Example of Too Few Classes

Vehicle Selling Price ($)	Number of Vehicles
15,000 up to 24,000	48
24,000 up to 33,000	30
33,000 up to 42,000	2
Total	80

A useful recipe to determine the number of classes (*k*) is the "2 to the *k* rule." This guide suggests you select the smallest number (*k*) for the number of classes such that 2^k (in words, 2 raised to the power of *k*) is greater than the number of observations (*n*).

In the Whitner Autoplex example, 80 vehicles were sold. So *n* = 80. If we try *k* = 6, which means we would use 6 classes, then $2^6 = 64$, somewhat less than 80. Hence, 6 is not enough classes. If we let *k* = 7, then $2^7 = 128$, which is greater than 80. So the recommended number of classes is 7.

Step 2: Determine the class interval or width. Generally the **class interval** or **width** should be the same for all classes. The classes all taken together must cover at least the distance from the lowest value in the data up to the highest value. Expressing these words in a formula:

$$i \geq \frac{H - L}{k}$$

where i is the class interval, H is the highest observed value, L is the lowest observed value, and k is the number of classes.

In the Whitner Autoplex case, the lowest value is \$15,546 and the highest value is \$35,925. If we need 7 classes, the interval should be at least (\$35,925 − \$15,546)/7 = \$2,911. In practice this interval size is usually rounded up to some convenient number, such as a multiple of 10 or 100. The value of \$3,000 might readily be used in this case.

Unequal class intervals present problems in graphically portraying the distribution and in doing some of the computations, which we will see in later chapters. Unequal class intervals, however, may be necessary in certain situations to avoid a large number of empty, or almost empty, classes. Such is the case in Table 2–6. The Internal Revenue Service used unequal-sized class intervals to report the adjusted gross income on individual tax returns. Had they used an equal-sized interval of, say, \$1,000, more than 1,000 classes would have been required to describe all the incomes. A frequency distribution with 1,000 classes would be difficult to interpret. In this case the distribution is easier to understand in spite of the unequal classes. Note also that the number of income tax returns or "frequencies" is reported in thousands in this particular table. This also makes the information easier to understand.

TABLE 2–6 Adjusted Gross Income for Individuals Filing Income Tax Returns

Adjusted Gross Income			Number of Returns (in thousands)
No adjusted gross income			178.2
$ 1 up to	$	5,000	1,204.6
5,000 up to		10,000	2,595.5
10,000 up to		15,000	3,142.0
15,000 up to		20,000	3,191.7
20,000 up to		25,000	2,501.4
25,000 up to		30,000	1,901.6
30,000 up to		40,000	2,502.3
40,000 up to		50,000	1,426.8
50,000 up to		75,000	1,476.3
75,000 up to		100,000	338.8
100,000 up to		200,000	223.3
200,000 up to		500,000	55.2
500,000 up to		1,000,000	12.0
1,000,000 up to		2,000,000	5.1
2,000,000 up to		10,000,000	3.4
10,000,000 or more			0.6

Step 3: Set the individual class limits. State clear class limits so you can put each observation into only one category. This means you must avoid overlapping or unclear class limits. For example, classes such as "\$1,300–\$1,400" and "\$1,400–\$1,500" should not be used because it is not clear whether the value \$1,400 is in the first or second class. Classes stated as "\$1,300–\$1,400" and "\$1,500–\$1,600" are frequently used, but may also be confusing without the additional common convention of rounding all data at

or above $1,450 up to the second class and data below $1,450 down to the first class. In this text we will generally use the format $1,300 up to $1,400 and $1,400 up to $1,500 and so on. With this format it is clear that $1,399 goes into the first class and $1,400 in the second.

Because we round the class interval up to get a convenient class size, we cover a larger than necessary range. For example, 7 classes of width $3,000 in the Whitner Autoplex case result in a range of $7(\$3,000) = \$21,000$. The actual range is $20,379, found by $35,925 − $15,546. Comparing that value to $21,000 we have an excess of $621. Because we need to cover only the distance $(H - L)$, it is natural to put approximately equal amounts of the excess in each of the two tails. Of course, we should also select convenient class limits. A guideline is to make the lower limit of the first class a multiple of the class interval. Sometimes this is not possible, but the lower limit should at least be rounded. So here are the classes we could use for this data.

$15,000 up to $18,000
18,000 up to 21,000
21,000 up to 24,000
24,000 up to 27,000
27,000 up to 30,000
30,000 up to 33,000
33,000 up to 36,000

Step 4: Tally the vehicle selling prices into the classes. To begin, the selling price of the first vehicle in Table 2–4 is $23,197. It is tallied in the $21,000 up to $24,000 class. The second selling price in the first column of Table 2–4 is $18,021. It is tallied in the $18,000 up to $21,000 class. The other selling prices are tallied in a similar manner. When all the selling prices are tallied, the table would appear as:

Class	Tallies
$15,000 up to $18,000	ЖІ ІІІ
18,000 up to 21,000	ЖІ ЖІ ЖІ ЖІ ІІІ
21,000 up to 24,000	ЖІ ЖІ ЖІ ІІ
24,000 up to 27,000	ЖІ ЖІ ЖІ ІІІ
27,000 up to 30,000	ЖІ ІІІ
30,000 up to 33,000	ІІІІ
33,000 up to 36,000	ІІ

Step 5: Count the number of items in each class. The number of observations in each class is called the **class frequency.** In the $15,000 up to $18,000 class there are 8 observations, and in the $18,000 up to $21,000 class there are 23 observations. Therefore, the class frequency in the first class is 8 and the class frequency in the second class is 23. There is a total of 80 observations or frequencies in the entire set of data.

Often it is useful to express the data in thousands, or some convenient units, rather than the actual data. Table 2–7, for example, reports the vehicle selling prices in thousands of dollars, rather than dollars.

Now that we have organized the data into a frequency distribution, we can summarize the pattern in the selling prices of the vehicles for the AutoUSA lot of Whitner Autoplex in Raytown, Missouri. Observe the following:

1. The selling prices ranged from about $15,000 up to about $36,000.
2. The selling prices are concentrated between $18,000 and $27,000. A total of 58, or 72.5 percent, of the vehicles sold within this range.

TABLE 2–7 Frequency Distribution of Selling Prices at Whitner Autoplex Last Month

Selling Prices ($ thousands)	Frequency
15 up to 18	8
18 up to 21	23
21 up to 24	17
24 up to 27	18
27 up to 30	8
30 up to 33	4
33 up to 36	2
Total	80

3. The largest concentration, or highest frequency, is in the $18,000 up to $21,000 class. The middle of this class is $19,500. So we say that a typical selling price is $19,500.

By presenting this information to Ms. Ball, we give her a clear picture of the distribution of selling prices for last month.

We admit that arranging the information on selling prices into a frequency distribution does result in the loss of some detailed information. That is, by organizing the data into a frequency distribution, we cannot pinpoint the exact selling price, such as $23,197 or $26,237. Further, we cannot tell that the actual selling price for the least expensive vehicle was $15,546 and for the most expensive $35,925. However, the lower limit of the first class and the upper limit of the largest class convey essentially the same meaning. Likely, Ms. Ball will make the same judgment if she knows the lowest price is about $15,000 that she will if she knows the exact price is $15,546. The advantages of condensing the data into a more understandable and organized form more than offset this disadvantage.

Self-Review 2–2

The commissions earned for the first quarter of last year by the 11 members of the sales staff at Master Chemical Company are:

$1,650	$1,475	$1,510	$1,670	$1,595	$1,760	$1,540	$1,495	$1,590	$1,625	$1,510

(a) What are the values such as $1,650 and $1,475 called?
(b) Using $1,400 up to $1,500 as the first class, $1,500 up to $1,600 as the second class, and so forth, organize the quarterly commissions into a frequency distribution.
(c) What are the numbers in the right column of your frequency distribution called?
(d) Describe the distribution of quarterly commissions, based on the frequency distribution. What is the largest concentration of commissions earned? What is the smallest, and the largest? What is the typical amount earned?

Class Intervals and Class Midpoints

We will use two other terms frequently: **class midpoint** and **class interval.** The midpoint is halfway between the lower limits of two consecutive classes. It is computed by adding the lower limits of consecutive classes and dividing the result by 2. Referring to Table 2–7, the lower class limit for the first class is $15,000 and the next limit is $18,000. The class midpoint is $16,500, found by ($15,000 + $18,000)/2. The midpoint of $16,500 best represents, or is typical of, the selling price of the vehicles in that class.

To determine the class interval, subtract the lower limit of the class from the lower limit of the next class. The class interval of the vehicle selling price data is

$3,000, which we find by subtracting the lower limit of the first class, $15,000, from the lower limit of the next class; that is, $18,000 − $15,000 = $3,000. You can also determine the class interval by finding the difference between consecutive mid-points. The midpoint of the first class is $16,500 and the midpoint of the second class is $19,500. The difference is $3,000.

A Software Example

As we mentioned in Chapter 1, there are many software packages that perform statistical calculations. Throughout this text we will show the output from Microsoft Excel; from MegaStat, which is an add-in to Microsoft Excel; and from MINITAB. The commands necessary to generate the outputs are given in the **Software Commands** section at the end of each chapter.

    The following is a frequency distribution, produced by MegaStat, showing the prices of the 80 vehicles sold last month at the Whitner Autoplex lot in Raytown, Missouri. The form of the output is somewhat different than the frequency distribution of Table 2–7, but the overall conclusions are the same.

Whitner Distribution

Frequency Distribution - Quantitative

Price (lower)		(upper)	midpoint	width	frequency	percent	cumulative frequency	cumulative percent
15,000	<	18,000	16,500	3,000	8	10.0	8	10.0
18,000	<	21,000	19,500	3,000	23	28.8	31	38.8
21,000	<	24,000	22,500	3,000	17	21.3	48	60.0
24,000	<	27,000	25,500	3,000	18	22.5	66	82.5
27,000	<	30,000	28,500	3,000	8	10.0	74	92.5
30,000	<	33,000	31,500	3,000	4	5.0	78	97.5
33,000	<	36,000	34,500	3,000	2	2.5	80	100.0
					80	100.0		

Self-Review 2–3

Barry Bonds of the San Francisco Giants established a new single season home run record by hitting 73 home runs during the 2001 season. The longest of these home runs traveled 488 feet and the shortest 320 feet. You need to construct a frequency distribution of these home run lengths.
(a) How many classes would you use?
(b) What class interval would you suggest?
(c) What actual classes would you suggest?

Relative Frequency Distribution

A relative frequency distribution converts the frequency to a percent.

It may be desirable as we did earlier with qualitative data to convert class frequencies to relative class frequencies to show the fraction of the total number of observations in each class. In our vehicle sales example, we may want to know what percent of the vehicle prices are in the $21,000 up to $24,000 class. In another study, we may want to know what percent of the employees used 5 up to 10 personal leave days last year.

    To convert a frequency distribution to a *relative* frequency distribution, each of the class frequencies is divided by the total number of observations. From the distribution of vehicle selling prices (Table 2–7, where the selling price is reported in thousands of dollars), the relative frequency for the $15,000 up to $18,000 class is 0.10, found by dividing 8 by 80. That is, the price of 10 percent of the vehicles sold at Whitner Autoplex is between $15,000 and $18,000. The relative frequencies for the remaining classes are shown in Table 2–8.

TABLE 2–8 Relative Frequency Distribution of the Prices of Vehicles Sold Last Month at Whitner Autoplex

Selling Price ($ thousands)	Frequency	Relative Frequency	Found by
15 up to 18	8	0.1000 ◄———	8/80
18 up to 21	23	0.2875	23/80
21 up to 24	17	0.2125	17/80
24 up to 27	18	0.2250	18/80
27 up to 30	8	0.1000	8/80
30 up to 33	4	0.0500	4/80
33 up to 36	2	0.0250	2/80
Total	80	1.0000	

Self-Review 2–4

Refer to Table 2–8, which shows the relative frequency distribution for the vehicles sold last month at Whitner Autoplex.
(a) How many vehicles sold for $18,000 up to $21,000?
(b) What percent of the vehicles sold for a price between $18,000 and $21,000?
(c) What percent of the vehicles sold for $30,000 or more?

Exercises

connect™

7. A set of data consists of 38 observations. How many classes would you recommend for the frequency distribution?
8. A set of data consists of 45 observations between $0 and $29. What size would you recommend for the class interval?
9. A set of data consists of 230 observations between $235 and $567. What class interval would you recommend?
10. A set of data contains 53 observations. The lowest value is 42 and the largest is 129. The data are to be organized into a frequency distribution.
    a. How many classes would you suggest?
    b. What would you suggest as the lower limit of the first class?
11. Wachesaw Manufacturing, Inc., produced the following number of units in the last 16 days.

27	27	27	28	27	25	25	28
26	28	26	28	31	30	26	26

The information is to be organized into a frequency distribution.
    a. How many classes would you recommend?
    b. What class interval would you suggest?
    c. What lower limit would you recommend for the first class?
    d. Organize the information into a frequency distribution and determine the relative frequency distribution.
    e. Comment on the shape of the distribution.
12. The Quick Change Oil Company has a number of outlets in the metropolitan Seattle area. The daily number of oil changes at the Oak Street outlet in the past 20 days are:

65	98	55	62	79	59	51	90	72	56
70	62	66	80	94	79	63	73	71	85

The data are to be organized into a frequency distribution.
a. How many classes would you recommend?
b. What class interval would you suggest?
c. What lower limit would you recommend for the first class?
d. Organize the number of oil changes into a frequency distribution.
e. Comment on the shape of the frequency distribution. Also determine the relative frequency distribution.

13. The manager of the BiLo Supermarket in Mt. Pleasant, Rhode Island, gathered the following information on the number of times a customer visits the store during a month. The responses of 51 customers were:

5	3	3	1	4	4	5	6	4	2	6	6	6	7	1
1	14	1	2	4	4	4	5	6	3	5	3	4	5	6
8	4	7	6	5	9	11	3	12	4	7	6	5	15	1
1	10	8	9	2	12									

a. Starting with 0 as the lower limit of the first class and using a class interval of 3, organize the data into a frequency distribution.
b. Describe the distribution. Where do the data tend to cluster?
c. Convert the distribution to a relative frequency distribution.

14. The food services division of Cedar River Amusement Park, Inc., is studying the amount families who visit the amusement park spend per day on food and drink. A sample of 40 families who visited the park yesterday revealed they spent the following amounts:

$77	$18	$63	$84	$38	$54	$50	$59	$54	$56	$36	$26	$50	$34	$44
41	58	58	53	51	62	43	52	53	63	62	62	65	61	52
60	60	45	66	83	71	63	58	61	71					

a. Organize the data into a frequency distribution, using seven classes and 15 as the lower limit of the first class. What class interval did you select?
b. Where do the data tend to cluster?
c. Describe the distribution.
d. Determine the relative frequency distribution.

Graphic Presentation of a Frequency Distribution

Sales managers, stock analysts, hospital administrators, and other busy executives often need a quick picture of the trends in sales, stock prices, or hospital costs. These trends can often be depicted by the use of charts and graphs. Three charts that will help portray a frequency distribution graphically are the histogram, the frequency polygon, and the cumulative frequency polygon.

Histogram

LO4 Present a frequency distribution for quantitative data using histograms, frequency polygons, and cumulative frequency polygons.

A **histogram** for a frequency distribution based on quantitative data is very similar to the bar chart showing the distribution of qualitative data. The classes are marked on the horizontal axis and the class frequencies on the vertical axis. The class frequencies are represented by the heights of the bars. However, there is one important difference based on the nature of the data. When qualitative data are measured using scales that are continuous, not discrete, the horizontal axis represents all possible values, and the bars are drawn adjacent to each other to show the continuous nature of the data.

HISTOGRAM A graph in which the classes are marked on the horizontal axis and the class frequencies on the vertical axis. The class frequencies are represented by the heights of the bars and the bars are drawn adjacent to each other.

We summarized the selling prices—a continuous variable—of the 80 vehicles sold last month at Whitner Autoplex with a frequency distribution. We construct a histogram to illustrate this frequency distribution.

Example

Below is the frequency distribution.

Selling Prices ($ thousands)	Frequency
15 up to 18	8
18 up to 21	23
21 up to 24	17
24 up to 27	18
27 up to 30	8
30 up to 33	4
33 up to 36	2
Total	80

Construct a histogram. What conclusions can you reach based on the information presented in the histogram?

Solution

The class frequencies are scaled along the vertical axis (*Y*-axis) and either the class limits or the class midpoints along the horizontal axis. To illustrate the construction of the histogram, the first three classes are shown in Chart 2–3.

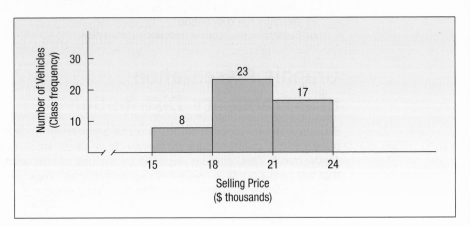

CHART 2–3 Construction of a Histogram

From Chart 2–3 we note that there are eight vehicles in the $15,000 up to $18,000 class. Therefore, the height of the column for that class is 8. There are 23 vehicles in the $18,000 up to $21,000 class. So, logically, the height of that column is 23. The height of the bar represents the number of observations in the class.

This procedure is continued for all classes. The complete histogram is shown in Chart 2–4. Note that there is no space between the bars. This is an important feature of the histogram. Why is this important? Because the variable plotted on the horizontal axis is quantitative and of the interval, or in this case the ratio, scale of measurement. In bar charts, as described previously, the vertical bars are separated.

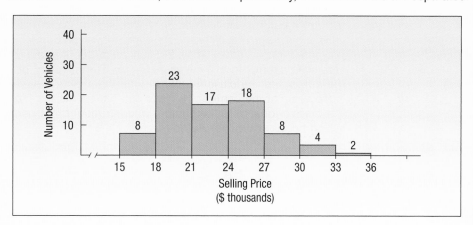

CHART 2–4 Histogram of the Selling Prices of 80 Vehicles at Whitner Autoplex

From the histogram in Chart 2–4, we conclude:

1. The lowest selling price is about $15,000, and the highest is about $36,000.
2. The largest class frequency is the $18,000 up to $21,000 class. A total of 23 of the 80 vehicles sold are within this price range.
3. Fifty-eight of the vehicles, or 72.5 percent, had a selling price between $18,000 and $27,000.

Thus, the histogram provides an easily interpreted visual representation of a frequency distribution. We should also point out that we would have reached the same conclusions and the shape of the histogram would have been the same had we used a relative frequency distribution instead of the actual frequencies. That is, if we had used the relative frequencies of Table 2–8, found on page 34, we would have had a histogram of the same shape as Chart 2–4. The only difference is that the vertical axis would have been reported in percent of vehicles instead of the number of vehicles.

We use the Microsoft Excel system to produce the histogram for the Whitner Autoplex vehicle sales data (which is shown on page 29). Note that class midpoints are used as the labels for the classes. The software commands to create this output are given in the **Software Commands** section at the end of the chapter.

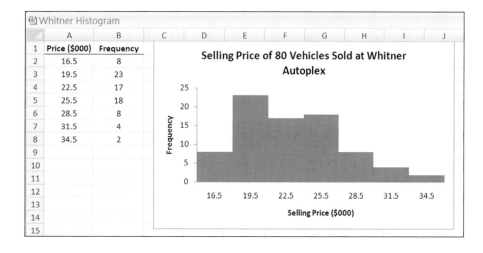

Frequency Polygon

A **frequency polygon** also shows the shape of a distribution and is similar to a histogram. It consists of line segments connecting the points formed by the intersections of the class midpoints and the class frequencies. The construction of a frequency polygon is illustrated in Chart 2–5 (on page 39). We use the vehicle prices for the cars sold last month at Whitner Autoplex. The midpoint of each class is scaled on the X-axis and the class frequencies on the Y-axis. Recall that the class midpoint is the value at the center of a class and represents the typical values in that class. The class frequency is the number of observations in a particular class. The vehicle selling prices at Whitner Autoplex are:

Selling Price ($ thousands)	Midpoint	Frequency
15 up to 18	16.5	8
18 up to 21	19.5	23
21 up to 24	22.5	17
24 up to 27	25.5	18
27 up to 30	28.5	8
30 up to 33	31.5	4
33 up to 36	34.5	2
Total		80

Statistics in Action

Florence Nightingale is known as the founder of the nursing profession. However, she also saved many lives by using statistical analysis. When she encountered an unsanitary condition or an undersupplied hospital, she improved the conditions and then used statistical data to document the improvement. Thus, she was able to convince others of the need for medical reform, particularly in the area of sanitation. She developed original graphs to demonstrate that, during the Crimean War, more soldiers died from unsanitary conditions than were killed in combat. The adjacent graph by Nightingale is a polar-area graph showing the relative monthly proportions of causes of death from April 1854 to March 1855.

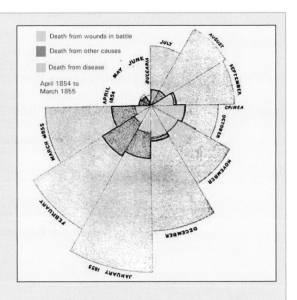

As noted previously, the $15,000 up to $18,000 class is represented by the midpoint $16,500. To construct a frequency polygon, move horizontally on the graph to the midpoint, $16.5, and then vertically to 8, the class frequency, and place a dot. The X and the Y values of this point are called the *coordinates*. The coordinates of the next point are X = $19.5 and Y = 23. The process is continued for all classes. Then the points are connected in order. That is, the point representing the lowest class is joined to the one representing the second class and so on.

Note in Chart 2–5 that, to complete the frequency polygon, midpoints of $13.5 and $37.5 are added to the X-axis to "anchor" the polygon at zero frequencies. These two values, $13.5 and $37.5, were derived by subtracting the class interval of $3.0 from the lowest midpoint ($16.5) and by adding $3.0 to the highest midpoint ($34.5) in the frequency distribution.

CHART 2–5 Frequency Polygon of the Selling Prices of 80 Vehicles at Whitner Autoplex

Both the histogram and the frequency polygon allow us to get a quick picture of the main characteristics of the data (highs, lows, points of concentration, etc.). Although the two representations are similar in purpose, the histogram has the advantage of depicting each class as a rectangle, with the height of the rectangular bar representing the number in each class. The frequency polygon, in turn, has an advantage over the histogram. It allows us to compare directly two or more frequency distributions. Suppose Ms. Ball of AutoUSA wants to compare the Whitner Autoplex lot in Raytown, Missouri, with a similar lot, Fowler Auto Mall in Grayling, Michigan. To do this, two frequency polygons are constructed, one on top of the other, as in Chart 2–6. It is clear from Chart 2–6 that the typical vehicle selling price is higher at the Fowler Auto Mall.

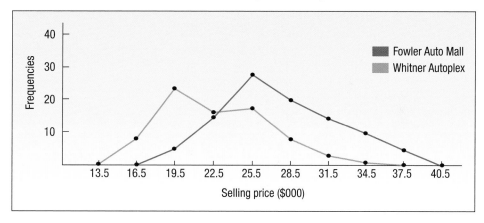

CHART 2–6 Distribution of Vehicle Selling Prices at Whitner Autoplex and Fowler Auto Mall

The total number of frequencies at the two dealerships is about the same, so a direct comparison is possible. If the difference in the total number of frequencies is quite large, converting the frequencies to relative frequencies and then plotting the two distributions would allow a clearer comparison.

Self-Review 2–5

The annual imports of a selected group of electronic suppliers are shown in the following frequency distribution.

Imports ($ millions)	Number of Suppliers	Imports ($ millions)	Number of Suppliers
2 up to 5	6	11 up to 14	10
5 up to 8	13	14 up to 17	1
8 up to 11	20		

(a) Portray the imports as a histogram.
(b) Portray the imports as a relative frequency polygon.
(c) Summarize the important facets of the distribution (such as classes with the highest and lowest frequencies).

Exercises

connect™

15. Molly's Candle Shop has several retail stores in the coastal areas of North and South Carolina. Many of Molly's customers ask her to ship their purchases. The following chart shows the number of packages shipped per day for the last 100 days.

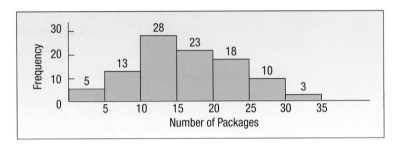

a. What is this chart called?
b. What is the total number of packages shipped?
c. What is the class interval?
d. What is the class frequency for the 10 up to 15 class?
e. What is the relative frequency of the 10 up to 15 class?
f. What is the midpoint of the 10 up to 15 class?
g. On how many days were 25 or more packages shipped?

16. The following chart shows the number of patients admitted daily to Memorial Hospital through the emergency room.

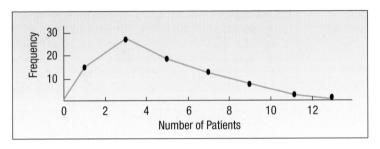

a. What is the midpoint of the 2 up to 4 class?
b. How many days were 2 up to 4 patients admitted?
c. Approximately how many days were studied?
d. What is the class interval?
e. What is this chart called?

17. The following frequency distribution reports the number of frequent flier miles, reported in thousands, for employees of Brumley Statistical Consulting, Inc., during the most recent quarter.

Frequent Flier Miles (000)	Number of Employees
0 up to 3	5
3 up to 6	12
6 up to 9	23
9 up to 12	8
12 up to 15	2
Total	50

    a. How many employees were studied?
    b. What is the midpoint of the first class?
    c. Construct a histogram.
    d. A frequency polygon is to be drawn. What are the coordinates of the plot for the first class?
    e. Construct a frequency polygon.
    f. Interpret the frequent flier miles accumulated using the two charts.
18. Ecommerce.com, a large Internet retailer, is studying the lead time (elapsed time between when an order is placed and when it is filled) for a sample of recent orders. The lead times are reported in days.

Lead Time (days)	Frequency
0 up to 5	6
5 up to 10	7
10 up to 15	12
15 up to 20	8
20 up to 25	7
Total	40

    a. How many orders were studied?
    b. What is the midpoint of the first class?
    c. What are the coordinates of the first class for a frequency polygon?
    d. Draw a histogram.
    e. Draw a frequency polygon.
    f. Interpret the lead times using the two charts.

Cumulative Frequency Distributions

Consider once again the distribution of the selling prices of vehicles at Whitner Autoplex. Suppose we were interested in the number of vehicles that sold for less than $21,000, or the value below which 40 percent of the vehicles sold. These numbers can be approximated by developing a **cumulative frequency distribution** and portraying it graphically in a **cumulative frequency polygon.**

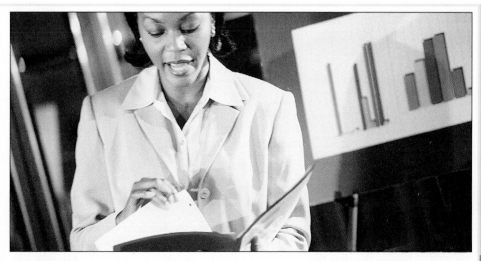

Example   The frequency distribution of the vehicle selling prices at Whitner Autoplex is repeated from Table 2–7.

Selling Price ($ thousands)	Frequency
15 up to 18	8
18 up to 21	23
21 up to 24	17
24 up to 27	18
27 up to 30	8
30 up to 33	4
33 up to 36	2
Total	80

Construct a cumulative frequency polygon. Fifty percent of the vehicles were sold for less than what amount? Twenty-five of the vehicles were sold for less than what amount?

Solution

As the name implies, a cumulative frequency distribution and a cumulative frequency polygon require *cumulative frequencies*. To construct a cumulative frequency distribution, refer to the preceding table and note that eight vehicles were sold for less than $18,000. Those 8 vehicles, plus the 23 in the next higher class, for a total of 31, were sold for less than $21,000. The cumulative frequency for the next higher class is 48, found by 8 + 23 + 17. This process is continued for all the classes. All the vehicles were sold for less than $36,000. (See Table 2–9.)

To plot a cumulative frequency distribution, scale the upper limit of each class along the X-axis and the corresponding cumulative frequencies along the Y-axis. To provide additional information, you can label the vertical axis on the left in units and the vertical axis on the right in percent. In the Whitner Autoplex example, the vertical axis on the left is labeled from 0 to 80 and on the right from 0 to 100 percent. The value of 50 percent corresponds to 40 vehicles sold.

TABLE 2–9 Cumulative Frequency Distribution for Vehicle Selling Price

Selling Price ($ thousands)	Frequency	Cumulative Frequency	Found by
15 up to 18	8	8	
18 up to 21	23	31	←——— 8 + 23
21 up to 24	17	48	8 + 23 + 17
24 up to 27	18	66	8 + 23 + 17 + 18
27 up to 30	8	74	⋮
30 up to 33	4	78	
33 up to 36	2	80	
Total	80		

To begin the plotting, 8 vehicles sold for less than $18,000, so the first plot is at X = 18 and Y = 8. The coordinates for the next plot are X = 21 and Y = 31. The rest of the points are plotted and then the dots connected (see the green line) to form the chart that follows.

CHART 2–7 Cumulative Frequency Distribution for Vehicle Selling Price

To find the selling price below which half the cars sold, we draw a horizontal line from the 50 percent mark on the right-hand vertical axis over to the polygon, then drop down to the X-axis and read the selling price. The value on the X-axis is about 22.5, so we estimate that 50 percent of the vehicles sold for less than $22,500.

　　To find the price below which 25 of the vehicles sold, we locate the value of 25 on the left-hand vertical axis. Next, we draw a horizontal line from the value of 25 to the polygon, and then drop down to the X-axis and read the price. It is about 20.5, so we estimate that 25 of the vehicles sold for less than $20,500. We can also make estimates of the percent of vehicles that sold for less than a particular amount. To explain, suppose we want to estimate the percent of vehicles that sold for less than $28,500. We begin by locating the value of 28.5 on the X-axis, move vertically to the polygon, and then horizontally to the vertical axis on the right. The value is about 87 percent, so we conclude that 87 percent of the vehicles sold for less than $28,500.

Self-Review 2–6

A sample of the hourly wages of 15 employees at Home Depot in Brunswick, Georgia, was organized into the following table.

Hourly Wages	Number of Employees
$ 8 up to $10	3
10 up to 12	7
12 up to 14	4
14 up to 16	1

(a) What is the table called?
(b) Develop a cumulative frequency distribution and portray the distribution in a cumulative frequency polygon.
(c) On the basis of the cumulative frequency polygon, how many employees earn $11 an hour or less? Half of the employees earn an hourly wage of how much or more? Four employees earn how much or less?

Exercises

connect

19. The following chart shows the hourly wages of a sample of certified welders in the Atlanta, Georgia area.

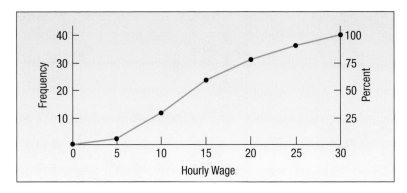

  a. How many welders were studied?
  b. What is the class interval?
  c. About how many welders earn less than $10.00 per hour?
  d. About 75 percent of the welders make less than what amount?
  e. Ten of the welders studied made less than what amount?
  f. What percent of the welders make less than $20.00 per hour?

20. The following chart shows the selling price ($000) of houses sold in the Billings, Montana area.

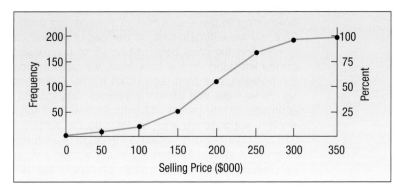

  a. How many homes were studied?
  b. What is the class interval?
  c. One hundred homes sold for less than what amount?
  d. About 75 percent of the homes sold for less than what amount?
  e. Estimate the number of homes in the $150,000 up to $200,000 class.
  f. About how many homes sold for less than $225,000?

21. The frequency distribution representing the number of frequent flier miles accumulated by employees at Brumley Statistical Consulting Company is repeated from Exercise 17.

Frequent Flier Miles (000)	Frequency
0 up to 3	5
3 up to 6	12
6 up to 9	23
9 up to 12	8
12 up to 15	2
Total	50

   a. How many employees accumulated less than 3,000 miles?
   b. Convert the frequency distribution to a cumulative frequency distribution.
   c. Portray the cumulative distribution in the form of a cumulative frequency polygon.
   d. Based on the cumulative frequency polygon, about 75 percent of the employees accumulated how many miles or less?

22. The frequency distribution of order lead time at Ecommerce.com from Exercise 18 is repeated below.

Lead Time (days)	Frequency
0 up to 5	6
5 up to 10	7
10 up to 15	12
15 up to 20	8
20 up to 25	7
Total	$\overline{40}$

   a. How many orders were filled in less than 10 days? In less than 15 days?
   b. Convert the frequency distribution to a cumulative frequency distribution.
   c. Develop a cumulative frequency polygon.
   d. About 60 percent of the orders were filled in less than how many days?

Chapter Summary

   I. A frequency table is a grouping of qualitative data into mutually exclusive classes showing the number of observations in each class.
   II. A relative frequency table shows the fraction of the number of frequencies in each class.
   III. A bar chart is a graphic representation of a frequency table.
   IV. A pie chart shows the proportion each distinct class represents of the total number of frequencies.
   V. A frequency distribution is a grouping of data into mutually exclusive classes showing the number of observations in each class.
      A. The steps in constructing a frequency distribution are:
         1. Decide on the number of classes.
         2. Determine the class interval.
         3. Set the individual class limits.
         4. Tally the raw data into classes.
         5. Count the number of tallies in each class.
      B. The class frequency is the number of observations in each class.
      C. The class interval is the difference between the limits of two consecutive classes.
      D. The class midpoint is halfway between the limits of consecutive classes.
   VI. A relative frequency distribution shows the percent of observations in each class.
   VII. There are three methods for graphically portraying a frequency distribution.
      A. A histogram portrays the number of frequencies in each class in the form of a rectangle.
      B. A frequency polygon consists of line segments connecting the points formed by the intersection of the class midpoint and the class frequency.
      C. A cumulative frequency distribution shows the number or percent of observations below given values.

Chapter Exercises

connect™

23. Describe the similarities and differences of qualitative and quantitative variables. Be sure to include:
   a. What level of measurement is required for each variable type?
   b. Can both types be used to describe both samples and populations?

24. Describe the similarities and differences of a frequency table and a frequency distribution. Be sure to include which requires qualitative data and which requires quantitative data.

25. Alexandra Damonte will be building a new resort in Myrtle Beach, South Carolina. She must decide how to design the resort based on the type of activities that the resort will offer to its customers. A recent poll of 300 potential customers showed the following results about customers' preferences for planned resort activities:

Like planned activities	63
Do not like planned activities	135
Not sure	78
No answer	24

a. What is the table called?
b. Draw a bar chart to portray the survey results.
c. Draw a pie chart for the survey results.
d. If you are preparing to present the results to Ms. Damonte as part of a report, which graph would you prefer to show? Why?

26. Speedy Swift is a package delivery service that serves the greater Atlanta, Georgia metropolitan area. To maintain customer loyalty, one of Speedy Swift's performance objectives is on-time delivery. To monitor its performance, each delivery is measured on the following scale: early (package delivered before the promised time), on-time (package delivered within 5 minutes of the promised time), late (package delivered more than 5 minutes past the promised time), lost (package never delivered). Speedy Swift's objective is to deliver 99 percent of all packages either early or on-time. Another objective is never to lose a package.

Speedy collected the following data for last month's performance:

On-time	On-time	Early	Late	On-time	On-time	On-time	On-time	Late	On-time
Early	On-time	On-time	Early	On-time	On-time	On-time	On-time	On-time	On-time
Early	On-time	Early	On-time	On-time	On-time	Early	On-time	On-time	On-time
Early	On-time	On-time	Late	Early	Early	On-time	On-time	On-time	Early
On-time	Late	Late	On-time	On-time	On-time	On-time	On-time	On-time	On-time
On-time	Late	Early	On-time	Early	On-time	Lost	On-time	On-time	On-time
Early	Early	On-time	On-time	Late	Early	Lost	On-time	On-time	On-time
On-time	On-time	Early	On-time	Early	On-time	Early	On-time	Late	On-time
On-time	Early	On-time	On-time	On-time	Late	On-time	Early	On-time	On-time
On-time	On-time	On-time	On-time	On-time	Early	Early	On-time	On-time	On-time

a. What scale is used to measure delivery performance? What kind of variable is delivery performance?
b. Construct a frequency table for delivery performance for last month.
c. Construct a relative frequency table for delivery performance last month.
d. Construct a bar chart of the frequency table for delivery performance for last month.
e. Construct a pie chart of on-time delivery performance for last month.
f. Analyze the data summaries and write an evaluation of last month's delivery performance as it relates to Speedy Swift's performance objectives. Write a general recommendation for further analysis.

27. A data set consists of 83 observations. How many classes would you recommend for a frequency distribution?

28. A data set consists of 145 observations that range from 56 to 490. What size class interval would you recommend?

29. The following is the number of minutes to commute from home to work for a group of automobile executives.

28	25	48	37	41	19	32	26	16	23	23	29	36
31	26	21	32	25	31	43	35	42	38	33	28	

a. How many classes would you recommend?
b. What class interval would you suggest?

    c. What would you recommend as the lower limit of the first class?
    d. Organize the data into a frequency distribution.
    e. Comment on the shape of the frequency distribution.

30. The following data give the weekly amounts spent on groceries for a sample of households.

$271	$363	$159	$ 76	$227	$337	$295	$319	$250
279	205	279	266	199	177	162	232	303
192	181	321	309	246	278	50	41	335
116	100	151	240	474	297	170	188	320
429	294	570	342	279	235	434	123	325

    a. How many classes would you recommend?
    b. What class interval would you suggest?
    c. What would you recommend as the lower limit of the first class?
    d. Organize the data into a frequency distribution.

31. A social scientist is studying the use of iPods by college students. A sample of 45 students revealed they played the following number of songs yesterday.

4	6	8	7	9	6	3	7	7	6	7	1	4	7	7
4	6	4	10	2	4	6	3	4	6	8	4	3	3	6
8	8	4	6	4	6	5	5	9	6	8	8	6	5	10

Organize the above information into a frequency distribution.
    a. How many classes would you suggest?
    b. What is the most suitable class interval?
    c. What is the lower limit of the initial class?
    d. Create the frequency distribution.
    e. Describe the profile of the distribution.

32. David Wise handles his own investment portfolio, and has done so for many years. Listed below is the holding time (recorded to the nearest whole year) between purchase and sale for his collection of stocks.

8	8	6	11	11	9	8	5	11	4	8	5	14	7	12	8	6	11	9	7
9	15	8	8	12	5	9	8	5	9	10	11	3	9	8	6				

    a. How many classes would you propose?
    b. What class interval would you suggest?
    c. What quantity would you use for the lower limit of the initial class?
    d. Using your responses to parts (a), (b), and (c), create a frequency distribution.
    e. Describe the essential elements or features of the frequency distribution.

33. You are exploring the music in your iTunes library. The total play counts over the past year for the songs on your "smart playlist" are shown below. Make a frequency distribution of the counts and describe its shape. It is often claimed that a small fraction of a person's songs will account for most of their total plays. Does this seem to be the case here?

128	56	54	91	190	23	160	298	445	50
578	494	37	677	18	74	70	868	108	71
466	23	84	38	26	814	17			

34. The *Journal of Finance* made its content available on the Internet starting in July of 2005. The table below shows the number of times a monthly version was downloaded and the number of articles that were viewed during each month. Suppose you wish to make a frequency distribution of the number of downloads.

312	2,753	2,595	6,057	7,624	6,624	6,362	6,575	7,760	7,085	7,272
5,967	5,256	6,160	6,238	6,709	7,193	5,631	6,490	6,682	7,829	7,091
6,871	6,230	7,253	5,507	5,676	6,974	6,915	4,999	5,689	6,143	7,086

    a. How many classes would you propose?
    b. What class interval would you suggest?
    c. What quantity would you use for the lower limit of the initial class?
    d. Using your responses to parts (a), (b), and (c), create a frequency distribution.
    e. Describe the essential elements or features of the frequency distribution.

35. The following histogram shows the scores on the first exam for a statistics class.

    a. How many students took the exam?
    b. What is the class interval?
    c. What is the class midpoint for the first class?
    d. How many students earned a score of less than 70?

36. The following chart summarizes the selling price of homes sold last month in the Sarasota, Florida, area.

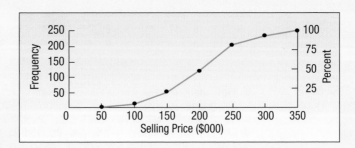

    a. What is the chart called?
    b. How many homes were sold during the last month?
    c. What is the class interval?
    d. About 75 percent of the houses sold for less than what amount?
    e. One hundred seventy-five of the homes sold for less than what amount?

37. A chain of sport shops catering to beginning skiers, headquartered in Aspen, Colorado, plans to conduct a study of how much a beginning skier spends on his or her initial purchase of equipment and supplies. Based on these figures, it wants to explore the possibility of offering combinations, such as a pair of boots and a pair of skis, to induce customers to buy more. A sample of cash register receipts revealed these initial purchases:

$140	$ 82	$265	$168	$ 90	$114	$172	$230	$142
86	125	235	212	171	149	156	162	118
139	149	132	105	162	126	216	195	127
161	135	172	220	229	129	87	128	126
175	127	149	126	121	118	172	126	

   a. Arrive at a suggested class interval. Use six classes, and let the lower limit of the first class be $70.

   b. What would be a better class interval?

   c. Organize the data into a frequency distribution using a lower limit of $80.

   d. Interpret your findings.

38. Following is the number of shareholders for a selected group of large companies (in thousands):

Company	Number of Shareholders (thousands)	Company	Number of Shareholders (thousands)
Southwest Airlines	144	Standard Oil (Indiana)	173
General Public Utilities	177	Home Depot	195
Occidental Petroleum	266	Detroit Edison	220
Middle South Utilities	133	Eastman Kodak	251
DaimlerChrysler	209	Dow Chemical	137
Standard Oil of California	264	Pennsylvania Power	150
Bethlehem Steel	160	American Electric Power	262
Long Island Lighting	143	Ohio Edison	158
RCA	246	Transamerica Corporation	162
Greyhound Corporation	151	Columbia Gas System	165
Pacific Gas & Electric	239	International Telephone &	
Niagara Mohawk Power	204	Telegraph	223
E. I. du Pont de Nemours	204	Union Electric	158
Westinghouse Electric	195	Virginia Electric and Power	162
Union Carbide	176	Public Service Electric & Gas	225
BankAmerica	175	Consumers Power	161
Northeast Utilities	200		

The shareholder numbers are to be organized into a frequency distribution and several graphs drawn to portray the distribution.

   a. Using seven classes and a lower limit of 130, construct a frequency distribution.

   b. Portray the distribution as a frequency polygon.

   c. Portray the distribution in a cumulative frequency polygon.

   d. According to the polygon, three out of four (75 percent) of the companies have how many shareholders or less?

   e. Write a brief analysis of the number of shareholders based on the frequency distribution and graphs.

39. A recent survey showed that the typical American car owner spends $2,950 per year on operating expenses. Below is a breakdown of the various expenditure items. Draw an appropriate chart to portray the data and summarize your findings in a brief report.

Expenditure Item	Amount
Fuel	$ 603
Interest on car loan	279
Repairs	930
Insurance and license	646
Depreciation	492
Total	$2,950

40. Midland National Bank selected a sample of 40 student checking accounts. Below are their end-of-the-month balances.

$404	$ 74	$234	$149	$279	$215	$123	$ 55	$ 43	$321
87	234	68	489	57	185	141	758	72	863
703	125	350	440	37	252	27	521	302	127
968	712	503	489	327	608	358	425	303	203

a. Tally the data into a frequency distribution using $100 as a class interval and $0 as the starting point.
b. Draw a cumulative frequency polygon.
c. The bank considers any student with an ending balance of $400 or more a "preferred customer." Estimate the percentage of preferred customers.
d. The bank is also considering a service charge to the lowest 10 percent of the ending balances. What would you recommend as the cutoff point between those who have to pay a service charge and those who do not?

41. Residents of the state of South Carolina earned a total of $69.5 billion in adjusted gross income. Seventy-three percent of the total was in wages and salaries; 11 percent in dividends, interest, and capital gains; 8 percent in IRAs and taxable pensions; 3 percent in business income pensions; 2 percent in Social Security, and the remaining 3 percent from other sources. Develop a pie chart depicting the breakdown of adjusted gross income. Write a paragraph summarizing the information.

42. A recent study of home technologies reported the number of hours of personal computer usage per week for a sample of 60 persons. Excluded from the study were people who worked out of their home and used the computer as a part of their work.

9.3	5.3	6.3	8.8	6.5	0.6	5.2	6.6	9.3	4.3
6.3	2.1	2.7	0.4	3.7	3.3	1.1	2.7	6.7	6.5
4.3	9.7	7.7	5.2	1.7	8.5	4.2	5.5	5.1	5.6
5.4	4.8	2.1	10.1	1.3	5.6	2.4	2.4	4.7	1.7
2.0	6.7	1.1	6.7	2.2	2.6	9.8	6.4	4.9	5.2
4.5	9.3	7.9	4.6	4.3	4.5	9.2	8.5	6.0	8.1

a. Organize the data into a frequency distribution. How many classes would you suggest? What value would you suggest for a class interval?
b. Draw a histogram. Interpret your result.

43. Merrill Lynch, a subsidiary of Bank of America, recently completed a study regarding the size of investment portfolios (stocks, bonds, mutual funds, and certificates of deposit) for a sample of clients in the 40- to 50-year-old age group. Listed following is the value of all the investments in thousands of dollars for the 70 participants in the study.

$669.9	$ 7.5	$ 77.2	$ 7.5	$125.7	$516.9	$ 219.9	$645.2
301.9	235.4	716.4	145.3	26.6	187.2	315.5	89.2
136.4	616.9	440.6	408.2	34.4	296.1	185.4	526.3
380.7	3.3	363.2	51.9	52.2	107.5	82.9	63.0
228.6	308.7	126.7	430.3	82.0	227.0	321.1	403.4
39.5	124.3	118.1	23.9	352.8	156.7	276.3	23.5
31.3	301.2	35.7	154.9	174.3	100.6	236.7	171.9
221.1	43.4	212.3	243.3	315.4	5.9	1,002.2	171.7
295.7	437.0	87.8	302.1	268.1	899.5		

a. Organize the data into a frequency distribution. How many classes would you suggest? What value would you suggest for a class interval?
b. Draw a histogram. Interpret your result.

44. A total of 5.9 percent of the prime time viewing audience watched shows on ABC, 7.6 percent watched shows on CBS, 5.5 percent on Fox, 6.0 percent on NBC, 2.0 percent on Warner Brothers, and 2.2 percent on UPN. A total of 70.8 percent of the audience watched shows on other cable networks, such as CNN and ESPN. You can find the latest information on TV viewing from the following website: http://tv.zap2it.com/news/ratings. Develop a pie chart or a bar chart to depict this information. Write a paragraph summarizing your findings.

45. The American Heart Association reported the following percentage breakdown of expenses. Draw a pie chart depicting the information. Interpret.

Category	Percent
Research	32.3
Public Health Education	23.5
Community Service	12.6
Fund Raising	12.1
Professional and Educational Training	10.9
Management and General	8.6

46. Annual revenues, by type of tax, for the state of Georgia are as follows. Develop an appropriate chart or graph and write a brief report summarizing the information.

Type of Tax	Amount ($000)
Sales	$2,812,473
Income (Individual)	2,732,045
License	185,198
Corporate	525,015
Property	22,647
Death and Gift	37,326
Total	$6,314,704

47. Annual imports from selected Canadian trading partners are listed below. Develop an appropriate chart or graph and write a brief report summarizing the information.

Partner	Annual Imports ($ millions)
Japan	$9,550
United Kingdom	4,556
South Korea	2,441
China	1,182
Australia	618

48. Farming has changed from the early 1900s. In the early 20th century, machinery gradually replaced animal power. For example, in 1910 U.S. farms used 24.2 million horses and mules and only about 1,000 tractors. By 1960, 4.6 million tractors were used and only 3.2 million horses and mules. In 1920 there were over 6 million farms in the United States. Today there are less than 2 million. Listed below is the number of farms, in thousands, for each of the 50 states. Write a paragraph summarizing your findings.

47	1	8	46	76	26	4	3	39	45
4	21	80	63	100	65	91	29	7	15
7	52	87	39	106	25	55	2	3	8
14	38	59	33	76	71	37	51	1	24
35	86	185	13	7	43	36	20	79	9

49. One of the most popular candies in the United States is M&M's, which are produced by the Mars Company. In the beginning M&M's were all brown; more recently they were produced in red, green, blue, orange, brown, and yellow. You can read about the history of the product, find ideas for baking, purchase the candies in the colors of your school or favorite team, and learn the percent of each color in the standard bags at www.m-ms.com. Recently the purchase of a 14-ounce bag of M&M's Plain had 444 candies with the following breakdown by color: 130 brown, 98 yellow, 96 red, 35 orange, 52 blue, and 33 green. Develop a chart depicting this information and write a paragraph summarizing the results.

50. The following graph shows the total wages paid by software and aircraft companies in the state of Washington from 1997 until 2005. Write a brief report summarizing this information.

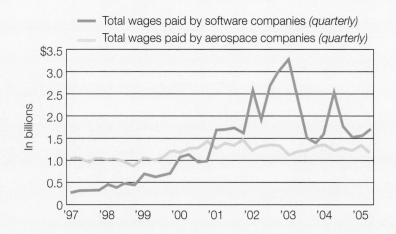

51. A pie chart shows the market shares of cola products. The "slice" for Pepsi-Cola has a central angle of 90 degrees. What is its market share?

52. The number of families who used the Minneapolis YWCA day care service was recorded over a 30-day period. The results are as follows: 31, 49, 19, 62, 24, 45, 23, 51, 55, 60, 40, 35, 54, 26, 57, 37, 43, 65, 18, 41, 50, 56, 4, 54, 39, 52, 35, 51, 63, and 42.
   a. Construct a cumulative frequency distribution of this data.
   b. Sketch a graph of the cumulative frequency polygon.
   c. How many days saw fewer than 30 families utilize the day care center?
   d. How busy were the highest 80 percent of the days?

Data Set Exercises

53. Refer to the Real Estate data at the end of the book, which reports information on homes sold in the Phoenix, Arizona, area during the last year.
   a. Organize the data on number of bedrooms into a frequency distribution.
      1. What is the typical number of bedrooms?
      2. What are the fewest and the most number of bedrooms offered in the market?
   b. Select an appropriate class interval and organize the selling prices into a frequency distribution.
      1. Around what values do the data tend to cluster?
      2. What is the largest selling price? What is the smallest selling price?

      c. Draw a cumulative frequency distribution based on the frequency distribution developed in part (b).

        1. How many homes sold for less than $200,000?

        2. Estimate the percent of the homes that sold for more than $220,000.

        3. What percent of the homes sold for less than $125,000?

      d. Write a report summarizing the selling prices of the homes.

54. Refer to the Baseball 2008 data, which reports information on the 30 Major League Baseball teams for the 2008 season.

      a. Organize the information on the team salaries into a frequency distribution. Select an appropriate class interval.

        1. What is a typical team salary? What is the range of salaries?

        2. Comment on the shape of the distribution. Does it appear that any of the team salaries are out of line with the others?

      b. Draw a cumulative frequency distribution based on the frequency distribution developed in part (a).

        1. Forty percent of the teams are paying less than what amount in total team salary?

        2. About how many teams have total salaries of less than $80,000,000?

        3. Below what amount do the lowest five teams pay in total salary?

      c. Organize the information on the size of the various stadiums into a frequency distribution.

        1. What is a typical stadium size? Where do the stadium sizes tend to cluster?

        2. Comment on the shape of the distribution. Does it appear that any of the stadium sizes are out of line with the others?

      d. Organize the information on the year in which the 30 major league stadiums were built into a frequency distribution. (You could also create a new variable called "age" by subtracting the year in which the stadium was built from the current year.)

        1. What is the year in which the typical stadium was built? Where do these years tend to cluster?

        2. Comment on the shape of the distribution. Does it appear that any of the stadium ages are out of line with the others? If so, which ones?

55. Refer to the Wage data, which reports information on annual wages for a sample of 100 workers. Also included are variables relating to industry, years of education, and gender for each worker. Draw a bar chart of the variable occupation. Write a brief report summarizing your findings.

Practice Test

Part I Objective

1. A grouping of qualitative data into mutually exclusive classes showing the number of observations in each class is known as a _____ .

2. A grouping of quantitative data into mutually exclusive classes showing the number of observations in each class is known as a _____ .

3. A graph in which the classes for qualitative data are reported on the horizontal axis and the class frequencies (proportional to the heights of the bars) on the vertical axis is called _____ .

4. A _____ chart shows the proportion or percent that each class represents of the total.

5. A graph in which the classes of a quantitative data set are marked on the horizontal axis and the class frequencies on the vertical axis is called a _____

6. A set of data contained 70 observations. How many classes would you suggest to construct a frequency distribution? _____

7. The distance between successive lower class limits is called the _____ .

8. The average of the respective class limits of two consecutive classes is the _____ .

9. In a relative frequency distribution, the class frequencies are divided by _____ .

10. A cumulative frequency polygon is created by line segments connecting the _____ and the corresponding cumulative frequencies.

Part II Problems

1. Consider these data on the selling prices ($000) of homes in the city of Warren, Pennsylvania, last year.

Sales Price	Frequency
$120 up to $150	4
150 up to 180	18
180 up to 210	30
210 up to 240	20
240 up to 270	17
270 up to 300	10
300 up to 330	6

a. How large is the class interval?
b. How many homes were sold last year?
c. How many homes sold for less than $210,000?
d. What is the relative frequency for the $210 up to 240 class?
e. What is the midpoint of the $150 up to 180 class?
f. What were the maximum and minimum selling prices?
g. Construct a histogram of these data.
h. Make a frequency polygon of these data.

Software Commands

1. The Excel commands for the pie chart on page 26 are:
   a. Set cell *A1* as the active cell and type the words *Use of Sales.* In cells *A2* through *A5* type *Prizes, Education, Bonuses, and Expense.*
   b. Set *B1* as the active cell and type *Amount ($ Millions)* and in cells *B2* through *B5* enter the data. When finished entering data in B5, hit the enter button.
   c. From the top row of tabs, select **Insert.** In the Chart tool bar, select **Pie.** Select the top-left **2-D** pie chart. A blank chart will appear.

   d. In Excel's top row, a **Chart Tools** tab will appear. Select the **Design** option. Select the **Select Data** option from the tool bar. A **Select Data** window will appear. For the **Chart Data Range,** using the mouse, select all cells from A1 to B5. Click OK.
   e. Click on the pie chart. Right click for the options menu. Select **Add Data Labels.** Click on the pie chart again. Right click for the options menu. Select **Format Data Labels** then uncheck any boxes currently checked in the dialog box. Next select **Category, Percent, and Leader Lines.** Then click **Close.**
   f. Double click on the chart title and rename **Ohio State Lottery Expenses.**
2. The MegaStat commands for the frequency distribution on page 33 are:
   a. Open Excel and from the CD provided, select **Data Sets,** and select the Excel format; go to

Chapter 2, and select **Whitner.** Click on **Mega-Stat, Frequency Distribution,** and select **Quantitative.**
   b. In the dialog box, input the range from *A1:A81,* select **Equal width intervals,** use *3,000* as the interval width, *15,000* as the lower boundary of the first interval, select **Histogram,** and then click **OK.**
3. The Excel commands for the histogram on page 37 are:
   a. In cell A1 indicate that the column of data is the selling price and in B1 that it is the frequency. In cells A2 to A8 insert the midpoints of the selling prices in $000. In B2 to B8 record the class frequencies. When finished entering data in cell B8, hit the enter key.
   b. With your mouse, highlight cells B2 through B8.
   c. From the tabs, select **Insert.** From the Charts, select **Column,** then **2-D column** and pick the first chart type. A graph will appear.
   d. When the graph area is active, a **Chart Tools** tab appears at the top of the screen. Select the **Design** tab, and then select **Data.** Under **Horizontal (Category) Axis Labels,** click **Edit,** then use the mouse to select cells A2 through A8 and click **OK** twice. The horizontal axis now shows the class midpoints.
   e. With the **Chart Tools** displayed at the top, select the **Design** tab. Select **Chart Layout.** Select the

layout:
   f. With **Chart Tools** displayed at the top, select the **Layout** tab. Double click on the **Chart Title** and

type in *Selling price of 80 Vehicles Sold at the Whitner Autoplex Lot.* Next, under the same **Layout** tab, select **Axis Titles**. Using **Primary Vertical Axis Title,** name the vertical axis *Frequency* and delete the words *vertical axis.* Using the **Primary Horizontal Axis Title,** name the horizontal axis *Sales Dollars ($000).* Next select **Legend** and select **None.**

g. Double click one of the columns in the graph. Then from the Tabs across the top select **Layout.** On the left-hand side of the tool bar click the words **Format Selection.** A dialog box will appear. Under *Series Option,* change the

Gap Width to 0% by moving the arrow all the way to the left, and then click the **Close** button at the bottom of the dialog box.

Chapter 2   Answers to Self-Review

2–1 **a.** Qualitative data, because the customers' response to the taste test is the name of a beverage.
  b. Frequency table. It shows the number of people who prefer each beverage.
  c.

  d.

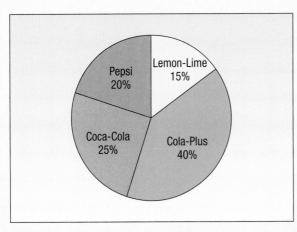

2–2 **a.** The raw data or ungrouped data.
  b.

Commission	Number of Salespeople
$1,400 up to $1,500	2
1,500 up to 1,600	5
1,600 up to 1,700	3
1,700 up to 1,800	1
Total	$\overline{11}$

  c. Class frequencies.
  d. The largest concentration of commissions is $1,500 up to $1,600. The smallest commission is about $1,400 and the largest is about $1,800. The typical amount earned is $15,500.

2–3 **a.** $2^6 = 64 < 73 < 128 = 2^7$. So 7 classes are recommended.
  b. The interval width should be at least $(488 - 320)/7 = 24$. Class intervals of 25 or 30 feet are both reasonable.
  c. If we use a class interval of 25 feet and begin with a lower limit of 300 feet, eight classes would be necessary. A class interval of 30 feet beginning with 300 feet is also reasonable. This alternative requires only seven classes.

2–4 **a.** 23
  b. 28.75%, found by (23/80) × 100
  c. 7.5%, found by (6/80) × 100

2–5 **a.**

b.

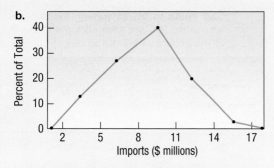

The plots are: (3.5, 12), (6.5, 26), (9.5, 40), (12.5, 20), and (15.5, 2).

c. The smallest annual volume of imports by a supplier is about $2 million, the largest about $17 million. The highest frequency is between $8 million and $11 million.

2–6 **a.** A frequency distribution.

b.

Hourly Wages	Cumulative Number
Less than $8	0
Less than $10	3
Less than $12	10
Less than $14	14
Less than $16	15

c. About seven employees earn $11.00 or less. About half the employees earn $11.25 or more. About four employees earn $10.25 or less.

Describing Data:

Numerical Measures

U.S. housing prices reached their peak in July of 2006. Based on the data given in the table, showing the ratio of the prices reported in a recent month to the July 2006 figure, find the mean, median, and mode of these statistics. (Exercise 65, LO1)

Learning Objectives

When you have completed this chapter you will be able to:

LO1 Calculate the *arithmetic mean, weighted mean, median,* and *mode.*

LO2 Explain the characteristics, uses, advantages, and disadvantages of each *measure of location.*

LO3 Identify the position of the mean, median, and mode for both *symmetric* and *skewed distributions.*

LO4 Compute and interpret the *range, mean deviation, variance,* and *standard deviation.*

LO5 Understand the characteristics, uses, advantages, and disadvantages of each *measure of dispersion.*

LO6 Understand *Chebyshev's theorem* and the *Empirical Rule* as they relate to a set of observations.

Introduction

Chapter 2 began our study of descriptive statistics. To transform a mass of raw data into a meaningful form, we organized quantitative data into a frequency distribution and portrayed it graphically in a histogram. We also looked at other graphical techniques such as pie charts to portray qualitative data and frequency polygons to portray quantitative data.

Statistics in Action

Did you ever meet the "average" American? Well, his name is Robert (that is the nominal level of measurement), he is 31 years old (that is the ratio level), he is 69.5 inches tall (again the ratio level of measurement), weighs 172 pounds, wears a size 9½ shoe, has a 34-inch waist, and wears a size 40 suit. In addition, the average man eats 4 pounds of potato chips, and eats 26 pounds of bananas each year and also sleeps 7.7 hours per night.

The average American woman is 5′ 4″ tall and weighs 140 pounds, while the average American model is 5′ 11″ tall and weighs 117 pounds. On any given day, almost half of the women in the United States are on a diet. Idolized in the 1950s, Marilyn Monroe would be considered overweight by today's standards. She fluctuated between a size 14 and 18 dress, and was a healthy and attractive woman.

This chapter is concerned with two numerical ways of describing quantitative data, namely, **measures of location** and **measures of dispersion.** Measures of location are often referred to as **averages.** The purpose of a measure of location is to pinpoint the center of a set of values.

You are familiar with the concept of an average. An average is a measure of location that shows the central value of the data. Averages appear daily on TV, in the newspaper, and other journals. Here are some examples:

- The average U.S. home changes ownership every 11.8 years.
- An American receives an average of 568 pieces of mail per year.
- The average American home has more TV sets than people. There are 2.73 TV sets and 2.55 people in the typical home.
- In 2008 the typical (median) weekly earnings for those with a bachelor's degree were $978.
- The average American couple spends $28,732 for their wedding, while their budget is 50 percent less. This does not include the cost of a honeymoon or engagement ring.
- In Chicago the mean high temperature is 84 degrees in July and 31 degrees in January. The mean amount of precipitation is 3.80 inches in July and 1.90 inches in January.

If we consider only the measures of location in a set of data, or if we compare several sets of data using central values, we may draw an erroneous conclusion. In addition to the measures of location, we should consider the **dispersion**—often called the *variation* or the *spread*—in the data. As an illustration, suppose the average annual income of executives for Internet-related companies is $80,000, and the average income for executives in pharmaceutical firms is also $80,000. If we looked only at the average incomes, we might wrongly conclude that the two salary distributions are identical or nearly identical. A look at the salary ranges indicates that this conclusion is not correct. The salaries for the executives in the Internet firms range from $70,000 to $90,000, but salaries for the marketing executives in pharmaceuticals range from $40,000 to $120,000. Thus, we conclude that although the average salaries are the same for the two industries, there is much more spread or dispersion in salaries for the pharmaceutical executives. To describe the dispersion we will consider the range, the mean deviation, the variance, and the standard deviation.

We begin by discussing measures of location. There is not just one measure of location; in fact, there are many. We will consider four: the arithmetic mean, the weighted mean, the median, and the mode. The arithmetic mean is the most widely used and widely reported measure of location. We study the mean as both a population parameter and a sample statistic.

The Population Mean

Many studies involve all the values in a population. For example, there are 39 exits on I-75 through the state of Kentucky. The mean distance between these state exits is 4.76 miles. This is an example of a population parameter because we have studied the distance between *all* the exits. There are 12 sales associates employed at the Reynolds Road outlet of Carpets by Otto. The mean amount of commission they earned last month was $345. This is a population value because we considered the commission of *all* the sales associates. Other examples of a population mean would be: the mean closing price for Johnson & Johnson stock for the last 5 days is $61.27; and the mean number of hours of overtime worked last week by the six welders in the welding department of Butts Welding, Inc., is 6.45 hours.

For raw data, that is, data that has not been grouped in a frequency distribution, the population mean is the sum of all the values in the population divided by the number of values in the population. To find the population mean, we use the following formula.

$$\text{Population mean} = \frac{\text{Sum of all the values in the population}}{\text{Number of values in the population}}$$

LO1 Calculate the arithmetic mean, weighted mean, median, and mode.

Instead of writing out in words the full directions for computing the population mean (or any other measure), it is more convenient to use the shorthand symbols of mathematics. The mean of a population using mathematical symbols is:

POPULATION MEAN	$\mu = \dfrac{\Sigma X}{N}$	**[3–1]**

where:

    μ represents the population mean. It is the Greek lowercase letter "mu."
    N is the number of values in the population.
    X represents any particular value.
    Σ is the Greek capital letter "sigma" and indicates the operation of adding.
    ΣX is the sum of the X values in the population.

Any measurable characteristic of a population is called a **parameter.** The mean of a population is a parameter.

PARAMETER A characteristic of a population.

Example

There are 12 high schools in the Corry County School District. Listed below is the number of students enrolled in each.

School	Students	School	Students
St. James	1048	Springfield	1095
Waccamaw	1072	Anthony Wayne	983
Aynor	951	Sheffield	818
Loris	1066	Carvers Bay	734
Darlington	1025	Start	776
Youngsville	891	Woodward	701

Is this information a sample or a population? What is the arithmetic mean number of students per high school?

Solution

This is a population because we are considering *all* the high schools in the Corry County School District. To determine the arithmetic mean, we add the number of students for each high school and then divide this total by 12. The total number of students in the 12 high schools is 11,160. So the arithmetic mean is 930, found by 11,160/12. From formula (3–1):

$$\mu = \frac{\Sigma X}{n} = \frac{1048 + 1072 + \cdots + 701}{12} = \frac{11,160}{12} = 930$$

How do we interpret the value of 930? The typical number of students in a high school in the Corry County School District is 930. Because we considered all high schools in the district, this is a population.

The Sample Mean

As explained in Chapter 1, we often select a sample from the population to find something about a specific characteristic of the population. The quality assurance department, for example, needs to be assured that the ball bearings being produced have an acceptable outside diameter. It would be very expensive and time consuming to check the outside diameter of all the bearings produced. Therefore, a sample of five bearings is selected and the mean outside diameter of the five bearings is calculated to estimate the mean diameter of all the bearings.

For raw data, that is, ungrouped data, *the mean is the sum of all the sampled values divided by the total number of sampled values*. To find the mean for a sample:

Mean of ungrouped sample data

$$\text{Sample mean} = \frac{\text{Sum of all the values in the sample}}{\text{Number of values in the sample}}$$

The mean of a sample and the mean of a population are computed in the same way, but the shorthand notation used is different. The formula for the mean of a *sample* is:

SAMPLE MEAN	$\overline{X} = \dfrac{\Sigma X}{n}$	[3–2]

where:
$\overline{X}$ is the sample mean. It is read "X bar."
n is the number of values in the sample.

The mean of a sample, or any other measure based on sample data, is called a **statistic.** If the mean outside diameter of a sample of five ball bearings is 0.625 inches, this is an example of a statistic.

STATISTIC A characteristic of a sample.

Example

SunCom is studying the number of minutes used by clients in a particular cell phone rate plan. A random sample of 12 clients showed the following number of minutes used last month.

90	77	94	89	119	112
91	110	92	100	113	83

What is the arithmetic mean number of minutes used?

Solution

Using formula (3–2), the sample mean is:

$$\text{Sample mean} = \frac{\text{Sum of all values in the sample}}{\text{Number of values in the sample}}$$

$$\bar{X} = \frac{\Sigma X}{n} = \frac{90 + 77 + \cdots + 83}{12} = \frac{1170}{12} = 97.5$$

The arithmetic mean number of minutes used last month by the sample of cell phone users is 97.5 minutes.

Properties of the Arithmetic Mean

LO2 Explain the characteristics, uses, advantages, and disadvantages of each measure of location.

The arithmetic mean is a widely used measure of location. It has several important properties:

1. **Every set of interval- or ratio-level data has a mean.** Recall from Chapter 1 that ratio-level data include such data as ages, incomes, and weights, with the distance between numbers being constant.
2. **All the values are included in computing the mean.**
3. **The mean is unique.** That is, there is only one mean in a set of data. Later in the chapter we will discover an average that might appear twice, or more than twice, in a set of data.
4. **The sum of the deviations of each value from the mean is zero.** Expressed symbolically:

$$\Sigma(X - \bar{X}) = 0$$

As an example, the mean of 3, 8, and 4 is 5. Then:

$$\Sigma(X - \bar{X}) = (3 - 5) + (8 - 5) + (4 - 5)$$

$$= -2 + 3 - 1$$

$$= 0$$

Mean as a balance point

Thus, we can consider the mean as a balance point for a set of data. To illustrate, we have a long board with the numbers 1, 2, 3, . . . , 9 evenly spaced on it. Suppose three bars of equal weight were placed on the board at numbers 3, 4, and 8, and the balance point was set at 5, the mean of the three numbers. We would find that the board is balanced perfectly! The deviations below the mean (−3) are equal to the deviations above the mean (+3). Shown schematically:

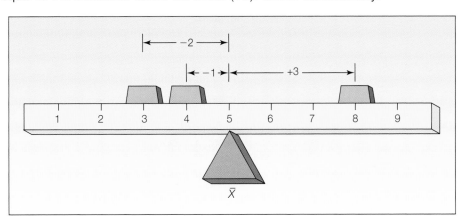

Mean unduly affected by unusually large or small values

The mean does have a weakness. Recall that the mean uses the value of every item in a sample, or population, in its computation. If one or two of these values are either extremely large or extremely small compared to the majority of data, the mean might not be an appropriate average to represent the data. For example, suppose the annual incomes of a sample of real estate agents are $62,900, $61,600, $62,500, $60,800, and $1,200,000. The mean income is $289,560. Obviously, it is not representative of this group, because all but one agent has an income in the $60,000 to $63,000 range. One income ($1.2 million) is unduly affecting the mean.

Self-Review 3–1

1. The annual incomes of a sample of middle-management employees at Westinghouse are: $62,900, $69,100, $58,300, and $76,800.
   (a) Give the formula for the sample mean.
   (b) Find the sample mean.
   (c) Is the mean you computed in (b) a statistic or a parameter? Why?
   (d) What is your best estimate of the population mean?
2. All the students in advanced Computer Science 411 are a population. Their course grades are 92, 96, 61, 86, 79, and 84.
   (a) Give the formula for the population mean.
   (b) Compute the mean course grade.
   (c) Is the mean you computed in (b) a statistic or a parameter? Why?

Exercises

The answers to the odd-numbered exercises are at the end of the book.

1. Compute the mean of the following population values: 6, 3, 5, 7, 6.
2. Compute the mean of the following population values: 7, 5, 7, 3, 7, 4.
3. **a.** Compute the mean of the following sample values: 5, 9, 4, 10.
   b. Show that $\Sigma(X - \bar{X}) = 0$.
4. **a.** Compute the mean of the following sample values: 1.3, 7.0, 3.6, 4.1, 5.0.
   b. Show that $\Sigma(X - \bar{X}) = 0$.
5. Compute the mean of the following sample values: 16.25, 12.91, 14.58.
6. Compute the mean hourly wage paid to carpenters who earned the following hourly wages: $15.40, $20.10, $18.75, $22.76, $30.67, $18.00.

For Exercises 7–10, (a) compute the arithmetic mean and (b) indicate whether it is a statistic or a parameter.

7. There are 10 salespeople employed by Midtown Ford. The number of new cars sold last month by the respective salespeople were: 15, 23, 4, 19, 18, 10, 10, 8, 28, 19.
8. The accounting department at a mail-order company counted the following numbers of incoming calls per day to the company's toll-free number during the first 7 days in May: 14, 24, 19, 31, 36, 26, 17.
9. The Cambridge Power and Light Company selected a random sample of 20 residential customers. Following are the amounts, to the nearest dollar, the customers were charged for electrical service last month:

54	48	58	50	25	47	75	46	60	70
67	68	39	35	56	66	33	62	65	67

10. The Human Relations Director at DuPont began a study of the overtime hours in the Inspection Department. A sample of 15 workers showed they worked the following number of overtime hours last month.

13	13	12	15	7	15	5	12
6	7	12	10	9	13	12	

11. AAA Heating and Air Conditioning completed 30 jobs last month with a mean revenue of $5,430 per job. The president wants to know the total revenue for the month. Based on the limited information, can you compute the total revenue? What is it?

12. A large pharmaceutical company hires business administration graduates to sell its products. The company is growing rapidly and dedicates only one day of sales training for new salespeople. The company's goal for new salespeople is $10,000 per month. The goal is based on the current mean sales for the entire company, which is $10,000 per month. After reviewing the retention rates of new employees, the company finds that only 1 in 10 new employees stays longer than three months. Comment on using the current mean sales per month as a sales goal for new employees. Why do new employees leave the company?

The Weighted Mean

The weighted mean is a special case of the arithmetic mean. It occurs when there are several observations of the same value. To explain, suppose the nearby Wendy's Restaurant sold medium, large, and Biggie-sized soft drinks for $.90, $1.25, and $1.50, respectively. Of the last 10 drinks sold, 3 were medium, 4 were large, and 3 were Biggie-sized. To find the mean price of the last 10 drinks sold, we could use formula (3–2).

$$\overline{X} = \frac{\$.90 + \$.90 + \$.90 + \$1.25 + \$1.25 + \$1.25 + \$1.25 + \$1.50 + \$1.50 + \$1.50}{10}$$

$$\overline{X} = \frac{\$12.20}{10} = \$1.22$$

The mean selling price of the last 10 drinks is $1.22.

An easier way to find the mean selling price is to determine the weighted mean. That is, we multiply each observation by the number of times it happens. We will refer to the weighted mean as $\overline{X}_w$. This is read "X bar sub w."

$$\overline{X}_w = \frac{3(\$0.90) + 4(\$1.25) + 3(\$1.50)}{10} = \frac{\$12.20}{10} = \$1.22$$

In this case the weights are frequency counts. However, any measure of importance could be used as a weight. In general the weighted mean of a set of numbers designated X_1, X_2, X_3, . . . , X_n with the corresponding weights w_1, w_2, w_3, . . . , w_n is computed by:

WEIGHTED MEAN $$\qquad \overline{X}_w = \frac{w_1X_1 + w_2X_2 + w_3X_3 + \cdots + w_nX_n}{w_1 + w_2 + w_3 + \cdots + w_n} \qquad \textbf{[3–3]}$$

This may be shortened to:

$$\overline{X}_w = \frac{\Sigma(wX)}{\Sigma w}$$

Note that the denominator of a weighted mean is always the sum of the weights.

Example

The Carter Construction Company pays its hourly employees $16.50, $19.00, or $25.00 per hour. There are 26 hourly employees, 14 of which are paid at the $16.50 rate, 10 at the $19.00 rate, and 2 at the $25.00 rate. What is the mean hourly rate paid the 26 employees?

Solution

To find the mean hourly rate, we multiply each of the hourly rates by the number of employees earning that rate. From formula (3–3), the mean hourly rate is

$$\overline{X}_w = \frac{14(\$16.50) + 10(\$19.00) + 2(\$25.00)}{14 + 10 + 2} = \frac{\$471.00}{26} = \$18.1154$$

The weighted mean hourly wage is rounded to $18.12.

Self-Review 3–2   Springers sold 95 Antonelli men's suits for the regular price of $400. For the spring sale the suits were reduced to $200 and 126 were sold. At the final clearance, the price was reduced to $100 and the remaining 79 suits were sold.
(a)   What was the weighted mean price of an Antonelli suit?
(b)   Springers paid $200 a suit for the 300 suits. Comment on the store's profit per suit if a salesperson receives a $25 commission for each one sold.

Exercises

connect™

13. In June an investor purchased 300 shares of Oracle (an information technology company) stock at $20 per share. In August she purchased an additional 400 shares at $25 per share. In November she purchased an additional 400 shares, but the stock declined to $23 per share. What is the weighted mean price per share?

14. The Bookstall, Inc., is a specialty bookstore concentrating on used books sold via the Internet. Paperbacks are $1.00 each, and hardcover books are $3.50. Of the 50 books sold last Tuesday morning, 40 were paperback and the rest were hardcover. What was the weighted mean price of a book?

15. The Loris Healthcare System employs 200 persons on the nursing staff. Fifty are nurse's aides, 50 are practical nurses, and 100 are registered nurses. Nurse's aides receive $8 an hour, practical nurses $15 an hour, and registered nurses $24 an hour. What is the weighted mean hourly wage?

16. Andrews and Associates specialize in corporate law. They charge $100 an hour for researching a case, $75 an hour for consultations, and $200 an hour for writing a brief. Last week one of the associates spent 10 hours consulting with her client, 10 hours researching the case, and 20 hours writing the brief. What was the weighted mean hourly charge for her legal services?

The Median

We have stressed that, for data containing one or two very large or very small values, the arithmetic mean may not be representative. The center for such data can be better described by a measure of location called the **median.**

To illustrate the need for a measure of location other than the arithmetic mean, suppose you are seeking to buy a condominium in Palm Aire. Your real estate agent says that the typical price of the units currently available is $110,000. Would you still want to look? If you had budgeted your maximum purchase price at $75,000, you might think they are out of your price range. However, checking the prices of the individual units might change your mind. They are $60,000, $65,000, $70,000, and $80,000, and a superdeluxe penthouse costs $275,000. The arithmetic mean price is $110,000, as the real estate agent reported, but one price ($275,000) is pulling the arithmetic mean upward, causing it to be an unrepresentative average. It does seem that a price around $70,000 is a more typical or representative average, and it is. In cases such as this, the median provides a more valid measure of location.

> **MEDIAN** The midpoint of the values after they have been ordered from the smallest to the largest, or the largest to the smallest.

The median price of the units available is $70,000. To determine this, we order the prices from low ($60,000) to high ($275,000) and select the middle value ($70,000). For the median, the data must be at least an ordinal level of measurement.

Prices Ordered from Low to High		Prices Ordered from High to Low
$ 60,000		$275,000
65,000		80,000
70,000	← Median →	70,000
80,000		65,000
275,000		60,000

Median less affected by extreme values

Note that there is the same number of prices below the median of $70,000 as above it. The median is, therefore, unaffected by extremely low or high prices. Had the highest price been $90,000, or $300,000, or even $1 million, the median price would still be $70,000. Likewise, had the lowest price been $20,000 or $50,000, the median price would still be $70,000.

In the previous illustration there is an *odd* number of observations (five). How is the median determined for an *even* number of observations? As before, the observations are ordered. Then by convention to obtain a unique value we calculate the mean of the two middle observations. So for an even number of observations, the median may not be one of the given values.

Example

The five-year annualized total returns of the 10 top-performing diversified mutual funds for the period ending March 2009 are listed below.

Fund Name	Symbol	Annualized Return
Oppenheimer Developing Markets A	ODMAX	9.46%
Oppenheimer Developing Markets N	ODVNX	9.04
Lazard Emerging Markets Equity Instl	LZEMX	8.87
Evergreen Emerging Markets Growth I	EMGYX	8.82
Oppenheimer Developing Markets C	ODVCX	8.65
Oppenheimer Developing Markets B	ODVBX	8.60
Lazard Emerging Markets Equity Open	LZOEX	8.60
Evergreen Emerging Markets Growth A	EMGAX	8.52
DFA Emerging Markets Value I	DFEVX	8.28
Eaton Vance Tax-Managed Emg Mkts I	EITEX	8.01

What is the median annualized return of these funds?

Solution

The number of mutual funds listed is an even number (10). These funds are already ordered from largest to smallest, so we can easily find the middle two returns. The middle two funds are the Oppenheimer Developing Markets C (8.65%) and Oppenheimer Developing Markets B (8.60%). The arithmetic mean of these two funds is 8.625%, found by (8.65 + 8.60)/2. So the median five-year return of the 10 funds is 8.625%. Notice that:

- The median is not one of the original data values.
- Half of the returns are larger than the median and half are smaller.

LO2 Explain the characteristics, uses, advantages, and disadvantages of each measure of location.

Median can be determined for all levels of data except nominal

The major properties of the median are:

1. **It is not affected by extremely large or small values.** Therefore the median is a valuable measure of location when such values do occur.
2. **It can be computed for ordinal-level data or higher.** Recall from Chapter 1 that ordinal-level data can be ranked from low to high—such as the responses "excellent," "very good," "good," "fair," and "poor" to a question on a marketing survey. To use a simple illustration, suppose five people rated a new fudge bar. One person thought it was excellent, one rated it very good, one called it good, one rated it fair, and one considered it poor. The median response is "good." Half of the responses are above "good"; the other half are below it.

The Mode

The **mode** is another measure of location.

> **MODE** The value of the observation that appears most frequently.

The mode is especially useful in summarizing nominal-level data. As an example of its use for nominal-level data, a company has developed five bath oils. The bar chart in Chart 3–1 shows the results of a marketing survey designed to find which bath oil consumers prefer. The largest number of respondents favored Lamoure, as evidenced by the highest bar. Thus, Lamoure is the mode.

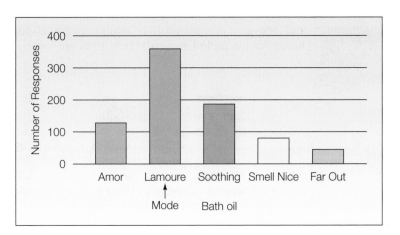

CHART 3–1 Number of Respondents Favoring Various Bath Oils

Example	The annual salaries of quality-control managers in selected states are shown below. What is the modal annual salary?

State	Salary	State	Salary	State	Salary
Arizona	$65,000	Illinois	$88,000	Ohio	$ 80,000
California	79,100	Louisiana	90,000	Tennessee	90,000
Colorado	90,000	Maryland	90,000	Texas	101,400
Florida	90,000	Massachusetts	70,000	West Virginia	90,000
Idaho	70,000	New Jersey	95,000	Wyoming	85,000

Solution	A perusal of the salaries reveals that the annual salary of $90,000 appears more often (six times) than any other salary. The mode is, therefore, $90,000.

LO2 Explain the characteristics, uses, advantages, and disadvantages of each measure of location.

Disadvantages of the mode

In summary, we can determine the mode for all levels of data—nominal, ordinal, interval, and ratio. The mode also has the advantage of not being affected by extremely high or low values.

The mode does have disadvantages, however, that cause it to be used less frequently than the mean or median. For many sets of data, there is no mode because no value appears more than once. For example, there is no mode for this set of price data: $19, $21, $23, $20, and $18. Since every value is different, however, it could be argued that every value is the mode. Conversely, for some data sets there is more than one mode. Suppose the ages of the individuals in a stock investment club are 22, 26, 27, 27, 31, 35, and 35. Both the ages 27 and 35 are modes. Thus, this grouping of ages is referred to as *bimodal* (having two modes). One would question the use of two modes to represent the location of this set of age data.

Self-Review 3–3

1. A sample of single persons in Towson, Texas, receiving Social Security payments revealed these monthly benefits: $852, $598, $580, $1,374, $960, $878, and $1,130.
   (a) What is the median monthly benefit?
   (b) How many observations are below the median? Above it?
2. The number of work stoppages in the automobile industry for selected months are 6, 0, 10, 14, 8, and 0.
   (a) What is the median number of stoppages?
   (b) How many observations are below the median? Above it?
   (c) What is the modal number of work stoppages?

Exercises

connect

17. What would you report as the modal value for a set of observations if there were a total of:
   a. 10 observations and no two values were the same?
   b. 6 observations and they were all the same?
   c. 6 observations and the values were 1, 2, 3, 3, 4, and 4?

For Exercises 18–20, determine the (a) mean, (b) median, and (c) mode.

18. The following is the number of oil changes for the last 7 days at the Jiffy Lube located at the corner of Elm Street and Pennsylvania Avenue.

41	15	39	54	31	15	33

19. The following is the percent change in net income from last year to this year for a sample of 12 construction companies in Denver.

5	1	−10	−6	5	12	7	8	2	5	−1	11

20. The following are the ages of the 10 people in the video arcade at the Southwyck Shopping Mall at 10 A.M.

12	8	17	6	11	14	8	17	10	8

21. Several indicators of long-term economic growth in the United States are listed below.

Economic Indicator	Percent Change	Economic Indicator	Percent Change
Inflation	4.5%	Real GNP	2.9%
Exports	4.7	Investment (residential)	3.6
Imports	2.3	Investment (nonresidential)	2.1
Real disposable income	2.9	Productivity (total)	1.4
Consumption	2.7	Productivity (manufacturing)	5.2

   a. What is the median percent change?
   b. What is the modal percent change?

22. Reported below are the per capita state lottery sales (rounded to the nearest $10) for a recent year in selected states. Find the median and the mode of this lottery information.

State	Amount	State	Amount	State	Amount
Arizona	$ 70	Florida	$230	Indiana	$120
California	90	Kentucky	180	Iowa	80
Colorado	100	Georgia	360	Kansas	90
Connecticut	270	Idaho	90	Louisiana	80
Delaware	880	Illinois	160		

23. The accounting firm of Rowatti and Koppel specializes in income tax returns for self-employed professionals, such as physicians, dentists, architects, and lawyers. The firm employs 11 accountants who prepare the returns. For last year the number of returns prepared by each accountant was:

58	75	31	58	46	65	60	71	45	58	80

Find the mean, median, and mode for the number of returns prepared by each accountant. If you could report only one, which measure of location would you recommend reporting?

24. The demand for the video games provided by Mid-Tech Video Games, Inc., has exploded in the last several years. Hence, the owner needs to hire several new technical people to keep up with the demand. Mid-Tech gives each applicant a special test that Dr. McGraw, the designer of the test, believes is closely related to the ability to create video games. For the general population the mean on this test is 100. Below are the scores on this test for the applicants.

95	105	120	81	90	115	99	100	130	10

The president is interested in the overall quality of the job applicants based on this test. Compute the mean and the median score for the ten applicants. What would you report to the president? Does it seem that the applicants are better than the general population?

Software Solution

We can use a statistical software package to find many measures of location.

Example

Table 2–4 on page 29 shows the prices of the 80 vehicles sold last month at Whitner Autoplex in Raytown, Missouri. Determine the mean and the median selling price.

Solution

The mean and the median selling prices are reported in the following Excel output. (Remember: The instructions to create the output appear in the **Software Commands** section at the end of the chapter.) There are 80 vehicles in the study. So the calculations with a calculator would be tedious and prone to error.

	A	B	C	D	E	F	G	H
1	Price	Price($000)	Age	Type		*Price*		
2	23197	23.197	46	0				
3	23372	23.372	48	0		Mean	23218.1625	
4	20454	20.454	40	1		Standard Error	486.8409474	
5	23591	23.591	40	0		Median	22831	
6	26651	26.651	46	1		Mode	20642	
7	27453	27.453	37	1		Standard Deviation	4354.43781	
8	17266	17.266	32	1		Sample Variance	18961128.64	
9	18021	18.021	29	1		Kurtosis	0.5433087	
10	28683	28.683	38	1		Skewness	0.72681585	
11	30872	30.872	43	0		Range	20379	
12	19587	19.587	32	0		Minimum	15546	
13	23169	23.169	47	0		Maximum	35925	
14	35851	35.851	56	0		Sum	1857453	
15	19251	19.251	42	1		Count	80	
16	20047	20.047	28	1				

Whitner Mean Median

The mean selling price is $23,218 and the median is $22,831. These two values are less than $400 apart. So either value is reasonable. We can also see from the Excel output that there were 80 vehicles sold and their total price is $1,857,453. We will describe the meaning of standard error, standard deviation, and other measures later.

What can we conclude? The typical vehicle sold for about $23,000. Ms. Ball of AutoUSA might use this value in her revenue projections. For example, if the dealership could increase the number sold in a month from 80 to 90, this would result in an additional estimated $230,000 of revenue, found by 10 × $23,000.

The Relative Positions of the Mean, Median, and Mode

LO3 Identify the position of the mean, median, and mode for both symmetric and skewed distributions.

Refer to the histogram in Chart 3–2. It is a symmetric distribution, which is also mound-shaped. This distribution *has the same shape on either side of the center.* If the polygon were folded in half, the two halves would be identical. For any symmetric unimodal distribution, the mode, median, and mean are located at the center and are always equal. They are all equal to 20 years in Chart 3–2. We should point out that there are symmetric distributions that are not mound-shaped.

For a symmetric, mound-shaped distribution, mean, median, and mode are equal.

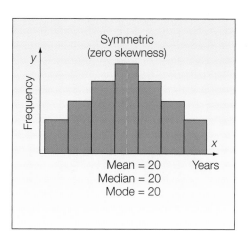

CHART 3–2 A Symmetric Distribution

The number of years corresponding to the highest point of the curve is the *mode* (20 years). Because the distribution is symmetrical, the *median* corresponds to the point where the distribution is cut in half (20 years). The total number of frequencies representing many years is offset by the total number representing few years, resulting in an *arithmetic mean* of 20 years. Logically, any of the three measures would be appropriate to represent the distribution's center.

A skewed distribution is not symmetrical.

If a distribution is nonsymmetrical, or **skewed,** the relationship among the three measures changes. In a **positively skewed distribution,** the arithmetic mean is the largest of the three measures. Why? Because the mean is influenced more than the median or mode by a few extremely high values. The median is generally the next largest measure in a positively skewed frequency distribution. The mode is the smallest of the three measures.

If the distribution is highly skewed, such as the weekly incomes in Chart 3–3, the mean would not be a good measure to use. The median and mode would be more representative.

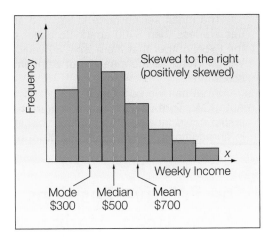

CHART 3–3 A Positively Skewed Distribution

Conversely, if a distribution is **negatively skewed,** the mean is the lowest of the three measures. The mean is, of course, influenced by a few extremely low observations. The median is greater than the arithmetic mean, and the modal value is the largest of the three measures. Again, if the distribution is highly skewed, such as the distribution of tensile strengths shown in Chart 3–4, the mean should not be used to represent the data.

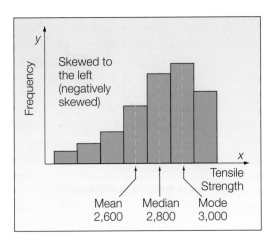

CHART 3–4 A Negatively Skewed Distribution

Self-Review 3–4   The weekly sales from a sample of Hi-Tec electronic supply stores were organized into a frequency distribution. The mean of weekly sales was computed to be $105,900, the median $105,000, and the mode $104,500.
(a) Sketch the sales in the form of a smoothed frequency polygon. Note the location of the mean, median, and mode on the X-axis.
(b) Is the distribution symmetrical, positively skewed, or negatively skewed? Explain.

Exercises

connect

25. The unemployment rate in the state of Alaska by month is given in the table below:

Jan	Feb	Mar	Apr	May	Jun	Jul	Aug	Sep	Oct	Nov	Dec
8.7	8.8	8.7	7.8	7.3	7.8	6.6	6.5	6.5	6.8	7.3	7.6

   a. What is the arithmetic mean of the Alaska unemployment rates?
   b. Find the median and the mode for the unemployment rates.
   c. Compute the arithmetic mean and median for just the winter (Dec–Mar) months. Is it much different?

26. Big Orange Trucking is designing an information system for use in "in-cab" communications. It must summarize data from eight sites throughout a region to describe typical conditions. Compute an appropriate measure of central location for each of the three variables shown in the table below:

City	Wind Direction	Temperature	Pavement
Anniston, AL	West	89	Dry
Atlanta, GA	Northwest	86	Wet
Augusta, GA	Southwest	92	Wet
Birmingham, AL	South	91	Dry
Jackson, MS	Southwest	92	Dry
Meridian, MS	South	92	Trace
Monroe, LA	Southwest	93	Wet
Tuscaloosa, AL	Southwest	93	Trace

Statistics in Action

The United States Postal Service has tried to become more "user friendly" in the last several years. A recent survey showed that customers were interested in more *consistency* in the time it takes to make a delivery. Under the old conditions, a local letter might take only one day to deliver, or it might take several. "Just tell me how many days ahead I need to mail the birthday card to Mom so it gets there on her birthday, not early, not late," was a common complaint. The level of consistency is measured by the standard deviation of the delivery times.

Why Study Dispersion?

A measure of location, such as the mean or the median, only describes the center of the data. It is valuable from that standpoint, but it does not tell us anything about the spread of the data. For example, if your nature guide told you that the river ahead averaged 3 feet in depth, would you want to wade across on foot without additional information? Probably not. You would want to know something about the variation in the depth. Is the maximum depth of the river 3.25 feet and the minimum 2.75 feet? If that is the case, you would probably agree to cross. What if you learned the river depth ranged from 0.50 feet to 5.5 feet? Your decision would probably be not to cross. Before making a decision about crossing the river, you want information on both the typical depth and the dispersion in the depth of the river.

A small value for a measure of dispersion indicates that the data are clustered closely, say, around the arithmetic mean. The mean is therefore considered representative of the data. Conversely, a large measure of dispersion indicates that the mean is not reliable. Refer to Chart 3–5. The 100 employees of Hammond Iron Works, Inc., a steel fabricating company, are organized into a histogram based on the number of years of employment with the company. The mean is 4.9 years, but the spread of the data is from 6 months to 16.8 years. The mean of 4.9 years is not very representative of all the employees.

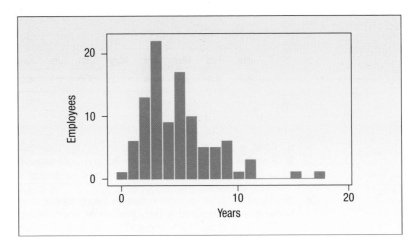

CHART 3–5 Histogram of Years of Employment at Hammond Iron Works, Inc.

A second reason for studying the dispersion in a set of data is to compare the spread in two or more distributions. Suppose, for example, that the new Vision Quest LCD computer monitor is assembled in Baton Rouge and also in Tucson. The arithmetic mean hourly output in both the Baton Rouge plant and the Tucson plant is 50. Based on the two means, you might conclude that the distributions of the hourly outputs are identical. Production records for 9 hours at the two plants, however, reveal that this conclusion is not correct (see Chart 3–6). Baton Rouge production varies from 48 to 52 assemblies per hour. Production at the Tucson plant is more erratic, ranging from 40 to 60 per hour. Therefore, the hourly output for Baton Rouge is clustered near the mean of 50; the hourly output for Tucson is more dispersed.

The average is not representative because of the large spread.

A measure of dispersion can be used to evaluate the reliability of two or more measures of location.

CHART 3–6 Hourly Production of Computer Monitors at the Baton Rouge and Tucson Plants

Measures of Dispersion

We will consider several measures of dispersion. The range is based on the largest and the smallest values in the data set, that is, only two values are considered. The mean deviation, the variance, and the standard deviation use all the values in a data set and are all based on deviations from the arithmetic mean.

Range

LO4 Compute and interpret the range, mean deviation, variance, and standard deviation.

The simplest measure of dispersion is the **range.** It is the difference between the largest and the smallest values in a data set. In the form of an equation:

RANGE	Range = Largest value − Smallest value	[3–4]

The range is widely used in statistical process control (SPC) applications because it is very easy to calculate and understand.

Example

Refer to Chart 3–6 on the previous page. Find the range in the number of computer monitors produced per hour for the Baton Rouge and the Tucson plants. Interpret the two ranges.

Solution

The range of the hourly production of computer monitors at the Baton Rouge plant is 4, found by the difference between the largest hourly production of 52 and the smallest of 48. The range in the hourly production for the Tucson plant is 20 computer monitors, found by 60 − 40. We therefore conclude that (1) there is less dispersion in the hourly production in the Baton Rouge plant than in the Tucson plant because the range of 4 computer monitors is less than a range of 20 computer monitors, and (2) the production is clustered more closely around the mean of 50 at the Baton Rouge plant than at the Tucson plant (because a range of 4 is less than a range of 20). Thus, the mean production in the Baton Rouge plant (50 computer monitors) is a more representative measure of location than the mean of 50 computer monitors for the Tucson plant.

Mean Deviation

A defect of the range is that it is based on only two values, the highest and the lowest; it does not take into consideration all of the values. The **mean deviation** does. It measures the mean amount by which the values in a population, or sample, vary from their mean. In terms of a definition:

MEAN DEVIATION The arithmetic mean of the absolute values of the deviations from the arithmetic mean.

In terms of a formula, the mean deviation, designated *MD*, is computed for a sample by:

MEAN DEVIATION	$MD = \dfrac{\Sigma|X - \bar{X}|}{n}$	[3–5]

where:
    X is the value of each observation.
    $\bar{X}$ is the arithmetic mean of the values.
    n is the number of observations in the sample.
    $\|\ \|$ indicates the absolute value.

Why do we ignore the signs of the deviations from the mean? If we didn't, the positive and negative deviations from the mean would exactly offset each other, and the mean deviation would always be zero. Such a measure (zero) would be a useless statistic.

Example

Solution

The number of cappuccinos sold at the Starbucks location in the Orange County Airport between 4 and 7 p.m. for a sample of 5 days last year were 20, 40, 50, 60, and 80. In the LAX airport in Los Angeles, the number of cappuccinos sold at a Starbucks location between 4 and 7 p.m. for a sample of 5 days last year were 20, 49, 50, 51, and 80. Determine the mean, median, range, and mean deviation for each location. Compare the differences.

For the Orange County location the mean, median, and range are:

Mean	50 cappuccinos per day
Median	50 cappuccinos per day
Range	60 cappuccinos per day

The mean deviation is the mean of the absolute differences between individual observations and the arithmetic mean. For Orange County, the mean number of cappuccinos sold is 50, found by (20 + 40 + 50 + 60 + 80)/5. Next we find the differences between each observation and the mean. Then we sum these differences, ignoring the signs, and divide the sum by the number of observations. The result is the mean difference between the observations and the mean.

Number of Cappuccinos Sold Daily	$(X - \bar{X})$	Absolute Deviation
20	(20 − 50) = −30	30
40	(40 − 50) = −10	10
50	(50 − 50) = 0	0
60	(60 − 50) = 10	10
80	(80 − 50) = 30	30
		Total 80

$$MD = \frac{\Sigma\,|X - \bar{X}|}{n} = \frac{80}{5} = 16$$

The mean deviation is 16 cappuccinos per day and shows that the number of cappuccinos sold deviates, on average, by 16 from the mean of 50 cappuccinos per day.
    The summary of the mean, median, range, and mean deviation for LAX follows. You should perform the calculations to verify the results.

Mean	50 cappuccinos per day
Median	50 cappuccinos per day
Range	60 cappuccinos per day
Mean Deviation	12.4 cappuccinos per day

Recall in the previous chapter that we described data using graphical methods. In this chapter, we describe data using numerical measures. When we use numerical measures, it is very important to always report measures of location and dispersion.

Let's interpret and compare the results of our measures for the Starbucks locations. The mean and median of the two locations are exactly the same, 50 cappuccinos per day. Therefore, the location of both distributions is the same. The range for both locations is also the same, 60. However, recall that the range provides limited information about the dispersion of the distribution.

Notice that the mean deviations are not the same because they are based on the differences between all observations and the arithmetic mean, which show the relative closeness or clustering of the data relative to the mean or center of the distribution. Compare the mean deviation for Orange County of 16 to the mean deviation for LAX of 12.4. Based on the mean deviation, we can say that the dispersion for the sales distribution of the LAX Starbucks is more concentrated near the mean of 50 than the Orange County location.

LO5 Understand the characteristics, uses, advantages, and disadvantages of each measure of dispersion.

The mean deviation has two advantages. First, it uses all the values in the computation. Recall that the range uses only the highest and the lowest values. Second, it is easy to understand—it is the average amount by which values deviate from the mean. However, its drawback is the use of absolute values. Generally, absolute values are difficult to work with and to explain, so the mean deviation is not used as frequently as other measures of dispersion, such as the standard deviation.

Self-Review 3–5

The weights of containers being shipped to Ireland are (in thousands of pounds):

95	103	105	110	104	105	112	90

(a)   What is the range of the weights?
(b)   Compute the arithmetic mean weight.
(c)   Compute the mean deviation of the weights.

Exercises

connect™

For Exercises 27–30, calculate the (a) arithmetic mean, (b) range and (c) mean deviation. Interpret your values.

27. There were five customer service representatives on duty at the Electronic Super Store during last weekend's sale. The numbers of HDTVs these representatives sold are: 5, 8, 4, 10, and 3.
28. The Department of Statistics at Western State University offers eight sections of basic statistics. Following are the numbers of students enrolled in these sections: 34, 46, 52, 29, 41, 38, 36, and 28.
29. Dave's Automatic Door installs automatic garage door openers. The following list indicates the number of minutes needed to install a sample of 10 door openers: 28, 32, 24, 46, 44, 40, 54, 38, 32, and 42.

30. A sample of eight companies in the aerospace industry was surveyed as to their return on investment last year. The results are (in percent): 10.6, 12.6, 14.8, 18.2, 12.0, 14.8, 12.2, and 15.6.

31. Ten randomly selected young adults living in California rated the taste of a newly developed sushi pizza topped with tuna, rice, and kelp on a scale of 1 to 50, with 1 indicating they did not like the taste and 50 that they did. The ratings were:

34	39	40	46	33	31	34	14	15	45

In a parallel study 10 randomly selected young adults in Iowa rated the taste of the same pizza. The ratings were:

28	25	35	16	25	29	24	26	17	20

As a market researcher, compare the potential markets for sushi pizza.

32. A sample of the personnel files of eight employees at the Pawnee location of Acme Carpet Cleaners, Inc., revealed that during the last six-month period they lost the following number of days due to illness:

2	0	6	3	10	4	1	2

A sample of eight employees during the same period at the Chickpee location of Acme Carpets revealed they lost the following number of days due to illness.

2	0	1	0	5	0	1	0

As the director of human relations, compare the two locations. What would you recommend?

Variance and Standard Deviation

Variance and standard deviation are based on squared deviations from the mean.

The **variance** and **standard deviation** are also based on the deviations from the mean. However, instead of using the absolute value of the deviations, the variance and the standard deviation square the deviations.

> **VARIANCE** The arithmetic mean of the squared deviations from the mean.

The variance is nonnegative and is zero only if all observations are the same.

> **STANDARD DEVIATION** The square root of the variance.

Population Variance   The formulas for the population variance and the sample variance are slightly different. The population variance is considered first. (Recall that a population is the totality of all observations being studied.) The **population variance** is found by:

POPULATION VARIANCE	$\sigma^2 = \dfrac{\Sigma(X - \mu)^2}{N}$	[3–6]

Where:

σ^2 is the population variance (σ is the lowercase Greek letter sigma). It is read as "sigma squared."

X is the value of an observation in the population.

μ is the arithmetic mean of the population.

N is the number of observations in the population.

Note the process of computing the variance.

- We begin by finding the mean.
- Next we find the difference between each observation and the mean, and square that difference.
- Then we sum all the squared differences.
- And finally we divide the sum of the squared differences by the number of items in the population.

LO5 Understand the characteristics, uses, advantages, and disadvantages of each measure of dispersion.

So you might think of the population variance as the mean of the squared difference between each value and the mean. For populations whose values are near the mean, the variance will be small. For populations whose values are dispersed from the mean, the population variance will be large.

The variance overcomes the weakness of the range by using all the values in the population, whereas the range uses only the largest and the smallest. We overcome the issue where $\Sigma(X - \mu) = 0$ by squaring the differences, instead of using the absolute values. Squaring the differences will always result in non-negative values.

Example

The number of traffic citations issued last year by month in Beaufort County, South Carolina, is reported below.

Month	January	February	March	April	May	June	July	August	September	October	November	December
Citations	19	17	22	18	28	34	45	39	38	44	34	10

Determine the population variance.

Solution

Because we are studying all the citations for a year, the data is a population. To determine the population variance, we use formula [3–6]. The table below details the calculations.

Month	Citations (X)	$X - \mu$	$(X - \mu)^2$
January	19	−10	100
February	17	−12	144
March	22	−7	49
April	18	−11	121
May	28	−1	1
June	34	5	25
July	45	16	256
August	39	10	100
September	38	9	81
October	44	15	225
November	34	5	25
December	10	−19	361
Total	348	0	1,488

1. We begin by determining the arithmetic mean of the population. The total number of citations issued for the year is 348, so the mean number issued per month is 29.

$$\mu = \frac{\Sigma X}{N} = \frac{19 + 17 + \cdots + 10}{12} = \frac{348}{12} = 29$$

2. Next we find the difference between each observation and the mean. This is shown in the third column of the table. Recall that earlier in the chapter (page 61) we indicated that the sum of the differences between each value and the mean is 0. From the table, the sum of the differences between the mean and the number of citations each month is 0.

3. The next step is to square the difference between each monthly value. That is shown in the fourth column of the table. By squaring the differences, we convert both the positive and the negative values to a plus sign. Hence, each difference will be positive.

4. The squared differences are totaled. The total of the fourth column is 1,488. That is the term $\Sigma(X - \mu)^2$.

5. Finally, we divide the squared differences by N, the number of observations in the population.

$$\sigma^2 = \frac{\Sigma(X - \mu)^2}{N} = \frac{1488}{12} = 124$$

So, the population variation for the number of citations is 124.

Like the range and the mean deviation, the variance can be used to compare dispersion in two or more sets of observations. For example, the variance for the number of citations issued in Beaufort County was just computed to be 124. If the variance in the number of citations issued in Marlboro County, South Carolina, is 342.9, we conclude that (1) there is less dispersion in the distribution of the number of citations issued in Beaufort County than in Marlboro County (because 124 is less than 342.9); and (2) the number of citations in Beaufort County is more closely clustered around the mean of 29 than for the number of citations issued in Marlboro County. Thus the mean number of citations issued in Beaufort County is a more representative measure of location than the mean number of citations in Marlboro County.

Variance is difficult to interpret because the units are squared.

Population Standard Deviation   Both the range and the mean deviation are easy to interpret. The range is the difference between the high and low values of a set of data, and the mean deviation is the mean of the deviations from the mean. However, the variance is difficult to interpret for a single set of observations. The variance of 124 for the number of citations issued is not in terms of citations, but citations squared.

Standard deviation is in the same units as the data.

There is a way out of this difficulty. By taking the square root of the population variance, we can transform it to the same unit of measurement used for the original data. The square root of 124 citations-squared is 11.14 citations. The units are now simply citations. The square root of the population variance is the **population standard deviation**.

| POPULATION STANDARD DEVIATION | $\sigma = \sqrt{\dfrac{\Sigma(X - \mu)^2}{N}}$ | [3–7] |

Self-Review 3–6

The Philadelphia office of PricewaterhouseCoopers LLP hired five accounting trainees this year. Their monthly starting salaries were: $3,536; $3,173; $3,448; $3,121; and $3,622.
(a) Compute the population mean.
(b) Compute the population variance.
(c) Compute the population standard deviation.
(d) The Pittsburgh office hired six trainees. Their mean monthly salary was $3,550, and the standard deviation was $250. Compare the two groups.

Exercises

connect

33. Consider these five values a population: 8, 3, 7, 3, and 4.
    a. Determine the mean of the population.
    b. Determine the variance.
34. Consider these six values a population: 13, 3, 8, 10, 8, and 6.
    a. Determine the mean of the population.
    b. Determine the variance.
35. The annual report of Dennis Industries cited these primary earnings per common share for the past 5 years: $2.68, $1.03, $2.26, $4.30, and $3.58. If we assume these are population values, what is:
    a. The arithmetic mean primary earnings per share of common stock?
    b. The variance?
36. Referring to Exercise 35, the annual report of Dennis Industries also gave these returns on stockholder equity for the same five-year period (in percent): 13.2, 5.0, 10.2, 17.5, and 12.9.
    a. What is the arithmetic mean return?
    b. What is the variance?
37. Plywood, Inc., reported these returns on stockholder equity for the past 5 years: 4.3, 4.9, 7.2, 6.7, and 11.6. Consider these as population values.
    a. Compute the range, the arithmetic mean, the variance, and the standard deviation.
    b. Compare the return on stockholder equity for Plywood, Inc., with that for Dennis Industries cited in Exercise 36.
38. The annual incomes of the five vice presidents of TMV Industries are: $125,000; $128,000; $122,000; $133,000; and $140,000. Consider this a population.
    a. What is the range?
    b. What is the arithmetic mean income?
    c. What is the population variance? The standard deviation?
    d. The annual incomes of officers of another firm similar to TMV Industries were also studied. The mean was $129,000 and the standard deviation $8,612. Compare the means and dispersions in the two firms.

Sample Variance   The formula for the population mean is $\mu = \Sigma X/N$. We just changed the symbols for the sample mean; that is, $\overline{X} = \Sigma X/n$. Unfortunately, the conversion from the population variance to the sample variance is not as direct. It requires a change in the denominator. Instead of substituting n (number in the sample) for N (number in the population), the denominator is $n - 1$. Thus the formula for the **sample variance** is:

SAMPLE VARIANCE	$s^2 = \dfrac{\Sigma(X - \overline{X})^2}{n - 1}$	[3–8]

where:
> s^2 is the sample variance.
> X is the value of each observation in the sample.
> $\overline{X}$ is the mean of the sample.
> n is the number of observations in the sample.

Why is this change made in the denominator? Although the use of n is logical since $\overline{X}$ is used to estimate μ, it tends to underestimate the population variance, σ^2. The use of $(n - 1)$ in the denominator provides the appropriate correction for this tendency. Because the primary use of sample statistics like s^2 is to estimate population parameters like σ^2, $(n - 1)$ is preferred to n in defining the sample variance. We will also use this convention when computing the sample standard deviation.

Example

The hourly wages for a sample of part-time employees at Home Depot are: $12, $20, $16, $18, and $19. What is the sample variance?

Solution

The sample variance is computed by using formula (3–8).

$$\overline{X} = \frac{\Sigma X}{n} = \frac{\$85}{5} = \$17$$

Hourly Wage (X)	X − X̄	(X − X̄)²
$12	−$5	25
20	3	9
16	−1	1
18	1	1
19	2	4
$85	0	40

$$s^2 = \frac{\Sigma(X - \overline{X})^2}{n - 1} = \frac{40}{5 - 1}$$

$$= 10 \text{ in dollars squared}$$

Sample Standard Deviation   The sample standard deviation is used as an estimator of the population standard deviation. As noted previously, the population standard deviation is the square root of the population variance. Likewise, the *sample standard deviation is the square root of the sample variance*. The sample standard deviation is most easily determined by:

SAMPLE STANDARD DEVIATION $$s = \sqrt{\frac{\Sigma(X - \overline{X})^2}{n - 1}}$$ [3–9]

Example

The sample variance in the previous example involving hourly wages was computed to be 10. What is the sample standard deviation?

Solution

The sample standard deviation is $3.16, found by $\sqrt{10}$. Note again that the sample variance is in terms of dollars squared, but taking the square root of 10 gives us $3.16, which is in the same units (dollars) as the original data.

Software Solution

On page 68 we used Excel to determine the mean and median of the Whitner Autoplex sales data. You will also note that it outputs the sample standard deviation. Excel, like most other statistical software, assumes the data are from a sample.

Another software package that we will use in this text is MINITAB. This package uses a spreadsheet format, much like Excel, but produces a wider variety of statistical output. The information for the Whitner Autoplex selling prices follows. Note that a histogram (although the default is to use a class interval of $2,000 and 11 classes) is included as well as the mean, sample standard deviation and the number of observations. A graph of the normal curve is superimposed on the frequency distribution. We will explain the normal curve in Chapter 7.

Self-Review 3–7

The years of service for a sample of seven employees at a State Farm Insurance claims office in Cleveland, Ohio, are: 4, 2, 5, 4, 5, 2, and 6. What is the sample variance? Compute the sample standard deviation.

Exercises

For Exercises 39–44, do the following:

  a. Compute the sample variance.
  b. Determine the sample standard deviation.

39. Consider these values a sample: 7, 2, 6, 2, and 3.
40. The following five values are a sample: 11, 6, 10, 6, and 7.

41. Dave's Automatic Door, referred to in Exercise 29, installs automatic garage door openers. Based on a sample, following are the times, in minutes, required to install 10 door openers: 28, 32, 24, 46, 44, 40, 54, 38, 32, and 42.
42. The sample of eight companies in the aerospace industry, referred to in Exercise 28, was surveyed as to their return on investment last year. The results are: 10.6, 12.6, 14.8, 18.2, 12.0, 14.8, 12.2, and 15.6.
43. The Houston, Texas, Motel Owner Association conducted a survey regarding weekday motel rates in the area. Listed below is the room rate for business-class guests for a sample of 10 motels.

| $101 | $97 | $103 | $110 | $78 | $87 | $101 | $80 | $106 | $88 |

44. A consumer watchdog organization is concerned about credit card debt. A survey of 10 young adults with credit card debt of more than $2,000 showed they paid an average of just over $100 per month against their balances. Listed below is the amounts each young adult paid last month.

| $110 | $126 | $103 | $93 | $99 | $113 | $87 | $101 | $109 | $100 |

Interpretation and Uses of the Standard Deviation

The standard deviation is commonly used as a measure to compare the spread in two or more sets of observations. For example, the standard deviation of the biweekly amounts invested in the Dupree Paint Company profit-sharing plan is computed to be $7.51. Suppose these employees are located in Georgia. If the standard deviation for a group of employees in Texas is $10.47, and the means are about the same, it indicates that the amounts invested by the Georgia employees are not dispersed as much as those in Texas (because $7.51 < $10.47). Because the amounts invested by the Georgia employees are clustered more closely about the mean, the mean for the Georgia employees is a more reliable measure than the mean for the Texas group.

Chebyshev's Theorem

We have stressed that a small standard deviation for a set of values indicates that these values are located close to the mean. Conversely, a large standard deviation reveals that the observations are widely scattered about the mean. The Russian mathematician P. L. Chebyshev (1821–1894) developed a theorem that allows us to determine the minimum proportion of the values that lie within a specified number of standard deviations of the mean. For example, according to **Chebyshev's theorem,** at least three of four values, or 75 percent, must lie between the mean plus two standard deviations and the mean minus two standard deviations. This relationship applies regardless of the shape of the distribution. Further, at least eight of nine values, or 88.9 percent, will lie between plus three standard deviations and minus three standard deviations of the mean. At least 24 of 25 values, or 96 percent, will lie between plus and minus five standard deviations of the mean.

Chebyshev's theorem states:

> **CHEBYSHEV'S THEOREM** For any set of observations (sample or population), the proportion of the values that lie within k standard deviations of the mean is at least $1 - 1/k^2$, where k is any constant greater than 1.

Statistics in Action

Most colleges report the "average class size." This information can be misleading because average class size can be found several ways. If we find the number of students *in each class* at a particular university, the result is the mean number of students per class. If we compile a list of the class sizes for each student and find the mean class size, we might find the mean to be quite different. One school found the mean number of students in each of its 747 classes to be 40. But when it found the mean from a list of the class sizes of each student it was 147. Why the disparity? Because there are few students in the small classes and a larger number of students in the larger classes, which has the effect of increasing the mean class size when it is calculated this way. A school could reduce this mean class size for each student by reducing the number of students in each class. That is, cut out the large freshman lecture classes.

Example	The arithmetic mean biweekly amount contributed by the Dupree Paint employees to the company's profit-sharing plan is $51.54, and the standard deviation is $7.51. At least what percent of the contributions lie within plus 3.5 standard deviations and minus 3.5 standard deviations of the mean?
Solution	About 92 percent, found by $$1 - \frac{1}{k^2} = 1 - \frac{1}{(3.5)^2} = 1 - \frac{1}{12.25} = 0.92$$

The Empirical Rule

LO6 Understand *Chebyshev's theorem* and the *Empirical Rule* as they relate to a set of observation.

The Empirical Rule applies only to symmetrical, bell-shaped distributions.

Chebyshev's theorem is concerned with any set of values; that is, the distribution of values can have any shape. However, for a symmetrical, bell-shaped distribution such as the one in Chart 3–7, we can be more precise in explaining the dispersion about the mean. These relationships involving the standard deviation and the mean are described by the **Empirical Rule,** sometimes called the **Normal Rule.**

EMPIRICAL RULE For a symmetrical, bell-shaped frequency distribution, approximately 68 percent of the observations will lie within plus and minus one standard deviation of the mean; about 95 percent of the observations will lie within plus and minus two standard deviations of the mean; and practically all (99.7 percent) will lie within plus and minus three standard deviations of the mean.

These relationships are portrayed graphically in Chart 3–7 for a bell-shaped distribution with a mean of 100 and a standard deviation of 10.

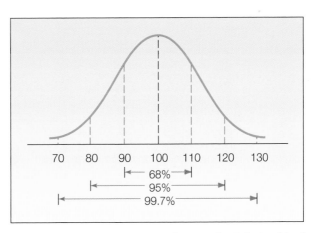

CHART 3–7 A Symmetrical, Bell-Shaped Curve Showing the Relationships between the Standard Deviation and the Observations

It has been noted that if a distribution is symmetrical and bell-shaped, practically all of the observations lie between the mean plus and minus three standard deviations. Thus, if $\overline{X} = 100$ and $s = 10$, practically all the observations lie between $100 + 3(10)$ and $100 - 3(10)$, or 70 and 130. The estimated range is therefore 60, found by $130 - 70$.

Conversely, if we know that the range is 60, we can approximate the standard deviation by dividing the range by 6. For this illustration: range ÷ 6 = 60 ÷ 6 = 10, the standard deviation.

Example

A sample of the rental rates at University Park Apartments approximates a symmetrical, bell-shaped distribution. The sample mean is $500; the standard deviation is $20. Using the Empirical Rule, answer these questions:

1. About 68 percent of the monthly food expenditures are between what two amounts?
2. About 95 percent of the monthly food expenditures are between what two amounts?
3. Almost all of the monthly expenditures are between what two amounts?

Solution

1. About 68 percent are between $480 and $520, found by $\bar{X} \pm 1s = \$500 \pm 1(\$20)$.
2. About 95 percent are between $460 and $540, found by $\bar{X} \pm 2s = \$500 \pm 2(\$20)$.
3. Almost all (99.7 percent) are between $440 and $560, found by $\bar{X} \pm 3s = \$500 \pm 3(\$20)$.

Self-Review 3–8

The Pitney Pipe Company is one of several domestic manufacturers of PVC pipe. The quality control department sampled 600 10-foot lengths. At a point 1 foot from the end of the pipe they measured the outside diameter. The mean was 14.0 inches and the standard deviation 0.1 inches.
(a) If the shape of the distribution is not known, at least what percent of the observations will be between 13.85 inches and 14.15 inches?
(b) If we assume that the distribution of diameters is symmetrical and bell-shaped, about 95 percent of the observations will be between what two values?

Exercises

connect

45. According to Chebyshev's theorem, at least what percent of any set of observations will be within 1.8 standard deviations of the mean?
46. The mean income of a group of sample observations is $500; the standard deviation is $40. According to Chebyshev's theorem, at least what percent of the incomes will lie between $400 and $600?
47. The distribution of the weights of a sample of 1,400 cargo containers is symmetric and bell-shaped. According to the Empirical Rule, what percent of the weights will lie:
    a. Between $\bar{X} - 2s$ and $\bar{X} + 2s$?
    b. Between $\bar{X}$ and $\bar{X} + 2s$? Below $\bar{X} - 2s$?
48. The following graph portrays the distribution of the number of Biggie-sized soft drinks sold at a nearby Wendy's for the last 141 days. The mean number of drinks sold per day is 91.9 and the standard deviation is 4.67.

If we use the Empirical Rule, sales will be between what two values on 68 percent of the days? Sales will be between what two values on 95 percent of the days?

Ethics and Reporting Results

In Chapter 1, we discussed the ethical and unbiased reporting of statistical results. While you are learning about how to organize, summarize, and interpret data using statistics, it is also important to understand statistics so that you can be an intelligent consumer of information.

In this chapter, we learned how to compute numerical descriptive statistics. Specifically, we showed how to compute and interpret measures of location for a data set: the mean, median, and mode. We also discussed the advantages and disadvantages for each statistic. For example, if a real estate developer tells a client that the average home in a particular subdivision sold for $150,000, we assume that $150,000 is a representative selling price for all the homes. But suppose that the client also asks what the median sales price is, and the median is $60,000. Why was the developer only reporting the mean price? This information is extremely important to a person's decision making when buying a home. Knowing the advantages and disadvantages of the mean, median, and mode is important as we report statistics and as we use statistical information to make decisions.

We also learned how to compute measures of dispersion: range, mean deviation, and standard deviation. Each of these statistics also has advantages and disadvantages. Remember that the range provides information about the overall spread of a distribution. However, it does not provide any information about how the data is clustered or concentrated around the center of the distribution.

As we learn more about statistics, we need to remember that when we use statistics we must maintain an independent and principled point of view. Any statistical report requires objective and honest communication of the results.

Statistics in Action

Chipper Jones of the Atlanta Braves had the highest batting average, at .364, during the 2008 season. Tony Gwynn hit .394 in the strike-shortened season of 1994, and Ted Williams hit .406 in 1941. No one has hit over .400 since 1941. The mean batting average has remained constant at about .260 for more than 100 years, but the standard deviation declined from .049 to .031. This indicates less dispersion in the batting averages today and helps explain the lack of any .400 hitters in recent times.

Chapter Summary

I. A measure of location is a value used to describe the center of a set of data.

   A. The arithmetic mean is the most widely reported measure of location.

   1. It is calculated by adding the values of the observations and dividing by the total number of observations.

   a. The formula for a population mean of ungrouped or raw data is

$$\mu = \frac{\Sigma X}{N}$$

[3–1]

   b. The formula for the mean of a sample is

$$\bar{X} = \frac{\Sigma X}{n}$$

[3–2]

   2. The major characteristics of the arithmetic mean are:

   a. At least the interval scale of measurement is required.

   b. All the data values are used in the calculation.

      c. A set of data has only one mean. That is, it is unique.

      d. The sum of the deviations from the mean equals 0.

B. The weighted mean is found by multiplying each observation by its corresponding weight.

   1. The formula for determining the weighted mean is

$$\bar{X}_w = \frac{w_1 X_1 + w_2 X_2 + w_3 X_3 + \cdots + w_n X_n}{w_1 + w_2 + w_3 + \cdots + w_n} \qquad \textbf{[3–3]}$$

   2. It is a special case of the arithmetic mean.

C. The median is the value in the middle of a set of ordered data.

   1. To find the median, sort the observations from smallest to largest and identify the middle value.

   2. The major characteristics of the median are:

      a. It requires at least the ordinal scale of measurement.

      b. It is not influenced by extreme values.

      c. Fifty percent of the observations are larger than the median.

      d. It is unique to a set of data.

D. The mode is the value that occurs most often in a set of data.

   1. The mode can be found for nominal-level data.

   2. A set of data can have more than one mode.

II. The dispersion is the variation or spread in a set of data.

A. The range is the difference between the largest and the smallest value in a set of data.

   1. The formula for the range is

$$\text{Range} = \text{Largest value} - \text{Smallest value} \qquad \textbf{[3–4]}$$

   2. The major characteristics of the range are:

      a. Only two values are used in its calculation.

      b. It is influenced by extreme values.

      c. It is easy to compute and to understand.

B. The mean absolute deviation is the sum of the absolute values of the deviations from the mean divided by the number of observations.

   1. The formula for computing the mean absolute deviation is

$$MD = \frac{\Sigma |X - \bar{X}|}{n} \qquad \textbf{[3–5]}$$

   2. The major characteristics of the mean absolute deviation are:

      a. It is not unduly influenced by large or small values.

      b. All observations are used in the calculation.

      c. The absolute values are difficult to work with.

C. The variance is the mean of the squared deviations from the arithmetic mean.

   1. The formula for the population variance is

$$\sigma^2 = \frac{\Sigma (X - \mu)^2}{N} \qquad \textbf{[3–6]}$$

   2. The formula for the sample variance is

$$s^2 = \frac{\Sigma (X - \bar{X})^2}{n - 1} \qquad \textbf{[3–8]}$$

   3. The major characteristics of the variance are:

      a. All observations are used in the calculation.

      b. It is not unduly influenced by extreme observations.

      c. The units are difficult to work with; they are the original units squared.

D. The standard deviation is the square root of the variance.

   1. The major characteristics of the standard deviation are:

      a. It is in the same units as the original data.

      b. It is the square root of the average squared distance from the mean.

    c. It cannot be negative.

    d. It is the most widely reported measure of dispersion.

  2. The formula for the sample standard deviation is

$$s = \sqrt{\frac{\Sigma(X - \overline{X})^2}{n - 1}}$$ **[3–9]**

III. We interpret the standard deviation using two measures.

  A. Chebyshev's theorem states that regardless of the shape of the distribution, at least $1 - 1/k^2$ of the observations will be within k standard deviations of the mean, where k is greater than 1.

  B. The Empirical Rule states that for a bell-shaped distribution about 68 percent of the values will be within one standard deviation of the mean, 95 percent within two, and virtually all within three.

Pronunciation Key

SYMBOL	MEANING	PRONUNCIATION
μ	Population mean	*mu*
Σ	Operation of adding	*sigma*
ΣX	Adding a group of values	*sigma X*
$\overline{X}$	Sample mean	*X bar*
$\overline{X}_w$	Weighted mean	*X bar sub w*
σ^2	Population variance	*sigma squared*
σ	Population standard deviation	*sigma*

Chapter Exercises

connect™

49. The accounting firm of Crawford and Associates has five senior partners. Yesterday the senior partners saw six, four, three, seven, and five clients, respectively.

  a. Compute the mean number and median number of clients seen by the partners.

  b. Is the mean a sample mean or a population mean?

  c. Verify that $\Sigma(X - \mu) = 0$.

50. Owens Orchards sells apples in a large bag by weight. A sample of seven bags contained the following numbers of apples: 23, 19, 26, 17, 21, 24, 22.

  a. Compute the mean number and median number of apples in a bag.

  b. Verify that $\Sigma(X - \overline{X}) = 0$.

51. A sample of households that subscribe to United Bell Phone Company for land line phone service revealed the following number of calls received per household last week. Determine the mean and the median number of calls received.

52	43	30	38	30	42	12	46	39	37
34	46	32	18	41	5				

52. The Citizens Banking Company is studying the number of times the ATM located in a Loblaws Supermarket at the foot of Market Street is used per day. Following are the number of times the machine was used daily over each of the last 30 days. Determine the mean number of times the machine was used per day.

83	64	84	76	84	54	75	59	70	61
63	80	84	73	68	52	65	90	52	77
95	36	78	61	59	84	95	47	87	60

53. The Canadian government wants to know the relative age of its workforce. As the baby boom generation becomes older, the government is concerned about the availability of younger qualified workers. To become more informed, the government surveyed many industries regarding employee ages. The mean and median age for two industries, communication and retail trade, for six different job types are listed in the following table.

	Communication and Other Utilities		Retail Trade and Consumer Services	
	Mean	Median	Mean	Median
Managers	42.6	43	38.6	38
Professionals	40.8	40	40.0	39
Technical/Trades	41.4	42	37.1	37
Marketing/Sales	NA	NA	33.7	31
Clerical/Administrative	40.8	41	38.0	38
Production Workers	37.2	40	32.0	24

Comment on the distribution of age. Which industry appears to have older workers? Younger workers? In each industry, which job types show the greatest difference between mean and median age?

54. Trudy Green works for the True-Green Lawn Company. Her job is to solicit lawn-care business via the telephone. Listed below is the number of appointments she made in each of the last 25 hours of calling. What is the arithmetic mean number of appointments she made per hour? What is the median number of appointments per hour? Write a brief report summarizing the findings.

9	5	2	6	5	6	4	4	7	2	3	6	3
4	4	7	8	4	4	5	5	4	8	3	3	

55. The Split-A-Rail Fence Company sells three types of fence to homeowners in suburban Seattle, Washington. Grade A costs $5.00 per running foot to install, Grade B costs $6.50 per running foot, and Grade C, the premium quality, costs $8.00 per running foot. Yesterday, Split-A-Rail installed 270 feet of Grade A, 300 feet of Grade B, and 100 feet of Grade C. What was the mean cost per foot of fence installed?

56. Rolland Poust is a sophomore in the College of Business at Scandia Tech. Last semester he took courses in statistics and accounting, 3 hours each, and earned an A in both. He earned a B in a five-hour history course and a B in a two-hour history of jazz course. In addition, he took a one-hour course dealing with the rules of basketball so he could get his license to officiate high school basketball games. He got an A in this course. What was his GPA for the semester? Assume that he receives 4 points for an A, 3 for a B, and so on. What measure of location did you just calculate?

57. The table below shows the percent of the labor force that is unemployed and the size of the labor force for three counties in Northwest Ohio. Jon Elsas is the Regional Director of Economic Development. He must present a report to several companies that are considering locating in Northwest Ohio. What would be an appropriate unemployment rate to show for the entire region?

County	Percent Unemployed	Size of Workforce
Wood	4.5	15,300
Ottawa	3.0	10,400
Lucas	10.2	150,600

58. The manager of Tri-Town Motors checks the age of vehicles traded in at his dealership. Here are the values for a sample of 15 cars:

9	9	5	9	3	4	3	5
10	5	7	6	13	4	4	

a. What is the mean age of the trade-ins?
b. Find the median age.
c. What is the modal age?

59. The ages of a sample of Canadian tourists flying from Toronto to Hong Kong were: 32, 21, 60, 47, 54, 17, 72, 55, 33, and 41.
   a. Compute the range.
   b. Compute the mean deviation.
   c. Compute the standard deviation.
60. The weights (in pounds) of a sample of five boxes being sent by UPS are: 12, 6, 7, 3, and 10.
   a. Compute the range.
   b. Compute the mean deviation.
   c. Compute the standard deviation.
61. The Apollo space program lasted from 1967 until 1972 and included 13 missions. The missions lasted from as little as 7 hours to as long as 301 hours. The duration of each flight is listed below.

9	195	241	301	216	260	7	244	192	147
10	295	142							

   a. Explain why the flight times are a population.
   b. Find the mean and median of the flight times.
   c. Find the range and the standard deviation of the flight times.
62. Creek Ratz is a very popular restaurant located along the coast of northern Florida. They serve a variety of steak and seafood dinners. During the summer beach season, they do not take reservations or accept "call ahead" seating. Management of the restaurant is concerned with the time a patron must wait before being seated for dinner. Listed below is the wait time, in minutes, for the 25 tables seated last Saturday night.

28	39	23	67	37	28	56	40	28	50
51	45	44	65	61	27	24	61	34	44
64	25	24	27	29					

   a. Explain why the times are a population.
   b. Find the mean and median of the times.
   c. Find the range and the standard deviation of the times.
63. A sample of 25 undergraduates reported the following dollar amounts of entertainment expenses last year:

684	710	688	711	722	698	723	743	738	722	696	721	685
763	681	731	736	771	693	701	737	717	752	710	697	

   a. Find the mean, median and mode of this information.
   b. What are the range and standard deviation?
   c. Use the Empirical Rule to establish an interval which includes about 95 percent of the observations.
64. The EPA recently released the following air quality indexes for selected metropolitan areas.

Index	Metropolitan Area	Index	Metropolitan Area
41	Allentown–Bethlehem–Easton, PA	29	Monroe, LA
45	Athens, GA	48	New York, NY
44	Bergen–Passaic, NJ	34	Oakland, CA
39	Buffalo–Niagara Falls, NY	31	Pittsfield, MA
32	Cedar Rapids, IA	36	Reading, PA
42	Cleveland–Lorain–Elyria, OH	31	Rochester, NY
37	Florence, AL	38	San Antonio, TX
41	Fort Worth–Arlington, TX	42	Savannah, GA
37	Goldsboro, NC	35	Scranton–Wilkes Barre–Hazleton, PA
38	Huntsville, AL	36	Vineland–Millville–Bridgeton, NJ
38	Jacksonville, FL	54	Visalia–Tulare–Porterville, CA
33	Johnstown, PA	47	Wheeling, WV–OH
20	Mayaguez, PR		

    a. Find the mean, median, and mode of this data set.
    b. What are the range and standard deviation of the readings?
    c. Use the Empirical Rule to establish an interval which includes about 95 percent of the observations.

65. U.S. housing prices reached their peak in July of 2006. The following data shows the ratio of the prices reported in a recent month to the July 2006 figure. These are to be used to represent typical amounts of decline from that peak for 20 cities.

Phoenix	Los Angeles	San Diego	San Francisco	Denver	Washington	Miami	Tampa	Atlanta	Chicago
0.760	0.784	0.764	0.802	0.909	0.828	0.786	0.792	0.933	0.915

Boston	Detroit	Minneapolis	Charlotte	Las Vegas	New York	Cleveland	Portland	Dallas	Seattle
0.902	0.792	0.855	1.025	0.756	0.922	0.865	0.981	0.939	0.999

    a. Find the mean, median, and mode of these statistics.
    b. What are the range and standard deviation of the values? (Assume this to be sample information.)
    c. Use the Empirical Rule to determine an interval which contains approximately 95 percent of the observations.

66. The Kentucky Derby is held the first Saturday in May at Churchill Downs in Louisville, KY. The racing track is one and one-quarter miles. The following table shows the winners since 1990, their margin of victory, the winning time, and the payoff on a $2 bet.

Year	Winner	Margin (lengths)	Time (minutes)	Payoffs for $2 Bets
1990	Unbridled	3.5	2.03333	10.80
1991	Strike the Gold	1.75	2.05000	4.80
1992	Lil E. Tee	1	2.05000	16.80
1993	Sea Hero	2.5	2.04000	12.90
1994	Go For Gin	2	2.06000	9.10
1995	Thunder Gulch	2.25	2.02000	24.50
1996	Grindstone	Nose	2.01667	5.90
1997	Silver Charm	Head	2.04000	4.00
1998	Real Quiet	0.5	2.03667	8.40
1999	Charismatic	Neck	2.05333	31.30
2000	Fusaichi Pegasus	1.5	2.02000	2.30
2001	Monarchos	4.75	1.99667	10.50
2002	War Emblem	4	2.01667	20.50
2003	Funny Cide	1.75	2.01667	12.80
2004	Smarty Jones	2.75	2.06667	4.10
2005	Giacomo	0.5	2.04583	50.30
2006	Barbaro	6.5	2.03933	6.10
2007	Street Sense	2.25	2.03617	4.90
2008	Big Brown	4.75	2.03033	6.80
2009	Mine that Bird	6.75	2.04433	103.20

    a. Obtain the mean and median for the variables winning time and payoff on a $2 bet.
    b. Determine the range and standard deviation of the variables time and payoff.
    c. Refer to the variable winning margin. What is the level of measurement? What measure of location would be most appropriate?

67. The manager of the local Walmart Super Store is studying the number of items purchased by customers in the evening hours. Listed below is the number of items for a sample of 30 customers.

15	8	6	9	9	4	18	10	10	12
12	4	7	8	12	10	10	11	9	13
5	6	11	14	5	6	6	5	13	5

a. Find the mean and the median of the number of items.
b. Find the range and the standard deviation of the number of items.

Data Set Exercises

68. Refer to the Real Estate data, which reports information on homes sold in the Phoenix, Arizona, area last year.
  a. Select the variable selling price.
    1. Find the mean, median, and the standard deviation.
    2. Write a brief summary of the distribution of selling prices.
  b. Select the variable referring to the area of the home in square feet.
    1. Find the mean, median, and the standard deviation.
    2. Write a brief summary of the distribution of the area of homes.
69. Refer to the Baseball 2008 data, which reports information on the 30 major league teams for the 2008 baseball season.
  a. Select the variable team salary and find the mean, median, and the standard deviation.
  b. Select the variable that refers to the age the stadium was built. (Hint: Subtract the year in which the stadium was built from the current year to find the stadium age and work with that variable.) Find the mean, median, and the standard deviation.
  c. Select the variable that refers to the seating capacity of the stadium. Find the mean, median, and the standard deviation.

Practice Test

Part I Objective
  1. An observable characteristic of a population is called a _____.
  2. A measure, such as the mean, based on sample data is called a _____.
  3. The sum of the differences between each value and the mean is always equal to _____.
  4. The midpoint of a set of values after they have been ordered from the smallest to the largest is called the _____.
  5. What percentage of the values in every data set are larger than the median?
  6. The value of the observation that appears most frequently in a data set is called the _____.
  7. The _____ is the difference between the largest and the smallest values in a data set.
  8. The _____ is the arithmetic mean of the squared deviations from the mean.
  9. The square of the standard deviation is the _____.
  10. The standard deviation assumes a negative value when (all the values are negative, at least half the values are negative, or never—pick one) _____.
  11. Which of the following is least affected by an outlier? (mean, median, or range—pick one) _____.

12. The _____ states that for any symmetrical, bell-shaped frequency distribution, approximately 68 percent of the observations will lie within plus and minus one standard deviation of the mean.

Part II Problems

1. A sample of college students reported they owned the following number of CDs.

| 52 | 76 | 64 | 79 | 80 | 74 | 66 | 69 |

   a. What is the mean number of CDs owned?
   b. What is the median number of CDs owned?
   c. What is the range of the number of CDs owned?
   d. What is the standard deviation of the number of CDs owned?

2. An investor purchased 200 shares of the Blair Company for $36 each in July of 2008, 300 shares at $40 each in September 2008, and 500 shares at $50 each in January 2009. What is the investor's weighted mean price per share?

3. The *Wall Street Journal* regularly surveys a group of about 50 economists. The mean of their forecasts for the change in the domestic gross national product (GNP) is -0.88. That indicates they predict a decline of almost nine tenths of a percent. If the standard deviation is 1.41, use the Empirical Rule to estimate the range that includes 95 percent of all the anticipated values for the GNP.

Software Commands

1. The Excel Commands for the descriptive statistics on page 68 are:
   a. From the CD retrieve the Whitner data file, which is called **Whitner.**
   b. From the menu bar select **Data** and then **Data Analysis.** Select **Descriptive Statistics** and then click **OK.**
   c. For the **Input Range,** type *A1:A81,* indicate that the data are grouped by column and that the labels are in the first row. Click on **Output Range,** indicate that the output should go in *H1* (or any place you wish), click on **Summary statistics,** then click **OK.**
   d. After you get your results, double-check the count in the output to be sure it contains the correct number of items.

2. The MINITAB commands for the descriptive summary on page 81 are:
   a. From the CD retrieve the Whitner data, which is called **Whitner.**
   b. Select **Stat, Basic Statistics,** and then **Display Descriptive Statistics.** In the dialog box select

Price as the variable and then click on **Graphs** in the lower right-hand corner. Within the new dialog box select **Histogram of data, with normal curve** and click **OK.** Click **OK** in the next dialog box.

Chapter 3   Answers to Self-Review

3–1   1. a. $\bar{X} = \dfrac{\Sigma X}{n}$

   b. $\bar{X} = \dfrac{\$267,100}{4} = \$66,775$

   c. Statistic, because it is a sample value.

   d. $66,775. The sample mean is our best estimate of the population mean.

   2. a. $\mu = \dfrac{\Sigma X}{N}$

   b. $\mu = \dfrac{498}{6} = 83$

   c. Parameter, because it was computed using all the population values.

3–2   a. $237, found by:
$$\frac{(95 \times \$400) + (126 \times \$200) + (79 \times \$100)}{95 + 126 + 79} = \$237.00$$

   b. The profit per suit is $12, found by $237 − $200 cost − $25 commission. The total profit for the 300 suits is $3,600, found by 300 × $12.

3–3   1. a. $878
   b. 3, 3
   2. a. 7, found by (6 + 8)/2 = 7
   b. 3, 3
   c. 0

3–4   a.

Weekly Sales

   b. Positively skewed, because the mean is the largest average and the mode is the smallest.

3–5 **a.** 22 thousands of pounds, found by $112 - 90$

b. $\overline{X} = \dfrac{824}{8} = 103$ thousands of pounds

c.

X	$|X - \overline{X}|$	Absolute Deviation
95	$|-8|$	8
103	$|0|$	0
105	$|+2|$	2
110	$|+7|$	7
104	$|+1|$	1
105	$|+2|$	2
112	$|+9|$	9
90	$|-13|$	13
		Total 42

$MD = \dfrac{42}{8} = 5.25$ thousands of pounds

3–6 **a.** $\mu = \dfrac{\$16,900}{5} = \$3,380$

b. $\sigma^2 = \dfrac{(3536 - 3380)^2 + \cdots + (3622 - 3380)^2}{5}$

$= \dfrac{\begin{array}{c}(156)^2 + (-207)^2 + (68)^2 \\ + (-259)^2 + (242)^2\end{array}}{5}$

$= \dfrac{197,454}{5} = 39,490.8$

c. $\sigma = \sqrt{39,490.8} = 198.72$

d. There is more variation in the Pittsburgh office because the standard deviation is larger. The mean is also larger in the Pittsburgh office.

3–7 2.33, found by:

$\overline{X} = \dfrac{\Sigma X}{n} = \dfrac{28}{7} = 4$

X	$X - \overline{X}$	$(X - \overline{X})^2$
4	0	0
2	-2	4
5	1	1
4	0	0
5	1	1
2	-2	4
6	2	4
28	0	14

$s^2 = \dfrac{\Sigma(X - \overline{X})^2}{n - 1}$

$= \dfrac{14}{7 - 1}$

$= 2.33$

$s = \sqrt{2.33} = 1.53$

3–8 **a.** $k = \dfrac{14.15 - 14.00}{.10} = 1.5$

$k = \dfrac{13.85 - 14.0}{.10} = -1.5$

$1 - \dfrac{1}{(1.5)^2} = 1 - .44 = .56$

b. 13.8 and 14.2

Describing Data:

Displaying and Exploring Data

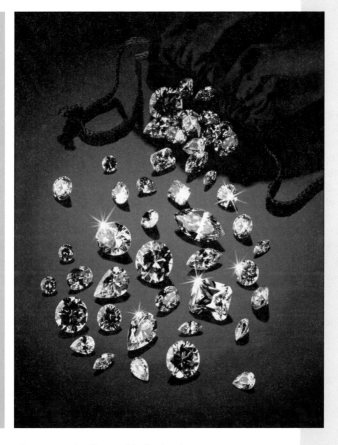

McGivern Jewelers recently ran an advertisement in the local newspaper reporting the shape, size, price, and cut grade for 33 of its diamonds in stock. Using the data provided in Exercise 27, develop a box plot of the variable price and comment on the result. (LO3)

Learning Objectives
When you have completed this chapter, you will be able to:

LO1 Develop and interpret a *dot plot.*

LO2 Compute and understand *quartiles, deciles,* and *percentiles.*

LO3 Construct and interpret *box plots.*

LO4 Compute and understand the *coefficient of skewness.*

LO5 Draw and interpret a *scatter diagram.*

LO6 Construct and interpret a *contingency table.*

Introduction

Chapter 2 began our study of descriptive statistics. In order to transform raw or ungrouped data into a meaningful form, we organize the data into a frequency distribution. We present the frequency distribution in graphic form as a histogram or a frequency polygon. This allows us to visualize where the data tends to cluster, the largest and the smallest values, and the general shape of the data.

In Chapter 3 we first computed several measures of location, such as the mean and the median. These measures of location allow us to report a typical value in the set of observations. We also computed several measures of dispersion, such as the range and the standard deviation. These measures of dispersion allow us to describe the variation or the spread in a set of observations.

We continue our study of descriptive statistics in this chapter. We study (1) dot plots, (2) percentiles, and (3) box plots. These charts and statistics give us additional insight into where the values are concentrated as well as the general shape of the data. Then we consider bivariate data. In bivariate data we observe two variables for each individual or observation selected. Examples include: the number of hours a student studied and the points earned on an examination; whether a sampled product is acceptable or not and the shift on which it is manufactured; and the amount of electricity used in a month by a homeowner and the mean daily high temperature in the region for the month.

Dot Plots

LO1 Develop and interpret a *dot plot*.

A histogram groups data into classes. Recall in the Whitner Autoplex data from Table 2–4 that 80 observations were condensed into seven classes. When we organized the data into the seven classes we lost the exact value of the observations. A **dot plot,** on the other hand, groups the data as little as possible and we do not lose the identity of an individual observation. To develop a dot plot we simply display a dot for each observation along a horizontal number line indicating the possible values of the data. If there are identical observations or the observations are too close to be shown individually, the dots are "piled" on top of each other. This allows us to see the shape of the distribution, the value about which the data tend to cluster, and the largest and smallest observations. Dot plots are most useful for smaller data sets, whereas histograms tend to be most useful for large data sets. An example will show how to construct and interpret dot plots.

Example

Recall in Table 2–4 on page 29 we presented data on the selling price of 80 vehicles sold last month at Whitner Autoplex in Raytown, Missouri. Whitner is one of the many dealerships owned by AutoUSA. AutoUSA has many other dealerships located in small towns throughout the United States. Reported below are the number of vehicles sold in the last 24 months at Smith Ford Mercury Jeep, Inc., in Kane, Pennsylvania, and Brophy Honda Volkswagen in Greenville, Ohio. Construct dot plots and report summary statistics for the two small-town AutoUSA lots.

Smith Ford Mercury Jeep, Inc.									
23	27	30	27	32	31	32	32	35	33
28	39	32	29	35	36	33	25	35	37
26	28	36	30						

Brophy Honda Volkswagen									
31	44	30	36	37	34	43	38	37	35
36	34	31	32	40	36	31	44	26	30
37	43	42	33						

Solution

The MINITAB system provides a dot plot and calculates the mean, median, maximum, and minimum values, and the standard deviation for the number of cars sold at each of the dealerships over the last 24 months.

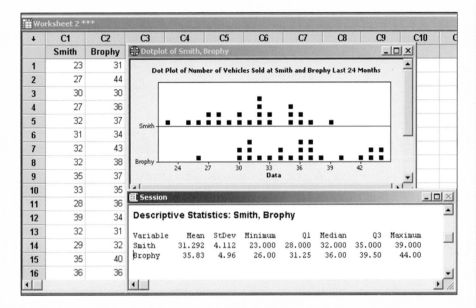

From the descriptive statistics we see that Brophy sold a mean of 35.83 vehicles per month and Smith a mean of 31.292. So Brophy typically sells 4.54 more vehicles per month. There is also more dispersion or variation in the monthly Brophy sales than in the Smith sales. How do we know this? The standard deviation is larger at Brophy (4.96 cars per month) than at Smith (4.112 cars per month).

The dot plot, shown in the center of the software output, graphically illustrates the distributions for both dealerships. The plots show the difference in the location and dispersion of the observations. By looking at the plots, we can see that Brophy's sales are more widely dispersed and have a larger mean than Smith's sales. Several other features of the monthly sales are apparent:

- Smith sold the fewest cars in any month, 23.
- Brophy sold 26 cars in its lowest month, which is 4 cars less than the next lowest month.
- Smith sold exactly 32 cars in four different months.
- The monthly sales cluster is around 32 for Smith and 36 for Brophy.

Self-Review 4–1

The number of employees at each of the 142 Home Depot Stores in the Southeast region is shown in the following dot plot.

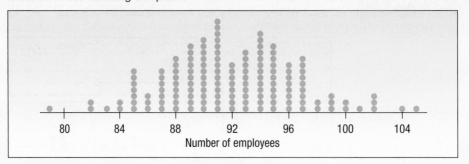

(a) What are the maximum and minimum numbers of employees per store?
(b) How many stores employ 91 people?
(c) Around what values does the number of employees per store tend to cluster?

Exercises

connect

1. Consider the following chart.

   a. What is this chart called?
   b. How many observations are in the study?
   c. What are the maximum and the minimum values?
   d. Around what values do the observations tend to cluster?
2. The following chart reports the number of cell phones sold at Radio Shack for the last 26 days.

   a. What are the maximum and the minimum number of cell phones sold in a day?
   b. What is a typical number of cell phones sold?

Other Measures of Dispersion

The standard deviation is the most widely used measure of dispersion. However, there are other ways of describing the variation or spread in a set of data. One method is to determine the *location* of values that divide a set of observations into equal parts. These measures include **quartiles, deciles,** and **percentiles.**

   Quartiles divide a set of observations into four equal parts. To explain further, think of any set of values arranged from smallest to largest. In Chapter 3 we called the middle value of a set of data arranged from smallest to largest the median. That is, 50 percent of the observations are larger than the median and 50 percent are smaller. The median is a measure of location because it pinpoints the center of the data. In a similar fashion **quartiles** divide a set of observations into four equal parts. The first quartile, usually labeled Q_1, is the value below which 25 percent of the observations occur, and the third quartile, usually labeled Q_3, is the value below which 75 percent of the observations occur. Logically, Q_2 is the median. Q_1 can be thought of as the "median" of the lower half of the data and Q_3 the "median" of the upper half of the data.

In a similar fashion **deciles** divide a set of observations into 10 equal parts and **percentiles** into 100 equal parts. So if you found that your GPA was in the 8th decile at your university, you could conclude that 80 percent of the students had a GPA lower than yours and 20 percent had a higher GPA. A GPA in the 33rd percentile means that 33 percent of the students have a lower GPA and 67 percent have a higher GPA. Percentile scores are frequently used to report results on such national standardized tests as the SAT, ACT, GMAT (used to judge entry into many master of business administration programs), and LSAT (used to judge entry into law school).

Quartiles, Deciles, and Percentiles

LO2 Compute and understand *quartiles, deciles,* and *percentiles.*

To formalize the computational procedure, let L_p refer to the location of a desired percentile. So if we want to find the 33rd percentile we would use L_{33} and if we wanted the median, the 50th percentile, then L_{50}. The number of observations is n, so if we want to locate the median, its position is at $(n + 1)/2$, or we could write this as $(n + 1)(P/100)$, where P is the desired percentile.

LOCATION OF A PERCENTILE	$L_p = (n + 1)\dfrac{P}{100}$	[4–1]

An example will help to explain further.

Example

Listed below are the commissions earned last month by a sample of 15 brokers at Salomon Smith Barney's Oakland, California office. Salomon Smith Barney is an investment company with offices located throughout the United States.

$2,038	$1,758	$1,721	$1,637	$2,097	$2,047	$2,205	$1,787	$2,287
1,940	2,311	2,054	2,406	1,471	1,460			

Locate the median, the first quartile, and the third quartile for the commissions earned.

Solution

The first step is to sort the data from the smallest commission to the largest.

$1,460	$1,471	$1,637	$1,721	$1,758	$1,787	$1,940	$2,038
2,047	2,054	2,097	2,205	2,287	2,311	2,406	

The median value is the observation in the center. The center value or L_{50} is located at $(n + 1)(50/100)$, where n is the number of observations. In this case that is position number 8, found by $(15 + 1)(50/100)$. The eighth largest commission is $2,038. So we conclude this is the median and that half the brokers earned commissions more than $2,038 and half earned less than $2,038.

Recall the definition of a quartile. Quartiles divide a set of observations into four equal parts. Hence 25 percent of the observations will be less than the first quartile. Seventy-five percent of the observations will be less than the third quartile. To locate the first quartile, we use formula (4–1), where $n = 15$ and $P = 25$:

$$L_{25} = (n + 1)\frac{P}{100} = (15 + 1)\frac{25}{100} = 4$$

and to locate the third quartile, $n = 15$ and $P = 75$:

$$L_{75} = (n + 1)\frac{P}{100} = (15 + 1)\frac{75}{100} = 12$$

Therefore, the first and third quartile values are located at positions 4 and 12, respectively. The fourth value in the ordered array is $1,721 and the twelfth is $2,205. These are the first and third quartiles.

In the above example the location formula yielded a whole number. That is, we wanted to find the first quartile and there were 15 observations, so the location formula indicated we should find the fourth ordered value. What if there were 20 observations in the sample, that is $n = 20$, and we wanted to locate the first quartile? From the location formula (4–1):

$$L_{25} = (n + 1)\frac{P}{100} = (20 + 1)\frac{25}{100} = 5.25$$

We would locate the fifth value in the ordered array and then move .25 of the distance between the fifth and sixth values and report that as the first quartile. Like the median, the quartile does not need to be one of the actual values in the data set.

To explain further, suppose a data set contained the six values: 91, 75, 61, 101, 43, and 104. We want to locate the first quartile. We order the values from smallest to largest: 43, 61, 75, 91, 101, and 104. The first quartile is located at

$$L_{25} = (n + 1)\frac{P}{100} = (6 + 1)\frac{25}{100} = 1.75$$

The position formula tells us that the first quartile is located between the first and the second value and that it is .75 of the distance between the first and the second values. The first value is 43 and the second is 61. So the distance between these two values is 18. To locate the first quartile, we need to move .75 of the distance between the first and second values, so .75(18) = 13.5. To complete the procedure, we add 13.5 to the first value and report that the first quartile is 56.5.

We can extend the idea to include both deciles and percentiles. To locate the 23rd percentile in a sample of 80 observations, we would look for the 18.63 position.

$$L_{23} = (n + 1)\frac{P}{100} = (80 + 1)\frac{23}{100} = 18.63$$

To find the value corresponding to the 23rd percentile, we would locate the 18th value and the 19th value and determine the distance between the two values. Next, we would multiply this difference by 0.63 and add the result to the smaller value. The result would be the 23rd percentile.

With a statistical software package, it is quite easy to sort the data from smallest to largest and to locate percentiles and deciles. Both MINITAB and Excel output summary statistics. Listed below is the MINITAB output. The data are reported in $000. It includes the first and third quartiles, as well as the mean, median, and standard deviation for the Whitner Autoplex data (see Table 2–4). We conclude that 25 percent of the vehicles sold for less than $20,074 and that 75 percent sold for less than $25,795.

The following Excel output includes the same information regarding the mean, median, and standard deviation. It will also output the quartiles, but the method of calculation is not as precise. To find the quartiles, we multiply the sample size by the desired percentile and report the integer of that value. To explain, in the Whitner Autoplex data there are 80 observations, and we wish to locate the 25th percentile. We multiply $n + 1 = 80 + 1 = 81$ by .25; the result is 20.25. Excel will not allow us to enter a fractional value, so we use 20 and request the location of the largest 20 values and the smallest 20 values. The result is a good approximation of the 25th and 75th percentiles.

ꂆ Whitner Quartiles							
	A	B	C	D	E	F	G	H
1	Price	Price($000)	Age	Type		Price($000)		
2	23197	23.197	46	0				
3	23372	23.372	48	0		Mean	23.2181625	
4	20454	20.454	40	1		Standard Error	0.486840947	
5	23591	23.591	40	0		Median	22.831	
6	26651	26.651	46	1		Mode	20.642	
7	27453	27.453	37	1		Standard Deviation	4.35443781	
8	17266	17.266	32	1		Sample Variance	18.96112864	
9	18021	18.021	29	1		Kurtosis	0.5433087	
10	28683	28.683	38	1		Skewness	0.72681585	
11	30872	30.872	43	0		Range	20.379	
12	19587	19.587	32	0		Minimum	15.546	
13	23169	23.169	47	0		Maximum	35.925	
14	35851	35.851	56	0		Sum	1857.453	
15	19251	19.251	42	1		Count	80	
16	20047	20.047	28	1		Largest(20)	25.799	
17	24285	24.285	56	0		Smallest(20)	20.047	
18	24324	24.324	50	1				

Self-Review 4–2

The Quality Control department of Plainsville Peanut Company is responsible for checking the weight of the 8-ounce jar of peanut butter. The weights of a sample of nine jars produced last hour are:

7.69	7.72	7.8	7.86	7.90	7.94	7.97	8.06	8.09

(a) What is the median weight?
(b) Determine the weights corresponding to the first and third quartiles.

Exercises

connect™

3. Determine the median and the values corresponding to the first and third quartiles in the following data.

46	47	49	49	51	53	54	54	55	55	59

4. Determine the median and the values corresponding to the first and third quartiles in the following data.

5.24	6.02	6.67	7.30	7.59	7.99	8.03	8.35	8.81	9.45
9.61	10.37	10.39	11.86	12.22	12.71	13.07	13.59	13.89	15.42

5. The Thomas Supply Company, Inc., is a distributor of gas-powered generators. As with any business, the length of time customers take to pay their invoices is important. Listed below, arranged from smallest to largest, is the time, in days, for a sample of The Thomas Supply Company, Inc., invoices.

13	13	13	20	26	27	31	34	34	34	35	35	36	37	38
41	41	41	45	47	47	47	50	51	53	54	56	62	67	82

  a. Determine the first and third quartiles.
  b. Determine the second decile and the eighth decile.
  c. Determine the 67th percentile.

6. Kevin Horn is the national sales manager for National Textbooks, Inc. He has a sales staff of 40 who visit college professors all over the United States. Each Saturday morning he requires his sales staff to send him a report. This report includes, among other things, the number of professors visited during the previous week. Listed below, ordered from smallest to largest, is the number of visits last week.

38	40	41	45	48	48	50	50	51	51	52	52	53	54	55	55	55	56	56	57
59	59	59	62	62	62	63	64	65	66	66	67	67	69	69	71	77	78	79	79

  a. Determine the median number of calls.
  b. Determine the first and third quartiles.
  c. Determine the first decile and the ninth decile.
  d. Determine the 33rd percentile.

Box Plots

LO3 Construct and interpret *box plots*.

A **box plot** is a graphical display, based on quartiles, that helps us picture a set of data. To construct a box plot, we need only five statistics: the minimum value, Q_1 (the first quartile), the median, Q_3 (the third quartile), and the maximum value. An example will help to explain.

Example

Alexander's Pizza offers free delivery of its pizza within 15 miles. Alex, the owner, wants some information on the time it takes for delivery. How long does a typical delivery take? Within what range of times will most deliveries be completed? For a sample of 20 deliveries, he determined the following information:

$$\text{Minimum value} = 13 \text{ minutes}$$

$$Q_1 = 15 \text{ minutes}$$

$$\text{Median} = 18 \text{ minutes}$$

$$Q_3 = 22 \text{ minutes}$$

$$\text{Maximum value} = 30 \text{ minutes}$$

Develop a box plot for the delivery times. What conclusions can you make about the delivery times?

Solution

The first step in drawing a box plot is to create an appropriate scale along the horizontal axis. Next, we draw a box that starts at Q_1 (15 minutes) and ends at Q_3 (22 minutes). Inside the box we place a vertical line to represent the median (18 minutes). Finally, we extend horizontal lines from the box out to the minimum value (13 minutes) and the maximum value (30 minutes). These horizontal lines outside of the box are sometimes called "whiskers" because they look a bit like a cat's whiskers.

The box plot shows that the middle 50 percent of the deliveries take between 15 minutes and 22 minutes. The distance between the ends of the box, 7 minutes, is the **interquartile range.** The interquartile range is the distance between the first and the third quartile. It shows the spread or dispersion of the majority of deliveries.

The box plot also reveals that the distribution of delivery times is positively skewed. Recall from page 69 in Chapter 3 that we defined skewness as the lack of symmetry in a set of data. How do we know this distribution is positively skewed? In this case there are actually two pieces of information that suggest this. First, the dashed line to the right of the box from 22 minutes (Q_3) to the maximum time of 30 minutes is longer than the dashed line from the left of 15 minutes (Q_1) to the minimum value of 13 minutes. To put it another way, the 25 percent of the data larger than the third quartile is more spread out than the 25 percent less than the first quartile. A second indication of positive skewness is that the median is not in the center of the box. The distance from the first quartile to the median is smaller than the distance from the median to the third quartile. We know that the number of delivery times between 15 minutes and 18 minutes is the same as the number of delivery times between 18 minutes and 22 minutes.

Example

Refer to the Whitner Autoplex data in Table 2–4. Develop a box plot of the data. What can we conclude about the distribution of the vehicle selling prices?

Solution

The MINITAB statistical software system was used to develop the following chart.

	C1	C2	
	Price	Price($000)	
1	23197	23.197	
2	23372	23.372	
3	20454	20.454	
4	23591	23.591	
5	26651	26.651	
6	27453	27.453	
7	17266	17.266	
8	18021	18.021	
9	28683	28.683	
10	30872	30.872	
11	19587	19.587	
12	23169	23.169	
13	35851	35.851	
14	19251	19.251	
15	20047	20.047	
16	24285	24.285	
17	24324	24.324	
18	24609	24.609	

We conclude that the median vehicle selling price is about $23,000, that about 25 percent of the vehicles sell for less than $20,000, and that about 25 percent sell for more than $26,000. About 50 percent of the vehicles sell for between $20,000 and $26,000. The distribution is positively skewed because the solid line above $26,000 is somewhat longer than the line below $20,000.

There is an asterisk (*) above the $35,000 selling price. An asterisk indicates an **outlier.** An outlier is a value that is inconsistent with the rest of the data. An outlier is defined as a value that is more than 1.5 times the interquartile range smaller than Q_1 or larger than Q_3. In this example, an outlier would be a value larger than $35,000, found by

$$\text{Outlier} > Q_3 + 1.5(Q_3 - Q_1) = \$26,000 + 1.5(\$26,000 - \$20,000) = \$35,000$$

A value less than $11,000 is also an outlier.

$$\text{Outlier} < Q_1 - 1.5(Q_3 - Q_1) = \$20,000 - 1.5(\$26,000 - \$20,000) = \$11,000$$

The MINITAB box plot indicates that there is only one value larger than $35,000. However, if you look at the actual data in Table 2–4 on page 29 you will notice that there are actually two values ($35,851 and $35,925). The software was not able to graph two data points so close together, so it shows only one asterisk.

Self-Review 4–3

The following box plot shows the assets in millions of dollars for credit unions in Seattle, Washington.

What are the smallest and largest values, the first and third quartiles, and the median? Would you agree that the distribution is symmetrical?

Exercises

7. The box plot below shows the amount spent for books and supplies per year by students at four-year public colleges.

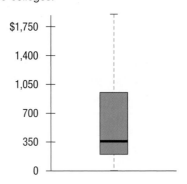

   a. Estimate the median amount spent.
   b. Estimate the first and third quartiles for the amount spent.
   c. Estimate the interquartile range for the amount spent.
   d. Beyond what point is a value considered an outlier?
   e. Identify any outliers and estimate their value.
   f. Is the distribution symmetrical or positively or negatively skewed?
8. The box plot shows the undergraduate in-state charge per credit hour at four-year public colleges.

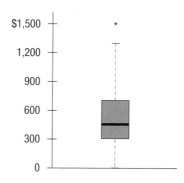

a. Estimate the median.
b. Estimate the first and third quartiles.
c. Determine the interquartile range.
d. Beyond what point is a value considered an outlier?
e. Identify any outliers and estimate their value.
f. Is the distribution symmetrical or positively or negatively skewed?

9. In a study of the gasoline mileage of model year 2007 automobiles, the mean miles per gallon was 27.5 and the median was 26.8. The smallest value in the study was 12.70 miles per gallon, and the largest was 50.20. The first and third quartiles were 17.95 and 35.45 miles per gallon, respectively. Develop a box plot and comment on the distribution. Is it a symmetric distribution?

10. A sample of 28 time shares in the Orlando, Florida, area revealed the following daily charges for a one-bedroom suite. For convenience the data are ordered from smallest to largest. Construct a box plot to represent the data. Comment on the distribution. Be sure to identify the first and third quartiles and the median.

$116	$121	$157	$192	$207	$209	$209
229	232	236	236	239	243	246
260	264	276	281	283	289	296
307	309	312	317	324	341	353

Skewness

In Chapter 3 we described measures of central location for a set of observations by reporting the mean, median, and mode. We also described measures that show the amount of spread or variation in a set of data, such as the range and the standard deviation.

LO4 Compute and understand the *coefficient of skewness.*

Another characteristic of a set of data is the shape. There are four shapes commonly observed: symmetric, positively skewed, negatively skewed, and bimodal. In a **symmetric** set of observations the mean and median are equal and the data values are evenly spread around these values. The data values below the mean and median are a mirror image of those above. A set of values is **skewed to the right** or **positively skewed** if there is a single peak and the values extend much further to the right of the peak than to the left of the peak. In this case the mean is larger than the median. In a **negatively skewed** distribution there is a single peak but the observations extend further to the left, in the negative direction, than to the right. In a negatively skewed distribution the mean is smaller than the median. Positively skewed distributions are more common. Salaries often follow this pattern. Think of the salaries of those employed in a small company of about 100 people. The president and a few top executives would have very large salaries relative to the other workers and hence the distribution of salaries would exhibit positive skewness. A **bimodal distribution** will have two or more peaks. This is often the case when the values are from two or more populations. This information is summarized in Chart 4–1.

CHART 4–1 Shapes of Frequency Distributions

There are several formulas in statistical literature used to calculate skewness. The simplest, developed by Professor Karl Pearson (1857–1936), is based on the difference between the mean and the median.

$$\textbf{PEARSON'S COEFFICIENT OF SKEWNESS} \qquad sk = \frac{3(\overline{X} - \text{Median})}{s} \qquad \textbf{[4–2]}$$

Using this relationship the coefficient of skewness can range from -3 up to 3. A value near -3, such as -2.57, indicates considerable negative skewness. A value such as 1.63 indicates moderate positive skewness. A value of 0, which will occur when the mean and median are equal, indicates the distribution is symmetrical and that there is no skewness present.

In this text we present output from the statistical software packages MINITAB and Excel. Both of these software packages compute a value for the coefficient of skewness that is based on the cubed deviations from the mean. The formula is:

$$\textbf{SOFTWARE COEFFICIENT OF SKEWNESS} \qquad sk = \frac{n}{(n-1)(n-2)}\left[\sum\left(\frac{X-\overline{X}}{s}\right)^3\right] \qquad \textbf{[4–3]}$$

Formula (4–3) offers an insight into skewness. The right-hand side of the formula is the difference between each value and the mean, divided by the standard deviation. That is the portion $(X - \overline{X})/s$ of the formula. This idea is called **standardizing.** We will discuss the idea of standardizing a value in more detail in Chapter 7 when we describe the normal probability distribution. At this point, observe that the result takes into consideration the difference between each value and the mean in units of the standard deviation. If this difference is positive, the particular value is larger than the mean; if the variation is negative, the standardized quantity is smaller than the mean. When we cube these values, we retain the information on the direction of the difference. Recall that in the formula for the standard deviation [see formula (3–9)] we squared the difference between each value and the mean, so that the result was all non-negative values.

If the set of data values under consideration is symmetric, when we cube the standardized values and sum over all the values the result would be near zero. If there are several large values, clearly separate from the others, the sum of the cubed differences would be a large positive value. Several values much smaller will result in a negative cubed sum.

An example will illustrate the idea of skewness.

Example

Following are the earnings per share for a sample of 15 software companies for the year 2009. The earnings per share are arranged from smallest to largest.

$0.09	$0.13	$0.41	$0.51	$ 1.12	$ 1.20	$ 1.49	$3.18
3.50	6.36	7.83	8.92	10.13	12.99	16.40	

Compute the mean, median, and standard deviation. Find the coefficient of skewness using Pearson's estimate and the software methods. What is your conclusion regarding the shape of the distribution?

Solution

These are sample data, so we use formula (3–2) to determine the mean

$$\overline{X} = \frac{\Sigma X}{n} = \frac{\$74.26}{15} = \$4.95$$

The median is the middle value in a set of data, arranged from smallest to largest. In this case the middle value is $3.18, so the median earnings per share is $3.18. We use formula (3–9) on page 80 to determine the sample standard deviation.

$$s = \sqrt{\frac{\Sigma(X - \overline{X})^2}{n - 1}} = \sqrt{\frac{(\$0.09 - \$4.95)^2 + \cdots + (\$16.40 - \$4.95)^2}{15 - 1}} = \$5.22$$

Pearson's coefficient of skewness is 1.017, found by

$$sk = \frac{3(\overline{X} - \text{Median})}{s} = \frac{3(\$4.95 - \$3.18)}{\$5.22} = 1.017$$

This indicates there is moderate positive skewness in the earnings per share data.
We obtain a similar, but not exactly the same, value from the software method. The details of the calculations are shown in Table 4–1. To begin we find the difference

TABLE 4–1 Calculation of the Coefficient of Skewness

Earnings per Share	$\dfrac{(X - \overline{X})}{s}$	$\left(\dfrac{X - \overline{X}}{s}\right)^3$
0.09	−0.9310	−0.8070
0.13	−0.9234	−0.7873
0.41	−0.8697	−0.6579
0.51	−0.8506	−0.6154
1.12	−0.7337	−0.3950
1.20	−0.7184	−0.3708
1.49	−0.6628	−0.2912
3.18	−0.3391	−0.0390
3.50	−0.2778	−0.0214
6.36	0.2701	0.0197
7.83	0.5517	0.1679
8.92	0.7605	0.4399
10.13	0.9923	0.9772
12.99	1.5402	3.6539
16.40	2.1935	10.5537
		11.8274

between each earnings per share value and the mean and divide this result by the standard deviation. Recall that we referred to this as standardizing. Next, we cube, that is, raise to the third power, the result of the first step. Finally, we sum the cubed values. The details for the first company, that is, the company with an earnings per share of $0.09, are:

$$\left(\frac{X - \overline{X}}{s}\right)^3 = \left(\frac{0.09 - 4.95}{5.22}\right)^3 = (-0.9310)^3 = -0.8070$$

When we sum the 15 cubed values, the result is 11.8274. That is, the term $\Sigma[(X - \overline{X})/s]^3 = 11.8274$. To find the coefficient of skewness, we use formula (4–3), with $n = 15$.

$$sk = \frac{n}{(n - 1)(n - 2)} \Sigma\left(\frac{X - \overline{X}}{s}\right)^3 = \frac{15}{(15 - 1)(15 - 2)} (11.8274) = 0.975$$

We conclude that the earnings per share values are somewhat positively skewed. The following chart, from MINITAB, reports the descriptive measures, such as the mean, median, and standard deviation of the earnings per share data. Also included are the coefficient of skewness and a histogram with a bell-shaped curve superimposed.

Self-Review 4–4

A sample of five data entry clerks employed in the Horry County Tax Office revised the following number of tax records last hour: 73, 98, 60, 92, and 84.
(a)   Find the mean, median, and the standard deviation.
(b)   Compute the coefficient of skewness using Pearson's method.
(c)   Calculate the coefficient of skewness using the software method.
(d)   What is your conclusion regarding the skewness of the data?

Exercises

connect

For Exercises 11–14:

a. Determine the mean, median, and the standard deviation.
b. Determine the coefficient of skewness using Pearson's method.
c. Determine the coefficient of skewness using the software method.

11. The following values are the starting salaries, in $000, for a sample of five accounting graduates who accepted positions in public accounting last year.

36.0	26.0	33.0	28.0	31.0

12. Listed below are the salaries, in $000, for a sample of 15 chief financial officers in the electronics industry.

$516.0	$548.0	$566.0	$534.0	$586.0	$529.0
546.0	523.0	538.0	523.0	551.0	552.0
486.0	558.0	574.0			

13. Listed below are the commissions earned ($000) last year by the sales representatives at Furniture Patch, Inc.

$ 3.9	$ 5.7	$ 7.3	$10.6	$13.0	$13.6	$15.1	$15.8	$17.1
17.4	17.6	22.3	38.6	43.2	87.7			

14. Listed below are the salaries for the New York Yankees for the year 2009.

Player	Salary ($000)	Player	Salary ($000)
Alex Rodriguez	$33,000.0	Chien-Ming Wang	$5,000.0
Derek Jeter	21,600.0	Damaso Marte	3,750.0
Mark Teixeira	20,625.0	Jose Molina	2,125.0
A.J. Burnett	16,500.0	Melky Cabrera	1,400.0
CC Sabathia	15,285.7	Brian Bruney	1,250.0
Mariano Rivera	15,000.0	Cody Ransom	455.1
Jorge Posada	13,100.0	Jose Veras	433.0
Johnny Damon	13,000.0	Joba Chamberlain	432.6
Hideki Matsui	13,000.0	Edwar Ramirez	422.5
Xavier Nady	6,550.0	Brett Gardner	414.0
Robinson Cano	6,000.0	Phil Coke	403.3
Andy Pettitte	5,500.0	Jonathan Albaladejo	403.1
Nick Swisher	5,400.0	Ramiro Pena	400.0

Describing the Relationship between Two Variables

In Chapter 2 and the first section of this chapter we presented graphical techniques to summarize the distribution of a single variable. We used a histogram in Chapter 2 to summarize the prices of vehicles sold at Whitner Autoplex. Earlier in this chapter we used dot plots to visually summarize a set of data. Because we are studying a single variable we refer to this as **univariate** data.

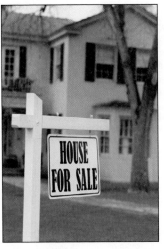

There are situations where we wish to study and visually portray the relationship between two variables. When we study the relationship between two variables we refer to the data as **bivariate.** Data analysts frequently wish to understand the relationship between two variables. Here are some examples:

- Tybo and Associates is a law firm that advertises extensively on local TV. The partners are considering increasing their advertising budget. Before doing so, they would like to know the relationship between the amount spent per month on advertising and the total amount of billings for that month. To put it another way, will increasing the amount spent on advertising result in an increase in billings?
- Coastal Realty is studying the selling prices of homes. What variables seem to be related to the selling price of homes? For example, do larger homes sell for more than smaller ones? Probably. So Coastal might study the relationship between the area in square feet and the selling price.
- Dr. Stephen Givens is an expert in human development. He is studying the relationship between the height of fathers and the height of their sons. That is, do tall fathers tend to have tall children? Would you expect Shaquille O'Neal, the 7'1", 335-pound professional basketball player, to have relatively tall sons?

LO5 Draw and interpret a *scatter diagram.*

One graphical technique we use to show the relationship between variables is called a **scatter diagram.**

To draw a scatter diagram we need two variables. We scale one variable along the horizontal axis (*X*-axis) of a graph and the other variable along the vertical axis (*Y*-axis). Usually one variable depends to some degree on the other. In the third example above, the height of the son *depends* on the height of the father. So we scale the height of the father on the horizontal axis and that of the son on the vertical axis.

We can use statistical software, such as Excel, to perform the plotting function for us. *Caution:* you should always be careful of the scale. By changing the scale of either the vertical or the horizontal axis, you can affect the apparent visual strength of the relationship.

Following are three scatter diagrams (Chart 4–2). The one on the left shows a rather strong positive relationship between the age in years and the maintenance cost last year for a sample of 10 buses owned by the city of Cleveland, Ohio. Note that as the age of the bus increases the yearly maintenance cost also increases. The example in the center, for a sample of 20 vehicles, shows a rather strong indirect

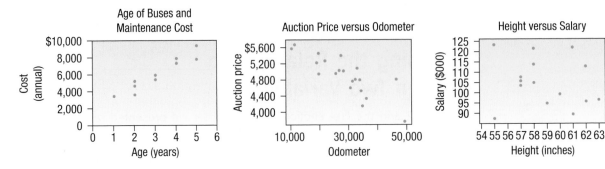

CHART 4–2 Three Examples of Scatter Diagrams.

relationship between the odometer reading and the auction price. That is, as the number of miles driven increases, the auction price decreases. The example on the right depicts the relationship between the height and yearly salary for a sample of 15 shift supervisors. This graph indicates there is little relationship between their height and yearly salary.

Example

In the Introduction to Chapter 2 we presented data from AutoUSA. In this case the information concerned the prices of 80 vehicles sold last month at the Whitner Autoplex lot in Raytown, Missouri. The data shown on page 22 include the selling price of the vehicle as well as the age of the purchaser. Is there a relationship between the selling price of a vehicle and the age of the purchaser? Would it be reasonable to conclude that the more expensive vehicles are purchased by older buyers?

Solution

We can investigate the relationship between vehicle selling price and the age of the buyer with a scatter diagram. We scale age on the horizontal, or X-axis, and the selling price on the vertical, or Y-axis. We use Microsoft Excel to develop the scatter diagram. The Excel commands necessary for the output are shown in the **Software Commands** section at the end of the chapter.

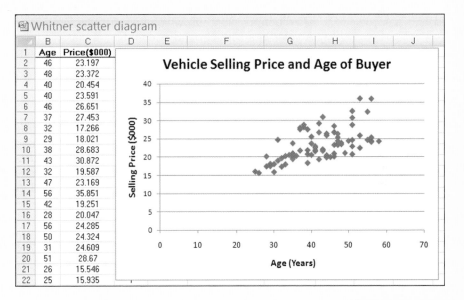

The scatter diagram shows a positive relationship between the variables. In fact, older buyers tend to buy more expensive cars. In Chapter 13 we will study the relationship between variables more extensively, even calculating several numerical measures to express the relationship between variables.

In the Whitner Autoplex example there is a positive or direct relationship between the variables. That is, as age increased, the vehicle selling price also increased. There are, however, many instances where there is a relationship between the variables, but that relationship is inverse or negative. For example:

- The value of a vehicle and the number of miles driven. As the number of miles increases, the value of the vehicle decreases.
- The premium for auto insurance and the age of the driver. Auto rates tend to be the highest for young adults and less for older people.

- For many law enforcement personnel as the number of years on the job increases, the number of traffic citations decreases. This may be because personnel become more liberal in their interpretations or they may be in supervisor positions and not in a position to issue as many citations. But in any event as age increases, the number of citations decreases.

A scatter diagram requires that both of the variables be at least interval scale. In the Whitner Autoplex example both age and selling price are ratio scale variables. Height is also ratio scale as used in the discussion of the relationship between the height of fathers and the height of their sons. What if we wish to study the relationship between two variables when one or both are nominal or ordinal scale? In this case we tally the results in a **contingency table.**

LO6 Construct and interpret a *contingency table.*

> **CONTINGENCY TABLE** A table used to classify observations according to two identifiable characteristics.

A contingency table is a cross-tabulation that simultaneously summarizes two variables of interest. For example:

- Students at a university are classified by gender and class rank.
- A product is classified as acceptable or unacceptable and by the shift (day, afternoon, or night) on which it is manufactured.
- A voter in a school bond referendum is classified as to party affiliation (Democrat, Republican, other) and the number of children that voter has attending school in the district (0, 1, 2, etc.).

Example

A manufacturer of preassembled windows produced 50 windows yesterday. This morning the quality assurance inspector reviewed each window for all quality aspects. Each was classified as acceptable or unacceptable and by the shift on which it was produced. Thus we reported two variables on a single item. The two variables are shift and quality. The results are reported in the following table.

	Shift			
	Day	**Afternoon**	**Night**	**Total**
Defective	3	2	1	6
Acceptable	17	13	14	44
Total	20	15	15	50

Compare the quality levels on each shift.

Solution

The level of measurement for both variables is nominal. That is, the variables shift and quality are such that a particular unit can only be classified or assigned into groups. By organizing the information into a contingency table we can compare the quality on the three shifts. For example, on the day shift, 3 out of 20 windows or 15 percent are defective. On the afternoon shift, 2 of 15 or 13 percent are defective and on the night shift 1 out of 15 or 7 percent are defective. Overall 12 percent of the windows are defective. Observe also that 40 percent of the windows are produced on the day shift, found by (20/50)(100). We will return to the study of contingency tables in Chapter 5 during the study of probability and in Chapter 15 during the study of chi-square applications.

Self-Review 4–5   The rock group Blue String Beans is touring the United States. The following chart shows the relationship between concert seating capacity and revenue in $000 for a sample of concerts.

(a) What is the diagram called?
(b) How many concerts were studied?
(c) Estimate the revenue for the concert with the largest seating capacity.
(d) How would you characterize the relationship between revenue and seating capacity? Is it strong or weak, direct or inverse?

Exercises

connect

15. Develop a scatter diagram for the following sample data. How would you describe the relationship between the values?

X-Value	Y-Value	X-Value	Y-Value
10	6	11	6
8	2	10	5
9	6	7	2
11	5	7	3
13	7	11	7

16. Silver Springs Moving and Storage, Inc., is studying the relationship between the number of rooms in a move and the number of labor hours required for the move. As part of the analysis the CFO of Silver Springs developed the following scatter diagram.

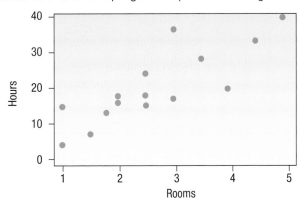

a. How many moves are in the sample?
b. Does it appear that more labor hours are required as the number of rooms increases, or do labor hours decrease as the number of rooms increases?

17. The Director of Planning for Devine Dining, Inc., wishes to study the relationship between the gender of a guest and whether the guest orders dessert. To investigate the relationship the manager collected the following information on 200 recent customers.

Dessert Ordered	Gender		Total
	Male	Female	
Yes	32	15	47
No	68	85	153
Total	100	100	200

   a. What is the level of measurement of the two variables?
   b. What is the above table called?
   c. Does the evidence in the table suggest men are more likely to order dessert than women? Explain why.

18. Ski Resorts of Vermont, Inc., is considering a merger with Gulf Shores, Inc., of Alabama. The board of directors surveyed 50 stockholders concerning their position on the merger. The results are reported below.

Number of Shares Held	Opinion			Total
	Favor	Oppose	Undecided	
Under 200	8	6	2	16
200 up to 1,000	6	8	1	15
Over 1,000	6	12	1	19
Total	20	26	4	50

   a. What level of measurement is used in this table?
   b. What is this table called?
   c. What group seems most strongly opposed to the merger?

Chapter Summary

I. A dot plot shows the range of values on the horizontal axis and a dot is placed above each of the values.
   A. Dot plots report the details of each observation.
   B. They are useful for comparing two or more data sets.
II. Measures of location also describe the shape of a set of observations.
   A. Quartiles divide a set of observations into four equal parts.
      1. Twenty-five percent of the observations are less than the first quartile, 50 percent are less than the second quartile, and 75 percent are less than the third quartile.
      2. The interquartile range is the difference between the third and the first quartile.
   B. Deciles divide a set of observations into ten equal parts and percentiles into 100 equal parts.
   C. A box plot is a graphic display of a set of data.
      1. A box is drawn enclosing the regions between the first and third quartiles.
         a. A line is drawn inside the box at the median value.
         b. Dotted line segments are drawn from the third quartile to the largest value to show the highest 25 percent of the values and from the first quartile to the smallest value to show the lowest 25 percent of the values.
      2. A box plot is based on five statistics: the maximum and minimum values, the first and third quartiles, and the median.
III. The coefficient of skewness is a measure of the symmetry of a distribution.
   A. There are two formulas for the coefficient of skewness.
      1. The formula developed by Pearson is:

$$sk = \frac{3(\overline{X} - \text{Median})}{s}$$
[4–2]

2. The coefficient of skewness computed by statistical software is:

$$sk = \frac{n}{(n-1)(n-2)}\left[\sum\left(\frac{X-\bar{X}}{s}\right)^3\right] \qquad \textbf{[4–3]}$$

IV. A scatter diagram is a graphic tool to portray the relationship between two variables.
  A. Both variables are measured with interval or ratio scales.
  B. If the scatter of points moves from the lower left to the upper right, the variables under consideration are directly or positively related.
  C. If the scatter of points moves from the upper left to the lower right, the variables are inversely or negatively related.
V. A contingency table is used to classify nominal-scale observations according to two characteristics.

Pronunciation Key

SYMBOL	MEANING	PRONUNCIATION
L_p	Location of percentile	L sub p
Q_1	First quartile	Q sub 1
Q_3	Third quartile	Q sub 3

Chapter Exercises

connect

19. A sample of students attending Southeast Florida University is asked the number of social activities in which they participated last week. The chart below was prepared from the sample data.

  a. What is the name given to this chart?
  b. How many students were in the study?
  c. How many students reported attending no social activities?

20. Doctor's Care is a walk-in clinic, with locations in Georgetown, Monks Corners, and Aynor, at which patients may receive treatment for minor injuries, colds, and flu, as well as physical examinations. The following charts report the number of patients treated in each of the three locations last month.

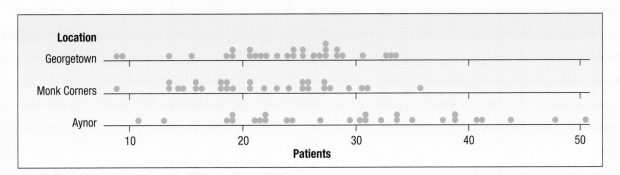

Describe the number of patients served at the three locations each day. What are the maximum and minimum numbers of patients served at each of the locations?

21. In recent years, due to low interest rates, many homeowners refinanced their home mortgages. Linda Lahey is a mortgage officer at Down River Federal Savings and Loan. Below is the amount refinanced for 20 loans she processed last week. The data are reported in thousands of dollars and arranged from smallest to largest.

59.2	59.5	61.6	65.5	66.6	72.9	74.8	77.3	79.2
83.7	85.6	85.8	86.6	87.0	87.1	90.2	93.3	98.6
100.2	100.7							

a. Find the median, first quartile, and third quartile.
b. Find the 26th and 83rd percentiles.
c. Draw a box plot of the data.

22. A study is made by the recording industry in the United States of the number of music CDs owned by senior citizens and young adults. The information is reported below.

Seniors									
28	35	41	48	52	81	97	98	98	99
118	132	133	140	145	147	153	158	162	174
177	180	180	187	188					

Young Adults									
81	107	113	147	147	175	183	192	202	209
233	251	254	266	283	284	284	316	372	401
417	423	490	500	507	518	550	557	590	594

a. Find the median and the first and third quartiles for the number of CDs owned by senior citizens. Develop a box plot for the information.
b. Find the median and the first and third quartiles for the number of CDs owned by young adults. Develop a box plot for the information.
c. Compare the number of CDs owned by the two groups.

23. The corporate headquarters of *Bank.com,* a new Internet company that performs all banking transactions via the Internet, is located in downtown Philadelphia. The director of human resources is making a study of the time it takes employees to get to work. The city is planning to offer incentives to each downtown employer if they will encourage their employees to use public transportation. Below is a listing of the time to get to work this morning according to whether the employee used public transportation or drove a car.

Public Transportation									
23	25	25	30	31	31	32	33	35	36
37	42								

Private									
32	32	33	34	37	37	38	38	38	39
40	44								

  a. Find the median and the first and third quartiles for the time it took employees using public transportation. Develop a box plot for the information.
  b. Find the median and the first and third quartiles for the time it took employees who drove their own vehicle. Develop a box plot for the information.
  c. Compare the times of the two groups.
24. The following box plot shows the number of daily newspapers published in each state and the District of Columbia. Write a brief report summarizing the number published. Be sure to include information on the values of the first and third quartiles, the median, and whether there is any skewness. If there are any outliers, estimate their value.

Number of Newspapers

25. Walter Gogel Company is an industrial supplier of fasteners, tools, and springs. The amounts of its invoices vary widely, from less than $20.00 to more than $400.00. During the month of January the company sent out 80 invoices. Here is a box plot of these invoices. Write a brief report summarizing the invoice amounts. Be sure to include information on the values of the first and third quartiles, the median, and whether there is any skewness. If there are any outliers, approximate the value of these invoices.

Invoice Amount

26. National Muffler Company claims it will change your muffler in less than 30 minutes. An investigative reporter for WTOL Channel 11 monitored 30 consecutive muffler changes at the National outlet on Liberty Street. The number of minutes to perform changes is reported below.

44	12	22	31	26	22	30	26	18	28	12
40	17	13	14	17	25	29	15	30	10	28
16	33	24	20	29	34	23	13			

  a. Develop a box plot for the time to change a muffler.
  b. Does the distribution show any outliers?
  c. Summarize your findings in a brief report.
27. McGivern Jewelers is located in the Levis Square Mall just south of Toledo, Ohio. Recently it ran an advertisement in the local newspaper reporting the shape, size,

price, and cut grade for 33 of its diamonds currently in stock. The information is reported below.

Shape	Size (carats)	Price	Cut Grade	Shape	Size (carats)	Price	Cut Grade
Princess	5.03	$44,312	Ideal cut	Round	0.77	$ 2,828	Ultra ideal cut
Round	2.35	20,413	Premium cut	Oval	0.76	3,808	Premium cut
Round	2.03	13,080	Ideal cut	Princess	0.71	2,327	Premium cut
Round	1.56	13,925	Ideal cut	Marquise	0.71	2,732	Good cut
Round	1.21	7,382	Ultra ideal cut	Round	0.70	1,915	Premium cut
Round	1.21	5,154	Average cut	Round	0.66	1,885	Premium cut
Round	1.19	5,339	Premium cut	Round	0.62	1,397	Good cut
Emerald	1.16	5,161	Ideal cut	Round	0.52	2,555	Premium cut
Round	1.08	8,775	Ultra ideal cut	Princess	0.51	1,337	Ideal cut
Round	1.02	4,282	Premium cut	Round	0.51	1,558	Premium cut
Round	1.02	6,943	Ideal cut	Round	0.45	1,191	Premium cut
Marquise	1.01	7,038	Good cut	Princess	0.44	1,319	Average cut
Princess	1.00	4,868	Premium cut	Marquise	0.44	1,319	Premium cut
Round	0.91	5,106	Premium cut	Round	0.40	1,133	Premium cut
Round	0.90	3,921	Good cut	Round	0.35	1,354	Good cut
Round	0.90	3,733	Premium cut	Round	0.32	896	Premium cut
Round	0.84	2,621	Premium cut				

a. Develop a box plot of the variable price and comment on the result. Are there any outliers? What is the median price? What is the value of the first and the third quartile?

b. Develop a box plot of the variable size and comment on the result. Are there any outliers? What is the median price? What is the value of the first and the third quartile?

c. Develop a scatter diagram between the variables price and size. Be sure to put price on the vertical axis and size on the horizontal axis. Does there seem to be an association between the two variables? Is the association direct or indirect? Does any point seem to be different from the others?

d. Develop a contingency table for the variables shape and cut grade. What is the most common cut grade? What is the most common shape? What is the most common combination of cut grade and shape?

28. Listed below is the amount of commissions earned last month for the eight members of the sales staff at Best Electronics. Calculate the coefficient of skewness using both methods. *Hint:* Use of a spreadsheet will expedite the calculations.

980.9	1,036.5	1,099.5	1,153.9	1,409.0	1,456.4	1,718.4	1,721.2

29. Listed below is the number of car thefts in a large city over the last week. Calculate the coefficient of skewness using both methods. *Hint:* Use of a spreadsheet will expedite the calculations.

3	12	13	7	8	3	8

30. The manager of Information Services at Wilkin Investigations, a private investigation firm, is studying the relationship between the age (in months) of a combination printer, copy, and fax machine and its monthly maintenance cost. For a sample of 15 machines the manager developed the following chart. What can the manager conclude about the relationship between the variables?

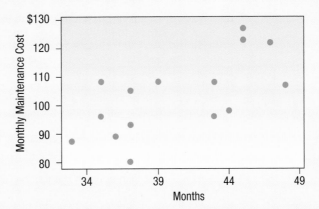

31. An auto insurance company reported the following information regarding the age of a driver and the number of accidents reported last year. Develop a scatter diagram for the data and write a brief summary.

Age	Accidents	Age	Accidents
16	4	23	0
24	2	27	1
18	5	32	1
17	4	22	3

32. Wendy's offers eight different condiments (mustard, catsup, onion, mayonnaise, pickle, lettuce, tomato, and relish) on hamburgers. A store manager collected the following information on the number of condiments ordered and the age group of the customer. What can you conclude regarding the information? Who tends to order the most or least number of condiments?

	Age			
Number of Condiments	**Under 18**	**18 up to 40**	**40 up to 60**	**60 or older**
0	12	18	24	52
1	21	76	50	30
2	39	52	40	12
3 or more	71	87	47	28

33. Listed below is a table showing the number of employed and unemployed workers 20 years or older by gender in the United States in 2006.

	Number of Workers (000)	
Gender	**Employed**	**Unemployed**
Men	70,415	4,209
Women	61,402	3,314

   a. How many workers were studied?
   b. What percent of the workers were unemployed?
   c. Compare the percent unemployed for the men and the women.

Data Set Exercises

34. Refer to the Real Estate data, which report information on homes sold in the Phoenix, Arizona, area last year. Select the variable selling price.
   a. Develop a box plot. Estimate the first and the third quartiles. Are there any outliers?
   b. Develop a scatter diagram with price on the vertical axis and the size of the home on the horizontal. Does there seem to be a relationship between these variables? Is the relationship direct or inverse?

   c. Develop a scatter diagram with price on the vertical axis and distance from the center of the city on the horizontal axis. Does there seem to be a relationship between these variables? Is the relationship direct or inverse?

35. Refer to the Baseball 2008 data, which report information on the 30 Major League Baseball teams for the 2008 season.

   a. Select the variable that refers to the year in which the stadium was built. (*Hint:* Subtract the year in which the stadium was built from the current year to find the age of the stadium and work with this variable.) Develop a box plot. Are there any outliers?

   b. Select the variable team salary and draw a box plot. Are there any outliers? What are the quartiles? Write a brief summary of your analysis. How do the salaries of the New York Yankees compare with the other teams?

   c. Draw a scatter diagram with the number of games won on the vertical axis and the team salary on the horizontal axis. What are your conclusions?

   d. Select the variable wins. Draw a dot plot. What can you conclude from this plot?

36. Refer to the Wage data, which report information on annual wages for a sample of 100 workers. Also included are variables relating to industry, years of education, and gender for each worker.

   a. Develop a box plot for the variable annual wage. Are there any outliers? Write a brief summary of your findings.

   b. Develop a box plot for the variable years of education. Are there any outliers? Write a brief summary of your findings.

   c. Draw a bar chart of the variable occupation. Write a brief report summarizing your findings.

Practice Test

Part I Objective

  1. A graph for displaying data in which each individual value is represented along a number line is called a _____ .

  2. A _____ is a graphical display based on five statistics: the maximum and minimum values, the first and third quartiles, and the median.

  3. A _____ is a graphical technique used to show the relationship between two variables.

  4. A _____ table is used to classify observations according to two identifiable characteristics.

  5. A _____ divides a set of observations into four equal parts.

  6. A _____ divides a set of observations into 100 equal parts.

  7. The coefficient of _____ is a measure of the symmetry.

  8. The _____ is the point below which one-fourth of the ranked values lie.

  9. The _____ is the difference between the first and third quartiles.

Part II Problems

  1. The market capitalization at the end of the most recent fiscal year for 11 companies in the property and casualty insurance industry is (in millions of dollars):

15	17	23	26	27	35	72	88	91	98	102

   a. Draw a dot plot of the data.

   b. Determine the median.

   c. Compute the first quartile.

   d. Find the 75th percentile.

   e. Make a box plot of the data.

2. A Texas farm cooperative held a health screening for its members. The results for blood pressure screening are summarized by the different age groups in the following table.

Blood Pressure	Age			Total
	Under 30	30 to 60	Over 60	
Low	21	29	37	87
Medium	45	82	91	218
High	23	46	75	144
Total	89	157	203	449

a. What fraction of the members have high blood pressure?
b. What fraction of the "Under 30" members have low blood pressure?
c. Is there a relationship between age and blood pressure? Describe what it is.

Software Commands

1. The MINITAB commands for the dot plot on page 97 are:
   a. Enter the vehicles sold at Smith Ford Mercury Jeep in column *C1* and Brophy Honda Volkswagen in *C2*. Name the variables accordingly.
   b. Select **Graph** and **Dotplot**. In the first dialog box select **Multiple Y's, Simple** in the lower left corner and click **OK**. In the next dialog box select **Smith** and **Brophy** as the variables to **Graph**, click on **Labels** and write an appropriate title. Then click **OK.**
   c. To calculate the descriptive statistics shown in the output select **Stat, Basic statistics,** and then **Display Descriptive statistics.** In the dialog box select **Smith** and **Brophy** as the **Variables,** click on **Statistics** and select the desired statistics to be output, and finally click **OK** twice.

2. The MINITAB commands for the descriptive summary on page 100 are:
   a. Import the Whitner Autoplex data from the CD. The file name is **Whitner.** Select the variable **Price.**
   b. From the toolbar select **Stat, Basic Statistics,** and **Display Descriptive Statistics.** In the dialog

box select **Price** as the **Variable,** in the lower right click on **Graphs.** In this box select **Graphs,** click on **Histogram of data,** and then click **OK** twice.

3. The Excel Commands for the descriptive statistics on page 101 are:

a. From the CD retrieve the Whitner Autoplex data file, which is **Whitner.**

b. From the menu bar select **Data,** and then **Data Analysis.** Select **Descriptive Statistics** and then click **OK.**

c. For the **Input Range,** type *B1:B81,* indicate that the data are grouped by column and that the labels are in the first row. Click on **Output Range,** indicate that the output should go into *F1* (or any place you wish), and click on **Summary statistics.**

d. In the lower left, click on **Kth Largest** and put *20* in the box and click on **Kth Smallest** and put *20* in that box.

e. After you get your results, double-check the count in the output to be sure it contains the correct number of values.

4. The MINITAB commands for the box plot on page 103 are:

a. Import the data from the CD. The file name is **Table2–1.**

b. Select **Graph** and then **Boxplot.** In the dialog box select **Simple** in the upper left corner and click **OK.** Select **Price ($000)** as the **Graph variable,** click on **Labels** and include an appropriate heading, and then click **OK.**

5. The MINITAB commands for the descriptive summary on page 108 are:

a. Enter the data in the first column. In the cell below C1, enter the variable *Earnings.*

b. Select **Stat, Basic Statistics,** and then click on **Graphical Summary.** Select **Earnings** as the variable, and then click **OK.**

6. The Excel commands for the scatter diagram on page 111 are:

a. Retrieve the data from **Whitner** on the CD.

b. You will need to copy the variables to other columns on the spreadsheet with age in a column and price ($000) in the next column. This will allow you to place price on the vertical axis and age on the horizontal axis.

c. Using the mouse, highlight the column of age and price ($000). Include the first row.

d. Select the **Insert** tab. Select **Scatter** from the **Chart** options. Select the top left option. The scatter plot will appear.

e. With **Chart Tools** displayed at the top, select the **Layout** tab. Select **Chart Title** and type in a title for the plot. Next, under the same **Layout** tab, select **Axis Titles.** Using **Primary Vertical Axis Title,** name the vertical axis *Price ($000).* Using the **Primary Horizontal Axis Title,** name the horizontal axis *Price ($000).* Next select **Legend** and select **None.**

Chapter 4   Answers to Self-Review

4–1 **a.** 79, 105
   b. 15
   c. From 88 to 97; 75 percent of the stores are in this range.

4–2 **a.** 7.9
   b. $Q_1 = 7.76$, $Q_3 = 8.015$

4–3 The smallest value is 10 and the largest 85; the first quartile is 25 and the third 60. About 50 percent of the values are between 25 and 60. The median value is 40. The distribution is positively skewed.

4–4 **a.** $\bar{X} = \dfrac{407}{5} = 81.4$, Median = 84

$$s = \sqrt{\frac{923.2}{5-1}} = 15.19$$

   b. $sk = \dfrac{3(81.4 - 84.0)}{15.19} = -0.51$

   c.

X	$\dfrac{X - \bar{X}}{s}$	$\left[\dfrac{X - \bar{X}}{s}\right]^3$
73	−0.5530	−0.1691
98	1.0928	1.3051
60	−1.4088	−2.7962
92	0.6978	0.3398
84	0.1712	0.0050
		−1.3154

$$sk = \frac{5}{(4)(3)}[-1.3154]$$

$$= -0.5481$$

   d. The distribution is somewhat negatively skewed.

4–5 **a.** Scatter diagram
   b. 16
   c. $7,500
   d. Strong and direct

5

A Survey of Probability Concepts

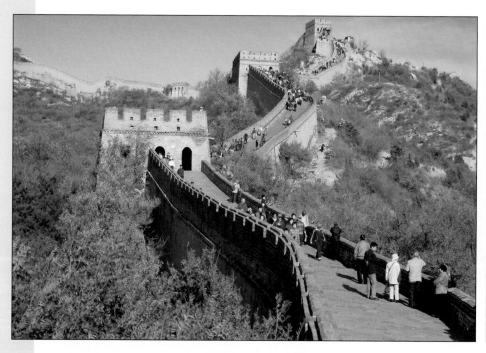

It was found that 60 percent of the tourists to China visited the Forbidden City, the Temple of Heaven, the Great Wall, and other historical sites in or near Beijing. Forty percent visited Xi'an and its magnificent terracotta soldiers, horses, and chariots, which lay buried for over 2,000 years. Thirty percent of the tourists went to both Beijing and Xi'an. What is the probability that a tourist visited at least one of these places? (Exercise 68, LO5)

Introduction

The emphasis in Chapters 2, 3, and 4 is on descriptive statistics. In Chapter 2 we organize the prices of 80 vehicles sold last month at the Whitner Autoplex location of AutoUSA into a frequency distribution. This frequency distribution shows the smallest and the largest selling prices and where the largest concentration of data occurs. In Chapter 3 we use numerical measures of location and dispersion to locate a typical selling price and to examine the variation in the data. We describe the variation in the selling prices with such measures of dispersion as the range and the standard deviation. In Chapter 4 we develop charts and graphs, such as a scatter diagram, to further describe the data graphically.

Descriptive statistics is concerned with summarizing data collected from past events. For example, we described the vehicle selling prices last month at Whitner Autoplex. We now turn to the second facet of statistics, namely, *computing the chance that something will occur in the future*. This facet of statistics is called **statistical inference** or **inferential statistics.**

Seldom does a decision maker have complete information to make a decision. For example:

- Toys and Things, a toy and puzzle manufacturer, recently developed a new game based on sports trivia. It wants to know whether sports buffs will purchase the game. "Slam Dunk" and "Home Run" are two of the names under consideration. One way to minimize the risk of making an incorrect decision is to hire a market research firm to select a sample of 2,000 consumers from the population and ask each respondent for a reaction to the new game and its proposed titles. Using the sample results the company can estimate the proportion of the population that will purchase the game.
- The quality assurance department of a Bethlehem Steel mill must assure management that the quarter-inch wire being produced has an acceptable tensile strength. Obviously, not all the wire produced can be tested for tensile strength because testing requires the wire to be stretched until it breaks—thus destroying

it. So a random sample of 10 pieces is selected and tested. Based on the test results, all the wire produced is deemed to be either acceptable or unacceptable.
- Other questions involving uncertainty are: Should the daytime drama "Days of Our Lives" be discontinued immediately? Will a newly developed mint-flavored cereal be profitable if marketed? Will Charles Linden be elected to county auditor in Batavia County?

Statistical inference deals with conclusions about a population based on a sample taken from that population. (The populations for the preceding illustrations are: all consumers who like sports trivia games, all the quarter-inch steel wire produced, all television viewers who watch soaps, all who purchase breakfast cereal, and so on.)

Because there is uncertainty in decision making, it is important that all the known risks involved be scientifically evaluated. Helpful in this evaluation is *probability theory,* which has often been referred to as the science of uncertainty. The use of probability theory allows the decision maker with only limited information to analyze the risks and minimize the gamble inherent, for example, in marketing a new product or accepting an incoming shipment possibly containing defective parts.

Because probability concepts are so important in the field of statistical inference (to be discussed starting with Chapter 8), this chapter introduces the basic language of probability, including such terms as *experiment, event, subjective probability,* and *addition* and *multiplication rules.*

What Is a Probability?

No doubt you are familiar with terms such as *probability, chance,* and *likelihood.* They are often used interchangeably. The weather forecaster announces that there is a 70 percent chance of rain for Super Bowl Sunday. Based on a survey of consumers who tested a newly developed pickle with a banana taste, the probability is .03 that, if marketed, it will be a financial success. (This means that the chance of the banana-flavor pickle being accepted by the public is rather remote.) What is a probability? In general, it is a number that describes the chance that something will happen.

LO1 Define *probability.*

> **PROBABILITY** A value between zero and one, inclusive, describing the relative possibility (chance or likelihood) an event will occur.

A probability is frequently expressed as a decimal, such as .70, .27, or .50. However, it may be given as a fraction such as 7/10, 27/100, or 1/2. It can assume any number from 0 to 1, inclusive. If a company has only five sales regions, and each region's name or number is written on a slip of paper and the slips put in a hat, the probability of selecting one of the five regions is 1. The probability of selecting from the hat a slip of paper that reads "Pittsburgh Steelers" is 0. Thus, the probability of 1 represents something that is certain to happen, and the probability of 0 represents something that cannot happen. The closer a probability is to 0, the more improbable it is the event will happen. The closer the probability is to 1, the more sure we are it will happen.

Three key words are used in the study of probability: **experiment, outcome,** and **event.** These terms are used in our everyday language, but in statistics they have specific meanings.

LO3 Explain the terms *experiment, event, outcome, permutations,* and *combinations.*

> **EXPERIMENT** A process that leads to the occurrence of one and only one of several possible observations.

This definition is more general than the one used in the physical sciences, where we picture someone manipulating test tubes or microscopes. In reference to probability, an experiment has two or more possible results, and it is uncertain which will occur.

> **OUTCOME** A particular result of an experiment.

For example, the tossing of a coin is an experiment. You may observe the toss of the coin, but you are unsure whether it will come up "heads" or "tails." Similarly, asking 500 college students whether they would purchase a new Dell computer system at a particular price is an experiment. If the coin is tossed, one particular outcome is a "head." The alternative outcome is a "tail." In the computer purchasing experiment, one possible outcome is that 273 students indicate they would purchase the computer. Another outcome is that 317 students would purchase the computer. Still another outcome is that 423 students indicate that they would purchase it. When one or more of the experiment's outcomes are observed, we call this an event.

EVENT A collection of one or more outcomes of an experiment.

Examples to clarify the definitions of the terms *experiment, outcome,* and *event* are presented in the following figure.

In the die-rolling experiment there are six possible outcomes, but there are many possible events. When counting the number of members of the board of directors for Fortune 500 companies over 60 years of age, the number of possible outcomes can be anywhere from zero to the total number of members. There are an even larger number of possible events in this experiment.

Experiment	Roll a die	Count the number of members of the board of directors for Fortune 500 companies who are over 60 years of age
All possible outcomes	Observe a 1 Observe a 2 Observe a 3 Observe a 4 Observe a 5 Observe a 6	None are over 60 One is over 60 Two are over 60 ... 29 are over 60 ... ... 48 are over 60 ...
Some possible events	Observe an even number Observe a number greater than 4 Observe a number 3 or less	More than 13 are over 60 Fewer than 20 are over 60

Self-Review 5–1 Video Games, Inc., recently developed a new video game. Its playability is to be tested by 80 veteran game players.
(a) What is the experiment?
(b) What is one possible outcome?
(c) Suppose 65 players tried the new game and said they liked it. Is 65 a probability?
(d) The probability that the new game will be a success is computed to be −1.0. Comment.
(e) Specify one possible event.

Approaches to Assigning Probabilities

LO2 Describe the *classical, empirical,* and *subjective* approaches to probability.

Two approaches to assigning probabilities to an event will be discussed, namely, the *objective* and the *subjective* viewpoints. **Objective probability** is subdivided into (1) *classical probability* and (2) *empirical probability*.

Classical Probability

Classical probability is based on the assumption that the outcomes of an experiment are *equally likely*. Using the classical viewpoint, the probability of an event happening is computed by dividing the number of favorable outcomes by the number of possible outcomes:

> **CLASSICAL PROBABILITY** $\dfrac{\text{Probability}}{\text{of an event}} = \dfrac{\text{Number of favorable outcomes}}{\text{Total number of possible outcomes}}$ **[5–1]**

Example

Consider an experiment of rolling a six-sided die. What is the probability of the event "an even number of spots appear face up"?

Solution

The possible outcomes are:

There are three "favorable" outcomes (a two, a four, and a six) in the collection of six equally likely possible outcomes. Therefore:

$$\text{Probability of an even number} = \frac{3}{6} \quad \begin{array}{l} \leftarrow \\ \leftarrow \end{array} \quad \boxed{\begin{array}{l}\text{Number of favorable outcomes} \\ \hline \text{Total number of possible outcomes}\end{array}}$$

$$= .5$$

The mutually exclusive concept appeared earlier in our study of frequency distributions in Chapter 2. Recall that we create classes so that a particular value is included in only one of the classes and there is no overlap between classes. Thus, only one of several events can occur at a particular time.

> **MUTUALLY EXCLUSIVE** The occurrence of one event means that none of the other events can occur at the same time.

The variable "gender" presents mutually exclusive outcomes, male and female. An employee selected at random is either male or female but cannot be both. A manufactured part is acceptable or unacceptable. The part cannot be both acceptable and unacceptable at the same time. In a sample of manufactured parts, the event of selecting an unacceptable part and the event of selecting an acceptable part are mutually exclusive.

If an experiment has a set of events that includes every possible outcome, such as the events "an even number" and "an odd number" in the die-tossing experiment, then the set of events is **collectively exhaustive.** For the die-tossing experiment, every outcome will be either even or odd. So the set is collectively exhaustive.

> **COLLECTIVELY EXHAUSTIVE** At least one of the events must occur when an experiment is conducted.

Sum of probabilities = 1

If the set of events is collectively exhaustive and the events are mutually exclusive, the sum of the probabilities is 1. Historically, the classical approach to probability was developed and applied in the 17th and 18th centuries to games of chance, such as cards and dice. It is unnecessary to do an experiment to determine the probability of an event occurring using the classical approach because the total number of outcomes is known before the experiment. The flip of a coin has two possible outcomes; the roll of a die has six possible outcomes. We can logically arrive at the probability of getting a tail on the toss of one coin or three heads on the toss of three coins.

The classical approach to probability can also be applied to lotteries. In South Carolina, one of the games of the Education Lottery is "Pick 3." A person buys a lottery ticket and selects three numbers between 0 and 9. Once per week, the three numbers are randomly selected from a machine that tumbles three containers each with balls numbered 0 through 9. One way to win is to match the numbers and the order of the numbers. Given that 1,000 possible outcomes exist (000 through 999), the probability of winning with any three-digit number is 0.001, or 1 in 1,000.

Empirical Probability

Empirical or **relative frequency** is the second type of objective probability. It is based on the number of times an event occurs as a proportion of a known number of trials.

> **EMPIRICAL PROBABILITY** The probability of an event happening is the fraction of the time similar events happened in the past.

In terms of a formula:

$$\text{Empirical probability} = \frac{\text{Number of times the event occurs}}{\text{Total number of observations}}$$

The empirical approach to probability is based on what is called the law of large numbers. The key to establishing probabilities empirically is that more observations will provide a more accurate estimate of the probability.

> **LAW OF LARGE NUMBERS** Over a large number of trials the empirical probability of an event will approach its true probability.

To explain the law of large numbers, suppose we toss a fair coin. The result of each toss is either a head or a tail. With just one toss of the coin the empirical probability for heads is either zero or one. If we toss the coin a great number of times, the probability of the outcome of heads will approach .5. The following table reports the results of an experiment of flipping a fair coin 1, 10, 50, 100, 500, 1,000 and 10,000 times and then computing the relative frequency of heads. Note as we increase the number of trials the empirical probability of a head appearing approaches .5, which is its value based on the classical approach to probability.

Number of Trials	Number of Heads	Relative Frequency of Heads
1	0	.00
10	3	.30
50	26	.52
100	52	.52
500	236	.472
1,000	494	.494
10,000	5,027	.5027

What have we demonstrated? Based on the classical definition of probability the likelihood of obtaining a head in a single toss of a fair coin is .5. Based on the empirical or relative frequency approach to probability, the probability of the event happening approaches the same value based on the classical definition of probability.

This reasoning allows us to use the empirical or relative frequency approach to finding a probability. Here are some examples.

- Last semester 80 students registered for Business Statistics 101 at Scandia University. Twelve students earned an A. Based on this information and the empirical approach to assigning a probability, we estimate the likelihood a student will earn an A is .15.
- Kobe Bryant of the Los Angles Lakers made 483 out of 564 free throw attempts during the 2008–09 NBA season. Based on the empirical rule of probability the likelihood of him making his next free throw attempt is .856.

Life insurance companies rely on past data to determine the acceptability of an applicant as well as the premium to be charged. Mortality tables list the likelihood a person of a particular age will die within the upcoming year. For example, the likelihood a 20-year-old female will die within the next year is .00105.

The empirical concept is illustrated with the following example.

Example

On February 1, 2003, the Space Shuttle Columbia exploded. This was the second disaster in 123 space missions for NASA. On the basis of this information, what is the probability that a future mission is successfully completed?

Solution

To simplify, letters or numbers may be used. P stands for probability, and in this case $P(A)$ stands for the probability a future mission is successfully completed.

$$\text{Probability of a successful flight} = \frac{\text{Number of successful flights}}{\text{Total number of flights}}$$

$$P(A) = \frac{121}{123} = .98$$

We can use this as an estimate of probability. In other words, based on past experience, the probability is .98 that a future space shuttle mission will be successfully completed.

Subjective Probability

If there is little or no experience or information on which to base a probability, it may be arrived at subjectively. Essentially, this means an individual evaluates the available opinions and information and then estimates or assigns the probability. This probability is aptly called a **subjective probability.**

SUBJECTIVE CONCEPT OF PROBABILITY The likelihood (probability) of a particular event happening that is assigned by an individual based on whatever information is available.

Illustrations of subjective probability are:

1. Estimating the likelihood the New England Patriots will play in the Super Bowl next year.
2. Estimating the likelihood you will be married before the age of 30.
3. Estimating the likelihood the U.S. budget deficit will be reduced by half in the next 10 years.

The types of probability are summarized in Chart 5–1. A probability statement always assigns a likelihood to an event that has not yet occurred. There is, of course, a considerable latitude in the degree of uncertainty that surrounds this probability, based primarily on the knowledge possessed by the individual concerning the underlying process. The individual possesses a great deal of knowledge about the toss of a die and can state that the probability that a one-spot will appear face up on the toss of a true die is one-sixth. But we know very little concerning the acceptance in the marketplace of a new and untested product. For example, even though a market research director tests a newly developed product in 40 retail stores and states that there is a 70 percent chance that the product will have sales of more than 1 million units, she has limited knowledge of how consumers will react when it is marketed nationally. In both cases (the case of the person rolling a die and the testing of a new product) the individual is assigning a probability value to an event of interest, and a difference exists only in the predictor's confidence in the precision of the estimate. However, regardless of the viewpoint, the same laws of probability (presented in the following sections) will be applied.

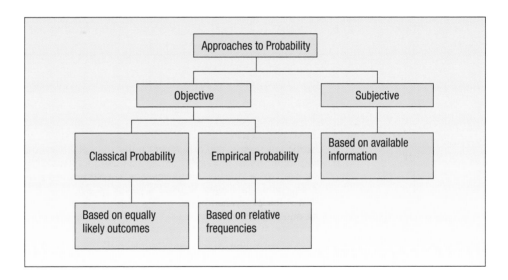

CHART 5–1 Summary of Approaches to Probability

Self-Review 5–2

1. One card will be randomly selected from a standard 52-card deck. What is the probability the card will be a queen? Which approach to probability did you use to answer this question?
2. The Center for Child Care reports on 539 children and the marital status of their parents. There are 333 married, 182 divorced, and 24 widowed. What is the probability a particular child chosen at random will have a parent who is divorced? Which approach did you use?
3. What is the probability that the Dow Jones Industrial Average will exceed 12,000 during the next 12 months? Which approach to probability did you use to answer this question?

Exercises

1. Some people are in favor of reducing federal taxes to increase consumer spending and others are against it. Two persons are selected and their opinions are recorded. Assuming no one is undecided, list the possible outcomes.

2. A quality control inspector selects a part to be tested. The part is then declared acceptable, repairable, or scrapped. Then another part is tested. List the possible outcomes of this experiment regarding two parts.

3. A survey of 34 students at the Wall College of Business showed the following majors:

Accounting	10
Finance	5
Economics	3
Management	6
Marketing	10

   Suppose you select a student and observe his or her major.
   a. What is the probability he or she is a management major?
   b. Which concept of probability did you use to make this estimate?

4. A large company that must hire a new president prepares a final list of five candidates, all of whom are equally qualified. Two of these candidates are members of a minority group. To avoid bias in the selection of the candidate, the company decides to select the president by lottery.
   a. What is the probability one of the minority candidates is hired?
   b. Which concept of probability did you use to make this estimate?

5. In each of the following cases, indicate whether classical, empirical, or subjective probability is used.
   a. A baseball player gets a hit in 30 out of 100 times at bat. The probability is .3 that he gets a hit in his next at bat.
   b. A seven-member committee of students is formed to study environmental issues. What is the likelihood that any one of the seven is chosen as the spokesperson?
   c. You purchase one of 5 million tickets sold for Lotto Canada. What is the likelihood you will win the $1 million jackpot?
   d. The probability of an earthquake in northern California in the next 10 years above 5.0 on the Richter Scale is .80.

6. A firm will promote two employees out of a group of six men and three women.
   a. List the chances of this experiment if there is particular concern about gender equity.
   b. Which concept of probability would you use to estimate these probabilities?

7. A sample of 40 oil industry executives was selected to test a questionnaire. One question about environmental issues required a yes or no answer.
   a. What is the experiment?
   b. List one possible event.
   c. Ten of the 40 executives responded yes. Based on these sample responses, what is the probability that an oil industry executive will respond yes?
   d. What concept of probability does this illustrate?
   e. Are each of the possible outcomes equally likely and mutually exclusive?

8. A sample of 2,000 licensed drivers revealed the following number of speeding violations.

Number of Violations	Number of Drivers
0	1,910
1	46
2	18
3	12
4	9
5 or more	5
Total	2,000

   a. What is the experiment?
   b. List one possible event.

    c. What is the probability that a particular driver had exactly two speeding violations?

    d. What concept of probability does this illustrate?

9. Bank of America customers select their own three-digit personal identification number (PIN) for use at ATMs.

    a. Think of this as an experiment and list four possible outcomes.

    b. What is the probability Mr. Jones and Mrs. Smith select the same PIN?

    c. Which concept of probability did you use to answer (b)?

10. An investor buys 100 shares of AT&T stock and records its price change daily.

    a. List several possible events for this experiment.

    b. Estimate the probability for each event you described in (a).

    c. Which concept of probability did you use in (b)?

Some Rules for Computing Probabilities

LO5 Calculate probabilities using the *rules of addition* and *rules of multiplication.*

Now that we have defined probability and described the different approaches to probability, we turn our attention to computing the probability of two or more events by applying rules of addition and multiplication.

Rules of Addition

There are two rules of addition, the special rule of addition and the general rule of addition. We begin with the special rule of addition.

Mutually exclusive events cannot both happen.

Special Rule of Addition To apply the **special rule of addition,** the events must be *mutually exclusive.* Recall that mutually exclusive means that when one event occurs, none of the other events can occur at the same time. An illustration of mutually exclusive events in the die-tossing experiment is the events "a number 4 or larger" and "a number 2 or smaller." If the outcome is in the first group {4, 5, and 6}, then it cannot also be in the second group {1 and 2}. Another illustration is a product coming off the assembly line cannot be defective and satisfactory at the same time.

    If two events *A* and *B* are mutually exclusive, the special rule of addition states that the probability of one *or* the other event's occurring equals the sum of their probabilities. This rule is expressed in the following formula:

SPECIAL RULE OF ADDITION	$P(A \text{ or } B) = P(A) + P(B)$	[5–2]

For three mutually exclusive events designated *A*, *B*, and *C*, the rule is written:

$$P(A \text{ or } B \text{ or } C) = P(A) + P(B) + P(C)$$

An example will help to show the details.

Example

An automatic Shaw machine fills plastic bags with a mixture of beans, broccoli, and other vegetables. Most of the bags contain the correct weight, but because of the variation in the size of the beans and other vegetables, a package might be underweight or overweight. A check of 4,000 packages filled in the past month revealed:

Weight	Event	Number of Packages	Probability of Occurrence	
Underweight	A	100	.025	← $\dfrac{100}{4{,}000}$
Satisfactory	B	3,600	.900	
Overweight	C	300	.075	
		4,000	1.000	

Solution

What is the probability that a particular package will be either underweight or overweight?

The outcome "underweight" is the event A. The outcome "overweight" is the event C. Applying the special rule of addition:

$$P(A \text{ or } C) = P(A) + P(C) = .025 + .075 = .10$$

Note that the events are mutually exclusive, meaning that a package of mixed vegetables cannot be underweight, satisfactory, and overweight at the same time. They are also collectively exhaustive; that is, a selected package must be either underweight, satisfactory, or overweight.

A Venn diagram is a useful tool to depict addition or multiplication rules.

English logician J. Venn (1834–1923) developed a diagram to portray graphically the outcome of an experiment. The *mutually exclusive* concept and various other rules for combining probabilities can be illustrated using this device. To construct a Venn diagram, a space is first enclosed representing the total of all possible outcomes. This space is usually in the form of a rectangle. An event is then represented by a circular area which is drawn inside the rectangle proportional to the probability of the event. The following Venn diagram represents the *mutually exclusive* concept. There is no overlapping of events, meaning that the events are mutually exclusive. In the following diagram assume the events A, B, and C are about equally likely.

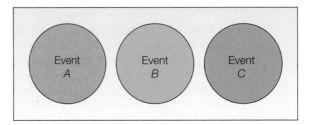

Complement Rule The probability that a bag of mixed vegetables selected is underweight, $P(A)$, plus the probability that it is not an underweight bag, written $P(\sim A)$ and read "not A," must logically equal 1. This is written:

$$P(A) + P(\sim A) = 1$$

This can be revised to read:

COMPLEMENT RULE	$P(A) = 1 - P(\sim A)$	[5–3]

This is the **complement rule.** It is used to determine the probability of an event occurring by subtracting the probability of the event not occurring from 1. This rule is useful because sometimes it is easier to calculate the probability of an event happening by determining the probability of it not happening and subtracting the result from 1. Notice that the events A and $\sim A$ are mutually exclusive and collectively exhaustive. Therefore, the probabilities of A and $\sim A$ sum to 1. A Venn diagram illustrating the complement rule is shown as:

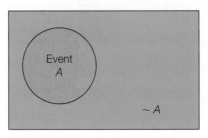

Example

Recall the probability a bag of mixed vegetables is underweight is .025 and the probability of an overweight bag is .075. Use the complement rule to show the probability of a satisfactory bag is .900. Show the solution using a Venn diagram.

Solution

The probability the bag is unsatisfactory equals the probability the bag is overweight plus the probability it is underweight. That is, $P(A \text{ or } C) = P(A) + P(C) = .025 + .075 = .100$. The bag is satisfactory if it is not underweight or overweight, so $P(B) = 1 - [P(A) + P(C)] = 1 - [.025 + .075] = 0.900$. The Venn diagram portraying this situation is:

A
.025

C
.075

not A or C
.90

Self-Review 5–3

A sample of employees of Worldwide Enterprises is to be surveyed about a new health care plan. The employees are classified as follows:

Classification	Event	Number of Employees
Supervisors	A	120
Maintenance	B	50
Production	C	1,460
Management	D	302
Secretarial	E	68

(a) What is the probability that the first person selected is:
    (i) either in maintenance or a secretary?
    (ii) not in management?
(b) Draw a Venn diagram illustrating your answers to part (a).
(c) Are the events in part (a)(i) complementary or mutually exclusive or both?

The General Rule of Addition The outcomes of an experiment may not be mutually exclusive. Suppose, for illustration, that the Florida Tourist Commission selected a sample of 200 tourists who visited the state during the year. The survey revealed that 120 tourists went to Disney World and 100 went to Busch Gardens near Tampa. What is the probability that a person selected visited either Disney World or Busch Gardens? If the special rule of addition is used, the probability of selecting a tourist who went to Disney World is .60, found by 120/200. Similarly, the probability of a tourist going to Busch Gardens is .50. The sum of these probabilities is 1.10. We know, however, that this probability cannot be greater than 1. The explanation is that many tourists visited both attractions and are being counted twice! A check of the survey responses revealed that 60 out of 200 sampled did, in fact, visit both attractions.

To answer our question, "What is the probability a selected person visited either Disney World or Busch Gardens?" (1) add the probability that a tourist visited Disney

World and the probability he or she visited Busch Gardens, and (2) subtract the probability of visiting both. Thus:

$$P(\text{Disney or Busch}) = P(\text{Disney}) + P(\text{Busch}) - P(\text{both Disney and Busch})$$
$$= .60 + .50 - .30 = .80$$

When two events both occur, the probability is called a **joint probability.** The probability that a tourist visits both attractions (.30) is an example of a joint probability.

The following Venn diagram shows two events that are not mutually exclusive. The two events overlap to illustrate the joint event that some people have visited both attractions.

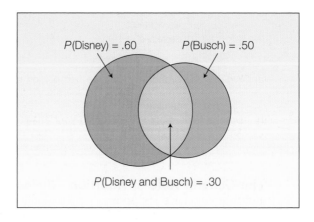

$P(\text{Disney}) = .60$ $P(\text{Busch}) = .50$

$P(\text{Disney and Busch}) = .30$

LO4 Define the terms *conditional probability* and *joint probability.*

JOINT PROBABILITY A probability that measures the likelihood two or more events will happen concurrently.

This rule for two events designated A and B is written:

GENERAL RULE OF ADDITION $P(A \text{ or } B) = P(A) + P(B) - P(A \text{ and } B)$ **[5–4]**

For the expression $P(A \text{ or } B)$, the word *or* suggests that A may occur or B may occur. This also includes the possibility that A and B may occur. This use of *or* is sometimes called an **inclusive.** You could also write $P(A \text{ or } B \text{ or both})$ to emphasize that the union of the events includes the intersection of A and B.

If we compare the general and special rules of addition, the important difference is determining if the events are mutually exclusive. If the events *are* mutually exclusive, then the joint probability $P(A \text{ and } B)$ is 0 and we could use the special rule of addition. Otherwise we must account for the joint probability and use the general rule of addition.

Example	What is the probability that a card chosen at random from a standard deck of cards will be either a king or a heart?

Solution	We may be inclined to add the probability of a king and the probability of a heart. But this creates a problem. If we do that, the king of hearts is counted with the kings and also with the hearts. So, if we simply add the probability of a king (there are 4 in a deck of 52 cards) to the probability of a heart (there are 13 in a deck of 52 cards) and report that 17 out of 52 cards meet the requirement, we have counted the king of hearts twice. We need to subtract 1 card from the 17 so the king of hearts is counted only once. Thus, there are 16 cards that are either hearts or kings. So the probability is $16/52 = .3077$.

Card	Probability		Explanation
King	$P(A)$	$= 4/52$	4 kings in a deck of 52 cards
Heart	$P(B)$	$= 13/52$	13 hearts in a deck of 52 cards
King of Hearts	$P(A \text{ and } B) =$	$1/52$	1 king of hearts in a deck of 52 cards

From formula (5–4):

$$P(A \text{ or } B) = P(A) + P(B) - P(A \text{ and } B)$$

$$= 4/52 + 13/52 - 1/52$$

$$= 16/52, \text{ or } .3077$$

A Venn diagram portrays these outcomes, which are not mutually exclusive.

Self-Review 5–4

Routine physical examinations are conducted annually as part of a health service program for General Concrete, Inc., employees. It was discovered that 8 percent of the employees need corrective shoes, 15 percent need major dental work, and 3 percent need both corrective shoes and major dental work.
(a) What is the probability that an employee selected at random will need either corrective shoes or major dental work?
(b) Show this situation in the form of a Venn diagram.

Exercises

connect™

11. The events *A* and *B* are mutually exclusive. Suppose $P(A) = .30$ and $P(B) = .20$. What is the probability of either *A* or *B* occurring? What is the probability that neither *A* nor *B* will happen?

12. The events *X* and *Y* are mutually exclusive. Suppose $P(X) = .05$ and $P(Y) = .02$. What is the probability of either *X* or *Y* occurring? What is the probability that neither *X* nor *Y* will happen?

13. A study of 200 advertising firms revealed their income after taxes:

Income after Taxes	Number of Firms
Under $1 million	102
$1 million to $20 million	61
$20 million or more	37

   a. What is the probability an advertising firm selected at random has under $1 million in income after taxes?
   b. What is the probability an advertising firm selected at random has either an income between $1 million and $20 million, or an income of $20 million or more? What rule of probability was applied?

14. The chair of the board of directors says, "There is a 50 percent chance this company will earn a profit, a 30 percent chance it will break even, and a 20 percent chance it will lose money next quarter."
   a. Use an addition rule to find the probability the company will not lose money next quarter.
   b. Use the complement rule to find the probability it will not lose money next quarter.

15. Suppose the probability you will get an A in this class is .25 and the probability you will get a B is .50. What is the probability your grade will be above a C?

16. Two coins are tossed. If *A* is the event "two heads" and *B* is the event "two tails," are *A* and *B* mutually exclusive? Are they complements?

17. The probabilities of the events *A* and *B* are .20 and .30, respectively. The probability that both *A* and *B* occur is .15. What is the probability of either *A* or *B* occurring?

18. Let $P(X) = .55$ and $P(Y) = .35$. Assume the probability that they both occur is .20. What is the probability of either *X* or *Y* occurring?

19. Suppose the two events *A* and *B* are mutually exclusive. What is the probability of their joint occurrence?

20. A student is taking two courses, history and math. The probability the student will pass the history course is .60, and the probability of passing the math course is .70. The probability of passing both is .50. What is the probability of passing at least one?

21. A survey of grocery stores in the Southeast revealed 40 percent had a pharmacy, 50 percent had a floral shop, and 70 percent had a deli. Suppose 10 percent of the stores have all three departments, 30 percent have both a pharmacy and a deli, 25 percent have both a floral shop and deli, and 20 percent have both a pharmacy and floral shop.
   a. What is the probability of selecting a store at random and finding it has both a pharmacy and a floral shop?
   b. What is the probability of selecting a store at random and finding it has both a pharmacy and a deli?

    c. Are the events "select a store with a deli" and "select a store with a pharmacy" mutually exclusive?

    d. What is the name given to the event of "selecting a store with a pharmacy, a floral shop, and a deli?"

    e. What is the probability of selecting a store that does *not* have all three departments?

22. A study by the National Park Service revealed that 50 percent of vacationers going to the Rocky Mountain region visit Yellowstone Park, 40 percent visit the Tetons, and 35 percent visit both.

    a. What is the probability a vacationer will visit at least one of these attractions?

    b. What is the probability .35 called?

    c. Are the events mutually exclusive? Explain.

Rules of Multiplication

When we use the rules of addition in the previous section we find the likelihood of combining two events. In this section we find the likelihood that two events both happen. For example, a marketing firm may want to estimate the likelihood that a person is 21 years old or older *and* buys a Hummer. Venn diagrams illustrate this as the intersection of two events. To find the likelihood of two events happening we use the rules of multiplication. There are two rules of multiplication, the special rule and the general rule.

Special Rule of Multiplication The special rule of multiplication requires that two events A and B are independent. Two events are independent if the occurrence of one event does not alter the probability of the occurrence of the other event.

> **INDEPENDENCE** The occurrence of one event has no effect on the probability of the occurrence of another event.

One way to think about independence is to assume that events A and B occur at different times. For example, when event B occurs after event A occurs, does A have any effect on the likelihood that event B occurs? If the answer is no, then A and B are independent events. To illustrate independence, suppose two coins are tossed. The outcome of a coin toss (head or tail) is unaffected by the outcome of any other prior coin toss (head or tail).

For two independent events A and B, the probability that A and B will both occur is found by multiplying the two probabilities. This is the **special rule of multiplication** and is written symbolically as:

SPECIAL RULE OF MULTIPLICATION	$P(A \text{ and } B) = P(A)P(B)$	**[5–5]**

For three independent events, A, B, and C, the special rule of multiplication used to determine the probability that all three events will occur is:

$$P(A \text{ and } B \text{ and } C) = P(A)P(B)P(C)$$

Example

A survey by the American Automobile Association (AAA) revealed 60 percent of its members made airline reservations last year. Two members are selected at random. What is the probability both made airline reservations last year?

Solution

The probability the first member made an airline reservation last year is .60, written $P(R_1) = .60$, where R_1 refers to the fact that the first member made a reservation.

The probability that the second member selected made a reservation is also .60, so $P(R_2) = .60$. Since the number of AAA members is very large, you may assume that R_1 and R_2 are independent. Consequently, using formula (5–5), the probability they both make a reservation is .36, found by:

$$P(R_1 \text{ and } R_2) = P(R_1)P(R_2) = (.60)(.60) = .36$$

All possible outcomes can be shown as follows. R means a reservation is made, and NR means no reservation was made.

   With the probabilities and the complement rule, we can compute the joint probability of each outcome. For example, the probability that neither member makes a reservation is .16. Further, the probability of the first or the second member (special addition rule) making a reservation is .48 (.24 + .24). You can also observe that the outcomes are mutually exclusive and collectively exhaustive. Therefore, the probabilities sum to 1.00.

Outcomes	Joint Probability	
R_1 R_2	$(.60)(.60) =$	.36
R_1 NR_2	$(.60)(.40) =$	.24
NR_1 R_2	$(.40)(.60) =$	.24
NR_1 NR_2	$(.40)(.40) =$	.16
Total		1.00

Self-Review 5–5

From experience, Teton Tire knows the probability is .95 that a particular XB-70 tire will last 60,000 miles before it becomes bald or fails. An adjustment is made on any tire that does not last 60,000 miles. You purchase four XB-70s. What is the probability all four tires will last at least 60,000 miles?

General Rule of Multiplication   If two events are not independent, they are referred to as **dependent.** To illustrate dependency, suppose there are 10 cans of soda in a cooler, seven are regular and three are diet. A can is selected from the cooler. The probability of selecting a can of diet soda is 3/10, and the probability of selecting a can of regular soda is 7/10. Then a second can is selected from the cooler, without returning the first. The probability the second is diet depends on whether the first one selected was diet or not. The probability that the second is diet is:

   2/9, if the first can is diet. (Only two cans of diet soda remain in the cooler.)
   3/9, if the first can selected is regular. (All three diet sodas are still in the cooler.)

The fraction 2/9 (or 3/9) is aptly called a **conditional probability** because its value is conditional on (dependent on) whether a diet or regular soda was the first selection from the cooler.

> **CONDITIONAL PROBABILITY** The probability of a particular event occurring, given that another event has occurred.

We use the general rule of multiplication to find the joint probability of two events when the events are not independent. For example, when event B occurs after event A occurs, and A has an effect on the likelihood that event B occurs, then A and B are not independent.

The general rule of multiplication states that for two events, A and B, the joint probability that both events will happen is found by multiplying the probability that event A will happen by the conditional probability of event B occurring given that A has occurred. Symbolically, the joint probability, $P(A \text{ and } B)$, is found by:

GENERAL RULE OF MULTIPLICATION	$P(A \text{ and } B) = P(A)P(B|A)$	[5–6]

Example

A golfer has 12 golf shirts in his closet. Suppose 9 of these shirts are white and the others blue. He gets dressed in the dark, so he just grabs a shirt and puts it on. He plays golf two days in a row and does not do laundry. What is the likelihood both shirts selected are white?

Solution

The event that the first shirt selected is white is W_1. The probability is $P(W_1) = 9/12$ because 9 of the 12 shirts are white. The event that the second shirt selected is also white is identified as W_2. The conditional probability that the second shirt selected is white, given that the first shirt selected is also white, is $P(W_2|W_1) = 8/11$. Why is this so? Because after the first shirt is selected there are only 11 shirts remaining in the closet and 8 of these are white. To determine the probability of 2 white shirts being selected we use formula (5–6).

$$P(W_1 \text{ and } W_2) = P(W_1)P(W_2|W_1) = \left(\frac{9}{12}\right)\left(\frac{8}{11}\right) = .55$$

So the likelihood of selecting two shirts and finding them both to be white is .55.

Incidentally, it is assumed that this experiment was conducted *without replacement*. That is, the first shirt was not laundered and put back in the closet before the second was selected. So the outcome of the second event is conditional or dependent on the outcome of the first event.

We can extend the general rule of multiplication to more than two events. For three events A, B, and C the formula is:

$$P(A \text{ and } B \text{ and } C) = P(A)P(B|A)P(C|A \text{ and } B)$$

In the case of the golf shirt example, the probability of selecting three white shirts without replacement is:

$$P(W_1 \text{ and } W_2 \text{ and } W_3) = P(W_1)P(W_2|W_1)P(W_3|W_1 \text{ and } W_2) = \left(\frac{9}{12}\right)\left(\frac{8}{11}\right)\left(\frac{7}{10}\right) = .38$$

So the likelihood of selecting three shirts without replacement and all being white is .38.

Self-Review 5–6

The board of directors of Tarbell Industries consists of eight men and four women. A four-member search committee is to be chosen at random to conduct a nationwide search for a new company president.
(a) What is the probability all four members of the search committee will be women?
(b) What is the probability all four members will be men?
(c) Does the sum of the probabilities for the events described in parts (a) and (b) equal 1? Explain.

Statistics in Action

In 2000 George W. Bush won the U.S. presidency by the slimmest of margins. Many election stories resulted, some involving voting irregularities, others raising interesting election questions. In a local Michigan election there was a tie between two candidates for an elected position. To break the tie the candidates drew a slip of paper from a box that contained two slips of paper, one marked "Winner" and the other unmarked. To determine which candidate drew first, election officials flipped a coin. The winner of the coin flip also drew the winning slip of paper. But was the coin flip really necessary? No, because the two events are independent. Winning the coin flip did not alter the probability of either candidate drawing the winning slip of paper.

Contingency Tables

Often we tally the results of a survey in a two-way table and use these results of this tally to determine various probabilities. We described this idea beginning on page 112 in Chapter 4. To review, we refer to a two-way table as a contingency table.

> **CONTINGENCY TABLE** A table used to classify sample observations according to two or more identifiable characteristics.

A contingency table is a cross-tabulation that simultaneously summarizes two variables of interest and their relationship. The level of measurement can be nominal. Below are several examples.

- A survey of 150 adults classified each as to gender and the number of movies attended last month. Each respondent is classified according to two criteria—the number of movies attended and gender.

Movies Attended	Gender		Total
	Men	Women	
0	20	40	60
1	40	30	70
2 or more	10	10	20
Total	70	80	150

- The American Coffee Producers Association reports the following information on age and the amount of coffee consumed in a month.

Age (Years)	Coffee Consumption			Total
	Low	Moderate	High	
Under 30	36	32	24	92
30 up to 40	18	30	27	75
40 up to 50	10	24	20	54
50 and over	26	24	29	79
Total	90	110	100	300

According to this table each of the 300 respondents is classified according to two criteria: (1) age and (2) the amount of coffee consumed.

The following example shows how the rules of addition and multiplication are used when we employ contingency tables.

Example

A sample of executives were surveyed about loyalty to their company. One of the questions was, "If you were given an offer by another company equal to or slightly better than your present position, would you remain with the company or take the other position?" The responses of the 200 executives in the survey were cross-classified with their length of service with the company. (See Table 5–1.)

TABLE 5–1 Loyalty of Executives and Length of Service with Company

| | Length of Service | | | | |
| | Less than 1 Year, B_1 | 1–5 Years, B_2 | 6–10 Years, B_3 | More than 10 Years, B_4 | |
Loyalty					Total
Would remain, A_1	10	30	5	75	120
Would not remain, A_2	25	15	10	30	80
	35	45	15	105	200

What is the probability of randomly selecting an executive who is loyal to the company (would remain) and who has more than 10 years of service?

Solution

Note that two events occur at the same time—the executive would remain with the company, and he or she has more than 10 years of service.

1. Event A_1 happens if a randomly selected executive will remain with the company despite an equal or slightly better offer from another company. To find the probability that event A_1 will happen, refer to Table 5–1. Note there are 120 executives out of the 200 in the survey who would remain with the company, so $P(A_1) = 120/200$, or .60.
2. Event B_4 happens if a randomly selected executive has more than 10 years of service with the company. Thus, $P(B_4|A_1)$ is the conditional probability that an executive with more than 10 years of service would remain with the company despite an equal or slightly better offer from another company. Referring to the contingency table, Table 5–1, 75 of the 120 executives who would remain have more than 10 years of service, so $P(B_4|A_1) = 75/120$.

Solving for the probability that an executive randomly selected will be one who would remain with the company and who has more than 10 years of service with the company, using the general rule of multiplication in formula (5–6), gives:

$$P(A_1 \text{ and } B_4) = P(A_1)P(B_4|A_1) = \left(\frac{120}{200}\right)\left(\frac{75}{120}\right) = \frac{9,000}{24,000} = .375$$

To find the probability of selecting an executive who would remain with the company *or* has less than 1 year of experience we use the general rule of addition, formula (5–4).

1. Event A_1 refers to executives who would remain with the company. So $P(A_1) = 120/200 = .60$.
2. Event B_1 refers to executives who have been with the company less than 1 year. The probability of B_1 is $P(B_1) = 35/200 = .175$.
3. The events A_1 and B_1 are not mutually exclusive. That is, an executive can both be willing to remain with the company and have less than 1 year of experience.

We write this probability, which is called the joint probability, as $P(A_1 \text{ and } B_1)$. There are 10 executives who would both stay with the company and have less than 1 year of service, so $P(A_1 \text{ and } B_1) = 10/200 = .05$. These 10 people are in both groups, those who would remain with the company and those with less than 1 year with the company. They are actually being counted twice, so we need to subtract out this value.

4. We insert these values in formula (5–4) and the result is as follows.

$$P(A_1 \text{ or } B_1) = P(A_1) + P(B_1) - P(A_1 \text{ and } B_1)$$
$$= .60 + .175 - .05 = .725$$

So the likelihood that a selected executive would either remain with the company or has been with the company less than 1 year is .725.

Self-Review 5–7

Refer to Table 5–1 on page 143 to find the following probabilities.
(a) What is the probability of selecting an executive with more than 10 years of service?
(b) What is the probability of selecting an executive who would not remain with the company, given that he or she has more than 10 years of service?
(c) What is the probability of selecting an executive with more than 10 years of service or one who would not remain with the company?

Tree Diagrams

LO6 Apply a *tree diagram* to organize and compute probabilities.

The **tree diagram** is a graph that is helpful in organizing calculations that involve several stages. Each segment in the tree is one stage of the problem. The branches of a tree diagram are weighted by probabilities. We will use the data in Table 5–1 to show the construction of a tree diagram.

Steps in constructing a tree diagram

1. To construct a tree diagram, we begin by drawing a heavy dot on the left to represent the root of the tree (see Chart 5–2).
2. For this problem, two main branches go out from the root, the upper one representing "would remain" and the lower one "would not remain." Their probabilities are written on the branches, namely, 120/200 and 80/200. These probabilities could also be denoted $P(A_1)$ and $P(A_2)$.
3. Four branches "grow" out of each of the two main branches. These branches represent the length of service—less than 1 year, 1–5 years, 6–10 years, and more than 10 years. The conditional probabilities for the upper branch of the tree, 10/120, 30/120, 5/120, and so on are written on the appropriate branches. These are $P(B_1|A_1)$, $P(B_2|A_1)$, $P(B_3|A_1)$, and $P(B_4|A_1)$, where B_1 refers to less than 1 year of service, B_2 1 to 5 years, B_3 6 to 10 years, and B_4 more than 10 years. Next, write the conditional probabilities for the lower branch.
4. Finally, joint probabilities, that the events A_1 and B_i or the events A_2 and B_i will occur together, are shown on the right side. For example, the joint probability of randomly selecting an executive who would remain with the company and who has less than 1 year of service, from formula (5–6), is:

$$P(A_1 \text{ and } B_1) = P(A_1)P(B_1|A_1) = \left(\frac{120}{200}\right)\left(\frac{10}{120}\right) = .05$$

Because the joint probabilities represent all possible outcomes (would remain, 6–10 years service; would not remain, more than 10 years of service; etc.), they must sum to 1.00 (see Chart 5–2).

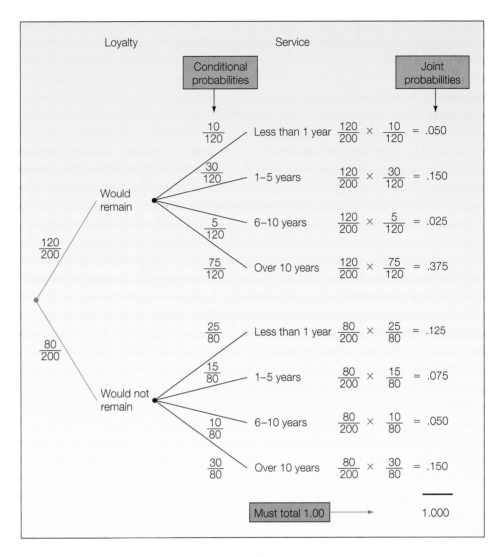

CHART 5–2 Tree Diagram Showing Loyalty and Length of Service

Self-Review 5–8

Consumers were surveyed on the relative number of visits to a Best Buy store (often, occasional, and never) and if the store was located in an enclosed mall (yes and no). When variables are measured nominally, such as these data, the results are usually summarized in a contingency table.

	Enclosed Mall		
Visits	**Yes**	**No**	**Total**
Often	60	20	80
Occasional	25	35	60
Never	5	50	55
	90	105	195

(a) Are the number of visits and enclosed mall variables independent? Why? Interpret your conclusion.
(b) Draw a tree diagram and determine the joint probabilities.

Exercises

connect™

23. Suppose $P(A) = .40$ and $P(B|A) = .30$. What is the joint probability of A and B?
24. Suppose $P(X_1) = .75$ and $P(Y_2|X_1) = .40$. What is the joint probability of X_1 and Y_2?
25. A local bank reports that 80 percent of its customers maintain a checking account, 60 percent have a savings account, and 50 percent have both. If a customer is chosen at random, what is the probability the customer has either a checking or a savings account? What is the probability the customer does not have either a checking or a savings account?
26. All Seasons Plumbing has two service trucks that frequently need repair. If the probability the first truck is available is .75, the probability the second truck is available is .50, and the probability that both trucks are available is .30, what is the probability neither truck is available?
27. Refer to the following table.

Second Event	First Event			Total
	A_1	A_2	A_3	
B_1	2	1	3	6
B_2	1	2	1	4
Total	3	3	4	10

   a. Determine $P(A_1)$.
   b. Determine $P(B_1|A_2)$.
   c. Determine $P(B_2 \text{ and } A_3)$.
28. Three defective electric toothbrushes were accidentally shipped to a drugstore by Cleanbrush Products along with 17 nondefective ones.
   a. What is the probability the first two electric toothbrushes sold will be returned to the drugstore because they are defective?
   b. What is the probability the first two electric toothbrushes sold will not be defective?
29. Each salesperson at Puchett, Sheets, and Hogan Insurance Agency is rated either below average, average, or above average with respect to sales ability. Each salesperson is also rated with respect to his or her potential for advancement—either fair, good, or excellent. These traits for the 500 salespeople were cross-classified into the following table.

Sales Ability	Potential for Advancement		
	Fair	Good	Excellent
Below average	16	12	22
Average	45	60	45
Above average	93	72	135

   a. What is this table called?
   b. What is the probability a salesperson selected at random will have above average sales ability and excellent potential for advancement?
   c. Construct a tree diagram showing all the probabilities, conditional probabilities, and joint probabilities.
30. An investor owns three common stocks. Each stock, independent of the others, has equally likely chances of (1) increasing in value, (2) decreasing in value, or (3) remaining the same value. List the possible outcomes of this experiment. Estimate the probability at least two of the stocks increase in value.
31. The board of directors of a small company consists of five people. Three of those are "strong leaders." If they buy an idea, the entire board will agree. The other "weak" members have no influence. Three salespeople are scheduled, one after the other, to make sales presentations to a board member of the salesperson's choice. The salespeople are

convincing but do not know who the "strong leaders" are. However, they will know who the previous salespeople spoke to. The first salesperson to find a strong leader will win the account. Do the three salespeople have the same chance of winning the account? If not, find their respective probabilities of winning.

32. If you ask three strangers about their birthdays, what is the probability: (a) All were born on Wednesday? (b) All were born on different days of the week? (c) None were born on Saturday?

Statistics in Action

A recent study by the National Collegiate Athletic Association (NCAA) reported that of 150,000 senior boys playing on their high school basketball team, 64 would make a professional team. To put it another way, the odds of a high school senior basketball player making a professional team are 1 in 2,344. From the same study:

1. The odds of a high school senior basketball player playing some college basketball are about 1 in 40.

2. The odds of a high school senior playing college basketball as a senior in college are about 1 in 60.

3. If you play basketball as a senior in college, the odds of making a professional team are about 1 in 37.5.

Principles of Counting

If the number of possible outcomes in an experiment is small, it is relatively easy to count them. There are six possible outcomes, for example, resulting from the roll of a die, namely:

If, however, there are a large number of possible outcomes, such as the number of heads and tails for an experiment with 10 tosses, it would be tedious to count all the possibilities. They could have all heads, one head and nine tails, two heads and eight tails, and so on. To facilitate counting, we discuss three formulas: the **multiplication formula** (not to be confused with the multiplication *rule* described earlier in the chapter), the **permutation formula,** and the **combination formula.**

The Multiplication Formula

We begin with the multiplication formula.

> **MULTIPLICATION FORMULA** If there are m ways of doing one thing and n ways of doing another thing, there are $m \times n$ ways of doing both.

In terms of a formula:

> **MULTIPLICATION FORMULA**   Total number of arrangements = $(m)(n)$ **[5–7]**

This can be extended to more than two events. For three events m, n, and o:

$$\text{Total number of arrangements} = (m)(n)(o)$$

Example

An automobile dealer wants to advertise that for $29,999 you can buy a convertible, a two-door sedan, or a four-door model with your choice of either wire wheel covers or solid wheel covers. How many different arrangements of models and wheel covers can the dealer offer?

Solution

Of course the dealer could determine the total number of arrangements by picturing and counting them. There are six.

Convertible with wire wheels

Convertible with solid wheels

Two-door with wire wheels

Two-door with solid wheels

Four-door with wire wheels

Four-door with solid wheels

We can employ the multiplication formula as a check (where m is the number of models and n the wheel cover type). From formula (5–7):

$$\text{Total possible arrangements} = (m)(n) = (3)(2) = 6$$

It was not difficult to count all the possible model and wheel cover combinations in this example. Suppose, however, that the dealer decided to offer eight models and six types of wheel covers. It would be tedious to picture and count all the possible alternatives. Instead, the multiplication formula can be used. In this case, there are $(m)(n) = (8)(6) = 48$ possible arrangements.

Note in the preceding applications of the multiplication formula that there were *two or more groupings from which you made selections*. The automobile dealer, for example, offered a choice of models and a choice of wheel covers. If a home builder offered you four different exterior styles of a home to choose from and three interior floor plans, the multiplication formula would be used to find how many different arrangements were possible. There are 12 possibilities.

Self-Review 5–9

1. The Women's Shopping Network on cable TV offers sweaters and slacks for women. The sweaters and slacks are offered in coordinating colors. If sweaters are available in five colors and the slacks are available in four colors, how many different outfits can be advertised?
2. Pioneer manufactures three models of stereo receivers, two MP3 docking stations, four speakers, and three CD carousels. When the four types of components are sold together, they form a "system." How many different systems can the electronics firm offer?

The Permutation Formula

As noted, the multiplication formula is applied to find the number of possible arrangements for two or more groups. The **permutation formula** is applied to find the possible number of arrangements when there is only *one* group of objects. Illustrations of this type of problem are:

- Three electronic parts are to be assembled into a plug-in unit for a television set. The parts can be assembled in any order. The question involving counting is: In how many different ways can the three parts be assembled?
- A machine operator must make four safety checks before starting his machine. It does not matter in which order the checks are made. In how many different ways can the operator make the checks?

One order for the first illustration might be: the transistor first, the LEDs second, and the synthesizer third. This arrangement is called a **permutation.**

PERMUTATION Any arrangement of *r* objects selected from a single group of *n* possible objects.

Note that the arrangements *a b c* and *b a c* are different permutations. The formula to count the total number of different permutations is:

PERMUTATION FORMULA $$_nP_r = \frac{n!}{(n-r)!}$$ [5–8]

where:
  n is the total number of objects.
  r is the number of objects selected.

Before we solve the two problems illustrated, note that permutations and combinations (to be discussed shortly) use a notation called *n factorial*. It is written *n!* and means the product of $n(n-1)(n-2)(n-3)\cdots(1)$. For instance, $5! = 5 \cdot 4 \cdot 3 \cdot 2 \cdot 1 = 120$.

Many of your calculators have a button with *x!* that will perform this calculation for you. It will save you a great deal of time. For example the Texas Instrument TI-36X calculator has the following key:

It is the "third function" so check your users' manual or the Internet for instructions.

The factorial notation can also be canceled when the same number appears in both the numerator and the denominator, as shown below.

$$\frac{6!3!}{4!} = \frac{6 \cdot 5 \cdot \cancel{4} \cdot \cancel{3} \cdot \cancel{2} \cdot \cancel{1}(3 \cdot 2 \cdot 1)}{\cancel{4} \cdot \cancel{3} \cdot \cancel{2} \cdot \cancel{1}} = 180$$

By definition, zero factorial, written 0!, is 1. That is, $0! = 1$.

Example

Referring to the group of three electronic parts that are to be assembled in any order, in how many different ways can they be assembled?

Solution

There are three electronic parts to be assembled, so $n = 3$. Because all three are to be inserted in the plug-in unit, $r = 3$. Solving using formula (5–8) gives:

$$_nP_r = \frac{n!}{(n-r)!} = \frac{3!}{(3-3)!} = \frac{3!}{0!} = \frac{3!}{1} = 6$$

We can check the number of permutations arrived at by using the permutation formula. We determine how many "spaces" have to be filled and the possibilities for each "space." In the problem involving three electronic parts, there are three locations in the plug-in unit for the three parts. There are three possibilities for the first place, two for the second (one has been used up), and one for the third, as follows:

$$(3)(2)(1) = 6 \text{ permutations}$$

The six ways in which the three electronic parts, lettered *A, B, C,* can be arranged are:

ABC	*BAC*	*CAB*	*ACB*	*BCA*	*CBA*

In the previous example we selected and arranged all the objects, that is $n = r$. In many cases, only some objects are selected and arranged from the n possible objects. We explain the details of this application in the following example.

Example

Betts Machine Shop, Inc., has eight screw machines but only three spaces available in the production area for the machines. In how many different ways can the eight machines be arranged in the three spaces available?

Solution

There are eight possibilities for the first available space in the production area, seven for the second space (one has been used up), and six for the third space. Thus:

$$(8)(7)(6) = 336,$$

that is, there are a total of 336 different possible arrangements. This could also be found by using formula (5–8). If $n = 8$ machines, and $r = 3$ spaces available, the formula leads to

$$_nP_r = \frac{n!}{(n-r)!} = \frac{8!}{(8-3)!} = \frac{8!}{5!} = \frac{(8)(7)(6)5!}{5!} = 336$$

The Combination Formula

If the order of the selected objects is *not* important, any selection is called a **combination**. The formula to count the number of r object combinations from a set of n objects is:

> **COMBINATION FORMULA**
> $$_nC_r = \frac{n!}{r!(n-r)!}$$
> **[5–9]**

For example, if executives Able, Baker, and Chauncy are to be chosen as a committee to negotiate a merger, there is only one possible combination of these three; the committee of Able, Baker, and Chauncy is the same as the committee of Baker, Chauncy, and Able. Using the combination formula:

$$_nC_r = \frac{n!}{r!(n-r)!} = \frac{3 \cdot 2 \cdot 1}{3 \cdot 2 \cdot 1(1)} = 1$$

Example

The marketing department has been given the assignment of designing color codes for the 42 different lines of compact disks sold by Goody Records. Three colors are to be used on each CD, but a combination of three colors used for one CD cannot be rearranged and used to identify a different CD. This means that if green, yellow, and violet were used to identify one line, then yellow, green, and violet (or any other combination of these three colors) cannot be used to identify another line. Would seven colors taken three at a time be adequate to color-code the 42 lines?

Solution

According to formula (5–9), there are 35 combinations, found by

$$_7C_3 = \frac{n!}{r!(n-r)!} = \frac{7!}{3!(7-3)!} = \frac{7!}{3!4!} = 35$$

The seven colors taken three at a time (i.e., three colors to a line) would not be adequate to color-code the 42 different lines because they would provide only 35 combinations. Eight colors taken three at a time would give 56 different combinations. This would be more than adequate to color-code the 42 different lines.

When the number of permutations or combinations is large, the calculations are tedious. Computer software and handheld calculators have "functions" to compute these numbers. The Excel output for the location of the eight screw machines in the production area of Betts Machine Shop, Inc., is shown below. There are a total of 336 arrangements.

Below is the output for the color codes at Goody Records. Three colors are chosen from among seven possible. The number of combinations possible is 35.

Self-Review 5–10

1. A musician wants to write a score based on only five chords: B-flat, C, D, E, and G. However, only three chords out of the five will be used in succession, such as C, B-flat, and E. Repetitions, such as B-flat, B-flat, and E, will not be permitted.
   (a) How many permutations of the five chords, taken three at a time, are possible?
   (b) Using formula (5–8), how many permutations are possible?

2. A machine operator must make four safety checks before machining a part. It does not matter in which order the checks are made. In how many different ways can the operator make the checks?

3. The 10 numbers 0 through 9 are to be used in code groups of four to identify an item of clothing. Code 1083 might identify a blue blouse, size medium; the code group 2031 might identify a pair of pants, size 18; and so on. Repetitions of numbers are not permitted. That is, the same number cannot be used twice (or more) in a total sequence. For example, 2256, 2562, or 5559 would not be permitted. How many different code groups can be designed?

4. In the above example involving Goody Records, we said that eight colors taken three at a time would give 56 different combinations.
   (a) Use formula (5–9) to show this is true.
   (b) As an alternative plan for color-coding the 42 different lines, it has been suggested that only two colors be placed on a disk. Would 10 colors be adequate to color-

code the 42 different lines? (Again, a combination of two colors could be used only once—that is, if pink and blue were coded for one line, blue and pink could not be used to identify a different line.)

5. In a lottery game, three numbers are randomly selected from a tumbler of balls numbered 1 through 50.
    (a) How many permutations are possible?
    (b) How many combinations are possible?

Exercises

connect

33. Solve the following:
   a. 40!/35!
   b. $_7P_4$
   c. $_5C_2$

34. Solve the following:
   a. 20!/17!
   b. $_9P_3$
   c. $_7C_2$

35. A pollster randomly selected 4 of 10 available people. How many different groups of 4 are possible?

36. A telephone number consists of seven digits, the first three representing the exchange. How many different telephone numbers are possible within the 537 exchange?

37. An overnight express company must include five cities on its route. How many different routes are possible, assuming that it does not matter in which order the cities are included in the routing?

38. A representative of the Environmental Protection Agency (EPA) wants to select samples from 10 landfills. The director has 15 landfills from which she can collect samples. How many different samples are possible?

39. A national pollster has developed 15 questions designed to rate the performance of the president of the United States. The pollster will select 10 of these questions. How many different arrangements are there for the order of the 10 selected questions?

40. A company is creating three new divisions and seven managers are eligible to be appointed head of a division. How many different ways could the three new heads be appointed? Hint: Assume the division assignment makes a difference.

Chapter Summary

I. A probability is a value between 0 and 1 inclusive that represents the likelihood a particular event will happen.
   A. An experiment is the observation of some activity or the act of taking some measurement.
   B. An outcome is a particular result of an experiment.
   C. An event is the collection of one or more outcomes of an experiment.

II. There are three definitions of probability.
   A. The classical definition applies when there are *n* equally likely outcomes to an experiment.
   B. The empirical definition occurs when the number of times an event happens is divided by the number of observations.
   C. A subjective probability is based on whatever information is available.

III. Two events are mutually exclusive if by virtue of one event happening the other cannot happen.

IV. Events are independent if the occurrence of one event does not affect the occurrence of another event.

V. The rules of addition refer to the union of events.
    A. The special rule of addition is used when events are mutually exclusive.

$$P(A \text{ or } B) = P(A) + P(B) \qquad \text{[5–2]}$$

    B. The general rule of addition is used when the events are not mutually exclusive.

$$P(A \text{ or } B) = P(A) + P(B) - P(A \text{ and } B) \qquad \text{[5–4]}$$

    C. The complement rule is used to determine the probability of an event happening by subtracting the probability of the event not happening from 1.

$$P(A) = 1 - P(\sim A) \qquad \text{[5–3]}$$

VI. The rules of multiplication refer to the product of events.
    A. The special rule of multiplication refers to events that are independent.

$$P(A \text{ and } B) = P(A)P(B) \qquad \text{[5–5]}$$

    B. The general rule of multiplication refers to events that are not independent.

$$P(A \text{ and } B) = P(A)P(B|A) \qquad \text{[5–6]}$$

    C. A joint probability is the likelihood that two or more events will happen at the same time.
    D. A conditional probability is the likelihood that an event will happen, given that another event has already happened.

VII. There are three counting rules that are useful in determining the number of outcomes in an experiment.
    A. The multiplication rule states that if there are m ways one event can happen and n ways another event can happen, then there are mn ways the two events can happen.

$$\text{Number of arrangements} = (m)(n) \qquad \text{[5–7]}$$

    B. A permutation is an arrangement in which the order of the objects selected from a specific pool of objects is important.

$$_nP_r = \frac{n!}{(n-r)!} \qquad \text{[5–8]}$$

    C. A combination is an arrangement where the order of the objects selected from a specific pool of objects is not important.

$$_nC_r = \frac{n!}{r!(n-r)!} \qquad \text{[5–9]}$$

Pronunciation Key

SYMBOL	MEANING	PRONUNCIATION
$P(A)$	Probability of A	P of A
$P(\sim A)$	Probability of not A	P of not A
$P(A \text{ and } B)$	Probability of A and B	P of A and B
$P(A \text{ or } B)$	Probability of A or B	P of A or B
$P(A|B)$	Probability of A given B has happened	P of A given B
$_nP_r$	Permutation of n items selected r at a time	Pnr
$_nC_r$	Combination of n items selected r at a time	Cnr

Chapter Exercises

connect

41. The marketing research department at Vernors plans to survey teenagers about a newly developed soft drink. Each will be asked to compare it with his or her favorite soft drink.
   a. What is the experiment?
   b. What is one possible event?

42. The number of times a particular event occurred in the past is divided by the number of occurrences. What is this approach to probability called?

43. The probability that the cause and the cure for all cancers will be discovered before the year 2020 is .20. What viewpoint of probability does this statement illustrate?

44. Berdine's Chicken Factory has several stores in the Hilton Head, South Carolina, area. When interviewing applicants for server positions, the owner would like to include information on the amount of tip a server can expect to earn per check (or bill). A study of 500 recent checks indicated the server earned the following amounts in tips per 8-hour shift.

Amount of Tip	Number
$0 up to $ 20	200
20 up to 50	100
50 up to 100	75
100 up to 200	75
200 or more	50
Total	500

   a. What is the probability of a tip of $200 or more?
   b. Are the categories "$0 up to $20," "$20 up to $50," and so on considered mutually exclusive?
   c. If the probabilities associated with each outcome were totaled, what would that total be?
   d. What is the probability of a tip of up to $50?
   e. What is the probability of a tip of less than $200?

45. Winning all three "Triple Crown" races is considered the greatest feat of a pedigree racehorse. After a successful Kentucky Derby, Big Brown is a 1 to 2 favorite to win the Preakness Stakes.
   a. If he is a 1 to 2 favorite to win the Belmont Stakes as well, what is his probability of winning the Triple Crown?
   b. What do his chances for the Preakness Stakes have to be in order for him to be "even money" to earn the Triple Crown?

46. The first card selected from a standard 52-card deck is a king.
   a. If it is returned to the deck, what is the probability that a king will be drawn on the second selection?
   b. If the king is not replaced, what is the probability that a king will be drawn on the second selection?
   c. What is the probability that a king will be selected on the first draw from the deck and another king on the second draw (assuming that the first king was not replaced)?

47. Armco, a manufacturer of traffic light systems, found that under accelerated-life tests, 95 percent of the newly developed systems lasted 3 years before failing to change signals properly.
   a. If a city purchased four of these systems, what is the probability all four systems would operate properly for at least 3 years?
   b. Which rule of probability does this illustrate?
   c. Using letters to represent the four systems, write an equation to show how you arrived at the answer to part (a).

48. Refer to the following picture.

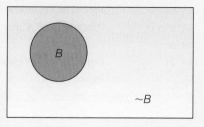

    a. What is the picture called?

    b. What rule of probability is illustrated?

    c. *B* represents the event of choosing a family that receives welfare payments. What does $P(B) + P(\sim B)$ equal?

49. In a management trainee program at Claremont Enterprises, 80 percent of the trainees are female and 20 percent male. Ninety percent of the females attended college, and 78 percent of the males attended college.

    a. A management trainee is selected at random. What is the probability that the person selected is a female who did not attend college?

    b. Are gender and attending college independent? Why?

    c. Construct a tree diagram showing all the probabilities, conditional probabilities, and joint probabilities.

    d. Do the joint probabilities total 1.00? Why?

50. Assume the likelihood that any flight on Northwest Airlines arrives within 15 minutes of the scheduled time is .90. We select four flights from yesterday for study.

    a. What is the likelihood all four of the selected flights arrived within 15 minutes of the scheduled time?

    b. What is the likelihood that none of the selected flights arrived within 15 minutes of the scheduled time?

    c. What is the likelihood at least one of the selected flights did not arrive within 15 minutes of the scheduled time?

51. There are 100 employees at Kiddie Carts International. Fifty-seven of the employees are production workers, 40 are supervisors, 2 are secretaries, and the remaining employee is the president. Suppose an employee is selected:

    a. What is the probability the selected employee is a production worker?

    b. What is the probability the selected employee is either a production worker or a supervisor?

    c. Refer to part (b). Are these events mutually exclusive?

    d. What is the probability the selected employee is neither a production worker nor a supervisor?

52. Chipper Jones of the Atlanta Braves had the highest batting average in the 2008 Major League Baseball season. His average was .364. So assume the probability of getting a hit was .364 for each time he batted. In a particular game assume he batted three times.

    a. This is an example of what type of probability?

    b. What was the probability of getting three hits in a particular game?

    c. What was the probability of not getting any hits in a game?

    d. What was the probability of getting at least one hit?

53. Four sports teams remain in a single-elimination playoff competition. If one team is favored in its semi-final match by odds of 2 to 1 and another squad is favored in its contest by odds of 3 to 1, what is the probability that:

    a. Both favored teams win their games?

    b. Neither favored team wins its game?

    c. At least one of the favored teams wins its game?

54. There are three clues labeled "daily double" on the game show *Jeopardy*. If three equally matched contenders play, what is the probability that:

    a. A single contestant finds all three "daily doubles"?

    b. The returning champion gets all three of the "daily doubles"?

    c. Each of the players selects precisely one of the "daily doubles"?

55. Brooks Insurance, Inc., wishes to offer life insurance to men age 60 via the Internet. Mortality tables indicate the likelihood of a 60-year-old man surviving another year is .98. If the policy is offered to five men age 60:

    a. What is the probability all five men survive the year?

    b. What is the probability at least one does not survive?

56. Forty percent of the homes constructed in the Quail Creek area include a security system. Three homes are selected at random:

    a. What is the probability all three of the selected homes have a security system?

    b. What is the probability none of the three selected homes have a security system?

    c. What is the probability at least one of the selected homes has a security system?

    d. Did you assume the events to be dependent or independent?

57. Refer to Exercise 56, but assume there are 10 homes in the Quail Creek area and four of them have a security system. Three homes are selected at random:

    a. What is the probability all three of the selected homes have a security system?

    b. What is the probability none of the three selected homes have a security system?

    c. What is the probability at least one of the selected homes has a security system?
    d. Did you assume the events to be dependent or independent?

58. There are 20 families living in the Willbrook Farms Development. Of these families 10 prepared their own federal income taxes for last year, 7 had their taxes prepared by a local professional, and the remaining 3 by H&R Block.
    a. What is the probability of selecting a family that prepared their own taxes?
    b. What is the probability of selecting two families, both of which prepared their own taxes?
    c. What is the probability of selecting three families, all of which prepared their own taxes?
    d. What is the probability of selecting two families, neither of which had their taxes prepared by H&R Block?

59. The board of directors of Saner Automatic Door Company consists of 12 members, 3 of whom are women. A new policy and procedures manual is to be written for the company. A committee of 3 is randomly selected from the board to do the writing.
    a. What is the probability that all members of the committee are men?
    b. What is the probability that at least 1 member of the committee is a woman?

60. A recent survey reported in *BusinessWeek* dealt with the salaries of CEOs at large corporations and whether company shareholders made money or lost money.

	CEO Paid More Than $1 Million	CEO Paid Less Than $1 Million	Total
Shareholders made money	2	11	13
Shareholders lost money	4	3	7
Total	6	14	20

If a company is randomly selected from the list of 20 studied, what is the probability:
    a. the CEO made more than $1 million?
    b. the CEO made more than $1 million or the shareholders lost money?
    c. the CEO made more than $1 million given the shareholders lost money?
    d. of selecting 2 CEOs and finding they both made more than $1 million?

61. Althoff and Roll, an investment firm in Augusta, Georgia, advertises extensively in the *Augusta Morning Gazette,* the newspaper serving the region. The *Gazette* marketing staff estimates that 60 percent of Althoff and Roll's potential market read the newspaper. It is further estimated that 85 percent of those who read the *Gazette* remember the Althoff and Roll advertisement.
    a. What percent of the investment firm's potential market sees and remembers the advertisement?
    b. What percent of the investment firm's potential market sees, but does not remember the advertisement?

62. An Internet company located in Southern California has season tickets to the Los Angeles Lakers basketball games. The company president always invites one of the four vice presidents to attend games with him, and claims he selects the person to attend at random. One of the four vice presidents has not been invited to attend any of the last five Lakers home games. What is the likelihood this could be due to chance?

63. A computer-supply retailer purchased a batch of 1,000 CD-R disks and attempted to format them for a particular application. There were 857 perfect CDs, 112 CDs were usable but had bad sectors, and the remainder could not be used at all.
    a. What is the probability a randomly chosen CD is not perfect?
    b. If the disk is not perfect, what is the probability it cannot be used at all?

64. An investor purchased 100 shares of Fifth Third Bank stock and 100 shares of Santee Electric Cooperative stock. The probability the bank stock will appreciate over a year is .70. The probability the electric utility will increase over the same period is .60.
    a. What is the probability both stocks appreciate during the period?
    b. What is the probability the bank stock appreciates but the utility does not?
    c. What is the probability at least one of the stocks appreciates?

65. With each purchase of a large pizza at Tony's Pizza, the customer receives a coupon that can be scratched to see if a prize will be awarded. The odds of winning a free soft drink are 1 in 10, and the odds of winning a free large pizza are 1 in 50. You plan to eat lunch tomorrow at Tony's. What is the probability:
    a. That you will win either a large pizza or a soft drink?
    b. That you will not win a prize?
    c. That you will not win a prize on three consecutive visits to Tony's?
    d. That you will win at least one prize on one of your next three visits to Tony's?

66. For the daily lottery game in Illinois, participants select three numbers between 0 and 9. A number cannot be selected more than once, so a winning ticket could be, say, 307 but not 337. Purchasing one ticket allows you to select one set of numbers. The winning numbers are announced on TV each night.
    a. How many different outcomes (three-digit numbers) are possible?
    b. If you purchase a ticket for the game tonight, what is the likelihood you will win?
    c. Suppose you purchase three tickets for tonight's drawing and select a different number for each ticket. What is the probability that you will not win with any of the tickets?

67. Several years ago Wendy's Hamburgers advertised that there are 256 different ways to order your hamburger. You may choose to have, or omit, any combination of the following on your hamburger: mustard, ketchup, onion, pickle, tomato, relish, mayonnaise, and lettuce. Is the advertisement correct? Show how you arrive at your answer.

68. It was found that 60 percent of the tourists to China visited the Forbidden City, the Temple of Heaven, the Great Wall, and other historical sites in or near Beijing. Forty percent visited Xi'an with its magnificent terracotta soldiers, horses, and chariots, which lay buried for over 2,000 years. Thirty percent of the tourists went to both Beijing and Xi'an. What is the probability that a tourist visited at least one of these places?

69. A new chewing gum has been developed that is helpful to those who want to stop smoking. If 60 percent of those people chewing the gum are successful in stopping smoking, what is the probability that in a group of four smokers using the gum at least one quits smoking?

70. Reynolds Construction Company has agreed not to erect all "look-alike" homes in a new subdivision. Five exterior designs are offered to potential home buyers. The builder has standardized three interior plans that can be incorporated in any of the five exteriors. How many different ways can the exterior and interior plans be offered to potential home buyers?

71. A new sports car model has defective brakes 15 percent of the time and a defective steering mechanism 5 percent of the time. Let's assume (and hope) that these problems occur independently. If one or the other of these problems is present, the car is called a "lemon." If both of these problems are present, the car is a "hazard." Your instructor purchased one of these cars yesterday. What is the probability it is:
    a. A lemon?
    b. A hazard?

72. The state of Maryland has license plates with three numbers followed by three letters. How many different license plates are possible?

73. There are four people being considered for the position of chief executive officer of Dalton Enterprises. Three of the applicants are over 60 years of age. Two are female, of which only one is over 60.
    a. What is the probability that a candidate is over 60 and female?
    b. Given that the candidate is male, what is the probability he is less than 60?
    c. Given that the person is over 60, what is the probability the person is female?

74. Tim Bleckie is the owner of Bleckie Investment and Real Estate Company. The company recently purchased four tracts of land in Holly Farms Estates and six tracts in Newburg Woods. The tracts are all equally desirable and sell for about the same amount.
    a. What is the probability that the next two tracts sold will be in Newburg Woods?
    b. What is the probability that of the next four sold at least one will be in Holly Farms?
    c. Are these events independent or dependent?

75. A computer password consists of four characters. The characters can be one of the 26 letters of the alphabet. Each character may be used more than once. How many different passwords are possible?

76. A case of 24 cans contains 1 can that is contaminated. Three cans are to be chosen randomly for testing.
    a. How many different combinations of 3 cans could be selected?
    b. What is the probability that the contaminated can is selected for testing?

77. A puzzle in the newspaper presents a matching problem. The names of 10 U.S. presidents are listed in one column, and their vice presidents are listed in random order in the second column. The puzzle asks the reader to match each president with his vice president. If you make the matches randomly, how many matches are possible? What is the probability all 10 of your matches are correct?

78. Two components, A and B, operate in series. Being in series means that for the system to operate, both components A and B must work. Assume the two components are independent. What is the probability the system works under these conditions? The probability A works is .90 and the probability B functions is also .90.

79. You take a trip by air that involves three independent flights. If there is an 80 percent chance each specific leg of the trip is done on time, what is the probability all three flights arrive on time?

80. The probability a HP network server is down is .05. If you have three independent servers, what is the probability that at least one of them is operational?

81. Twenty-two percent of all liquid crystal displays (LCDs) are manufactured by Samsung. What is the probability that in a collection of three independent LCD purchases, at least one is a Samsung?

Data Set Exercises

82. Refer to the Real Estate data, which reports information on homes sold in the Phoenix, Arizona, area during the last year.
  a. Sort the data into a table that shows the number of homes that have a pool versus the number that don't have a pool in each of the five townships. If a home is selected at random, compute the following probabilities.
  1. The home is in Township 1 or has a pool.
  2. Given that it is in Township 3, that it has a pool.
  3. Has a pool and is in Township 3.
  b. Sort the data into a table that shows the number of homes that have a garage attached versus those that don't in each of the five townships. If a home is selected at random, compute the following probabilities:
  1. The home has a garage attached.
  2. Given that it is in Township 5, that it does not have a garage attached.
  3. The home has a garage attached and is in Township 3.
  4. Does not have a garage attached or is in Township 2.

83. Refer to the Baseball 2008 data, which reports information on the 30 Major League Baseball teams for the 2008 season. Set up a variable that divides the teams into two groups, those that had a winning season and those that did not. That is, create a variable to count the teams that won 81 games or more, and those that won 80 or less. Next create a new variable for attendance, using three categories: attendance less than 2.0 million, attendance of 2.0 million up to 3.0 million, and attendance of 3.0 million or more.
  a. Create a table that shows the number of teams with a winning season versus those with a losing season by the three categories of attendance. If a team is selected at random, compute the following probabilities:
  1. Having a winning season.
  2. Having a winning season or attendance of more than 3.0 million.
  3. Given attendance of more than 3.0 million, having a winning season.
  4. Having a losing season and drawing less than 2.0 million.
  b. Create a table that shows the number of teams that play on artificial surfaces and natural surfaces by winning and losing records. If a team is selected at random, compute the following probabilities:
  1. Selecting a team with a home field that has a natural surface.
  2. Is the likelihood of selecting a team with a winning record larger for teams with natural or artificial surfaces?
  3. Having a winning record or playing on an artificial surface.

Practice Test

Part I Objective

1. A _____ is a value between zero and one, inclusive, describing the relative chance or likelihood an event will occur.

2. An _____ is a process that leads to the occurrence of one and only one of several possible observations.

3. An _____ is a collection of one or more outcomes of an experiment.

4. Using the _____ viewpoint, the probability of an event happening is the fraction of the time similar events happened in the past.

5. Using the _____ viewpoint, an individual evaluates the available opinions and information and then estimates or assigns the probability.

6. Using the _____ viewpoint, the probability of an event happening is computed by dividing the number of favorable outcomes by the number of possible outcomes.

7. If several events are described as _____ , then the occurrence of one event means that none of the other events can occur at the same time.

8. If an experiment has a set of events that includes every possible outcome, then the set of events is described as _____ .

9. If two events A and B are _____ , the special rule of addition states that the probability of one or the other events occurring equals the sum of their probabilities.

10. The _____ is used to determine the probability of an event occurring by subtracting the probability of the event not occurring from 1.

11. A probability that measures the likelihood two or more events will happen concurrently is called a _____ .

12. The special rule of multiplication requires that two events A and B are _____ .

Part II Problems

1. Fred Friendly, CPA, has 20 tax returns to prepare before the April 15th deadline. It is late at night, so he decides to do two more before going home. In his stack of accounts, 12 are for individuals, 5 are for businesses, and 3 are for charitable organizations. If he selects the two returns at random, what is the probability that:
   a. Both are businesses?
   b. At least one is a business?

2. Fred exercises regularly. He jogs 30 percent of the time, rides a bike 20 percent of the time, and does both 12 percent of the time. What is the probability that on a typical day he does at least one of these two types of exercise?

3. Fred works in a tax office with four other CPAs. There are five parking spots beside the office. If they all drive to work, how many different ways can the cars belonging to the CPAs be arranged in the five spots?

Software Commands

1. The Excel Commands to determine the number of permutations shown on page 151 are:

   a. Click on the **Formulas** tab in the top menu, then, on the far left, select **Insert Function** *fx*.

   b. In the **Insert Function** box select **Statistical** as the category, then scroll down to **PERMUT** in the **Select a function list.** Click **OK.**
   c. In the **PERM** box after **Number** enter *8* and the **Number_chosen** box enter *3*. The correct answer of *336* appears twice in the box.

2. The Excel Commands to determine the number of combinations shown on page 151 are:

    a. Click on the **Formulas** tab in the top menu, then, on the far left, select **Insert Function** *fx*.

    b. In the **Insert Function** box select **Math & Trig** as the category, then scroll down to **COMBIN** in the **Select a function list**. Click **OK.**

    c. In the **COMBIN** box after **Number** enter *7* and the **Number_chosen** box enter *3*. The correct answer of *35* appears twice in the box.

Chapter 5   Answers to Self-Review

5–1 **a.** Count the number who think the new game is playable.

    b. Seventy-three players found the game playable. Many other answers are possible.

    c. No. Probability cannot be greater than 1. The probability that the game, if put on the market, will be successful is 65/80, or .8125.

    d. Cannot be less than 0. Perhaps a mistake in arithmetic.

    e. More than half of the players testing the game liked it. (Of course, other answers are possible.)

5–2 **1.** $\dfrac{4 \text{ queens in deck}}{52 \text{ cards total}} = \dfrac{4}{52} = .0769$

      Classical.

    2. $\dfrac{182}{539} = .338$ Empirical.

    3. The author's view when writing the text of the chance that the DJIA will climb to 12,000 is .25. You may be more optimistic or less optimistic. Subjective.

5–3 **a.** **i.** $\dfrac{(50 + 68)}{2,000} = .059$

      ii. $1 - \dfrac{302}{2,000} = .849$

  b.

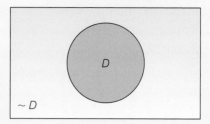

c. They are not complementary, but are mutually exclusive.

5–4 **a.** Need for corrective shoes is event A. Need for major dental work is event B.

$$P(A \text{ or } B) = P(A) + P(B) - P(A \text{ and } B)$$
$$= .08 + .15 - .03$$
$$= .20$$

b. One possibility is:

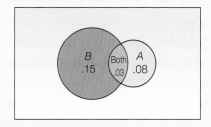

5–5 $(.95)(.95)(.95)(.95) = .8145$

5–6 **a.** .002, found by:

$$\left(\frac{4}{12}\right)\left(\frac{3}{11}\right)\left(\frac{2}{10}\right)\left(\frac{1}{9}\right) = \frac{24}{11,880} = .002$$

b. .14, found by:

$$\left(\frac{8}{12}\right)\left(\frac{7}{11}\right)\left(\frac{6}{10}\right)\left(\frac{5}{9}\right) = \frac{1,680}{11,880} = .1414$$

c. No, because there are other possibilities, such as three women and one man.

5–7 **a.** $P(B_4) = \dfrac{105}{200} = .525$

b. $P(A_2 | B_4) = \dfrac{30}{105} = .286$

c. $P(A_2 \text{ or } B_4) = \dfrac{80}{200} + \dfrac{105}{200} - \dfrac{30}{200} = \dfrac{155}{200} = .775$

5–8 **a.** Independence requires that $P(A|B) = P(A)$. One possibility is:

$$P(\text{visit often} | \text{yes enclosed mall}) = $$
$$P(\text{visit often})$$

Does $60/90 = 80/195$? No, the two variables are *not* independent.

Therefore, any joint probability in the table must be computed by using the general rule of multiplication.

b.

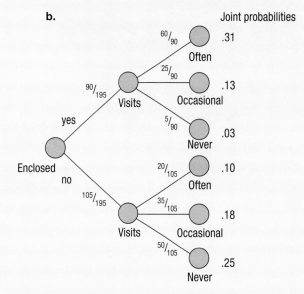

5–9 **1.** $(5)(4) = 20$
 2. $(3)(2)(4)(3) = 72$
5–10 **1.** **a.** 60, found by $(5)(4)(3)$.
 b. 60, found by:

$$\frac{5!}{(5-3)!} = \frac{5 \cdot 4 \cdot 3 \cdot \cancel{2 \cdot 1}}{\cancel{2 \cdot 1}}$$

 2. 24, found by:

$$\frac{4!}{(4-4)!} = \frac{4!}{0!} = \frac{4!}{1} = \frac{4 \cdot 3 \cdot 2 \cdot 1}{1}$$

 3. 5,040, found by:

$$\frac{10!}{(10-4)!} = \frac{10 \cdot 9 \cdot 8 \cdot 7 \cdot \cancel{6 \cdot 5 \cdot 4 \cdot 3 \cdot 2 \cdot 1}}{\cancel{6 \cdot 5 \cdot 4 \cdot 3 \cdot 2 \cdot 1}}$$

 4. **a.** 56 is correct, found by:

$$_8C_3 = \frac{n!}{r!(n-r)!} = \frac{8!}{3!(8-3)!} = 56$$

 b. Yes. There are 45 combinations, found by:

$$_{10}C_2 = \frac{n!}{r!(n-r)!} = \frac{10!}{2!(10-2)!} = 45$$

 5. **a.** $_{50}P_3 = \dfrac{50!}{(50-3)!} = 117,600$

 b. $_{50}C_3 = \dfrac{50!}{3!\,(50-3)!} = 19,600$

6

Discrete Probability Distributions

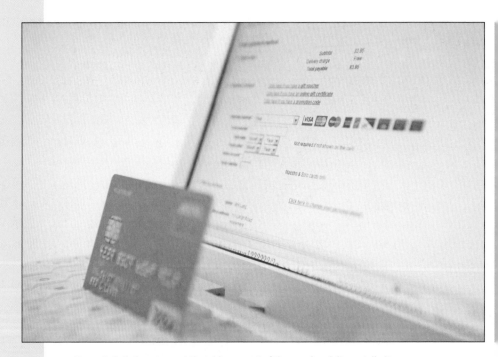

Recent statistics suggest that 15 percent of those who visit a retail site on the Web make a purchase. A retailer wished to verify this claim. To do so, she selected a sample of 16 "hits" to her site and found that 4 had actually made a purchase. What is the likelihood of exactly four purchases? How many purchases should she expect? What is the likelihood that four or more "hits" result in a purchase? (Exercise 43, LO4)

Introduction

Chapters 2 through 4 are devoted to descriptive statistics. We describe raw data by organizing it into a frequency distribution and portraying the distribution in tables, graphs, and charts. Also, we compute a measure of location—such as the arithmetic mean, median, or mode—to locate a typical value near the center of the distribution. The range and the standard deviation are used to describe the spread in the data. These chapters focus on describing *something that has already happened.*

Starting with Chapter 5, the emphasis changes—we begin examining *something that would probably happen.* We note that this facet of statistics is called *statistical inference.* The objective is to make inferences (statements) about a population based on a number of observations, called a sample, selected from the population. In Chapter 5, we state that a probability is a value between 0 and 1 inclusive, and we examine how probabilities can be combined using rules of addition and multiplication.

This chapter will begin the study of **probability distributions.** A probability distribution gives the entire range of values that can occur based on an experiment. A probability distribution is similar to a relative frequency distribution. However, instead of describing the past, it describes a likely future event. For example, a drug manufacturer may claim a treatment will cause weight loss for 80 percent of the population. A consumer protection agency may test the treatment on a sample of six people. If the manufacturer's claim is true, it is *almost impossible* to have an outcome where no one in the sample loses weight and it is *most likely* that 5 out of the 6 do lose weight.

In this chapter we discuss the mean, variance, and standard deviation of a probability distribution. We also discuss two frequently occurring probability distributions: the binomial and the Poisson.

What Is a Probability Distribution?

LO1 Define the terms *probability distribution* and *random variable.*

A probability distribution shows the possible outcomes of an experiment and the probability of each of these outcomes.

> **PROBABILITY DISTRIBUTION** A listing of all the outcomes of an experiment and the probability associated with each outcome.

Below are the major characteristics of a probability distribution.

> **CHARACTERISTICS OF A PROBABILITY DISTRIBUTION**
> 1. The probability of a particular outcome is between 0 and 1 inclusive.
> 2. The outcomes are mutually exclusive events.
> 3. The list is exhaustive. So the sum of the probabilities of the various events is equal to 1.

How can we generate a probability distribution? The following example will explain.

Example

Suppose we are interested in the number of heads showing face up on three tosses of a coin. This is the experiment. The possible results are: zero heads, one head, two heads, and three heads. What is the probability distribution for the number of heads?

Solution

There are eight possible outcomes. A tail might appear face up on the first toss, another tail on the second toss, and another tail on the third toss of the coin. Or we might get a tail, tail, and head, in that order. We use the multiplication formula for counting outcomes (5–7). There are (2)(2)(2) or 8 possible results. These results are on the next page.

Possible Result	Coin Toss			Number of Heads
	First	Second	Third	
1	T	T	T	0
2	T	T	H	1
3	T	H	T	1
4	T	H	H	2
5	H	T	T	1
6	H	T	H	2
7	H	H	T	2
8	H	H	H	3

Note that the outcome "zero heads" occurred only once, "one head" occurred three times, "two heads" occurred three times, and the outcome "three heads" occurred only once. That is, "zero heads" happened one out of eight times. Thus, the probability of zero heads is one-eighth, the probability of one head is three-eighths, and so on. The probability distribution is shown in Table 6–1. Because one of these outcomes must happen, the total of the probabilities of all possible events is 1.000. This is always true. The same information is shown in Chart 6–1.

TABLE 6–1 Probability Distribution for the Events of Zero, One, Two, and Three Heads Showing Face Up on Three Tosses of a Coin

Number of Heads, x	Probability of Outcome, $P(x)$
0	$\frac{1}{8} = .125$
1	$\frac{3}{8} = .375$
2	$\frac{3}{8} = .375$
3	$\frac{1}{8} = .125$
Total	$\frac{8}{8} = 1.000$

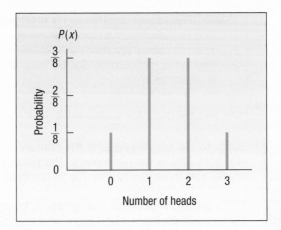

CHART 6–1 Graphical Presentation of the Number of Heads Resulting from Three Tosses of a Coin and the Corresponding Probability

Refer to the coin-tossing example in Table 6–1. We write the probability of x as $P(x)$. So the probability of zero heads is $P(0 \text{ heads}) = .125$ and the probability of one head is $P(1 \text{ head}) = .375$ and so forth. The sum of these mutually exclusive probabilities is 1; that is, from Table 6–1, $0.125 + 0.375 + 0.375 + 0.125 = 1.00$.

Self-Review 6–1

The possible outcomes of an experiment involving the roll of a six-sided die are a one-spot, a two-spot, a three-spot, a four-spot, a five-spot, and a six-spot.
(a)   Develop a probability distribution for the number of possible spots.
(b)   Portray the probability distribution graphically.
(c)   What is the sum of the probabilities?

Random Variables

In any experiment of chance, the outcomes occur randomly. So the numerical value associated with an outcome is often called a *random variable*. For example, rolling a single die is an experiment: any one of six possible outcomes can occur. Some experiments result in outcomes that are quantitative (such as dollars, weight, or number of children), and others result in qualitative outcomes (such as color or religious preference). Each value of the random variable is associated with a probability to indicate the chance of a particular outcome. A few examples will further illustrate what is meant by a **random variable.**

- If we count the number of employees absent from the day shift on Monday, the number might be 0, 1, 2, 3, . . . The number absent is the random variable.
- If we weigh four steel ingots, the weights might be 2,492 pounds, 2,497 pounds, 2,506 pounds, and so on. The weight is the random variable.
- If we toss two coins and count the number of heads, there could be zero, one, or two heads. Because the number of heads resulting from this experiment is due to chance, the number of heads appearing is the random variable.
- Other random variables might be the number of defective lightbulbs produced in an hour at the Cleveland Company, Inc., the grade level (9, 10, 11, or 12) of the members of the St. James girls' basketball team, the number of runners in the Boston Marathon for the 2008 race, and the daily number of drivers charged with driving under the influence of alcohol in Texas.

> **RANDOM VARIABLE** A quantity resulting from an experiment that, by chance, can assume different values.

The following diagram illustrates the terms *experiment, outcome, event,* and *random variable.* First, for the experiment where a coin is tossed three times, there are eight possible outcomes. In this experiment, we are interested in the event that one head occurs in the three tosses. The random variable is the number of heads. In terms of probability, we want to know the probability of the event that the random variable equals 1. The result is $P(1 \text{ head in 3 tosses}) = 0.375$.

Possible *outcomes* for three coin tosses

The *event* {one head} occurs and the *random variable* $x = 1$.

A random variable may be either *discrete* or *continuous.*

Discrete Random Variable

A discrete random variable can assume only a certain number of separated values. If there are 100 employees, then the count of the number absent on Monday can only be 0, 1, 2, 3, . . . , 100. A discrete random variable is usually the result of counting something. By way of definition:

LO2 Distinguish between *discrete* and *continuous probability distributions.*

> **DISCRETE RANDOM VARIABLE** A random variable that can assume only certain clearly separated values.

A discrete random variable can, in some cases, assume fractional or decimal values. It may also assume a negative value. These values must be separated, that is, have distance between them. As an example, the scores awarded by judges for technical competence and artistic form in figure skating are decimal values, such as 7.2, 8.9, and 9.7. Such values are discrete because there is distance between scores of, say, 8.3 and 8.4. A score cannot be 8.34 or 8.347, for example.

Continuous Random Variable

On the other hand, if the random variable is continuous, then the distribution is a continuous probability distribution. If we measure something such as the width of a room, the height of a person, or the pressure in an automobile tire, the variable is a *continuous random variable.* It can assume one of an infinitely large number of values, within certain limitations. As examples:

- The times of commercial flights between Atlanta and Los Angeles are 4.67 hours, 5.13 hours, and so on. The random variable is the time in hours.
- Tire pressure, measured in pounds per square inch (psi), for a new Chevy Trailblazer might be 32.78 psi, 31.62 psi, 33.07 psi, and so on. In other words, any values between 28 and 35 could reasonably occur. The random variable is the tire pressure.
- The waiting time for customers to receive their order at a Starbucks in the Oakland Town Center Mall is recorded to the nearest hundredth of a minute. The random variable is the time, which may be reported as 2.17 minutes, 3.86 minutes, and so on.

Logically, if we organize a set of possible values from a random variable into a probability distribution, the result is a **probability distribution.** So what is the difference between a probability distribution and a random variable? A random variable reports the particular outcome of an experiment. A probability distribution reports all the possible outcomes as well as the corresponding probability.

The tools used, as well as the probability interpretations, are different for discrete and continuous probability distributions. This chapter is limited to the discussion and interpretation of discrete distributions. In the next chapter we discuss continuous distributions. How do you tell the difference between the two types of distributions? Usually a discrete distribution is the result of counting something, such as:

- The number of heads appearing when a coin is tossed 3 times.
- The number of students earning an A in this class.
- The number of production employees absent from the second shift today.
- The number of 30-second commercials on NBC from 8 to 11 P.M. tonight.

Continuous distributions are usually the result of some type of measurement, such as:

- The length of each song on the latest Linkin Park CD.
- The weight of each student in this class.

- The temperature outside as you are reading this book.
- The amount of money earned by each of the more than 750 players currently on Major League Baseball team rosters.

The Mean, Variance, and Standard Deviation of a Probability Distribution

LO3 Calculate the mean, variance, and standard deviation of a discrete probability distribution.

In Chapter 3 we discussed measures of location and variation for a frequency distribution. The mean reports the central location of the data, and the variance describes the spread in the data. In a similar fashion, a probability distribution is summarized by its mean and variance. We identify the mean of a probability distribution by the lowercase Greek letter mu (μ) and the standard deviation by the lowercase Greek letter sigma (σ).

Mean

The mean is a typical value used to represent the central location of a probability distribution. It also is the long-run average value of the random variable. The mean of a probability distribution is also referred to as its **expected value.** It is a weighted average where the possible values of a random variable are weighted by their corresponding probabilities of occurrence.

The mean of a discrete probability distribution is computed by the formula:

MEAN OF A PROBABILITY DISTRIBUTION	$\mu = \Sigma[xP(x)]$	**[6–1]**

where $P(x)$ is the probability of a particular value x. In other words, multiply each x value by its probability of occurrence, and then add these products.

Variance and Standard Deviation

As noted, the mean is a typical value used to summarize a discrete probability distribution. However, it does not describe the amount of spread (variation) in a distribution. The variance does this. The formula for the variance of a probability distribution is:

VARIANCE OF A PROBABILITY DISTRIBUTION	$\sigma^2 = \Sigma[(x - \mu)^2 P(x)]$	**[6–2]**

The computational steps are

1. Subtract the mean from each value, and square this difference.
2. Multiply each squared difference by its probability.
3. Sum the resulting products to arrive at the variance.

The standard deviation, σ, is found by taking the positive square root of σ^2; that is, $\sigma = \sqrt{\sigma^2}$.

An example will help explain the details of the calculation and interpretation of the mean and standard deviation of a probability distribution.

Example

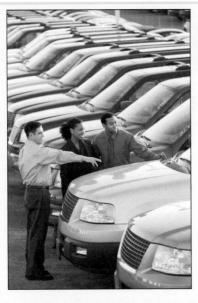

John Ragsdale sells new cars for Pelican Ford. John usually sells the largest number of cars on Saturday. He has developed the following probability distribution for the number of cars he expects to sell on a particular Saturday.

Number of Cars Sold, x	Probability, P(x)
0	.10
1	.20
2	.30
3	.30
4	.10
Total	1.00

1. What type of distribution is this?
2. On a typical Saturday, how many cars does John expect to sell?
3. What is the variance of the distribution?

Solution

The solution to each of these questions follows.

1. This is a discrete probability distribution for the random variable called "number of cars sold." Note that John expects to sell only within a certain range of cars; he does not expect to sell 5 cars, 50 cars, or −2 cars. Further, he cannot sell half a car. He can sell only 0, 1, 2, 3, or 4 cars. Also, the outcomes are mutually exclusive—he cannot sell a total of both 3 and 4 cars on the same Saturday. The sum of the possible outcomes totals 1. Hence, these circumstances qualify as a probability distribution.

2. The mean number of cars sold is computed by weighting the number of cars sold by the probability of selling that number and adding or summing the products, using formula (6–1):

$$\mu = \Sigma[xP(x)]$$

$$= 0(.10) + 1(.20) + 2(.30) + 3(.30) + 4(.10)$$

$$= 2.1$$

These calculations are summarized in the following table.

Number of Cars Sold, x	Probability, P(x)	x · P(x)
0	.10	0.00
1	.20	0.20
2	.30	0.60
3	.30	0.90
4	.10	0.40
Total	1.00	μ = 2.10

How do we interpret a mean of 2.1? This value indicates that, over a large number of Saturdays, John Ragsdale expects to sell a mean of 2.1 cars a day. Of course, it is not possible for him to sell *exactly* 2.1 cars on any particular Saturday. However, the expected value can be used to predict the arithmetic mean number of cars sold on Saturdays in the long run. For example, if John works 50 Saturdays during a year, he can expect to sell (50)(2.1) or 105 cars just on Saturdays. Thus, the mean is sometimes called the expected value.

3. Again, a table is useful for systemizing the computations for the variance, which is 1.290.

Number of Cars Sold, x	Probability, $P(x)$	$(x - \mu)$	$(x - \mu)^2$	$(x - \mu)^2 P(x)$
0	.10	0 − 2.1	4.41	0.441
1	.20	1 − 2.1	1.21	0.242
2	.30	2 − 2.1	0.01	0.003
3	.30	3 − 2.1	0.81	0.243
4	.10	4 − 2.1	3.61	0.361
				$\sigma^2 = 1.290$

Recall that the standard deviation, σ, is the positive square root of the variance. In this example, $\sqrt{\sigma^2} = \sqrt{1.290} = 1.136$ cars. How do we interpret a standard deviation of 1.136 cars? If salesperson Rita Kirsch also sold a mean of 2.1 cars on Saturdays, and the standard deviation in her sales was 1.91 cars, we would conclude that there is more variability in the Saturday sales of Ms. Kirsch than in those of Mr. Ragsdale (because 1.91 > 1.136).

Self-Review 6–2

The Pizza Palace offers three sizes of cola—small, medium, and large—to go with its pizza. The colas are sold for $0.80, $0.90, and $1.20, respectively. Thirty percent of the orders are for small, 50 percent are for medium, and 20 percent are for the large sizes. Organize the size of the colas and the probability of a sale into a probability distribution.
(a) Is this a discrete probability distribution? Indicate why or why not.
(b) Compute the mean amount charged for a cola.
(c) What is the variance in the amount charged for a cola? The standard deviation?

Exercises

connect

1. Compute the mean and variance of the following discrete probability distribution.

x	$P(x)$
0	.2
1	.4
2	.3
3	.1

2. Compute the mean and variance of the following discrete probability distribution.

x	$P(x)$
2	.5
8	.3
10	.2

3. The three tables below show "random variables" and their "probabilities." However, only one of these is actually a probability distribution.
   a. Which is it?

x	P(x)
5	.3
10	.3
15	.2
20	.4

x	P(x)
5	.1
10	.3
15	.2
20	.4

x	P(x)
5	.5
10	.3
15	−.2
20	.4

   b. Using the correct probability distribution, find the probability that x is:
   (1) Exactly 15.   **(2)** No more than 10.   **(3)** More than 5.
   c. Compute the mean, variance, and standard deviation of this distribution.

4. Which of these variables are discrete and which are continuous random variables?
   a. The number of new accounts established by a salesperson in a year.
   b. The time between customer arrivals to a bank ATM.
   c. The number of customers in Big Nick's barber shop.
   d. The amount of fuel in your car's gas tank.
   e. The number of minorities on a jury.
   f. The outside temperature today.

5. The information below is the number of daily emergency service calls made by the volunteer ambulance service of Walterboro, South Carolina, for the last 50 days. To explain, there were 22 days on which there were 2 emergency calls, and 9 days on which there were 3 emergency calls.

Number of Calls	Frequency
0	8
1	10
2	22
3	9
4	1
Total	50

   a. Convert this information on the number of calls to a probability distribution.
   b. Is this an example of a discrete or continuous probability distribution?
   c. What is the mean number of emergency calls per day?
   d. What is the standard deviation of the number of calls made daily?

6. The director of admissions at Kinzua University in Nova Scotia estimated the distribution of student admissions for the fall semester on the basis of past experience. What is the expected number of admissions for the fall semester? Compute the variance and the standard deviation of the number of admissions.

Admissions	Probability
1,000	.6
1,200	.3
1,500	.1

7. Belk Department Store is having a special sale this weekend. Customers charging purchases of more than $50 to their Belk credit card will be given a special Belk Lottery card. The customer will scratch off the card, which will indicate the amount to be taken off the total amount of the purchase. Listed below are the amount of the prize and the percent of the time that amount will be deducted from the total amount of the purchase.

Prize Amount	Probability
$ 10	.50
25	.40
50	.08
100	.02

a. What is the mean amount deducted from the total purchase amount?
b. What is the standard deviation of the amount deducted from the total purchase?

8. The Downtown Parking Authority of Tampa, Florida, reported the following information for a sample of 250 customers on the number of hours cars are parked and the amount they are charged.

Number of Hours	Frequency	Amount Charged
1	20	$ 3.00
2	38	6.00
3	53	9.00
4	45	12.00
5	40	14.00
6	13	16.00
7	5	18.00
8	36	20.00
	250	

a. Convert the information on the number of hours parked to a probability distribution. Is this a discrete or a continuous probability distribution?
b. Find the mean and the standard deviation of the number of hours parked. How would you answer the question: How long is a typical customer parked?
c. Find the mean and the standard deviation of the amount charged.

Binomial Probability Distribution

LO4 Describe the characteristics of and compute probabilities using the *binomial probability distribution.*

The **binomial probability distribution** is a widely occurring discrete probability distribution. One characteristic of a binomial distribution is that there are only two possible outcomes on a particular trial of an experiment. For example, the statement in a true/false question is either true or false. The outcomes are mutually exclusive, meaning that the answer to a true/false question cannot be both true and false at the same time. As other examples, a product is classified as either acceptable or not acceptable by the quality control department, a worker is classified as employed or unemployed, and a sales call results in the customer either purchasing the product or not purchasing the product. Frequently, we classify the two possible outcomes as "success" and "failure." However, this classification does *not* imply that one outcome is good and the other is bad.

Another characteristic of the binomial distribution is that the random variable is the result of counts. That is, we count the number of successes in the total number of trials. We flip a fair coin five times and count the number of times a head appears, we select 10 workers and count the number who are over 50 years of age, or we select 20 boxes of Kellogg's Raisin Bran and count the number that weigh more than the amount indicated on the package.

A third characteristic of a binomial distribution is that the probability of a success remains the same from one trial to another. That is, there is constant probability of a success. Two examples are:

• The probability you will guess the first question of a true/false test correctly (a success) is one-half. This is the first "trial." The probability that you will guess correctly on the second question (the second trial) is also one-half, the probability of success on the third trial is one-half, and so on.

- If past experience revealed the swing bridge over the Intracoastal Waterway in Socastee was raised one out of every 20 times you approach it, then the probability is one-twentieth that it will be raised (a "success") the next time you approach it, one-twentieth the following time, and so on.

The final characteristic of a binomial probability distribution is that each trial is *independent* of any other trial. Independent means that there is no pattern to the trials. The outcome of a particular trial does not affect the outcome of any other trial. Two examples are:

- A young family has two children, both boys. The probability of a third birth being a boy is still .50. That is, the gender of the third child is independent of the other two.
- Suppose 20 percent of the patients served in the emergency room at Waccamaw Hospital do not have insurance. If the second patient served on the afternoon shift today did not have insurance, that does not affect the probability the third, the tenth, or any of the other patients will or will not have insurance.

Binomial characteristics

> **BINOMIAL PROBABILITY EXPERIMENT**
> 1. An outcome on each trial of an experiment is classified into one of two mutually exclusive categories—a success or a failure.
> 2. The random variable counts the number of successes in a fixed number of trials.
> 3. The probability of success and failure stay the same for each trial.
> 4. The trials are independent, meaning that the outcome of one trial does not affect the outcome of any other trial.

How Is a Binomial Probability Computed?

To construct a particular binomial probability, we use (1) the number of trials and (2) the probability of success on each trial. For example, if an examination at the conclusion of a management seminar consists of 20 multiple-choice questions, the number of trials is 20. If each question has five choices and only one choice is correct, the probability of success on each trial is .20. Thus, the probability is .20 that a person with no knowledge of the subject matter will guess the answer to a question correctly. So the conditions of the binomial distribution just noted are met.

A binomial probability is computed by the formula:

> **BINOMIAL PROBABILITY FORMULA** $P(x) = {}_nC_x \pi^x(1 - \pi)^{n-x}$ **[6–3]**

where:

C denotes a combination.
n is the number of trials.
x is the random variable defined as the number of successes.
π is the probability of a success on each trial.

We use the Greek letter π (pi) to denote a binomial population parameter. Do not confuse it with the mathematical constant 3.1416.

Example

There are five flights daily from Pittsburgh via US Airways into the Bradford, Pennsylvania, Regional Airport. Suppose the probability that any flight arrives late is .20. What is the probability that none of the flights are late today? What is the probability that exactly one of the flights is late today?

Solution

We can use formula (6–3). The probability that a particular flight is late is .20, so let $\pi = .20$. There are five flights, so $n = 5$, and *x*, the random variable, refers to the number of successes. In this case a "success" is a flight that arrives late. Because there are no late arrivals $x = 0$.

$$P(0) = {}_nC_x(\pi)^x(1 - \pi)^{n - x}$$
$$= {}_5C_0(.20)^0(1 - .20)^{5 - 0} = (1)(1)(.3277) = .3277$$

The probability that exactly one of the five flights will arrive late today is .4096, found by

$$P(1) = {}_nC_x(\pi)^x(1 - \pi)^{n-x}$$
$$= {}_5C_1(.20)^1(1 - .20)^{5-1} = (5)(.20)(.4096) = .4096$$

The entire binomial probability distribution with $\pi = .20$ and $n = 5$ is shown in the following Excel bar chart. We can observe that the probability of exactly 3 late flights is .0512 and from the bar chart that the distribution of the number of late arrivals is positively skewed. The Excel instructions to compute these probabilities are the same as for the Excel output on page 176. These instructions are detailed in the Software Commands section on page 192 near the end of the chapter.

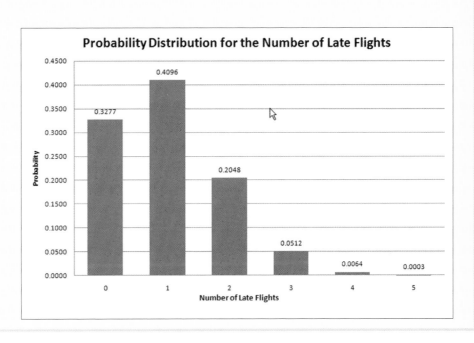

The mean (μ) and the variance (σ^2) of a binomial distribution can be computed in a "shortcut" fashion by:

MEAN OF A BINOMIAL DISTRIBUTION $\mu = n\pi$ **[6–4]**

VARIANCE OF A BINOMIAL DISTRIBUTION $\sigma^2 = n\pi(1 - \pi)$ **[6–5]**

For the example regarding the number of late flights, recall that $\pi = .20$ and $n = 5$. Hence:

$$\mu = n\pi = (5)(.20) = 1.0$$
$$\sigma^2 = n\pi(1 - \pi) = 5(.20)(1 - .20) = .80$$

The mean of 1.0 and the variance of .80 can be verified from formulas (6–1) and (6–2). The probability distribution from the Excel output on the previous page and the details of the calculations are shown below.

Number of Late Flights, x	P(x)	xP(x)	x − μ	(x − μ)²	(x − μ)²P(x)
0	0.3277	0.0000	−1	1	0.3277
1	0.4096	0.4096	0	0	0
2	0.2048	0.4096	1	1	0.2048
3	0.0512	0.1536	2	4	0.2048
4	0.0064	0.0256	3	9	0.0576
5	0.0003	0.0015	4	16	0.0048
		μ = 1.0000			σ² = 0.7997

Binomial Probability Tables

Formula (6–3) can be used to build a binomial probability distribution for any value of n and π. However, for a larger n, the calculations take more time. For convenience, the tables in Appendix B.9 show the result of using the formula for various values of n and π. Table 6–2 shows part of Appendix B.9 for $n = 6$ and various values of π.

TABLE 6–2 Binomial Probabilities for $n = 6$ and Selected Values of π

x\π	.05	.1	.2	.3	.4	.5	.6	.7	.8	.9	.95
0	.735	.531	.262	.118	.047	.016	.004	.001	.000	.000	.000
1	.232	.354	.393	.303	.187	.094	.037	.010	.002	.000	.000
2	.031	.098	.246	.324	.311	.234	.138	.060	.015	.001	.000
3	.002	.015	.082	.185	.276	.313	.276	.185	.082	.015	.002
4	.000	.001	.015	.060	.138	.234	.311	.324	.246	.098	.031
5	.000	.000	.002	.010	.037	.094	.187	.303	.393	.354	.232
6	.000	.000	.000	.001	.004	.016	.047	.118	.262	.531	.735

Example

Five percent of the worm gears produced by an automatic, high-speed Carter-Bell milling machine are defective. What is the probability that out of six gears selected at random none will be defective? Exactly one? Exactly two? Exactly three? Exactly four? Exactly five? Exactly six out of six?

Solution

The binomial conditions are met: (a) there are only two possible outcomes (a particular gear is either defective or acceptable), (b) there is a fixed number of trials (6), (c) there is a constant probability of success (.05), and (d) the trials are independent.

Refer to Table 6–2 above for the probability of exactly zero defective gears. Go down the left margin to an x of 0. Now move horizontally to the column headed by a π of .05 to find the probability. It is .735.

The probability of exactly one defective in a sample of six worm gears is .232. The complete binomial probability distribution for $n = 6$ and $\pi = .05$ is:

Number of Defective Gears, x	Probability of Occurrence, $P(x)$	Number of Defective Gears, x	Probability of Occurrence, $P(x)$
0	.735	4	.000
1	.232	5	.000
2	.031	6	.000
3	.002		

Of course, there is a slight chance of getting exactly five defective gears out of six random selections. It is .00000178, found by inserting the appropriate values in the binomial formula:

$$P(5) = {}_6C_5(.05)^5(.95)^1 = (6)(.05)^5(.95) = .00000178$$

For six out of the six, the exact probability is .000000016. Thus, the probability is very small that five or six defective gears will be selected in a sample of six.

We can compute the mean or expected value of the distribution of the number defective:

$$\mu = n\pi = (6)(.05) = 0.30$$

$$\sigma^2 = n\pi(1 - \pi) = 6(.05)(.95) = 0.285$$

MegaStat software will also compute the probabilities for a binomial distribution. Below is the output for the previous example. In MegaStat p is used to represent the probability of success rather than π. The cumulative probability, expected value, variance, and standard deviation are also reported.

Self-Review 6–3

Eighty percent of the employees at the General Mills plant on Laskey Road have their bimonthly wages sent directly to their bank by electronic funds transfer. This is also called direct deposit. Suppose we select a random sample of seven recipients.
(a) Does this situation fit the assumptions of the binomial distribution?
(b) What is the probability that all seven employees use direct deposit?
(c) Use formula (6–3) to determine the exact probability that four of the seven sampled employees use direct deposit.
(d) Use Appendix B.9 to verify your answers to parts (b) and (c).

	A	B
1	**Success**	**Probability**
2	0	0.0230
3	1	0.0910
4	2	0.1754
5	3	0.2198
6	4	0.2011
7	5	0.1432
8	6	0.0826
9	7	0.0397
10	8	0.0162
11	9	0.0057
12	10	0.0017
13	11	0.0005
14	12	0.0001
15	13	0.0000
16	14	0.0000
17	15	0.0000

Excel

Appendix B.9 is limited. It gives probabilities for n values from 1 to 15 and π values of .05, .10, . . . , .90, and .95. A software program can generate the probabilities for a specified number of successes, given n and π. The Excel output to the left shows the probability when $n = 40$ and $\pi = .09$. Note that the number of successes stops at 15 because the probabilities for 16 to 40 are very close to 0.

Several additional points should be made regarding the binomial probability distribution.

1. If n remains the same but π increases from .05 to .95, the shape of the distribution changes. Look at Table 6–3 and Chart 6–2. The probabilities for a π of .05 are positively skewed. As π approaches .50, the distribution becomes symmetrical. As π goes beyond .50 and moves toward .95, the probability distribution becomes negatively skewed. Table 6–3 highlights probabilities for $n = 10$ and π of .05, .10, .20, .50, and .70. The graphs of these probability distributions are shown in Chart 6–2.

TABLE 6–3 Probability of 0, 1, 2, . . . Successes for a π of .05, .10, .20, .50, and .70 and an n of 10

$x\backslash\pi$	.05	.1	.2	.3	.4	.5	.6	.7	.8	.9	.95
0	.599	.349	.107	.028	.006	.001	.000	.000	.000	.000	.000
1	.315	.387	.268	.121	.040	.010	.002	.000	.000	.000	.000
2	.075	.194	.302	.233	.121	.044	.011	.001	.000	.000	.000
3	.010	.057	.201	.267	.215	.117	.042	.009	.001	.000	.000
4	.001	.011	.088	.200	.251	.205	.111	.037	.006	.000	.000
5	.000	.001	.026	.103	.201	.246	.201	.103	.026	.001	.000
6	.000	.000	.006	.037	.111	.205	.251	.200	.088	.011	.001
7	.000	.000	.001	.009	.042	.117	.215	.267	.201	.057	.010
8	.000	.000	.000	.001	.011	.044	.121	.233	.302	.194	.075
9	.000	.000	.000	.000	.002	.010	.040	.121	.268	.387	.315
10	.000	.000	.000	.000	.000	.001	.006	.028	.107	.349	.599

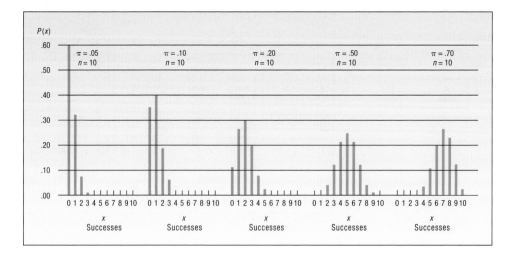

CHART 6–2 Graphing the Binomial Probability Distribution for a π of .05, .10, .20, .50, and .70 and an n of 10

2. If π, the probability of success, remains the same but n becomes larger, the shape of the binomial distribution becomes more symmetrical. Chart 6–3 shows a situation where π remains constant at .10 but n increases from 7 to 40.

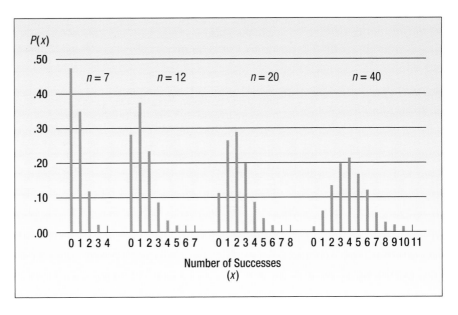

CHART 6–3 Chart Representing the Binomial Probability Distribution for a π of .10 and an n of 7, 12, 20, and 40

Exercises

9. In a binomial situation $n = 4$ and $\pi = .25$. Determine the probabilities of the following events using the binomial formula.
  a. $x = 2$
  b. $x = 3$
10. In a binomial situation $n = 5$ and $\pi = .40$. Determine the probabilities of the following events using the binomial formula.
  a. $x = 1$
  b. $x = 2$
11. Assume a binomial distribution where $n = 3$ and $\pi = .60$.
  a. Refer to Appendix B.9, and list the probabilities for values of x from 0 to 3.
  b. Determine the mean and standard deviation of the distribution from the general definitions given in formulas (6–1) and (6–2).
12. Assume a binomial distribution where $n = 5$ and $\pi = .30$.
  a. Refer to Appendix B.9, and list the probabilities for values of x from 0 to 5.
  b. Determine the mean and standard deviation of the distribution from the general definitions given in formulas (6–1) and (6–2).
13. An American Society of Investors survey found 30 percent of individual investors have used a discount broker. In a random sample of nine individuals, what is the probability:
  a. Exactly two of the sampled individuals have used a discount broker?
  b. Exactly four of them have used a discount broker?
  c. None of them have used a discount broker?
14. The United States Postal Service reports 95 percent of first class mail within the same city is delivered within two days of the time of mailing. Six letters are randomly sent to different locations.
  a. What is the probability that all six arrive within two days?
  b. What is the probability that exactly five arrive within two days?
  c. Find the mean number of letters that will arrive within two days.
  d. Compute the variance and standard deviation of the number that will arrive within two days.
15. Industry standards suggest that 10 percent of new vehicles require warranty service within the first year. Jones Nissan in Sumter, South Carolina, sold 12 Nissans yesterday.
  a. What is the probability that none of these vehicles requires warranty service?
  b. What is the probability exactly one of these vehicles requires warranty service?

connect

    c. Determine the probability that exactly two of these vehicles require warranty service.

    d. Compute the mean and standard deviation of this probability distribution.

16. A telemarketer makes six phone calls per hour and is able to make a sale on 30 percent of these contacts. During the next two hours, find:

    a. The probability of making exactly four sales.

    b. The probability of making no sales.

    c. The probability of making exactly two sales.

    d. The mean number of sales in the two-hour period.

17. A recent survey by the American Accounting Association revealed 23 percent of students graduating with a major in accounting select public accounting. Suppose we select a sample of 15 recent graduates.

    a. What is the probability two select public accounting?

    b. What is the probability five select public accounting?

    c. How many graduates would you expect to select public accounting?

18. It is reported that 16 percent of American households use a cell phone exclusively for their telephone service. In a sample of eight households, find the probability that:

    a. None use a cell phone as their exclusive service.

    b. At least one uses the cell exclusively.

    c. At least five use the cell phone.

Cumulative Binomial Probability Distributions

We may wish to know the probability of correctly guessing the answers to 6 *or more* true/false questions out of 10. Or we may be interested in the probability of *selecting less than two* defectives at random from production during the previous hour. In these cases we need cumulative frequency distributions similar to the ones developed in Chapter 2. See page 41. The following example will illustrate.

Example

A 2006 study by the Illinois Department of Transportation concluded that 76.2 percent of front seat occupants used seat belts. That means that both occupants of the front seat were using their seat belts. Suppose we decide to compare that information with current usage. We select a sample of 12 vehicles.

1. What is the probability the front seat occupants in exactly 7 of the 12 vehicles selected are wearing seat belts?
2. What is the probability the front seat occupants in at least 7 of the 12 vehicles are wearing seat belts?

Solution

This situation meets the binomial requirements.

- In a particular vehicle both the front seat occupants are either wearing seat belts or they are not. There are only two possible outcomes.
- There are a fixed number of trials, 12 in this case, because 12 vehicles are checked.
- The probability of a "success" (occupants wearing seat belts) is the same from one vehicle to the next: 76.2 percent.
- The trials are independent. If the fourth vehicle selected in the sample has all the occupants wearing their seat belts, this does not have any effect on the results for the fifth or tenth vehicle.

To find the likelihood the occupants of *exactly* 7 of the sampled vehicles are wearing seat belts we use formula (6–3). In this case $n = 12$ and $\pi = .762$.

$$P(x = 7 \mid n = 12 \text{ and } \pi = .762)$$
$$= {}_{12}C_7(.762)^7(1 - .762)^{12-7} = 792(.149171)(.000764) = .0902$$

So we conclude the likelihood that the occupants of exactly 7 of the 12 sampled vehicles will be wearing their seat belts is about 9 percent. We often use, as we did in this equation, a bar "|" to mean "given that." So in this equation we want to know the probability that x is equal to 7 "given that the number of trials is 12 and the probability of a success is .762."

To find the probability that the occupants in 7 or more of the vehicles will be wearing seat belts we use formula (6–3) from this chapter as well as the special rule of addition from the previous chapter. See formula (5–2) on page 133.

Because the events are mutually exclusive (meaning that a particular sample of 12 vehicles cannot have both a *total* of 7 and a *total* of 8 vehicles where the occupants are wearing seat belts), we find the probability of 7 vehicles where the occupants are wearing seat belts, the probability of 8 and so on up to the probability that occupants of all 12 sample vehicles are wearing seat belts. The probability of each of these outcomes is then totaled.

$P(x \geq 7 \mid n = 12 \text{ and } \pi = .762)$

$= P(x = 7) + P(x = 8) + P(x = 9) + P(x = 10) + P(x = 11) + P(x = 12)$

$= .0902 + .1805 + .2569 + .2467 + .1436 + .0383$

$= .9562$

So the probability of selecting 12 cars and finding that the occupants of 7 or more vehicles were wearing seat belts is .9562. This information is shown on the following Excel spreadsheet. There is a slight difference in the software answer due to rounding. The Excel commands are similar to those detailed in the Software Commands section on page 192, number 2.

Excel

Self-Review 6–4

For a case where $n = 4$ and $\pi = .60$, determine the probability that:
(a) $x = 2$.
(b) $x \leq 2$.
(c) $x > 2$.

Exercises

19. In a binomial distribution $n = 8$ and $\pi = .30$. Find the probabilities of the following events.
  a. $x = 2$.
  b. $x \leq 2$ (the probability that x is equal to or less than 2).
  c. $x \geq 3$ (the probability that x is equal to or greater than 3).
20. In a binomial distribution $n = 12$ and $\pi = .60$. Find the following probabilities.
  a. $x = 5$.
  b. $x \leq 5$.
  c. $x \geq 6$.
21. In a recent study 90 percent of the homes in the United States were found to have large-screen TVs. In a sample of nine homes, what is the probability that:
  a. All nine have large-screen TVs?
  b. Less than five have large-screen TVs?
  c. More than five have large-screen TVs?
  d. At least seven homes have large-screen TVs?
22. A manufacturer of window frames knows from long experience that 5 percent of the production will have some type of minor defect that will require an adjustment. What is the probability that in a sample of 20 window frames:
  a. None will need adjustment?
  b. At least one will need adjustment?
  c. More than two will need adjustment?
23. The speed with which utility companies can resolve problems is very important. GTC, the Georgetown Telephone Company, reports it can resolve customer problems the same day they are reported in 70 percent of the cases. Suppose the 15 cases reported today are representative of all complaints.
  a. How many of the problems would you expect to be resolved today? What is the standard deviation?
  b. What is the probability 10 of the problems can be resolved today?
  c. What is the probability 10 or 11 of the problems can be resolved today?
  d. What is the probability more than 10 of the problems can be resolved today?
24. It is asserted that 80 percent of the cars approaching an individual toll both in New Jersey are equipped with an E-ZPass transponder. Find the probability that in a sample of six cars:
  a. All six will have the transponder.
  b. At least three will have the transponder.
  c. None will have a transponder.

Poisson Probability Distribution

LO5 Describe the characteristics of and compute probabilities using the *Poisson probability distribution.*

The **Poisson probability distribution** describes the number of times some event occurs during a specified interval. The interval may be time, distance, area, or volume.

The distribution is based on two assumptions. The first assumption is that the probability is proportional to the length of the interval. The second assumption is that the intervals are independent. To put it another way, the longer the interval, the larger the probability, and the number of occurrences in one interval does not affect the other intervals. This distribution is also a limiting form of the binomial distribution when the probability of a success is small and n is large. It is often referred to as the "law of improbable events," meaning that the probability, π, of a particular event happening is quite small. The Poisson distribution is a discrete probability distribution because it is formed by counting.

In summary, a Poisson probability distribution has these characteristics:

> **POISSON PROBABILITY EXPERIMENT**
> 1. The random variable is the number of times some event occurs during a defined interval.
> 2. The probability of the event is proportional to the size of the interval.
> 3. The intervals do not overlap and are independent.

This distribution has many applications. It is used as a model to describe the distribution of errors in data entry, the number of scratches and other imperfections in newly painted car panels, the number of defective parts in outgoing shipments, the number of customers waiting to be served at a restaurant or waiting to get into an attraction at Disney World, and the number of accidents on I–75 during a three-month period.

The Poisson distribution is described mathematically by the formula:

Statistics in Action

Near the end of World War II, the Germans developed rocket bombs, which were fired at the city of London. The Allied military command didn't know whether these bombs were fired at random or whether they had an aiming device. To investigate, the city of London was divided into 586 square regions. The distribution of hits in each square was recorded as follows:

Hits					
0	1	2	3	4	5
Regions					
229	221	93	35	7	1

To interpret, the above chart indicates that 229 regions were not hit with one of the bombs. Seven regions were hit four times. Using the Poisson distribution, with a mean of 0.93 hits per region, the expected number of hits is as follows:

Hits					
0	1	2	3	4	5 or more
Regions					
231.2	215.0	100.0	31.0	7.2	1.6

Because the actual number of hits was close to the expected number of hits, the military command

(continued)

POISSON DISTRIBUTION	$P(x) = \dfrac{\mu^x e^{-\mu}}{x!}$	[6–6]

where:

μ (mu) is the mean number of occurrences (successes) in a particular interval.
    e is the constant 2.71828 (base of the Napierian logarithmic system).
    x is the number of occurrences (successes).
$P(x)$ is the probability for a specified value of x.

The mean number of successes, μ, is determined by $n\pi$, where n is the total number of trials and π the probability of success.

MEAN OF A POISSON DISTRIBUTION	$\mu = n\pi$	[6–7]

The variance of the Poisson is also equal to its mean. If, for example, the probability that a check cashed by a bank will bounce is .0003, and 10,000 checks are cashed, the mean and the variance for the number of bad checks is 3.0, found by $\mu = n\pi = 10,000(.0003) = 3.0$.

Recall that for a binomial distribution there is a fixed number of trials. For example, for a four-question multiple-choice test there can only be zero, one, two, three, or four successes (correct answers). The random variable, x, for a Poisson distribution, however, can assume an *infinite number of values*—that is, 0, 1, 2, 3, 4, 5, . . . However, *the probabilities become very small after the first few occurrences* (successes).

To illustrate the Poisson probability computation, assume baggage is rarely lost by Northwest Airlines. Most flights do not experience any mishandled bags; some have one bag lost; a few have two bags lost; rarely a flight will have three lost bags; and so on. Suppose a random sample of 1,000 flights shows a total of 300 bags were lost. Thus, the arithmetic mean number of lost bags per flight is 0.3, found by 300/1,000. If the number of lost bags per flight follows a Poisson distribution with $\mu = 0.3$, we can compute the various probabilities using formula (6–6):

$$P(x) = \frac{\mu^x e^{-\mu}}{x!}$$

For example, the probability of not losing any bags is:

$$P(0) = \frac{(0.3)^0 (e^{-0.3})}{0!} = 0.7408$$

concluded that the
bombs were falling
at random. The Ger-
mans had not devel-
oped a bomb with an
aiming device.

In other words, 74 percent of the flights will have no lost baggage. The probability of exactly one lost bag is:

$$P(1) = \frac{(0.3)^1(e^{-0.3})}{1!} = 0.2222$$

Thus, we would expect to find exactly one lost bag on 22 percent of the flights. Poisson probabilities can also be found in the table in Appendix B.5.

Example

Recall from the previous illustration that the number of lost bags follows a Poisson distribution with a mean of 0.3. Use Appendix B.5 to find the probability that no bags will be lost on a particular flight. What is the probability exactly one bag will be lost on a particular flight? When should the supervisor become suspicious that a flight is having too many lost bags?

Solution

Part of Appendix B.5 is repeated as Table 6–4. To find the probability of no lost bags, locate the column headed "0.3" and read down that column to the row labeled "0." The probability is .7408. That is the probability of no lost bags. The probability of one lost bag is .2222, which is in the next row of the table, in the same column. The probability of two lost bags is .0333, in the row below; for three lost bags it is .0033; and for four lost bags it is .0003. Thus, a supervisor should not be surprised to find one lost bag but should expect to see more than one lost bag infrequently.

TABLE 6–4 Poisson Table for Various Values of μ (from Appendix B.5)

					μ				
x	**0.1**	**0.2**	**0.3**	**0.4**	**0.5**	**0.6**	**0.7**	**0.8**	**0.9**
0	0.9048	0.8187	0.7408	0.6703	0.6065	0.5488	0.4966	0.4493	0.4066
1	0.0905	0.1637	0.2222	0.2681	0.3033	0.3293	0.3476	0.3595	0.3659
2	0.0045	0.0164	0.0333	0.0536	0.0758	0.0988	0.1217	0.1438	0.1647
3	0.0002	0.0011	0.0033	0.0072	0.0126	0.0198	0.0284	0.0383	0.0494
4	0.0000	0.0001	0.0003	0.0007	0.0016	0.0030	0.0050	0.0077	0.0111
5	0.0000	0.0000	0.0000	0.0001	0.0002	0.0004	0.0007	0.0012	0.0020
6	0.0000	0.0000	0.0000	0.0000	0.0000	0.0000	0.0001	0.0002	0.0003
7	0.0000	0.0000	0.0000	0.0000	0.0000	0.0000	0.0000	0.0000	0.0000

These probabilities can also be found using the MINITAB system. The commands necessary are reported at the end of the chapter.

Worksheet 1 ***						
↓	**C1**	**C2**	**C3**	**C4**	**C5**	**C6**
	Success	Probability				
1	0	0.740818				
2	1	0.222245				
3	2	0.033337				
4	3	0.003334				
5	4	0.000250				
6	5	0.000015				
7						

Earlier in this section we mentioned that the Poisson probability distribution is a limiting form of the binomial. That is, we could estimate a binomial probability using the Poisson.

The Poisson probability distribution is characterized by the number of times an event happens during some interval or continuum. Examples include:

- The number of misspelled words per page in a newspaper.
- The number of calls per hour received by Dyson Vacuum Cleaner Company.
- The number of vehicles sold per day at Hyatt Buick GMC in Durham, North Carolina.
- The number of goals scored in a college soccer game.

In each of these examples there is some type of continuum—misspelled words per page, calls per hour, vehicles per day, or goals per game.

In the previous example we investigated the number of bags lost per flight, so the continuum was a "flight." We knew the mean number of bags of luggage lost per flight, but we did not know the number of passengers or the probability of a bag being lost. We suspected the number of passengers was fairly large and the probability of a passenger losing his or her bag of luggage was small. In the following example we use the Poisson distribution to estimate a binomial probability when n, the number of trials, is large and π, the probability of a success, small.

Example

Coastal Insurance Company underwrites insurance for beachfront properties along the Virginia, North and South Carolina, and Georgia coasts. It uses the estimate that the probability of a named Category III hurricane (sustained winds of more than 110 miles per hour) or higher striking a particular region of the coast (for example, St. Simons Island, Georgia) in any one year is .05. If a homeowner takes a 30-year mortgage on a recently purchased property in St. Simons, what is the likelihood that the owner will experience at least one hurricane during the mortgage period?

Solution

To use the Poisson probability distribution we begin by determining the mean or expected number of storms meeting the criterion hitting St. Simons during the 30-year period. That is:

$$\mu = n\pi = 30(.05) = 1.5$$

where:

> n is the number of years, 30 in this case.
> π is the probability a hurricane meeting the strength criteria comes ashore.
> μ is the mean or expected number of storms in a 30-year period.

To find the probability of at least one storm hitting St. Simons Island, Georgia, we first find the probability of no storms hitting the coast and subtract that value from 1.

$$P(x \geq 1) = 1 - P(x = 0) = 1 - \frac{\mu^0 e^{-1.5}}{0!} = 1 - .2231 = .7769$$

We conclude that the likelihood a hurricane meeting the strength criteria will strike the beachfront property at St. Simons during the 30-year period when the mortgage is in effect is .7769. To put it another way, the probability St. Simons will be hit by a Category III or higher hurricane during the 30-year period is a little more than 75 percent.

We should emphasize that the continuum, as previously described, still exists. That is, there are expected to be 1.5 storms hitting the coast per 30-year period. The continuum is the 30-year period.

In the above case we are actually using the Poisson distribution as an estimate of the binomial. Note that we've met the binomial conditions outlined on page 172.

- There are only two possible outcomes: a hurricane hits the St. Simons area or it does not.
- There is a fixed number of trials, in this case 30 years.
- There is a constant probability of success; that is, the probability of a hurricane hitting the area is .05 each year.
- The years are independent. That means if a named storm strikes in the fifth year, that has no effect on any other year.

To find the probability of at least one storm striking the area in a 30-year period using the binomial distribution:

$$P(x \geq 1) = 1 - P(x = 0) = 1 - {}_{30}C_0(.05)^0(.95)^{30} = 1 - (1)(1)(.2146) = .7854$$

The probability of at least one hurricane hitting the St. Simons area during the 30-year period using the binomial distribution is .7854.

Which answer is correct? Why should we look at the problem both ways? The binomial is the more "technically correct" solution. The Poisson can be thought of as an approximation for the binomial, when n, the number of trials is large, and π, the probability of a success, is small. We look at the problem using both distributions to emphasize the convergence of the two discrete distributions. In some instances using the Poisson may be the quicker solution, and as you see there is little practical difference in the answers. In fact, as n gets larger and π smaller, the differences between the two distributions gets smaller.

The Poisson probability distribution is always positively skewed and the random variable has no specific upper limit. The Poisson distribution for the lost bags illustration, where $\mu = 0.3$, is highly skewed. As μ becomes larger, the Poisson distribution becomes more symmetrical. For example, Chart 6–4 shows the distributions of the number of transmission services, muffler replacements, and oil changes per day at Avellino's Auto Shop. They follow Poisson distributions with means of 0.7, 2.0, and 6.0, respectively.

CHART 6–4 Poisson Probability Distributions for Means of 0.7, 2.0, and 6.0

Only μ needed to construct Poisson

In summary, the Poisson distribution is actually a family of discrete distributions. All that is needed to construct a Poisson probability distribution is the mean number of defects, errors, and so on—designated as μ.

Self-Review 6–5 From actuary tables Washington Insurance Company determined the likelihood that a man age 25 will die within the next year is .0002. If Washington Insurance sells 4,000 policies to 25-year-old men this year, what is the probability they will pay on exactly one policy?

Exercises

25. In a Poisson distribution $\mu = 0.4$.
   a. What is the probability that $x = 0$?
   b. What is the probability that $x > 0$?
26. In a Poisson distribution $\mu = 4$.
   a. What is the probability that $x = 2$?
   b. What is the probability that $x \leq 2$?
   c. What is the probability that $x > 2$?
27. Ms. Bergen is a loan officer at Coast Bank and Trust. From her years of experience, she estimates that the probability is .025 that an applicant will not be able to repay his or her installment loan. Last month she made 40 loans.
   a. What is the probability that 3 loans will be defaulted?
   b. What is the probability that at least 3 loans will be defaulted?
28. Automobiles arrive at the Elkhart exit of the Indiana Toll Road at the rate of two per minute. The distribution of arrivals approximates a Poisson distribution.
   a. What is the probability that no automobiles arrive in a particular minute?
   b. What is the probability that at least one automobile arrives during a particular minute?
29. It is estimated that 0.5 percent of the callers to the Customer Service department of Dell, Inc., will receive a busy signal. What is the probability that of today's 1,200 callers, at least 5 received a busy signal?
30. In the past, schools in Los Angeles County have closed an average of three days each year for weather emergencies. What is the probability that schools in Los Angeles County will close for four days next year?

Chapter Summary

I. A random variable is a numerical value determined by the outcome of an experiment.
II. A probability distribution is a listing of all possible outcomes of an experiment and the probability associated with each outcome.
   A. A discrete probability distribution can assume only certain values. The main features are:
      1. The sum of the probabilities is 1.00.
      2. The probability of a particular outcome is between 0.00 and 1.00.
      3. The outcomes are mutually exclusive.
   B. A continuous distribution can assume an infinite number of values within a specific range.
III. The mean and variance of a probability distribution are computed as follows.
   A. The mean is equal to:

$$\mu = \Sigma[xP(x)] \qquad\qquad \text{[6–1]}$$

   B. The variance is equal to:

$$\sigma^2 = \Sigma[(x - \mu)^2 P(x)] \qquad\qquad \text{[6–2]}$$

IV. The binomial distribution has the following characteristics.
   A. Each outcome is classified into one of two mutually exclusive categories.
   B. The distribution results from a count of the number of successes in a fixed number of trials.

C. The probability of a success remains the same from trial to trial.
D. Each trial is independent.
E. A binomial probability is determined as follows:

$$P(x) = {}_nC_x\,\pi^x(1 - \pi)^{n-x}$$ [6–3]

F. The mean is computed as:

$$\mu = n\pi$$ [6–4]

G. The variance is

$$\sigma^2 = n\pi(1 - \pi)$$ [6–5]

V. The Poisson distribution has the following characteristics.
   A. It describes the number of times some event occurs during a specified interval.
   B. The probability of a "success" is proportional to the length of the interval.
   C. Nonoverlapping intervals are independent.
   D. It is a limiting form of the binomial distribution when n is large and π is small.
   E. A Poisson probability is determined from the following equation:

$$P(x) = \frac{\mu^x e^{-\mu}}{x!}$$ [6–6]

F. The mean and the variance are:

$$\mu = n\pi$$ [6–7]
$$\sigma^2 = n\pi$$

Chapter Exercises

connect™

31. What is the difference between a random variable and a probability distribution?
32. For each of the following indicate whether the random variable is discrete or continuous.
   a. The length of time to get a haircut.
   b. The number of cars a jogger passes each morning while running.
   c. The number of hits for a team in a high school girls' softball game.
   d. The number of patients treated at the South Strand Medical Center between 6 and 10 P.M. each night.
   e. The distance your car traveled on the last fill-up.
   f. The number of customers at the Oak Street Wendy's who used the drive-through facility.
   g. The distance between Gainesville, Florida, and all Florida cities with a population of at least 50,000.
33. An investment will be worth $1,000, $2,000, or $5,000 at the end of the year. The probabilities of these values are .25, .60, and .15, respectively. Determine the mean and variance of the worth of the investment.
34. The Human Resources Director at Cumberland Pig Iron Company is studying the number of on-the-job accidents over a period of one month. He developed the following probability distribution. Compute the mean, variance, and standard deviation of the number of accidents in a month.

Number of Accidents	Probability
0	.40
1	.20
2	.20
3	.10
4	.10

35. Croissant Bakery, Inc., offers special decorated cakes for birthdays, weddings, and other occasions. It also has regular cakes available in its bakery. The following table gives the total number of cakes sold per day and the corresponding probability. Compute the mean, variance, and standard deviation of the number of cakes sold per day.

Number of Cakes Sold in a Day	Probability
12	.25
13	.40
14	.25
15	.10

36. The payouts for the Powerball lottery and their corresponding odds and probabilities of occurrence are shown below. The price of a ticket is $1.00. Find the mean and standard deviation of the payout. Hint: Don't forget to include the cost of the ticket and its corresponding probability.

Divisions	Payout	Odds	Probability
Five plus Powerball	$50,000,000	146,107,962	0.000000006844
Match 5	200,000	3,563,609	0.000000280614
Four plus Powerball	10,000	584,432	0.000001711060
Match 4	100	14,255	0.000070145903
Three plus Powerball	100	11,927	0.000083836351
Match 3	7	291	0.003424657534
Two plus Powerball	7	745	0.001340482574
One plus Powerball	4	127	0.007812500000
Zero plus Powerball	3	69	0.014285714286

37. In a recent survey 35 percent indicated chocolate was their favorite flavor of ice cream. Suppose we select a sample of 10 people and ask them to name their favorite flavor of ice cream.
    a. How many of those in the sample would you expect to name chocolate?
    b. What is the probability exactly four of those in the sample name chocolate?
    c. What is the probability four or more name chocolate?

38. Thirty percent of the population in a southwestern community are Spanish-speaking Americans. A Spanish-speaking person is accused of killing a non-Spanish-speaking American and goes to trial. Of the first 12 potential jurors, only 2 are Spanish-speaking Americans, and 10 are not. The defendant's lawyer challenges the jury selection, claiming bias against her client. The government lawyer disagrees, saying that the probability of this particular jury composition is common. Compute the probability and discuss the assumptions.

39. An auditor for Health Maintenance Services of Georgia reports 40 percent of policyholders 55 years or older submit a claim during the year. Fifteen policyholders are randomly selected for company records.
    a. How many of the policyholders would you expect to have filed a claim within the last year?
    b. What is the probability that 10 of the selected policyholders submitted a claim last year?
    c. What is the probability that 10 or more of the selected policyholders submitted a claim last year?
    d. What is the probability that more than 10 of the selected policyholders submitted a claim last year?

40. Tire and Auto Supply is considering a 2-for-1 stock split. Before the transaction is finalized, at least two-thirds of the 1,200 company stockholders must approve the proposal. To evaluate the likelihood the proposal will be approved, the CFO selected a sample of 18 stockholders. He contacted each and found 14 approved of the

proposed split. What is the likelihood of this event, assuming two-thirds of the stock-holders approve?

41. A federal study reported that 7.5 percent of the U.S. workforce has a drug problem. A drug enforcement official for the State of Indiana wished to investigate this state-ment. In her sample of 20 employed workers:
   a. How many would you expect to have a drug problem? What is the standard deviation?
   b. What is the likelihood that *none* of the workers sampled has a drug problem?
   c. What is the likelihood *at least one* has a drug problem?

42. The Bank of Hawaii reports that 7 percent of its credit card holders will default at some time in their life. The Hilo branch just mailed out 12 new cards today.
   a. How many of these new cardholders would you expect to default? What is the stan-dard deviation?
   b. What is the likelihood that *none* of the cardholders will default?
   c. What is the likelihood *at least one* will default?

43. Recent statistics suggest that 15 percent of those who visit a retail site on the World Wide Web make a purchase. A retailer wished to verify this claim. To do so, she selected a sample of 16 "hits" to her site and found that 4 had actually made a purchase.
   a. What is the likelihood of exactly four purchases?
   b. How many purchases should she expect?
   c. What is the likelihood that four or more "hits" result in a purchase?

44. Acceptance sampling is used to monitor the quality of incoming raw materials. Suppose a purchaser of electronic components allows 1 percent of the components to be defec-tive. To ensure the quality of incoming parts, a purchaser or manufacturer normally sam-ples 20 parts and allows 1 defect.
   a. What is the likelihood of accepting a lot that is 1 percent defective?
   b. If the quality of the incoming lot was actually 2 percent, what is the likelihood of accepting it?
   c. If the quality of the incoming lot was actually 5 percent, what is the likelihood of accepting it?

45. Colgate-Palmolive, Inc., recently developed a new toothpaste flavored with honey. It tested a group of ten people. Six of the group said they liked the new flavor, and the remaining four indicated they definitely did not. Four of the ten are selected to participate in an in-depth interview. What is the probability that of those selected for the in-depth interview two liked the new flavor and two did not?

46. Dr. Richmond, a psychologist, is studying the daytime television viewing habits of college students. She believes 45 percent of college students watch soap operas during the after-noon. To further investigate, she selects a sample of 10.
   a. Develop a probability distribution for the number of students in the sample who watch soap operas.
   b. Find the mean and the standard deviation of this distribution.
   c. What is the probability of finding exactly four watch soap operas?
   d. What is the probability less than half of the students selected watch soap operas?

47. A recent study conducted by Penn, Shone, and Borland, on behalf of LastMinute.com, revealed that 52 percent of business travelers plan their trips less than two weeks before departure. The study is to be replicated in the tri-state area with a sample of 12 frequent business travelers.
   a. Develop a probability distribution for the number of travelers who plan their trips within two weeks of departure.
   b. Find the mean and the standard deviation of this distribution.
   c. What is the probability exactly 5 of the 12 selected business travelers plan their trips within two weeks of departure?
   d. What is the probability 5 or fewer of the 12 selected business travelers plan their trips within two weeks of departure?

48. Most software manufacturers offer a free help line that allows customers to call an 800 number to receive assistance with their problems. Because of the volume of calls, often customers are put on hold. Greeting Card Art, Inc. is proud of the fact that 93 percent of their calls for assistance are answered directly by a technician who can solve the cus-tomer's problem. To monitor this service claim, suppose Greeting Card Art selects a ran-dom sample of 25 recent calls.
   a. Explain why this situation fits the binomial distribution.

b. What is the probability exactly 20 of the calls are answered directly by a technician?

c. What is the probability at least one of the calls is put on hold?

49. The sales of Lexus automobiles in the Detroit area follow a Poisson distribution with a mean of 3 per day.

a. What is the probability that no Lexus is sold on a particular day?

b. What is the probability that for five consecutive days at least one Lexus is sold?

50. Suppose 1.5 percent of the antennas on new Nokia cell phones are defective. For a random sample of 200 antennas, find the probability that:

a. None of the antennas is defective.

b. Three or more of the antennas are defective.

51. A study of the checkout lines at the Safeway Supermarket in the South Strand area revealed that between 4 and 7 P.M. on weekdays there is an average of four customers waiting in line. What is the probability that you visit Safeway today during this period and find:

a. No customers are waiting?

b. Four customers are waiting?

c. Four or fewer are waiting?

d. Four or more are waiting?

52. An internal study by the Technology Services department at Lahey Electronics revealed company employees receive an average of two emails per hour. Assume the arrival of these emails is approximated by the Poisson distribution.

a. What is the probability Linda Lahey, company president, received exactly 1 email between 4 P.M. and 5 P.M. yesterday?

b. What is the probability she received 5 or more emails during the same period?

c. What is the probability she did not receive any email during the period?

53. Recent crime reports indicate that 3.1 motor vehicle thefts occur each minute in the United States. Assume that the distribution of thefts per minute can be approximated by the Poisson probability distribution.

a. Calculate the probability exactly *four* thefts occur in a minute.

b. What is the probability there are *no* thefts in a minute?

c. What is the probability there is *at least one* theft in a minute?

54. New Process, Inc., a large mail-order supplier of women's fashions, advertises same-day service on every order. Recently the movement of orders has not gone as planned, and there were a large number of complaints. Bud Owens, director of customer service, has completely redone the method of order handling. The goal is to have fewer than five unfilled orders on hand at the end of 95 percent of the working days. Frequent checks of the unfilled orders at the end of the day reveal that the distribution of the unfilled orders follows a Poisson distribution with a mean of two orders.

a. Has New Process, Inc., lived up to its internal goal? Cite evidence.

b. Draw a histogram representing the Poisson probability distribution of unfilled orders.

55. The National Aeronautics and Space Administration (NASA) has experienced two disasters. The Challenger exploded over the Atlantic Ocean in 1986 and the Columbia exploded over East Texas in 2003. There have been a total of 123 space missions. Assume failures continue to occur at the same rate and consider the next 23 missions. What is the probability of exactly two failures? What is the probability of no failures?

56. According to the "January theory," if the stock market is up for the month of January, it will be up for the year. If it is down in January, it will be down for the year. According to an article in *The Wall Street Journal,* this theory held for 29 out of the last 34 years. Suppose there is no truth to this theory; that is, the probability it is either up or down is .50. What is the probability this could occur by chance? You will probably need a software package such as Excel or MINITAB.

57. During the second round of the 1989 U.S. Open golf tournament, four golfers scored a hole in one on the sixth hole. The odds of a professional golfer making a hole in one are estimated to be 3,708 to 1, so the probability is 1/3,709. There were 155 golfers participating in the second round that day. Estimate the probability that four golfers would score a hole in one on the sixth hole.

58. Suppose the National Hurricane Center forecasts that hurricanes will hit the strike area with a .95 probability. Answer the following questions:

a. What probability distribution does this follow?

b. What is the probability that 10 hurricanes reach landfall in the strike area?

c. What is the probability at least one of 10 hurricanes reaches land outside the strike area?

STORM CONTINUES NORTHWEST
Position : **27.8 N, 71.4 W**
Movement: **NNW at 8 mph**
Sustained winds: **105 mph**
As of 11 p.m. EDT Tuesday

━━━ Hurricane watch
━━━ Tropical storm watch

59. A recent CBS News survey reported that 67 percent of adults felt the U.S. Treasury should continue making pennies.

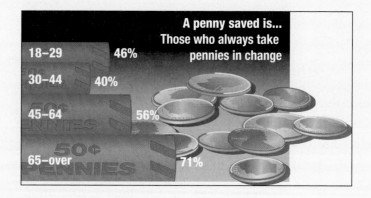

Suppose we select a sample of 15 adults.

a. How many of the 15 would we expect to indicate that the Treasury should continue making pennies? What is the standard deviation?

b. What is the likelihood that exactly 8 adults would indicate the Treasury should continue making pennies?

c. What is the likelihood at least 8 adults would indicate the Treasury should continue making pennies?

Data Set Exercises

60. Refer to the Real Estate data, which report information on homes sold in the Phoenix, Arizona, area last year.

a. Create a probability distribution for the number of bedrooms. Compute the mean and the standard deviation of this distribution.

b. Create a probability distribution for the number of bathrooms. Compute the mean and the standard deviation of this distribution.

Practice Test

Part I Objective

1. A listing of the possible outcomes of an experiment and the probability associated with each outcome is called a _____.
2. The essential difference between a discrete random variable and a discrete probability distribution is a discrete probability distribution includes the _____.
3. In a discrete probability distribution, the sum of the possible probabilities is always equal to _____.
4. The expected value of a probability distribution is also called the _____.
5. How many outcomes are there in a particular binomial trial? _____.
6. Under what conditions will the probability of a success change from trial to trial in a binomial experiment? _____.
7. In a Poisson experiment, the mean and variance are _____.
8. The Poisson distribution is a limiting case of the _____ probability distribution when n is large and π is small.
9. Suppose 5 percent of patients who take a certain drug suffer undesirable side effects. If we select 10 patients currently taking the drug, what is the probability exactly two suffer undesirable side effects?
10. The mean number of work-related accidents per month in a manufacturing plant is 1.70. What is the probability there will be no work-related accidents in a particular month?

Part II Problems

1. The IRS reports that 15 percent of the tax returns where the adjusted gross income is more than $1,000,000 will be subject to computer audit. For a particular year a CPA completed 16 returns where the adjusted gross income was more than $1,000,000.
   a. Which probability model does this situation follow?
   b. What is the probability exactly one of these returns is audited?
   c. What is the probability at least one of these returns is audited?
2. Under certain conditions, the IRS will compute the amount of refund due a taxpayer. Suppose the Cincinnati office of the IRS completes an average of three of this type of return per hour.
   a. Which probability model does this situation follow?
   b. What is the probability the IRS completes exactly three of this type of return in a particular hour?
   c. What is the probability the IRS does not complete any of this type of return in an hour?
   d. What is the probability the IRS completes at least one of these returns in a particular hour?
3. A CPA studied the number of exemptions claimed on tax returns. The data are summarized in the following table.

Exemptions	Percent
1	20
2	50
3	20
4	10

   a. What is the mean number of exemptions claimed?
   b. What is the variance of the number of exemptions claimed?

Software Commands

1. The MegaStat commands to create the binomial probability distribution on page 175 are:
   a. Select the **Add-Ins** tab in the top menu. On the far left, select the **MegaStat** pull-down menu. Click on **probability,** and **Discrete Probability Distributions.** Enter **n, number of trials,** and **p, probability of occurrence,** and click **OK.**

   b. In the dialog box select the **Binomial** tab. The number of trials is *6,* the probability of a success is *.05.* If you wish to see a graph, click on **display graph.**
2. The Excel commands necessary to determine the binomial probability distribution on page 176 are:
   a. On a blank Excel worksheet write the word *Success* in cell A1 and the word *Probability* in B1. In cells A2 through A17 write the integers *0* to *15.* Click on *B2* as the active cell.
   b. Click on the **Formulas** tab in the top menu, then, on the far left, select **Insert Function fx.**
   c. In the first dialog box select **Statistical** in the function category and **BINOMDIST** in the function name category, then click **OK.**
   d. In the second dialog box enter the four items necessary to compute a binomial probability.
      1. Enter *0* for the number of successes.
      2. Enter *40* for the number of trials.
      3. Enter *.09* for the probability of a success.
      4. Enter the word *false* or the number *0* for the individual probabilities and click on **OK.**
      5. Excel will compute the probability of 0 successes in 40 trials, with a .09 probability of success. The result, .02299618, is stored in cell B2.
   e. To complete the probability distribution for successes of 1 through 15, double-click on cell **B2.** The binomial function should appear. Replace the **0** to the right of the open parentheses with the cell reference **A2.**
   f. Move the mouse to the lower right corner of cell B2 till a solid black + symbol appears, then click and hold and highlight the B column to cell B17. The probability of a success for the various values of the random variable will appear.

3. The MINITAB commands to generate the Poisson distribution on page 182 are:
   a. Label column C1 as *Successes* and C2 as *Probability.* Enter the integers 0 though 5 in the first column.
   b. Select **Calc,** then **Probability Distributions,** and **Poisson.**
   c. In the dialog box click on **Probability,** set the mean equal to *.3,* and select *C1* as the Input column. Designate *C2* as Optional storage, and then click **OK.**

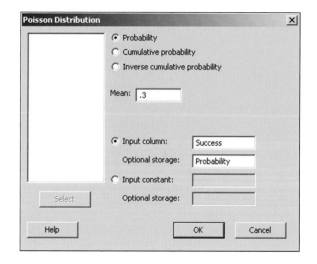

Chapter 6   Answers to Self-Review

6–1 a.

Number of Spots	Probability
1	$\frac{1}{6}$
2	$\frac{1}{6}$
3	$\frac{1}{6}$
4	$\frac{1}{6}$
5	$\frac{1}{6}$
6	$\frac{1}{6}$
Total	$\frac{6}{6} = 1.00$

b.

c. $\frac{6}{6}$ or 1.

6–2 a. It is discrete, because the value $0.80, $0.90, and $1.20 are clearly separated from each other. Also the sum of the probabilities is 1.00, and the outcomes are mutually exclusive.

b.

x	$P(x)$	$xP(x)$
$ .80	.30	0.24
.90	.50	0.45
1.20	.20	0.24
		0.93

The mean is 93 cents.

c.

x	$P(x)$	$(x - \mu)$	$(x - \mu)^2 P(x)$
$0.80	.30	−0.13	.00507
0.90	.50	−0.03	.00045
1.20	.20	0.27	.01458
			.02010

The variance is .02010, and the standard deviation is 14 cents.

6–3 a. It is reasonable because each employee either uses direct deposit or does not; employees are independent; the probability of using direct deposit is .80 for all; and we count the number using the service out of 7.

b. $P(7) = {}_7C_7 (.80)^7 (.20)^0 = .2097$

c. $P(4) = {}_7C_4 (.80)^4 (.20)^3 = .1147$

d. Answers are in agreement.

6–4 $n = 4, \pi = .60$

a. $P(x = 2) = .346$

b. $P(x \le 2) = .526$

c. $P(x > 2) = 1 - .526 = .474$

6–5 $\mu = 4,000(.0002) = 0.8$

$$P(1) = \frac{0.8^1 e^{-0.8}}{1!} = .3595$$

7

Continuous Probability Distributions

Many retail stores offer their own credit cards. At the time of the credit application, the customer may be given a 10 percent discount on his or her purchase. The time it takes to fill out the credit application form follows a uniform distribution with the times ranging from 4 to 10 minutes. What is the standard deviation for the process time? (See LO2 and Exercise 33.)

Introduction

Chapter 6 began our study of probability distributions. We consider two *discrete* probability distributions: binomial and Poisson. These distributions are based on discrete random variables, which can assume only clearly separated values. For example, we select for study 10 small businesses that began operations during the year 2005. The number still operating in 2010 can be 0, 1, 2, . . . , 10. There cannot be 3.7, 12, or −7 still operating in 2010. In this example, only certain outcomes are possible and these outcomes are represented by clearly separated values. In addition, the result is usually found by counting the number of successes. We count the number of the businesses in the study that are still in operation in 2010.

LO1 Understand the difference between discrete and continuous probability distributions.

In this chapter, we continue our study of probability distributions by examining *continuous* probability distributions. A continuous probability distribution usually results from measuring something, such as the distance from the dormitory to the classroom, the weight of an individual, or the amount of bonus earned by CEOs. Suppose we select five students and find the distance, in miles, they travel to attend class as 12.2, 8.9, 6.7, 3.6, and 14.6. When examining a continuous distribution we are usually interested in information such as the percent of students who travel less than 10 miles or the percent who travel more than 8 miles. In other words, for a continuous distribution we may wish to know the percent of observations that occur within a certain range. It is important to realize that a continuous random variable has an infinite number of values within a particular range. So you think of the probability a variable will have a value within a specified range, rather than the probability for a specific value.

We consider two families of continuous probability distributions, the **uniform probability distribution** and the **normal probability distribution.** These distributions describe the likelihood that a continuous random variable that has an infinite number of possible values will fall within a specified range. For example, suppose the time to access the McGraw-Hill Web page (www.mhhe.com) is uniformly distributed with a minimum time of 20 milliseconds and a maximum time of 60 milliseconds. Then we can determine the probability the page can be accessed in 30 milliseconds or less. The access time is measured on a continuous scale.

The second continuous distribution discussed in this chapter is the normal probability distribution. The normal distribution is described by its mean and standard deviation. For example, assume the operating life of an Energizer C-size battery follows a normal distribution with a mean of 45 hours and a standard deviation of 10 hours when used in a particular toy. We can determine the likelihood the battery will last more than 50 hours, between 35 and 62 hours, or less than 39 hours. The life of the battery is measured on a continuous scale.

The Family of Uniform Probability Distributions

The uniform probability distribution is perhaps the simplest distribution for a continuous random variable. This distribution is rectangular in shape and is defined by minimum and maximum values. Here are some examples that follow a uniform distribution.

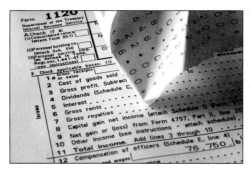

- The time to fly via a commercial airliner from Orlando, Florida, to Atlanta, Georgia, ranges from 60 minutes to 120 minutes. The random variable is the flight time within this interval. Note the variable of interest, flight time in minutes, is continuous in the interval from 60 minutes to 120 minutes.
- Volunteers at the Grand Strand Public Library prepare federal income tax forms. The time to prepare form 1040-EZ follows a uniform distribution over the interval between 10 minutes and 30 minutes. The random variable is the number of minutes to complete the form, and it can assume any value between 10 and 30.

A uniform distribution is shown in Chart 7–1. The distribution's shape is rectangular and has a minimum value of *a* and a maximum of *b*. Also notice in Chart 7–1 the height of the distribution is constant or uniform for all values between *a* and *b*.

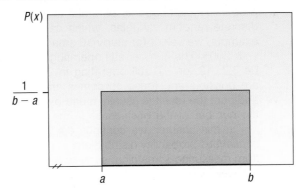

CHART 7–1 A Continuous Uniform Distribution

The mean of a uniform distribution is located in the middle of the interval between the minimum and maximum values. It is computed as:

LO2 Compute the mean and the standard deviation for a *uniform probability distribution.*

MEAN OF THE UNIFORM DISTRIBUTION	$\mu = \dfrac{a+b}{2}$	**[7–1]**

The standard deviation describes the dispersion of a distribution. In the uniform distribution, the standard deviation is also related to the interval between the maximum and minimum values.

STANDARD DEVIATION OF THE UNIFORM DISTRIBUTION	$\sigma = \sqrt{\dfrac{(b-a)^2}{12}}$	**[7–2]**

The equation for the uniform probability distribution is:

UNIFORM DISTRIBUTION	$P(x) = \dfrac{1}{b-a}$	if $a \le x \le b$ and 0 elsewhere	**[7–3]**

As described in Chapter 6, probability distributions are useful for making probability statements concerning the values of a random variable. For distributions describing a continuous random variable, areas within the distribution represent probabilities. In the uniform distribution, its rectangular shape allows us to apply the area formula for a rectangle. Recall we find the area of a rectangle by multiplying its length by its height. For the uniform distribution the height of the rectangle is $P(x)$, which is $1/(b-a)$. The length or base of the distribution is $b-a$. Notice that if we multiply the height of the distribution by its entire range to find the area, the result is always 1.00. To put it another way, the total area within a continuous probability distribution is equal to 1.00. In general

$$\text{Area} = (\text{height})(\text{base}) = \frac{1}{(b-a)}(b-a) = 1.00$$

So if a uniform distribution ranges from 10 to 15, the height is 0.20, found by $1/(15-10)$. The base is 5, found by $15-10$. The total area is:

$$\text{Area} = (\text{height})(\text{base}) = \frac{1}{(15-10)}(15-10) = 1.00$$

An example will illustrate the features of a uniform distribution and how we calculate probabilities using it.

Example

Southwest Arizona State University provides bus service to students while they are on campus. A bus arrives at the North Main Street and College Drive stop every 30 minutes between 6 A.M. and 11 P.M. during weekdays. Students arrive at the bus stop at random times. The time that a student waits is uniformly distributed from 0 to 30 minutes.

1. Draw a graph of this distribution.
2. Show that the area of this uniform distribution is 1.00.
3. How long will a student "typically" have to wait for a bus? In other words what is the mean waiting time? What is the standard deviation of the waiting times?
4. What is the probability a student will wait more than 25 minutes?
5. What is the probability a student will wait between 10 and 20 minutes?

Solution

In this case the random variable is the length of time a student must wait. Time is measured on a continuous scale, and the wait times may range from 0 minutes up to 30 minutes.

1. The graph of the uniform distribution is shown in Chart 7–2. The horizontal line is drawn at a height of .0333, found by 1/(30 − 0). The range of this distribution is 30 minutes.

CHART 7–2 Uniform Probability Distribution of Student Waiting Times

2. The times students must wait for the bus is uniform over the interval from 0 minutes to 30 minutes, so in this case a is 0 and b is 30.

$$\text{Area} = (\text{height})(\text{base}) = \frac{1}{(30 - 0)}(30 - 0) = 1.00$$

3. To find the mean, we use formula (7–1).

$$\mu = \frac{a + b}{2} = \frac{0 + 30}{2} = 15$$

The mean of the distribution is 15 minutes, so the typical wait time for bus service is 15 minutes.

To find the standard deviation of the wait times, we use formula (7–2).

$$\sigma = \sqrt{\frac{(b - a)^2}{12}} = \sqrt{\frac{(30 - 0)^2}{12}} = 8.66$$

The standard deviation of the distribution is 8.66 minutes. This measures the variation in the student wait times.

LO3 Compute probabilities by using the uniform probability distribution.

4. The area within the distribution for the interval 25 to 30 represents this particular probability. From the area formula:

$$P(25 < \text{wait time} < 30) = (\text{height})(\text{base}) = \frac{1}{(30 - 0)}(5) = .1667$$

So the probability a student waits between 25 and 30 minutes is .1667. This conclusion is illustrated by the following graph.

5. The area within the distribution for the interval 10 to 20 represents the probability.

$$P(10 < \text{wait time} < 20) = (\text{height})(\text{base}) = \frac{1}{(30 - 0)}(10) = .3333$$

We can illustrate this probability as follows.

Self-Review 7–1

Australian sheepdogs have a relatively short life. The length of their life follows a uniform distribution between 8 and 14 years.
(a) Draw this uniform distribution. What are the height and base values?
(b) Show the total area under the curve is 1.00.
(c) Calculate the mean and the standard deviation of this distribution.
(d) What is the probability a particular dog lives between 10 and 14 years?
(e) What is the probability a dog will live less than 9 years?

Exercises

connect™

1. A uniform distribution is defined over the interval from 6 to 10.
   a. What are the values for *a* and *b*?
   b. What is the mean of this uniform distribution?
   c. What is the standard deviation?
   d. Show that the total area is 1.00.
   e. Find the probability of a value more than 7.
   f. Find the probability of a value between 7 and 9.
2. A uniform distribution is defined over the interval from 2 to 5.
   a. What are the values for *a* and *b*?
   b. What is the mean of this uniform distribution?
   c. What is the standard deviation?
   d. Show that the total area is 1.00.
   e. Find the probability of a value more than 2.6.
   f. Find the probability of a value between 2.9 and 3.7.
3. The closing price of Schnur Sporting Goods, Inc., common stock is uniformly distributed between $20 and $30 per share. What is the probability that the stock price will be:
   a. More than $27?
   b. Less than or equal to $24?

4. According to the Insurance Institute of America, a family of four spends between $400 and $3,800 per year on all types of insurance. Suppose the money spent is uniformly distributed between these amounts.
   a. What is the mean amount spent on insurance?
   b. What is the standard deviation of the amount spent?
   c. If we select a family at random, what is the probability they spend less than $2,000 per year on insurance per year?
   d. What is the probability a family spends more than $3,000 per year?

5. The April rainfall in Flagstaff, Arizona, follows a uniform distribution between 0.5 and 3.00 inches.
   a. What are the values for *a* and *b*?
   b. What is the mean amount of rainfall for the month? What is the standard deviation?
   c. What is the probability of less than an inch of rain for the month?
   d. What is the probability of *exactly* 1.00 inch of rain?
   e. What is the probability of more than 1.50 inches of rain for the month?

6. Customers experiencing technical difficulty with their Internet cable hookup may call an 800 number for technical support. It takes the technician between 30 seconds to 10 minutes to resolve the problem. The distribution of this support time follows the uniform distribution.
   a. What are the values for *a* and *b* in minutes?
   b. What is the mean time to resolve the problem? What is the standard deviation of the time?
   c. What fraction of the problems take more than 5 minutes to resolve?
   d. Suppose we wish to find the middle 50 percent of the problem-solving times. What are the end points of these two times?

The Family of Normal Probability Distributions

Next we consider the normal probability distribution. Unlike the uniform distribution [see formula (7–3)], the normal probability distribution has a very complex formula.

NORMAL PROBABILITY DISTRIBUTION	$P(x) = \dfrac{1}{\sigma\sqrt{2\pi}}\, e^{-\left[\frac{(X-\mu)^2}{2\sigma^2}\right]}$	**[7–4]**

However, do not be bothered by how complex this formula looks. You are already familiar with many of the values. The symbols μ and σ refer to the mean and the standard deviation, as usual. The Greek symbol π is a natural mathematical constant and its value is approximately 22/7 or 3.1416. The letter *e* is also a mathematical constant. It is the base of the natural log system and is equal to 2.718. *X* is the value of a continuous random variable. So a normal distribution is based on—that is, it is defined by—its mean and standard deviation.

You will not need to make any calculations from formula (7–4). Instead you will be using a table, which is given as Appendix B.1, to look up the various probabilities.

The normal probability distribution has the following major characteristics.

LO4 List the characteristics of the *normal probability distribution.*

1. It is **bell-shaped** and has a single peak at the center of the distribution. The arithmetic mean, median, and mode are equal and located in the center of the distribution. The total area under the curve is 1.00. Half the area under the normal curve is to the right of this center point and the other half to the left of it.
2. It is **symmetrical** about the mean. If we cut the normal curve vertically at the center value, the two halves will be mirror images.
3. It falls off smoothly in either direction from the central value. Also, the distribution is **asymptotic** (i.e., the curve gets closer and closer to the *X*-axis but never actually touches it). To put it another way, the tails of the curve extend indefinitely in both directions.
4. The location of a normal distribution is determined by the mean, μ. The dispersion or spread of the distribution is determined by the standard deviation, σ.

These characteristics are shown graphically in Chart 7–3.

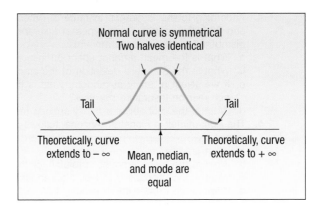

CHART 7–3 Characteristics of a Normal Distribution

There is not just one normal probability distribution, but rather a "family" of them. For example, in Chart 7–4 the probability distributions of length of employee service in three different plants can be compared. In the Camden plant, the mean is 20 years and the standard deviation is 3.1 years. There is another normal probability distribution for the length of service in the Dunkirk plant, where $\mu = 20$ years and $\sigma = 3.9$ years. In the Elmira plant, $\mu = 20$ years and $\sigma = 5.0$ years. Note that the means are the same but the standard deviations are different.

Equal means, unequal standard deviations

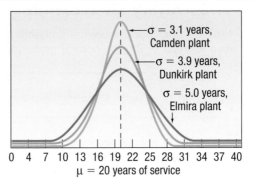

CHART 7–4 Normal Probability Distributions with Equal Means but Different Standard Deviations

Chart 7–5 shows the distribution of box weights of three different cereals. The weights follow a normal distribution with different means but identical standard deviations.

Unequal means, equal standard deviations

CHART 7–5 Normal Probability Distributions Having Different Means but Equal Standard Deviations

Finally, Chart 7–6 shows three normal distributions having different means and standard deviations. They show the distribution of tensile strengths, measured in pounds per square inch (psi), for three types of cables.

Unequal means, unequal standard deviations

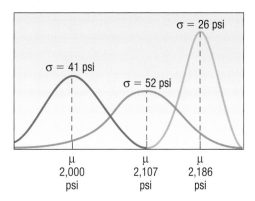

CHART 7–6 Normal Probability Distributions with Different Means and Standard Deviations

In Chapter 6, recall that discrete probability distributions show the specific likelihood a discrete value will occur. For example, starting on page 172, the binomial distribution is used to calculate the probability that none of the five flights arriving at the Bradford Pennsylvania Regional Airport would be late.

With a continuous probability distribution, areas below the curve define probabilities. The total area under the normal curve is 1.0. This accounts for all possible outcomes. Because a normal probability distribution is symmetric, the area under the curve to the left of the mean is 0.5, and the area under the curve to the right of the mean is 0.5. Apply this to the distribution of Sugar Yummies in Chart 7–5. It is normally distributed with a mean of 283 grams. Therefore, the probability of filling a box with more than 283 grams is 0.5 and the probability of filling a box with less than 283 grams is 0.5. We can also determine the probability that a box weighs between 280 and 286 grams. However, to determine this probability we need to know about the standard normal probability distribution.

The Standard Normal Probability Distribution

The number of normal distributions is unlimited, each having a different mean (μ), standard deviation (σ), or both. While it is possible to provide probability tables for discrete distributions such as the binomial and the Poisson, providing tables for the infinite number of normal distributions is impossible. Fortunately, one member of the family can be used to determine the probabilities for all normal probability distributions. It is called the **standard normal probability distribution,** and it is unique because it has a mean of 0 and a standard deviation of 1.

Any *normal probability distribution* can be converted into a *standard normal probability distribution* by subtracting the mean from each observation and dividing this difference by the standard deviation. The results are called **z values** or **z scores.**

LO5 Define and calculate z values.

> **z VALUE** The signed distance between a selected value, designated X, and the mean, μ, divided by the standard deviation, σ.

So, a z value is the distance from the mean, measured in units of the standard deviation.

In terms of a formula:

STANDARD NORMAL VALUE	$z = \dfrac{X - \mu}{\sigma}$	[7–5]

LO6 Determine the probability an observation is between two points on a normal probability distribution.

where:

X is the value of any particular observation or measurement.
μ is the mean of the distribution.
σ is the standard deviation of the distribution.

As noted in the above definition, a z value expresses the distance or difference between a particular value of X and the arithmetic mean in units of the standard deviation. Once the normally distributed observations are standardized, the z values are normally distributed with a mean of 0 and a standard deviation of 1. So the z distribution has all the characteristics of any normal probability distribution. These characteristics are listed on page 199. The table in Appendix B.1 (also on the inside back cover) lists the probabilities for the standard normal probability distribution.

TABLE 7–1 Areas under the Normal Curve

z	0.00	0.01	0.02	0.03	0.04	0.05	...
1.3	0.4032	0.4049	0.4066	0.4082	0.4099	0.4115	
1.4	0.4192	0.4207	0.4222	0.4236	0.4251	0.4265	
1.5	0.4332	0.4345	0.4357	0.4370	0.4382	0.4394	
1.6	0.4452	0.4463	0.4474	0.4484	0.4495	0.4505	
1.7	0.4554	0.4564	0.4573	0.4582	0.4591	0.4599	
1.8	0.4641	0.4649	0.4656	0.4664	0.4671	0.4678	
1.9	0.4713	0.4719	0.4726	0.4732	0.4738	0.4744	

To explain, suppose we wish to compute the probability that boxes of Sugar Yummies weigh between 283 and 285.4 grams. From Chart 7–5, we know that the box weight of Sugar Yummies follows the normal distribution with a mean of 283 grams and a standard deviation of 1.6 grams. We want to know the probability or area under the curve between the mean, 283 grams, and 285.4 grams. We can also express this problem using probability notation, similar to the style used in the previous chapter: $P(283 < \text{weight} < 285.4)$. To find the probability, it is necessary to convert both 283 grams and 285.4 grams to z values using formula (7–5). The z value corresponding to 283 is 0, found by $(283 - 283)/1.6$. The z value corresponding to 285.4 is 1.50 found by $(285.4 - 283)/1.6$. Next we go to the table in Appendix B.1. A portion of the table is repeated as Table 7–1. Go down the column of the table headed by the letter z to 1.5. Then move horizontally to the right and read the probability under the column headed 0.00. It is 0.4332. This means the area under the curve between 0.00 and 1.50 is 0.4332. This is the probability that a randomly selected box of Sugar Yummies will weigh between 283 and 285.4 grams. This is illustrated in the following graph.

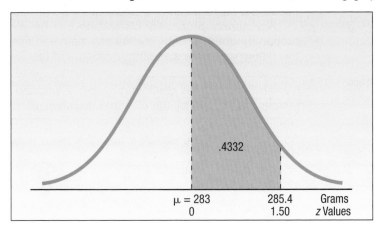

Applications of the Standard Normal Distribution

What is the area under the curve between the mean and X for the following z values? Check your answers against those given. You will need to use Appendix B.1 or the table located on the inside back cover of the text.

Computed z Value	Area under Curve
2.84	.4977
1.00	.3413
0.49	.1879

Now we will compute the z value given the population mean, μ, the population standard deviation, σ, and a selected X.

Example

The weekly incomes of shift foremen in the glass industry follow the normal probability distribution with a mean of $1,000 and a standard deviation of $100. What is the z value for the income, let's call it X, of a foreman who earns $1,100 per week? For a foreman who earns $900 per week?

Solution

Using formula (7–5), the z values for the two X values ($1,100 and $900) are:

For $X = \$1,100$:

$$z = \frac{X - \mu}{\sigma}$$

$$= \frac{\$1,100 - \$1,000}{\$100}$$

$$= 1.00$$

For $X = \$900$:

$$z = \frac{X - \mu}{\sigma}$$

$$= \frac{\$900 - \$1,000}{\$100}$$

$$= -1.00$$

The z of 1.00 indicates that a weekly income of $1,100 is one standard deviation above the mean, and a z of -1.00 shows that a $900 income is one standard deviation below the mean. Note that both incomes ($1,100 and $900) are the same distance ($100) from the mean.

Self-Review 7–2

Using the information in the preceding example ($\mu = \$1,000$, $\sigma = \$100$), convert:
(a) The weekly income of $1,225 to a z value.
(b) The weekly income of $775 to a z value.

The Empirical Rule

Before examining further applications of the standard normal probability distribution, we will consider three areas under the normal curve that will be used extensively in the following chapters. These facts were called the Empirical Rule in Chapter 3 (see page 83).

1. About 68 percent of the area under the normal curve is within one standard deviation of the mean. This can be written as $\mu \pm 1\sigma$.
2. About 95 percent of the area under the normal curve is within two standard deviations of the mean, written $\mu \pm 2\sigma$.
3. Practically all of the area under the normal curve is within three standard deviations of the mean, written $\mu \pm 3\sigma$.

This information is summarized in the following graph.

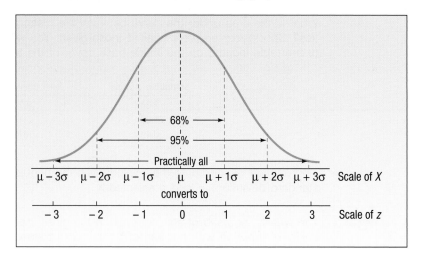

Transforming measurements to standard normal deviates changes the scale. The conversions are also shown in the graph. For example, $\mu + 1\sigma$ is converted to a z value of 1.00. Likewise, $\mu - 2\sigma$ is transformed to a z value of -2.00. Note that the center of the z distribution is zero, indicating no deviation from the mean, μ.

Example

As part of its quality assurance program, the Autolite Battery Company conducts tests on battery life. For a particular D-cell alkaline battery, the mean life is 19 hours. The useful life of the battery follows a normal distribution with a standard deviation of 1.2 hours. Answer the following questions.

1. About 68 percent of the batteries failed between what two values?
2. About 95 percent of the batteries failed between what two values?
3. Virtually all of the batteries failed between what two values?

Solution

We can use the results of the Empirical Rule to answer these questions.

1. About 68 percent of the batteries will fail between 17.8 and 20.2 hours, found by $19.0 \pm 1(1.2)$ hours.
2. About 95 percent of the batteries will fail between 16.6 and 21.4 hours, found by $19.0 \pm 2(1.2)$ hours.
3. Practically all failed between 15.4 and 22.6 hours, found by $19.0 \pm 3(1.2)$ hours.

This information is summarized on the following chart.

Self-Review 7–3

The distribution of the annual incomes of a group of middle-management employees at Compton Plastics approximates a normal distribution with a mean of $47,200 and a standard deviation of $800.
(a)   About 68 percent of the incomes lie between what two amounts?
(b)   About 95 percent of the incomes lie between what two amounts?
(c)   Virtually all of the incomes lie between what two amounts?
(d)   What are the median and the modal incomes?
(e)   Is the distribution of incomes symmetrical?

Exercises

connect™

7.   Explain what is meant by this statement: "There is not just one normal probability distribution but a 'family' of them."
8.   List the major characteristics of a normal probability distribution.
9.   The mean of a normal probability distribution is 500; the standard deviation is 10.
   a.   About 68 percent of the observations lie between what two values?
   b.   About 95 percent of the observations lie between what two values?
   c.   Practically all of the observations lie between what two values?
10.   The mean of a normal probability distribution is 60; the standard deviation is 5.
   a.   About what percent of the observations lie between 55 and 65?
   b.   About what percent of the observations lie between 50 and 70?
   c.   About what percent of the observations lie between 45 and 75?
11.   The Kamp family has twins, Rob and Rachel. Both Rob and Rachel graduated from college 2 years ago, and each is now earning $50,000 per year. Rachel works in the retail industry, where the mean salary for executives with less than 5 years' experience is $35,000 with a standard deviation of $8,000. Rob is an engineer. The mean salary for engineers with less than 5 years' experience is $60,000 with a standard deviation of $5,000. Compute the z values for both Rob and Rachel and comment on your findings.
12.   A recent article in the *Cincinnati Enquirer* reported that the mean labor cost to repair a heat pump is $90 with a standard deviation of $22. Monte's Plumbing and Heating Service completed repairs on two heat pumps this morning. The labor cost for the first was $75 and it was $100 for the second. Assume the distribution of labor costs follows the normal probability distribution. Compute z values for each and comment on your findings.

LO7 Determine the probability an observation is above (or below) a point on a normal probability distribution.

Finding Areas under the Normal Curve

The next application of the standard normal distribution involves finding the area in a normal distribution between the mean and a selected value, which we identify as X. The following example will illustrate the details.

Example

Recall in an earlier example (see page 203) we reported that the mean weekly income of a shift foreman in the glass industry is normally distributed with a mean of $1,000 and a standard deviation of $100. That is, $\mu = \$1,000$ and $\sigma = \$100$. What is the likelihood of selecting a foreman whose weekly income is between $1,000 and $1,100? We write this question in probability notation as: $P(\$1,000 < \text{weekly income} < \$1,100)$.

Solution

We have already converted $1,100 to a z value of 1.00 using formula (7–5). To repeat:

$$z = \frac{X - \mu}{\sigma} = \frac{\$1,100 - \$1,000}{\$100} = 1.00$$

The probability associated with a *z* of 1.00 is available in Appendix B.1. A portion of Appendix B.1 follows. To locate the probability, go down the left column to 1.0, and then move horizontally to the column headed .00. The value is .3413.

z	0.00	0.01	0.02
.	.	.	.
.	.	.	.
.	.	.	.
0.7	.2580	.2611	.2642
0.8	.2881	.2910	.2939
0.9	.3159	.3186	.3212
1.0	.3413	.3438	.3461
1.1	.3643	.3665	.3686
.	.	.	.
.	.	.	.
.	.	.	.

The area under the normal curve between $1,000 and $1,100 is .3413. We could also say 34.13 percent of the shift foremen in the glass industry earn between $1,000 and $1,100 weekly, or the likelihood of selecting a foreman and finding his or her income is between $1,000 and $1,100 is .3413.

This information is summarized in the following diagram.

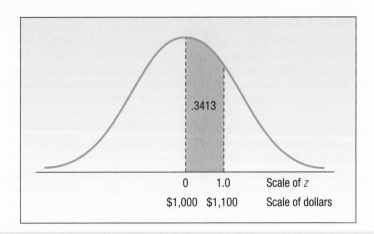

.3413

0   1.0   Scale of *z*

$1,000 $1,100   Scale of dollars

In the example just completed, we are interested in the probability between the mean and a given value. Let's change the question. Instead of wanting to know the probability of selecting at random a foreman who earned between $1,000 and $1,100, suppose we wanted the probability of selecting a foreman who earned less than $1,100. In probability notation we write this statement as *P*(weekly income < $1,100). The method of solution is the same. We find the probability of selecting a foreman who earns between $1,000, the mean, and $1,100. This probability is .3413. Next, recall that half the area, or probability, is above the mean and half is below. So the probability of selecting a foreman earning less than $1,000 is .5000. Finally, we add the two probabilities, so .3413 + .5000 = .8413. About 84 percent of the foremen in the glass industry earn less than $1,100 per month. See the following diagram.

Statistics in Action

Many processes, such as filling soda bottles and canning fruit, are normally distributed. Manufacturers must guard against both over- and underfilling. If they put too much in the can or bottle, they are giving away their product. If they put too little in, the customer may feel cheated and the government may question the label description. "Control charts," with limits drawn three standard deviations above and below the mean, are routinely used to monitor this type of production process.

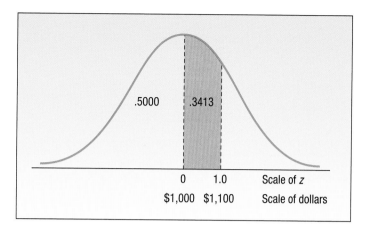

Excel will calculate this probability. The necessary commands are in the **Software Commands** section at the end of the chapter. The answer is .8413, the same as we calculated.

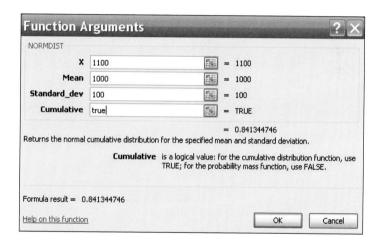

Example

Refer to the information regarding the weekly income of shift foremen in the glass industry. The distribution of weekly incomes follows the normal probability distribution, with a mean of $1,000 and a standard deviation of $100. What is the probability of selecting a shift foreman in the glass industry whose income is:

1. Between $790 and $1,000?
2. Less than $790?

Solution

We begin by finding the z value corresponding to a weekly income of $790. From formula (7–5):

$$z = \frac{X - \mu}{\sigma} = \frac{\$790 - \$1,000}{\$100} = -2.10$$

See Appendix B.1. Move down the left margin to the row 2.1 and across that row to the column headed 0.00. The value is .4821. So the area under the standard normal curve corresponding to a z value of 2.10 is .4821. However, because the normal distribution is symmetric, the area between 0 and a negative z value is the same as that between 0 and the corresponding positive z value. The likelihood of finding a foreman earning between $790 and $1,000 is .4821. In probability notation we write $P(\$790 < \text{weekly income} < \$1000) = .4821$.

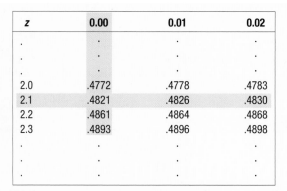

z	0.00	0.01	0.02
.	.	.	.
.	.	.	.
.	.	.	.
2.0	.4772	.4778	.4783
2.1	.4821	.4826	.4830
2.2	.4861	.4864	.4868
2.3	.4893	.4896	.4898
.	.	.	.
.	.	.	.
.	.	.	.

The mean divides the normal curve into two identical halves. The area under the half to the left of the mean is .5000, and the area to the right is also .5000. Because the area under the curve between $790 and $1,000 is .4821, the area below $790 is .0179, found by .5000 − .4821. In probability notation we write P(weekly income < $790) = .0179.

This means that 48.21 percent of the foremen have weekly incomes between $790 and $1,000. Further, we can anticipate that 1.79 percent earn less than $790 per week. This information is summarized in the following diagram.

Self-Review 7–4

Jose's Delivery Service delivers small packages to amusement and recreational parks in the Orlando and Kissimmee, Florida, area. The number of miles driven per day by Jose's fleet of trucks follows the normal probability distribution with a mean of 400 miles per day and a standard deviation of 50 miles per day.

(a) What is the area under the normal curve between 400 and 482? Write this area in probability notation.
(b) What is the area under the normal curve greater than 482 miles? Write this area in probability notation.
(c) Show the facets of this problem in a chart.

Exercises

13. A normal population has a mean of 20.0 and a standard deviation of 4.0.
   a. Compute the z value associated with 25.0.
   b. What proportion of the population is between 20.0 and 25.0?
   c. What proportion of the population is less than 18.0?
14. A normal population has a mean of 12.2 and a standard deviation of 2.5.
   a. Compute the z value associated with 14.3.
   b. What proportion of the population is between 12.2 and 14.3?
   c. What proportion of the population is less than 10.0?

15. A recent study of the hourly wages of maintenance crew members for major airlines showed that the mean hourly salary was $20.50, with a standard deviation of $3.50. Assume the distribution of hourly wages follows the normal probability distribution. If we select a crew member at random, what is the probability the crew member earns:
 a. Between $20.50 and $24.00 per hour?
 b. More than $24.00 per hour?
 c. Less than $19.00 per hour?

16. The mean of a normal probability distribution is 400 pounds. The standard deviation is 10 pounds.
 a. What is the area between 415 pounds and the mean of 400 pounds?
 b. What is the area between the mean and 395 pounds?
 c. What is the probability of selecting a value at random and discovering that it has a value of less than 395 pounds?

Another application of the normal distribution involves combining two areas, or probabilities. One of the areas is to the right of the mean and the other to the left.

Example

Recall the distribution of weekly incomes of shift foremen in the glass industry. The weekly incomes follow the normal probability distribution, with a mean of $1,000 and a standard deviation of $100. What is the area under this normal curve between $840 and $1,200?

Solution

The problem can be divided into two parts. For the area between $840 and the mean of $1,000:

$$z = \frac{\$840 - \$1,000}{\$100} = \frac{-\$160}{\$100} = -1.60$$

For the area between the mean of $1,000 and $1,200:

$$z = \frac{\$1,200 - \$1,000}{\$100} = \frac{\$200}{\$100} = 2.00$$

The area under the curve for a z of -1.60 is .4452 (from Appendix B.1). The area under the curve for a z of 2.00 is .4772. Adding the two areas: .4452 + .4772 = .9224. Thus, the probability of selecting an income between $840 and $1,200 is .9224. In probability notation we write $P(\$840 < \text{weekly income} < \$1,200) = .4452 + .4772 = .9224$. To summarize, 92.24 percent of the foremen have weekly incomes between $840 and $1,200. This is shown in a diagram:

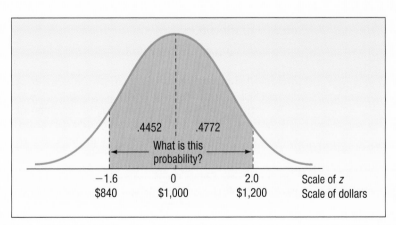

Another application of the normal distribution involves determining the area between values on the *same* side of the mean.

Example

Returning to the weekly income distribution of shift foremen in the glass industry ($\mu = $1,000$, $\sigma = 100), what is the area under the normal curve between $1,150 and $1,250?

Solution

The situation is again separated into two parts, and we use formula (7–5). First, we find the z value associated with a weekly salary of $1,250:

$$z = \frac{\$1,250 - \$1,000}{\$100} = 2.50$$

Next we find the z value for a weekly salary of $1,150:

$$z = \frac{\$1,150 - \$1,000}{\$100} = 1.50$$

From Appendix B.1 the area associated with a z value of 2.50 is .4938. So the probability of a weekly salary between $1,000 and $1,250 is .4938. Similarly, the area associated with a z value of 1.50 is .4332, so the probability of a weekly salary between $1,000 and $1,150 is .4332. We find the probability of a weekly salary between $1,150 and $1,250 by subtracting the area associated with a z value of 1.50 (.4332) from that associated with a z of 2.50 (.4938). Thus, the probability of a weekly salary between $1,150 and $1,250 is .0606. In probability notation we write $P(\$1,150 < \text{weekly income} < \$1,250) = .4938 - .4332 = .0606$.

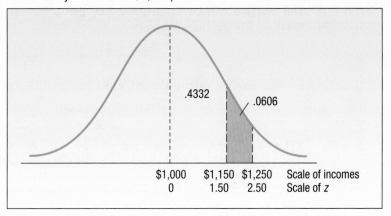

	.4332	.0606	
$1,000	$1,150	$1,250	Scale of incomes
0	1.50	2.50	Scale of z

In brief, there are four situations for finding the area under the standard normal probability distribution.

1. To find the area between 0 and z or ($-z$), look up the probability directly in the table.
2. To find the area beyond z or ($-z$), locate the probability of z in the table and subtract that probability from .5000.
3. To find the area between two points on different sides of the mean, determine the z values and add the corresponding probabilities.
4. To find the area between two points on the same side of the mean, determine the z values and subtract the smaller probability from the larger.

Self-Review 7–5

Refer to the previous example, where the distribution of weekly incomes follows the normal distribution with a mean of $1,000 and the standard deviation is $100.
(a) What fraction of the shift foremen earn a weekly income between $750 and $1,225? Draw a normal curve and shade the desired area on your diagram.
(b) What fraction of the shift foremen earn a weekly income between $1,100 and $1,225? Draw a normal curve and shade the desired area on your diagram.

Exercises

17. A normal distribution has a mean of 50 and a standard deviation of 4.
   a. Compute the probability of a value between 44.0 and 55.0.
   b. Compute the probability of a value greater than 55.0.
   c. Compute the probability of a value between 52.0 and 55.0.

18. A normal population has a mean of 80.0 and a standard deviation of 14.0.
   a. Compute the probability of a value between 75.0 and 90.0.
   b. Compute the probability of a value 75.0 or less.
   c. Compute the probability of a value between 55.0 and 70.0.

19. According to the Internal Revenue Service, the mean tax refund for the year 2007 was $2,708. Assume the standard deviation is $650 and that the amounts refunded follow a normal probability distribution.
   a. What percent of the refunds are more than $3,000?
   b. What percent of the refunds are more than $3,000 but less than $3,500?
   c. What percent of the refunds are more than $2,500 but less than $3,500?

20. The number of viewers of *American Idol* has a mean of 29 million with a standard deviation of 5 million. Assume this distribution follows a normal distribution. What is the probability that next week's show will:
   a. Have between 30 and 34 million viewers?
   b. Have at least 23 million viewers?
   c. Exceed 40 million viewers?

21. WNAE, an all-news AM station, finds that the distribution of the lengths of time listeners are tuned to the station follows the normal distribution. The mean of the distribution is 15.0 minutes and the standard deviation is 3.5 minutes. What is the probability that a particular listener will tune in:
   a. More than 20 minutes?
   b. For 20 minutes or less?
   c. Between 10 and 12 minutes?

22. Among U.S. cities with a population of more than 250,000 the mean one-way commute to work is 24.3 minutes. The longest one-way travel time is New York City, where the mean time is 38.3 minutes. Assume the distribution of travel times in New York City follows the normal probability distribution and the standard deviation is 7.5 minutes.
   a. What fraction of the New York City commutes are for less than 30 minutes?
   b. What fraction are between 30 and 35 minutes?
   c. What fraction are between 30 and 40 minutes?

LO8 Determine the point on a normal distribution for a given probability.

Previous examples require finding the percent of the observations located between two observations or the percent of the observations above, or below, a particular observation X. A further application of the normal distribution involves finding the value of the observation X when the percent above or below the observation is given. An example will illustrate the problem.

Example

Layton Tire and Rubber Company wishes to set a minimum mileage guarantee on its new MX100 tire. Tests reveal the mean mileage is 67,900 with a standard deviation of 2,050 miles and that the distribution of miles follows the normal probability distribution. Layton wants to set the minimum guaranteed mileage so that no more than 4 percent of the tires will have to be replaced. What minimum guaranteed mileage should Layton announce?

Solution

The facets of this case are shown in the following diagram, where X represents the minimum guaranteed mileage.

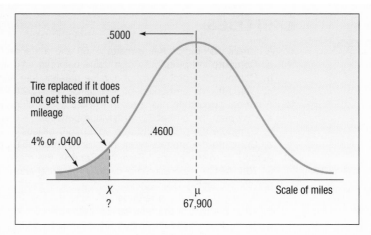

Inserting the mean and the standard deviation in formula (7–5) for z gives:

$$z = \frac{X - \mu}{\sigma} = \frac{X - 67{,}900}{2{,}050}$$

Notice that there are two unknowns, z and X. To find X, we first find z, and then solve for X. Notice the area under the normal curve to the left of μ is .5000. The area between μ and X is .4600, found by .5000 − .0400. Now refer to Appendix B.1. Search the body of the table for the area closest to .4600. The closest area is .4599. Move to the margins from this value and read the z value of 1.75. Because the value is to the left of the mean, it is actually −1.75. These steps are illustrated in Table 7–2.

TABLE 7–2   Selected Areas under the Normal Curve

z ...	.03	.04	.05	.06
.	.	.	.	.
.	.	.	.	.
.	.	.	.	.
1.5	.4370	.4382	.4394	.4406
1.6	.4484	.4495	.4505	.4515
1.7	.4582	.4591	.4599	.4608
1.8	.4664	.4671	.4678	.4686

Knowing that the distance between μ and X is -1.75σ or $z = -1.75$, we can now solve for X (the minimum guaranteed mileage):

$$z = \frac{X - 67{,}900}{2{,}050}$$

$$-1.75 = \frac{X - 67{,}900}{2{,}050}$$

$$-1.75(2{,}050) = X - 67{,}900$$

$$X = 67{,}900 - 1.75(2{,}050) = 64{,}312$$

So Layton Tire and Rubber Company can advertise that it will replace for free any tire that wears out before it reaches 64,312 miles, and the company will know that only 4 percent of the tires will be replaced under this plan.

Excel will also find the mileage value. See the following output. The necessary commands are given in the **Software Commands** section at the end of the chapter.

Self-Review 7–6

An analysis of the final test scores for Introduction to Business reveals the scores follow the normal probability distribution. The mean of the distribution is 75 and the standard deviation is 8. The professor wants to award an A to students whose score is in the highest 10 percent. What is the dividing point for those students who earn an A and those earning a B?

Exercises

23. A normal distribution has a mean of 50 and a standard deviation of 4. Determine the value below which 95 percent of the observations will occur.
24. A normal distribution has a mean of 80 and a standard deviation of 14. Determine the value above which 80 percent of the values will occur.
25. Assume that the mean hourly cost to operate a commercial airplane follows the normal distribution with a mean of $2,100 per hour and a standard deviation of $250. What is the operating cost for the lowest 3 percent of the airplanes?
26. The monthly sales of mufflers in the Richmond, Virginia, area follow the normal distribution with a mean of 1,200 and a standard deviation of 225. The manufacturer would like to establish inventory levels such that there is only a 5 percent chance of running out of stock. Where should the manufacturer set the inventory levels?
27. According to media research, the typical American listened to 195 hours of music in the last year. This is down from 290 hours four years earlier. Dick Trythall is a big country and western music fan. He listens to music while working around the house, reading, and riding in his truck. Assume the number of hours spent listening to music follows a normal probability distribution with a standard deviation of 8.5 hours.
    a. If Dick is in the top 1 percent in terms of listening time, how many hours does he listen per year?
    b. Assume that the distribution of times four years earlier also follows the normal probability distribution with a standard deviation of 8.5 hours. How many hours did the 1 percent who listen to the *least* music actually listen?
28. For the most recent year available the mean annual cost to attend a private university in the United States was $26,889. Assume the distribution of annual costs follows a normal probability distribution and the standard deviation is $4,500. Ninety-five percent of all students at private universities pay less than what amount?
29. The newsstand at the corner of East 9th Street and Euclid Avenue in downtown Cleveland sells the daily edition of the *Cleveland Plain Dealer*. The number of papers sold each day follows a normal probability distribution with a mean of 200 copies and a standard deviation of 17 copies. How many copies should the owner of the newsstand order, so that he only runs out of papers on 20 percent of the days?

30. The manufacturer of a laser printer reports the mean number of pages a cartridge will print before it needs replacing is 12,200. The distribution of pages printed per cartridge closely follows the normal probability distribution and the standard deviation is 820 pages. The manufacturer wants to provide guidelines to potential customers as to how long they can expect a cartridge to last. How many pages should the manufacturer advertise for each cartridge if it wants to be correct 99 percent of the time?

Chapter Summary

I. The uniform distribution is a continuous probability distribution with the following characteristics.
   A. It is rectangular in shape.
   B. The mean and the median are equal.
   C. It is completely described by its minimum value a and its maximum value b.
   D. It is also described by the following equation for the region from a to b:

$$P(x) = \frac{1}{b - a} \qquad \text{[7–3]}$$

   E. The mean and standard deviation of a uniform distribution are computed as follows:

$$\mu = \frac{(a + b)}{2} \qquad \text{[7–1]}$$

$$\sigma = \sqrt{\frac{(b - a)^2}{12}} \qquad \text{[7–2]}$$

II. The normal probability distribution is a continuous distribution with the following characteristics.
   A. It is bell-shaped and has a single peak at the center of the distribution.
   B. The distribution is symmetric.
   C. It is asymptotic, meaning the curve approaches but never touches the X-axis.
   D. It is completely described by its mean and standard deviation.
   E. There is a family of normal probability distributions.
      1. Another normal probability distribution is created when either the mean or the standard deviation changes.
      2. The normal probability distribution is described by the following formula:

$$P(x) = \frac{1}{\sigma\sqrt{2\pi}} e^{-\left[\frac{(x - \mu)^2}{2\sigma^2}\right]} \qquad \text{[7–4]}$$

III. The standard normal probability distribution is a particular normal distribution.
   A. It has a mean of 0 and a standard deviation of 1.
   B. Any normal probability distribution can be converted to the standard normal probability distribution by the following formula.

$$z = \frac{X - \mu}{\sigma} \qquad \text{[7–5]}$$

   C. By standardizing a normal probability distribution, we can report the distance of a value from the mean in units of the standard deviation.

Chapter Exercises

connect

31. The amount of cola in a 12-ounce can is uniformly distributed between 11.96 ounces and 12.05 ounces.
   a. What is the mean amount per can?
   b. What is the standard deviation amount per can?
   c. What is the probability of selecting a can of cola and finding it has less than 12 ounces?

d. What is the probability of selecting a can of cola and finding it has more than 11.98 ounces?

e. What is the probability of selecting a can of cola and finding it has more than 11.00 ounces?

32. A tube of Listerine Tartar Control toothpaste contains 4.2 ounces. As people use the toothpaste, the amount remaining in any tube is random. Assume the amount of toothpaste left in the tube follows a uniform distribution. From this information, we can determine the following information about the amount remaining in a toothpaste tube without invading anyone's privacy.

a. How much toothpaste would you expect to be remaining in the tube?

b. What is the standard deviation of the amount remaining in the tube?

c. What is the likelihood there is less than 3.0 ounces remaining in the tube?

d. What is the probability there is more than 1.5 ounces remaining in the tube?

33. Many retail stores offer their own credit cards. At the time of the credit application the customer is given a 10 percent discount on the purchase. The time required for the credit application process follows a uniform distribution with the times ranging from 4 minutes to 10 minutes.

a. What is the mean time for the application process?

b. What is the standard deviation of the process time?

c. What is the likelihood a particular application will take less than 6 minutes?

d. What is the likelihood an application will take more than 5 minutes?

34. The time patrons at the Grande Dunes Hotel in the Bahamas spend waiting for an elevator follows a uniform distribution between 0 and 3.5 minutes.

a. Show that the area under the curve is 1.00.

b. How long does the typical patron wait for elevator service?

c. What is the standard deviation of the waiting time?

d. What fraction of the patrons wait for less than a minute?

e. What fraction of the patrons wait more than 2 minutes?

35. The net sales and the number of employees for aluminum fabricators with similar characteristics are organized into frequency distributions. Both are normally distributed. For the net sales, the mean is $180 million and the standard deviation is $25 million. For the number of employees, the mean is 1,500 and the standard deviation is 120. Clarion Fabricators had sales of $170 million and 1,850 employees.

a. Convert Clarion's sales and number of employees to z values.

b. Locate the two z values.

c. Compare Clarion's sales and number of employees with those of the other fabricators.

36. The accounting department at Weston Materials, Inc., a national manufacturer of unattached garages, reports that it takes two construction workers a mean of 32 hours and a standard deviation of 2 hours to erect the Red Barn model. Assume the assembly times follow the normal distribution.

a. Determine the z values for 29 and 34 hours. What percent of the garages take between 32 hours and 34 hours to erect?

b. What percent of the garages take between 29 hours and 34 hours to erect?

c. What percent of the garages take 28.7 hours or less to erect?

d. Of the garages, 5 percent take how many hours or more to erect?

37. A recent report in *USA Today* indicated a typical family of four spends $490 per month on food. Assume the distribution of food expenditures for a family of four follows the normal distribution, with a mean of $490 and a standard deviation of $90.

a. What fraction of the families spend more than $30 but less than $490 per month on food?

b. What fraction of the families spend less than $430 per month on food?

c. What fraction spend between $430 and $600 per month on food?

d. What fraction spend between $500 and $600 per month on food?

38. A study of long-distance phone calls made from the corporate offices of Pepsi Bottling Group, Inc., in Somers, New York, revealed the length of the calls, in minutes, follows the normal probability distribution. The mean length of time per call was 4.2 minutes and the standard deviation was 0.60 minutes.

a. What fraction of the calls last between 4.2 and 5 minutes?

b. What fraction of the calls last more than 5 minutes?

c. What fraction of the calls last between 5 and 6 minutes?

d. What fraction of the calls last between 4 and 6 minutes?

e. As part of her report to the president, the director of communications would like to report the length of the longest (in duration) 4 percent of the calls. What is this time?

39. Shaver Manufacturing, Inc., offers dental insurance to its employees. A recent study by the human resource director shows the annual cost per employee per year followed the normal probability distribution, with a mean of $1,280 and a standard deviation of $420 per year.
  a. What fraction of the employees cost more than $1,500 per year for dental expenses?
  b. What fraction of the employees cost between $1,500 and $2,000 per year?
  c. Estimate the percent that did not have any dental expense.
  d. What was the cost for the 10 percent of employees who incurred the highest dental expense?

40. The annual commissions earned by sales representatives of Machine Products, Inc., a manufacturer of light machinery, follow the normal probability distribution. The mean yearly amount earned is $40,000 and the standard deviation is $5,000.
  a. What fraction of the sales representatives earn more than $42,000 per year?
  b. What fraction of the sales representatives earn between $32,000 and $42,000?
  c. What fraction of the sales representatives earn between $32,000 and $35,000?
  d. The sales manager wants to award the sales representatives who earn the largest commissions a bonus of $1,000. He can award a bonus to 20 percent of the representatives. What is the cutoff point between those who earn a bonus and those who do not?

41. According to the South Dakota Department of Health, the mean number of hours of TV viewing per week is higher among adult women than men. A recent study showed women spent an average of 34 hours per week watching TV and men 29 hours per week. Assume that the distribution of hours watched follows the normal distribution for both groups, and that the standard deviation among the women is 4.5 hours and is 5.1 hours for the men.
  a. What percent of the women watch TV less than 40 hours per week?
  b. What percent of the men watch TV more than 25 hours per week?
  c. How many hours of TV do the one percent of women who watch the most TV per week watch? Find the comparable value for the men.

42. According to a government study among adults in the 25- to 34-year age group, the mean amount spent per year on reading and entertainment is $1,994. Assume that the distribution of the amounts spent follows the normal distribution with a standard deviation of $450.
  a. What percent of the adults spend more than $2,500 per year on reading and entertainment?
  b. What percent spend between $2,500 and $3,000 per year on reading and entertainment?
  c. What percent spend less than $1,000 per year on reading and entertainment?

43. Management at Gordon Electronics is considering adopting a bonus system to increase production. One suggestion is to pay a bonus on the highest 5 percent of production based on past experience. Past records indicate weekly production follows the normal distribution. The mean of this distribution is 4,000 units per week and the standard deviation is 60 units per week. If the bonus is paid on the upper 5 percent of production, the bonus will be paid on how many units or more?

44. Fast Service Truck Lines uses the Ford Super Duty F-750 exclusively. Management made a study of the maintenance costs and determined the number of miles traveled during the year followed the normal distribution. The mean of the distribution was 60,000 miles and the standard deviation 2,000 miles.
  a. What percent of the Ford Super Duty F-750s logged 65,200 miles or more?
  b. What percent of the trucks logged more than 57,060 but less than 58,280 miles?
  c. What percent of the Fords traveled 62,000 miles or less during the year?
  d. Is it reasonable to conclude that any of the trucks were driven more than 70,000 miles? Explain.

45. Best Electronics, Inc., offers a "no hassle" returns policy. The number of items returned per day follows the normal distribution. The mean number of customer returns is 10.3 per day and the standard deviation is 2.25 per day.
  a. In what percent of the days are there 8 or fewer customers returning items?
  b. In what percent of the days are between 12 and 14 customers returning items?
  c. Is there any chance of a day with no returns?

46. The funds dispensed at the ATM machine located near the checkout line at the Kroger's in Union, Kentucky, follows a normal probability distribution with a mean of $4,200 per day and a standard deviation of $720 per day. The machine is programmed to notify the nearby bank if the amount dispensed is very low (less than $2,500) or very high (more than $6,000).

    a. What percent of the days will the bank be notified because the amount dispensed is very low?

    b. What percent of the time will the bank be notified because the amount dispensed is high?

    c. What percent of the time will the bank not be notified regarding the amount of funds dispersed?

47. The weights of canned hams processed at Henline Ham Company follow the normal distribution, with a mean of 9.20 pounds and a standard deviation of 0.25 pounds. The label weight is given as 9.00 pounds.

    a. What proportion of the hams actually weigh less than the amount claimed on the label?

    b. The owner, Glen Henline, is considering two proposals to reduce the proportion of hams below label weight. He can increase the mean weight to 9.25 and leave the standard deviation the same, or he can leave the mean weight at 9.20 and reduce the standard deviation from 0.25 pounds to 0.15. Which change would you recommend?

48. The *Cincinnati Enquirer*, in its Sunday business supplement, reported that the mean number of hours worked per week by those employed full time is 43.9. The article further indicated that about one-third of those employed full time work less than 40 hours per week.

    a. Given this information and assuming that number of hours worked follows the normal distribution, what is the standard deviation of the number of hours worked?

    b. The article also indicated that 20 percent of those working full time work more than 49 hours per week. Determine the standard deviation with this information. Are the two estimates of the standard deviation similar? What would you conclude?

49. Most four-year automobile leases allow up to 60,000 miles. If the lessee goes beyond this amount, a penalty of 20 cents per mile is added to the lease cost. Suppose the distribution of miles driven on four-year leases follows the normal distribution. The mean is 52,000 miles and the standard deviation is 5,000 miles.

    a. What percent of the leases will yield a penalty because of excess mileage?

    b. If the automobile company wanted to change the terms of the lease so that 25 percent of the leases went over the limit, where should the new upper limit be set?

    c. One definition of a low-mileage car is one that is 4 years old and has been driven less than 45,000 miles. What percent of the cars returned are considered low-mileage?

50. The price of shares of Bank of Florida at the end of trading each day for the last year followed the normal distribution. Assume there were 240 trading days in the year. The mean price was $42.00 per share and the standard deviation was $2.25 per share.

    a. What percent of the days was the price over $45.00? How many days would you estimate?

    b. What percent of the days was the price between $38.00 and $40.00?

    c. What was the stock's price on the *highest* 15 percent of days?

51. The annual sales of romance novels follow the normal distribution. However, the mean and the standard deviation are unknown. Forty percent of the time sales are more than 470,000, and 10 percent of the time sales are more than 500,000. What are the mean and the standard deviation?

52. In establishing warranties on HDTV sets, the manufacturer wants to set the limits so that few will need repair at the manufacturer's expense. On the other hand, the warranty period must be long enough to make the purchase attractive to the buyer. For a new HDTV the mean number of months until repairs are needed is 36.84 with a standard deviation of 3.34 months. Where should the warranty limits be set so that only 10 percent of the HDTVs need repairs at the manufacturer's expense?

53. According to the *2009 Statistical Abstract of the United States,* Table 676, the mean income for families where the head of the household is between 35 and 44 years of age is $83,900. Assume this distribution follows a normal distribution with a standard deviation of $30,000.

    a. What percent of the families in this income group earn more than $100,000?

    b. Is there much chance a family in this income group is earning more than $200,000?

    c. What is the income of families in the highest 3 percent of incomes?

Data Set Exercises

54. Refer to the Real Estate data, which report information on homes sold in the Phoenix, Arizona, area during the last year.
    a. The mean selling price (in $ thousands) of the homes was computed earlier to be $221.10, with a standard deviation of $47.11. Use the normal distribution to estimate the percent of homes selling for more than $280.0. Compare this to the actual results. Does the normal distribution yield a good approximation of the actual results?
    b. The mean distance from the center of the city is 14.629 miles with a standard deviation of 4.874 miles. Use the normal distribution to estimate the number of homes 18 or more miles but less than 22 miles from the center of the city. Compare this to the actual results. Does the normal distribution yield a good approximation of the actual results?
55. Refer to the Baseball 2008 data, which report information on the 30 Major League Baseball teams for the 2008 season.
    a. The mean attendance per team for the season was 2,620,000 with a standard deviation of 751,000. Use the normal distribution to estimate the number of teams with attendance of more than 3.5 million. Compare that estimate with the actual number. Comment on the accuracy of your estimate.
    b. The mean team salary was $89.91 million with a standard deviation of $37.84 million. Use the normal distribution to estimate the number of teams with a team salary of more than $50 million. Compare that estimate with the actual number. Comment on the accuracy of the estimate.

Practice Test

Part I Objective

1. For a continuous probability distribution, the total area under the curve is equal to _____ .
2. For a uniform distribution that ranges from 10 to 20, how many values can be in that range? (1, 10, 100, infinite—pick one) _____ .
3. Which of the following is *NOT* a characteristic of the normal distribution? (bell-shaped, symmetrical, discrete, asymptotic) _____ .
4. For a normal distribution, the mean and the median are _____ (always equal, mean is twice the median, equal to the standard deviation, none of these is true). _____ .
5. How many normal distributions are there? (1, 10, 30, infinite) _____ .
6. How many standard normal distributions are there? (1, 10, 30, infinite) _____ .
7. The signed difference between a selected value and the mean divided by the standard deviation is called a _____ . (z score, z value, standardized value, any of these)
8. What is the probability of a z value between 0 and -0.76? _____ .
9. What is the probability of a z value between -2.03 and 1.76? _____ .
10. What is the probability of a z value between -1.86 and -1.43? _____ .

Part II Problems

1. In a memo to all those involved in tax preparation, the IRS indicated the mean amount of refund was $1,600. The distribution of tax returns follows a normal distribution with a standard deviation of $850.
    a. What percent of the returns are between $1,600 and $2000?
    b. What percent of the returns are between $900 and $2000?
    c. What percent of the returns are between $1,800 and $2000?
    d. Ninety-five percent of the returns are for less than what amount?

Software Commands

1. The Excel commands necessary to produce the output on page 207 are:
   a. Click on the **Formulas** tab in the top menu, then, on the far left, select **Insert Function fx.** Then from the category box select **Statistical** and below that **NORMDIST** and click **OK.**
   b. In the dialog box put *1100* in the box for **X**, *1000* for the **Mean**, *100* for the **Standard_dev**, *True* in the **Cumulative** box, and click **OK.**
   c. The result will appear in the dialog box. If you click **OK,** the answer appears in your spreadsheet.
2. The Excel Commands necessary to produce the output on page 213 are:
   a. Click the **Formulas** tab in the top menu, then, on the far left, select **Insert Function fx.** Then from the category box select **Statistical** and below that **NORMINV** and click **OK.**
   b. In the dialog box, set the **Probability** to *.04*, the **Mean** to *67900*, and the **Standard_dev** to *2050*.
   c. The results will appear in the dialog box. Note that the answer is different from page 213 because of rounding error. If you click **OK,** the answer also appears in your spreadsheet.
   d. Try entering a **Probability** of *.04*, a **Mean** of *0*, and a **Standard_dev** of *1*. The *z* value will be computed.

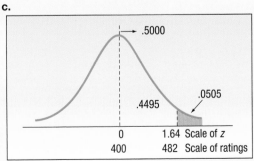

Chapter 7 Answers to Self-Review

7–1 a. $P(x)$

.167

8   14

b. $P(x)$ = (height)(base)

$$= \left(\frac{1}{14 - 8}\right)(14 - 8)$$

$$= \left(\frac{1}{6}\right)(6) = 1.00$$

c. $\mu = \dfrac{a + b}{2} = \dfrac{14 + 8}{2} = \dfrac{22}{2} = 11$

$\sigma = \sqrt{\dfrac{(b - a)^2}{12}} = \sqrt{\dfrac{(14 - 8)^2}{12}} = \sqrt{\dfrac{36}{12}} = \sqrt{3}$

$= 1.73$

d. $P(10 < x < 14)$ = (height)(base)

$$= \left(\frac{1}{14 - 8}\right)(14 - 10)$$

$$= \frac{1}{6}(4)$$

$$= .667$$

e. $P(x < 9)$ = (height)(base)

$$= \left(\frac{1}{14 - 8}\right)(9 - 8)$$

$$= 0.167$$

7–2 a. 2.25, found by:

$$z = \frac{\$1{,}225 - \$1{,}000}{\$100} = \frac{\$225}{\$100} = 2.25$$

b. −2.25, found by:

$$z = \frac{\$775 - \$1{,}000}{\$100} = \frac{-\$225}{\$100} = -2.25$$

7–3 a. $46,400 and $48,000, found by $47,200 ± 1($800).

b. $45,600 and $48,800, found by $47,200 ± 2($800).

c. $44,800 and $49,600, found by $47,200 ± 3($800).

d. $47,200. The mean, median, and mode are equal for a normal distribution.

e. Yes, a normal distribution is symmetrical.

7–4 a. Computing *z*:

$$z = \frac{482 - 400}{50} = +1.64$$

Referring to Appendix B.1, the area is .4495.
$P(400 < \text{miles} < 482)$ = .4495

b. .0505, found by .5000 − .4495
$P(\text{miles} > 482)$ = .5000 − .4495 = .0505

c.

.5000

.4495   .0505

0   1.64 Scale of z
400   482 Scale of ratings

7–5   **a.** .9816, found by 0.4938 + 0.4878.

750   1,000   1,225 ⟵ $ scale
−2.50   0   2.25 ⟵ z scale

  b. .1465, found by 0.4878 − 0.3413.

1,000   1,100   1,225 ⟵ $ scale
0   1.00   2.25 ⟵ z scale

7–6   85.24 (instructor would no doubt make it 85). The closest area to .4000 is .3997; z is 1.28. Then:

$$1.28 = \frac{X - 75}{8}$$
$$10.24 = X - 75$$
$$X = 85.24$$

Sampling Methods and the Central Limit Theorem

The Nike annual report says that the average American buys 6.5 pairs of sports shoes per year. Suppose the population standard deviation is 2.1 and that a sample of 81 customers will be examined next year. What is the standard error of the mean in this experiment? (See LO5 and Exercise 43.)

Learning Objectives

When you have completed this chapter, you will be able to:

LO1 Explain why a sample is often the only feasible way to learn something about a population.

LO2 Describe methods to select a sample.

LO3 Define and construct a sampling distribution of the sample mean.

LO4 Understand and explain the *central limit theorem.*

LO5 Use the central limit theorem to find probabilities of selecting possible sample means from a specified population.

Statistics in Action

With the significant role played by inferential statistics in all branches of science, the availability of large sources of random numbers has become a necessity. The first book of random numbers, containing 41,600 random digits generated by L. Tippett, was published in 1927. In 1938, R. A. Fisher and F. Yates published 15,000 random digits generated using two decks of cards. In 1955, RAND Corporation published a million random digits, generated by the random frequency pulses of an electronic roulette wheel. By 1970, applications of sampling required billions of random numbers. Methods have since been developed for generating, using a computer, digits that are "almost" random and hence are called *pseudo-random*. The question of whether a computer program can be used to generate numbers that are truly random remains a debatable issue.

Introduction

Chapters 2 through 4 emphasize techniques to describe data. To illustrate these techniques, we organize the prices for the 80 vehicles sold last month at Whitner Autoplex into a frequency distribution and compute various measures of location and dispersion. Such measures as the mean and the standard deviation describe the typical selling price and the spread in the selling prices. In these chapters the emphasis is on describing the condition of the data. That is, we describe something that has already happened.

Chapter 5 starts to lay the foundation for statistical inference with the study of probability. Recall that in statistical inference our goal is to determine something about a *population* based only on the *sample*. The population is the entire group of individuals or objects under consideration, and the sample is a part or subset of that population. Chapter 6 extends the probability concepts by describing two discrete probability distributions: the binomial and the Poisson. Chapter 7 describes the uniform probability distribution and the normal probability distribution. Both of these are continuous distributions. Probability distributions encompass all possible outcomes of an experiment and the probability associated with each outcome. We use probability distributions to evaluate the likelihood something occurs in the future.

This chapter begins our study of sampling. Sampling is a tool to infer something about a population. We begin this chapter by discussing methods of selecting a sample from a population. Next, we construct a distribution of the sample mean to understand how the sample means tend to cluster around the population mean. Finally, we show that for any population the shape of this sampling distribution tends to follow the normal probability distribution.

Sampling Methods

In Chapter 1, we said the purpose of inferential statistics is to find something about a population based on a sample. A sample is a portion or part of the population of interest. In many cases, sampling is more feasible than studying the entire population. In this section, we discuss the major reasons for sampling, and then several methods for selecting a sample.

Reasons to Sample

When studying characteristics of a population, there are many practical reasons why we prefer to select portions or samples of a population to observe and measure. Here are some of the reasons for sampling:

1. **To contact the whole population would be time consuming.** A candidate for a national office may wish to determine her chances for election. A sample poll using the regular staff and field interviews of a professional polling firm would take only 1 or 2 days. Using the same staff and interviewers and working 7 days a week, it would take nearly 200 years to contact all the voting population! Even if a large staff of interviewers could be assembled, the benefit of contacting all of the voters would probably not be worth the time.

2. **The cost of studying all the items in a population may be prohibitive.** Public opinion polls and consumer testing organizations, such as Gallup Polls and Harris Polls, usually contact fewer than 2,000 of the nearly 60 million families in the United States. One consumer panel–type organization charges about $40,000 to mail samples and tabulate responses in order to test a product (such as breakfast cereal, cat food, or perfume). The same product test using all 60 million families would cost about $1 billion.

3. **The physical impossibility of checking all items in the population.** Some populations are infinite. It would be impossible to check all the water in Lake Erie for bacterial levels, so we select samples at various locations. The populations of fish, birds, snakes, mosquitoes, and the like are large and are constantly moving, being born, and dying. Instead of even attempting to count all the ducks in Canada or all the fish in Lake Pontchartrain, we make estimates using various techniques—such as counting all the ducks on a pond picked at random, making creel checks, or setting nets at predetermined places in the lake.

4. **The destructive nature of some tests.** If the wine tasters at the Sutter Home Winery in California drank all the wine to evaluate the vintage, they would consume the entire crop, and none would be available for sale. In the area of industrial production, steel plates, wires, and similar products must have a certain minimum tensile strength. To ensure that the product meets the minimum standard, the Quality Assurance Department selects a sample from the current production. Each piece is stretched until it breaks and the breaking point (usually measured in pounds per square inch) recorded. Obviously, if all the wire or all the plates were tested for tensile strength, none would be available for sale or use. For the same reason, only a few seeds are tested for germination by Burpee Seeds, Inc., prior to the planting season.

5. **The sample results are adequate.** Even if funds were available, it is doubtful the additional accuracy of a 100 percent sample—that is, studying the entire population—is essential in most problems. For example, the federal government uses a sample of grocery stores scattered throughout the United States to determine the monthly index of food prices. The prices of bread, beans, milk, and other major food items are included in the index. It is unlikely that the inclusion of all grocery stores in the United States would significantly affect the index, since the prices of milk, bread, and other major foods usually do not vary by more than a few cents from one chain store to another.

Simple Random Sampling

The most widely used type of sampling is a **simple random sample.**

> **SIMPLE RANDOM SAMPLE** A sample selected so that each item or person in the population has the same chance of being included.

To illustrate simple random sampling and selection, suppose a population consists of 845 employees of Nitra Industries. A sample of 52 employees is to be selected from that population. One way of ensuring that every employee in the population has the same chance of being chosen is to first write the name of each employee on a small slip of paper and deposit all of the slips in a box. After they have been thoroughly mixed, the first selection is made by drawing a slip out of the box without looking at it. This process is repeated until the sample of 52 employees is chosen.

A more convenient method of selecting a random sample is to use the identification number of each employee and a **table of random numbers** such as the one in Appendix B.6. As the name implies, these numbers have been generated by a random process (in this case, by a computer). For each digit of a number, the probability of 0, 1, 2, . . . , 9 is the same. Thus, the probability that employee number 011 will be selected is the same as for employee 722 or employee 382. By using random numbers to select employees, bias is eliminated from the selection process.

A portion of a table of random numbers is shown in the following illustration. To select a sample of employees, you first choose a starting point in the table. Any starting point will do. Suppose the time is 3:04. You might look at the third column and then move down to the fourth set of numbers. The number is 03759. Since there are only 845 employees, we will use the first three digits of a five-digit random number. Thus, 037 is the number of the first employee to be a member of the sample. Another way of selecting the starting point is to close your eyes and point at a number in the table. To continue selecting employees, you could move in any direction. Suppose you move right. The first three digits of the number to the right of 03759 are 447—the number of the employee selected to be the second member of the sample. The next three-digit number to the right is 961. You skip 961 because there are only 845 employees. You continue to the right and select employee 784, then 189, and so on.

5 0 5 2 5	5 7 4 5 4	2 8 4 5 5	6 8 2 2 6	3 4 6 5 6	3 8 8 8 4	3 9 0 1 8
7 2 5 0 7	5 3 3 8 0	5 3 8 2 7	4 2 4 8 6	5 4 4 6 5	7 1 8 1 9	9 1 1 9 9
3 4 9 8 6	7 4 2 9 7	0 0 1 4 4	3 8 6 7 6	8 9 9 6 7	9 8 8 6 9	3 9 7 4 4
6 8 8 5 1	2 7 3 0 5	0 3 7 5 9	4 4 7 2 3	9 6 1 0 8	7 8 4 8 9	1 8 9 1 0
0 6 7 3 8	6 2 8 7 9	0 3 9 1 0	1 7 3 5 0	4 9 1 6 9	0 3 8 5 0	1 8 9 1 0
1 1 4 4 8	1 0 7 3 4	0 5 8 3 7	2 4 3 9 7	1 0 4 2 0	1 6 7 1 2	9 4 4 9 6
		Starting point	Second employee		Third employee	Fourth employee

Most statistical software packages have available a routine that will select a simple random sample. The following example uses the Excel System to select a random sample.

Example

Jane and Joe Miley operate the Foxtrot Inn, a bed and breakfast in Tryon, North Carolina. There are eight rooms available for rent at this B&B. Listed below is the number of these eight rooms rented each day during June 2009. Use Excel to select a sample of five nights during the month of June.

June	Rentals	June	Rentals	June	Rentals
1	0	11	3	21	3
2	2	12	4	22	2
3	3	13	4	23	3
4	2	14	4	24	6
5	3	15	7	25	0
6	4	16	0	26	4
7	2	17	5	27	1
8	3	18	3	28	1
9	4	19	6	29	3
10	7	20	2	30	3

Solution

Excel will select the random sample and report the results. On the first sampled date there were four of the eight rooms rented. On the second sampled date in June, seven of the eight rooms were rented. The information is reported in column D of the Excel spreadsheet. The Excel steps are listed in the **Software Commands** section at the end of the chapter. The Excel system performs the sampling *with* replacement. This means it is possible for the same day to appear more than once in a sample.

	A	B	C	D	E
1	June	Rentals		Sample	
2	1	0		4	
3	2	2		7	
4	3	3		4	
5	4	2		3	
6	5	3		1	
7	6	4			
8	7	2			
9	8	3			
10	9	4			
11	10	7			
12	11	3			
13	12	4			
14	13	4			
15	14	4			

Self-Review 8–1

The following class roster lists the students enrolling in an introductory course in business statistics. Three students are to be randomly selected and asked various questions regarding course content and method of instruction.
(a) The numbers 00 through 45 are handwritten on slips of paper and placed in a bowl. The three numbers selected are 31, 7, and 25. Which students would be included in the sample?
(b) Now use the table of random digits, Appendix B.6, to select your own sample.
(c) What would you do if you encountered the number 59 in the table of random digits?

```
                    CSPM 264 01 BUSINESS & ECONOMIC STAT
                      8:00 AM 9:40 AM MW ST 118 LIND D
```

RANDOM NUMBER	NAME	CLASS RANK	RANDOM NUMBER	NAME	CLASS RANK
00	ANDERSON, RAYMOND	SO	23	MEDLEY, CHERYL ANN	SO
01	ANGER, CHERYL RENEE	SO	24	MITCHELL, GREG R	FR
02	BALL, CLAIRE JEANETTE	FR	25	MOLTER, KRISTI MARIE	SO
03	BERRY, CHRISTOPHER G	FR	26	MULCAHY, STEPHEN ROBERT	SO
04	BOBAK, JAMES PATRICK	SO	27	NICHOLAS, ROBERT CHARLES	JR
05	BRIGHT, M. STARR	JR	28	NICKENS, VIRGINIA	SO
06	CHONTOS, PAUL JOSEPH	SO	29	PENNYWITT, SEAN PATRICK	SO
07	DETLEY, BRIAN HANS	JR	30	POTEAU, KRIS E	JR
08	DUDAS, VIOLA	SO	31	PRICE, MARY LYNETTE	SO
09	DULBS, RICHARD ZALFA	JR	32	RISTAS, JAMES	SR
10	EDINGER, SUSAN KEE	SR	33	SAGER, ANNE MARIE	SO
11	FINK, FRANK JAMES	SR	34	SMILLIE, HEATHER MICHELLE	SO
12	FRANCIS, JAMES P	JR	35	SNYDER, LEISHA KAY	SR
13	GAGHEN, PAMELA LYNN	JR	36	STAHL, MARIA TASHERY	SO
14	GOULD, ROBYN KAY	SO	37	ST. JOHN, AMY J	SO
15	GROSENBACHER, SCOTT ALAN	SO	38	STURDEVANT, RICHARD K	SO
16	HEETFIELD, DIANE MARIE	SO	39	SWETYE, LYNN MICHELE	SO
17	KABAT, JAMES DAVID	JR	40	WALASINSKI, MICHAEL	SO
18	KEMP, LISA ADRIANE	FR	41	WALKER, DIANE ELAINE	SO
19	KILLION, MICHELLE A	SO	42	WARNOCK, JENNIFER MARY	SO
20	KOPERSKI, MARY ELLEN	SO	43	WILLIAMS, WENDY A	SO
21	KOPP, BRIDGETTE ANN	SO	44	YAP, HOCK BAN	SO
22	LEHMANN, KRISTINA MARIE	JR	45	YODER, ARLAN JAY	JR

Systematic Random Sampling

The simple random sampling procedure may be awkward in some research situations. For example, suppose the sales division of Computer Graphic, Inc., needs to quickly estimate the mean dollar revenue per sale during the past month. It finds that 2,000 sales invoices were recorded and stored in file drawers, and decides to select 100 invoices to estimate the mean dollar revenue. Simple random sampling requires the numbering of each invoice before using the random number table to select the 100 invoices. The numbering process would be a very time-consuming task. Instead, we use **systematic random sampling.**

> **SYSTEMATIC RANDOM SAMPLE** A random starting point is selected, and then every kth member of the population is selected.

First, k is calculated as the population size divided by the sample size. For Computer Graphic, Inc., we would select every 20th (2,000/100) invoice from the file drawers; in so doing the numbering process is avoided. If k is not a whole number, then round down.

Random sampling is used in the selection of the first invoice. For example, a number from a random number table between 1 and k, or 20, would be selected. Say the random number was 18. Then, starting with the 18th invoice, every 20th invoice (18, 38, 58, etc.) would be selected as the sample.

Before using systematic random sampling, we should carefully observe the physical order of the population. When the physical order is related to the population characteristic, then systematic random sampling should not be used. For example, if the invoices in the example were filed in order of increasing sales, systematic random sampling would not guarantee a random sample. Other sampling methods should be used.

Stratified Random Sampling

When a population can be clearly divided into groups based on some characteristic, we may use **stratified random sampling.** It guarantees each group is represented in the sample. The groups are also called **strata.** For example, college students can be grouped as full time or part time, male or female, or traditional or nontraditional. Once the strata are defined, we can apply simple random sampling within each group or stratum to collect the sample.

> **STRATIFIED RANDOM SAMPLE** A population is divided into subgroups, called strata, and a sample is randomly selected from each stratum.

For instance, we might study the advertising expenditures for the 352 largest companies in the United States. Suppose the objective of the study is to determine whether firms with high returns on equity (a measure of profitability) spent more of each sales dollar on advertising than firms with a low return or deficit. To make sure that the sample is a fair representation of the 352 companies, the companies are grouped on percent return on equity. Table 8–1 shows the strata and the relative frequencies. If simple random sampling was used, observe that firms in the 3rd and 4th strata have a high chance of selection (probability of 0.87) while firms in the other strata have a low chance of selection (probability of 0.13). We might not select any firms in stratum 1 or 5 *simply by chance*. However, stratified random sampling will guarantee that at least one firm in strata 1 and 5 are represented in the sample. Let's say that 50 firms are selected for intensive study. Then 1 (0.02 × 50) firm from stratum 1 would be randomly selected, 5 (0.10 × 50) firms from stratum 2 would be randomly selected, and so on. In this case, the number of firms sampled from each stratum is proportional to the stratum's relative frequency in the population. Stratified sampling has the advantage, in some cases, of more accurately reflecting the characteristics of the population than does simple random or systematic random sampling.

TABLE 8–1 Number Selected for a Proportional Stratified Random Sample

Stratum	Profitability (return on equity)	Number of Firms	Relative Frequency	Number Sampled
1	30 percent and over	8	0.02	1*
2	20 up to 30 percent	35	0.10	5*
3	10 up to 20 percent	189	0.54	27
4	0 up to 10 percent	115	0.33	16
5	Deficit	5	0.01	1
Total		352	1.00	50

*0.02 of 50 = 1, 0.10 of 50 = 5, etc.

Cluster Sampling

Another common type of sampling is **cluster sampling.** It is often employed to reduce the cost of sampling a population scattered over a large geographic area.

> **CLUSTER SAMPLE** A population is divided into clusters using naturally occurring geographic or other boundaries. Then, clusters are randomly selected and a sample is collected by randomly selecting from each cluster.

Suppose you want to determine the views of residents in Oregon about state and federal environmental protection policies. Selecting a random sample of residents in Oregon and personally contacting each one would be time consuming and very expensive. Instead, you could employ cluster sampling by subdividing the state into small units—either counties or regions. These are often called *primary units*.

Suppose you divided the state into 12 primary units, then selected at random four regions—2, 7, 4, and 12—and concentrated your efforts in these primary units. You could take a random sample of the residents in each of these regions and interview them. (Note that this is a combination of cluster sampling and simple random sampling.)

Many other sampling methods

The discussion of sampling methods in the preceding sections did not include all the sampling methods available to a researcher. Should you become involved in a major research project in marketing, finance, accounting, or other areas, you would need to consult books devoted solely to sample theory and sample design.

Self-Review 8–2

Refer to Self-Review 8–1 and the class roster on page 225. Suppose a systematic random sample will select every ninth student enrolled in the class. Initially, the fourth student on the list was selected at random. That student is numbered 03. Remembering that the random numbers start with 00, which students will be chosen to be members of the sample?

Exercises

connect™

1. The following is a list of Marco's Pizza stores in Lucas County. Also noted is whether the store is corporate-owned (C) or manager-owned (M). A sample of four locations is to be selected and inspected for customer convenience, safety, cleanliness, and other features.

ID No.	Address	Type	ID No.	Address	Type
00	2607 Starr Av	C	12	2040 Ottawa River Rd	C
01	309 W Alexis Rd	C	13	2116 N Reynolds Rd	C
02	2652 W Central Av	C	14	3678 Rugby Dr	C
03	630 Dixie Hwy	M	15	1419 South Av	C
04	3510 Dorr St	C	16	1234 W Sylvania Av	C
05	5055 Glendale Av	C	17	4624 Woodville Rd	M
06	3382 Lagrange St	M	18	5155 S Main	M
07	2525 W Laskey Rd	C	19	106 E Airport Hwy	C
08	303 Louisiana Av	C	20	6725 W Central	M
09	149 Main St	C	21	4252 Monroe	C
10	835 S McCord Rd	M	22	2036 Woodville Rd	C
11	3501 Monroe St	M	23	1316 Michigan Av	M

a. The random numbers selected are 08, 18, 11, 54, 02, 41, and 54. Which stores are selected?

b. Use the table of random numbers to select your own sample of locations.

c. A sample is to consist of every seventh location. The number 03 is the starting point. Which locations will be included in the sample?

d. Suppose a sample is to consist of three locations, of which two are corporate-owned and one is manager-owned. Select a sample accordingly.

2. The following is a list of hospitals in the Cincinnati (Ohio) and Northern Kentucky Region. Also included is whether the hospital is a general medical/surgical hospital (M/S) or a specialty hospital (S). We are interested in estimating the average number of full- and part-time nurses employed in the area hospitals.

a. A sample of five hospitals is to be randomly selected. The random numbers are 09, 16, 00, 49, 54, 12, and 04. Which hospitals are included in the sample?

b. Use a table of random numbers to develop your own sample of five hospitals.

ID Number	Name	Address	Type	ID Number	Name	Address	Type
00	Bethesda North	10500 Montgomery Cincinnati, Ohio 45242	M/S	10	Christ Hospital	2139 Auburn Avenue Cincinnati, Ohio 45219	M/S
01	Ft. Hamilton-Hughes	630 Eaton Avenue Hamilton, Ohio 45013	M/S	11	Deaconess Hospital	311 Straight Street Cincinnati, Ohio 45219	M/S
02	Jewish Hospital-Kenwood	4700 East Galbraith Rd. Cincinnati, Ohio 45236	M/S	12	Good Samaritan Hospital	375 Dixmyth Avenue Cincinnati, Ohio 45220	M/S
03	Mercy Hospital-Fairfield	3000 Mack Road Fairfield, Ohio 45014	M/S	13	Jewish Hospital	3200 Burnet Avenue Cincinnati, Ohio 45229	M/S
04	Mercy Hospital-Hamilton	100 Riverfront Plaza Hamilton, Ohio 45011	M/S	14	University Hospital	234 Goodman Street Cincinnati, Ohio 45267	M/S
05	Middletown Regional	105 McKnight Drive Middletown, Ohio 45044	M/S	15	Providence Hospital	2446 Kipling Avenue Cincinnati, Ohio 45239	M/S
06	Clermont Mercy Hospital	3000 Hospital Drive Batavia, Ohio 45103	M/S	16	St. Francis-St. George Hospital	3131 Queen City Avenue Cincinnati, Ohio 45238	M/S
07	Mercy Hospital-Anderson	7500 State Road Cincinnati, Ohio 45255	M/S	17	St. Elizabeth Medical Center, North Unit	401 E. 20th Street Covington, Kentucky 41014	M/S
08	Bethesda Oak Hospital	619 Oak Street Cincinnati, Ohio 45206	M/S	18	St. Elizabeth Medical Center, South Unit	One Medical Village Edgewood, Kentucky 41017	M/S
09	Children's Hospital Medical Center	3333 Burnet Avenue Cincinnati, Ohio 45229	M/S	19	St. Luke's Hospital West	7380 Turfway Drive Florence, Kentucky 41075	M/S

ID Number	Name	Address	Type	ID Number	Name	Address	Type
20	St. Luke's Hospital East	85 North Grand Avenue Ft. Thomas, Kentucky 41042	M/S	25	Drake Center Rehab—Long Term	151 W. Galbraith Road Cincinnati, Ohio 45216	S
21	Care Unit Hospital	3156 Glenmore Avenue Cincinnati, Ohio 45211	S	26	No. Kentucky Rehab Hospital—Short Term	201 Medical Village Edgewood, Kentucky	S
22	Emerson Behavioral Science	2446 Kipling Avenue Cincinnati, Ohio 45239	S	27	Shriners Burns Institute	3229 Burnet Avenue Cincinnati, Ohio 45229	S
23	Pauline Warfield Lewis Center for Psychiatric Treat.	1101 Summit Road Cincinnati, Ohio 45237	S	28	VA Medical Center	3200 Vine Cincinnati, Ohio 45220	S
24	Children's Psychiatric No. Kentucky	502 Farrell Drive Covington, Kentucky 41011	S				

    c. A sample is to consist of every fifth location. We select 02 as the starting point. Which hospitals will be included in the sample?

    d. A sample is to consist of four medical and surgical hospitals and one specialty hospital. Select an appropriate sample.

3. Listed below are the 35 members of the Metro Toledo Automobile Dealers Association. We would like to estimate the mean revenue from dealer service departments.

ID Number	Dealer	ID Number	Dealer	ID Number	Dealer
00	Dave White Acura	11	Thayer Chevrolet/Toyota	23	Kistler Ford, Inc.
01	Autofair Nissan	12	Spurgeon Chevrolet Motor Sales, Inc.	24	Lexus of Toledo
02	Autofair Toyota-Suzuki	13	Dunn Chevrolet	25	Mathews Ford Oregon, Inc.
03	George Ball's Buick GMC Truck	14	Don Scott Chevrolet-Pontiac	26	Northtowne Chevrolet
04	Yark Automotive Group	15	Dave White Chevrolet Co.	27	Quality Ford Sales, Inc.
05	Bob Schmidt Chevrolet	16	Dick Wilson Pontiac	28	Rouen Chrysler Jeep Eagle
06	Bowling Green Lincoln Mercury Jeep Eagle	17	Doyle Pontiac Buick	29	Saturn of Toledo
07	Brondes Ford	18	Franklin Park Lincoln Mercury	30	Ed Schmidt Pontiac Jeep Eagle
08	Brown Honda	19	Genoa Motors	31	Southside Lincoln Mercury
09	Brown Mazda	20	Great Lakes Ford Nissan	32	Valiton Chrysler
10	Charlie's Dodge	21	Grogan Towne Chrysler	33	Vin Divers
		22	Hatfield Motor Sales	34	Whitman Ford

    a. We want to select a random sample of five dealers. The random numbers are: 05, 20, 59, 21, 31, 28, 49, 38, 66, 08, 29, and 02. Which dealers would be included in the sample?

    b. Use the table of random numbers to select your own sample of five dealers.

    c. A sample is to consist of every seventh dealer. The number 04 is selected as the starting point. Which dealers are included in the sample?

4. Listed below are the 27 Nationwide Insurance agents in the Toledo, Ohio, metropolitan area. We would like to estimate the mean number of years employed with Nationwide.

ID Number	Agent	ID Number	Agent	ID Number	Agent
00	**Bly Scott** 3332 W Laskey Rd	10	**Heini Bernie** 7110 W Centra	19	**Riker Craig** 2621 N Reynolds Rd
01	**Coyle Mike** 5432 W Central Av	11	**Hinckley Dave** 14 N Holland Sylvania Rd	20	**Schwab Dave** 572 W Dussel Dr
02	**Denker Brett** 7445 Airport Hwy			21	**Seibert John H** 201 S Main
03	**Denker Rollie** 7445 Airport Hwy	12	**Joehlin Bob** 3358 Navarre Av	22	**Smithers Bob** 229 Superior St
04	**Farley Ron** 1837 W Alexis Rd	13	**Keisser David** 3030 W Sylvania Av	23	**Smithers Jerry** 229 Superior St
05	**George Mark** 7247 W Central Av	14	**Keisser Keith** 5902 Sylvania Av	24	**Wright Steve** 105 S Third St
06	**Gibellato Carlo** 6616 Monroe St	15	**Lawrence Grant** 342 W Dussel Dr	25	**Wood Tom** 112 Louisiana Av
07	**Glemser Cathy** 5602 Woodville Rd	16	**Miller Ken** 2427 Woodville Rd	26	**Yoder Scott** 6 Willoughby Av
08	**Green Mike** 4149 Holland Sylvania Rd	17	**O'Donnell Jim** 7247 W Central Av		
09	**Harris Ev** 2026 Albon Rd	18	**Priest Harvey** 5113 N Summit St		

  a. We want to select a random sample of four agents. The random numbers are: 02, 59, 51, 25, 14, 29, 77, 69, and 18. Which dealers would be included in the sample?
  b. Use the table of random numbers to select your own sample of four agents.
  c. A sample is to consist of every seventh dealer. The number 04 is selected as the starting point. Which agents will be included in the sample?

Sampling "Error"

In the previous section we discussed sampling methods that are used to select a sample that is a fair and unbiased representation of the population. In each method, it is important to note that the selection of every possible sample of a specified size from a population has a known chance or probability. This is another way to describe an unbiased sampling method.

Samples are used to estimate population characteristics. For example, the mean of a sample is used to estimate the population mean. However, since the sample is a part or portion of the population, it is unlikely that the sample mean would be *exactly equal* to the population mean. Similarly, it is unlikely that the sample standard deviation would be *exactly equal* to the population standard deviation. We can therefore expect a difference between a *sample statistic* and its corresponding *population parameter*. This difference is called **sampling error.**

> **SAMPLING ERROR** The difference between a sample statistic and its corresponding population parameter.

The following example clarifies the idea of sampling error.

Example

Refer to the previous example on page 224 where we studied the number of rooms rented at the Foxtrot Inn bed and breakfast in Tryon, North Carolina. The population is the number of rooms rented each of the 30 days in June 2009. Find the mean of the population. Use Excel or other statistical software to select three random samples of five days. Calculate the mean of each sample and compare it to the population mean. What is the sampling error in each case?

Solution

During the month there were a total of 94 rentals. So the mean number of units rented per night is 3.13. This is the population mean. Hence we designate this value with the Greek letter μ.

$$\mu = \frac{\Sigma X}{N} = \frac{0 + 2 + 3 + \cdots + 3}{30} = \frac{94}{30} = 3.13$$

The first random sample of five nights resulted in the following number of rooms rented: 4, 7, 4, 3, and 1. The mean of this sample of five nights is 3.8 rooms, which we designate as $\overline{X}_1$. The bar over the X reminds us that it is a sample mean and the subscript 1 indicates it is the mean of the first sample.

$$\overline{X}_1 = \frac{\Sigma X}{n} = \frac{4 + 7 + 4 + 3 + 1}{5} = \frac{19}{5} = 3.80$$

The sampling error for the first sample is the difference between the population mean (3.13) and the first sample mean (3.80). Hence, the sampling error is $(\overline{X}_1 - \mu = 3.80 - 3.13 = 0.67)$. The second random sample of five days from the population of all 30 days in June revealed the following number of rooms rented: 3, 3, 2, 3, and 6. The mean of these five values is 3.4, found by

$$\overline{X}_2 = \frac{\Sigma X}{n} = \frac{3 + 3 + 2 + 3 + 6}{5} = 3.4$$

The sampling error is $(\overline{X}_2 - \mu = 3.4 - 3.13 = 0.27)$.

In the third random sample the mean was 1.8 and the sampling error was −1.33.

Each of these differences, 0.67, 0.27, and −1.33, is the sampling error made in estimating the population mean. Sometimes these errors are positive values, indicating that the sample mean overestimated the population mean; other times they are negative values, indicating the sample mean was less than the population mean.

	A	B	C	D	E	F	G	H
	June	Rentals			Sample 1	Sample 2	Sample 3	
1	June	Rentals			Sample 1	Sample 2	Sample 3	
2	1	0			4	3	0	
3	2	2			7	3	0	
4	3	3			4	2	3	
5	4	2			3	3	3	
6	5	3			1	6	3	
7	6	4		Totals	19	17	9	
8	7	2		Sample means	3.8	3.4	1.8	
9	8	3						
10	9	4						
11	10	7						
12	11	3						
13	12	4						
14	13	4						
15	14	4						
16	15	7						

Random Samples

In this case where we have a population of 30 values and samples of 5 values there is a very large number of possible samples—142,506 to be exact! To find this value use the combination formula (5–9) on page 150. Each of the 142,506 different samples has the same chance of being selected. Each sample may have a different sample mean and therefore a different sampling error. The value of the sampling error is based on the particular one of the 142,506 different possible samples selected. Therefore, the sampling errors are random and occur by chance. If you were to determine the sum of these sampling errors over a large number of samples the result would be very close to zero. This is true because the sample mean is an *unbiased estimator* of the population mean.

Sampling Distribution of the Sample Mean

LO3 Define and construct a sampling distribution of the sample mean.

Now that we have discovered the possibility of a sampling error when sample results are used to estimate a population parameter, how can we make an accurate prediction about the possible success of a newly developed toothpaste or other product, based only on sample results? How can the quality-assurance department in a mass-production firm release a shipment of microchips based only on a sample of 10 chips? How can the CNN/*USA Today* or ABC News/*Washington Post* polling organizations make an accurate prediction about a presidential race based on a sample of 1,200 registered voters out of a voting population of nearly 90 million? To answer these questions, we first develop a *sampling distribution of the sample mean.*

Sample means vary from sample to sample.

The sample means in the previous example varied from one sample to the next. The mean of the first sample of 5 days was 3.80 rooms, and the second sample was 3.40 rooms. The population mean was 3.13 rooms. If we organized the means of all possible samples of 5 days into a probability distribution, the result is called the **sampling distribution of the sample mean.**

> **SAMPLING DISTRIBUTION OF THE SAMPLE MEAN** A probability distribution of all possible sample means of a given sample size.

The following example illustrates the construction of a sampling distribution of the sample mean.

Example

Tartus Industries has seven production employees (considered the population). The hourly earnings of each employee are given in Table 8–2.

TABLE 8–2 Hourly Earnings of the Production Employees of Tartus Industries

Employee	Hourly Earnings	Employee	Hourly Earnings
Joe	$7	Jan	$7
Sam	7	Art	8
Sue	8	Ted	9
Bob	8		

1. What is the population mean?
2. What is the sampling distribution of the sample mean for samples of size 2?
3. What is the mean of the sampling distribution?
4. What observations can be made about the population and the sampling distribution?

Solution

Here are the solutions to the questions.

1. The population mean is $7.71, found by:

$$\mu = \frac{\Sigma X}{N} = \frac{\$7 + \$7 + \$8 + \$8 + \$7 + \$8 + \$9}{7} = \$7.71$$

   We identify the population mean with the Greek letter μ. Our policy, stated in Chapters 1, 3, and 4, is to identify population parameters with Greek letters.

2. To arrive at the sampling distribution of the sample mean, we need to select all possible samples of 2 without replacement from the population, then compute the mean of each sample. There are 21 possible samples, found by using formula (5–9) on page 150.

$$_NC_n = \frac{N!}{n!(N-n)!} = \frac{7!}{2!(7-2)!} = 21$$

   where $N = 7$ is the number of items in the population and $n = 2$ is the number of items in the sample.

   The 21 sample means from all possible samples of 2 that can be drawn from the population are shown in Table 8–3. These 21 sample means are used to construct a probability distribution. This is the sampling distribution of the sample mean, and it is summarized in Table 8–4.

TABLE 8–3 Sample Means for All Possible Samples of 2 Employees

Sample	Employees	Hourly Earnings	Sum	Mean	Sample	Employees	Hourly Earnings	Sum	Mean
1	Joe, Sam	$7, $7	$14	$7.00	12	Sue, Bob	$8, $8	$16	$8.00
2	Joe, Sue	7, 8	15	7.50	13	Sue, Jan	8, 7	15	7.50
3	Joe, Bob	7, 8	15	7.50	14	Sue, Art	8, 8	16	8.00
4	Joe, Jan	7, 7	14	7.00	15	Sue, Ted	8, 9	17	8.50
5	Joe, Art	7, 8	15	7.50	16	Bob, Jan	8, 7	15	7.50
6	Joe, Ted	7, 9	16	8.00	17	Bob, Art	8, 8	16	8.00
7	Sam, Sue	7, 8	15	7.50	18	Bob, Ted	8, 9	17	8.50
8	Sam, Bob	7, 8	15	7.50	19	Jan, Art	7, 8	15	7.50
9	Sam, Jan	7, 7	14	7.00	20	Jan, Ted	7, 9	16	8.00
10	Sam, Art	7, 8	15	7.50	21	Art, Ted	8, 9	17	8.50
11	Sam, Ted	7, 9	16	8.00					

TABLE 8–4 Sampling Distribution of the Sample Mean for $n = 2$

Sample Mean	Number of Means	Probability
$7.00	3	.1429
7.50	9	.4285
8.00	6	.2857
8.50	3	.1429
	21	1.0000

3. The mean of the sampling distribution of the sample mean is obtained by summing the various sample means and dividing the sum by the number of samples. The mean of all the sample means is usually written $\mu_{\bar{X}}$. The μ reminds us that it is a population value because we have considered all possible samples. The subscript $\bar{X}$ indicates that it is the sampling distribution of the sample mean.

Population mean is equal to the mean of the sample means

$$\mu_{\bar{X}} = \frac{\text{Sum of all sample means}}{\text{Total number of samples}} = \frac{\$7.00 + \$7.50 + \cdots + \$8.50}{21}$$

$$= \frac{\$162}{21} = \$7.71$$

4. Refer to Chart 8–1, which shows both the population distribution and the distribution of the sample mean. These observations can be made:
   a. The mean of the distribution of the sample mean ($7.71) is equal to the mean of the population: $\mu = \mu_{\bar{X}}$.
   b. The spread in the distribution of the sample mean is less than the spread in the population values. The sample mean ranges from $7.00 to $8.50, while the population values vary from $7.00 up to $9.00. Notice, as we increase the size of the sample, the spread of the distribution of the sample mean becomes smaller.
   c. The shape of the sampling distribution of the sample mean and the shape of the frequency distribution of the population values are different. The distribution of the sample mean tends to be more bell-shaped and to approximate the normal probability distribution.

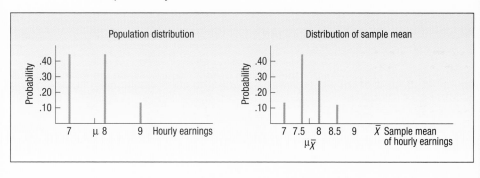

CHART 8–1 Distributions of Population Values and Sample Mean

In summary, we took all possible random samples from a population and for each sample calculated a sample statistic (the mean amount earned). This example illustrates important relationships between the population distribution and the sampling distribution of the sample mean:

1. The mean of the sample means is exactly equal to the population mean.
2. The dispersion of the sampling distribution of sample means is narrower than the population distribution.
3. The sampling distribution of sample means tends to become bell-shaped and to approximate the normal probability distribution.

Given a bell-shaped or normal probability distribution, we will be able to apply concepts from Chapter 7 to determine the probability of selecting a sample with a specified sample mean. In the next section, we will show the importance of sample size as it relates to the sampling distribution of sample means.

Self-Review 8–3   The lengths of service of all the executives employed by Standard Chemicals are:

Name	Years
Mr. Snow	20
Ms. Tolson	22
Mr. Kraft	26
Ms. Irwin	24
Mr. Jones	28

(a) Using the combination formula, how many samples of size 2 are possible?
(b) List all possible samples of 2 executives from the population and compute their means.
(c) Organize the means into a sampling distribution.
(d) Compare the population mean and the mean of the sample means.
(e) Compare the dispersion in the population with that in the distribution of the sample mean.
(f) A chart portraying the population values follows. Is the distribution of population values normally distributed (bell-shaped)?

(g) Is the distribution of the sample mean computed in part (c) starting to show some tendency toward being bell-shaped?

Exercises

connect

5. A population consists of the following four values: 12, 12, 14, and 16.
   a. List all samples of size 2, and compute the mean of each sample.
   b. Compute the mean of the distribution of the sample mean and the population mean. Compare the two values.
   c. Compare the dispersion in the population with that of the sample mean.
6. A population consists of the following five values: 2, 2, 4, 4, and 8.
   a. List all samples of size 2, and compute the mean of each sample.
   b. Compute the mean of the distribution of sample means and the population mean. Compare the two values.
   c. Compare the dispersion in the population with that of the sample means.
7. A population consists of the following five values: 12, 12, 14, 15, and 20.
   a. List all samples of size 3, and compute the mean of each sample.
   b. Compute the mean of the distribution of sample means and the population mean. Compare the two values.
   c. Compare the dispersion in the population with that of the sample means.
8. A population consists of the following five values: 0, 0, 1, 3, 6.
   a. List all samples of size 3, and compute the mean of each sample.
   b. Compute the mean of the distribution of sample means and the population mean. Compare the two values.
   c. Compare the dispersion in the population with that of the sample means.
9. In the law firm Tybo and Associates, there are six partners. Listed below is the number of cases each associate actually tried in court last month.

Associate	Number of Cases
Ruud	3
Wu	6
Sass	3
Flores	3
Wilhelms	0
Schueller	1

    a. How many different samples of 3 are possible?

    b. List all possible samples of size 3, and compute the mean number of cases in each sample.

    c. Compare the mean of the distribution of sample means to the population mean.

    d. On a chart similar to Chart 8–1, compare the dispersion in the population with that of the sample means.

10. There are five sales associates at Mid-Motors Ford. The five representatives and the number of cars they sold last week are:

Sales Representative	Cars Sold
Peter Hankish	8
Connie Stallter	6
Juan Lopez	4
Ted Barnes	10
Peggy Chu	6

    a. How many different samples of size 2 are possible?

    b. List all possible samples of size 2, and compute the mean of each sample.

    c. Compare the mean of the sampling distribution of sample means with that of the population.

    d. On a chart similar to Chart 8–1, compare the dispersion in sample means with that of the population.

The Central Limit Theorem

LO4 Understand and explain the *central limit theorem.*

In this section, we examine the **central limit theorem.** Its application to the sampling distribution of the sample mean, introduced in the previous section, allows us to use the normal probability distribution to create confidence intervals for the population mean (described in Chapter 9) and perform tests of hypothesis (described in Chapter 10). The central limit theorem states that, for large random samples, the shape of the sampling distribution of the sample mean is close to the normal probability distribution. The approximation is more accurate for large samples than for small samples. This is one of the most useful conclusions in statistics. We can reason about the distribution of the sample mean with absolutely no information about the shape of the population distribution from which the sample is taken. In other words, the central limit theorem is true for all distributions.

A formal statement of the central limit theorem follows.

> **CENTRAL LIMIT THEOREM** If all samples of a particular size are selected from any population, the sampling distribution of the sample mean is approximately a normal distribution. This approximation improves with larger samples.

If the population follows a normal probability distribution, then for any sample size the sampling distribution of the sample mean will also be normal. If the population distribution is symmetrical (but not normal), you will see the normal shape of the distribution of the sample mean emerge with samples as small as 10. On the other hand, if you start with a distribution that is skewed or has thick tails, it may require samples of 30 or more to observe the normality feature. This concept is summarized in Chart 8–2

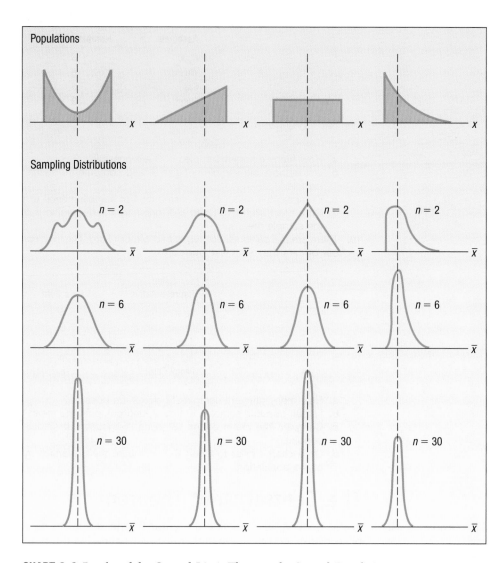

CHART 8–2 Results of the Central Limit Theorem for Several Populations

for various population shapes. Observe the convergence to a normal distribution regardless of the shape of the population distribution. Most statisticians consider a sample of 30 or more to be large enough for the central limit theorem to be employed.

The idea that the distribution of the sample means from a population that is not normal will converge to normality is illustrated in Charts 8–3, 8–4, and 8–5. We will discuss this example in more detail shortly, but Chart 8–3 is a graph of a discrete probability distribution that is positively skewed. There are many possible samples of 5 that might be selected from this population. Suppose we randomly select 25 samples of size 5 each and compute the mean of each sample. These results are shown in Chart 8–4. Notice that the shape of the distribution of sample means has changed from the shape of the original population even though we selected only 25 of the many possible samples. To put it another way, we selected 25 random samples of 5 each from a population that is positively skewed and found the distribution of sample means has changed from the shape of the population. As we take larger samples, that is, $n = 20$ instead of $n = 5$, we will find the distribution of the sample mean will approach the normal distribution. Chart 8–5 shows the results of 25 random samples of 20 observations each from the same population. Observe the clear trend toward the normal probability distribution. This is the point of the central limit theorem. The following example will underscore this condition.

Example

Ed Spence began his sprocket business 20 years ago. The business has grown over the years and now employs 40 people. Spence Sprockets, Inc., faces some major decisions regarding health care for these employees. Before making a final decision on what health care plan to purchase, Ed decides to form a committee of five representative employees. The committee will be asked to study the health care issue carefully and make a recommendation as to what plan best fits the employees' needs. Ed feels the views of newer employees toward health care may differ from those of more experienced employees. If Ed randomly selects this committee, what can he expect in terms of the mean years with Spence Sprockets for those on the committee? How does the shape of the distribution of years of experience of all employees (the population) compare with the shape of the sampling distribution of the mean? The lengths of service (rounded to the nearest year) of the 40 employees currently on the Spence Sprockets, Inc., payroll are as follows.

11	4	18	2	1	2	0	2	2	4
3	4	1	2	2	3	3	19	8	3
7	1	0	2	7	0	4	5	1	14
16	8	9	1	1	2	5	10	2	3

Solution

Chart 8–3 shows the distribution of the years of experience for the population of 40 current employees. This distribution of lengths of service is positively skewed because there are a few employees who have worked at Spence Sprockets for a longer period of time. Specifically, six employees have been with the company 10 years or more. However, because the business has grown, the number of employees has increased in the last few years. Of the 40 employees, 18 have been with the company two years or less.

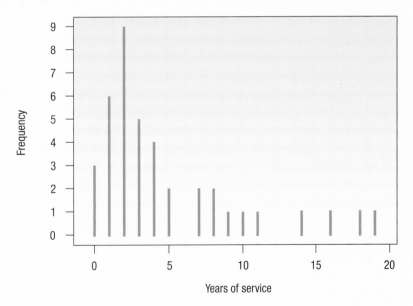

CHART 8–3 Length of Service for Spence Sprockets, Inc., Employees

Let's consider the first of Ed Spence's problems. He would like to form a committee of five employees to look into the health care question and suggest what type of health care coverage would be most appropriate for the majority of workers. How should he select the committee? If he selects the committee randomly, what might he expect in terms of mean length of service for those on the committee?

To begin, Ed writes the length of service for each of the 40 employees on pieces of paper and puts them into an old baseball hat. Next, he shuffles the pieces of paper around and randomly selects five slips of paper. The lengths of service for these five employees are 1, 9, 0, 19, and 14 years. Thus, the mean length of service for these five sampled employees is 8.60 years. How does that compare with the population mean? At this point Ed does not know the population mean, but the number of employees in the population is only 40, so he decides to calculate the mean length of service for *all* his employees. It is 4.8 years, found by adding the lengths of service for *all* the employees and dividing the total by 40.

$$\mu = \frac{11 + 4 + 18 + \cdots + 2 + 3}{40} = 4.80$$

The difference between the sample mean $(\overline{X})$ and the population mean (μ) is called **sampling error.** In other words, the difference of 3.80 years between the population mean of 4.80 and the sample mean of 8.60 is the sampling error. It is due to chance. Thus, if Ed selected these five employees to constitute the committee, their mean length of service would be larger than the population mean.

What would happen if Ed put the five pieces of paper back into the baseball hat and selected another sample? Would you expect the mean of this second sample to be exactly the same as the previous one? Suppose he selects another sample of five employees and finds the lengths of service in this sample to be 7, 4, 4, 1, and 3. This sample mean is 3.80 years. The result of selecting 25 samples of five employees each is shown in Table 8–5 and Chart 8–4. There are actually 658,008 possible samples of 5 from the population of 40 employees, found by the combination formula (5–9) for 40 things taken 5 at a time. Notice the difference in the shape of the population and

TABLE 8–5 Twenty-Five Random Samples of Five Employees

Sample I.D.			Sample Data			Sample Mean
A	1	9	0	19	14	8.6
B	7	4	4	1	3	3.8
C	8	19	8	2	1	7.6
D	4	18	2	0	11	7.0
E	4	2	4	7	18	7.0
F	1	2	0	3	2	1.6
G	2	3	2	0	2	1.8
H	11	2	9	2	4	5.6
I	9	0	4	2	7	4.4
J	1	1	1	11	1	3.0
K	2	0	0	10	2	2.8
L	0	2	3	2	16	4.6
M	2	3	1	1	1	1.6
N	3	7	3	4	3	4.0
O	1	2	3	1	4	2.2
P	19	0	1	3	8	6.2
Q	5	1	7	14	9	7.2
R	5	4	2	3	4	3.6
S	14	5	2	2	5	5.6
T	2	1	1	4	7	3.0
U	3	7	1	2	1	2.8
V	0	1	5	1	2	1.8
W	0	3	19	4	2	5.6
X	4	2	3	4	0	2.6
Y	1	1	2	3	2	1.8

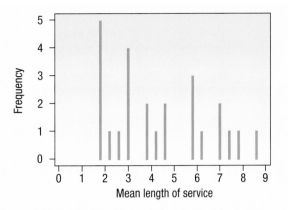

CHART 8–4 Histogram of Mean Lengths of Service for 25 Samples of Five Employees

the distribution of these sample means. The population of the lengths of service for employees (Chart 8–3) is positively skewed, but the distribution of these 25 sample means does not reflect the same positive skew. There is also a difference in the range of the sample means versus the range of the population. The population ranged from 0 to 19 years, whereas the sample means range from 1.6 to 8.6 years.

Table 8–6 reports the result of selecting 25 samples of 20 employees each and computing their sample means. These sample means are shown graphically in Chart 8–5. Compare the shape of this distribution to the population (Chart 8–3) and to the distribution of sample means where the sample is $n = 5$ (Chart 8–4). You should observe two important features:

TABLE 8–6 Random Samples and Sample Means of 25 Samples of 20 Spence Sprocket, Inc., Employees

Sample Number	Sample Data (Length of Service)																				Sample Mean
A	3	8	3	0	2	1	2	3	11	5	1	3	4	2	7	1	1	2	4	16	3.95
B	2	3	8	2	1	5	2	0	3	1	0	7	1	4	3	11	4	4	3	1	3.25
C	14	5	0	3	2	14	11	9	2	2	1	2	19	1	0	1	4	2	19	8	5.95
D	9	2	1	1	4	10	0	8	4	3	2	1	0	8	1	14	5	10	1	3	4.35
E	18	1	2	2	4	3	2	8	2	1	0	19	4	19	0	1	4	0	3	14	5.35
F	10	4	4	18	3	3	1	0	0	2	2	4	7	10	2	0	3	4	2	1	4.00
G	5	7	11	8	11	18	1	1	16	2	2	16	2	3	2	16	2	2	2	4	6.55
H	3	0	2	0	5	4	5	3	8	3	2	5	1	1	2	9	8	3	16	5	4.25
I	0	0	18	2	1	7	4	1	3	0	3	2	11	7	2	8	5	1	2	3	4.00
J	2	7	2	4	1	3	3	2	5	10	0	1	1	2	9	3	2	19	3	2	4.05
K	7	4	5	3	3	0	18	2	0	4	2	7	2	7	4	2	10	1	1	2	4.20
L	0	3	10	5	9	2	1	4	1	2	1	8	18	1	4	3	3	2	0	4	4.05
M	4	1	2	1	7	3	9	14	8	19	4	4	1	2	0	3	1	2	1	2	4.40
N	3	16	1	2	4	4	4	2	1	5	2	3	5	3	4	7	16	1	11	1	4.75
O	2	19	2	0	2	2	16	2	3	11	9	2	8	0	8	2	7	3	2	2	5.10
P	2	18	16	5	2	2	19	0	1	2	11	4	2	2	1	4	2	0	4	3	5.00
Q	3	2	3	11	10	1	1	5	19	16	7	10	3	1	1	1	2	2	3	1	5.10
R	2	3	1	2	7	4	3	19	9	2	2	1	1	2	2	2	1	8	0	2	3.65
S	2	14	19	1	19	2	8	4	2	2	14	2	8	16	4	7	2	9	0	7	7.10
T	0	1	3	3	2	2	3	1	1	0	3	2	3	5	2	10	14	4	2	0	3.05
U	1	0	1	2	16	1	1	2	5	1	4	1	2	2	2	2	2	8	9	3	3.25
V	1	9	4	4	2	8	7	1	14	18	1	5	10	11	19	0	3	7	2	11	6.85
W	8	1	9	19	3	19	0	5	2	1	5	3	3	4	1	5	3	1	8	7	5.35
X	4	2	0	3	1	16	1	11	3	3	2	18	2	0	1	5	0	7	2	5	4.30
Y	1	2	1	2	0	2	7	2	4	8	19	2	5	3	3	0	19	2	1	18	5.05

1. The shape of the distribution of the sample mean is different from that of the population. In Chart 8–3 the distribution of all employees is positively skewed. However, as we select random samples from this population, the shape of the distribution of the sample mean changes. As we increase the size of the sample, the distribution of the sample mean approaches the normal probability distribution. This illustrates the central limit theorem.
2. There is less dispersion in the sampling distribution of sample means than in the population distribution. In the population the lengths of service ranged from 0 to 19 years. When we selected samples of 5, the sample means ranged from 1.6 to 8.6 years, and when we selected samples of 20, the means ranged from 3.05 to 7.10 years.

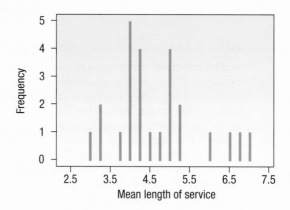

CHART 8–5 Histogram of Mean Lengths of Service for 25 Samples of 20 Employees

We can also compare the mean of the sample means to the population mean. The mean of the 25 samples of 20 employees reported in Table 8–6 is 4.676 years.

$$\mu_{\bar{X}} = \frac{3.95 + 3.25 + \cdots + 4.30 + 5.05}{25} = 4.676$$

We use the symbol $\mu_{\bar{X}}$ to identify the mean of the distribution of the sample mean. The subscript reminds us that the distribution is of the sample mean. It is read "mu sub X bar." We observe that the mean of the sample means, 4.676 years, is very close to the population mean of 4.80.

What should we conclude from this example? The central limit theorem indicates that, regardless of the shape of the population distribution, the sampling distribution of the sample mean will move toward the normal probability distribution. The larger the number of observations in each sample, the stronger the convergence. The Spence Sprockets, Inc., example shows how the central limit theorem works. We began with a positively skewed population (Chart 8–3). Next, we selected 25 random samples of 5 observations, computed the mean of each sample, and finally organized these 25 sample means into a graph (Chart 8–4). We observe a change in the shape of the sampling distribution of the sample mean from that of the population. The movement is from a positively skewed distribution to a distribution that has the shape of the normal probability distribution.

To further illustrate the effects of the central limit theorem, we increased the number of observations in each sample from 5 to 20. We selected 25 samples of 20 observations each and calculated the mean of each sample. Finally, we organized these sample means into a graph (Chart 8–5). The shape of the histogram in Chart 8–5 is clearly moving toward the normal probability distribution.

If you go back to Chapter 6, where several binomial distributions with a "success" proportion of .10 are shown in Chart 6–4, you can see yet another demonstration of the central limit theorem. Observe as *n* increases from 7 through 12 and 20 up to 40 that the profile of the probability distributions moves closer and closer to a normal probability distribution. Chart 8–5 on the previous page also shows the convergence to normality as *n* increases. This again reinforces the fact that, as more observations are sampled from any population distribution, the shape of the sampling distribution of the sample mean will get closer and closer to a normal distribution.

The central limit theorem itself (reread the definition on page 235) does not say anything about the dispersion of the sampling distribution of the sample mean or about the comparison of the mean of the sampling distribution of the sample mean to the mean of the population. However, in our Spence Sprockets example we did observe that there was less dispersion in the distribution of the sample mean than in the population distribution by noting the difference in the range in the population and the range of the sample means. We observe that the mean of the sample means is close to the mean of the population. It can be demonstrated that the mean of the sampling distribution is the population mean, i.e., $\mu_{\bar{X}} = \mu$, and if the standard deviation in the population is σ, the standard deviation of the sample means is $\sigma/\sqrt{n}$, where *n* is the number of observations in each sample. We refer to $\sigma/\sqrt{n}$ as the **standard error of the mean.** Its longer name is actually the *standard deviation of the sampling distribution of the sample mean*.

STANDARD ERROR OF THE MEAN	$\sigma_{\bar{X}} = \dfrac{\sigma}{\sqrt{n}}$	[8–1]

In this section we also came to other important conclusions.

1. The mean of the distribution of sample means will be *exactly* equal to the population mean if we are able to select all possible samples of the same size from a given population. That is:

$$\mu = \mu_{\bar{X}}$$

Even if we do not select all samples, we can expect the mean of the distribution of sample means to be close to the population mean.
2. There will be less dispersion in the sampling distribution of the sample mean than in the population. If the standard deviation of the population is σ, the standard deviation of the distribution of sample means is $\sigma/\sqrt{n}$. Note that when we increase the size of the sample the standard error of the mean decreases.

Self-Review 8–4

Refer to the Spence Sprockets, Inc., data on page 237. Select 10 random samples of 5 employees each. Use the methods described earlier in the chapter and the Table of Random Numbers (Appendix B.6) to find the employees to include in the sample. Compute the mean of each sample and plot the sample means on a chart similar to Chart 8–3. What is the mean of your 10 sample means?

Exercises

connect™

11. Appendix B.6 is a table of random numbers. Hence, each digit from 0 to 9 has the same likelihood of occurrence.
    a. Draw a graph showing the population distribution. What is the population mean?

b. Following are the first 10 rows of five digits from Appendix B.6. Assume that these are 10 random samples of five values each. Determine the mean of each sample and plot the means on a chart similar to Chart 8–3. Compare the mean of the sampling distribution of the sample means with the population mean.

0	2	7	1	1
9	4	8	7	3
5	4	9	2	1
7	7	6	4	0
6	1	5	4	5
1	7	1	4	7
1	3	7	4	8
8	7	4	5	5
0	8	9	9	9
7	8	8	0	4

12. Scrapper Elevator Company has 20 sales representatives who sell its product throughout the United States and Canada. The number of units sold last month by each representative is listed below. Assume these sales figures to be the population values.

2	3	2	3	3	4	2	4	3	2	2	7	3	4	5	3	3	3	3	5

   a. Draw a graph showing the population distribution.
   b. Compute the mean of the population.
   c. Select five random samples of 5 each. Compute the mean of each sample. Use the methods described in this chapter and Appendix B.6 to determine the items to be included in the sample.
   d. Compare the mean of the sampling distribution of the sample means to the population mean. Would you expect the two values to be about the same?
   e. Draw a histogram of the sample means. Do you notice a difference in the shape of the distribution of sample means compared to the shape of the population distribution?

13. Consider all of the coins (pennies, nickels, quarters, etc.) in your pocket or purse as a population. Make a frequency table beginning with the current year and counting backward to record the ages (in years) of the coins. For example, if the current year is 2010, then a coin with 2007 stamped on it is 3 years old.
   a. Draw a histogram or other graph showing the population distribution.
   b. Randomly select five coins and record the mean age of the sampled coins. Repeat this sampling process 20 times. Now draw a histogram or other graph showing the distribution of the sample means.
   c. Compare the shapes of the two histograms.

14. Consider the digits in the phone numbers on a randomly selected page of your local phone book a population. Make a frequency table of the final digit of 30 randomly selected phone numbers. For example, if a phone number is 555-9704, record a 4.
   a. Draw a histogram or other graph of this population distribution. Using the uniform distribution, compute the population mean and the population standard deviation.
   b. Also record the sample mean of the final four digits (9704 would lead to a mean of 5). Now draw a histogram or other graph showing the distribution of the sample means.
   c. Compare the shapes of the two histograms.

Using the Sampling Distribution of the Sample Mean

The previous discussion is important because most business decisions are made on the basis of sampling results. Here are some examples.

1. Arm and Hammer Company wants to ensure that its laundry detergent actually contains 100 fluid ounces, as indicated on the label. Historical summaries from

the filling process indicate the mean amount per container is 100 fluid ounces and the standard deviation is 2 fluid ounces. The quality technician in her 10 A.M. check of 40 containers finds the mean amount per container is 99.8 fluid ounces. Should the technician shut down the filling operation or is the sampling error reasonable?

2. A. C. Nielsen Company provides information to organizations advertising on television. Prior research indicates that adult Americans watch an average of 6.0 hours per day of television. The standard deviation is 1.5 hours. For a sample of 50 adults in the greater Boston area, would it be reasonable that we could randomly select a sample and find that they watch an average of 6.5 hours of television per day?

3. Haughton Elevator Company wishes to develop specifications for the number of people who can ride in a new oversized elevator. Suppose the mean weight for an adult is 160 pounds and the standard deviation is 15 pounds. However, the distribution of weights does not follow the normal probability distribution. It is positively skewed. What is the likelihood that for a sample of 30 adults their mean weight is 170 pounds or more?

In each of these situations we have a population about which we have some information. We take a sample from that population and wish to conclude whether the sampling error, that is, the difference between the population parameter and the sample statistic, is due to chance.

Using ideas discussed in the previous section, we can compute the probability that a sample mean will fall within a certain range. We know that the sampling distribution of the sample mean will follow the normal probability distribution under two conditions:

1. When the samples are taken from populations known to follow the normal distribution. In this case the size of the sample is not a factor.

2. When the shape of the population distribution is not known or the shape is known to be nonnormal, but our sample contains at least 30 observations. In this case, the central limit theorem guarantees the sampling distribution of the mean follows a normal distribution.

We can use formula (7–5) from the previous chapter to convert any normal distribution to the standard normal distribution. We also refer to this as a z value. Then we can use the standard normal table, Appendix B.1, to find the probability of selecting an observation that would fall within a specific range. The formula for finding a z value is:

$$z = \frac{X - \mu}{\sigma}$$

LO5 Use the central limit theorem to find probabilities of selecting possible sample means from a specified population.

In this formula X is the value of the random variable, μ is the population mean, and σ the population standard deviation.

However, most business decisions refer to a sample—not just one observation. So we are interested in the distribution of $\overline{X}$, the sample mean, instead of X, the value of one observation. That is the first change we make in formula (7–5). The second is that we use the standard error of the mean of n observations instead of the population standard deviation. That is, we use $\sigma/\sqrt{n}$ in the denominator rather than σ. Therefore, to find the likelihood of a sample mean with a specified range, we first use the following formula to find the corresponding z value. Then we use Appendix B.1 to locate the probability.

FINDING THE z VALUE OF $\overline{X}$ WHEN THE POPULATION STANDARD DEVIATION IS KNOWN	$z = \dfrac{\overline{X} - \mu}{\sigma/\sqrt{n}}$	[8–2]

The following example will show the application.

Example

The Quality Assurance Department for Cola, Inc., maintains records regarding the amount of cola in its Jumbo bottle. The actual amount of cola in each bottle is critical, but varies a small amount from one bottle to the next. Cola, Inc., does not wish to underfill the bottles, because it will have a problem with truth in labeling. On the other hand, it cannot overfill each bottle, because it would be giving cola away, hence reducing its profits. Its records indicate that the amount of cola follows the normal probability distribution. The mean amount per bottle is 31.2 ounces and the population standard deviation is 0.4 ounces. At 8 A.M. today the quality technician randomly selected 16 bottles from the filling line. The mean amount of cola contained in the bottles is 31.38 ounces. Is this an unlikely result? Is it likely the process is putting too much soda in the bottles? To put it another way, is the sampling error of 0.18 ounces unusual?

Solution

We can use the results of the previous section to find the likelihood that we could select a sample of 16 (n) bottles from a normal population with a mean of 31.2 (μ) ounces and a population standard deviation of 0.4 (σ) ounces and find the sample mean to be 31.38($\overline{X}$). We use formula (8–2) to find the value of z.

$$z = \frac{\overline{X} - \mu}{\sigma/\sqrt{n}} = \frac{31.38 - 31.20}{0.4/\sqrt{16}} = 1.80$$

The numerator of this equation, $\overline{X} - \mu = 31.38 - 31.20 = .18$, is the sampling error. The denominator, $\sigma/\sqrt{n} = 0.4/\sqrt{16} = 0.1$, is the standard error of the sampling distribution of the sample mean. So the z values express the sampling error in standard units, in other words, the standard error.

Next, we compute the likelihood of a z value greater than 1.80. In Appendix B.1 locate the probability corresponding to a z value of 1.80. It is .4641. The likelihood of a z value greater than 1.80 is .0359, found by .5000 − .4641.

What do we conclude? It is unlikely, less than a 4 percent chance, we could select a sample of 16 observations from a normal population with a mean of 31.2 ounces and a population standard deviation of 0.4 ounces and find the sample mean equal to or greater than 31.38 ounces. We conclude the process is putting too much cola in the bottles. The quality technician should contact the production supervisor about reducing the amount of soda in each bottle. This information is summarized in Chart 8–6.

.0359

.4641

| 31.20 | 31.38 | Ounces ($\overline{X}$) |
| 0 | 1.80 | z value |

CHART 8–6 Sampling Distribution of the Mean Amount of Cola in a Jumbo Bottle

| Self-Review 8–5 | Refer to the Cola, Inc., information. Suppose the quality technician selected a sample of 16 Jumbo bottles that averaged 31.08 ounces. What can you conclude about the filling process? |

Exercises

connect

15. A normal population has a mean of 60 and a standard deviation of 12. You select a random sample of 9. Compute the probability the sample mean is:
    a. Greater than 63.
    b. Less than 56.
    c. Between 56 and 63.

16. A normal population has a mean of 75 and a standard deviation of 5. You select a sample of 40. Compute the probability the sample mean is:
    a. Less than 74.
    b. Between 74 and 76.
    c. Between 76 and 77.
    d. Greater than 77.

17. The rent for a one-bedroom apartment in Southern California follows the normal distribution with a mean of $2,200 per month and a standard deviation of $250 per month. The distribution of the monthly costs does not follow the normal distribution. In fact, it is positively skewed. What is the probability of selecting a sample of 50 one-bedroom apartments and finding the mean to be at least $1,950 per month?

18. According to an IRS study, it takes a mean of 330 minutes for taxpayers to prepare, copy, and electronically file a 1040 tax form. This distribution of times follows the normal distribution and the standard deviation is 80 minutes. A consumer watchdog agency selects a random sample of 40 taxpayers.
    a. What is the standard error of the mean in this example?
    b. What is the likelihood the sample mean is greater than 320 minutes?
    c. What is the likelihood the sample mean is between 320 and 350 minutes?
    d. What is the likelihood the sample mean is greater than 350 minutes?

Chapter Summary

I. There are many reasons for sampling a population.
  A. The results of a sample may adequately estimate the value of the population parameter, thus saving time and money.
  B. It may be too time consuming to contact all members of the population.
  C. It may be impossible to check or locate all the members of the population.
  D. The cost of studying all the items in the population may be prohibitive.
  E. Often testing destroys the sampled item and it cannot be returned to the population.
II. In an unbiased or probability sample all members of the population have a chance of being selected for the sample. There are several probability sampling methods.
  A. In a simple random sample all members of the population have the same chance of being selected for the sample.
  B. In a systematic sample a random starting point is selected, and then every *k*th item thereafter is selected for the sample.
  C. In a stratified sample the population is divided into several groups, called strata, and then a random sample is selected from each stratum.
  D. In cluster sampling the population is divided into primary units, then samples are drawn from the primary units.

III. The sampling error is the difference between a population parameter and a sample statistic.

IV. The sampling distribution of the sample mean is a probability distribution of all possible sample means of the same sample size.

    A. For a given sample size, the mean of all possible sample means selected from a population is equal to the population mean.

    B. There is less variation in the distribution of the sample mean than in the population distribution.

    C. The standard error of the mean measures the variation in the sampling distribution of the sample mean. The standard error is found by:

$$\sigma_{\bar{X}} = \frac{\sigma}{\sqrt{n}} \qquad \text{[8–1]}$$

    D. If the population follows a normal distribution, the sampling distribution of the sample mean will also follow the normal distribution for samples of any size. Assume the population standard deviation is known. To determine the probability that a sample mean falls in a particular region, use the following formula.

$$z = \frac{\bar{X} - \mu}{\sigma/\sqrt{n}} \qquad \text{[8–2]}$$

Pronunciation Key

SYMBOL	MEANING	PRONUNCIATION
$\mu_{\bar{X}}$	Mean of the sampling distribution of the sample mean	*mu sub X bar*
$\sigma_{\bar{X}}$	Population standard error of the sample mean	*sigma sub X bar*

Chapter Exercises

connect

19. The retail stores located in the North Towne Square Mall are:

00	Elder-Beerman	09	Lion Store	18	County Seat
01	Sears	10	Bootleggers	19	Kid Mart
02	Deb Shop	11	Formal Man	20	Lerner
03	Frederick's of Hollywood	12	Leather Ltd.	21	Coach House Gifts
04	Petries	13	B Dalton Bookseller	22	Spencer Gifts
05	Easy Dreams	14	Pat's Hallmark	23	CPI Photo Finish
06	Summit Stationers	15	Things Remembered	24	Regis Hairstylists
07	E. B. Brown Opticians	16	Pearle Vision Express		
08	Kay-Bee Toy & Hobby	17	Dollar Tree		

    a. If the following random numbers are selected, which retail stores should be contacted for a survey? 11, 65, 86, 62, 06, 10, 12, 77, and 04

    b. Select a random sample of four retail stores. Use Appendix B.6.

    c. A systematic sampling procedure is to be used. The first store is to be contacted and then every third store. Which stores will be contacted?

20. Medical Mutual Insurance is investigating the cost of a routine office visit to family-practice physicians in the Rochester, New York, area. The following is a list of family-practice physicians in the region. Physicians are to be randomly selected and contacted regarding their charges. The 39 physicians have been coded from 00 to 38. Also noted is whether they are in practice by themselves (S), have a partner (P), or are in a group practice (G).

Number	Physician	Type of Practice	Number	Physician	Type of Practice
00	R. E. Scherbarth, M.D.	S	20	Gregory Yost, M.D.	P
01	Crystal R. Goveia, M.D.	P	21	J. Christian Zona, M.D.	P
02	Mark D. Hillard, M.D.	P	22	Larry Johnson, M.D.	P
03	Jeanine S. Huttner, M.D.	P	23	Sanford Kimmel, M.D.	P
04	Francis Aona, M.D.	P	24	Harry Mayhew, M.D.	S
05	Janet Arrowsmith, M.D.	P	25	Leroy Rodgers, M.D.	S
06	David DeFrance, M.D.	S	26	Thomas Tafelski, M.D.	S
07	Judith Furlong, M.D.	S	27	Mark Zilkoski, M.D.	G
08	Leslie Jackson, M.D.	G	28	Ken Bertka, M.D.	G
09	Paul Langenkamp, M.D.	S	29	Mark DeMichiei, M.D.	G
10	Philip Lepkowski, M.D.	S	30	John Eggert, M.D.	P
11	Wendy Martin, M.D.	S	31	Jeanne Fiorito, M.D.	P
12	Denny Mauricio, M.D.	P	32	Michael Fitzpatrick, M.D.	P
13	Hasmukh Parmar, M.D.	P	33	Charles Holt, D.O.	P
14	Ricardo Pena, M.D.	P	34	Richard Koby, M.D.	P
15	David Reames, M.D.	P	35	John Meier, M.D.	P
16	Ronald Reynolds, M.D.	G	36	Douglas Smucker, M.D.	S
17	Mark Steinmetz, M.D.	G	37	David Weldy, M.D.	P
18	Geza Torok, M.D.	S	38	Cheryl Zaborowski, M.D.	P
19	Mark Young, M.D.	P			

    a. The random numbers obtained from Appendix B.6 are: 31, 94, 43, 36, 03, 24, 17, and 09. Which physicians should be contacted?

    b. Select a random sample of four physicians using the random numbers of Appendix B.6.

    c. A sample is to consist of every fifth physician. The number 04 is selected as the starting point. Which physicians will be contacted?

    d. A sample is to consist of two physicians in solo practice (S), two in partnership (P), and one in group practice (G). Select a sample accordingly. Explain your procedure.

21. A population consists of the following three values: 1, 2, and 3.

    a. List all possible samples of size 2 (including possible repeats) and compute the mean of every sample.

    b. Find the means of the distribution of the sample mean and the population mean. Compare the two values.

    c. Compare the dispersion of the population with that of the sample mean.

    d. Describe the shapes of the two distributions.

22. In the Department of Education at UR University, student records suggest that the population of students spends an average of 5.5 hours per week playing organized sports. The population's standard deviation is 2.2 hours per week. Based on a sample of 121 students, Healthy Lifestyles Incorporated (HLI) would like to apply the central limit theorem to make various estimates.

    a. Compute the standard error of the sample mean.

    b. What is the chance HLI will find a sample mean between 5 and 6 hours?

    c. Calculate the probability that the sample mean will be between 5.3 and 5.7 hours.

    d. How strange would it be to obtain a sample mean greater than 6.5 hours?

23. The manufacturer of eMachines, an economy-priced computer, recently completed the design for a new laptop model. eMachine's top management would like some assistance in pricing the new laptop. Two market research firms were contacted and asked to prepare a pricing strategy. Marketing-Gets-Results tested the new eMachines laptop with 50 randomly selected consumers, who indicated they plan to purchase a laptop within the next year. The second marketing research firm, called Marketing-Reaps-Profits, test-marketed the new eMachines laptop with 200 current laptop owners. Which of the marketing research companies' test results will be more useful? Discuss why.

24. Answer the following questions in one or two well-constructed sentences.
  a. What happens to the standard error of the mean if the sample size is increased?
  b. What happens to the distribution of the sample means if the sample size in increased?
  c. When using the distribution of sample means to estimate the population mean, what is the benefit of using larger sample sizes?
25. There are 25 motels in Goshen, Indiana. The number of rooms in each motel follows:

90 72 75 60 75 72 84 72 88 74 105 115 68 74 80 64 104 82 48 58 60 80 48 58 100

  a. Using a table of random numbers (Appendix B.6), select a random sample of five motels from this population.
  b. Obtain a systematic sample by selecting a random starting point among the first five motels and then select every fifth motel.
  c. Suppose the last five motels are "cut-rate" motels. Describe how you would select a random sample of three regular motels and two cut-rate motels.
26. As a part of their customer-service program, United Airlines randomly selected 10 passengers from today's 9 A.M. Chicago–Tampa flight. Each sampled passenger is to be interviewed in depth regarding airport facilities, service, and so on. To identify the sample, each passenger was given a number on boarding the aircraft. The numbers started with 001 and ended with 250.
  a. Select 10 usable numbers at random using Appendix B.6.
  b. The sample of 10 could have been chosen using a systematic sample. Choose the first number using Appendix B.6, and then list the numbers to be interviewed.
  c. Evaluate the two methods by giving the advantages and possible disadvantages.
  d. In what other way could a random sample be selected from the 250 passengers?
27. Suppose your statistics instructor gave six examinations during the semester. You received the following grades (percent correct): 79, 64, 84, 82, 92, and 77. Instead of averaging the six scores, the instructor indicated he would randomly select two grades and compute the final percent correct based on the two percents.
  a. How many different samples of two test grades are possible?
  b. List all possible samples of size two and compute the mean of each.
  c. Compute the mean of the sample means and compare it to the population mean.
  d. If you were a student, would you like this arrangement? Would the result be different from dropping the lowest score? Write a brief report.
28. At the downtown office of First National Bank there are five tellers. Last week the tellers made the following number of errors each: 2, 3, 5, 3, and 5.
  a. How many different samples of 2 tellers are possible?
  b. List all possible samples of size 2 and compute the mean of each.
  c. Compute the mean of the sample means and compare it to the population mean.
29. The Quality Control Department employs five technicians during the day shift. Listed below is the number of times each technician instructed the production foreman to shut down the manufacturing process last week.

Technician	Shutdowns	Technician	Shutdowns
Taylor	4	Rousche	3
Hurley	3	Huang	2
Gupta	5		

  a. How many different samples of two technicians are possible from this population?
  b. List all possible samples of two observations each and compute the mean of each sample.
  c. Compare the mean of the sample means with the population mean.
  d. Compare the shape of the population distribution with the shape of the distribution of the sample means.

30. The Appliance Center has six sales representatives at its North Jacksonville outlet. Listed below is the number of refrigerators sold by each last month.

Sales Representative	Number Sold	Sales Representative	Number Sold
Zina Craft	54	Jan Niles	48
Woon Junge	50	Molly Camp	50
Ernie DeBrul	52	Rachel Myak	52

    a. How many samples of size 2 are possible?
    b. Select all possible samples of size 2 and compute the mean number sold.
    c. Organize the sample means into a frequency distribution.
    d. What is the mean of the population? What is the mean of the sample means?
    e. What is the shape of the population distribution?
    f. What is the shape of the distribution of the sample mean?

31. Mattel Corporation produces a remote-controlled car that requires three AA batteries. The mean life of these batteries in this product is 35.0 hours. The distribution of the battery lives closely follows the normal probability distribution with a standard deviation of 5.5 hours. As a part of its testing program Sony tests samples of 25 batteries.
    a. What can you say about the shape of the distribution of the sample mean?
    b. What is the standard error of the distribution of the sample mean?
    c. What proportion of the samples will have a mean useful life of more than 36 hours?
    d. What proportion of the sample will have a mean useful life greater than 34.5 hours?
    e. What proportion of the sample will have a mean useful life between 34.5 and 36.0 hours?

32. CRA CDs, Inc., wants the mean lengths of the "cuts" on a CD to be 135 seconds (2 minutes and 15 seconds). This will allow the disk jockeys to have plenty of time for commercials within each 10-minute segment. Assume the distribution of the length of the cuts follows the normal distribution with a population standard deviation of 8 seconds. Suppose we select a sample of 16 cuts from various CDs sold by CRA CDs, Inc.
    a. What can we say about the shape of the distribution of the sample mean?
    b. What is the standard error of the mean?
    c. What percent of the sample means will be greater than 140 seconds?
    d. What percent of the sample means will be greater than 128 seconds?
    e. What percent of the sample means will be greater than 128 but less than 140 seconds?

33. Recent studies indicate that the typical 50-year-old woman spends $350 per year for personal-care products. The distribution of the amounts spent follows a normal distribution with a standard deviation of $45 per year. We select a random sample of 40 women. The mean amount spent for those sampled is $335. What is the likelihood of finding a sample mean this large or larger from the specified population?

34. Information from the American Institute of Insurance indicates the mean amount of life insurance per household in the United States is $110,000. This distribution follows the normal distribution with a standard deviation of $40,000.
    a. If we select a random sample of 50 households, what is the standard error of the mean?
    b. What is the expected shape of the distribution of the sample mean?
    c. What is the likelihood of selecting a sample with a mean of at least $112,000?
    d. What is the likelihood of selecting a sample with a mean of more than $100,000?
    e. Find the likelihood of selecting a sample with a mean of more than $100,000 but less than $112,000.

35. The mean age at which men in the United States marry for the first time follows the normal distribution with a mean of 24.8 years. The standard deviation of the distribution is 2.5 years. For a random sample of 60 men, what is the likelihood that the age at which they were married for the first time is less than 25.1 years?

36. A recent study by the Greater Los Angeles Taxi Drivers Association showed that the mean fare charged for service from Hermosa Beach to Los Angeles International Airport is $18.00 and the standard deviation is $3.50. We select a sample of 15 fares.
    a. What is the likelihood that the sample mean is between $17.00 and $20.00?
    b. What must you assume to make the above calculation?

37. Crossett Trucking Company claims that the mean weight of its delivery trucks when they are fully loaded is 6,000 pounds and the standard deviation is 150 pounds. Assume that the population follows the normal distribution. Forty trucks are randomly selected and weighed. Within what limits will 95 percent of the sample means occur?

38. The mean amount purchased by a typical customer at Churchill's Grocery Store is $23.50 with a standard deviation of $5.00. Assume the distribution of amounts purchased follows the normal distribution. For a sample of 50 customers, answer the following questions.
    a. What is the likelihood the sample mean is at least $25.00?
    b. What is the likelihood the sample mean is greater than $22.50 but less than $25.00?
    c. Within what limits will 90 percent of the sample means occur?

39. The mean SAT score for Division I student-athletes is 947 with a standard deviation of 205. If you select a random sample of 60 of these students, what is the probability the mean is below 900?

40. Suppose we roll a fair die two times.
    a. How many different samples are there?
    b. List each of the possible samples and compute the mean.
    c. On a chart similar to Chart 8–1, compare the distribution of sample means with the distribution of the population.
    d. Compute the mean and the standard deviation of each distribution and compare them.

41. Over the past decade the mean number of members of the Information Systems Security Association who have experienced a denial-of-service attack each year is 510 with a standard deviation of 14.28 attacks. Suppose nothing in this environment changes.
    a. What is the likelihood this group will suffer an average of more than 600 attacks in the next 10 years?
    b. Compute the probability the mean number of attacks over the next 10 years is between 500 and 600.
    c. What is the possibility they will experience an average of less than 500 attacks over the next 10 years?

42. The Oil Price Information Center reports the mean price per gallon of regular gasoline is $3.79 with a population standard deviation of $0.18. Assume a random sample of 40 gasoline stations is selected and their mean cost for regular gasoline is computed.
    a. What is the standard error of the mean in this experiment?
    b. What is the probability that the sample mean is between $3.77 and $3.81?
    c. What is the probability that the difference between the sample mean and the population mean is less than 0.01?
    d. What is the likelihood the sample mean is greater than $3.87?

43. Nike's annual report says that the average American buys 6.5 pairs of sports shoes per year. Suppose the population standard deviation is 2.1 and that a sample of 81 customers will be examined next year.
    a. What is the standard error of the mean in this experiment?
    b. What is the probability that the sample mean is between 6 and 7 pairs of sports shoes?
    c. What is the probability that the difference between the sample mean and the population mean is less than 0.25 pairs?
    d. What is the likelihood the sample mean is greater than 7 pairs?

Data Set Exercises

44. Refer to the Real Estate data, which report information on the homes sold in the Phoenix, Arizona, area last year.
    a. Compute the mean and the standard deviation of the distribution of the selling prices for the homes. Assume this to be the population. Develop a histogram of the data. Would it seem reasonable from this histogram to conclude that the population of selling prices follows the normal distribution?
    b. Let's assume a normal population. Select a sample of 10 homes. Compute the mean and the standard deviation of the sample. Determine the likelihood of finding a sample mean this large or larger from the population.

Practice Test

Part I Objective

1. In a _____ each item in the population has the same chance of being included in the sample.
2. A sample should have at least how many observations? (10, 30, 100, 1,000, no size restriction) _____
3. When a population is divided into groups based on some characteristic, such as region of the country, the groups are called _____.
4. The difference between a sample mean and the population mean is the _____.
5. A probability distribution of all possible samples means for a particular sample size is the _____.
6. Suppose a population consisted of 10 items and we wished to list all possible samples of size 3. How many samples are there? _____
7. What is the name given to the standard deviation of the distribution of sample means? _____
8. The mean of all possible sample means is _____ the population mean. (always larger than, always smaller than, always equal to, or not a constant relationship with)
9. If we increase the sample size from 10 to 20, the standard error of the mean will _____. (increase, decrease, stay the same, or the result is not predictable)
10. If a population follows the normal distribution, what will be the shape of the distribution of sample means? _____

Part II Problems

1. Americans spend an average (mean) of 12.2 minutes (per day) in the shower. The distribution of times follows the normal distribution with a population standard deviation of 2.3 minutes. What is the likelihood that the mean time in the shower per day for a sample of 12 Americans is 11 minutes or less?

Software Commands

1. The Excel commands to select a simple random sample on page 225 are:
   a. Select the **Data** tab on the top of the menu. Then on the far right select **Data Analysis,** then **Sampling** and **OK.**
   b. For **Input Range** insert *B1:B31*. Since the column is named, click the **Labels** box. Select **Random,** and enter the sample size for the **Number of Samples,** in this case 5. Click on **Output Range** and indicate the place in the spreadsheet you want the sample information. Note that your sample results will differ from those in the text. Also recall that Excel samples with replacement, so it is possible for a population value to appear more than once in the sample.

Chapter 8   Answers to Self-Review

8–1 **a.** Students selected are Price, Detley, and Molter.
     b. Answers will vary.
     c. Skip it and move to the next random number.

8–2 The students selected are Berry, Francis, Kopp, Poteau, and Swetye.

8–3 **a.** 10, found by:

$$_5C_2 = \frac{5!}{2!(5-2)!}$$

     b.

	Service	Sample Mean
Snow, Tolson	20, 22	21
Snow, Kraft	20, 26	23
Snow, Irwin	20, 24	22
Snow, Jones	20, 28	24
Tolson, Kraft	22, 26	24
Tolson, Irwin	22, 24	23
Tolson, Jones	22, 28	25
Kraft, Irwin	26, 24	25
Kraft, Jones	26, 28	27
Irwin, Jones	24, 28	26

     c.

Mean	Number	Probability
21	1	.10
22	1	.10
23	2	.20
24	2	.20
25	2	.20
26	1	.10
27	1	.10
	10	1.00

     d. Identical: population mean, μ, is 24, and mean of sample means, $\mu_{\bar{X}}$, is also 24.

     e. Sample means range from 21 to 27. Population values go from 20 to 28.

     f. Nonnormal.

     g. Yes.

8–4 The answers will vary. Here is one solution.

	Sample Number									
	1	**2**	**3**	**4**	**5**	**6**	**7**	**8**	**9**	**10**
	8	2	2	19	3	4	0	4	1	2
	19	1	14	9	2	5	8	2	14	4
	8	3	4	2	4	4	1	14	4	1
	0	3	2	3	1	2	16	1	2	3
	2	1	7	2	19	18	18	16	3	7
Total	37	10	29	35	29	33	43	37	24	17
$\bar{X}$	7.4	2	5.8	7.0	5.8	6.6	8.6	7.4	4.8	3.4

Mean of the 10 sample means is 5.88.

8–5 $z = \dfrac{31.08 - 31.20}{0.4/\sqrt{16}} = -1.20$

The probability that z is greater than -1.20 is $.5000 + .3849 = .8849$. There is more than an 88 percent chance the filling operation will produce bottles with at least 31.08 ounces.

Estimation and Confidence Intervals

Learning Objectives

When you have completed this chapter you will be able to:

LO1 Define a *point estimate*.

LO2 Define *level of confidence*.

LO3 Construct a confidence interval for the population mean when the population standard deviation is known.

LO4 Construct a confidence interval for a population mean when the population standard deviation is unknown.

LO5 Construct a confidence interval for a population proportion.

LO6 Determine the required sample size for either an attribute or a variable.

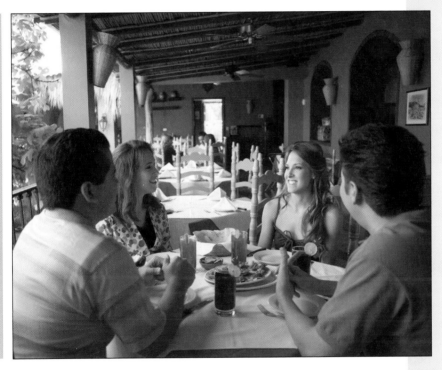

The American Restaurant Association collected information on the number of meals eaten outside the home per week by young married couples. A survey of 60 couples showed the sample mean number of meals eaten outside the home was 2.76 meals per week, with a standard deviation of 0.75 meals per week. Construct a 97 percent confidence interval for the population mean. (See LO3 and Exercise 36.)

Introduction

The previous chapter began our discussion of statistical inference. It introduced both the reasons for, and the methods of, sampling. The reasons for sampling were:

- To contact the entire population is too time consuming.
- The cost of studying all the items in the population is often too expensive.
- The sample results are usually adequate.
- Certain tests are destructive.
- Checking all the items is physically impossible.

There are several methods of sampling. Simple random sampling is the most widely used method. With this type of sampling, each member of the population has the same chance of being selected to be a part of the sample. Other methods of sampling include systematic sampling, stratified sampling, and cluster sampling.

Chapter 8 assumes information about the population, such as the mean, the standard deviation, or the shape of the population. In most business situations, such information is not available. In fact, the purpose of sampling may be to estimate some of these values. For example, you select a sample from a population and use the mean of the sample to estimate the mean of the population.

This chapter considers several important aspects of sampling. We begin by studying **point estimates.** A point estimate is a single value (point) derived from a sample and used to estimate a population value. For example, suppose we select a sample of 50 junior executives and ask each the number of hours they worked last week. Compute the mean of this sample of 50 and use the value of the sample mean as a point estimate of the unknown population mean. However, a point estimate is a single value. A more informative approach is to present a range of values in which we expect the population parameter to occur. Such a range of values is called a **confidence interval.**

Frequently in business we need to determine the size of a sample. How many voters should a polling organization contact to forecast the election outcome? How many products do we need to examine to ensure our quality level? This chapter also develops a strategy for determining the appropriate number of observations in the sample.

Point Estimates and Confidence Intervals for a Mean

We begin the study of point estimates and confidence intervals by studying estimates of the population mean. We will consider two cases, where

- The population standard deviation (σ) is known,
- The population standard deviation is unknown. In this case we substitute the sample standard deviation (s) for the population standard deviation (σ).

There are important distinctions in the assumptions between these two situations. We consider the case where σ is known first.

Population Standard Deviation, Known σ

In the previous chapter, the data on the length of service of Spence Sprockets employees, presented in the example on page 237, is a population because we present the length of service for all 40 employees. In that case we can easily compute the population mean. We have all the data and the population is not too large. In most situations, however, the population is large or it is difficult to identify all members of the population, so we need to rely on sample information. In other words, we do not know the population parameter and we therefore want to estimate the value from a sample statistic. Consider the following business situations.

1. Tourism is a major source of income for many Caribbean countries, such as Barbados. Suppose the Bureau of Tourism for Barbados wants an estimate of the mean amount spent by tourists visiting the country. It would not be feasible to contact each tourist. Therefore, 500 tourists are randomly selected as they depart the country and asked in detail about their spending while visiting the island. The mean amount spent by the sample of 500 tourists is an estimate of the unknown population parameter. That is, we let $\overline{X}$, the sample mean, serve as an estimate of μ, the population mean.

2. Centex Home Builders, Inc., builds quality homes in the southeastern region of the United States. One of the major concerns of new buyers is the date on which the home will be completed. In recent times Centex has been telling customers, "Your home will be completed 45 working days from the date we begin installing drywall." The customer relations department at Centex wishes to compare this pledge with recent experience. A sample of 50 homes completed this year revealed the mean number of working days from the start of drywall to the completion of the home was 46.7 days. Is it reasonable to conclude that the population mean is still 45 days and that the difference between the sample mean (46.7 days) and the proposed population mean is sampling error?

3. Recent medical studies indicate that exercise is an important part of a person's overall health. The director of human resources at OCF, a large glass manufacturer, wants an estimate of the number of hours per week employees spend exercising. A sample of 70 employees reveals the mean number of hours of exercise last week is 3.3. The sample mean of 3.3 hours estimates the unknown population mean, the mean hours of exercise for all employees.

A point estimate is a single statistic used to estimate a population parameter. Suppose Best Buy, Inc., wants to estimate the mean age of buyers of HD plasma televisions. They select a random sample of 50 recent purchasers, determine the age of each purchaser, and compute the mean age of the buyers in the sample. The mean of this sample is a point estimate of the mean of the population.

LO1 Define a *point estimate.*

> **POINT ESTIMATE** The statistic, computed from sample information, which is used to estimate the population parameter.

The sample mean, $\overline{X}$, is a point estimate of the population mean, μ; p, a sample proportion, is a point estimate of π, the population proportion; and s, the sample standard deviation, is a point estimate of σ, the population standard deviation.

A point estimate, however, tells only part of the story. While we expect the point estimate to be close to the population parameter, we would like to measure how close it really is. A confidence interval serves this purpose.

LO2 Define *level of confidence.*

> **CONFIDENCE INTERVAL** A range of values constructed from sample data so that the population parameter is likely to occur within that range at a specified probability. The specified probability is called the *level of confidence*.

For example, we estimate the mean yearly income for construction workers in the New York–New Jersey area is $105,000. The range of this estimate might be from $101,000 to $109,000. We can describe how confident we are that the population parameter is in the interval by making a probability statement. We might say, for instance, that we are 90 percent sure that the mean yearly income of construction workers in the New York–New Jersey area is between $101,000 and $109,000.

The information developed about the shape of a sampling distribution of the sample mean, that is, the sampling distribution of $\overline{X}$, allows us to locate an interval that has a specified probability of containing the population mean, μ. For a sample from a population that follows a normal distribution with σ known or a reasonably large sample from a population of any shape, the results of the central limit theorem allow us to state the following:

1. Ninety-five percent of the sample means selected from a population will be within 1.96 standard deviations of the population mean μ.
2. Ninety-nine percent of the sample means will lie within 2.58 standard deviations of the population mean.

The standard deviation discussed here is the standard deviation of the sampling distribution of the sample mean. It is usually called the *standard error*. Intervals computed in this fashion are called the **95 percent confidence interval** and the **99 percent confidence interval**. How are the values of 1.96 and 2.58 obtained? The *95 percent* and *99 percent* refer to the percent of similarly constructed intervals that would include the parameter being estimated. The *95 percent*, for example, refers to the middle 95 percent of the observations. Therefore, the remaining 5 percent are equally divided between the two tails.

See the following diagram.

We use Appendix B.1 to find the appropriate z values. Locate .4750 in the body of the table. Read the corresponding row and column values. The value is 1.96. Thus, the probability of finding a z value between 0 and 1.96 is .4750. Likewise, the probability of being in the interval between -1.96 and 0 is also .4750. When we combine these two, the probability of being in the interval -1.96 to 1.96 is .9500. Following is a portion of Appendix B.1. The z value for the 90 percent level of confidence is determined in a similar manner. It is 1.65. For a 99 percent level of confidence the z value is 2.58.

z	0.00	0.01	0.02	0.03	0.04	0.05	0.06	0.07	0.08	0.09
⋮	⋮	⋮	⋮	⋮	⋮	⋮	⋮	⋮	⋮	⋮
1.5	0.4332	0.4345	0.4357	0.4370	0.4382	0.4394	0.4406	0.4418	0.4429	0.4441
1.6	0.4452	0.4463	0.4474	0.4484	0.4495	0.4505	0.4515	0.4525	0.4535	0.4545
1.7	0.4554	0.4564	0.4573	0.4582	0.4591	0.4599	0.4608	0.4616	0.4625	0.4633
1.8	0.4641	0.4649	0.4656	0.4664	0.4671	0.4678	0.4686	0.4693	0.4699	0.4706
1.9	0.4713	0.4719	0.4726	0.4732	0.4738	0.4744	0.4750	0.4756	0.4761	0.4767
2.0	0.4772	0.4778	0.4783	0.4788	0.4793	0.4798	0.4803	0.4808	0.4812	0.4817
2.1	0.4821	0.4826	0.4830	0.4834	0.4838	0.4842	0.4846	0.4850	0.4854	0.4857
2.2	0.4861	0.4864	0.4868	0.4871	0.4875	0.4878	0.4881	0.4884	0.4887	0.4890
2.3	0.4893	0.4896	0.4898	0.4901	0.4904	0.4906	0.4909	0.4911	0.4913	0.4916
2.4	0.4918	0.4920	0.4922	0.4925	0.4927	0.4929	0.4931	0.4932	0.4934	0.4936

How do we determine a 95 percent confidence interval? The width of the interval is determined by the level of confidence and the size of the standard error of the mean. We've described above how to find the z value for a particular level of confidence. Recall from the previous chapter (see formula 8–1 on page 241) the standard error of the mean reports the variation in the distribution of sample means. It is really the standard deviation of the distribution of sample means. The formula is repeated below:

$$\sigma_{\bar{x}} = \frac{\sigma}{\sqrt{n}}$$

where

$\sigma_{\bar{x}}$ is the symbol for the standard error of the mean. We use a Greek letter because it is a population value, and the subscript $\bar{x}$ reminds us that it refers to a sampling distribution of the sample means.

σ is the population standard deviation.

n is the number of observations in the sample.

The size of the standard error is affected by two values. The first is the standard deviation of the population. The larger the population standard deviation, σ, the larger $\sigma/\sqrt{n}$. If the population is homogenous, resulting in a small population standard deviation, the standard error will also be small. However, the standard error is also affected by the number of observations in the sample. A large number of observations in the sample will result in a small standard error of estimate, indicating that there is less variability in the sample means.

To explain these ideas, consider the following example. Del Monte Foods distributes diced peaches in 4-ounce plastic cups. To be sure each cup contains at least the

required amount Del Monte sets the filling operation to dispense 4.01 ounces of peaches and gel in each cup. So 4.01 is the population mean. Of course not every cup will contain exactly 4.01 ounces of peaches and gel. Some cups will have more and others less. Suppose the standard deviation of the process is .02 ounces. Let's also assume that the process follows the normal probability distribution. Now, we select a random sample of 16 cups and determine the sample mean. It is 4.015 ounces of peaches and gel. The 95 percent confidence interval for the population mean of this particular sample is:

$$4.015 \pm 1.96(.02/\sqrt{16}) = 4.015 \pm .0098$$

The 95 percent confidence interval is between 4.0052 and 4.0248. Of course in this case we observe that the population mean of 4.01 ounces is in this interval. But that will not always be the case. Theoretically, if we selected 100 samples of 16 cups from the population, calculated the sample mean, and developed a confidence interval based on each *sample* mean, we would expect to find the *population* mean in about 95 of the 100 intervals.

We can summarize the following calculations for a 95 percent confidence interval in the following formula:

$$\bar{X} \pm 1.96 \frac{\sigma}{\sqrt{n}}$$

Similarly a 99 percent confidence interval is computed as follows.

$$\bar{X} \pm 2.58 \frac{\sigma}{\sqrt{n}}$$

As we discussed earlier, the values 1.96 and 2.58 are z values corresponding to the middle 95 percent and the middle 99 percent of the observations, respectively.

We are not restricted to the 95 and 99 percent levels of confidence. We can select any confidence level between 0 and 100 percent and find the corresponding value for z. In general, a confidence interval for the population mean when the population standard deviation is known is computed by:

LO3 Construct a confidence interval for the population mean when the population standard deviation is known.

CONFIDENCE INTERVAL FOR POPULATION MEAN WITH σ KNOWN	$\bar{X} \pm z \dfrac{\sigma}{\sqrt{n}}$	[9–1]

where z depends on the level of confidence. Thus for a 92 percent level of confidence, the value of z in formula (9–1) is 1.75. The value of z is from Appendix B.1. This table is based on half the normal distribution, so .9200/2 = .4600. The closest value in the body of the table is .4599 and the corresponding z value is 1.75.

Frequently, we also use the 90 percent level of confidence. In this case, we want the area between 0 and z to be .4500, found by .9000/2. To find the z value for this level of confidence, move down the left column of Appendix B.1 to 1.6 and then over to the columns headed 0.04 and 0.05. The area corresponding to a z value of 1.64 is .4495, and for 1.65 it is .4505. To be conservative, we use 1.65. Try looking up the following levels of confidence and check your answers with the corresponding z values given on the right.

Confidence Level	Nearest Half Probability	z Value
80 percent	.3997	1.28
94 percent	.4699	1.88
96 percent	.4798	2.05

The following example shows the details for calculating a confidence interval and interpreting the result.

Example

The American Retail Managers Association wishes to have information on the mean income of store managers in the retail industry. A random sample of 256 managers reveals a sample mean of $75,420. The standard deviation of this population is $2,050. The association would like answers to the following questions:

1. What is the population mean?
2. What is a reasonable range of values for the population mean?
3. How do we interpret these results?

Solution

Generally, distributions of salary and income are positively skewed, because a few individuals earn considerably more than others, thus skewing the distribution in the positive direction. Fortunately, the central limit theorem stipulates that if we select a large sample, the distribution of the sample means will follow the normal distribution. In this instance, a sample of 256 store managers is large enough that we can assume that the sampling distribution will follow the normal distribution. Now to answer the questions posed in the example.

1. **What is the population mean?** In this case, we do not know. We do know the sample mean is $75,420. Hence, our best estimate of the unknown population value is the corresponding sample statistic. Thus the sample mean of $75,420 is a *point estimate* of the unknown population mean.

2. **What is a reasonable range of values for the population mean?** The association decides to use the 95 percent level of confidence. To determine the corresponding confidence interval we use formula (9–1).

$$\bar{X} \pm z\frac{\sigma}{\sqrt{n}} = \$75{,}420 \pm 1.96\frac{\$2{,}050}{\sqrt{256}} = \$75{,}420 \pm \$251$$

The usual practice is to round these endpoints to \$75,169 and \$75,671. These endpoints are called the *confidence limits*. The degree of confidence or the *level of confidence* is 95 percent and the confidence interval is from \$75,169 to \$75,671. The ±\$251 is often referred to as the *margin of error*.

3. **How do we interpret these results?** Suppose we select many samples of 256 store managers, perhaps several hundred. For each sample, we compute the mean and then construct a 95 percent confidence interval, such as we did in the previous section. We could expect about 95 percent of these confidence intervals to contain the *population* mean. About 5 percent of the intervals would not contain the population mean annual income, which is μ. However, a particular confidence interval either contains the population parameter or it does not. The following diagram shows the results of selecting samples from the population of store managers in the retail industry, computing the mean of each and then, using formula (9–1), determining a 95 percent confidence interval for the population mean. Note that not all intervals include the population mean. Both the endpoints of the fifth sample are less than the population mean. We attribute this to sampling error, and it is the risk we assume when we select the level of confidence.

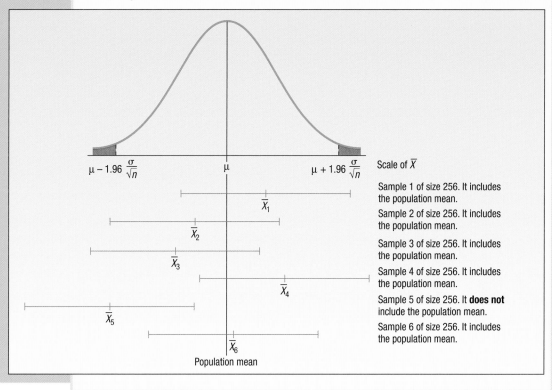

A Computer Simulation

With the aid of a computer, we can randomly select samples from a population, quickly compute the confidence interval, and show how confidence intervals usually, but not always, include the population parameter. The following example will help to explain.

Example

From many years in the automobile leasing business, Town Bank knows the mean distance driven on a four-year lease is 50,000 miles and the standard deviation is 5,000. These are population values. Suppose, using the MINITAB statistical software system, we want to find what proportion of the 95 percent confidence intervals will include the population mean of 50. To make the calculations easier to understand, we'll conduct the study in thousands of miles, instead of miles. We select 60 random samples of 30 observations from a population with a mean of 50 and a standard deviation of 5.

Solution

The results of 60 random samples of 30 automobiles each are summarized in the computer output below. Of the 60 confidence intervals with a 95 percent confidence level, 2, or 3.33 percent, did not include the population mean of 50. The intervals (C3 and C59) that do *not* include the population mean are highlighted. 3.33 percent is close to the estimate that 5 percent of the intervals will not include the population mean, and the 58 of 60, or 96.67 percent, is close to 95 percent.

To explain the first calculation in more detail: MINITAB began by selecting a random sample of 30 observations from a population with a mean of 50 and a standard deviation of 5. The mean of these 30 observations is 50.053. The sampling error is 0.053, found by $\bar{X} - \mu = 50.053 - 50.000$. The endpoints of the confidence interval are 48.264 and 51.842. These endpoints are determined by using formula (9–1):

$$\bar{X} \pm 1.96\,\frac{\sigma}{\sqrt{n}} = 50.053 \pm 1.96\,\frac{5}{\sqrt{30}} = 50.053 \pm 1.789$$

```
One-Sample Z:

The assumed sigma = 5

Variable      N      Mean     StDev     SE Mean        95.0% CI
C1           30     50.053    5.002      0.913     ( 48.264, 51.842)
C2           30     49.025    4.450      0.913     ( 47.236, 50.815)
C3           30     52.023    5.918      0.913     ( 50.234, 53.812)
C4           30     50.056    3.364      0.913     ( 48.267, 51.845)
C5           30     49.737    4.784      0.913     ( 47.948, 51.526)
C6           30     51.074    5.495      0.913     ( 49.285, 52.863)
C7           30     50.040    5.930      0.913     ( 48.251, 51.829)
C8           30     48.910    3.645      0.913     ( 47.121, 50.699)
C9           30     51.033    4.918      0.913     ( 49.244, 52.822)
C10          30     50.692    4.571      0.913     ( 48.903, 52.482)
C11          30     49.853    4.525      0.913     ( 48.064, 51.642)
C12          30     50.286    3.422      0.913     ( 48.497, 52.076)
C13          30     50.257    4.317      0.913     ( 48.468, 52.046)
C14          30     49.605    4.994      0.913     ( 47.816, 51.394)
C15          30     51.474    5.497      0.913     ( 49.685, 53.264)
C16          30     48.930    5.317      0.913     ( 47.141, 50.719)
C17          30     49.870    4.847      0.913     ( 48.081, 51.659)
C18          30     50.739    6.224      0.913     ( 48.950, 52.528)
C19          30     50.979    5.520      0.913     ( 49.190, 52.768)
C20          30     48.848    4.130      0.913     ( 47.059, 50.638)
C21          30     49.481    4.056      0.913     ( 47.692, 51.270)
C22          30     49.183    5.409      0.913     ( 47.394, 50.973)
C23          30     50.084    4.522      0.913     ( 48.294, 51.873)
C24          30     50.866    5.142      0.913     ( 49.077, 52.655)
C25          30     48.768    5.582      0.913     ( 46.979, 50.557)
C26          30     50.904    6.052      0.913     ( 49.115, 52.694)
C27          30     49.481    5.535      0.913     ( 47.691, 51.270)
C28          30     50.949    5.916      0.913     ( 49.160, 52.739)
C29          30     49.106    4.641      0.913     ( 47.317, 50.895)
C30          30     49.994    5.853      0.913     ( 48.205, 51.784)
C31          30     49.601    5.064      0.913     ( 47.811, 51.390)
C32          30     51.494    5.597      0.913     ( 49.705, 53.284)
C33          30     50.460    4.393      0.913     ( 48.671, 52.249)
C34          30     50.378    4.075      0.913     ( 48.589, 52.167)
C35          30     49.808    4.155      0.913     ( 48.019, 51.597)
C36          30     49.934    5.012      0.913     ( 48.145, 51.723)
```

Variable	N	Mean	StDev	SE Mean	95.0% CI
C37	30	50.017	4.082	0.913	(48.228, 51.806)
C38	30	50.074	3.631	0.913	(48.285, 51.863)
C39	30	48.656	4.833	0.913	(46.867, 50.445)
C40	30	50.568	3.855	0.913	(48.779, 52.357)
C41	30	50.916	3.775	0.913	(49.127, 52.705)
C42	30	49.104	4.321	0.913	(47.315, 50.893)
C43	30	50.308	5.467	0.913	(48.519, 52.097)
C44	30	49.034	4.405	0.913	(47.245, 50.823)
C45	30	50.399	4.729	0.913	(48.610, 52.188)
C46	30	49.634	3.996	0.913	(47.845, 51.424)
C47	30	50.479	4.881	0.913	(48.689, 52.268)
C48	30	50.529	5.173	0.913	(48.740, 52.318)
C49	30	51.577	5.822	0.913	(49.787, 53.366)
C50	30	50.403	4.893	0.913	(48.614, 52.192)
C51	30	49.717	5.218	0.913	(47.927, 51.506)
C52	30	49.796	5.327	0.913	(48.007, 51.585)
C53	30	50.549	4.680	0.913	(48.760, 52.338)
C54	30	50.200	5.840	0.913	(48.410, 51.989)
C55	30	49.138	5.074	0.913	(47.349, 50.928)
C56	30	49.667	3.843	0.913	(47.878, 51.456)
C57	30	49.603	5.614	0.913	(47.814, 51.392)
C58	30	49.441	5.702	0.913	(47.652, 51.230)
C59	30	47.873	4.685	0.913	(46.084, 49.662)
C60	30	51.087	5.162	0.913	(49.297, 52.876)

Self-Review 9–1

The Bun-and-Run is a franchise fast-food restaurant located in the Northeast specializing in half-pound hamburgers, fish sandwiches, and chicken sandwiches. Soft drinks and french fries are also available. The Planning Department of Bun-and-Run, Inc., reports that the distribution of daily sales for restaurants follows the normal distribution and that the standard deviation is $3,000. A sample of 40 restaurants showed the mean daily sales to be $20,000.
(a) What is the population mean?
(b) What is the best estimate of the population mean? What is this value called?
(c) Develop a 99 percent confidence interval for the population mean.
(d) Interpret the confidence interval.

Exercises

1. A sample of 49 observations is taken from a normal population with a standard deviation of 10. The sample mean is 55. Determine the 99 percent confidence interval for the population mean.
2. A sample of 81 observations is taken from a normal population with a standard deviation of 5. The sample mean is 40. Determine the 95 percent confidence interval for the population mean.
3. A sample of 10 observations is selected from a normal population for which the population standard deviation is known to be 5. The sample mean is 20.
   a. Determine the standard error of the mean.
   b. Explain why we can use formula (9–1) to determine the 95 percent confidence interval even though the sample is less than 30.
   c. Determine the 95 percent confidence interval for the population mean.
4. Suppose you want an 85 percent confidence level. What value would you use to multiply the standard error of the mean by?
5. A research firm conducted a survey to determine the mean amount steady smokers spend on cigarettes during a week. They found the distribution of amounts spent per week followed the normal distribution with a standard deviation of $5. A sample of 49 steady smokers revealed that $\bar{X} = \$20$.
   a. What is the point estimate of the population mean? Explain what it indicates.

    b. Using the 95 percent level of confidence, determine the confidence interval for μ. Explain what it indicates.

6. Refer to the previous exercise. Suppose that 64 smokers (instead of 49) were sampled. Assume the sample mean remained the same.

    a. What is the 95 percent confidence interval estimate of μ?

    b. Explain why this confidence interval is narrower than the one determined in the previous exercise.

7. Bob Nale is the owner of Nale's Texaco GasTown. Bob would like to estimate the mean number of gallons of gasoline sold to his customers. Assume the number of gallons sold follows the normal distribution with a standard deviation of 2.30 gallons. From his records, he selects a random sample of 60 sales and finds the mean number of gallons sold is 8.60.

    a. What is the point estimate of the population mean?

    b. Develop a 99 percent confidence interval for the population mean.

    c. Interpret the meaning of part (b).

8. Dr. Patton is a professor of English. Recently she counted the number of misspelled words in a group of student essays. She noted the distribution of misspelled words per essay followed the normal distribution with a standard deviation of 2.44 words per essay. For her 10 A.M. section of 40 students, the mean number of misspelled words was 6.05. Construct a 95 percent confidence interval for the mean number of misspelled words in the population of student essays.

Population Standard Deviation, σ Unknown

In the previous section we assumed the population standard deviation was known. In the case involving Del Monte 4-ounce cups of peaches and gel in each cup, there would likely be a long history of measurements in the filling process. Therefore, it is reasonable to assume the standard deviation of the population is available. However, in most sampling situations the population standard deviation (σ) is not known. Here are some examples where we wish to estimate the population means and it is unlikely we would know the population standard deviations. Suppose each of these studies involves students at West Virginia University.

- The Dean of the Business College wants to estimate the mean number of hours full-time students work at paying jobs each week. He selects a sample of 30 students, contacts each student and asks them how many hours they worked last week. From the sample information he can calculate the sample mean, but it is not likely he would know or be able to find the *population* (σ) standard deviation required in formula (9–1). He could calculate the standard deviation of the sample and use that as an estimate, but he would not likely know the population standard deviation.

- The Dean of Students wants to estimate the distance the typical commuter student travels to class. She selects a sample of 40 commuter students, contacts each, and determines the one-way distance from each student's home to the center of campus. From the sample data she calculates the mean travel distance, that is $\overline{X}$. It is unlikely the standard deviation of the population would be known or available, again making formula (9–1) unusable.

- The Director of Student Loans wants to know the mean amount owed on student loans at the time of his/her graduation. The director selects a sample of 20 graduating students and contacts each to find the information. From the sample information he can estimate the mean amount. However, to develop a confidence interval using formula (9–1), the population standard deviation is necessary. It is not likely this information is available.

Fortunately we can use the sample standard deviation to estimate the population standard deviation. That is, we use s, the sample standard deviation, to estimate σ, the population standard deviation. But in doing so, we cannot use formula

(9–1). Because we do not know σ we cannot use the z distribution. However, there is a remedy. We use the sample standard deviation and replace the z distribution with the t distribution.

The t distribution is a continuous probability distribution, with many similar characteristics to the z distribution. William Gosset, an English brewmaster, was the first to study the t distribution.

He was particularly concerned with the exact behavior of the distribution of the following statistic:

$$t = \frac{\overline{X} - \mu}{s/\sqrt{n}}$$

where s is an estimate of σ. He was especially worried about the discrepancy between s and σ when s was calculated from a very small sample. The t distribution and the standard normal distribution are shown graphically in Chart 9–1. Note particularly that the t distribution is flatter, more spread out, than the standard normal distribution. This is because the standard deviation of the t distribution is larger than the standard normal distribution.

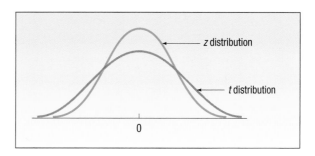

CHART 9–1 The Standard Normal Distribution and Student's t Distribution

The following characteristics of the t distribution are based on the assumption that the population of interest is normal, or nearly normal.

1.   It is, like the z distribution, a continuous distribution.
2.   It is, like the z distribution, bell-shaped and symmetrical.
3.   There is not one t distribution, but rather a family of t distributions. All t distributions have a mean of 0, but their standard deviations differ according to the sample size, n. There is a t distribution for a sample size of 20, another for a sample size of 22, and so on. The standard deviation for a t distribution with 5 observations is larger than for a t distribution with 20 observations.
4.   The t distribution is more spread out and flatter at the center than the standard normal distribution (see Chart 9–1). As the sample size increases, however, the t distribution approaches the standard normal distribution, because the errors in using s to estimate σ decrease with larger samples.

Because Student's t distribution has a greater spread than the z distribution, the value of t for a given level of confidence is larger in magnitude than the corresponding z value. Chart 9–2 shows the values of z for a 95 percent level of confidence and of t for the same level of confidence when the sample size is $n = 5$. How we obtained the actual value of t will be explained shortly. For now, observe that for the same level of confidence the t distribution is flatter or more spread out than the standard normal distribution.

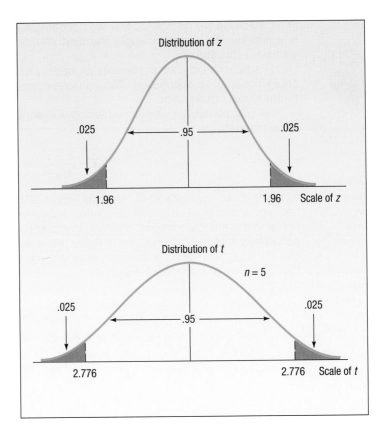

CHART 9–2 Values of z and t for the 95 Percent Level of Confidence

To develop a confidence interval for the population mean using the t distribution, we adjust formula (9–1) as follows.

LO4 Construct a confidence interval for a population mean when the population standard deviation is unknown.

| CONFIDENCE INTERVAL FOR THE POPULATION MEAN, σ UNKNOWN | $\bar{X} \pm t \dfrac{s}{\sqrt{n}}$ | **[9–2]** |

To develop a confidence interval for the population mean with an unknown standard deviation we:

1. Assume the sampled population is either normal or approximately normal.
2. Estimate the population standard deviation (σ) with the sample standard deviation (s).
3. Use the t distribution rather than the z distribution.

We should be clear at this point. We base the decision on whether to use the t or the z on whether or not we know σ, the population standard deviation. If we know the population standard deviation, then we use z. If we do not know the population standard deviation, then we must use t. Chart 9–3 summarizes the decision-making process.

The following example will illustrate a confidence interval for a population mean when the population standard deviation is unknown and how to find the appropriate value of t in a table.

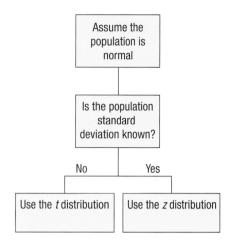

CHART 9–3 Determining When to Use the z Distribution or the t Distribution

Example

A tire manufacturer wishes to investigate the tread life of its tires. A sample of 10 tires driven 50,000 miles revealed a sample mean of 0.32 inch of tread remaining with a standard deviation of 0.09 inch. Construct a 95 percent confidence interval for the population mean. Would it be reasonable for the manufacturer to conclude that after 50,000 miles the population mean amount of tread remaining is 0.30 inches?

Solution

To begin, we assume the population distribution is normal. In this case, we don't have a lot of evidence, but the assumption is probably reasonable. We do not know the population standard deviation, but we know the sample standard deviation, which is .09 inches. We use formula (9–2):

$$\overline{X} \pm t \frac{s}{\sqrt{n}}$$

From the information given, $\overline{X} = 0.32$, $s = 0.09$, and $n = 10$. To find the value of t we use Appendix B.2, a portion of which is reproduced in Table 9–1. Appendix B.2 is also reproduced on the inside back cover of the text. The first step for locating t is to move across the columns identified for "Confidence Intervals" to the level of confidence requested. In this case we want the 95 percent level of confidence, so we move to the column headed "95%." The column on the left margin is identified as "df." This refers to the number of degrees of freedom. The number of degrees of freedom is the number of observations in the sample minus the number of samples, written $n - 1$. In this case it is $10 - 1 = 9$. Why did we decide there were 9 degrees of freedom? When sample statistics are being used, it is necessary to determine the number of values that are *free to vary*.

To illustrate the meaning of degrees of freedom: assume that the mean of four numbers is known to be 5. The four numbers are 7, 4, 1, and 8. The deviations of these numbers from the mean must total 0. The deviations of $+2$, -1, -4, and $+3$ do total 0. If the deviations of $+2$, -1, and -4 are known, then the value of $+3$ is fixed (restricted) in order to satisfy the condition that the sum of the deviations must equal 0. Thus, 1 degree of freedom is lost in a sampling problem involving the standard deviation of the sample because one number (the arithmetic mean) is known. For a 95 percent level of confidence and 9 degrees of freedom, we select the row with 9 degrees of freedom. The value of t is 2.262.

TABLE 9–1 A Portion of the t Distribution

	Confidence Intervals				
	80%	90%	95%	98%	99%
	Level of Significance for One-Tailed Test				
df	0.10	0.05	0.025	0.010	0.005
	Level of Significance for Two-Tailed Test				
	0.20	0.10	0.05	0.02	0.01
1	3.078	6.314	12.706	31.821	63.657
2	1.886	2.920	4.303	6.965	9.925
3	1.638	2.353	3.182	4.541	5.841
4	1.533	2.132	2.776	3.747	4.604
5	1.476	2.015	2.571	3.365	4.032
6	1.440	1.943	2.447	3.143	3.707
7	1.415	1.895	2.365	2.998	3.499
8	1.397	1.860	2.306	2.896	3.355
9	1.383	1.833	2.262	2.821	3.250
10	1.372	1.812	2.228	2.764	3.169

To determine the confidence interval we substitute the values in formula (9–2).

$$\bar{X} \pm t\frac{s}{\sqrt{n}} = 0.32 \pm 2.262\frac{0.09}{\sqrt{10}} = 0.32 \pm .064$$

The endpoints of the confidence interval are 0.256 and 0.384. How do we interpret this result? It is reasonable to conclude that the population mean is in this interval. The manufacturer can be reasonably sure (95 percent confident) that the mean remaining tread depth is between 0.256 and 0.384 inches. Because the value of 0.30 is in this interval, it is possible that the mean of the population is 0.30.

Here is another example to clarify the use of confidence intervals. Suppose an article in your local newspaper reported that the mean time to sell a residential property in the area is 60 days. You select a random sample of 20 homes sold in the last year and find the mean selling time is 65 days. Based on the sample data, you develop a 95 percent confidence interval for the population mean. You find that the endpoints of the confidence interval are 62 days and 68 days. How do you interpret this result? You can be reasonably confident the population mean is within this range. The value proposed for the population mean, that is, 60 days, is not included in the interval. It is not likely that the population mean is 60 days. The evidence indicates the statement by the local newspaper may not be correct. To put it another way, it seems unreasonable to obtain the sample you did from a population that had a mean selling time of 60 days.

The following example will show additional details for determining and interpreting a confidence interval. We used MINITAB to perform the calculations.

Example

The manager of the Inlet Square Mall, near Ft. Myers, Florida, wants to estimate the mean amount spent per shopping visit by customers. A sample of 20 customers reveals the following amounts spent.

$48.16	$42.22	$46.82	$51.45	$23.78	$41.86	$54.86
37.92	52.64	48.59	50.82	46.94	61.83	61.69
49.17	61.46	51.35	52.68	58.84	43.88	

What is the best estimate of the population mean? Determine a 95 percent confidence interval. Interpret the result. Would it be reasonable to conclude that the population mean is $50? What about $60?

Solution

The mall manager assumes that the population of the amounts spent follows the normal distribution. This is a reasonable assumption in this case. Additionally, the confidence interval technique is quite powerful and tends to commit any errors on the conservative side if the population is not normal. We should not make the normality assumption when the population is severely skewed or when the distribution has "thick tails."

The population standard deviation is not known. Hence, it is appropriate to use the t distribution and formula (9–2) to find the confidence interval. We use the MINITAB system to find the mean and standard deviation of this sample. The results are shown below.

9-Shopping.MTW ***		
↓	**C1**	C
	Amount	
3	46.82	
4	51.45	
5	23.78	
6	41.86	
7	54.86	
8	37.92	
9	52.64	
10	48.59	
11	50.82	
12	46.94	

Session

Descriptive Statistics: Amount

Variable	N	N*	Mean	SE Mean	StDev	Minimum	Q1	Median	Q3	Maximum
Amount	20	0	49.35	2.02	9.01	23.78	44.62	50.00	54.31	61.83

One-Sample T: Amount

Variable	N	Mean	StDev	SE Mean	95% CI
Amount	20	49.35	9.01	2.02	(45.13, 53.57)

The mall manager does not know the population mean. The sample mean is the best estimate of that value. From the pictured MINITAB output, the mean is $49.35, which is the best estimate, the *point estimate,* of the unknown population mean.

We use formula (9–2) to find the confidence interval. The value of t is available from Appendix B.2. There are $n - 1 = 20 - 1 = 19$ degrees of freedom. We move across the row with 19 degrees of freedom to the column for the 95 percent confidence level. The value at this intersection is 2.093. We substitute these values into formula (9–2) to find the confidence interval.

$$\bar{X} \pm t\frac{s}{\sqrt{n}} = \$49.35 \pm 2.093\frac{\$9.01}{\sqrt{20}} = \$49.35 \pm \$4.22$$

The endpoints of the confidence interval are $45.13 and $53.57. It is reasonable to conclude that the population mean is in that interval.

The manager of Inlet Square wondered whether the population mean could have been $50 or $60. The value of $50 is within the confidence interval. It is reasonable that the population mean could be $50. The value of $60 is not in the confidence interval. Hence, we conclude that the population mean is unlikely to be $60.

The calculations to construct a confidence interval are also available in Excel. The output follows. Note that the sample mean ($49.35) and the sample standard deviation ($9.01) are the same as those in the Minitab calculations. In the Excel information the last line of the output also includes the margin of error, which is the amount that is added and subtracted from the sample mean to form the endpoints of the confidence interval. This value is found from

$$t\frac{s}{\sqrt{n}} = 2.093\frac{\$9.01}{\sqrt{20}} = \$4.22.$$

	A	B	C	D	E
1	**Amount**		**Amount**		
2	48.16				
3	42.22		Mean	49.35	
4	46.82		Standard Error	2.02	
5	51.45		Median	50.00	
6	23.78		Mode	#N/A	
7	41.86		Standard Deviation	9.01	
8	54.86		Sample Variance	81.22	
9	37.92		Kurtosis	2.26	
10	52.64		Skewness	-1.00	
11	48.59		Range	38.05	
12	50.82		Minimum	23.78	
13	46.94		Maximum	61.83	
14	61.83		Sum	986.96	
15	61.69		Count	20.00	
16	49.17		Confidence Level(95.0%)	4.22	
17	61.46				
18	51.35				
19	52.68				
20	58.84				
21	43.88				
22					

Self-Review 9–2

Dottie Kleman is the "Cookie Lady." She bakes and sells cookies at 50 different locations in the Philadelphia area. Ms. Kleman is concerned about absenteeism among her workers. The information below reports the number of days absent for a sample of 10 workers during the last two-week pay period.

4	1	2	2	1	2	2	1	0	3

(a) Determine the mean and the standard deviation of the sample.
(b) What is the population mean? What is the best estimate of that value?
(c) Develop a 95 percent confidence interval for the population mean.
(d) Explain why the t distribution is used as a part of the confidence interval.
(e) Is it reasonable to conclude that the typical worker does not miss any days during a pay period?

Exercises

9. Use Appendix B.2 to locate the value of t under the following conditions.
 a. The sample size is 12 and the level of confidence is 95 percent.
 b. The sample size is 20 and the level of confidence is 90 percent.
 c. The sample size is 8 and the level of confidence is 99 percent.
10. Use Appendix B.2 to locate the value of t under the following conditions.
 a. The sample size is 15 and the level of confidence is 95 percent.
 b. The sample size is 24 and the level of confidence is 98 percent.
 c. The sample size is 12 and the level of confidence is 90 percent.
11. The owner of Britten's Egg Farm wants to estimate the mean number of eggs laid per chicken. A sample of 20 chickens shows they laid an average of 20 eggs per month with a standard deviation of 2 eggs per month.
 a. What is the value of the population mean? What is the best estimate of this value?
 b. Explain why we need to use the t distribution. What assumption do you need to make?
 c. For a 95 percent confidence interval, what is the value of t?
 d. Develop the 95 percent confidence interval for the population mean.

    e. Would it be reasonable to conclude that the population mean is 21 eggs? What about 25 eggs?

12. The American Sugar Producers Association wants to estimate the mean yearly sugar consumption. A sample of 16 people reveals the mean yearly consumption to be 60 pounds with a standard deviation of 20 pounds.

    a. What is the value of the population mean? What is the best estimate of this value?

    b. Explain why we need to use the *t* distribution. What assumption do you need to make?

    c. For a 90 percent confidence interval, what is the value of *t*?

    d. Develop the 90 percent confidence interval for the population mean.

    e. Would it be reasonable to conclude that the population mean is 63 pounds?

13. Taylor Industries and Caldwell Securities are two large employers in downtown Toledo, Ohio. They are considering jointly offering child care for their employees. As a part of the feasibility study, they wish to estimate the mean weekly child-care cost of their employees. A sample of 10 employees who use child care reveals the following amounts spent last week.

$107	$92	$97	$95	$105	$101	$91	$99	$95	$104

Develop a 90 percent confidence interval for the population mean. Interpret the result.

14. The Greater Pittsburgh Area Chamber of Commerce wants to estimate the mean time workers who are employed in the downtown area spend getting to work. A sample of 15 workers reveals the following number of minutes spent traveling.

29	38	38	33	38	21	45	34
40	37	37	42	30	29	35	

Develop a 98 percent confidence interval for the population mean. Interpret the result.

A Confidence Interval for a Proportion

The material presented so far in this chapter uses the ratio scale of measurement. That is, we use such variables as incomes, weights, distances, and ages. We now want to consider situations such as the following:

- The career services director at Southern Technical Institute reports that 80 percent of its graduates enter the job market in a position related to their field of study.
- A company representative claims that 45 percent of Burger King sales are made at the drive-through window.
- A survey of homes in the Chicago area indicated that 85 percent of the new construction had central air conditioning.
- A recent survey of married men between the ages of 35 and 50 found that 63 percent felt that both partners should earn a living.

These examples illustrate the nominal scale of measurement. When we measure with a nominal scale an observation is classified into one of two or more mutually exclusive groups. For example, a graduate of Southern Tech either entered the job market in a position related to his or her field of study or not. A particular Burger King customer either made a purchase at the drive-through window or did not make a purchase at the drive-through window. There are only two possibilities, and the outcome must be classified into one of the two groups.

Statistics in Action

Many survey results reported in newspapers, in news magazines, and on TV use confidence intervals. For example, a recent survey of 800 TV viewers in Toledo, Ohio, found 44 percent watched the evening news on the local CBS affiliate. The article went on to indicate the margin of error was 3.4 percent. The margin of error is actually the amount that is added and subtracted from the point estimate to find the endpoints of a confidence interval. From formula (9–4) and the 95 percent level of confidence:

$$z\sqrt{\frac{p(1-p)}{n}}$$

$$= 1.96\sqrt{\frac{.44(1-.44)}{800}}$$

$$= 0.034$$

> **PROPORTION** The fraction, ratio, or percent indicating the part of the sample or the population having a particular trait of interest.

As an example of a proportion, a recent survey indicated that 92 out of 100 surveyed favored the continued use of daylight savings time in the summer. The sample proportion is 92/100, or .92, or 92 percent. If we let p represent the sample proportion, X the number of "successes," and n the number of items sampled, we can determine a sample proportion as follows.

> **SAMPLE PROPORTION** $$p = \frac{X}{n}$$ [9–3]

The population proportion is identified by π. Therefore, π refers to the percent of successes in the population. Recall from Chapter 6 that π is the proportion of "successes" in a binomial distribution. This continues our practice of using Greek letters to identify population parameters and Roman letters to identify sample statistics.

To develop a confidence interval for a proportion, we need to meet the following assumptions.

1. The binomial conditions, discussed in Chapter 6, have been met. Briefly, these conditions are:
   a. The sample data is the result of counts.
   b. There are only two possible outcomes. (We usually label one of the outcomes a "success" and the other a "failure.")
   c. The probability of a success remains the same from one trial to the next.
   d. The trials are independent. This means the outcome on one trial does not affect the outcome on another.
2. The values $n\pi$ and $n(1 - \pi)$ should both be greater than or equal to 5. This condition allows us to invoke the central limit theorem and employ the standard normal distribution, that is, z, to complete a confidence interval.

Developing a point estimate for a population proportion and a confidence interval for a population proportion is similar to doing so for a mean. To illustrate, John Gail is running for Congress from the third district of Nebraska. From a random sample of 100 voters in the district, 60 indicate they plan to vote for him in the upcoming election. The sample proportion is .60, but the population proportion is unknown. That is, we do not know what proportion of voters in the *population* will vote for Mr. Gail. The sample value, .60, is the best estimate we have of the unknown population parameter. So we let p, which is .60, be an estimate of π, which is not known.

To develop a confidence interval for a population proportion, we use:

LO5 Construct a confidence interval for a population proportion.

> **CONFIDENCE INTERVAL FOR A POPULATION PROPORTION** $$p \pm z\sqrt{\frac{p(1-p)}{n}}$$ [9–4]

An example will help to explain the details of determining a confidence interval and the result.

Example

The union representing the Bottle Blowers of America (BBA) is considering a proposal to merge with the Teamsters Union. According to BBA union bylaws, at least three-fourths of the union membership must approve any merger. A random sample of 2,000 current BBA members reveals 1,600 plan to vote for the merger proposal. What is the estimate of the population proportion? Develop a 95 percent confidence interval for the population proportion. Basing your decision on this sample information, can you conclude that the necessary proportion of BBA members favor the merger? Why?

Solution

First, calculate the sample proportion from formula (9–3). It is .80, found by

$$p = \frac{X}{n} = \frac{1,600}{2,000} = .80$$

Thus, we estimate that 80 percent of the population favor the merger proposal. We determine the 95 percent confidence interval using formula (9–4). The z value corresponding to the 95 percent level of confidence is 1.96.

$$p \pm z \sqrt{\frac{p(1-p)}{n}} = .80 \pm 1.96 \sqrt{\frac{.80(1-.80)}{2,000}} = .80 \pm .018$$

The endpoints of the confidence interval are .782 and .818. The lower endpoint is greater than .75. Hence, we conclude that the merger proposal will likely pass because the interval estimate includes values greater than 75 percent of the union membership.

The interpretation of a confidence interval can be very useful in decision making and play a very important role especially on election night. For example, Cliff Obermeyer is running for Congress from the 6th District of New Jersey. Suppose 500 voters are contacted upon leaving the polls and 275 indicate they voted for Mr. Obermeyer. We will assume that the exit poll of 500 voters is a random sample of those voting in the 6th District. That means that 55 percent of those in the sample voted for Mr. Obermeyer. Based on formula (9–3):

$$p = \frac{X}{n} = \frac{275}{500} = .55$$

Now, to be assured of election, he must earn *more than* 50 percent of the votes in the population of those voting. At this point we know a point estimate, which is .55, of the population of voters that will vote for him. But we do not know the percent in the population that will vote for the candidate. So the question is could we take a sample of 500 voters from a population where 50 percent or less of the voters support Mr. Obermeyer and find that 55 percent of the sample support him? To put it another way, could the sampling error, which is $p - \pi = .55 - .50 = .05$ be due to chance, or is the population of voters who support Mr. Obermeyer greater than .50. If we develop a confidence interval for the sample proportion and find that .50 is *not* in the interval, then we conclude that the proportion of voters supporting Mr. Obermeyer is greater than .50. What does that mean? Well, it means he should be elected! What if .50 is in the interval? Then we conclude that it is possible that 50 percent or less of the voters support his candidacy and we cannot conclude that he will be elected based on the sample information. In this case using the 95 percent significance level and formula (9–4):

$$p \pm z \sqrt{\frac{p(1-p)}{n}} = .55 \pm 1.96 \sqrt{\frac{.55(1-.55)}{500}} = .55 \pm .044$$

So the endpoints of the confidence interval are $.55 - .044 = .506$ and $.55 + .044 = .594$. The value of .50 is not in this interval. So we conclude that probably *more than 50 percent* of the voters support Mr. Obermeyer and that is enough to get him elected.

Is this procedure ever used? Yes! It is exactly the procedure used by television networks, news magazines, and polling organizations on election night.

Self-Review 9–3

A market survey was conducted to estimate the proportion of homemakers who would recognize the brand name of a cleanser based on the shape and the color of the container. Of the 1,400 homemakers sampled, 420 were able to identify the brand by name.
(a) Estimate the value of the population proportion.
(b) Develop a 99 percent confidence interval for the population proportion.
(c) Interpret your findings.

Exercises

connect™

15. The owner of the West End Kwick Fill Gas Station wishes to determine the proportion of customers who use a credit card or debit card to pay at the pump. He surveys 100 customers and finds that 80 paid at the pump.
   a. Estimate the value of the population proportion.
   b. Develop a 95 percent confidence interval for the population proportion.
   c. Interpret your findings.
16. Ms. Maria Wilson is considering running for mayor of the town of Bear Gulch, Montana. Before completing the petitions, she decides to conduct a survey of voters in Bear Gulch. A sample of 400 voters reveals that 300 would support her in the November election.
   a. Estimate the value of the population proportion.
   b. Develop a 99 percent confidence interval for the population proportion.
   c. Interpret your findings.
17. The Fox TV network is considering replacing one of its prime-time crime investigation shows with a new family-oriented comedy show. Before a final decision is made, network executives commission a sample of 400 viewers. After viewing the comedy, 250 indicated they would watch the new show and suggested it replace the crime investigation show.
   a. Estimate the value of the population proportion.
   b. Develop a 99 percent confidence interval for the population proportion.
   c. Interpret your findings.
18. Schadek Silkscreen Printing, Inc., purchases plastic cups on which to print logos for sporting events, proms, birthdays, and other special occasions. Zack Schadek, the owner, received a large shipment this morning. To ensure the quality of the shipment, he selected a random sample of 300 cups. He found 15 to be defective.
   a. What is the estimated proportion defective in the population?
   b. Develop a 95 percent confidence interval for the proportion defective.
   c. Zack has an agreement with his supplier that he is to return lots that are 10 percent or more defective. Should he return this lot? Explain your decision.

Finite-Population Correction Factor

The populations we have sampled so far have been very large or infinite. What if the sampled population is not very large? We need to make some adjustments in the way we compute the standard error of the sample means and the standard error of the sample proportions.

A population that has a fixed upper bound is *finite*. For example, there are 12,179 students enrolled at Eastern Illinois University, there are 40 employees at Spence Sprockets, or there were 65 surgical patients at St. Rose Memorial Hospital in Sarasota yesterday. A finite population can be rather small; it could be all the students registered for this class. It can also be very large, such as all senior citizens living in Florida.

For a finite population, where the total number of objects or individuals is N and the number of objects or individuals in the sample is n, we need to adjust the standard errors in the confidence interval formulas. To put it another way, to find the confidence interval for the mean we adjust the standard error of the mean in formulas (9–1) and (9–2). If we are determining the confidence interval for a proportion, then we need to adjust the standard error of the proportion in formula (9–3).

This adjustment is called the **finite-population correction factor.** It is often shortened to *FPC* and is:

$$FPC = \sqrt{\frac{N-n}{N-1}}$$

Why is it necessary to apply a factor, and what is its effect? Logically, if the sample is a substantial percentage of the population, the estimate is more precise. Note the effect of the term $(N-n)/(N-1)$. Suppose the population is 1,000 and the sample is 100. Then this ratio is $(1{,}000-100)/(1{,}000-1)$, or 900/999. Taking the square root gives the correction factor, .9492. Multiplying this correction factor by the standard error *reduces* the standard error by about 5 percent $(1 - .9492 = .0508)$. This reduction in the size of the standard error yields a smaller range of values in estimating the population mean or the population proportion. If the sample is 200, the correction factor is .8949, meaning that the standard error has been reduced by more than 10 percent. Table 9–2 shows the effects of various sample sizes. Note that when the sample is less than about 5 percent of the population, the impact of the correction factor is quite small. The usual rule is if the ratio of n/N is less than .05, the correction factor is ignored.

TABLE 9–2 Finite-Population Correction Factor for Selected Samples When the Population Is 1,000

Sample Size	Fraction of Population	Correction Factor
10	.010	.9955
25	.025	.9879
50	.050	.9752
100	.100	.9492
200	.200	.8949
500	.500	.7075

So if we wished to develop a confidence interval for the mean from a finite population and the population standard deviation was unknown, we would adjust formula (9–2) as follows:

$$\bar{X} \pm t \frac{s}{\sqrt{n}} \left(\sqrt{\frac{N-n}{N-1}} \right)$$

We would make a similar adjustment to formula (9–3) in the case of a proportion.

The following example summarizes the steps to find a confidence interval for the mean.

Example

There are 250 families in Scandia, Pennsylvania. A random sample of 40 of these families revealed the mean annual church contribution was $450 and the standard deviation of this was $75. Could the population mean be $445 or $425?

1. What is the population mean? What is the best estimate of the population mean?
2. Discuss why the finite-population correction factor should be used.

3. Develop a 90 percent confidence interval for the population mean. What are the endpoints of the confidence interval?
4. Interpret the confidence interval.

Solution

First, note the population is finite. That is, there is a limit to the number of people in Scandia, in this case 250.

1. We do not know the population mean. This is the value we wish to estimate. The best estimate we have of the population mean is the sample mean, which is $450.
2. The sample is 16 percent of the population, found by $n/N = 40/250 = .16$. Because the sample constitutes more than .05 of the population, we should use the *FPC* to adjust the standard error in determining the confidence interval.
3. The formula to find the confidence interval for a population mean follows.

$$\bar{X} \pm t \frac{s}{\sqrt{n}} \left(\sqrt{\frac{N-n}{N-1}} \right)$$

In this case we know $\bar{X} = 450$, $s = 75$, $N = 250$, and that $n = 40$. We do not know the population standard deviation so we use the *t* distribution. To find the appropriate value of *t* we use Appendix B.2, and move across the top row to the column headed 90 percent. The degrees of freedom is $df = n - 1 = 40 - 1 = 39$, so we move to the cell where the *df* row of 39 intersects with the column headed 90 percent. The value is 1.685. Inserting these values in the formula:

$$\bar{X} \pm t \frac{s}{\sqrt{n}} \left(\sqrt{\frac{N-n}{N-1}} \right)$$

$$= \$450 \pm 1.685 \frac{\$75}{\sqrt{40}} \left(\sqrt{\frac{250-40}{250-1}} \right) = \$450 \pm \$19.98\sqrt{.8434} = \$450 \pm \$18.35$$

The endpoints of the confidence interval are $431.65 and $468.35.
4. It is likely that the population mean is more than $431.65 but less than $468.35. To put it another way, could the population mean be $445? Yes, but it is not likely that it is $425. Why is this so? Because the value $445 is within the confidence interval and $425 is not within the confidence interval.

Self-Review 9–4

The same study of church contributions in Scandia revealed that 15 of the 40 families sampled attend church regularly. Construct the 95 percent confidence interval for the proportion of families attending church regularly. Should the finite-population correction factor be used? Why or why not?

Exercises

connect

19. Thirty-six items are randomly selected from a population of 300 items. The sample mean is 35 and the sample standard deviation 5. Develop a 95 percent confidence interval for the population mean.
20. Forty-nine items are randomly selected from a population of 500 items. The sample mean is 40 and the sample standard deviation 9. Develop a 99 percent confidence interval for the population mean.
21. The attendance at the Savannah Colts minor league baseball game last night was 400. A random sample of 50 of those in attendance revealed that the mean number of soft

drinks consumed per person was 1.86 with a standard deviation of 0.50. Develop a 99 percent confidence interval for the mean number of soft drinks consumed per person.

22. There are 300 welders employed at Maine Shipyards Corporation. A sample of 30 welders revealed that 18 graduated from a registered welding course. Construct the 95 percent confidence interval for the proportion of all welders who graduated from a registered welding course.

Choosing an Appropriate Sample Size

A concern that usually arises when designing a statistical study is how many items should be in the sample. If a sample is too large, money is wasted collecting the data. Similarly, if the sample is too small, the resulting conclusions will be uncertain. The necessary sample size depends on three factors:

1. The level of confidence desired.
2. The margin of error the researcher will tolerate.
3. The variability in the population being studied.

The first factor is the *level of confidence*. Those conducting the study select the level of confidence. The 95 percent and the 99 percent levels of confidence are the most common, but any value between 0 and 100 percent is possible. The 95 percent level of confidence corresponds to a z value of 1.96, and a 99 percent level of confidence corresponds to a z value of 2.58. The higher the level of confidence selected, the larger the size of the corresponding sample.

The second factor is the *allowable error*. The maximum allowable error, designated as E, is the amount that is added and subtracted to the sample mean (or sample proportion) to determine the endpoints of the confidence interval. It is the amount of error those conducting the study are willing to tolerate. It is also one-half the width of the corresponding confidence interval. A small allowable error will require a larger sample. A large allowable error will permit a smaller sample.

The third factor in determining the size of a sample is the *population standard deviation*. If the population is widely dispersed, a large sample is required. On the other hand, if the population is concentrated (homogeneous), the required sample size will be smaller. However, it may be necessary to use an estimate for the population standard deviation. Here are three suggestions for finding that estimate.

1. **Use a comparable study.** Use this approach when there is an estimate of the dispersion available from another study. Suppose we want to estimate the number of hours worked per week by refuse workers. Information from certain state or federal agencies who regularly sample the workforce might be useful to provide an estimate of the standard deviation. If a standard deviation observed in a previous study is thought to be reliable, it can be used in the current study to help provide an approximate sample size.

2. **Use a range-based approach.** To use this approach we need to know or have an estimate of the largest and smallest values in the population. Recall from Chapter 3, where we described the Empirical Rule, that virtually all the observations could be expected to be within plus or minus 3 standard deviations of the mean, assuming that the distribution follows the normal distribution. Thus, the distance between the largest and the smallest values is 6 standard deviations. We could estimate the standard deviation as one-sixth of the range. For example, the director of operations at University Bank wants an estimate of the number of checks written per month by college students. She believes that the distribution of the number of checks written follows the normal distribution. The minimum number written per month is 2 and 50 is the most. The range of the number of checks written per month is 48, found by 50 − 2. The estimate of the standard deviation then would be 8 checks per month, 48/6.

3. **Conduct a pilot study.** This is the most common method. Suppose we want an estimate of the number of hours per week worked by students enrolled in

the College of Business at the University of Texas. To test the validity of our questionnaire, we use it on a small sample of students. From this small sample we compute the standard deviation of the number of hours worked and use this value to determine the appropriate sample size.

We can express the interaction among these three factors and the sample size in the following formula.

$$E = z \frac{\sigma}{\sqrt{n}}$$

Solving this equation for n yields the following result.

LO6 Determine the required sample size for either an attribute or a variable.

| SAMPLE SIZE FOR ESTIMATING THE POPULATION MEAN | $n = \left(\dfrac{z\sigma}{E}\right)^2$ | **[9–5]** |

where:
 n is the size of the sample.
 z is the standard normal value corresponding to the desired level of confidence.
 σ is the population standard deviation.
 E is the maximum allowable error.

The result of this calculation is not always a whole number. When the outcome is not a whole number, the usual practice is to round up *any* fractional result. For example, 201.22 would be rounded up to 202.

Example

A student in public administration wants to determine the mean amount members of city councils in large cities earn per month as remuneration for being a council member. The error in estimating the mean is to be less than $100 with a 95 percent level of confidence. The student found a report by the Department of Labor that estimated the standard deviation to be $1,000. What is the required sample size?

Solution

The maximum allowable error, E, is $100. The value of z for a 95 percent level of confidence is 1.96, and the estimate of the standard deviation is $1,000. Substituting these values into formula (9–5) gives the required sample size as:

$$n = \left(\frac{z\sigma}{E}\right)^2 = \left(\frac{(1.96)(\$1,000)}{\$100}\right)^2 = (19.6)^2 = 384.16$$

The computed value of 384.16 is rounded up to 385. A sample of 385 is required to meet the specifications. If the student wants to increase the level of confidence, for example to 99 percent, this will require a larger sample. The z value corresponding to the 99 percent level of confidence is 2.58.

$$n = \left(\frac{z\sigma}{E}\right)^2 = \left(\frac{(2.58)(\$1,000)}{\$100}\right)^2 = (25.8)^2 = 665.64$$

We recommend a sample of 666. Observe how much the change in the confidence level changed the size of the sample. An increase from the 95 percent to the 99 percent level of confidence resulted in an increase of 281 observations. This could greatly increase the cost of the study, both in terms of time and money. Hence, the level of confidence should be considered carefully.

The procedure just described can be adapted to determine the sample size for a proportion. Again, three items need to be specified:

1. The desired level of confidence.
2. The margin of error in the population proportion.
3. An estimate of the population proportion.

The formula to determine the sample size of a proportion is:

SAMPLE SIZE FOR THE POPULATION PROPORTION	$n = p(1 - p)\left(\dfrac{z}{E}\right)^2$	[9–6]

If an estimate of p is available from a pilot study or some other source, it can be used. Otherwise, .50 is used because the term $p(1 - p)$ can never be larger than when $p = .50$. For example, if $p = .30$, then $p(1 - p) = .3(1 - .3) = .21$, but when $p = .50$, $p(1 - p) = .5(1 - .5) = .25$

Example

The study in the previous example also estimates the proportion of cities that have private refuse collectors. The student wants the margin of error to be within .10 of the population proportion, the desired level of confidence is 90 percent, and no estimate is available for the population proportion. What is the required sample size?

Solution

The estimate of the population proportion is to be within .10, so $E = .10$. The desired level of confidence is .90, which corresponds to a z value of 1.65. Because no estimate of the population proportion is available, we use .50. The suggested number of observations is

$$n = (.5)(1 - .5)\left(\frac{1.65}{.10}\right)^2 = 68.0625$$

The student needs a random sample of 69 cities.

Self-Review 9–5

The registrar wants to estimate the arithmetic mean grade point average (GPA) of all graduating seniors during the past 10 years. GPAs range between 2.0 and 4.0. The mean GPA is to be estimated within plus or minus .05 of the population mean. The standard deviation is estimated to be 0.279. Use the 99 percent level of confidence. Will you assist the college registrar in determining how many transcripts to study?

Exercises

connect

23. A population is estimated to have a standard deviation of 10. We want to estimate the population mean within 2, with a 95 percent level of confidence. How large a sample is required?

24. We want to estimate the population mean within 5, with a 99 percent level of confidence. The population standard deviation is estimated to be 15. How large a sample is required?

25. The estimate of the population proportion is to be within plus or minus .05, with a 95 percent level of confidence. The best estimate of the population proportion is .15. How large a sample is required?

26. The estimate of the population proportion is to be within plus or minus .10, with a 99 percent level of confidence. The best estimate of the population proportion is .45. How large a sample is required?

27. A survey is being planned to determine the mean amount of time corporation executives watch television. A pilot survey indicated that the mean time per week is 12 hours, with a standard deviation of 3 hours. It is desired to estimate the mean viewing time within one-quarter hour. The 95 percent level of confidence is to be used. How many executives should be surveyed?

28. A processor of carrots cuts the green top off each carrot, washes the carrots, and inserts six to a package. Twenty packages are inserted in a box for shipment. To test the weight of the boxes, a few were checked. The mean weight was 20.4 pounds, the standard deviation 0.5 pounds. How many boxes must the processor sample to be 95 percent confident that the sample mean does not differ from the population mean by more than 0.2 pound?

29. Suppose the U.S. president wants an estimate of the proportion of the population who support his current policy toward revisions in the Social Security system. The president wants the estimate to be within .04 of the true proportion. Assume a 95 percent level of

confidence. The president's political advisors estimated the proportion supporting the current policy to be .60.

   a. How large a sample is required?

   b. How large a sample would be necessary if no estimate were available for the proportion supporting current policy?

30. Past surveys reveal that 30 percent of tourists going to Las Vegas to gamble during a weekend spend more than $1,000. Management wants to update this percentage.

   a. The new study is to use the 90 percent confidence level. The estimate is to be within 1 percent of the population proportion. What is the necessary sample size?

   b. Management said that the sample size determined above is too large. What can be done to reduce the sample? Based on your suggestion recalculate the sample size.

Chapter Summary

I. A point estimate is a single value (statistic) used to estimate a population value (parameter).

II. A confidence interval is a range of values within which the population parameter is expected to occur.

  A. The factors that determine the width of a confidence interval for a mean are:

    1. The number of observations in the sample, n.

    2. The variability in the population, usually estimated by the sample standard deviation, s.

    3. The level of confidence.

      a. To determine the confidence limits when the population standard deviation is known we use the z distribution. The formula is

$$\bar{X} \pm z \frac{\sigma}{\sqrt{n}} \qquad \text{[9–1]}$$

      b. To determine the confidence limits when the population standard deviation is unknown we use the t distribution. The formula is

$$\bar{X} \pm t \frac{s}{\sqrt{n}} \qquad \text{[9–2]}$$

III. The major characteristics of the t distribution are:

  A. It is a continuous distribution.

  B. It is mound-shaped and symmetrical.

  C. It is flatter, or more spread out, than the standard normal distribution.

  D. There is a family of t distributions, depending on the number of degrees of freedom.

IV. A proportion is a ratio, fraction, or percent that indicates the part of the sample or population that has a particular characteristic.

  A. A sample proportion is found by X, the number of successes, divided by n, the number of observations.

  B. We construct a confidence interval for a sample proportion from the following formula.

$$p \pm z \sqrt{\frac{p(1 - p)}{n}} \qquad \text{[9–4]}$$

V. For a finite population, the standard error is adjusted by the factor $\sqrt{\dfrac{N - n}{N - 1}}$.

VI. We can determine an appropriate sample size for estimating both means and proportions.

  A. There are three factors that determine the sample size when we wish to estimate the mean.

    1. The desired level of confidence, which is usually expressed by z.

    2. The maximum allowable error, E.

    3. The variation in the population, expressed by s.

    4. The formula to determine the sample size for the mean is

$$n = \left(\frac{z\sigma}{E} \right)^2 \qquad \text{[9–5]}$$

B. There are three factors that determine the sample size when we wish to estimate a proportion.
1. The desired level of confidence, which is usually expressed by *z*.
2. The maximum allowable error, *E*.
3. An estimate of the population proportion. If no estimate is available, use .50.
4. The formula to determine the sample size for a proportion is

$$n = p(1 - p)\left(\frac{z}{E}\right)^2 \qquad \textbf{[9–6]}$$

Chapter Exercises

connect™

31. A random sample of 85 group leaders, supervisors, and similar personnel at General Electric revealed that, on the average, they spent 6.5 years on the job before being promoted. The standard deviation of the sample was 1.7 years. Construct a 95 percent confidence interval.

32. A state meat inspector in Iowa has been given the assignment of estimating the mean net weight of packages of ground chuck labeled "3 pounds." Of course, he realizes that the weights cannot be precisely 3 pounds. A sample of 36 packages reveals the mean weight to be 3.01 pounds, with a standard deviation of 0.03 pounds.
    a. What is the estimated population mean?
    b. Determine a 95 percent confidence interval for the population mean.

33. A recent study of 50 self-service gasoline stations in the Greater Cincinnati–Northern Kentucky metropolitan area revealed that the mean price of unleaded gas was $2.029 per gallon. The sample standard deviation was $0.03 per gallon.
    a. Determine a 99 percent confidence interval for the population mean price.
    b. Would it be reasonable to conclude that the population mean was $1.50? Why or why not?

34. A recent survey of 50 executives who were laid off from their previous position revealed it took a mean of 26 weeks for them to find another position. The standard deviation of the sample was 6.2 weeks. Construct a 95 percent confidence interval for the population mean. Is it reasonable that the population mean is 28 weeks? Justify your answer.

35. Marty Rowatti recently assumed the position of director of the YMCA of South Jersey. He would like some current data on how long current members of the YMCA have been members. To investigate, suppose he selects a random sample of 40 current members. The mean length of membership of those included in the sample is 8.32 years and the standard deviation is 3.07 years.
    a. What is the mean of the population?
    b. Develop a 90 percent confidence interval for the population mean.
    c. The previous director, in the summary report she prepared as she retired, indicated the mean length of membership was now "almost 10 years." Does the sample information substantiate this claim? Cite evidence.

36. The American Restaurant Association collected information on the number of meals eaten outside the home per week by young married couples. A survey of 60 couples showed the sample mean number of meals eaten outside the home was 2.76 meals per week, with a standard deviation of 0.75 meals per week. Construct a 97 percent confidence interval for the population mean.

37. The National Collegiate Athletic Association (NCAA) reported that the mean number of hours spent per week on coaching and recruiting by college football assistant coaches during the season was 70. A random sample of 50 assistant coaches showed the sample mean to be 68.6 hours, with a standard deviation of 8.2 hours.
    a. Using the sample data, construct a 99 percent confidence interval for the population mean.
    b. Does the 99 percent confidence interval include the value suggested by the NCAA? Interpret this result.
    c. Suppose you decided to switch from a 99 to a 95 percent confidence interval. Without performing any calculations, will the interval increase, decrease, or stay the same? Which of the values in the formula will change?

38. The Human Relations Department of Electronics, Inc., would like to include a dental plan as part of the benefits package. The question is: How much does a typical employee and his or her family spend per year on dental expenses? A sample of 45 employees reveals the mean amount spent last year was $1,820, with a standard deviation of $660.

a. Construct a 95 percent confidence interval for the population mean.
b. The information from part (a) was given to the president of Electronics, Inc. He indicated he could afford $1,700 of dental expenses per employee. Is it possible that the population mean could be $1,700? Justify your answer.

39. A student conducted a study and reported that the 95 percent confidence interval for the mean ranged from 46 to 54. He is sure the sample mean was 50 and that the population standard deviation was 16, but cannot remember the sample size. Can you help him out?

40. A recent study by the American Automobile Dealers Association revealed the mean amount of profit per car sold for a sample of 20 dealers was $290, with a standard deviation of $125. Develop a 95 percent confidence interval for the population mean.

41. A study of 25 graduates of four-year colleges by the American Banker's Association revealed the mean amount owed by a student in student loans was $14,381. The standard deviation of the sample was $1,892. Construct a 90 percent confidence interval for the population mean. Is it reasonable to conclude that the mean of the population is actually $15,000? Tell why or why not.

42. An important factor in selling a residential property is the number of people who look through the home. A sample of 15 homes recently sold in the Buffalo, New York, area revealed the mean number looking through each home was 24 and the standard deviation of the sample was 5 people. Develop a 98 percent confidence interval for the population mean.

43. Warren County Telephone Company claims in its annual report that "the typical customer spends $60 per month on local and long-distance service." A sample of 12 subscribers revealed the following amounts spent last month.

$64	$66	$64	$66	$59	$62	$67	$61	$64	$58	$54	$66

a. What is the point estimate of the population mean?
b. Develop a 90 percent confidence interval for the population mean.
c. Is the company's claim that the "typical customer" spends $60 per month reasonable? Justify your answer.

44. The manufacturer of a new line of ink-jet printers would like to include as part of its advertising the number of pages a user can expect from a print cartridge. A sample of 10 cartridges revealed the following number of pages printed.

2,698	2,028	2,474	2,395	2,372	2,475	1,927	3,006	2,334	2,379

a. What is the point estimate of the population mean?
b. Develop a 95 percent confidence interval for the population mean.

45. Dr. Susan Benner is an industrial psychologist. She is currently studying stress among executives of Internet companies. She has developed a questionnaire that she believes measures stress. A score above 80 indicates stress at a dangerous level. A random sample of 15 executives revealed the following stress level scores.

94	78	83	90	78	99	97	90	97	90	93	94	100	75	84

a. Find the mean stress level for this sample. What is the point estimate of the population mean?
b. Construct a 95 percent confidence level for the population mean.
c. Is it reasonable to conclude that Internet executives have a mean stress level in the dangerous level, according to Dr. Benner's test?

46. As a condition of employment, Fashion Industries applicants must pass a drug test. Of the last 220 applicants 14 failed the test. Develop a 99 percent confidence interval for the proportion of applicants that fail the test. Would it be reasonable to conclude that more than 10 percent of the applicants are now failing the test? In addition to the testing of applicants, Fashion Industries randomly tests its employees throughout the year. Last year in the 400 random tests conducted, 14 employees failed the test. Would it be reasonable to conclude that less than 5 percent of the employees are not able to pass the random drug test?

47. There are 20,000 eligible voters in York County, South Carolina. A random sample of 500 York County voters revealed 350 plan to vote to return Louella Miller to the state senate. Construct a 99 percent confidence interval for the proportion of voters in the county who plan to vote for Ms. Miller. From this sample information, can you confirm she will be re-elected?

48. In a poll to estimate presidential popularity, each person in a random sample of 1,000 voters was asked to agree with one of the following statements:

1. The president is doing a good job.

2. The president is doing a poor job.

3. I have no opinion.

A total of 560 respondents selected the first statement, indicating they thought the president was doing a good job.

a. Construct a 95 percent confidence interval for the proportion of respondents who feel the president is doing a good job.

b. Based on your interval in part (a), is it reasonable to conclude that a majority (more than half) of the population believes the president is doing a good job?

49. Police Chief Edward Wilkin of River City reports 500 traffic citations were issued last month. A sample of 35 of these citations showed the mean amount of the fine was $54, with a standard deviation of $4.50. Construct a 95 percent confidence interval for the mean amount of a citation in River City.

50. The First National Bank of Wilson has 650 checking account customers. A recent sample of 50 of these customers showed 26 to have a Visa card with the bank. Construct the 99 percent confidence interval for the proportion of checking account customers who have a Visa card with the bank.

51. It is estimated that 60 percent of U.S. households subscribe to cable TV. You would like to verify this statement for your class in mass communications. If you want your estimate to be within 5 percentage points, with a 95 percent level of confidence, how large of a sample is required?

52. You need to estimate the mean number of travel days per year for outside salespeople. The mean of a small pilot study was 150 days, with a standard deviation of 14 days. If you must estimate the population mean within 2 days, how many outside salespeople should you sample? Use the 90 percent confidence level.

53. You are to conduct a sample survey to determine the mean family income in a rural area of central Florida. The question is, how many families should be sampled? In a pilot sample of 10 families, the standard deviation of the sample was $500. The sponsor of the survey wants you to use the 95 percent confidence level. The estimate is to be within $100. How many families should be interviewed?

54. *Families USA,* a monthly magazine that discusses issues related to health and health costs, surveyed 20 of its subscribers. It found that the annual health insurance premiums for a family with coverage through an employer averaged $10,979. The standard deviation of the sample was $1,000.

a. Based on this sample information, develop a 90 percent confidence interval for the population mean yearly premium.

b. How large a sample is needed to find the population mean within $250 at 99 percent confidence?

55. Passenger comfort is influenced by the amount of pressurization in an airline cabin. Higher pressurization permits a closer-to-normal environment and a more relaxed flight. A study by an airline user group recorded the corresponding air pressure on 30 randomly chosen flights. The study revealed a mean equivalent pressure of 8,000 feet with a standard deviation of 300 feet.

a. Develop a 99 percent confidence interval for the population mean equivalent pressure.

b. How large a sample is needed to find the population mean within 25 feet at 95 percent confidence?

56. A random sample of 25 people employed by the Florida state authority established they earned an average wage (including benefits) of $65.00 per hour. The sample standard deviation was $6.25 per hour.

a. What is the population mean? What is the best estimate of the population mean?

b. Develop a 99 percent confidence interval for the population mean wage (including benefits) for these employees.

c. How large a sample is needed to assess the population mean with an allowable error of $1.00 at 95 percent confidence?

57. A film alliance used a random sample of 50 U.S. citizens to estimate that the typical American spent 78 hours watching videos and DVDs last year. The standard deviation of this sample was 9 hours.

a. Develop a 95 percent confidence interval for the population mean number of hours spent watching videos and DVDs last year.

b. How large a sample should be used to be 90 percent confident the sample mean is within 1.0 hour of the population mean?

58. Dylan Jones kept careful records of the fuel efficiency of his new car. After the first nine times he filled up the tank, he found the mean was 23.4 miles per gallon (mpg) with a sample standard deviation of 0.9 mpg.
   a. Compute the 95 percent confidence interval for his mpg.
   b. How many times should he fill his gas tank to obtain a margin of error below 0.1 mpg?

59. A survey of 36 randomly selected "iPhone" owners showed that the purchase price has a mean of $416 with a sample standard deviation of $180.
   a. Compute the standard error of the sample mean.
   b. Compute the 95 percent confidence interval for the mean.
   c. How large a sample is needed to estimate the population mean within $10?

60. You plan to conduct a survey to find what proportion of the workforce has two or more jobs. You decide on the 95 percent confidence level and state that the estimated proportion must be within 2 percent of the population proportion. A pilot survey reveals that 5 of the 50 sampled hold two or more jobs. How many in the workforce should be interviewed to meet your requirements?

61. The proportion of public accountants who have changed companies within the last three years is to be estimated within 3 percent. The 95 percent level of confidence is to be used. A study conducted several years ago revealed that the percent of public accountants changing companies within three years was 21.
   a. To update this study, the files of how many public accountants should be studied?
   b. How many public accountants should be contacted if no previous estimates of the population proportion are available?

62. Huntington National Bank, like most other large banks, found that using automatic teller machines (ATMs) reduces the cost of routine bank transactions. Huntington installed an ATM in the corporate offices of Fun Toy Company. The ATM is for the exclusive use of Fun's 605 employees. After several months of operation, a sample of 100 employees revealed the following use of the ATM machine by Fun employees in a month.

Number of Times ATM Used	Frequency
0	25
1	30
2	20
3	10
4	10
5	5

   a. What is the estimate of the proportion of employees who do not use the ATM in a month?
   b. Develop a 95 percent confidence interval for this estimate. Can Huntington be sure that at least 40 percent of the employees of Fun Toy Company will use the ATM?
   c. How many transactions does the average Fun employee make per month?
   d. Develop a 95 percent confidence interval for the mean number of transactions per month.
   e. Is it possible that the population mean is .7? Explain.

63. In a recent Zogby poll of 1,000 adults nationwide, 613 said they believe other forms of life exist elsewhere in the universe. Construct the 99 percent confidence interval for the population proportion of those believing life exists elsewhere in the universe. Does your result imply that a majority of Americans believe life exists outside of Earth?

64. As part of an annual review of its accounts, a discount brokerage selects a random sample of 36 customers. Their accounts are reviewed for total account valuation, which showed a mean of $32,000, with a sample standard deviation of $8,200. What is a 90 percent confidence interval for the mean account valuation of the population of customers?

65. The National Weight Control Registry tries to mine secrets of success from people who have lost at least 30 pounds and kept it off for at least a year. It reports that out of 2,700 registrants 459 were on low-carbohydrate diets (less than 90 grams a day).
   a. Develop a 95 percent confidence interval for this fraction.
   b. Is it possible that the population percentage is 18 percent?
   c. How large a sample is needed to estimate the proportion within 0.5 percent?

66. Near the time of an election, a cable news service performs an opinion poll of 1,000 probable voters. It shows that the Republican contender has an advantage of 52 percent to 48 percent.

   a. Develop a 95 percent confidence interval for the proportion favoring the Republican candidate.
   b. Estimate the probability that the Democratic candidate is actually leading.
   c. Repeat the above analysis based on a sample of 3,000 probable voters.
67. A sample of 352 subscribers to *Wired* magazine shows the mean time spent using the Internet is 13.4 hours per week, with a sample standard deviation of 6.8 hours. Find the 95 percent confidence interval for the mean time *Wired* subscribers spend on the Internet.
68. The Tennessee Tourism Institute (TTI) plans to sample information center visitors entering the state to learn the fraction of visitors who plan to camp in the state. Current estimates are that 35 percent of visitors are campers. How large a sample would you take to estimate at a 95 percent confidence level the population proportion with an allowable error of 2 percent?

Data Set Exercises

69. Refer to the Real Estate data, which report information on the homes sold in Phoenix, Arizona, last year.
   a. Develop a 95 percent confidence interval for the mean selling price of the homes.
   b. Develop a 95 percent confidence interval for the mean distance the home is from the center of the city.
   c. Develop a 95 percent confidence interval for the proportion of homes with an attached garage.
70. Refer to the Baseball 2008 data, which report information on the 30 Major League Baseball teams for the 2008 season.
   a. Develop a 95 percent confidence interval for the mean number of home runs per team.
   b. Develop a 95 percent confidence interval for the mean number of errors committed by each team.
   c. Develop a 95 percent confidence interval for the mean number of stolen bases for each team.
71. Refer to the Wage data, which report information on annual wages for a sample of 100 workers. Also included are variables relating to industry, years of education, and gender for each worker.
   a. Develop a 95 percent confidence interval for the mean wage of the workers. Is it reasonable to conclude that the population mean is $35,000?
   b. Develop a 95 percent confidence interval for the mean years of education. Is it reasonable to conclude that the population mean is 13 years?
   c. Develop a 95 percent confidence interval for the mean age of the workers. Could the mean age be 40 years?

Practice Test

Part I Objective

   1. A _____ is a single value computed from sample information used to estimate a population parameter.
   2. A _____ is a range of values within which the population parameter is likely to occur.
   3. Assuming the same sample size and the same standard deviation, a 90 percent confidence interval will be _____ than a 95 percent confidence interval. (equal to, wider, narrower, can't tell)
   4. A _____ shows the fraction of a sample that has a particular characteristic.
   5. For a 95 percent confidence interval, approximately _____ percent of the similarly constructed intervals will include the population parameter being estimated.
   6. To construct a confidence interval for a mean, the z distribution is used only when the population _____ is known.
   7. To develop a confidence interval for a proportion, the four conditions of the _____ must be met.
   8. The finite population correction factor is used when the sample is more than _____ percent of the population. (5, 20, 50, 100)
   9. The _____ has no effect on the size of the sample. (level of confidence, margin of error, size of the population, variability in the population)
   10. To locate the appropriate *t* value, which is not necessary? (degrees of freedom, level of confidence, population mean) _____

Part II Problems

1. A recent study of 26 Conway, South Carolina, residents revealed they had lived at their current address for a mean of 9.3 years with a sample standard deviation of 2 years.
   a. What is the population mean?
   b. What is the best estimate of the population mean?
   c. What is the standard error of the mean?
   d. Develop a 90 percent confidence interval for the population mean.
2. A recent federal report indicated 27 percent of children ages 2 to 5 ate vegetables at least five times a week. How large a sample is necessary to estimate the true population proportion within 2 percent with a 98 percent level of confidence? Be sure to use the evidence in the federal report.
3. The Philadelphia Regional Transport Authority wishes to estimate the proportion of central city workers that use public transportation to get to work. A sample of 100 workers revealed 64 used public transportation. Develop a 95 percent confidence interval.

Software Commands

1. The MINITAB commands for the 60 columns of 30 random numbers used in the example/solution on page 260 are:
   a. Select **Calc, Random Data,** and then click on **Normal.**
   b. From the dialog box click in the **Generate** box and type *30* for the number of rows of data, **Store in column(s)** is *C1-C60,* **Mean** is *50,* **Standard deviation** is *5.0,* and finally click **OK.**

2. The MINITAB commands for the 60 confidence intervals on page 260 follow.
   a. Select **Stat, Basic Statistics,** and then click on **1-Sample Z.**
   b. In the dialog box indicate that the **Variables** are *C1-C60* and that **Standard Duration** is *5.* Next, click on **Options** in the lower right corner, and in the next dialog box indicate that the **Confidence level** is *95,* and then click **OK.** Click **OK** in the main dialog box.
3. The MINITAB commands for the descriptive statistics on page 267 follow. Enter the data in the first column and label this column *Amount.* On the Toolbar select **Stat, Basic Statistics,** and **Display Descriptive Statistics.** In the dialog box select *Amount* as the **Variable** and click **OK.**

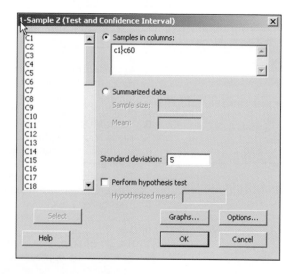

4. The MINITAB commands for the confidence interval for the amount spent at the Inlet Square Mall on page 267 are:
   a. Enter the 20 amounts spent in column *C1* and name the variable *Amount,* or locate the data on the student data disk. It is named **Shopping** and is found in the folder for Chapter 9.
   b. On the Toolbar select **Stat, Basic Statistics,** and click on **1-Sample t.**
   c. Select **Samples in columns:** and select **Amount** and click **OK.**

5. The Excel commands for the confidence interval for the amounts spent at the Inlet Square Mall on page 268 are:
   a. Select the **Data** tab on the top menu. Then, on the far right, select **Data Analysis,** and then **Descriptive Statistics** and click **OK.**
   b. For the **Input Range** type *A1:A21,* click on **Labels in first row,** type *C1* as the **Output Range,** click on **Summary statistics** and **Confidence Level for Mean,** and then on **OK.**

Chapter 9   Answers to Self-Review

9–1 a. Unknown. This is the value we wish to estimate.
   b. $20,000, point estimate.

   c. $20,000 \pm 2.58 \dfrac{\$3,000}{\sqrt{40}} = \$20,000 \pm \$1,224$

   d. The endpoints of the confidence interval are $18,776 and $21,224. About 99 percent of the intervals similarly constructed would include the population mean.

9–2 a. $\bar{X} = \dfrac{18}{10} = 1.8 \qquad s = \sqrt{\dfrac{11.6}{10-1}} = 1.1353$

   b. The population mean is not known. The best estimate is the sample mean, 1.8 days.

   c. $1.80 \pm 2.262 \dfrac{1.1353}{\sqrt{10}} = 1.80 \pm 0.81$

   The endpoints are 0.99 and 2.61
   d. *t* is used because the population standard deviation is unknown.
   e. The value of 0 is not in the interval. It is unreasonable to conclude that the mean

number of days of work missed is 0 per employee.

9–3 a. $p = \dfrac{420}{1,400} = .30$

   b. $.30 \pm 2.58(.0122) = .30 \pm .03$

   c. The interval is between .27 and .33. About 99 percent of the similarly constructed intervals would include the population mean.

9–4 $.375 \pm 1.96 \sqrt{\dfrac{.375(1-.375)}{40}} \sqrt{\dfrac{250-40}{250-1}} =$

   $.375 \pm 1.96(.0765)(.9184) = .375 \pm .138$

   The correction factor should be applied because $40/250 > .05$.

9–5 $n = \left(\dfrac{2.58(.279)}{.05}\right)^2 = 207.26$. The sample should be rounded to 208.

10

Learning Objectives

When you have completed this chapter you will be able to:

LO1 Define a *hypothesis* and *hypothesis testing*.

LO2 Describe the five-step hypothesis-testing procedure.

LO3 Distinguish between a *one-tailed* and a *two-tailed* test of hypothesis.

LO4 Conduct a test of hypothesis about a population mean.

LO5 Conduct a test of hypothesis about a population proportion.

LO6 Define *Type I* and *Type II* errors.

One-Sample Tests of Hypothesis

Dole Pineapple, Inc., is concerned that the 16-ounce can of sliced pineapple is being overfilled. Assume the standard deviation of the process is .03 ounces. The quality control department took a random sample of 50 cans and found that the arithmetic mean weight was 16.05 ounces. At the 5 percent level of significance, can we conclude that the mean weight is greater than 16 ounces? Determine the *p*-value. (Exercise 28, LO4)

Introduction

Chapter 8 began our study of statistical inference. We described how we could select a random sample and from this sample estimate the value of a population parameter. For example, we selected a sample of 5 employees at Spence Sprockets, found the number of years of service for each sampled employee, computed the mean years of service, and used the sample mean to estimate the mean years of service for all employees. In other words, we estimated a population parameter from a sample statistic.

Chapter 9 continued the study of statistical inference by developing a confidence interval. A confidence interval is a range of values within which we expect the population parameter to occur. In this chapter, rather than develop a range of values within which we expect the population parameter to occur, we develop a procedure to test the validity of a statement about a population parameter. Some examples of statements we might want to test are:

- The mean speed of automobiles passing milepost 150 on the West Virginia Turnpike is 68 miles per hour.
- The mean number of miles driven by those leasing a Chevy TrailBlazer for three years is 32,000 miles.
- The mean time an American family lives in a particular single-family dwelling is 11.8 years.
- The 2009 mean starting salary for a graduate of a four-year college with a degree in business administration is $46,973.
- Thirty-five percent of retirees in the upper Midwest sell their home and move to a warm climate within 1 year of their retirement.
- Eighty percent of those who regularly play the state lotteries never win more than $100 in any one play.

This chapter and several of the following chapters are concerned with statistical hypothesis testing. We begin by defining what we mean by a statistical hypothesis and statistical hypothesis testing. Next, we outline the steps in statistical hypothesis testing. Then we conduct tests of hypothesis for means and proportions. In the last section of the chapter, we describe possible errors due to sampling in hypothesis testing.

What Is a Hypothesis?

LO1 Define a *hypothesis* and *hypothesis testing*.

A hypothesis is a statement about a population. Data are then used to check the reasonableness of the statement. To begin we need to define the word *hypothesis*. In the United States legal system, a person is innocent until proven guilty. A jury hypothesizes that a person charged with a crime is innocent and subjects this hypothesis to verification by reviewing the evidence and hearing testimony before reaching a verdict. In a similar sense, a patient goes to a physician and reports various symptoms. On the basis of the symptoms, the physician will order certain diagnostic tests, then, according to the symptoms and the test results, determine the treatment to be followed.

A hypothesis is a statement about a population parameter.

In statistical analysis we make a claim, that is, state a hypothesis, collect data, then use the data to test the assertion. We define a statistical hypothesis as follows.

> **HYPOTHESIS** A statement about a population parameter subject to verification.

In most cases the population is so large that it is not feasible to study all the items, objects, or persons in the population. For example, it would not be possible to contact every systems analyst in the United States to find his or her monthly income. Likewise, the quality assurance department at Cooper Tire cannot check each tire produced to determine whether it will last more than 60,000 miles.

As noted in Chapter 8, an alternative to measuring or interviewing the entire population is to take a sample from the population. We can, therefore, test a statement to determine whether the sample does or does not support the statement concerning the population.

What Is Hypothesis Testing?

The terms *hypothesis testing* and *testing a hypothesis* are used interchangeably. Hypothesis testing starts with a statement, or assumption, about a population parameter—such as the population mean. As noted, this statement is referred to as a *hypothesis.* A hypothesis might be that the mean monthly commission of sales associates in retail electronics stores, such as Best Buy, is $2,000. We cannot contact all these sales associates to ascertain that the mean is in fact $2,000. The cost of locating and interviewing every electronics sales associate in the United States would be exorbitant. To test the validity of the assumption (μ = $2,000), we must select a sample from the population of all electronics sales associates, calculate sample statistics, and based on certain decision rules reject or do not reject the hypothesis. A sample mean of $1,000 for the electronics sales associates would certainly cause rejection of the hypothesis. However, suppose the sample mean is $1,995. Is that close enough to $2,000 for us to accept the assumption that the population mean is $2,000? Can we attribute the difference of $5 between the two means to sampling error, or is that difference statistically significant?

> **HYPOTHESIS TESTING** A procedure based on sample evidence and probability theory to determine whether the hypothesis is a reasonable statement.

Five-Step Procedure for Testing a Hypothesis

There is a five-step procedure that systematizes hypothesis testing; when we get to step 5, we are ready to reject or not reject the hypothesis. However, hypothesis testing as used by statisticians does not provide proof that something is true, in the manner in which a mathematician "proves" a statement. It does provide a kind of "proof beyond a reasonable doubt," in the manner of the court system. Hence, there are specific rules of evidence, or procedures, that are followed. The steps are shown in the following diagram. We will discuss in detail each of the steps.

Step 1: State the Null Hypothesis (H_0) and the Alternate Hypothesis (H_1)

LO2 Describe the five-step hypothesis-testing procedure.

The first step is to state the hypothesis being tested. It is called the **null hypothesis,** designated H_0, and read "*H sub zero.*" The capital letter H stands for hypothesis, and the subscript zero implies "no difference." There is usually a "not" or a "no" term in the null hypothesis, meaning that there is "no change." For example, the null hypothesis is that the mean number of miles driven on the steel-belted tire is not different from 60,000. The null hypothesis would be written H_0: $\mu = 60{,}000$. Generally speaking, the null hypothesis is developed for the purpose of testing. We either reject or fail to reject the null hypothesis. The null hypothesis is a statement that is not rejected unless our sample data provide convincing evidence that it is false.

We should emphasize that, if the null hypothesis is not rejected on the basis of the sample data, we cannot say that the null hypothesis is true. To put it another way, failing to reject the null hypothesis does not prove that H_0 is true, it means we have *failed to disprove* H_0. To prove without any doubt the null hypothesis is true, the population parameter would have to be known. To actually determine it, we would have to test, survey, or count every item in the population. This is usually not feasible. The alternative is to take a sample from the population.

State the null hypothesis and the alternative hypothesis.

We usually begin by stating the null hypothesis, such as "There is no *significant* difference between . . . ," or "The mean impact strength of the glass is not *significantly* different from. . . ." When we select a sample from a population, the sample statistic is usually numerically different from the hypothesized population parameter. As an illustration, suppose the hypothesized impact strength of a glass plate is 70 psi, and the mean impact strength of a sample of 12 glass plates is 69.5 psi. We must make a decision about the difference of 0.5 psi. Is it a true difference, that is, a significant difference, or is the difference between the sample statistic (69.5) and the hypothesized population parameter (70.0) due to chance (sampling)? As noted, to answer this question we conduct a test of significance, commonly referred to as a test of hypothesis. To define what is meant by a null hypothesis:

> **NULL HYPOTHESIS** A statement about the value of a population parameter developed for the purpose of testing numerical evidence.

The **alternate hypothesis** describes what you will conclude if you reject the null hypothesis. It is written H_1 and is read "*H sub one.*" It is also referred to as the research hypothesis. The alternate hypothesis is accepted if the sample data provide us with enough statistical evidence that the null hypothesis is false.

> **ALTERNATE HYPOTHESIS** A statement that is accepted if the sample data provide sufficient evidence that the null hypothesis is false.

The following example will help clarify what is meant by the null hypothesis and the alternate hypothesis. A recent article indicated the mean age of U.S. commercial aircraft is 15 years. To conduct a statistical test regarding this statement, the first step is to determine the null and the alternate hypotheses. The null hypothesis represents the current or reported condition. It is written H_0: $\mu = 15$. The alternate hypothesis is that the statement is not true, that is, H_1: $\mu \neq 15$. It is important to remember that no matter how the problem is stated, *the null hypothesis will always contain the equal sign.* The equal sign (=) will never appear in the alternate hypothesis. Why? Because the null hypothesis is the statement being tested, and we need a specific value to include in our calculations. We turn to the alternate hypothesis only if the data suggests the null hypothesis is untrue.

Step 2: Select a Level of Significance

After setting up the null hypothesis and alternate hypothesis, the next step is to state the level of significance.

> **LEVEL OF SIGNIFICANCE** The probability of rejecting the null hypothesis when it is true.

Select a level of significance or risk.

The level of significance is designated α, the Greek letter alpha. It is also sometimes called the level of risk. This may be a more appropriate term because it is the risk you take of rejecting the null hypothesis when it is really true.

There is no one level of significance that is applied to all tests. The .05 level (often stated as the 5 percent level), the .01 level, and the .10 level, are the most common levels of significance, but any value between 0 and 1 can be used. Traditionally, the .05 level is selected for consumer research projects, .01 for quality assurance, and .10 for political polling. You, the researcher, must decide on the level of significance *before* formulating a decision rule and collecting sample data.

To illustrate how it is possible to reject a true hypothesis, suppose a firm manufacturing personal computers uses a large number of printed circuit boards. Suppliers bid on the boards, and the one with the lowest bid is awarded a sizable contract. Suppose the contract specifies that the computer manufacturer's quality-assurance department will sample all incoming shipments of circuit boards. If more than 6 percent of the boards sampled are defective, the shipment is rejected. The null hypothesis is that the incoming shipment of boards contains 6 percent or less defective boards. The alternate hypothesis is that more than 6 percent of the boards are defective.

A sample of 50 circuit boards received July 21 from Allied Electronics revealed that 4 boards, or 8 percent, were defective. The shipment was rejected because it exceeded the maximum of 6 percent defective printed circuit boards. If the shipment actually failed to meet the criteria for acceptance, then the decision to return the boards to the supplier was correct. However, suppose the 4 defective printed circuit boards selected in the sample of 50 were the only ones in the shipment of 4,000 boards. Then only $\frac{1}{10}$ of 1 percent were defective (4/4,000 = .001). In that case, less than 6 percent of the entire shipment were defective, and rejecting the shipment was an error. In terms of hypothesis testing, we rejected the null hypothesis when we should have accepted the null hypothesis. By rejecting a true null hypothesis, we committed a Type I error. The probability of committing a Type I error is α.

> **TYPE I ERROR** Rejecting the null hypothesis, H_0, when it is true.

LO6 Define Type I and Type II errors.

The probability of committing another type of error, called a Type II error, is designated by the Greek letter beta (β).

> **TYPE II ERROR** Accepting the null hypothesis when it is false.

The firm manufacturing personal computers would commit a Type II error if, unknown to the manufacturer, an incoming shipment of printed circuit boards from Allied Electronics contained 15 percent substandard boards, yet the shipment was accepted. How could this happen? Suppose 2 of the 50 boards in the sample (4 percent) tested were defective, and 48 of the 50 were good boards. According to the stated procedure, because the sample contained less than 6 percent defective boards, the shipment was accepted. It could be that *by chance* the 48 good boards selected in the sample were the only acceptable ones in the entire shipment consisting of thousands of boards!

In retrospect, the researcher cannot study every item or individual in the population. Thus, there is a possibility of two types of error—a Type I error, wherein the null hypothesis is rejected when it should have been accepted, and a Type II error, wherein the null hypothesis is not rejected when it should have been rejected.

We often refer to the probability of these two possible errors as *alpha,* α, and *beta,* β. Alpha (α) is the probability of making a Type I error, and beta (β) is the probability of making a Type II error.

The following table summarizes the decisions the researcher could make and the possible consequences.

Null Hypothesis	Researcher	
	Does Not Reject H_0	Rejects H_0
H_0 is true	Correct decision	Type I error
H_0 is false	Type II error	Correct decision

Step 3: Select the Test Statistic

There are many test statistics. In this chapter we use both z and t as the test statistic. In later chapters we will use such test statistics as F and χ^2, called chi-square.

> **TEST STATISTIC** A value, determined from sample information, used to determine whether to reject the null hypothesis.

In hypothesis testing for the mean (μ) when σ is known, the test statistic z is computed by:

$$\text{TESTING A MEAN, } \sigma \text{ KNOWN} \qquad z = \frac{\overline{X} - \mu}{\sigma/\sqrt{n}} \qquad \textbf{[10–1]}$$

The z value is based on the sampling distribution of $\overline{X}$, which follows the normal distribution with a mean ($\mu_{\bar{x}}$) equal to μ, and a standard deviation $\sigma_{\bar{x}}$, which is equal to $\sigma/\sqrt{n}$. We can thus determine whether the difference between $\overline{X}$ and μ is statistically significant by finding the number of standard deviations $\overline{X}$ is from μ, using formula (10–1).

Step 4: Formulate the Decision Rule

The decision rule states the conditions when H_0 is rejected.

A decision rule is a statement of the specific conditions under which the null hypothesis is rejected and the conditions under which it is not rejected. The region or area of rejection defines the location of all those values that are so large or so small that the probability of their occurrence under a true null hypothesis is rather remote.

Chart 10–1 portrays the rejection region for a test of significance that will be conducted later in the chapter.

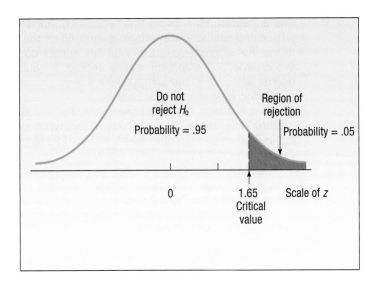

CHART 10–1 Sampling Distribution of the Statistic z, a Right-Tailed Test, .05 Level of Significance

Note in the chart that:

1. The area where the null hypothesis is not rejected is to the left of 1.65. We will explain how to get the 1.65 value shortly.
2. The area of rejection is to the right of 1.65.
3. A one-tailed test is being applied. (This will also be explained later.)
4. The .05 level of significance was chosen.
5. The sampling distribution of the statistic z follows the normal probability distribution.
6. The value 1.65 separates the regions where the null hypothesis is rejected and where it is not rejected.
7. The value 1.65 is the **critical value.**

> **CRITICAL VALUE** The dividing point between the region where the null hypothesis is rejected and the region where it is not rejected.

Step 5: Make a Decision

The fifth and final step in hypothesis testing is computing the test statistic, comparing it to the critical value, and making a decision to reject or not to reject the null hypothesis. Referring to Chart 10–1, if, based on sample information, z is computed to be 2.34, the null hypothesis is rejected at the .05 level of significance. The decision to reject H_0 was made because 2.34 lies in the region of rejection, that is, beyond 1.65. We would reject the null hypothesis, reasoning that it is highly improbable that a computed z value this large is due to sampling error (chance).

Had the computed value been 1.65 or less, say 0.71, the null hypothesis would not be rejected. It would be reasoned that such a small computed value could be attributed to chance, that is, sampling error.

As noted, only one of two decisions is possible in hypothesis testing—either accept or reject the null hypothesis. Instead of "accepting" the null hypothesis, H_0, some researchers prefer to phrase the decision as: "Do not reject H_0," "We fail to reject H_0," or "The sample results do not allow us to reject H_0."

It should be reemphasized that there is always a possibility that the null hypothesis is rejected when it should not be rejected (a Type I error). Also, there is a definable chance that the null hypothesis is accepted when it should be rejected (a Type II error).

> **SUMMARY OF THE STEPS IN HYPOTHESIS TESTING**
> 1. Establish the null hypothesis (H_0) and the alternate hypothesis (H_1).
> 2. Select the level of significance, that is α.
> 3. Select an appropriate test statistic.
> 4. Formulate a decision rule based on steps 1, 2, and 3 above.
> 5. Make a decision regarding the null hypothesis based on the sample information. Interpret the results of the test.

Before actually conducting a test of hypothesis, we will differentiate between a one-tailed test of significance and a two-tailed test.

One-Tailed and Two-Tailed Tests of Significance

LO3 Distinguish between a *one-tailed* and *a two-tailed test of hypothesis.*

Refer to Chart 10–1. It depicts a one-tailed test. The region of rejection is only in the right (upper) tail of the curve. To illustrate, suppose that the packaging department at General Foods Corporation is concerned that some boxes of Grape Nuts are significantly overweight. The cereal is packaged in 453-gram boxes, so the null hypothesis is H_0: $\mu \le 453$. This is read, "the population mean (μ) is equal to or less than 453." The alternate hypothesis is, therefore, H_1: $\mu > 453$. This is read, "μ is greater than 453." Note that the inequality sign in the alternate hypothesis ($>$) points to the region of rejection in the upper tail. (See Chart 10–1.) Also note that the null hypothesis includes the equal sign. That is, H_0: $\mu \le 453$. The equality condition always appears in H_0, never in H_1.

Chart 10–2 portrays a situation where the rejection region is in the left (lower) tail of the standard normal distribution. As an illustration, consider the problem of automobile manufacturers, large automobile leasing companies, and other organizations that purchase large quantities of tires. They want the tires to average, say, 60,000 miles of wear under normal usage. They will, therefore, reject a shipment of tires if tests reveal that the mean life of the tires is significantly below 60,000 miles. They gladly accept a shipment if the mean life is greater than 60,000 miles! They are not concerned with this possibility, however. They are concerned only if they have sample evidence to conclude that the tires will average less than 60,000 miles of useful life. Thus, the test is set up to satisfy the concern of the automobile manufacturers that *the mean life of*

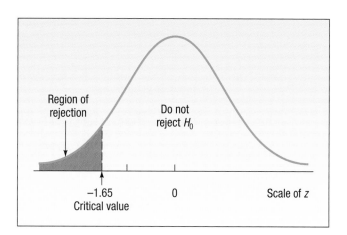

CHART 10–2 Sampling Distribution for the Statistic z, Left-Tailed Test, .05 Level of Significance

the tires is no less than 60,000 miles. This statement appears in the alternate hypothesis. The null and alternate hypotheses in this case are written:

Test is one-tailed if H_1 states $\mu >$ or $\mu <$.

$$H_0: \mu \geq 60,000$$
$$H_1: \mu < 60,000.$$

One way to determine the location of the rejection region is to look at the direction in which the inequality sign in the alternate hypothesis is pointing (either $<$ or $>$). In this problem it is pointing to the left, and the rejection region is therefore in the left tail.

If H_1 states a direction, test is one-tailed.

In summary, a test is *one-tailed* when the alternate hypothesis, H_1, states a direction, such as:

H_0: The mean income of women stockbrokers is *less than or equal to* $65,000 per year.
H_1: The mean income of women stockbrokers is *greater than* $65,000 per year.

If no direction is specified in the alternate hypothesis, we use a *two-tailed* test. Changing the previous problem to illustrate, we can say:

H_0: The mean income of women stockbrokers is $65,000 per year.
H_1: The mean income of women stockbrokers is *not equal to* $65,000 per year.

If the null hypothesis is rejected and H_1 accepted in the two-tailed case, the mean income could be significantly greater than $65,000 per year or it could be significantly less than $65,000 per year. To accommodate these two possibilities, the 5 percent area of rejection is divided equally into the two tails of the sampling distribution (2.5 percent each). Chart 10–3 shows the two areas and the critical values. Note that the total area in the normal distribution is 1.0000, found by .9500 + .0250 + .0250.

CHART 10–3 Regions of Nonrejection and Rejection for a Two-Tailed Test, .05 Level of Significance

Testing for a Population Mean: Known Population Standard Deviation

A Two-Tailed Test

LO4 Conduct a test of hypothesis about a population mean.

An example will show the details of the five-step hypothesis testing procedure. We also wish to use a two-tailed test. That is, we are *not* concerned whether the sample results are larger or smaller than the proposed population mean. Rather, we are interested in whether it is *different from* the proposed value for the population mean. We begin, as we did in the previous chapter, with a situation in which we have historical information about the population and in fact know its standard deviation.

Example

Jamestown Steel Company manufactures and assembles desks and other office equipment at several plants in western New York State. The weekly production of the Model A325 desk at the Fredonia Plant follows a normal probability distribution with a mean of 200 and a standard deviation of 16. Recently, because of market expansion, new production methods have been introduced and new employees hired. The vice president of manufacturing would like to investigate whether there has been a *change* in the weekly production of the Model A325 desk. Is the mean number of desks produced at the Fredonia Plant *different from* 200 at the .01 significance level?

Solution

We use the statistical hypothesis testing procedure to investigate whether the production rate has changed from 200 per week.

Step 1: State the null hypothesis and the alternate hypothesis. The null hypothesis is "The population mean is 200." The alternate hypothesis is "The mean is different from 200" or "The mean is not 200." These two hypotheses are written:

$$H_0: \mu = 200$$

$$H_1: \mu \neq 200$$

This is a *two-tailed test* because the alternate hypothesis does not state a direction. In other words, it does not state whether the mean production is greater than 200 or less than 200. The vice president wants only to find out whether the production rate is different from 200.

Step 2: Select the level of significance. As noted, the .01 level of significance is used. This is α, the probability of committing a Type I error, and it is the probability of rejecting a true null hypothesis.

Step 3: Select the test statistic. The test statistic for a mean when σ is known is z. It was discussed at length in Chapter 7. Transforming the production data to standard units (z values) permits their use not only in this problem but also in other hypothesis-testing problems. Formula (10–1) for z is repeated below with the various letters identified.

Formula for the test statistic

$$z = \frac{\bar{X} - \mu}{\sigma/\sqrt{n}} \quad [10\text{–}1]$$

Sample mean — Population mean

Standard deviation of population — Sample size

Step 4: Formulate the decision rule. The decision rule is formulated by finding the critical values of z from Appendix B.1. Since this is a two-tailed test, half of .01, or .005, is placed in each tail. The area where H_0 is not rejected, located between the two tails, is therefore .99. Appendix B.1 is based on half of the area under the curve, or .5000. Then, .5000 − .0050 is .4950, so .4950 is the area between 0 and the critical value. Locate .4950 in the body of the table. The value nearest to .4950 is .4951. Then read the critical value in the row and column corresponding to .4951. It is 2.58. For your convenience, Appendix B.1, Areas under the Normal Curve, is repeated in the inside back cover.

All the features of this problem are shown in the diagram in Chart 10–4.

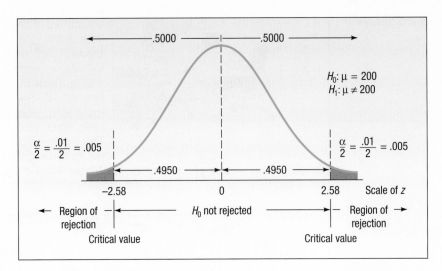

CHART 10–4 Decision Rule for the .01 Significance Level

The decision rule is, therefore: Reject the null hypothesis and accept the alternate hypothesis (which states that the population mean is not 200) if the computed value of z is not between -2.58 and $+2.58$. Do not reject the null hypothesis if z falls between -2.58 and $+2.58$.

Step 5: Make a decision and interpret the result. Take a sample from the population (weekly production), compute z, apply the decision rule, and arrive at a decision to reject H_0 or not to reject H_0. The mean number of desks produced last year (50 weeks, because the plant was shut down 2 weeks for vacation) is 203.5. The standard deviation of the population is 16 desks per week. Computing the z value from formula (10–1):

$$z = \frac{\overline{X} - \mu}{\sigma/\sqrt{n}} = \frac{203.5 - 200}{16/\sqrt{50}} = 1.55$$

Because 1.55 does not fall in the rejection region, H_0 is not rejected. We conclude that the population mean is *not* different from 200. So we would report to the vice president of manufacturing that the sample evidence does not show that the production rate at the Fredonia Plant has changed from 200 per week. The difference of 3.5 units between the historical weekly production rate and that last year can reasonably be attributed to sampling error. This information is summarized in the following chart.

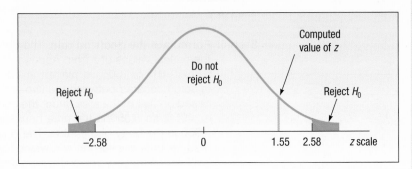

Did we prove that the assembly rate is still 200 per week? Not really. What we did, technically, was *fail to disprove the null hypothesis.* Failing to disprove the hypothesis that the population mean is 200 is not the same thing as proving it to be true. As we suggested in the chapter introduction, the conclusion is analogous to the American judicial system. To explain, suppose a person is accused of a crime but is acquitted by a jury. If a person is acquitted of a crime, the conclusion is that there was not enough evidence to prove the person guilty. The trial did not prove that the individual was innocent, only that there was not enough evidence to prove the defendant guilty. That is what we do in statistical hypothesis testing when we do not reject the null hypothesis. The correct interpretation is that we have failed to disprove the null hypothesis.

We selected the significance level, .01 in this case, before setting up the decision rule and sampling the population. This strategy is both ethical and fair. The significance level should be set by the investigator, but it should be determined *before* gathering the sample evidence and not changed based on the sample evidence.

Comparing confidence intervals and hypothesis testing.

How does the hypothesis testing procedure just described compare with that of confidence intervals discussed in the previous chapter? When we conducted the test of hypothesis regarding the production of desks we changed the units from desks per week to a z value. Then we compared the computed value of the test statistic (1.55) to that of the critical values (-2.58 and 2.58). Because the computed value was in the region where the null hypothesis was not rejected, we concluded that the population mean could be 200. To use the confidence interval approach, on the other hand, we would develop a confidence interval, based on formula (9–1). See page 258. The interval would be from 197.66 to 209.34, found by $203.5 \pm 2.58(16/\sqrt{50})$. Note that the proposed population value, 200, is within this interval. Hence, we would conclude that the population mean could reasonably be 200.

In general, H_0 is rejected if the confidence interval does not include the hypothesized value. If the confidence interval includes the hypothesized value, then H_0 is not rejected. So the "do not reject region" for a test of hypothesis is equivalent to the proposed population value occurring in the confidence interval. The primary difference between a confidence interval and the "do not reject" region for a hypothesis test is whether the interval is centered around the sample statistic, such as $\bar{X}$, as in the confidence interval, or around 0, as in the test of hypothesis.

Self-Review 10–1

Heinz, a manufacturer of ketchup, uses a particular machine to dispense 16 ounces of its ketchup into containers. From many years of experience with the particular dispensing machine, Heinz knows the amount of product in each container follows a normal distribution with a mean of 16 ounces and a standard deviation of 0.15 ounce. A sample of 50 containers filled last hour revealed the mean amount per container was 16.017 ounces. Does this evidence suggest that the mean amount dispensed is different from 16 ounces? Use the .05 significance level.

(a) State the null hypothesis and the alternate hypothesis.
(b) What is the probability of a Type I error?
(c) Give the formula for the test statistic.
(d) State the decision rule.
(e) Determine the value of the test statistic.
(f) What is your decision regarding the null hypothesis?
(g) Interpret, in a single sentence, the result of the statistical test.

A One-Tailed Test

In the previous example, we emphasized that we were concerned only with reporting to the vice president whether there had been a change in the mean number of desks assembled at the Fredonia Plant. We were not concerned with whether the change was an increase or a decrease in the production.

To illustrate a one-tailed test, let's change the problem. Suppose the vice president wants to know whether there has been an *increase* in the number of units assembled. Can we conclude, because of the improved production methods, that the mean number of desks assembled in the last 50 weeks was more than 200? Look at the difference in the way the problem is formulated. In the first case we wanted to know whether there was a *difference* in the mean number assembled, but now we want to know whether there has been an *increase*. Because we are investigating different questions, we will set our hypotheses differently. The biggest difference occurs in the alternate hypothesis. Before, we stated the alternate hypothesis as "different from"; now we want to state it as "greater than." In symbols:

A two–tailed test:

H_0: $\mu = 200$

H_1: $\mu \neq 200$

A one–tailed test:

H_0: $\mu \leq 200$

H_1: $\mu > 200$

The critical values for a one-tailed test are different from a two-tailed test at the same significance level. In the previous example, we split the significance level in half and put half in the lower tail and half in the upper tail. In a one-tailed test we put all the rejection region in one tail. See Chart 10–5.

For the one-tailed test, the critical value is 2.33, found by: (1) subtracting .01 from .5000 and (2) finding the z value corresponding to .4900.

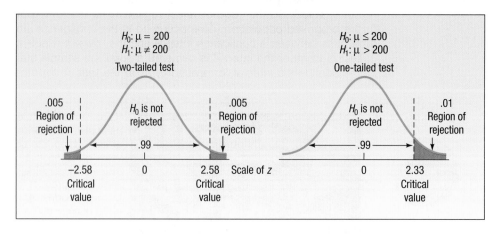

CHART 10–5 Rejection Regions for Two-Tailed and One-Tailed Tests, $\alpha = .01$

p-Value in Hypothesis Testing

In testing a hypothesis, we compare the test statistic to a critical value. A decision is made to either reject the null hypothesis or not to reject it. So, for example, if the critical value is 1.96 and the computed value of the test statistic is 2.19, the decision is to reject the null hypothesis.

In recent years, spurred by the availability of computer software, additional information is often reported on the strength of the rejection or acceptance. That is, how confident are we in rejecting the null hypothesis? This approach reports the probability (assuming that the null hypothesis is true) of getting a value of the test statistic at least as extreme as the value actually obtained. This process compares the probability, called the **p-value,** with the significance level. If the p-value is smaller than the significance level, H_0 is rejected. If it is larger than the significance level, H_0 is not rejected.

> **p-VALUE** The probability of observing a sample value as extreme as, or more extreme than, the value observed, given that the null hypothesis is true.

Determining the p-value not only results in a decision regarding H_0, but it gives us additional insight into the strength of the decision. A very small p-value, such as .0001, indicates that there is little likelihood the H_0 is true. On the other hand, a p-value of .2033 means that H_0 is not rejected, and there is little likelihood that it is false.

How do we compute the p-value? To illustrate we will use the example in which we tested the null hypothesis that the mean number of desks produced per week at Fredonia was 200. We did not reject the null hypothesis, because the z value of 1.55 fell in the region between −2.58 and 2.58. We agreed not to reject the null hypothesis if the computed value of z fell in this region. The probability of finding a z value of 1.55 or more is .0606, found by .5000 − .4394. To put it another way, the probability of obtaining an $\overline{X}$ greater than 203.5 if $\mu = 200$ is .0606. To compute the p-value, we need to be concerned with the region less than −1.55 as well as the values greater than 1.55 (because the rejection region is in both tails). The two-tailed p-value is .1212, found by 2(.0606). The p-value of .1212 is greater than the significance level of .01 decided upon initially, so H_0 is not rejected. The details are shown in the following graph. In general, the area is doubled in a two-sided test. Then the p-value can easily be compared with the significance level. The same decision rule is used as in the one-sided test.

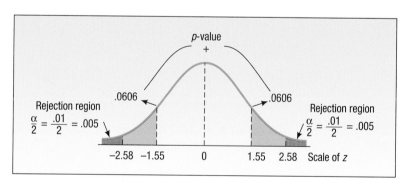

A p-value is a way to express the likelihood that H_0 is false. But how do we interpret a p-value? We have already said that if the p-value is less than the significance level, then we reject H_0; if it is greater than the significance level, then we do not reject H_0. Also, if the p-value is very large, then it is likely that H_0 is true. If the p-value is small, then it is likely that H_0 is not true. The following box will help to interpret p-values.

> **INTERPRETING THE WEIGHT OF EVIDENCE AGAINST H_0** If the p-value is less than
> (a) .10, we have *some* evidence that H_0 is not true.
> (b) .05, we have *strong* evidence that H_0 is not true.
> (c) .01, we have *very strong* evidence that H_0 is not true.
> (d) .001, we have *extremely strong* evidence that H_0 is not true.

Statistics in Action

There is a difference between *statistically significant* and *practically significant.* To explain, suppose we develop a new diet pill and test it on 100,000 people. We conclude that the typical person taking the pill for two years lost one pound. Do you think many people would be interested in taking the pill to lose one pound? The results of using the new pill were statistically significant but not practically significant.

Self-Review 10–2 Refer to Self-Review 10–1.
(a) Suppose the next to the last sentence is changed to read: Does this evidence suggest that the mean amount dispensed is *more than* 16 ounces? State the null hypothesis and the alternate hypothesis under these conditions.
(b) What is the decision rule under the new conditions stated in part (a)?
(c) A second sample of 50 filled containers revealed the mean to be 16.040 ounces. What is the value of the test statistic for this sample?
(d) What is your decision regarding the null hypothesis?
(e) Interpret, in a single sentence, the result of the statistical test.
(f) What is the *p*-value? What is your decision regarding the null hypothesis based on the *p*-value? Is this the same conclusion reached in part (d)?

Exercises

connect™

For Exercises 1–4 answer the questions: (a) Is this a one- or two-tailed test? (b) What is the decision rule? (c) What is the value of the test statistic? (d) What is your decision regarding H_0? (e) What is the *p*-value? Interpret it.

1. The following information is available.

$$H_0: \mu = 50$$
$$H_1: \mu \neq 50$$

The sample mean is 49, and the sample size is 36. The population standard deviation is 5. Use the .05 significance level.

2. The following information is available.

$$H_0: \mu \leq 10$$
$$H_1: \mu > 10$$

The sample mean is 12 for a sample of 36. The population standard deviation is 3. Use the .02 significance level.

3. A sample of 36 observations is selected from a normal population. The sample mean is 21, and the population standard deviation is 5. Conduct the following test of hypothesis using the .05 significance level.

$$H_0: \mu \leq 20$$
$$H_1: \mu > 20$$

4. A sample of 64 observations is selected from a normal population. The sample mean is 215, and the population standard deviation is 15. Conduct the following test of hypothesis using the .03 significance level.

$$H_0: \mu \geq 220$$
$$H_1: \mu < 220$$

For Exercises 5–8: (a) State the null hypothesis and the alternate hypothesis. (b) State the decision rule. (c) Compute the value of the test statistic. (d) What is your decision regarding H_0? (e) What is the *p*-value? Interpret it.

5. The manufacturer of the X-15 steel-belted radial truck tire claims that the mean mileage the tire can be driven before the tread wears out is 60,000 miles. The population standard deviation of the mileage is 5,000 miles. Crosset Truck Company bought 48 tires and found that the mean mileage for its trucks is 59,500 miles. Is Crosset's experience different from that claimed by the manufacturer at the .05 significance level?

6. The MacBurger restaurant chain claims that the mean waiting time of customers is 3 minutes with a population standard deviation of 1 minute. The quality-assurance department found in a sample of 50 customers at the Warren Road MacBurger that the mean waiting time was 2.75 minutes. At the .05 significance level, can we conclude that the mean waiting time is less than 3 minutes?

7. A recent national survey found that high school students watched an average (mean) of 6.8 DVDs per month with a population standard deviation of 0.5 hours. A random sample

of 36 college students revealed that the mean number of DVDs watched last month was 6.2. At the .05 significance level, can we conclude that college students watch fewer DVDs a month than high school students?

8. At the time she was hired as a server at the Grumney Family Restaurant, Beth Brigden was told, "You can average more than $80 a day in tips." Assume the standard deviation of the population distribution is $3.24. Over the first 35 days she was employed at the restaurant, the mean daily amount of her tips was $84.85. At the .01 significance level, can Ms. Brigden conclude that she is earning an average of more than $80 in tips?

Testing for a Population Mean: Population Standard Deviation Unknown

In the preceding example, we knew σ, the population standard deviation. In most cases, however, the population standard deviation is unknown. Thus, σ must be based on prior studies or estimated by the sample standard deviation, s. The population standard deviation in the following example is not known, so the sample standard deviation is used to estimate σ.

To find the value of the test statistic we use the t distribution and revise formula [10–1] as follows:

| TESTING A MEAN, σ UNKNOWN | $t = \dfrac{\overline{X} - \mu}{s/\sqrt{n}}$ | [10–2] |

with $n - 1$ degrees of freedom, where:

$\overline{X}$ is the sample mean.

μ is the hypothesized population mean.

s is the sample standard deviation.

n is the number of observations in the sample.

We encountered this same situation when constructing confidence intervals in the previous chapter. See pages 262–268 in Chapter 9. We summarized this problem in Chart 9–3 on page 265. Under these conditions the correct statistical procedure is to replace the standard normal distribution with the t distribution. To review, the major characteristics of the t distribution are:

1. It is a continuous distribution.
2. It is bell-shaped and symmetrical.
3. There is a family of t distributions. Each time the degrees of freedom change, a new distribution is created.
4. As the number of degrees of freedom increases the shape of the t distribution approaches that of the standard normal distribution.
5. The t distribution is flatter, or more spread out, than the standard normal distribution.

The following example shows the details.

Example

The McFarland Insurance Company Claims Department reports the mean cost to process a claim is $60. An industry comparison showed this amount to be larger than most other insurance companies, so the company instituted cost-cutting measures. To evaluate the effect of the cost-cutting measures, the Supervisor of the Claims Department selected a random sample of 26 claims processed last month. The sample information is reported on the next page.

$45	$49	$62	$40	$43	$61
48	53	67	63	78	64
48	54	51	56	63	69
58	51	58	59	56	57
38	76				

At the .01 significance level is it reasonable to conclude that mean cost to process a claim is now less than $60?

Solution

We will use the five-step hypothesis testing procedure.

Step 1: State the null hypothesis and the alternate hypothesis. The null hypothesis is that the population mean is at least $60. The alternate hypothesis is that the population mean is less than $60. We can express the null and alternate hypotheses as follows:

$$H_0: \mu \geq \$60$$

$$H_1: \mu < \$60$$

The test is *one*-tailed because we want to determine whether there has been a *reduction* in the cost. The inequality in the alternate hypothesis points to the region of rejection in the left tail of the distribution.

Step 2: Select the level of significance. We decided on the .01 significance level.

Step 3: Select the test statistic. The test statistic in this situation is the *t* distribution. Why? First it is reasonable to conclude that the distribution of the cost per claim follows the normal distribution. We can confirm this from the histogram in the center of the following MINITAB output. Observe the normal distribution superimposed on the frequency distribution.

We do not know the standard deviation of the population. So we substitute the sample standard deviation. The value of the test statistic is computed by formula (10–2):

$$t = \frac{\overline{X} - \mu}{s/\sqrt{n}}$$

Step 4: Formulate the decision rule. The critical values of t are given in Appendix B.2, a portion of which is shown in Table 10–1. Appendix B.2 is also repeated in the back inside cover of the text. The far left column of the table is labeled "*df*" for degrees of freedom. The number of degrees of freedom is the total number of observations in the sample minus the number of populations sampled, written $n - 1$. In this case the number of observations in the sample is 26, and we sampled 1 population, so there are $26 - 1 = 25$ degrees of freedom. To find the critical value, first locate the row with the appropriate degrees of freedom. This row is shaded in Table 10–1. Next, determine whether the test is one-tailed or two-tailed. In this case, we have a one-tailed test, so find the portion of the table that is labeled "one-tailed." Locate the column with the selected significance level. In this example, the significance level is .01. Move down the column labeled "0.01" until it intersects the row with 25 degrees of freedom. The value is 2.485. Because this is a one-sided test and the rejection region is in the left tail, the critical value is negative. The decision rule is to reject H_0 if the value of t is less than -2.485.

TABLE 10–1 A Portion of the t Distribution Table

	Confidence Intervals					
	80%	90%	95%	98%	99%	99.9%
	Level of Significance for One-Tailed Test, α					
df	0.10	0.05	0.025	0.01	0.005	0.0005
	Level of Significance for Two-Tailed Test, α					
	0.20	0.10	0.05	0.02	0.01	0.001
⋮	⋮	⋮	⋮	⋮	⋮	⋮
21	1.323	1.721	2.080	2.518	2.831	3.819
22	1.321	1.717	2.074	2.508	2.819	3.792
23	1.319	1.714	2.069	2.500	2.807	3.768
24	1.318	1.711	2.064	2.492	2.797	3.745
25	1.316	1.708	2.060	2.485	2.787	3.725
26	1.315	1.706	2.056	2.479	2.779	3.707
27	1.314	1.703	2.052	2.473	2.771	3.690
28	1.313	1.701	2.048	2.467	2.763	3.674
29	1.311	1.699	2.045	2.462	2.756	3.659
30	1.310	1.697	2.042	2.457	2.750	3.646

Step 5: Make a decision and interpret the result. From the MINITAB output, to the right of the histogram, the mean cost per claim for the sample of 26 observations is $56.42. The standard deviation of this sample is $10.04. We insert these values in formula (10–2) and compute the value of t:

$$t = \frac{\overline{X} - \mu}{s/\sqrt{n}} = \frac{\$56.42 - \$60}{\$10.04/\sqrt{26}} = -1.818$$

Because -1.818 lies in the region to the right of the critical value of -2.485, the null hypothesis is not rejected at the .01 significance level. We have not demonstrated that the cost-cutting measures reduced the mean cost per claim to less than $60. To put it another way, the difference of $3.58 ($56.42 − $60) between the sample mean and the population mean could be due to sampling error. The computed value of t is shown in Chart 10–6. It is in the region where the null hypothesis is *not* rejected.

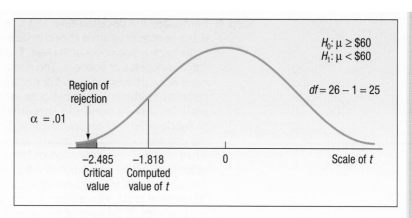

CHART 10–6 Rejection Region, *t* Distribution, .01 Significance Level

In the previous example the mean and the standard deviation were computed using MINITAB. The following example shows the details when the sample mean and sample standard deviation are calculated from sample data.

Example

The mean length of a small counterbalance bar is 43 millimeters. The production supervisor is concerned that the adjustments of the machine producing the bars have changed. He asks the Engineering Department to investigate. Engineering selects a random sample of 12 bars and measures each. The results are reported below in millimeters.

42	39	42	45	43	40	39	41	40	42	43	42

Is it reasonable to conclude that there has been a change in the mean length of the bars? Use the .02 significance level.

Solution

We begin by stating the null hypothesis and the alternate hypothesis.

$$H_0: \mu = 43$$
$$H_1: \mu \neq 43$$

The alternate hypothesis does not state a direction, so this is a two-tailed test. There are 11 degrees of freedom, found by $n - 1 = 12 - 1 = 11$. The t value is 2.718, found by referring to Appendix B.2 for a two-tailed test, using the .02 significance level, with 11 degrees of freedom. The decision rule is: Reject the null hypothesis if the computed t is to the left of -2.718 or to the right of 2.718. This information is summarized in Chart 10–7.

CHART 10–7 Regions of Rejection, Two-Tailed Test, Student's *t* Distribution, $\alpha = .02$

We calculate the standard deviation of the sample using formula (3–9). The mean, $\bar{X}$, is 41.5 millimeters, and the standard deviation, s, is 1.784 millimeters. The details are shown in Table 10–2.

TABLE 10–2 Calculations of the Sample Standard Deviation

X (mm)	$X - \bar{X}$	$(X - \bar{X})^2$
42	0.5	0.25
39	−2.5	6.25
42	0.5	0.25
45	3.5	12.25
43	1.5	2.25
40	−1.5	2.25
39	−2.5	6.25
41	−0.5	0.25
40	−1.5	2.25
42	0.5	0.25
43	1.5	2.25
42	0.5	0.25
498	0	35.00

$$\bar{X} = \frac{498}{12} = 41.5 \text{ mm}$$

$$s = \sqrt{\frac{\Sigma(X - \bar{X})^2}{n - 1}} = \sqrt{\frac{35}{12 - 1}} = 1.784$$

Now we are ready to compute the value of t, using formula (10–2).

$$t = \frac{\bar{X} - \mu}{s/\sqrt{n}} = \frac{41.5 - 43.0}{1.784/\sqrt{12}} = -2.913$$

The null hypothesis that the population mean is 43 millimeters is rejected because the computed t of −2.913 lies in the area to the left of −2.718. We accept the alternate hypothesis and conclude that the population mean is not 43 millimeters. The machine is out of control and needs adjustment.

Self-Review 10–3

The mean life of a battery used in a digital clock is 305 days. The lives of the batteries follow the normal distribution. The battery was recently modified to last longer. A sample of 20 of the modified batteries had a mean life of 311 days with a standard deviation of 12 days. Did the modification increase the mean life of the battery?
(a) State the null hypothesis and the alternate hypothesis.
(b) Show the decision rule graphically. Use the .05 significance level.
(c) Compute the value of t. What is your decision regarding the null hypothesis? Briefly summarize your results.

Exercises

connect

9. Given the following hypothesis:

$$H_0: \mu \leq 10$$
$$H_1: \mu > 10$$

For a random sample of 10 observations, the sample mean was 12 and the sample standard deviation 3. Using the .05 significance level:
a. State the decision rule.
b. Compute the value of the test statistic.
c. What is your decision regarding the null hypothesis?

10. Given the following hypothesis:

$$H_0: \mu = 400$$
$$H_1: \mu \neq 400$$

For a random sample of 12 observations, the sample mean was 407 and the sample standard deviation 6. Using the .01 significance level:
a. State the decision rule.
b. Compute the value of the test statistic.
c. What is your decision regarding the null hypothesis?

11. The Rocky Mountain district sales manager of Rath Publishing, Inc., a college textbook publishing company, claims that the sales representatives make an average of 40 sales calls per week on professors. Several reps say that this estimate is too low. To investigate, a random sample of 28 sales representatives reveals that the mean number of calls made last week was 42. The standard deviation of the sample is 2.1 calls. Using the .05 significance level, can we conclude that the mean number of calls per salesperson per week is more than 40?

12. The management of White Industries is considering a new method of assembling its golf cart. The present method requires 42.3 minutes, on the average, to assemble a cart. The mean assembly time for a random sample of 24 carts, using the new method, was 40.6 minutes, and the standard deviation of the sample was 2.7 minutes. Using the .10 level of significance, can we conclude that the assembly time using the new method is faster?

13. A spark plug manufacturer claimed that its plugs have a mean life in excess of 22,100 miles. Assume the life of the spark plugs follows the normal distribution. A fleet owner purchased a large number of sets. A sample of 18 sets revealed that the mean life was 23,400 miles and the standard deviation was 1,500 miles. Is there enough evidence to substantiate the manufacturer's claim at the .05 significance level?

14. Most air travelers now use e-tickets. Electronic ticketing allows passengers to not worry about a paper ticket, and it costs the airline companies less to handle than paper ticketing. However, in recent times the airlines have received complaints from passengers regarding their e-tickets, particularly when connecting flights and a change of airlines were involved. To investigate the problem an independent watchdog agency contacted a random sample of 20 airports and collected information on the number of complaints the airport had with e-tickets for the month of March. The information is reported below.

| 14 | 14 | 16 | 12 | 12 | 14 | 13 | 16 | 15 | 14 |
| 12 | 15 | 15 | 14 | 13 | 13 | 12 | 13 | 10 | 13 |

At the .05 significance level can the watchdog agency conclude the mean number of complaints per airport is less than 15 per month?

a. What assumption is necessary before conducting a test of hypothesis?

b. Plot the number of complaints per airport in a frequency distribution or a dot plot. Is it reasonable to conclude that the population follows a normal distribution?

c. Conduct a test of hypothesis and interpret the results.

A Software Solution

The MINITAB statistical software system, used in earlier chapters and the previous section, provides an efficient way of conducting a one-sample test of hypothesis for a population mean. The steps to generate the following output are shown in the **Software Commands** section at the end of the chapter.

An additional feature of most statistical software packages is to report the *p*-value, which gives additional information on the null hypothesis. The *p*-value is the probability of a *t* value as extreme as that computed, given that the null hypothesis is true. Using the data from the previous counterbalance bar example, the *p*-value of .014 is the likelihood of a *t* value of −2.91 or less plus the likelihood of a *t* value of 2.91 or larger, given a population mean of 43. Thus, comparing the p-value to the significance level tells us whether the null hypothesis was close to being rejected, barely rejected, and so on.

To explain further, refer to the diagram below. The p-value of .014 is the darker or shaded area and the significance level is the total shaded area. Because the p-value of .014 is less than the significance level of .02, the null hypothesis is rejected. Had the p-value been larger than the significance level—say, .06, .19, or .57—the null hypothesis would not be rejected. If the significance level had initially been selected as .01, the null hypothesis would not be rejected.

In the preceding example the alternate hypothesis was two-sided, so there were rejection areas in both the lower (left) tail and the upper (right) tail. To determine the p-value, it was necessary to determine the area to the left of −2.913 for a t distribution with 11 degrees of freedom and add to it the value of the area to the right of 2.913.

What if we were conducting a one-sided test, so that the entire rejection region would be in either the upper or the lower tail? In that case, we would report the area from only the one tail. In the counterbalance example, if H_1 were stated as μ < 43, the inequality would point to the left. Thus, we would have reported the p-value as the area to the left of −2.913. This value is .007, found by .014/2. Thus, the p-value for a one-tailed test would be .007.

How can we estimate a p-value without computer software? To illustrate, recall that, in the example regarding the length of a counterbalance, we rejected the null hypothesis that μ = 43 and accepted the alternate hypothesis that μ ≠ 43. The significance level was .02, so logically the p-value is less than .02. To estimate the p-value more accurately, go to Appendix B.2 and find the row with 11 degrees of freedom. The computed t value of 2.913 is between 2.718 and 3.106. (A portion of Appendix B.2 is reproduced as Table 10–3.) The two-tailed significance level

TABLE 10–3 A Portion of Student's t Distribution

	Confidence Intervals					
	80%	90%	95%	98%	99%	99.9%
	Level of Significance for One-Tailed Test, α					
df	0.10	0.05	.0025	0.01	0.005	0.0005
	Level of Significance for Two-Tailed Test, α					
	0.20	0.10	0.05	0.02	0.01	0.001
⋮	⋮	⋮	⋮	⋮	⋮	⋮
9	1.383	1.833	2.262	2.821	3.250	4.781
10	1.372	1.812	2.228	2.764	3.169	4.587
11	1.363	1.796	2.201	2.718	3.106	4.437
12	1.356	1.782	2.179	2.681	3.055	4.318
13	1.350	1.771	2.160	2.650	3.012	4.221
14	1.345	1.761	2.145	2.624	2.977	4.140
15	1.341	1.753	2.131	2.602	2.947	4.073

corresponding to 2.718 is .02, and for 3.106 it is .01. Therefore, the p-value is between .01 and .02. The usual practice is to report that the p-value is *less* than the larger of the two significance levels. So we would report, "the p-value is less than .02."

Self-Review 10–4

A machine is set to fill a small bottle with 9.0 grams of medicine. A sample of eight bottles revealed the following amounts (grams) in each bottle.

| 9.2 | 8.7 | 8.9 | 8.6 | 8.8 | 8.5 | 8.7 | 9.0 |

At the .01 significance level, can we conclude that the mean weight is less than 9.0 grams?
(a) State the null hypothesis and the alternate hypothesis.
(b) How many degrees of freedom are there?
(c) Give the decision rule.
(d) Compute the value of t. What is your decision regarding the null hypothesis?
(e) Estimate the p-value.

Exercises

connect

15. Given the following hypothesis:

$$H_0: \mu \geq 20$$
$$H_1: \mu < 20$$

A random sample of five resulted in the following values: 18, 15, 12, 19, and 21. Using the .01 significance level, can we conclude the population mean is less than 20?
a. State the decision rule.
b. Compute the value of the test statistic.
c. What is your decision regarding the null hypothesis?
d. Estimate the p-value.

16. Given the following hypothesis:

$$H_0: \mu = 100$$
$$H_1: \mu \neq 100$$

A random sample of six resulted in the following values: 118, 105, 112, 119, 105, and 111. Using the .05 significance level, can we conclude the mean is different from 100?
a. State the decision rule.
b. Compute the value of the test statistic.
c. What is your decision regarding the null hypothesis?
d. Estimate the p-value.

17. Experience raising New Jersey Red chickens revealed the mean weight of the chickens at five months is 4.35 pounds. The weights follow the normal distribution. In an effort to increase their weight, a special additive is added to the chicken feed. The subsequent weights of a sample of five-month-old chickens were (in pounds):

| 4.41 | 4.37 | 4.33 | 4.35 | 4.30 | 4.39 | 4.36 | 4.38 | 4.40 | 4.39 |

At the .01 level, has the special additive increased the mean weight of the chickens? Estimate the p-value.

18. The liquid chlorine added to swimming pools to combat algae has a relatively short shelf life before it loses its effectiveness. Records indicate that the mean shelf life of a 5-gallon jug of chlorine is 2,160 hours (90 days). As an experiment, Holdlonger was added to the chlorine to find whether it would increase the shelf life. A sample of nine jugs of chlorine had these shelf lives (in hours):

| 2,159 | 2,170 | 2,180 | 2,179 | 2,160 | 2,167 | 2,171 | 2,181 | 2,185 |

At the .025 level, has Holdlonger increased the shelf life of the chlorine? Estimate the p-value.

19. Wyoming fisheries contend that the mean number of cutthroat trout caught during a full day of fly-fishing on the Snake, Buffalo, and other rivers and streams in the Jackson Hole area is 4.0. To make their yearly update, the fishery personnel asked a sample of fly fishermen to keep a count of the number caught during the day. The numbers were: 4, 4, 3, 2, 6, 8, 7, 1, 9, 3, 1, and 6. At the .05 level, can we conclude that the mean number caught is greater than 4.0? Estimate the *p*-value.

20. Hugger Polls contends that an agent conducts a mean of 53 in-depth home surveys every week. A streamlined survey form has been introduced, and Hugger wants to evaluate its effectiveness. The number of in-depth surveys conducted during a week by a random sample of agents are:

53	57	50	55	58	54	60	52	59	62	60	60	51	59	56

At the .05 level of significance, can we conclude that the mean number of interviews conducted by the agents is more than 53 per week? Estimate the *p*-value.

Tests Concerning Proportions

LO5 Conduct a test of hypothesis about a population proportion.

In the previous chapter we discussed confidence intervals for proportions. We can also conduct a test of hypothesis for a proportion. Recall that a proportion is the ratio of the number of successes to the number of observations. We let X refer to the number of successes and n the number of observations, so the proportion of successes in a fixed number of trials is X/n. Thus, the formula for computing a sample proportion, p, is $p = X/n$. Consider the following potential hypothesis-testing situations.

- Historically, Wells Fargo Bank reports that 70 percent of leased vehicles are returned with less than 36,000 miles. A recent sample of 200 vehicles returned at the end of their lease showed 158 had less than 36,000 miles. Has the proportion increased?
- The American Association of Retired Persons (AARP) reports that 60 percent of retired people under the age of 65 would return to work on a full-time basis if a suitable job were available. A sample of 500 retirees under 65 revealed 315 would return to work. Can we conclude that more than 60 percent would return to work?
- Able Moving and Storage, Inc., advises its clients for long-distance residential moves that their household goods will be delivered in 3 to 5 days from the time they are picked up. Able's records show it is successful 90 percent of the time with this claim. A recent audit revealed it was successful 190 times out of 200. Can the company conclude its success rate has increased?

Some assumptions must be made and conditions met before testing a population proportion. To test a hypothesis about a population proportion, a random sample is chosen from the population. It is assumed that the binomial assumptions discussed in Chapter 6 are met. To review, these conditions are: (1) the sample data collected are the result of counts; (2) the outcome of an experiment is classified into one of two mutually exclusive categories—a "success" or a "failure"; (3) the probability of a success is the same for each trial; and (4) the trials are independent, meaning the outcome of one trial does not affect the outcome of any other trial. The test we will conduct shortly is appropriate when both $n\pi$ and $n(1 - \pi)$ are at least 5. n is the sample size, and π is the population proportion. It takes advantage of the fact that a binomial distribution can be approximated by the normal distribution.

$n\pi$ and $n(1 - \pi)$ must be at least 5.

Example

Suppose prior elections in a certain state indicated it is necessary for a candidate for governor to receive at least 80 percent of the vote in the northern section of the state to be elected. The incumbent governor is interested in assessing his chances of returning to office and plans to conduct a survey of 2,000 registered voters in the northern section of the state.

Using the hypothesis-testing procedure, assess the governor's chances of reelection.

Solution

This situation regarding the governor's reelection meets the binomial conditions.

- There are only two possible outcomes. That is, a sampled voter will either vote or not vote for the governor.
- The probability of a success is the same for each trial. In this case the likelihood a particular sampled voter will support reelection is .80.
- The trials are independent. This means, for example, the likelihood the 23rd voter sampled will support reelection is not affected by what the 24th or 52nd voter does.
- The sample data is the result of counts. We are going to count the number of voters who support reelection in the sample of 2,000.

We can use the normal approximation to the binomial distribution, discussed in Chapter 7, because both $n\pi$ and $n(1-\pi)$ exceed 5. In this case, $n = 2,000$ and $\pi = .80$ (π is the proportion of the vote in the northern part of the state, or 80 percent, needed to be elected).

Thus:

$$n\pi = 2,000(.80) = 1,600 \text{ and } n(1-\pi) = 2,000\,(1-.80) = 400$$

Both 1,600 and 400 are greater than 5.

Step 1: State the null hypothesis and the alternate hypothesis. The null hypothesis, H_0, is that the population proportion π is .80 or larger. The alternate hypothesis, H_1, is that the proportion is less than .80. From a practical standpoint, the incumbent governor is concerned only when the proportion is less than .80. If it is equal to or greater than .80, he will have no problem; that is, the sample data would indicate he will probably be reelected. These hypotheses are written symbolically as:

$$H_0: \pi \geq .80$$
$$H_1: \pi < .80$$

H_1 states a direction. Thus, as noted previously, the test is one-tailed with the inequality sign pointing to the tail of the distribution containing the region of rejection.

Step 2: Select the level of significance. The level of significance is .05. This is the likelihood that a true hypothesis will be rejected.

Step 3: Select the test statistic. z is the appropriate statistic, found by:

TEST OF HYPOTHESIS, ONE PROPORTION $z = \dfrac{p - \pi}{\sqrt{\dfrac{\pi(1-\pi)}{n}}}$ [10–3]

where:
π is the population proportion.
p is the sample proportion.
n is the sample size.

Finding the critical value

Step 4: Formulate the decision rule. The critical value or values of z form the dividing point or points between the regions where H_0 is rejected and where it is not rejected. Because the alternate hypothesis states a direction, this is a one-tailed test. The sign of the inequality points to the left, so only the left side of the curve is used. (See Chart 10–8.) The significance level was given as .05 in step 2. This probability is in the left tail and determines the region of rejection. The area between zero and the critical value is .4500, found by .5000 − .0500. Referring to Appendix B.1 and searching for .4500, we find the critical value of z is 1.65. The decision rule is, therefore: Reject the null hypothesis and accept the alternate hypothesis if the computed value of z falls to the left of −1.65; otherwise do not reject H_0.

Select a sample and make a decision regarding H_0.

Step 5: Make a decision and interpret the result. Select a sample and make a decision about H_0. A sample survey of 2,000 potential voters in the northern part of the state revealed that 1,550 planned to vote for the incumbent

CHART 10–8 Rejection Region for the .05 Level of Significance, One-Tailed Test

governor. Is the sample proportion of .775 (found by 1,550/2,000) close enough to .80 to conclude that the difference is due to sampling error? In this case:

p is .775, the proportion in the sample who plan to vote for the governor.

n is 2,000, the number of voters surveyed.

π is .80, the hypothesized population proportion.

z is a normally distributed test statistic when the hypothesis is true and the other assumptions are true.

Using formula (10–3) and computing z gives

$$z = \frac{p - \pi}{\sqrt{\dfrac{\pi(1 - \pi)}{n}}} = \frac{\dfrac{1{,}550}{2{,}000} - .80}{\sqrt{\dfrac{.80(1 - .80)}{2{,}000}}} = \frac{.775 - .80}{\sqrt{.00008}} = -2.80$$

The computed value of z (-2.80) is in the rejection region, so the null hypothesis is rejected at the .05 level. The difference of 2.5 percentage points between the sample percent (77.5 percent) and the hypothesized population percent in the northern part of the state necessary to carry the state (80 percent) is statistically significant. It is probably not due to sampling variation. To put it another way, the evidence at this point does not support the claim that the incumbent governor will return to the governor's mansion for another four years.

The p-value is the probability of finding a z value less than -2.80. From Appendix B.1, the probability of a z value between zero and -2.80 is .4974. So the p-value is .0026, found by $.5000 - .4974$. The governor cannot be confident of reelection because the p-value is less than the significance level.

Self-Review 10–5 A recent insurance industry report indicated that 40 percent of those persons involved in minor traffic accidents this year have been involved in a least one other traffic accident in the last five years. An advisory group decided to investigate this claim, believing it was too large. A sample of 200 traffic accidents this year showed 74 persons were also involved in another accident within the last five years. Use the .01 significance level.

(a) Can we use z as the test statistic? Tell why or why not.
(b) State the null hypothesis and the alternate hypothesis.
(c) Show the decision rule graphically.
(d) Compute the value of z and state your decision regarding the null hypothesis.
(e) Determine and interpret the p-value.

Exercises

21. The following hypotheses are given.

$$H_0: \pi \leq .70$$
$$H_1: \pi > .70$$

A sample of 100 observations revealed that $p = .75$. At the .05 significance level, can the null hypothesis be rejected?
a. State the decision rule.
b. Compute the value of the test statistic.
c. What is your decision regarding the null hypothesis?

22. The following hypotheses are given.

$$H_0: \pi = .40$$
$$H_1: \pi \neq .40$$

A sample of 120 observations revealed that $p = .30$. At the .05 significance level, can the null hypothesis be rejected?
a. State the decision rule.
b. Compute the value of the test statistic.
c. What is your decision regarding the null hypothesis?

Note: It is recommended that you use the five-step hypothesis-testing procedure in solving the following problems.

23. The National Safety Council reported that 52 percent of American turnpike drivers are men. A sample of 300 cars traveling southbound on the New Jersey Turnpike yesterday revealed that 170 were driven by men. At the .01 significance level, can we conclude that a larger proportion of men were driving on the New Jersey Turnpike than the national statistics indicate?

24. A recent article in *USA Today* reported that a job awaits only one in three new college graduates. The major reasons given were an overabundance of college graduates and a weak economy. A survey of 200 recent graduates from your school revealed that 80 students had jobs. At the .02 significance level, can we conclude that a larger proportion of students at your school have jobs?

25. Chicken Delight claims that 90 percent of its orders are delivered within 10 minutes of the time the order is placed. A sample of 100 orders revealed that 82 were delivered within the promised time. At the .10 significance level, can we conclude that less than 90 percent of the orders are delivered in less than 10 minutes?

26. Research at the University of Toledo indicates that 50 percent of students change their major area of study after their first year in a program. A random sample of 100 students in the College of Business revealed that 48 had changed their major area of study after their first year of the program. Has there been a significant decrease in the proportion of students who change their major after the first year in this program? Test at the .05 level of significance.

Chapter Summary

I. The objective of hypothesis testing is to check the validity of a statement about a population parameter.
II. The steps in conducting a test of hypothesis are:
   A. State the null hypothesis (H_0) and the alternate hypothesis (H_1).
   B. Select the level of significance.
      1. The level of significance is the likelihood of rejecting a true null hypothesis.
      2. The most frequently used significance levels are .01, .05, and .10, but any value between 0 and 1.00 is possible.
   C. Select the test statistic.
      1. A test statistic is a value calculated from sample information used to determine whether to reject the null hypothesis.
      2. Two test statistics were considered in this chapter.
         a. The standard normal distribution (the z distribution) is used when the population follows the normal distribution and the population standard deviation is known.

    b. The *t* distribution is used when the population follows the normal distribution and the population standard deviation is unknown.
  D. State the decision rule.
    1. The decision rule indicates the condition or conditions when the null hypothesis is rejected.
    2. In a two-tailed test, the rejection region is evenly split between the upper and lower tails.
    3. In a one-tailed test, all of the rejection region is in either the upper or the lower tail.
  E. Select a sample, compute the value of the test statistic, make a decision regarding the null hypothesis, and interpret the results.
III. A *p*-value is the probability that the value of the test statistic is as extreme as the value computed, when the null hypothesis is true.
IV. When testing a hypothesis about a population mean:
  A. If the population standard deviation, σ, is known, the test statistic is the standard normal distribution and is determined from:

$$z = \frac{\bar{X} - \mu}{\sigma/\sqrt{n}} \qquad \textbf{[10–1]}$$

  B. If the population standard deviation is not known, *s* is substituted for σ. The test statistic is the *t* distribution, and its value is determined from:

$$t = \frac{\bar{X} - \mu}{s/\sqrt{n}} \qquad \textbf{[10–2]}$$

  The major characteristics of the *t* distribution are:
  1. It is a continuous distribution.
  2. It is mound-shaped and symmetrical.
  3. It is flatter, or more spread out, than the standard normal distribution.
  4. There is a family of *t* distributions, depending on the number of degrees of freedom.
V. When testing about a population proportion:
  A. The binomial conditions must be met.
  B. Both $n\pi$ and $n(1 - \pi)$ must be at least 5.
  C. The test statistic is

$$z = \frac{p - \pi}{\sqrt{\dfrac{\pi(1 - \pi)}{n}}} \qquad \textbf{[10–3]}$$

Pronunciation Key

SYMBOL	MEANING	PRONUNCIATION
H_0	Null hypothesis	*H sub zero*
H_1	Alternate hypothesis	*H sub one*
$\alpha/2$	Two-tailed significance level	*Alpha over 2*

Chapter Exercises

connect™

27. According to the local union president, the mean gross income of plumbers in the Salt Lake City area follows the normal probability distribution with a population mean of $45,000 and a population standard deviation of $3,000. A recent investigative reporter for KYAK TV found, for a sample of 120 plumbers, the mean gross income was $45,500. At the .10 significance level, is it reasonable to conclude that the mean income is not equal to $45,000? Determine the *p*-value.

28. Rutter Nursery Company packages its pine bark mulch in 50-pound bags. From a long history, the production department reports that the distribution of the bag weights follows the normal distribution and the standard deviation of this process is 3 pounds per bag. At the end of each day, Jeff Rutter, the production manager, weighs 10 bags and computes the mean weight of the sample. Below are the weights of 10 bags from today's production.

45.6	47.7	47.6	46.3	46.2	47.4	49.2	55.8	47.5	48.5

    a. Can Mr. Rutter conclude that the mean weight of the bags is less than 50 pounds? Use the .01 significance level.

    b. In a brief report, tell why Mr. Rutter can use the z distribution as the test statistic.

    c. Compute the p-value.

29. A new weight-watching company, Weight Reducers International, advertises that those who join will lose, on the average, 10 pounds the first two weeks with a standard deviation of 2.8 pounds. A random sample of 50 people who joined the new weight reduction program revealed the mean loss to be 9 pounds. At the .05 level of significance, can we conclude that those joining Weight Reducers on average will lose less than 10 pounds? Determine the p-value.

30. Dole Pineapple, Inc., is concerned that the 16-ounce can of sliced pineapple is being overfilled. Assume the standard deviation of the process is .03 ounces. The quality-control department took a random sample of 50 cans and found that the arithmetic mean weight was 16.05 ounces. At the 5 percent level of significance, can we conclude that the mean weight is greater than 16 ounces? Determine the p-value.

31. According to a recent survey, Americans get a mean of 7 hours of sleep per night. A random sample of 50 students at West Virginia University revealed the mean number of hours slept last night was 6 hours and 48 minutes (6.8 hours). The standard deviation of the sample was 0.9 hours. Is it reasonable to conclude that students at West Virginia sleep less than the typical American? Compute the p-value.

32. A statewide real estate sales agency, Farm Associates, specializes in selling farm property in the state of Nebraska. Its records indicate that the mean selling time of farm property is 90 days. Because of recent drought conditions, the agency believes that the mean selling time is now greater than 90 days. A statewide survey of 100 farms sold recently revealed that the mean selling time was 94 days, with a standard deviation of 22 days. At the .10 significance level, has there been an increase in selling time?

33. A cable news network, in a segment on the price of gasoline, reported that the mean price nationwide is $3.75 per gallon for self-serve regular unleaded. A random sample of 35 stations in the Milwaukee, Wisconsin, area revealed that the mean price was $3.77 per gallon and that the standard deviation was $0.05 per gallon. At the .05 significance level, can we conclude that the price of gasoline is higher in the Milwaukee area? Determine the p-value.

34. A recent article in *Vitality* magazine reported that the mean amount of leisure time per week for American men is 40.0 hours. You believe this figure is too large and decide to conduct your own test. In a random sample of 60 men, you find that the mean is 37.8 hours of leisure per week and that the standard deviation of the sample is 12.2 hours. Can you conclude that the information in the article is untrue? Use the .05 significance level. Determine the p-value and explain its meaning.

35. In recent years the interest rate on home mortgages has declined to less than 6.0 percent. However, according to a study by the Federal Reserve Board the rate charged on credit card debt is more than 14 percent. Listed below is the interest rate charged on a sample of 10 credit cards.

14.6	16.7	17.4	17.0	17.8	15.4	13.1	15.8	14.3	14.5

Is it reasonable to conclude the mean rate charged is greater than 14 percent? Use the .01 significance level.

36. A recent article in *The Wall Street Journal* reported that the 30-year mortgage rate is now less than 6 percent. A sample of eight small banks in the Midwest revealed the following 30-year rates (in percent):

4.8	5.3	6.5	4.8	6.1	5.8	6.2	5.6

At the .01 significance level, can we conclude that the 30-year mortgage rate for small banks is less than 6 percent? Estimate the p-value.

37. According to the Coffee Research Organization (http://www.coffeeresearch.org) the typical American coffee drinker consumes an average of 3.1 cups per day. A sample of 12 senior citizens revealed they consumed the following amounts of coffee, reported in cups, yesterday.

3.1	3.3	3.5	2.6	2.6	4.3	4.4	3.8	3.1	4.1	3.1	3.2

At the .05 significance level does this sample data suggest there is a difference between the national average and the sample mean from senior citizens?

38. The postanesthesia care area (recovery room) at St. Luke's Hospital in Maumee, Ohio, was recently enlarged. The hope was that with the enlargement the mean number of patients per day would be more than 25. A random sample of 15 days revealed the following numbers of patients.

25	27	25	26	25	28	28	27	24	26	25	29	25	27	24

At the .01 significance level, can we conclude that the mean number of patients per day is more than 25? Estimate the p-value and interpret it.

39. www.golfsmith.com receives an average of 6.5 returns per day from online shoppers. For a sample of 12 days, it received the following number of returns.

0	4	3	4	9	4	5	9	1	6	7	10

At the .01 significance level, can we conclude the mean number of returns is less than 6.5?

40. During recent seasons, Major League Baseball has been criticized for the length of the games. A report indicated that the average game lasts 3 hours and 30 minutes. A sample of 17 games revealed the following times to completion. (Note that the minutes have been changed to fractions of hours, so that a game that lasted 2 hours and 24 minutes is reported at 2.40 hours.)

2.98	2.40	2.70	2.25	3.23	3.17	2.93	3.18	2.80
2.38	3.75	3.20	3.27	2.52	2.58	4.45	2.45	

Can we conclude that the mean time for a game is less than 3.50 hours? Use the .05 significance level.

41. Watch Corporation of Switzerland claims that its watches on average will neither gain nor lose time during a week. A sample of 18 watches provided the following gains (+) or losses (−) in seconds per week.

−0.38	−0.20	−0.38	−0.32	+0.32	−0.23	+0.30	+0.25	−0.10
−0.37	−0.61	−0.48	−0.47	−0.64	−0.04	−0.20	−0.68	+0.05

Is it reasonable to conclude that the mean gain or loss in time for the watches is 0? Use the .05 significance level. Estimate the p-value.

42. Listed below is the rate of return for one year (reported in percent) for a sample of 12 mutual funds that are classified as taxable money market funds.

4.63	4.15	4.76	4.70	4.65	4.52	4.70	5.06	4.42	4.51	4.24	4.52

Using the .05 significance level is it reasonable to conclude that the mean rate of return is more than 4.50 percent?

43. Many grocery stores and large retailers such as Walmart and Kmart have installed self-checkout systems so shoppers can scan their own items and cash out themselves. How do customers like this service and how often do they use it? Listed below is the number of customers using the service for a sample of 15 days at the Walmart on Highway 544 in Surfside, South Carolina.

120	108	120	114	118	91	118	92	104	104
112	97	118	108	117					

Is it reasonable to conclude that the mean number of customers using the self-checkout system is more than 100 per day? Use the .05 significance level.

44. For a recent year the mean fare to fly from Charlotte, North Carolina, to Seattle, Washington, on a discount ticket was $267. A random sample of round-trip discount fares on this route last month gives:

$321	$286	$290	$330	$310	$250	$270	$280	$299	$265	$291	$275	$281

   At the .01 significance level can we conclude that the mean fare has increased? What is the p-value?

45. The publisher of *Celebrity Living* claims that the mean sales for personality magazines that feature people such as Angelina Jolie or Paris Hilton are 1.5 million copies per week. A sample of 10 comparable titles shows a mean weekly sales last week of 1.3 million copies with a standard deviation of 0.9 million copies. Does this data contradict the publisher's claim? Use the 0.01 significance level.

46. A United Nations report shows the mean family income for Mexican migrants to the United States is $27,000 per year. A FLOC (Farm Labor Organizing Committee) evaluation of 25 Mexican family units reveals a mean to be $30,000 with a sample standard deviation of $10,000. Does this information disagree with the United Nations report? Apply the 0.01 significance level.

47. Traditionally, 2 percent of the citizens of the United States live in a foreign country because they are disenchanted with U.S. politics or social attitudes. In order to test if this proportion has increased since the September 11, 2001, terror attacks, U.S. consulates contacted a random sample of 400 of these expatriates. The sample yields 12 people who report they are living overseas because of political or social attitudes. Can you conclude this data shows the proportion of politically motivated expatriates has increased? Use the 0.05 significance level.

48. According to a study by the American Pet Food Dealers Association, 63 percent of U.S. households own pets. A report is being prepared for an editorial in the *San Francisco Chronicle*. As a part of the editorial a random sample of 300 households showed 210 own pets. Does this data disagree with the Pet Food Dealers Association data? Use a .05 level of significance.

49. Tina Dennis is the comptroller for Meek Industries. She believes that the current cash-flow problem at Meek is due to the slow collection of accounts receivable. She believes that more than 60 percent of the accounts are in arrears more than three months. A random sample of 200 accounts showed that 140 were more than three months old. At the .01 significance level, can she conclude that more than 60 percent of the accounts are in arrears for more than three months?

50. The policy of the Suburban Transit Authority is to add a bus route if more than 55 percent of the potential commuters indicate they would use the particular route. A sample of 70 commuters revealed that 42 would use a proposed route from Bowman Park to the downtown area. Does the Bowman-to-downtown route meet the STA criterion? Use the .05 significance level.

51. Past experience at the Crowder Travel Agency indicated that 44 percent of those persons who wanted the agency to plan a vacation for them wanted to go to Europe. During the most recent busy season, a sampling of 1,000 plans was selected at random from the files. It was found that 480 persons wanted to go to Europe on vacation. Has there been a significant shift upward in the percentage of persons who want to go to Europe? Test at the .05 significance level.

52. From past experience a television manufacturer found that 10 percent or less of its sets needed any type of repair in the first two years of operation. In a sample of 50 sets manufactured two years ago, 9 needed repair. At the .05 significance level, has the percent of sets needing repair increased? Determine the p-value.

53. An urban planner claims that, nationally, 20 percent of all families renting condominiums move during a given year. A random sample of 200 families renting condominiums in the Dallas Metroplex revealed that 56 had moved during the past year. At the .01 significance level, does this evidence suggest that a larger proportion of condominium owners moved in the Dallas area? Determine the p-value.

54. The cost of weddings in the United States has skyrocketed in recent years. As a result many couples are opting to have their weddings in the Caribbean. A Caribbean vacation resort recently advertised in *Bride Magazine* that the cost of a Caribbean wedding was less than $10,000. Listed below is a total cost in $000 for a sample of 8 Caribbean weddings.

| 9.7 | 9.4 | 11.7 | 9.0 | 9.1 | 10.5 | 9.1 | 9.8 |

At the .05 significance level is it reasonable to conclude the mean wedding cost is less than $10,000 as advertised?

55. The U.S. president's call for designing and building a missile defense system that ignores restrictions of the Anti-Ballistic Missile Defense System treaty (ABM) is supported by 483 of the respondents in a nationwide poll of 1,002 adults. Is it reasonable to conclude that the nation is evenly divided on the issue? Use the .05 significance level.

56. After a losing season there is a great uproar to fire the head football coach. In a random sample of 200 college alumni, 80 favor keeping the coach. Test at the .05 level of significance whether the proportion of alumni who support the coach is less than 50 percent.

57. During the 1990s the fatality rate for lung cancer was 80 per 100,000 people. After the turn of the century and the establishment of newer treatments and adjustment in public health advertising, a random sample of 10,000 people exhibits only six deaths due to lung cancer. Test at the .05 significance level whether that data is proof of a reduced fatality rate for lung cancer.

Data Set Exercises

58. Refer to the Real Estate data, which report information on homes sold in Phoenix, Arizona, last year.
    a. A recent article in *The Arizona Republic* indicated that the mean selling price of the homes in the area is more than $220,000. Can we conclude that the mean selling price in the Denver area is more than $220,000? Use the .01 significance level. What is the *p*-value?
    b. The same article reported the mean size was more than 2,100 square feet. Can we conclude that the mean size of homes sold in the Denver area is more than 2,100 square feet? Use the .01 significance level. What is the *p*-value?
    c. Determine the proportion of homes that have an attached garage. At the .05 significance level can we conclude that more than 60 percent of the homes sold in the Denver area had an attached garage? What is the *p*-value?
    d. Determine the proportion of homes that have a pool. At the .05 significance level, can we conclude that less than 40 percent of the homes sold in the Denver area had a pool? What is the *p*-value?

59. Refer to the Baseball 2008 data, which report information on the 30 Major League Baseball teams for the 2008 season.
    a. Conduct a test of hypothesis to determine whether the mean salary of the teams was different from $80.0 million. Use the .05 significance level.
    b. Conduct a test of hypothesis to determine whether the mean attendance was more than 2,000,000 per team.

60. Refer to the Wage data, which report information on the annual wages for a sample of 100 workers. Also included are variables relating to the industry, years of education, and gender for each worker.
    a. Conduct a test of hypothesis to determine if the mean annual wage is greater than $30,000. Use the .05 significance level. Determine the *p*-value and interpret the result.
    b. Conduct a test of hypothesis to determine if the mean years of experience is different from 20. Use the .05 significance level. Determine the *p*-value and interpret the result.
    c. Conduct a test of hypothesis to determine if the mean age is less than 40. Use the .05 significance level. Determine the *p*-value and interpret the result.
    d. Conduct a test of hypothesis to determine if the proportion of union workers is greater than 15 percent. Use the .05 significance level and report the *p*-value.

Practice Test

Part I Objective

1. The _____ is a statement about the value of a population parameter.
2. We commit a Type II error when we _____ the null hypothesis when it is actually false.
3. The probability of committing a Type I error is equal to the _____.
4. The _____, based on sample information, is used to determine whether to reject the null hypothesis.

5. The _____ value separates the region where the null hypothesis is rejected from the region where it is not rejected.
6. In a _____ -tailed test, the significance level is divided equally between the two tails. (one, two, neither)
7. When conducting a test of hypothesis for means (assuming a normal population), we use the standard normal distribution when the population _____ is known.
8. The _____ value is the probability of finding a value of the test statistic at least as extreme as the one observed, given that the null hypothesis is true.
9. The _____ conditions are necessary to conduct a test of hypothesis about a proportion.
10. To conduct a test of proportions, the value of $n\pi$ and $n(1 - \pi)$ must be at least _____. (1, 5, 30, 1000)

Part II Problems

For each of these problems, use the five-step hypothesis-testing procedure.
1. The Park Manager at Fort Fisher State Park in North Carolina believes the typical park visitor spends at least 90 minutes in the park during the summer months. A sample of 18 visitors during the summer months of 2009 revealed the mean time in the park was 96 minutes with a standard deviation of 12 minutes. At the .01 significance level, is it reasonable to conclude that the mean time in the park is greater than 90 minutes?
2. The weights of full boxes of Frosted Flakes breakfast cereal follow the normal probability distribution with a mean of 9.75 oz and a standard deviation of 0.27 oz. A sample of 25 boxes packed this morning showed the mean to be 9.85 oz. Can we conclude that the mean weight is more than 9.75 oz per box?
3. A recent newspaper article reported that 67 percent of young married couples consulted with and sought the approval of their spouse on any purchase of more than $500. A sample of 300 young married couples in Greater Chicago revealed 180 consulted with their spouse on their most recent purchase of more than $500. At the .05 significance level, can we conclude that less than 67 percent of those sampled in Chicago sought the approval of their spouse?

Software Commands

1. The MINITAB commands for the histogram and the descriptive statistics on page 302 are:
   a. Enter the 26 sample observations in column *C1* and name the variable *Cost*.
   b. From the menu bar select **Stat, Basic Statistics,** and **Graphical Summary.** In the dialog box select **Cost** as the variable and click **OK.**

2. The MINITAB commands for the one-sample *t* test on page 306 are:
   a. Enter the sample data into column *C1* and name the variable *Length.*
   b. From the menu bar select **Stat, Basic Statistics,** and **1-Sample *t*** and then hit **Enter.**
   c. Select **Length** as the variable, select **Test mean,** insert the number *43* and click **OK.**

Chapter 10 Answers to Self-Review

10–1 a. H_0: $\mu = 16.0$; H_1: $\mu \neq 16.0$

b. .05

c. $z = \dfrac{\bar{X} - \mu}{\sigma/\sqrt{n}}$

d. Reject H_0 if $z < -1.96$ or $z > 1.96$

e. $z = \dfrac{16.017 - 16.0}{0.15/\sqrt{50}} = \dfrac{0.0170}{0.0212} = 0.80$

f. Do not reject H_0

g. We cannot conclude the mean amount dispensed is different from 16.0 ounces.

10–2 a. H_0: $\mu \leq 16.0$; H_1: $\mu > 16.0$

b. Reject H_0 if $z > 1.65$

c. $z = \dfrac{16.040 - 16.0}{0.15/\sqrt{50}} = \dfrac{.0400}{.0212} = 1.89$

d. Reject H_0

e. The mean amount dispensed is more than 16.0 ounces.

f. p-value $= .5000 - .4706 = .0294$. The p-value is less than α (.05), so H_0 is rejected. It is the same conclusion as in part (d).

10–3 a. H_0: $\mu \leq 305$; H_1: $\mu > 305$.

b. $df = n - 1 = 20 - 1 = 19$

The decision rule is to reject H_0 if $t > 1.729$.

c. $t = \dfrac{\bar{X} - \mu}{s/\sqrt{n}} = \dfrac{311 - 305}{12/\sqrt{20}} = 2.236$

Reject H_0 because $2.236 > 1.729$. The modification increased the mean battery life to more than 305 days.

10–4 a. H_0: $\mu \geq 9.0$; H_1: $\mu < 9.0$.

b. 7, found by $n - 1 = 8 - 1 = 7$.

c. Reject H_0 if $t < -2.998$.

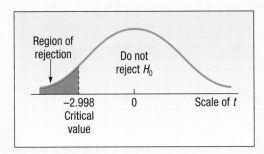

d. $t = -2.494$, found by:

$$s = \sqrt{\dfrac{0.36}{8 - 1}} = 0.2268$$

$$\bar{X} = \dfrac{70.4}{8} = 8.8$$

Then

$$t = \dfrac{8.8 - 9.0}{0.2268/\sqrt{8}} = -2.494$$

Since -2.494 lies to the right of -2.998, H_0 is not rejected. We have not shown that the mean is less than 9.0.

e. The p-value is between .025 and .010.

10–5 a. Yes, because both $n\pi$ and $n(1 - \pi)$ exceed 5:
$n\pi = 200(.40) = 80$, and
$n(1 - \pi) = 200(.60) = 120$.

b. H_0: $\pi \geq .40$
H_1: $\pi < .40$

c. Reject H_0 if $z < -2.33$

d. $z = -0.87$, found by:

$$z = \dfrac{.37 - .40}{\sqrt{\dfrac{.40(1 - .40)}{200}}} = \dfrac{-.03}{\sqrt{.0012}} = -0.87$$

Do not reject H_0.

e. The p-value is .1922, found by $.5000 - .3078$.

11

Two-Sample Tests of Hypothesis

Learning Objectives

When you have completed this chapter, you will be able to:

LO1 Conduct a test of a hypothesis about the difference between two independent population means.

LO2 Conduct a test of a hypothesis about the difference between two population proportions.

LO3 Conduct a test of a hypothesis about the mean difference between *dependent observations*.

LO4 Understand the difference between *dependent and independent samples*.

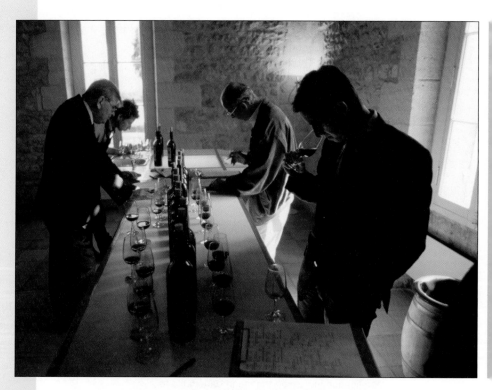

The Damon family owns a large grape vineyard in western New York along Lake Erie. The grapevines must be sprayed at the beginning of the growing season to protect against various insects and diseases. Two new insecticides have just been marketed, Pernod 5 and Action. When the grapes ripened, 400 of the vines treated with Pernod 5 were checked for infestation, and 400 of the vines treated with Action were checked. At the .05 significance level, can we conclude that there is a difference in the proportion of vines infested using Pernod 5 as opposed to Action? (Exercise 9, LO2)

Introduction

Chapter 10 began our study of hypothesis testing. We described the nature of hypothesis testing and conducted tests of a hypothesis in which we compared the results of a single sample to a population value. That is, we selected a single random sample from a population and conducted a test of whether the proposed population value was reasonable. Recall, in Chapter 10 we selected a sample of the number of desks assembled per week at Jamestown Steel Company to determine whether there was a change in the production rate. Similarly, we sampled voters in one area of a particular state to determine whether the population proportion that

would support the governor for reelection was less than .80. In both of these cases, we compared the results of a *single* sample statistic to a population parameter.

In this chapter we expand the idea of hypothesis testing to two samples. That is, we select random samples from two different populations to determine whether the population means or proportions are equal. Some questions we might want to test are:

1. Is there a difference in the mean value of residential real estate sold by male agents and female agents in south Florida?
2. Is there a difference in the mean number of defects produced on the day and the afternoon shifts at Kimble Products?
3. Is there a difference in the mean number of days absent between young workers (under 21 years of age) and older workers (more than 60 years of age) in the fast-food industry?
4. Is there a difference in the proportion of Ohio State University graduates and University of Cincinnati graduates who pass the state Certified Public Accountant Examination on their first attempt?
5. Is there an increase in the production rate if music is piped into the production area?

We begin this chapter with the case in which we select random samples from two independent populations and wish to investigate whether these populations have the same mean.

Two-Sample Tests of Hypothesis: Independent Samples

A city planner in Florida wishes to know whether there is a difference in the mean hourly wage rate of plumbers and electricians in central Florida. A financial accountant wishes to know whether the mean rate of return for high yield mutual funds is different from the mean rate of return on global mutual funds. In each of these cases there are two independent populations. In the first case, the plumbers represent one population and the electricians the other. In the second case, high-yield mutual funds are one population and global mutual funds the other.

In each of these cases, to investigate the question, we would select a random sample from each population and compute the mean of the two samples. If the two population means are the same, that is, the mean hourly rate is the same for the plumbers and the electricians, we would expect the *difference* between the two sample means to be zero. But what if our sample results yield a difference other than zero? Is that difference due to chance or is it because there is a real difference in the hourly earnings? A two-sample test of means will help to answer this question.

We do need to return to the results of Chapter 8. Recall we showed that a distribution of sample means would tend to approximate the normal distribution. We need to again assume a distribution of sample means will follow the normal distribution. It can be shown mathematically that the distribution of the differences between sample means for two normal distributions is also normal.

We can illustrate this theory in terms of the city planner in Tampa, Florida. To begin, let's assume some information that is not usually available. Suppose the population of plumbers has a mean of $30.00 per hour and a standard deviation of $5.00 per hour. The population of electricians has a mean of $29.00 and a standard deviation of $4.50. Now, from this information it is clear that the two population means are not the same. The plumbers actually earn $1.00 per hour more than the electricians. But we cannot expect to uncover this difference each time we sample the two populations.

Suppose we select a random sample of 40 plumbers and a random sample of 35 electricians and compute the mean of each sample. Then, we determine the difference between the sample means. It is this difference between the sample means that holds our interest. If the populations have the same mean, then we would expect the difference between the two sample means to be zero. If there is a difference between the population means, then we expect to find a difference between the sample means.

To understand the theory, we need to take several pairs of samples, compute the mean of each, determine the difference between the sample means, and study the distribution of the differences in the sample means. Because of our study of the distribution of sample means in Chapter 8, we know the distribution of the sample means follows the normal distribution. If the two distributions of sample means follow the normal distribution, then we can reason the distribution of their differences will also follow the normal distribution. This is the first hurdle.

The second hurdle refers to the mean of this distribution of differences. If we find the mean of this distribution is zero, this implies there is no difference in the two populations. On the other hand, if the mean of the distribution of differences is equal to some value other than zero, either positive or negative, then we conclude the two populations do not have the same mean.

To report some concrete results, let's return to the city planner in Tampa, Florida. Table 11–1 shows the result of selecting 20 different samples of 40 plumbers and 35 electricians, computing the mean of each sample, and finding the difference between the two sample means. In the first case the sample of 40 plumbers has a mean of $29.80, and for the 35 electricians the mean is $28.76. The difference between the sample means is $1.04. This process was repeated 19 more times. Observe that in 17 of the 20 cases the mean of the plumbers is larger than the mean of the electricians.

Our final hurdle is that we need to know something about the *variability* of the distribution of differences. To put it another way, what is the standard deviation of this distribution of differences? Statistical theory shows when we have independent populations, such as the case here, the distribution of the differences has a variance (standard deviation squared) equal to the sum of the two individual variances. This means that we can add the variances of the two sampling distributions. To put it another way, the variance of the difference in sample means $(\bar{X}_1 - \bar{X}_2)$ is equal to the sum of the variance of the plumber's mean hourly rate and the variance of the electrician's mean hourly rate.

VARIANCE OF THE DISTRIBUTION OF DIFFERENCES IN MEANS	$\sigma^2_{\bar{X}_1 - \bar{X}_2} = \dfrac{\sigma^2_1}{n_1} + \dfrac{\sigma^2_2}{n_2}$	**[11–1]**

TABLE 11–1 The Means of Random Samples of Plumbers and Electricians

Sample	Plumbers	Electricians	Difference
1	$29.80	$28.76	$1.04
2	30.32	29.40	0.92
3	30.57	29.94	0.63
4	30.04	28.93	1.11
5	30.09	29.78	0.31
6	30.02	28.66	1.36
7	29.60	29.13	0.47
8	29.63	29.42	0.21
9	30.17	29.29	0.88
10	30.81	29.75	1.06
11	30.09	28.05	2.04
12	29.35	29.07	0.28
13	29.42	28.79	0.63
14	29.78	29.54	0.24
15	29.60	29.60	0.00
16	30.60	30.19	0.41
17	30.79	28.65	2.14
18	29.14	29.95	−0.81
19	29.91	28.75	1.16
20	28.74	29.21	−0.47

LO1 Conduct a test of a hypothesis about the difference between two independent population means.

The term $\sigma^2_{\bar{X}_1-\bar{X}_2}$ looks complex but need not be difficult to interpret. The σ^2 portion reminds us that it is a variance, and the subscript $\bar{X}_1 - \bar{X}_2$ that it is a distribution of differences in the sample means.

We can put this equation in a more usable form by taking the square root, so that we have the standard deviation of the distribution or "standard error" of the differences. Finally, we standardize the distribution of the differences. The result is the following equation.

TWO-SAMPLE TEST OF MEANS—KNOWN σ	$z = \dfrac{\bar{X}_1 - \bar{X}_2}{\sqrt{\dfrac{\sigma_1^2}{n_1} + \dfrac{\sigma_2^2}{n_2}}}$	[11–2]

Before we present an example, let's review the assumptions necessary for using formula (11–2).

1. The two samples must be unrelated, that is, independent.
2. The standard deviations for both populations must be known.

Assumptions for testing independent sample means.

The following example shows the details of the test of hypothesis for two population means.

Example

Customers at FoodTown Supermarkets have a choice when paying for their groceries. They may check out and pay using the standard cashier-assisted checkout, or they may use the new Fast Lane procedure. In the standard procedure a FoodTown employee scans each item, puts it on a short conveyor where another employee puts it in a bag and then into the grocery cart. In the Fast Lane procedure the customer scans each item, bags it, and places the bags in the cart themselves.

The Fast Lane procedure is designed to reduce the time a customer spends in the checkout line.

The Fast Lane facility was recently installed at the Byrne Road FoodTown location. The store manager would like to know if the mean checkout time using the standard checkout method is longer than using the Fast Lane. She gathered the following sample information. The time is measured from when the customer enters the line until their bags are in the cart. Hence the time includes both waiting in line and checking out. What is the p-value?

Customer Type	Sample Mean	Population Standard Deviation	Sample Size
Standard	5.50 minutes	0.40 minutes	50
Fast Lane	5.30 minutes	0.30 minutes	100

Solution

We use the five-step hypothesis testing procedure to investigate the question.

Step 1: State the null hypothesis and the alternate hypothesis. The null hypothesis is that there is no difference in the mean checkout times for the two groups. In other words, the difference of 0.20 minutes between the mean checkout time for the standard method and the mean checkout time for Fast Lane is due to chance. The alternate hypothesis is that the mean checkout time is longer for those using the standard method. We will let μ_s refer to the mean checkout time for the population of standard customers and μ_f the mean checkout time for the Fast Lane customers. The null and alternative hypotheses are:

$$H_0: \mu_s \leq \mu_f$$
$$H_1: \mu_s > \mu_f$$

Step 2: Select the level of significance. The significance level is the probability that we reject the null hypothesis when it is actually true. This likelihood is determined prior to selecting the sample or performing any calculations. The .05 and .01 significance levels are the most common, but other values, such as .02 and .10, are also used. In theory, we may select any value between 0 and 1 for the significance level. In this case we selected the .01 significance level.

Step 3: Determine the test statistic. In Chapter 10 we used the standard normal distribution (that is z) and t as test statistics. In this case we use the z distribution as the test statistic because the standard deviations of both populations are known.

Step 4: Formulate a decision rule. The decision rule is based on the null and the alternate hypotheses (i.e., one-tailed or two-tailed test), the level of significance, and the test statistic used. We selected the .01 significance level and the z distribution as the test statistic, and we wish to determine whether the mean checkout time is longer using the standard method. We set the alternate hypothesis to indicate that the mean checkout time is longer for those using the standard method than the Fast Lane method. Hence, the rejection region is in the upper tail of the standard normal distribution (a one-tailed test). To find the critical value, place .01 of the total area in the upper tail. This means that .4900 (.5000 − .0100) of the area is located between the z value of 0 and the critical value. Next,

Statistics in Action

Do you live to work or work to live? A recent poll of 802 working Americans revealed that, among those who considered their work as a career, the mean number of hours worked per day was 8.7. Among those who considered their work as a job, the mean number of hours worked per day was 7.6.

we search the body of Appendix B.1 for a value located near .4900. It is 2.33, so our decision rule is to reject H_0 if the value computed from the test statistic exceeds 2.33. Chart 11–1 depicts the decision rule.

$H_0: \mu_s \leq \mu_f$
$H_1: \mu_s > \mu_f$

.5000   .4900   Region of rejection .01

0   2.33   Scale of z
         Critical value

CHART 11–1 Decision Rule for One-Tailed Test at .01 Significance Level

Step 5: Make the decision regarding H_0 and interpret the result. We use formula (11–2) to compute the value of the test statistic.

$$z = \frac{\bar{X}_s - \bar{X}_f}{\sqrt{\dfrac{\sigma_s^2}{n_s} + \dfrac{\sigma_f^2}{n_f}}} = \frac{5.5 - 5.3}{\sqrt{\dfrac{0.40^2}{50} + \dfrac{0.30^2}{100}}} = \frac{0.2}{0.064} = 3.13$$

The computed value of 3.13 is larger than the critical value of 2.33. Our decision is to reject the null hypothesis and accept the alternate hypothesis. The difference of .20 minutes between the mean checkout time using the standard method is too large to have occurred by chance. To put it another way, we conclude the Fast Lane method is faster.

What is the p-value for the test statistic? Recall that the p-value is the probability of finding a value of the test statistic this extreme when the null hypothesis is true. To calculate the p-value we need the probability of a z value larger than 3.13. From Appendix B.1 we cannot find the probability associated with 3.13. The largest value available is 3.09. The area corresponding to 3.09 is .4990. In this case we can report that the p-value is less than .0010, found by .5000 − .4990. We conclude that there is very little likelihood that the null hypothesis is true!

In summary, the criteria for using formula (11–2) are:

1. *The samples are from independent populations.* This means the checkout time for the Fast Lane customers is unrelated to the checkout time for the other customers. For example, Mr. Smith's checkout time does not affect any other customer's checkout time.
2. *Both population standard deviations are known.* In the FoodTown example, the population standard deviation of the Fast Lane times was 0.30 minutes. The standard deviation of the standard checkout times was 0.40 minutes.

Self-Review 11–1 Tom Sevits is the owner of the Appliance Patch. Recently Tom observed a difference in the dollar value of sales between the men and women he employs as sales associates. A sample of 40 days revealed the men sold a mean of $1,400 worth of appliances per day. For a sample of 50 days, the women sold a mean of $1,500 worth of appliances per day. Assume the population standard deviation for men is $200 and for women $250. At the .05 significance level can Mr. Sevits conclude that the mean amount sold per day is larger for the women?

(a) State the null hypothesis and the alternate hypothesis.
(b) What is the decision rule?
(c) What is the value of the test statistic?
(d) What is your decision regarding the null hypothesis?
(e) What is the *p*-value?
(f) Interpret the result.

Exercises

1. A sample of 40 observations is selected from one population with a population standard deviation of 5. The sample mean is 102. A sample of 50 observations is selected from a second population with a population standard deviation of 6. The sample mean is 99. Conduct the following test of hypothesis using the .04 significance level.

$$H_0: \mu_1 = \mu_2$$
$$H_1: \mu_1 \neq \mu_2$$

   a. Is this a one-tailed or a two-tailed test?
   b. State the decision rule.
   c. Compute the value of the test statistic.
   d. What is your decision regarding H_0?
   e. What is the *p*-value?

2. A sample of 65 observations is selected from one population with a population standard deviation of 0.75. The sample mean is 2.67. A sample of 50 observations is selected from a second population with a population standard deviation of 0.66. The sample mean is 2.59. Conduct the following test of hypothesis using the .08 significance level.

$$H_0: \mu_1 \leq \mu_2$$
$$H_1: \mu_1 > \mu_2$$

   a. Is this a one-tailed or a two-tailed test?
   b. State the decision rule.
   c. Compute the value of the test statistic.
   d. What is your decision regarding H_0?
   e. What is the *p*-value?

Note: Use the five-step hypothesis testing procedure to solve the following exercises.

3. Gibbs Baby Food Company wishes to compare the weight gain of infants using its brand versus its competitor's. A sample of 40 babies using the Gibbs products revealed a mean weight gain of 7.6 pounds in the first three months after birth. For the Gibbs brand the population standard deviation of the sample is 2.3 pounds. A sample of 55 babies using the competitor's brand revealed a mean increase in weight of 8.1 pounds. The population standard deviation is 2.9 pounds. At the .05 significance level, can we conclude that babies using the Gibbs brand gained less weight? Compute the *p*-value and interpret it.

4. As part of a study of corporate employees, the director of human resources for PNC, Inc., wants to compare the distance traveled to work by employees at its office in downtown Cincinnati with the distance for those in downtown Pittsburgh. A sample of 35 Cincinnati employees showed they travel a mean of 370 miles per month. A sample of 40 Pittsburgh employees showed they travel a mean of 380 miles per month. The population standard deviation for the Cincinnati and Pittsburgh employees

are 30 and 26 miles, respectively. At the .05 significance level, is there a difference in the mean number of miles traveled per month between Cincinnati and Pittsburgh employees?

5. A financial analyst wants to compare the turnover rates, in percent, for shares of oil-related stocks versus other stocks, such as GE and IBM. She selected 32 oil-related stocks and 49 other stocks. The mean turnover rate of oil-related stocks is 31.4 percent and the population standard deviation 5.1 percent. For the other stocks, the mean rate was computed to be 34.9 percent and the population standard deviation 6.7 percent. Is there a significant difference in the turnover rates of the two types of stock? Use the .01 significance level.

6. Mary Jo Fitzpatrick is the vice president for Nursing Services at St. Luke's Memorial Hospital. Recently she noticed in the job postings for nurses that those that are unionized seem to offer higher wages. She decided to investigate and gathered the following information.

Group	Mean Wage	Population Standard Deviation	Sample Size
Union	$20.75	$2.25	40
Nonunion	$19.80	$1.90	45

Would it be reasonable for her to conclude that union nurses earn more? Use the .02 significance level. What is the *p*-value?

Two-Sample Tests about Proportions

In the previous section, we considered a test involving population means. However, we are often interested also in whether two sample proportions come from populations that are equal. Here are several examples.

- The vice president of human resources wishes to know whether there is a difference in the proportion of hourly employees who miss more than 5 days of work per year at the Atlanta and the Houston plants.

LO2 Conduct a test of a hypothesis about the difference between two population proportions.

- Ford is considering a new design for the Mustang. The design is shown to a group of potential buyers under 30 years of age and another group over 60 years of age. Ford wishes to know whether there is a difference in the proportion of the two groups who like the new design.
- A consultant to the airline industry is investigating the fear of flying among adults. Specifically, the company wishes to know whether there is a difference in the proportion of men versus women who are fearful of flying.

In the above cases each sampled item or individual can be classified as a "success" or a "failure." That is, in the Ford Mustang example each potential buyer is classified as "liking the new design" or "not liking the new design." We then compare the proportion in the under 30 group with the proportion in the over 60 group who indicated they liked the new design. Can we conclude that the differences are due to chance? In this study there is no measurement obtained, only classifying the individuals or objects.

To conduct the test, we assume each sample is large enough that the normal distribution will serve as a good approximation of the binomial distribution. The test statistic follows the standard normal distribution. We compute the value of *z* from the following formula:

TWO-SAMPLE TEST OF PROPORTIONS

$$z = \frac{p_1 - p_2}{\sqrt{\dfrac{p_c(1 - p_c)}{n_1} + \dfrac{p_c(1 - p_c)}{n_2}}}$$

[11–3]

Formula (11–3) is formula (11–2) with the respective sample proportions replacing the sample means and $p_c(1 - p_c)$ replacing the two variances. In addition:

n_1 is the number of observations in the first sample.
n_2 is the number of observations in the second sample.
p_1 is the proportion in the first sample possessing the trait.
p_2 is the proportion in the second sample possessing the trait.
p_c is the pooled proportion possessing the trait in the combined samples. It is called the pooled estimate of the population proportion and is computed from the following formula.

POOLED PROPORTION $$p_c = \frac{X_1 + X_2}{n_1 + n_2}$$ **[11–4]**

where:
X_1 is the number possessing the trait in the first sample.
X_2 is the number possessing the trait in the second sample.

The following example will illustrate the two-sample test of proportions.

Example

Manelli Perfume Company recently developed a new fragrance that it plans to market under the name Heavenly. A number of market studies indicate that Heavenly has very good market potential. The Sales Department at Manelli is particularly interested in whether there is a difference in the proportions of younger and older women who would purchase Heavenly if it were marketed. There are two independent populations, a population consisting of the younger women and a population consisting of the older women. Each sampled woman will be asked to smell Heavenly and indicate whether she likes the fragrance well enough to purchase a bottle.

Solution

We will use the usual five-step hypothesis-testing procedure.

Step 1: State H_0 and H_1. In this case the null hypothesis is: "There is no difference in the proportion of young women and older women who prefer Heavenly." We designate π_1 as the proportion of young women who would purchase Heavenly and π_2 as the proportion of older women who would purchase. The alternate hypothesis is that the two proportions are not equal.

$$H_0: \pi_1 = \pi_2$$
$$H_1: \pi_1 \neq \pi_2$$

Step 2: Select the level of significance. We choose the .05 significance level in this example.

Step 3: Determine the test statistic. The test statistic follows the standard normal distribution. The value of the test statistic can be computed from formula (11–3).

Step 4: Formulate the decision rule. Recall that the alternate hypothesis from **Step 1** does not state a direction, so this is a two-tailed test. To determine the critical value, we divide the significance level in half and place this amount in each tail of the z distribution. Next, we subtract this amount from the total area to the right of zero. That is .5000 − .0250 = .4750. Finally, we search the body of the z table (Appendix B.1) for the closest value. It is 1.96. The critical values are −1.96 and +1.96. As before, if the computed z value falls in the region between $+1.96$ and -1.96, the null hypothesis is not rejected. If that does occur, it is assumed that any difference between the two sample proportions is due to chance variation. This information is summarized in Chart 11–2.

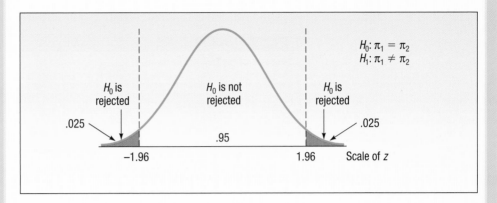

$$H_0: \pi_1 = \pi_2$$
$$H_1: \pi_1 \neq \pi_2$$

H_0 is rejected

H_0 is not rejected

H_0 is rejected

.025

.025

.95

-1.96 1.96   Scale of z

CHART 11–2 Decision Rules for Heavenly Fragrance Test, .05 Significance Level

Step 5: Select a sample and make a decision. A random sample of 100 young women revealed 19 liked the Heavenly fragrance well enough to purchase it. Similarly, a sample of 200 older women revealed 62 liked the fragrance well enough to make a purchase. We let p_1 refer to the young women and p_2 to the older women.

$$p_1 = \frac{X_1}{n_1} = \frac{19}{100} = .19 \qquad p_2 = \frac{X_2}{n_2} = \frac{62}{200} = .31$$

The research question is whether the difference of .12 in the two sample proportions is due to chance or whether there is a difference in the proportion of younger and older women who like the Heavenly fragrance.

Next, we combine or pool the sample proportions. We use formula (11–4).

$$p_c = \frac{X_1 + X_2}{n_1 + n_2} = \frac{19 + 62}{100 + 200} = \frac{81}{300} = 0.27$$

Note that the pooled proportion is closer to .31 than to .19 because more older women than younger women were sampled.

We use formula (11–3) to find the value of the test statistic.

$$z = \frac{p_1 - p_2}{\sqrt{\dfrac{p_c(1 - p_c)}{n_1} + \dfrac{p_c(1 - p_c)}{n_2}}} = \frac{.19 - .31}{\sqrt{\dfrac{.27(1 - .27)}{100} + \dfrac{.27(1 - .27)}{200}}} = -2.21$$

The computed value of -2.21 is in the area of rejection; that is, it is to the left of -1.96. Therefore, the null hypothesis is rejected at the .05 significance level. To put it another way, we reject the null hypothesis that the proportion of young women who would purchase Heavenly is equal to the proportion of older women who would purchase Heavenly. It is unlikely that the difference between the two sample proportions is due to chance. To find the p-value, go to Appendix B.1 and find the likelihood of a z value less than -2.21 or greater than 2.21. The z value corresponding to 2.21 is .4864. So the likelihood of finding the value of the test statistic to be less than -2.21 or greater than 2.21 is:

$$p\text{-value} = 2(.5000 - .4864) = 2(.0136) = .0272$$

The *p*-value of .0272 is less than the significance level of .05, so our decision is to reject the null hypothesis. Again, we conclude that there is a difference in the proportion of younger and older women who would purchase Heavenly.

The MINITAB system has a procedure to quickly determine the value of the test statistic and compute the *p*-value. The results follow.

```
Session                                                        _ □ ×

Test and CI for Two Proportions

Sample   X    N   Sample p              I
1       19  100  0.190000
2       62  200  0.310000


Difference = p (1) - p (2)
Estimate for difference:  -0.12
95% CI for difference:  (-0.220102, -0.0198978)
Test for difference = 0 (vs not = 0):   Z = -2.21   P-Value = 0.027

Fisher's exact test: P-Value = 0.028
```

Notice the MINITAB output includes the two sample proportions, the value of *z*, and the *p*-value.

Self-Review 11–2

Of 150 adults who tried a new peach-flavored Peppermint Pattie, 87 rated it excellent. Of 200 children sampled, 123 rated it excellent. Using the .10 level of significance, can we conclude that there is a significant difference in the proportion of adults and the proportion of children who rate the new flavor excellent?
(a)   State the null hypothesis and the alternate hypothesis.
(b)   What is the probability of a Type I error?
(c)   Is this a one-tailed or a two-tailed test?
(d)   What is the decision rule?
(e)   What is the value of the test statistic?
(f)   What is your decision regarding the null hypothesis?
(g)   What is the *p*-value? Explain what it means in terms of this problem.

Exercises

7. The null and alternate hypotheses are:

$$H_0: \pi_1 \leq \pi_2$$
$$H_1: \pi_1 > \pi_2$$

A sample of 100 observations from the first population indicated that X_1 is 70. A sample of 150 observations from the second population revealed X_2 to be 90. Use the .05 significance level to test the hypothesis.
a. State the decision rule.
b. Compute the pooled proportion.
c. Compute the value of the test statistic.
d. What is your decision regarding the null hypothesis?

8. The null and alternate hypotheses are:

$$H_0: \pi_1 = \pi_2$$
$$H_1: \pi_1 \neq \pi_2$$

A sample of 200 observations from the first population indicated that X_1 is 170. A sample of 150 observations from the second population revealed X_2 to be 110. Use the .05 significance level to test the hypothesis.

a. State the decision rule.

b. Compute the pooled proportion.

c. Compute the value of the test statistic.

d. What is your decision regarding the null hypothesis?

Note: Use the five-step hypothesis-testing procedure in solving the following exercises.

9. The Damon family owns a large grape vineyard in western New York along Lake Erie. The grapevines must be sprayed at the beginning of the growing season to protect against various insects and diseases. Two new insecticides have just been marketed: Pernod 5 and Action. To test their effectiveness, three long rows were selected and sprayed with Pernod 5, and three others were sprayed with Action. When the grapes ripened, 400 of the vines treated with Pernod 5 were checked for infestation. Likewise, a sample of 400 vines sprayed with Action were checked. The results are:

Insecticide	Number of Vines Checked (sample size)	Number of Infested Vines
Pernod 5	400	24
Action	400	40

At the .05 significance level, can we conclude that there is a difference in the proportion of vines infested using Pernod 5 as opposed to Action?

10. The GfK Custom Research America, formerly known as the Roper Organization, conducted identical surveys 5 years apart. One question asked of women was "Are most men basically kind, gentle, and thoughtful?" The earlier survey revealed that, of the 3,000 women surveyed, 2,010 said that they were. The latter revealed 1,530 of the 3,000 women surveyed thought that men were kind, gentle, and thoughtful. At the .05 level, can we conclude that women think men are less kind, gentle, and thoughtful in the later survey compared with the earlier one?

11. A nationwide sample of influential Republicans and Democrats was asked as a part of a comprehensive survey whether they favored lowering environmental standards so that high-sulfur coal could be burned in coal-fired power plants. The results were:

	Republicans	Democrats
Number sampled	1,000	800
Number in favor	200	168

At the .02 level of significance, can we conclude that there is a larger proportion of Democrats in favor of lowering the standards? Determine the *p*-value.

12. The research department at the home office of New Hampshire Insurance conducts on-going research on the causes of automobile accidents, the characteristics of the drivers, and so on. A random sample of 400 policies written on single persons revealed 120 had at least one accident in the previous three-year period. Similarly, a sample of 600 policies written on married persons revealed that 150 had been in at least one accident. At the .05 significance level, is there a significant difference in the proportions of single and married persons having an accident during a three-year period? Determine the *p*-value.

Comparing Population Means with Unknown Population Standard Deviations (the Pooled *t*-Test)

In the previous two sections we described conditions where the standard normal distribution, that is *z*, is used as the test statistic. In one case we were working with a variable (calculating the mean) and in the second an attribute (calculating a proportion). In the first case we wished to compare two sample means from independent populations to determine if they came from the same or equal populations. In that instance we assumed the population followed the normal probability distribution and that we knew the standard deviation of the population. In many cases, in fact in most cases, we do not know the population standard deviation. We can overcome this problem, as we did in the one sample case in the previous chapter, by substituting the sample standard deviation (s) for the population standard deviation (σ). See formula (10–2) on page 301.

This section describes another method for comparing the sample means of two independent populations to determine if the sampled populations could reasonably have the same mean. The method described does *not* require that we know the standard deviations of the populations. This gives us a great deal more flexibility when investigating the difference in sample means. There are two major differences in this test and the previous test described earlier in this chapter.

1. We assume the sampled populations have equal but unknown standard deviations. Because of this assumption we combine or "pool" the sample standard deviations.
2. We use the *t* distribution as the test statistic.

The formula for computing the value of the test statistic *t* is similar to (11–2), but an additional calculation is necessary. The two sample standard deviations are pooled to form a single estimate of the unknown population standard deviation. In essence we compute a weighted mean of the two sample standard deviations and use this value as an estimate of the unknown population standard deviation. The weights are the degrees of freedom that each sample provides. Why do we need to pool the sample standard deviations? Because we assume that the two populations have equal standard deviations, the best estimate we can make of that value is to combine or pool all the sample information we have about the value of the population standard deviation.

The following formula is used to pool the sample standard deviations. Notice that two factors are involved: the number of observations in each sample and the sample standard deviations themselves.

POOLED VARIANCE	$s_p^2 = \dfrac{(n_1 - 1)s_1^2 + (n_2 - 1)s_2^2}{n_1 + n_2 - 2}$	[11–5]

where:
  s_1^2 is the variance (standard deviation squared) of the first sample.
  s_2^2 is the variance of the second sample.

The value of *t* is computed from the following equation.

TWO-SAMPLE TEST OF MEANS—UNKNOWN σ'S	$t = \dfrac{\bar{X}_1 - \bar{X}_2}{\sqrt{s_p^2\left(\dfrac{1}{n_1} + \dfrac{1}{n_2}\right)}}$	[11–6]

where:
  $\bar{X}_1$ is the mean of the first sample.
  $\bar{X}_2$ is the mean of the second sample.
  n_1 is the number of observations in the first sample.
  n_2 is the number of observations in the second sample.
  s_p^2 is the pooled estimate of the population variance.

The number of degrees of freedom in the test is the total number of items sampled minus the total number of samples. Because there are two samples, there are $n_1 + n_2 - 2$ degrees of freedom.

To summarize, there are three requirements or assumptions for the test.

1. The sampled populations follow the normal distribution.
2. The sampled populations are independent.
3. The standard deviations of the two populations are equal.

The following example explains the details of the test.

Example

Owens Lawn Care, Inc., manufactures and assembles lawnmowers that are shipped to dealers throughout the United States and Canada. Two different procedures have been proposed for mounting the engine on the frame of the lawnmower. The question is: Is there a difference in the mean time to mount the engines on the frames of the lawnmowers? The first procedure was developed by longtime Owens employee Herb Welles (designated as procedure 1), and the other procedure was developed by Owens Vice President of Engineering William Atkins (designated as procedure 2). To evaluate the two methods, it was decided to conduct a time and motion study. A sample of five employees was timed using the Welles method and six using the Atkins method. The results, in minutes, are shown below. Is there a difference in the mean mounting times? Use the .10 significance level.

Welles (minutes)	Atkins (minutes)
2	3
4	7
9	5
3	8
2	4
	3

Solution

Following the five steps to test a hypothesis, the null hypothesis states that there is no difference in mean mounting times between the two procedures. The alternate hypothesis indicates that there is a difference.

$$H_0: \mu_1 = \mu_2$$
$$H_1: \mu_1 \neq \mu_2$$

The required assumptions are:

1. The observations in the Welles sample are *independent* of the observations in the Atkins sample.
2. The two populations follow the normal distribution.
3. The two populations have equal standard deviations.

Is there a difference between the mean assembly times using the Welles and the Atkins methods? The degrees of freedom are equal to the total number of items sampled minus the number of samples. In this case that is $n_1 + n_2 - 2$. Five assemblers used the Welles method and six the Atkins method. Thus, there are 9 degrees of freedom, found by $5 + 6 - 2$. The critical values of t, from Appendix B.2 for $df = 9$, a two-tailed test, and the .10 significance level, are -1.833 and 1.833. The decision rule is portrayed graphically in Chart 11–3. We reject the null hypothesis if the computed value of t is less than -1.833 or greater than 1.833.

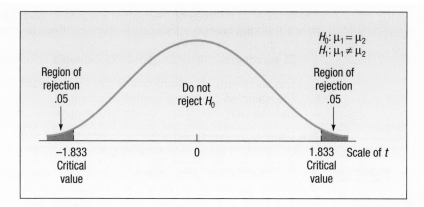

CHART 11–3 Regions of Rejection, Two-Tailed Test, $df = 9$, and .10 Significance Level

We use three steps to compute the value of t.

Step 1: Calculate the sample standard deviations. To compute the sample standard deviations, we use formula (3–9) from page 80. See the details below.

Welles Method		Atkins Method	
X_1	$(X_1 - \bar{X}_1)^2$	X_2	$(X_2 - \bar{X}_2)^2$
2	$(2 - 4)^2 = 4$	3	$(3 - 5)^2 = 4$
4	$(4 - 4)^2 = 0$	7	$(7 - 5)^2 = 4$
9	$(9 - 4)^2 = 25$	5	$(5 - 5)^2 = 0$
3	$(3 - 4)^2 = 1$	8	$(8 - 5)^2 = 9$
2	$(2 - 4)^2 = 4$	4	$(4 - 5)^2 = 1$
20	34	3	$(3 - 5)^2 = 4$
		30	22

$$\bar{X}_1 = \frac{\Sigma X_1}{n_1} = \frac{20}{5} = 4 \qquad\qquad \bar{X}_2 = \frac{\Sigma X_2}{n_2} = \frac{30}{6} = 5$$

$$s_1 = \sqrt{\frac{\Sigma(X_1 - \bar{X}_1)^2}{n_1 - 1}} = \sqrt{\frac{34}{5 - 1}} = 2.9155 \qquad s_2 = \sqrt{\frac{\Sigma(X_2 - \bar{X}_2)^2}{n_2 - 1}} = \sqrt{\frac{22}{6 - 1}} = 2.0976$$

Step 2: Pool the Sample Variances. We use formula (11–5) to pool the sample variances (standard deviations squared).

$$s_p^2 = \frac{(n_1 - 1)s_1^2 + (n_2 - 1)s_2^2}{n_1 + n_2 - 2} = \frac{(5 - 1)(2.9155)^2 + (6 - 1)(2.0976)^2}{5 + 6 - 2} = 6.2222$$

Step 3: Determine the value of t. The mean mounting time for the Welles method is 4.00 minutes, found by $\bar{X}_1 = 20/5$. The mean mounting time for the Atkins method is 5.00 minutes, found by $\bar{X}_2 = 30/6$. We use formula (11–6) to calculate the value of t.

$$t = \frac{\bar{X}_1 - \bar{X}_2}{\sqrt{s_p^2\left(\dfrac{1}{n_1} + \dfrac{1}{n_2}\right)}} = \frac{4.00 - 5.00}{\sqrt{6.2222\left(\dfrac{1}{5} + \dfrac{1}{6}\right)}} = -0.662$$

The decision is not to reject the null hypothesis, because −0.662 falls in the region between −1.833 and 1.833. We conclude that there is no difference in the mean times to mount the engine on the frame using the two methods.

We can also estimate the *p*-value using Appendix B.2. Locate the row with 9 degrees of freedom, and use the two-tailed test column. Find the *t* value, without regard to the sign, which is closest to our computed value of 0.662. It is 1.383, corresponding to a significance level of .20. Thus, even had we used the 20 percent significance level, we would not have rejected the null hypothesis of equal means. We can report that the *p*-value is greater than .20.

Excel has a procedure called "t-Test: Two Sample Assuming Equal Variances" that will perform the calculations of formulas (11–5) and (11–6) as well as find the sample means and sample variances. The details of the procedure are shown in the Software Commands section at the end of the chapter. The data are input in the first two columns of the Excel spreadsheet. They are labeled "Welles" and "Atkins." The output follows. The value of *t*, called the "t Stat," is −0.662, and the two-tailed *p*-value is .525. As we would expect, the *p*-value is larger than the significance level of .10. The conclusion is not to reject the null hypothesis.

Excel

welles and atkins

	A	B	C	D	E	F	G
1	Welles	Atkins		t-Test: Two-Sample Assuming Equal Variances			
2	2	3					
3	4	7			*Welles*	*Atkins*	
4	9	5		Mean	4.000	5.000	
5	3	8		Variance	8.500	4.400	
6	2	4		Observations	5.000	6.000	
7		3		Pooled Variance	6.222		
8				Hypothesized Mean Difference	0.000		
9				df	9.000		
10				t Stat	-0.662		
11				P(T<=t) one-tail	0.262		
12				t Critical one-tail	1.833		
13				P(T<=t) two-tail	0.525		
14				t Critical two-tail	2.262		
15							

Self-Review 11–3 The production manager at Bellevue Steel, a manufacturer of wheelchairs, wants to compare the number of defective wheelchairs produced on the day shift with the number on the afternoon shift. A sample of the production from 6 day shifts and 8 afternoon shifts revealed the following number of defects.

Day	5	8	7	6	9	7		
Afternoon	8	10	7	11	9	12	14	9

At the .05 significance level, is there a difference in the mean number of defects per shift?
(a) State the null hypothesis and the alternate hypothesis.
(b) What is the decision rule?
(c) What is the value of the test statistic?
(d) What is your decision regarding the null hypothesis?
(e) What is the *p*-value?
(f) Interpret the result.
(g) What are the assumptions necessary for this test?

Exercises

For Exercises 13 and 14: (a) state the decision rule, (b) compute the pooled estimate of the population variance, (c) compute the test statistic, (d) state your decision about the null hypothesis, and (e) estimate the p-value.

13. The null and alternate hypotheses are:

$$H_0: \mu_1 = \mu_2$$
$$H_1: \mu_1 \neq \mu_2$$

A random sample of 10 observations from one population revealed a sample mean of 23 and a sample deviation of 4. A random sample of 8 observations from another population revealed a sample mean of 26 and a sample standard deviation of 5. At the .05 significance level, is there a difference between the population means?

14. The null and alternate hypotheses are:

$$H_0: \mu_1 = \mu_2$$
$$H_1: \mu_1 \neq \mu_2$$

A random sample of 15 observations from the first population revealed a sample mean of 350 and a sample standard deviation of 12. A random sample of 17 observations from the second population revealed a sample mean of 342 and a sample standard deviation of 15. At the .10 significance level, is there a difference in the population means?

Note: Use the five-step hypothesis testing procedure for the following exercises.

15. A sample of scores on an examination given in Statistics 201 are:

Men	72	69	98	66	85	76	79	80	77
Women	81	67	90	78	81	80	76		

At the .01 significance level, is the mean grade of the women higher than that of the men?

16. A recent study compared the time spent together by single- and dual-earner couples. According to the records kept by the wives during the study, the mean amount of time spent together watching television among the single-earner couples was 61 minutes per day, with a standard deviation of 15.5 minutes. For the dual-earner couples, the mean number of minutes spent watching television was 48.4 minutes, with a standard deviation of 18.1 minutes. At the .01 significance level, can we conclude that the single-earner couples on average spend more time watching television together? There were 15 single-earner and 12 dual-earner couples studied.

17. Ms. Lisa Monnin is the budget director for Nexus Media, Inc. She would like to compare the daily travel expenses for the sales staff and the audit staff. She collected the following sample information.

Sales ($)	131	135	146	165	136	142	
Audit ($)	130	102	129	143	149	120	139

At the .10 significance level, can she conclude that the mean daily expenses are greater for the sales staff than the audit staff? What is the p-value?

18. The Tampa Bay (Florida) Area Chamber of Commerce wanted to know whether the mean weekly salary of nurses was larger than that of school teachers. To investigate, they collected the following information on the amounts earned last week by a sample of school teachers and nurses.

School Teachers ($)	845	826	827	875	784	809	802	820	829	830	842	832
Nurses ($)	841	890	821	771	850	859	825	829				

Is it reasonable to conclude that the mean weekly salary of nurses is higher? Use the .01 significance level. What is the p-value?

Two-Sample Tests of Hypothesis: Dependent Samples

On page 333, we tested the difference between the means from two independent samples. We compared the mean time required to mount an engine using the Welles method to the time to mount the engine using the Atkins method. The samples were *independent*, meaning that the sample of assembly times using the Welles method was in no way related to the sample of assembly times using the Atkins method.

There are situations, however, in which the samples are not independent. To put it another way, the samples are *dependent* or *related*. As an example, Nickel Savings and Loan employs two firms, Schadek Appraisals and Bowyer Real Estate, to appraise the value of the real estate properties on which it makes loans. It is important that these two firms be similar in their appraisal values. To review the consistency of the two appraisal firms, Nickel Savings randomly selects 10 homes and has both Schadek Appraisals and Bowyer Real Estate appraise the value of the selected homes. For each home, there will be a pair of appraisal values. That is, for

each home there will be an appraised value from both Schadek Appraisals and Bowyer Real Estate. The appraised values depend on, or are related to, the home selected. This is also referred to as a **paired sample.**

For hypothesis testing, we are interested in the distribution of the *differences* in the appraised value of each home. Hence, there is only one sample. To put it more formally, we are investigating whether the mean of the distribution of differences in the appraised values is 0. The sample is made up of the *differences* between the appraised values determined by Schadek Appraisals and the values from Bowyer Real Estate. If the two appraisal firms are reporting similar estimates, then sometimes Schadek Appraisals will be the higher value and sometimes Bowyer Real Estate will have the higher value. However, the mean of the distribution of differences will be 0. On the other hand, if one of the firms consistently reports the larger appraisal values, then the mean of the distribution of the differences will not be 0.

We will use the symbol μ_d to indicate the population mean of the distribution of differences. We assume the distribution of the population of differences follows the normal distribution. The test statistic follows the t distribution and we calculate its value from the following formula:

LO3 Conduct a test of a hypothesis about the mean difference between *dependent observations.*

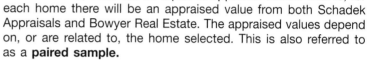

PAIRED t TEST	$t = \dfrac{\bar{d}}{s_d/\sqrt{n}}$	**[11–7]**

There are $n - 1$ degrees of freedom and

$\bar{d}$ is the mean of the difference between the paired or related observations.

s_d is the standard deviation of the differences between the paired or related observations.

n is the number of paired observations.

The standard deviation of the differences is computed by the familiar formula for the standard deviation (see formula 3–11), except d is substituted for X. The formula is:

$$s_d = \sqrt{\frac{\Sigma(d - \bar{d})^2}{n - 1}}$$

The following example illustrates this test.

Example

Recall that Nickel Savings and Loan wishes to compare the two companies it uses to appraise the value of residential homes. Nickel Savings selected a sample of 10 residential properties and scheduled both firms for an appraisal. The results, reported in $000, are:

Home	Schadek	Bowyer
1	235	228
2	210	205
3	231	219
4	242	240
5	205	198
6	230	223
7	231	227
8	210	215
9	225	222
10	249	245

At the .05 significance level, can we conclude there is a difference in the mean appraised values of the homes?

Solution

The first step is to state the null and the alternate hypotheses. In this case a two-tailed alternative is appropriate because we are interested in determining whether there is a *difference* in the appraised values. We are not interested in showing whether one particular firm appraises property at a higher value than the other. The question is whether the sample differences in the appraised values could have come from a population with a mean of 0. If the population mean of the differences is 0, then we conclude that there is no difference in the appraised values. The null and alternate hypotheses are:

$$H_0: \mu_d = 0$$
$$H_1: \mu_d \neq 0$$

There are 10 homes appraised by both firms, so $n = 10$, and $df = n - 1 = 10 - 1 = 9$. We have a two-tailed test, and the significance level is .05. To determine the critical value, go to Appendix B.2, move across the row with 9 degrees of freedom to the column for a two-tailed test and the .05 significance level. The value at the intersection is 2.262. This value appears in the box in Table 11–2. The decision rule is to reject the null hypothesis if the computed value of t is less than -2.262 or greater than 2.262. Here are the computational details.

Home	Schadek	Bowyer	Difference, d	$(d - \bar{d})$	$(d - \bar{d})^2$
1	235	228	7	2.4	5.76
2	210	205	5	0.4	0.16
3	231	219	12	7.4	54.76
4	242	240	2	−2.6	6.76
5	205	198	7	2.4	5.76
6	230	223	7	2.4	5.76
7	231	227	4	−0.6	0.36
8	210	215	−5	−9.6	92.16
9	225	222	3	−1.6	2.56
10	249	245	4	−0.6	0.36
			46	0	174.40

$$\overline{d} = \frac{\Sigma d}{n} = \frac{46}{10} = 4.60$$

$$s_d = \sqrt{\frac{\Sigma(d - \overline{d})^2}{n - 1}} = \sqrt{\frac{174.4}{10 - 1}} = 4.402$$

Using formula (11–7), the value of the test statistic is 3.305, found by

$$t = \frac{\overline{d}}{s_d/\sqrt{n}} = \frac{4.6}{4.402/\sqrt{10}} = 3.305$$

Because the computed t falls in the rejection region, the null hypothesis is rejected. The population distribution of differences does not have a mean of 0. We conclude that there is a difference in the mean appraised values of the homes. The largest difference of $12,000 is for Home 3. Perhaps that would be an appropriate place to begin a more detailed review.

To find the p-value, we use Appendix B.2 and the section for a two-tailed test. Move along the row with 9 degrees of freedom and find the values of t that are closest to our calculated value. For a .01 significance level, the value of t is 3.250. The computed value is larger than this value, but smaller than the value of 4.781 corresponding to the .001 significance level. Hence, the p-value is less than .01. This information is highlighted in Table 11–2.

TABLE 11–2 A Portion of the t Distribution from Appendix B.2

	Confidence Intervals					
	80%	90%	95%	98%	99%	99.9%
	Level of Significance for One-Tailed Test					
df	0.10	0.05	0.025	0.01	0.005	0.0005
	Level of Significance for Two-Tailed Test					
	0.20	0.10	0.05	0.02	0.01	0.001
1	3.078	6.314	12.706	31.821	63.657	636.619
2	1.886	2.920	4.303	6.965	9.925	31.599
3	1.638	2.353	3.182	4.541	5.841	12.924
4	1.533	2.132	2.776	3.747	4.604	8.610
5	1.476	2.015	2.571	3.365	4.032	6.869
6	1.440	1.943	2.447	3.143	3.707	5.959
7	1.415	1.895	2.365	2.998	3.499	5.408
8	1.397	1.860	2.306	2.896	3.355	5.041
9	1.383	1.833	2.262	2.821	3.250	4.781
10	1.372	1.812	2.228	2.764	3.169	4.587

Excel has a procedure called "t-Test: Paired Two-Sample for Means" that will perform the calculations of formula (11–7). The output from this procedure is given below.

The computed value of t is 3.305, and the two-tailed p-value is .009. Because the p-value is less than .05, we reject the hypothesis that the mean of the distribution of the differences between the appraised values is zero. In fact, this p-value is between .01 and .001. There is a small likelihood that the null hypothesis is true.

paired t test

	A	B	C	D	E	F	G
1	Home	Schadek	Bowyer		t-Test: Paired Two Sample for Means		
2	1	235	228				
3	2	210	205			*Schadek*	*Bowyer*
4	3	231	219		Mean	226.800	222.200
5	4	242	240		Variance	208.844	204.178
6	5	205	198		Observations	10.000	10.000
7	6	230	223		Pearson Correlation	0.953	
8	7	231	227		Hypothesized Mean Difference	0.000	
9	8	210	215		df	9.000	
10	9	225	222		t Stat	3.305	
11	10	249	245		P(T<=t) one-tail	0.005	
12					t Critical one-tail	1.833	
13					P(T<=t) two-tail	0.009	
14					t Critical two-tail	2.262	
15							

Comparing Dependent and Independent Samples

LO4 Understand the difference between *dependent* and *independent samples.*

Beginning students are often confused by the difference between tests for independent samples [formula (11–6)] and tests for dependent samples [formula (11–7)]. How do we tell the difference between dependent and independent samples? There are two types of dependent samples: (1) those characterized by a measurement, an intervention of some type, and then another measurement; and (2) a matching or pairing of the observations. To explain further:

1. The first type of dependent sample is characterized by a measurement followed by an intervention of some kind and then another measurement. This could be called a "before" and "after" study. Two examples will help to clarify. Suppose we want to show that, by placing speakers in the production area and playing soothing music, we are able to increase production. We begin by selecting a sample of workers and measuring their output under the current conditions. The speakers are then installed in the production area, and we again measure the output of the same workers. There are two measurements, before placing the speakers in the production area and after. The intervention is placing speakers in the production area.

   A second example involves an educational firm that offers courses designed to increase test scores and reading ability. Suppose the firm wants to offer a course that will help high school juniors increase their SAT scores. To begin, each student takes the SAT in the junior year in high school. During the summer between the junior and senior year, they participate in the course that gives them tips on taking tests. Finally, during the fall of their senior year in high school, they retake the SAT. Again, the procedure is characterized by a measurement (taking the SAT as a junior), an intervention (the summer workshops), and another measurement (taking the SAT during their senior year).

2. The second type of dependent sample is characterized by matching or pairing observations. Nickel Savings in the previous example is a dependent sample of this type. It selected a property for appraisal and then had two appraisals on the same property. As a second example, suppose an industrial psychologist wishes to study the intellectual similarities of newly married couples. She selects a sample of newlyweds. Next, she administers a standard intelligence test to both the man and woman to determine the difference in the scores. Notice the matching that occurred: comparing the scores that are paired or matched by marriage.

Why do we prefer dependent samples to independent samples? By using dependent samples, we are able to reduce the variation in the sampling distribution. To illustrate, we will use the Nickel Savings and Loan example just completed. Suppose we assume that we have two independent samples of real estate property for appraisal and conduct the following test of hypothesis, using formula (11–6). The null and alternate hypotheses are:

$$H_0: \mu_1 = \mu_2$$
$$H_1: \mu_1 \neq \mu_2$$

There are now two independent samples of 10 each. So the number of degrees of freedom is $10 + 10 - 2 = 18$. From Appendix B.2, for the .05 significance level, H_0 is rejected if t is less than -2.101 or greater than 2.101.

We use the same Excel commands as on page 93 in Chapter 3 to find the mean and the standard deviation of the two independent samples. We use the Excel commands on page 352 of this chapter to find the pooled variance and the value of the "t Stat." These values are highlighted in yellow.

Independent t test

	A	B	C	D	E	F	G	H
1	Home	Schadek	Bowyer		t-Test: Two-Sample Assuming Equal Variances			
2	1	235	228					
3	2	210	205			Schadek	Bowyer	
4	3	231	219		Mean	226.800	222.200	
5	4	242	240		Variance	208.844	204.178	
6	5	205	198		Observations	10.000	10.000	
7	6	230	223		Pooled Variance	206.511		
8	7	231	227		Hypothesized Mean Difference	0.000		
9	8	210	215		df	18.000		
10	9	225	222		t Stat	0.716		
11	10	249	245		P(T<=t) one-tail	0.242		
12					t Critical one-tail	1.734		
13	Mean =	226.80	222.20		P(T<=t) two-tail	0.483		
14	S =	14.45	14.29		t Critical two-tail	2.101		
15								

The mean of the appraised value of the 10 properties by Schadek is $226,800, and the standard deviation is $14,450. For Bowyer Real Estate the mean appraised value is $222,200, and the standard deviation is $14,290. To make the calculations easier, we use $000 instead of $. The value of the pooled estimate of the variance from formula (11–5) is

$$s_p^2 = \frac{(n_1 - 1)s_1^2 + (n_2 - 1)s_2^2}{n_1 + n_2 - 2} = \frac{(10 - 1)(14.45^2) + (10 - 1)(14.29)^2}{10 + 10 - 2} = 206.50$$

From formula (11–6), t is 0.716.

$$t = \frac{\overline{X}_1 - \overline{X}_2}{\sqrt{s_p^2\left(\dfrac{1}{n_1} + \dfrac{1}{n_2}\right)}} = \frac{226.8 - 222.2}{\sqrt{206.50\left(\dfrac{1}{10} + \dfrac{1}{10}\right)}} = \frac{4.6}{6.4265} = 0.716$$

The computed t (0.716) is less than 2.101, so the null hypothesis is not rejected. We cannot show that there is a difference in the mean appraisal value. That is not the same conclusion that we got before! Why does this happen? The numerator is the same in the paired observations test (4.6). However, the denominator is smaller. In the paired test the denominator is 1.3920 (see the calculations on page 339). In the case of the independent samples, the denominator is 6.4265. There is more variation or uncertainty. This accounts for the difference in the t values and the difference in the statistical decisions. The denominator measures the standard error of the statistic. When the samples are *not* paired, two kinds of variation are present: differences between the two appraisal firms and the difference in the value of the real estate. Properties numbered 4 and 10 have relatively high values, whereas number 5 is relatively low. These data show how different the values of the property are, but we are really interested in the difference between the two appraisal firms.

The trick is to pair the values to reduce the variation among the properties. The paired test uses only the difference between the two appraisal firms for the same property. Thus, the paired or dependent statistic focuses on the variation between Schadek Appraisals and Bowyer Real Estate. Thus, its standard error is always smaller. That, in turn, leads to a larger test statistic and a greater chance of rejecting the null hypothesis. So whenever possible you should pair the data.

There is a bit of bad news here. In the paired observations test, the degrees of freedom are half of what they are if the samples are not paired. For the real estate example, the degrees of freedom drop from 18 to 9 when the observations are paired. However, in most cases, this is a small price to pay for a better test.

Self-Review 11–4 Advertisements by Sylph Fitness Center claim that completing its course will result in losing weight. A random sample of eight recent participants showed the following weights before and after completing the course. At the .01 significance level, can we conclude the students lost weight?

Name	Before	After
Hunter	155	154
Cashman	228	207
Mervine	141	147
Massa	162	157
Creola	211	196
Peterson	164	150
Redding	184	170
Poust	172	165

(a) State the null hypothesis and the alternate hypothesis.
(b) What is the critical value of t?
(c) What is the computed value of t?
(d) Interpret the result. What is the p-value?
(e) What assumption needs to be made about the distribution of the differences?

Exercises

19. The null and alternate hypotheses are:

$$H_0: \mu_d \leq 0$$
$$H_1: \mu_d > 0$$

The following sample information shows the number of defective units produced on the day shift and the afternoon shift for a sample of four days last month.

	Day			
	1	2	3	4
Day shift	10	12	15	19
Afternoon shift	8	9	12	15

At the .05 significance level, can we conclude there are more defects produced on the afternoon shift?

20. The null and alternate hypotheses are:

$$H_0: \mu_d = 0$$
$$H_1: \mu_d \neq 0$$

The following paired observations show the number of traffic citations given for speeding by Officer Dhondt and Officer Meredith of the South Carolina Highway Patrol for the last five months.

	Day				
	May	**June**	**July**	**August**	**September**
Officer Dhondt	30	22	25	19	26
Officer Meredith	26	19	20	15	19

At the .05 significance level, is there a difference in the mean number of citations given by the two officers?

Note: Use the five-step hypothesis testing procedure to solve the following exercises.

21. The management of Discount Furniture, a chain of discount furniture stores in the Northeast, designed an incentive plan for salespeople. To evaluate this innovative plan, 12 salespeople were selected at random, and their weekly incomes before and after the plan were recorded.

Salesperson	**Before**	**After**
Sid Mahone	$320	$340
Carol Quick	290	285
Tom Jackson	421	475
Andy Jones	510	510
Jean Sloan	210	210
Jack Walker	402	500
Peg Mancuso	625	631
Anita Loma	560	560
John Cuso	360	365
Carl Utz	431	431
A. S. Kushner	506	525
Fern Lawton	505	619

Was there a significant increase in the typical salesperson's weekly income due to the innovative incentive plan? Use the .05 significance level. Estimate the *p*-value, and interpret it.

22. The federal government recently granted funds for a special program designed to reduce crime in high-crime areas. A study of the results of the program in eight high-crime areas of Miami, Florida, yielded the following results.

	Number of Crimes by Area							
	A	**B**	**C**	**D**	**E**	**F**	**G**	**H**
Before	14	7	4	5	17	12	8	9
After	2	7	3	6	8	13	3	5

Has there been a decrease in the number of crimes since the inauguration of the program? Use the .01 significance level. Estimate the *p*-value.

Chapter Summary

I. In comparing two population means we wish to know whether they could be equal.

 A. We are investigating whether the distribution of the difference between the means could have a mean of 0.

 B. The test statistic follows the standard normal distribution if the population standard deviations are known.

  1. No assumption about the shape of either population is required.

  2. The samples are from independent populations.

  3. The formula to compute the value of z is

$$z = \frac{\overline{X}_1 - \overline{X}_2}{\sqrt{\dfrac{\sigma_1^2}{n_1} + \dfrac{\sigma_2^2}{n_2}}} \qquad \text{[11–2]}$$

II. We can also test whether two samples came from populations with an equal proportion of successes.

 A. The two sample proportions are pooled using the following formula:

$$p_c = \frac{X_1 + X_2}{n_1 + n_2} \qquad \text{[11–4]}$$

 B. We compute the value of the test statistic from the following formula:

$$z = \frac{p_1 - p_2}{\sqrt{\dfrac{p_c(1 - p_c)}{n_1} + \dfrac{p_c(1 - p_c)}{n_2}}} \qquad \text{[11–3]}$$

III. The test statistic to compare two means is the t distribution if the population standard deviations are not known.

 A. Both populations must follow the normal distribution.

 B. The populations must have equal standard deviations.

 C. The samples are independent.

 D. Finding the value of t requires two steps.

  1. The first step is to pool the standard deviations according to the following formula:

$$s_p^2 = \frac{(n_1 - 1)s_1^2 + (n_2 - 1)s_2^2}{n_1 + n_2 - 2} \qquad \text{[11–5]}$$

  2. The value of t is computed from the following formula:

$$t = \frac{\overline{X}_1 - \overline{X}_2}{\sqrt{s_p^2\left(\dfrac{1}{n_1} + \dfrac{1}{n_2}\right)}} \qquad \text{[11–6]}$$

  3. The degrees of freedom for the test are $n_1 + n_2 - 2$.

IV. For dependent samples, we assume the distribution of the paired differences between the populations has a mean of 0.

 A. We first compute the mean and the standard deviation of the sample differences.

 B. The value of the test statistic is computed from the following formula:

$$t = \frac{\overline{d}}{s_d / \sqrt{n}} \qquad \text{[11–7]}$$

Pronunciation Key

SYMBOL	MEANING	PRONUNCIATION
p_c	Pooled proportion	p sub c
s_p^2	Pooled sample variance	s sub p squared
$\overline{X}_1$	Mean of the first sample	X bar sub 1
$\overline{X}_2$	Mean of the second sample	X bar sub 2

$\overline{d}$	Mean of the difference between dependent observations	d bar
s_d	Standard deviation of the difference between dependent observations	s sub d

Chapter Exercises

connect™

23. A recent study focused on the number of times men and women who live alone buy take-out dinner in a month. The information is summarized below.

Statistic	Men	Women
Sample mean	24.51	22.69
Sample standard deviation	4.48	3.86
Sample size	35	40

At the .01 significance level, is there a difference in the mean number of times men and women order take-out dinners in a month? What is the *p*-value?

24. Clark Heter is an industrial engineer at Lyons Products. He would like to determine whether there are more units produced on the night shift than on the day shift. Assume the population standard deviation for the number of units produced on the day shift is 21 and is 28 on the night shift. A sample of 54 day-shift workers showed that the mean number of units produced was 345. A sample of 60 night-shift workers showed that the mean number of units produced was 351. At the .05 significance level, is the number of units produced on the night shift larger?

25. Fry Brothers Heating and Air Conditioning, Inc., employs Larry Clark and George Murnen to make service calls to repair furnaces and air conditioning units in homes. Tom Fry, the owner, would like to know whether there is a difference in the mean number of service calls they make per day. Assume the population standard deviation for Larry Clark is 1.05 calls per day and 1.23 calls per day for George Murnen. A random sample of 40 days last year showed that Larry Clark made an average of 4.77 calls per day. For a sample of 50 days George Murnen made an average of 5.02 calls per day. At the .05 significance level, is there a difference in the mean number of calls per day between the two employees? What is the *p*-value?

26. A coffee manufacturer is interested in whether the mean daily consumption of regular-coffee drinkers is less than that of decaffeinated-coffee drinkers. Assume the population standard deviation for those drinking regular coffee is 1.20 cups per day and 1.36 cups per day for those drinking decaffeinated coffee. A random sample of 50 regular-coffee drinkers showed a mean of 4.35 cups per day. A sample of 40 decaffeinated-coffee drinkers showed a mean of 5.84 cups per day. Use the .01 significance level. Compute the *p*-value.

27. A cell phone company offers two plans to its subscribers. At the time new subscribers sign up, they are asked to provide some demographic information. The mean yearly income for a sample of 40 subscribers to Plan A is $57,000 with a standard deviation of $9,200. This distribution is positively skewed; the actual coefficient of skewness is 2.11. For a sample of 30 subscribers to Plan B the mean income is $61,000 with a standard deviation of $7,100. The distribution of Plan B subscribers is also positively skewed, but not as severely. The coefficient of skewness is 1.54. At the .05 significance level, is it reasonable to conclude the mean income of those selecting Plan B is larger? What is the *p*-value? Do the coefficients of skewness affect the results of the hypothesis test? Why?

28. A computer manufacturer offers a help line that purchasers can call for help 24 hours a day, 7 days a week. Clearing these calls for help in a timely fashion is important to the company's image. After telling the caller that resolution of the problem is important the caller is asked whether the issue is software or hardware related. The mean time it takes a technician to resolve a software issue is 18 minutes with a standard deviation of 4.2 minutes. This information was obtained from a sample of 35 monitored calls. For a study of 45 hardware issues, the mean time for the technician to resolve the problem was 15.5 minutes with a standard deviation of 3.9 minutes. This information was also obtained from monitored calls. At the .05 significance level does it take longer to resolve software issues? What is the *p*-value?

29. Suppose the manufacturer of Advil, a common headache remedy, recently developed a new formulation of the drug that is claimed to be more effective. To evaluate the new drug, a sample of 200 current users is asked to try it. After a one-month trial, 180 indicated the new drug was more effective in relieving a headache. At the same time a sample of 300 current Advil users is given the current drug but told it is the new formulation. From this group, 261 said it was an improvement. At the .05 significance level can we conclude that the new drug is more effective?

30. Each month the National Association of Purchasing Managers publishes the NAPM index. One of the questions asked on the survey to purchasing agents is: Do you think the economy is contracting? Last month, of the 300 responses, 160 answered yes to the question. This month, 170 of the 290 responses indicated they felt the economy was contracting. At the .05 significance level, can we conclude that a larger proportion of the agents believe the economy is contracting this month?

31. As part of a recent survey among dual-wage-earner couples, an industrial psychologist found that 990 men out of the 1,500 surveyed believed the division of household duties was fair. A sample of 1,600 women found 970 believed the division of household duties was fair. At the .01 significance level, is it reasonable to conclude that the proportion of men who believe the division of household duties is fair is larger? What is the p-value?

32. There are two major Internet providers in the Colorado Springs, Colorado, area, one called HTC and the other Mountain Communications. We want to investigate whether there is a difference in the proportion of times a customer is able to access the Internet. During a one-week period, 500 calls were placed at random times throughout the day and night to HTC. A connection was made to the Internet on 450 occasions. A similar one-week study with Mountain Communications showed the Internet to be available on 352 of 400 trials. At the .01 significance level, is there a difference in the percent of time that access to the Internet is successful?

33. In a poll recently conducted at Iowa State University, 68 out of 98 male students and 45 out of 85 female students expressed "at least some support" for implementing regulations to limit greenhouse gases. Test at the .05 significance level the null hypothesis that the population proportions are equal against the two-tailed alternative.

34. A study was conducted to determine if there was a difference in the humor content in British and American trade magazine advertisements. In an independent random sample of 270 American trade magazine advertisements, 56 were humorous. An independent random sample of 203 British trade magazines contained 52 humorous ads. Does this data provide evidence at the .05 significance level that there is a difference in the proportion of humorous ads in British versus American trade magazines?

35. Century Business Products tested 180 computers with 8-bit microcontrollers and found that 13 failed to perform adequately on a compliance test. The same test was applied to a sample of 67 32-bit CPUs and 7 of those failed. Use the 0.05 significance level to test if it is reasonable to conclude that the 32-bit machines are not performing as well as the 8-bit ones?

36. The National Basketball Association had 39 black top executives (presidents or vice presidents) among its 388 senior managers. Meanwhile Major League Baseball had only 11 blacks among its 307 top administrators. Test at the .05 significance level if this reveals the NBA has significantly more black participation in higher levels of management.

37. The owner of Bun 'N' Run Hamburgers wishes to compare the sales per day at two locations. The mean number sold for 10 randomly selected days at the Northside site was 83.55, and the standard deviation was 10.50. For a random sample of 12 days at the Southside location, the mean number sold was 78.80 and the standard deviation was 14.25. At the .05 significance level, is there a difference in the mean number of hamburgers sold at the two locations? What is the p-value?

38. Grand Strand Family Medical Center is specifically set up to treat minor medical emergencies for visitors to the Myrtle Beach area. There are two facilities, one in the Little River Area and the other in Murrells Inlet. The Quality Assurance Department wishes to compare the mean waiting time for patients at the two locations. Samples of the waiting times, reported in minutes, follow:

Location	Waiting Time										
Little River	31.73	28.77	29.53	22.08	29.47	18.60	32.94	25.18	29.82	26.49	
Murrells Inlet	22.93	23.92	26.92	27.20	26.44	25.62	30.61	29.44	23.09	23.10	26.69	22.31

At the .05 significance level, is there a difference in the mean waiting time?

39. Commercial Bank and Trust Company is studying the use of its automatic teller machines (ATMs). Of particular interest is whether young adults (under 25 years) use the machines more than senior citizens. To investigate further, samples of customers under 25 years of age and customers over 60 years of age were selected. The number of ATM transactions last month was determined for each selected individual, and the results are shown below. At the .01 significance level, can bank management conclude that younger customers use the ATMs more?

Under 25	10	10	11	15	7	11	10	9			
Over 60	4	8	7	7	4	5	1	7	4	10	5

40. A number of minor automobile accidents occur at various high-risk intersections in Teton County despite traffic lights. The Traffic Department claims that a modification in the type of light will reduce these accidents. The county commissioners have agreed to a proposed experiment. Eight intersections were chosen at random, and the lights at those intersections were modified. The numbers of minor accidents during a six-month period before and after the modifications were:

	Number of Accidents							
	A	B	C	D	E	F	G	H
Before modification	5	7	6	4	8	9	8	10
After modification	3	7	7	0	4	6	8	2

At the .01 significance level is it reasonable to conclude that the modification reduced the number of traffic accidents?

41. Lester Hollar is vice president for human resources for a large manufacturing company. In recent years he has noticed an increase in absenteeism that he thinks is related to the general health of the employees. Four years ago, in an attempt to improve the situation, he began a fitness program in which employees exercise during their lunch hour. To evaluate the program, he selected a random sample of eight participants and found the number of days each was absent in the six months before the exercise program began and in the last six months. Below are the results. At the .05 significance level, can he conclude that the number of absences has declined? Estimate the *p*-value.

Employee	Before	After
1	6	5
2	6	2
3	7	1
4	7	3
5	4	3
6	3	6
7	5	3
8	6	7

42. The president of the American Insurance Institute wants to compare the yearly costs of auto insurance offered by two leading companies. He selects a sample of 15 families, some with only a single insured driver, others with several teenage drivers, and pays each family a stipend to contact the two companies and ask for a price quote. To make the data comparable, certain features, such as the deductible amount and

limits of liability, are standardized. The sample information is reported below. At the .10 significance level, can we conclude that there is a difference in the amounts quoted?

Family	Progressive Car Insurance	GEICO Mutual Insurance
Becker	$2,090	$1,610
Berry	1,683	1,247
Cobb	1,402	2,327
Debuck	1,830	1,367
DuBrul	930	1,461
Eckroate	697	1,789
German	1,741	1,621
Glasson	1,129	1,914
King	1,018	1,956
Kucic	1,881	1,772
Meredith	1,571	1,375
Obeid	874	1,527
Price	1,579	1,767
Phillips	1,577	1,636
Tresize	860	1,188

43. Fairfield Homes is developing two parcels near Pigeon Fork, Tennessee. In order to test different advertising approaches, it uses different media to reach potential buyers. The mean annual family income for 15 people making inquiries at the first development is $150,000, with a standard deviation of $40,000. A corresponding sample of 25 people at the second development had a mean of $180,000, with a standard deviation of $30,000. Assume the population standard deviations are the same. At the .05 significance level, can Fairfield conclude that the population means are different?

44. The following data resulted from a taste test of two different chocolate bars. The first number is a rating of the taste, which could range from 0 to 5, with a 5 indicating the person liked the taste. The second number indicates whether a "secret ingredient" was present. If the ingredient was present a code of 1 was used and a 0 otherwise. Assume the population standard deviations are the same. At the .05 significance level, do these data show a difference in the taste ratings?

Rating	With/Without	Rating	With/Without
3	1	1	1
1	1	4	0
0	0	4	0
2	1	2	1
3	1	3	0
1	1	4	0

45. An investigation of the effectiveness of an antibacterial soap in reducing operating room contamination resulted in the accompanying table. The new soap was tested in a sample of eight operating rooms in the greater Seattle area during the last year.

	Operating Room							
	A	B	C	D	E	F	G	H
Before	6.6	6.5	9.0	10.3	11.2	8.1	6.3	11.6
After	6.8	2.4	7.4	8.5	8.1	6.1	3.4	2.0

At the 0.05 significance level, can we conclude the contamination measurements are lower after use of the new soap?

46. The following data on annual rates of return were collected from five stocks listed on the New York Stock Exchange ("the big board") and five stocks listed on NASDAQ. Assume the population standard deviations are the same. At the .10 significance level, can we conclude that the annual rates of return are higher on the big board?

NYSE	NASDAQ
17.16	15.80
17.08	16.28
15.51	16.21
8.43	17.97
25.15	7.77

47. The city of Laguna Beach operates two public parking lots. The one on Ocean Drive can accommodate up to 125 cars and the one on Rio Rancho can accommodate up to 130 cars. City planners are considering both increasing the size of the lots and changing the fee structure. To begin, the Planning Office would like some information on the number of cars in the lots at various times of the day. A junior planner officer is assigned the task of visiting the two lots at random times of the day and evening and counting the number of cars in the lots. The study lasted over a period of one month. Below is the number of cars in the lots for 25 visits of the Ocean Drive lot and 28 visits of the Rio Rancho lot. Assume the population standard deviations are equal.

Ocean Drive												
89	115	93	79	113	77	51	75	118	105	106	91	54
63	121	53	81	115	67	53	69	95	121	88	64	

Rio Rancho												
128	110	81	126	82	114	93	40	94	45	84	71	74
92	66	69	100	114	113	107	62	77	80	107	90	129
105	124											

Is it reasonable to conclude that there is a difference in the mean number of cars in the two lots? Use the .05 significance level.

48. The amount of income spent on housing is an important component of the cost of living. The total costs of housing for homeowners might include mortgage payments, property taxes, and utility costs (water, heat, electricity). An economist selected a sample of 20 homeowners in New England and then calculated these total housing costs as a percent of monthly income, five years ago and now. The information is reported below. Is it reasonable to conclude the percent is less now than five years ago?

Homeowner	Five Years Ago	Now	Homeowner	Five Years Ago	Now
1	17%	10%	11	35%	32%
2	20	39	12	16	32
3	29	37	13	23	21
4	43	27	14	33	12
5	36	12	15	44	40
6	43	41	16	44	42
7	45	24	17	28	22
8	19	26	18	29	19
9	49	28	19	39	35
10	49	26	20	22	12

Use this information to do exercises 49 and 50. The drivers, ages, odds against winning, row of their starting position, and car number for the 2008 Indianapolis 500 motorcar race are listed below. Use the .01 significance level.

Driver	Age	Odds	Row	Car Number	Driver	Age	Odds	Row	Car Number
Dixon	27	4	1	9	Hamilton	45	100	6	22
Wheldon	29	4	1	10	Lloyd	23	200	7	16
Briscoe	26	4	1	6	Hunter-Reay	27	100	7	17
Castroneves	33	4	2	3	Andretti, J	45	100	7	24
Patrick	26	8	2	7	Fisher	27	200	8	67
Kanaan	33	4	2	11	Power	27	100	8	8
Andretti, M	21	8	3	26	Simmons	31	200	8	41
Meira	31	25	3	4	Servia	33	150	9	5
Mutoh	25	20	3	27	Viso	23	200	9	33
Carpenter	27	50	4	20	Duno	36	200	9	23
Scheckter	27	45	4	12	Moraes	19	200	10	19
Bell	33	200	4	99	Bernoldi	29	200	10	36
Rahal	19	40	5	6	Camara	27	200	10	34
Manning	33	100	5	14	Foyt	24	150	11	2
Junqueira	31	75	5	18	Lazier	40	150	11	91
Wilson	29	50	6	2	Roth	49	300	11	25
Rice	32	50	6	15					

49. Is it reasonable to conclude that starting in the first five rows significantly reduces the odds against winning in contrast to the last four rows?

50. Does having a car number of 20 or below significantly change the odds of winning?

Data Set Exercises

51. Refer to the Real Estate data, which report information on the homes sold in Phoenix, Arizona, last year.

   a. At the .05 significance level, can we conclude that there is a difference in the mean selling price of homes with a pool and homes without a pool?

   b. At the .05 significance level, can we conclude that there is a difference in the mean selling price of homes with an attached garage and homes without an attached garage?

   c. At the .05 significance level, can we conclude that there is a difference in the mean selling price of homes in Township 1 and Township 2?

   d. Find the median selling price of the homes. Divide the homes into two groups, those that sold for more than (or equal to) the median price and those that sold for less. Is there a difference in the proportion of homes with a pool for those that sold at or above the median price versus those that sold for less than the median price? Use the .05 significance level.

52. Refer to the Baseball 2008 data, which report information on the 30 Major League Baseball teams for the 2008 season.

   a. At the .05 significance level, can we conclude that there is a difference in the mean salary of teams in the American League versus teams in the National League?

   b. At the .05 significance level, can we conclude that there is a difference in the mean home attendance of teams in the American League versus teams in the National League?

   c. Compute the mean and the standard deviation of the number of wins for the 10 teams with the highest salaries. Do the same for the 10 teams with the lowest salaries. At the .05 significance level is there a difference in the mean number of wins for the two groups?

53. Refer to the Wage data, which report information on annual wages for a sample of 100 workers. Also included are variables relating to industry, years of education, and gender for each worker.

   a. Conduct a test of hypothesis to determine if there is a difference in the mean annual wages of Southern residents versus non-Southern residents.

b. Conduct a test of hypothesis to determine if there is a difference in the mean annual wages of white and non-white wage earners.

c. Conduct a test of hypothesis to determine if there is a difference in the mean annual wages of Hispanic and non-Hispanic wage earners.

d. Conduct a test of hypothesis to determine if there is a difference in the mean annual wages of female and male wage earners.

e. Conduct a test of hypothesis to determine if there is a difference in the mean annual wages of married and nonmarried wage earners.

Practice Test

Part I Objective

1. The hypothesized difference between two population means is _____.
2. If the population standard deviations are known for a test of differences for two independent populations, the test statistic is _____.
3. When sampled items from two populations are classified as "success" or "failure," the hypothesis test is for differences in population _____.
4. For two independent populations, sample standard deviations are pooled to compute a single estimate of the _____. (population mean, population standard deviation, population proportion, z value.)
5. A hypothesis test of differences between two dependent populations is based on a single population of mean _____. (differences, populations, standard deviations, t values)
6. The test statistic for a hypothesis test of differences between two dependent populations follows the _____.
7. Degrees of freedom are calculated as the total number of observations less the number of _____.
8. For dependent samples, observations are matched or _____.
9. For independent samples, the two samples are different or _____.
10. In a statistics class, for each student the percent correct on Exam 2 is subtracted from the percent correct on Exam 1. This is a situation to apply a hypothesis test of differences between two _____.

Part II Problems

For each of these problems, use the five-step hypothesis testing procedure.

1. Is there a difference in the mean miles traveled per week by each of the two taxi cab companies operating in the Grand Strand area? The *Sun News,* the local newspaper, is investigating and obtained the following sample information. At the .05 significance level, is there a difference in the mean miles traveled?

Variable	Yellow Cab	Horse and Buggy Cab
Mean miles	837	797
Standard deviation	30	40
Sample size	14	12

2. Dial Soap Company developed a new soap for men that it wants to test in two cities. The sample information is reported below.

City	Liked New Soap	Number Sampled
Erie, PA	128	300
Tustin, CA	149	400

At the .05 significance level, can we conclude there is a difference in the proportion in the two cities that liked the new soap?

Software Commands

1. The MINITAB commands for the two-sample test of proportions on page 330 are:
   a. From the toolbar, select **Stat, Basic Statistics,** and then **2 Proportions.**
   b. In the next dialog box select **Summarized data,** in the row labeled **First** enter *100* for **Trials** and *19* for **Events.** In the row labeled **Second** put *200* for **Trials** and *62* for **Events.** Then click on **Options** and select **Use pooled estimate of p for test,** finally click **OK** twice.

2. The Excel commands for the two-sample *t*-test on page 335 are:
   a. Enter the data into columns A and B (or any other columns) in the spreadsheet. Use the first row of each column to enter the variable name.
   b. Select the **Data** tab on the top menu. Then, on the far right, select **Data Analysis.** Select **t-Test: Two Sample Assuming Equal Variances,** then click **OK.**
   c. In the dialog box indicate that the range of **Variable 1** is from *A1* to *A6* and **Variable 2** from *B1* to *B7,* the **Hypothesized Mean Difference** is *0,* click **Labels, Alpha** is *0.05,* and the **Output Range** is *D1.* Click **OK.**

3. The Excel commands for the paired *t*-test on page 340 are:
   a. Enter the data into columns B and C (or any other two columns) in the spreadsheet, with the variable names in the first row.
   b. Select the **Data** tab on the top menu. Then, on the far right, select **Data Analysis.** Select **t-Test: Paired Two Sample for Means,** then click **OK.**
   c. In the dialog box indicate that the range of **Variable 1** is from *B1* to *B11* and **Variable 2** from *C1* to *C11,* the **Hypothesized Mean Difference** is *0,* click **Labels, Alpha** is *.05,* and the **Output Range** is *E1.* Click **OK.**

Chapter 11   Answers to Self-Review

11–1 **a.** H_0: $\mu_W \leq \mu_M$
H_1: $\mu_W > \mu_M$
The subscript W refers to the women and M to the men.
b. Reject H_0 if $z > 1.65$
c. $z = \dfrac{\$1{,}500 - \$1{,}400}{\sqrt{\dfrac{(\$250)^2}{50} + \dfrac{(\$200)^2}{40}}} = 2.11$
d. Reject the null hypothesis
e. p-value $= .5000 - .4826 = .0174$
f. The mean amount sold per day is larger for women.

11–2 **a.** H_0: $\pi_1 = \pi_2$
H_1: $\pi_1 \neq \pi_2$
b. .10
c. Two-tailed
d. Reject H_0 if z is less than -1.65 or greater than 1.65.
e. $p_c = \dfrac{87 + 123}{150 + 200} = \dfrac{210}{350} = .60$

$p_1 = \dfrac{87}{150} = .58 \qquad p_2 = \dfrac{123}{200} = .615$

$z = \dfrac{.58 - .615}{\sqrt{\dfrac{.60(.40)}{150} + \dfrac{.60(.40)}{200}}} = -0.66$
f. Do not reject H_0.
g. p-value $= 2(.5000 - .2454) = .5092$
There is no difference in the proportion of adults and children that liked the proposed flavor.

11–3 **a.** H_0: $\mu_d = \mu_a$
H_1: $\mu_d \neq \mu_a$
b. $df = 6 + 8 - 2 = 12$
Reject H_0 if t is less than -2.179 or t is greater than 2.179.
c. $\overline{X}_1 = \dfrac{42}{6} = 7.00 \quad s_1 = \sqrt{\dfrac{10}{6 - 1}} = 1.4142$

$\overline{X}_2 = \dfrac{80}{8} = 10.00 \quad s_2 = \sqrt{\dfrac{36}{8 - 1}} = 2.2678$

$s_p^2 = \dfrac{(6 - 1)(1.4142)^2 + (8 - 1)(2.2678)^2}{6 + 8 - 2}$

$\quad = 3.8333$

$t = \dfrac{7.00 - 10.00}{\sqrt{3.8333\left(\dfrac{1}{6} + \dfrac{1}{8}\right)}} = -2.837$

d. Reject H_0 because -2.837 is less than the critical value.
e. The p-value is less than .02.
f. The mean number of defects is not the same on the two shifts.
g. Independent populations, populations follow the normal distribution, populations have equal standard deviations.

11–4 **a.** H_0: $\mu_d \leq 0$, H_1: $\mu_d > 0$.
b. Reject H_0 if $t > 2.998$
c.

Name	Before	After	d	$(d - \bar{d})$	$(d - \bar{d})^2$
Hunter	155	154	1	-7.875	62.0156
Cashman	228	207	21	12.125	147.0156
Mervine	141	147	-6	-14.875	221.2656
Massa	162	157	5	-3.875	15.0156
Creola	211	196	15	6.125	37.5156
Peterson	164	150	14	5.125	26.2656
Redding	184	170	14	5.125	26.2656
Poust	172	165	7	-1.875	3.5156
			71		538.8750

$\bar{d} = \dfrac{71}{8} = 8.875$

$s_d = \sqrt{\dfrac{538.875}{8 - 1}} = 8.774$

$t = \dfrac{8.875}{8.774/\sqrt{8}} = 2.861$

d. Do not reject H_0. We cannot conclude that the students lost weight. The p-value is less than .025 but larger than .01.
e. The distribution of the differences must follow a normal distribution.

12

Analysis of Variance

Learning Objectives

When you have completed this chapter, you will be able to:

LO1 List the characteristics of the *F* distribution.

LO2 Conduct a test of hypothesis to determine whether the variances of two populations are equal.

LO3 Discuss the concept of *analysis of variance*.

LO4 Conduct a test of hypothesis among three or more treatment means.

LO5 Organize data into a *one-way ANOVA table*.

LO6 Develop confidence intervals for the difference in treatment means.

A new computer is sold with innovative flash memory. When compared to computers with conventional memory, the new machine is clearly faster, but initial tests indicate there is more variation in processing time. A sample of 16 computer runs showed that the standard deviation of the processing time was 22 (hundredths of a second) for the new machine and 12 (hundredths of a second) for the current machine. At the .05 significance level, can we conclude that there is more variation in the processing time of the new machine? (Exercise 16, LO2.)

Introduction

In this chapter we continue our discussion of hypothesis testing. Recall that in Chapters 10 and 11 we examined the general theory of hypothesis testing. We described the case where a sample was selected from the population. We used the z distribution (the standard normal distribution) or the t distribution to determine whether it was reasonable to conclude that the population mean was equal to a specified value. We tested whether two population means are the same. We also conducted both one- and two-sample tests for population proportions, using the standard normal distribution as the distribution of the test statistic. In this chapter we expand our idea of hypothesis tests. We describe a test for variances and then a test that simultaneously compares several means to determine if they came from equal populations.

The *F* Distribution

The probability distribution used in this chapter is the *F* distribution. It was named to honor Sir Ronald Fisher, one of the founders of modern-day statistics. The test statistic for several situations follows this probability distribution. It is used to test whether two samples are from populations having equal variances, and it is also applied when we want to compare several population means simultaneously. The simultaneous comparison of several population means is called **analysis of variance (ANOVA).** In both of these situations, the populations must follow a normal distribution, and the data must be at least interval-scale.

What are the characteristics of the *F* distribution?

LO1 List the characteristics of the *F* distribution.

1. **There is a family of *F* distributions.** A particular member of the family is determined by two parameters: the degrees of freedom in the numerator and the degrees of freedom in the denominator. The shape of the distribution is illustrated by the following graph. There is one *F* distribution for the combination of 29 degrees of freedom in the numerator (*df*) and 28 degrees of freedom in the denominator. There is another *F* distribution for 19 degrees in the numerator and 6 degrees of freedom in the denominator. The final distribution shown has 6 degrees of freedom in the numerator and 6 degrees of freedom in the denominator. We will describe the concept of degrees of freedom later in the chapter. Note that the shapes of the distributions change as the degrees of freedom change.

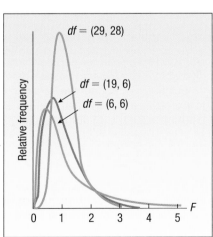

2. **The *F* distribution is continuous.** This means that it can assume an infinite number of values between zero and positive infinity.
3. **The *F* distribution cannot be negative.** The smallest value *F* can assume is 0.

4. **It is positively skewed.** The long tail of the distribution is to the right-hand side. As the number of degrees of freedom increases in both the numerator and denominator the distribution approaches a normal distribution.
5. **It is asymptotic.** As the values of X increase, the F distribution approaches the X-axis but never touches it. This is similar to the behavior of the normal probability distribution, described in Chapter 7.

Comparing Two Population Variances

The first application of the F distribution that we describe occurs when we test the hypothesis that the variance of one normal population equals the variance of another normal population. The following examples will show the use of the test:

LO2 Conduct a test of hypothesis to determine whether the variances of two populations are equal.

- Two Barth shearing machines are set to produce steel bars of the same length. The bars, therefore, should have the same mean length. We want to ensure that in addition to having the same mean length they also have similar variation.

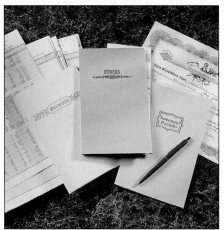

- The mean rate of return on two types of common stock may be the same, but there may be more variation in the rate of return in one than the other. A sample of 10 technology and 10 utility stocks shows the same mean rate of return, but there is likely more variation in the technology stocks.
- A study by the marketing department for a large newspaper found that men and women spent about the same amount of time per day surfing the Net. However, the same report indicated there was nearly twice as much variation in time spent per day among the men than the women.

The F distribution is also used to test assumptions for some statistical tests. Recall that in the previous chapter we used the t distribution to investigate whether the means of two independent populations differed. To conduct that test, we assume that the variances of two normal populations are the same. See this list of assumptions on page 333. The F distribution is used to test if the variances of two normal populations are equal.

Regardless of whether we want to determine whether one population has more variation than another population or validate an assumption for a statistical test, we first state the null hypothesis. The null hypothesis is that the variance of one normal population, σ_1^2, equals the variance of the other normal population, σ_2^2. The alternate hypothesis could be that the variances differ. In this instance the null hypothesis and the alternate hypothesis are:

$H_0: \sigma_1^2 = \sigma_2^2$
$H_1: \sigma_1^2 \neq \sigma_2^2$

To conduct the test, we select a random sample of n_1 observations from one population, and a random sample of n_2 observations from the second population. The test statistic is defined as follows.

TEST STATISTIC FOR COMPARING TWO VARIANCES	$F = \dfrac{s_1^2}{s_2^2}$	[12–1]

The terms s_1^2 and s_2^2 are the respective sample variances. If the null hypothesis is true, the test statistic follows the F distribution with $n_1 - 1$ and $n_2 - 1$ degrees of freedom. In order to reduce the size of the table of critical values, the *larger* sample variance is placed in the numerator; hence, the tabled F ratio is always larger than 1.00. Thus, the right-tail critical value is the only one required. The critical value of F for a two-tailed test is found by dividing the significance level in half ($\alpha/2$) and then referring to the appropriate degrees of freedom in Appendix B.4. An example will illustrate.

Example

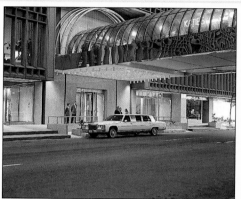

Lammers Limos offers limousine service from the city hall in Toledo, Ohio, to Metro Airport in Detroit. Sean Lammers, president of the company, is considering two routes. One is via U.S. 25 and the other via I-75. He wants to study the time it takes to drive to the airport using each route and then compare the results. He collected the following sample data, which is reported in minutes. Using the .10 significance level, is there a difference in the variation in the driving times for the two routes?

U.S. Route 25	Interstate 75
52	59
67	60
56	61
45	51
70	56
54	63
64	57
	65

Solution

The mean driving times along the two routes are nearly the same. The mean time is 58.29 minutes for the U.S. 25 route and 59.0 minutes along the I-75 route. However, in evaluating travel times, Mr. Lammers is also concerned about the variation in the travel times. The first step is to compute the two sample variances. We'll use formula (3–9) to compute the sample standard deviations. To obtain the sample variances, we square the standard deviations.

U.S. Route 25

$$\overline{X} = \frac{\Sigma X}{n} = \frac{408}{7} = 58.29 \qquad s = \sqrt{\frac{\Sigma(X - \overline{X})^2}{n-1}} = \sqrt{\frac{485.43}{7-1}} = 8.9947$$

Interstate 75

$$\overline{X} = \frac{\Sigma X}{n} = \frac{472}{8} = 59.00 \qquad s = \sqrt{\frac{\Sigma(X - \overline{X})^2}{n-1}} = \sqrt{\frac{134}{8-1}} = 4.3753$$

There is more variation, as measured by the standard deviation, in the U.S. 25 route than in the I-75 route. This is consistent with his knowledge of the two routes; the U.S. 25 route contains more stoplights, whereas I-75 is a limited-access interstate highway. However, the I-75 route is several miles longer. It is important that the service offered be both timely and consistent, so he decides to conduct a statistical test to determine whether there really is a difference in the variation of the two routes.

The usual five-step hypothesis-testing procedure will be employed.

Step 1: We begin by stating the null hypothesis and the alternate hypothesis. The test is two-tailed because we are looking for a difference in the variation of the two routes. We are *not* trying to show that one route has more variation than the other.

$$H_0: \sigma_1^2 = \sigma_2^2$$
$$H_1: \sigma_1^2 \neq \sigma_2^2$$

Step 2: We selected the .10 significance level.

Step 3: The appropriate test statistic follows the F distribution.

Step 4: The critical value is obtained from Appendix B.4, a portion of which is reproduced as Table 12–1. Because we are conducting a two-tailed test, the tabled significance level is .05, found by $\alpha/2 = .10/2 = .05$. There are $n_1 - 1 = 7 - 1 = 6$ degrees of freedom in the numerator, and $n_2 - 1 = 8 - 1 = 7$ degrees of freedom in the denominator. To find the critical value, move horizontally across the top portion of the F table (Table 12–1 or Appendix B.4) for the .05 significance level to 6 degrees of freedom in the numerator. Then move down that column to the critical value opposite 7 degrees of freedom in the denominator. The critical value is 3.87. Thus, the decision rule is: Reject the null hypothesis if the ratio of the sample variances exceeds 3.87.

TABLE 12–1 Critical Values of the F Distribution, $\alpha = .05$

Degrees of Freedom for Denominator	Degrees of Freedom for Numerator			
	5	6	7	8
1	230	234	237	239
2	19.3	19.3	19.4	19.4
3	9.01	8.94	8.89	8.85
4	6.26	6.16	6.09	6.04
5	5.05	4.95	4.88	4.82
6	4.39	4.28	4.21	4.15
7	3.97	3.87	3.79	3.73
8	3.69	3.58	3.50	3.44
9	3.48	3.37	3.29	3.23
10	3.33	3.22	3.14	3.07

Step 5: The final step is to take the ratio of the two sample variances, determine the value of the test statistic, and make a decision regarding the null hypothesis. Note that formula (12–1) refers to the sample *variances* but we calculated the sample *standard deviations*. We need to square the standard deviations to determine the variances.

$$F = \frac{s_1^2}{s_2^2} = \frac{(8.9947)^2}{(4.3753)^2} = 4.23$$

The decision is to reject the null hypothesis, because the computed F value (4.23) is larger than the critical value (3.87). We conclude that there is a difference in the variation of the travel times along the two routes.

As noted, the usual practice is to determine the F ratio by putting the larger of the two sample variances in the numerator. This will force the F ratio to be at least 1.00. This allows us to always use the right tail of the F distribution, thus avoiding the need for more extensive F tables.

A logical question arises: Is it possible to conduct one-tailed tests? For example, suppose in the previous example we suspected that the variance of the times using the U.S. 25 route is *larger* than the variance of the times along the I-75 route. We would state the null and the alternate hypothesis as

$$H_0: \sigma_1^2 \leq \sigma_2^2$$
$$H_1: \sigma_1^2 > \sigma_2^2$$

The test statistic is computed as s_1^2/s_2^2. Notice that we labeled the population with the suspected largest variance as population 1. So s_1^2 appears in the numerator. The F ratio will be larger than 1.00, so we can use the upper tail of the F distribution. Under these conditions, it is not necessary to divide the significance level in half. Because Appendix B.4 gives us only the .05 and .01 significance levels, we are restricted to these levels for one-tailed tests and .10 and .02 for two-tailed tests unless we consult a more complete table or use statistical software to compute the F statistic.

The Excel software system has a procedure to perform a test of variances. Below is the output. The computed value of F is the same as determined by using formula (12–1).

	A	B	C	D	E	F	G	H
	U. S. 25	Interstate 75		F-Test Two-Sample for Variances				
1								
2	52	59			U. S. 25	Interstate 75		
3	67	60		Mean	58.29	59.00		
4	56	61		Variance	80.90	19.14		
5	45	51		Observations	7.00	8.00		
6	70	56		df	6.00	7.00		
7	54	63		F	4.23			
8	64	57		P(F<=f) one-tail	0.04			
9		65		F Critical one-tail	3.87			
10								
11								

num 1 variance test

Self-Review 12–1 Steele Electric Products, Inc., assembles electrical components for cell phones. For the last 10 days Mark Nagy has averaged 9 rejects, with a standard deviation of 2 rejects per day. Debbie Richmond averaged 8.5 rejects, with a standard deviation of 1.5 rejects, over the same period. At the .05 significance level, can we conclude that there is more variation in the number of rejects per day attributed to Mark?

Exercises

connect

1. What is the critical F value for a sample of six observations in the numerator and four in the denominator? Use a two-tailed test and the .10 significance level.
2. What is the critical F value for a sample of four observations in the numerator and seven in the denominator? Use a one-tailed test and the .01 significance level.

3. The following hypotheses are given.

$$H_0: \sigma_1^2 = \sigma_2^2$$
$$H_1: \sigma_1^2 \neq \sigma_2^2$$

A random sample of eight observations from the first population resulted in a standard deviation of 10. A random sample of six observations from the second population resulted in a standard deviation of 7. At the .02 significance level, is there a difference in the variation of the two populations?

4. The following hypotheses are given.

$$H_0: \sigma_1^2 \leq \sigma_2^2$$
$$H_1: \sigma_1^2 > \sigma_2^2$$

A random sample of five observations from the first population resulted in a standard deviation of 12. A random sample of seven observations from the second population showed a standard deviation of 7. At the .01 significance level, is there more variation in the first population?

5. Arbitron Media Research, Inc., conducted a study of the iPod listening habits of men and women. One facet of the study involved the mean listening time. It was discovered that the mean listening time for men was 35 minutes per day. The standard deviation of the sample of the 10 men studied was 10 minutes per day. The mean listening time for the 12 women studied was also 35 minutes, but the standard deviation of the sample was 12 minutes. At the .10 significance level, can we conclude that there is a difference in the variation in the listening times for men and women?

6. A stockbroker at Critical Securities reported that the mean rate of return on a sample of 10 oil stocks was 12.6 percent with a standard deviation of 3.9 percent. The mean rate of return on a sample of 8 utility stocks was 10.9 percent with a standard deviation of 3.5 percent. At the .05 significance level, can we conclude that there is more variation in the oil stocks?

ANOVA Assumptions

Another use of the F distribution is the analysis of variance (ANOVA) technique in which we compare three or more population means to determine whether they could be equal. To use ANOVA, we assume the following:

1. The populations follow the normal distribution.
2. The populations have equal standard deviations (σ).
3. The populations are independent.

When these conditions are met, F is used as the distribution of the test statistic.

LO3 Discuss the concept of *analysis of variance.*

Using the *t* distribution leads to a buildup of Type I error.

Why do we need to study ANOVA? Why can't we just use the test of differences in population means discussed in the previous chapter? We could compare the population means two at a time. The major reason is the unsatisfactory buildup of Type I error. To explain further, suppose we have four different methods (A, B, C, and D) of training new recruits to be firefighters. We randomly assign each of the 40 recruits in this year's class to one of the four methods. At the end of the training program, we administer to the four groups a common test to measure understanding of firefighting techniques. The question is: Is there a difference in the mean test scores among the four groups? An answer to this question will allow us to compare the four training methods.

Using the *t* distribution to compare the four population means, we would have to conduct six different *t* tests. That is, we would need to compare the mean scores for the four methods as follows: A versus B, A versus C, A versus D, B versus C, B versus D, and C versus D. If we set the significance level at .05, the probability of a correct statistical decision is .95, found by $1 - .05$. Because we conduct six separate (independent) tests the probability that we do *not* make an incorrect decision due to sampling error in any of the six independent tests is:

$$P(All\ correct) = (.95)(.95)(.95)(.95)(.95)(.95) = .735$$

To find the probability of at least one error due to sampling, we subtract this result from 1. Thus, the probability of at least one incorrect decision due to sampling is $1 - .735 = .265$. To summarize, if we conduct six independent tests using the t distribution, the likelihood of rejecting a true null hypothesis because of sampling error is increased from .05 to an unsatisfactory level of .265. It is obvious that we need a better method than conducting six t tests. ANOVA will allow us to compare the treatment means simultaneously and avoid the buildup of Type I error.

ANOVA was first developed for applications in agriculture, and many of the terms related to that context remain. In particular the term *treatment* is used to identify the different populations being examined. For example, treatment refers to how a plot of ground was treated with a particular type of fertilizer. The following illustration will clarify the term *treatment* and demonstrate an application of ANOVA.

Example

Joyce Kuhlman manages a regional financial center. She wishes to compare the productivity, as measured by the number of customers served, among three employees. Four days are randomly selected and the number of customers served by each employee is recorded. The results are:

Wolfe	White	Korosa
55	66	47
54	76	51
59	67	46
56	71	48

Solution

Is there a difference in the mean number of customers served? Chart 12–1 illustrates how the populations would appear if there were a difference in the treatment means. Note that the populations follow the normal distribution and the variation in each population is the same. However, the means are *not* the same.

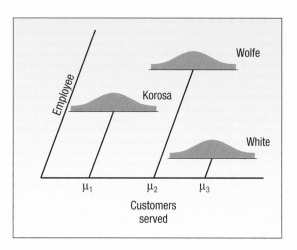

CHART 12–1 Case Where Treatment Means Are Different

Suppose the populations are the same. That is, there is no difference in the (treatment) means. This is shown in Chart 12–2. This would indicate that the population means are the same. Note again that the populations follow the normal distribution and the variation in each of the populations is the same.

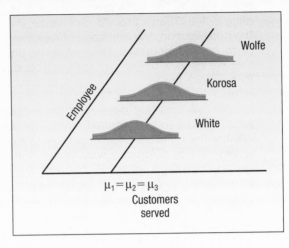

CHART 12–2 Case Where Treatment Means Are the Same

The ANOVA Test

How does the ANOVA test work? Recall that we want to determine whether the various sample means came from a single population or populations with different means. We actually compare these sample means through their variances. To explain, on page 360 we listed the assumptions required for ANOVA. One of those assumptions was that the standard deviations of the various normal populations had to be the same. We take advantage of this requirement in the ANOVA test. The underlying strategy is to estimate the population variance (standard deviation squared) two ways and then find the ratio of these two estimates. If this ratio is about 1, then logically the two estimates are the same, and we conclude that the population means are the same. If the ratio is quite different from 1, then we conclude that the population means are not the same. The F distribution serves as a referee by indicating when the ratio of the sample variances is too much greater than 1 to have occurred by chance.

Refer to the financial center example in the previous section. The manager wants to determine whether there is a difference in the mean number of customers served. To begin, find the overall mean of the 12 observations. It is 58, found by $(55 + 54 + \cdots + 48)/12$. Next, for each of the 12 observations find the difference between the particular value and the overall mean. Each of these differences is squared and these squares summed. This term is called the **total variation.**

> **TOTAL VARIATION** The sum of the squared differences between each observation and the overall mean.

In our example the total variation is 1,082, found by $(55 - 58)^2 + (54 - 58)^2 + \cdots + (48 - 58)^2$.

Next, break this total variation into two components: that which is due to the **treatments** and that which is **random.** To find these two components, determine the mean of each of the treatments. The first source of variation is due to the treatments.

> **TREATMENT VARIATION** The sum of the squared differences between each treatment mean and the grand or overall mean.

In the example, the variation due to the treatments is the sum of the squared differences between the mean number of customers served by each employee and the overall mean. This term is 992. To calculate it, we first find the mean of each of the three treatments. The mean for Wolfe is 56 customers, found by $(55 + 54 + 59 + 56)/4$. The other means are 70 and 48, respectively. The sum of the squares due to the treatments is:

$$(56 - 58)^2 + (56 - 58)^2 + \cdots + (48 - 58)^2 = 4(56 - 58)^2 + 4(70 - 58)^2 + 4(48 - 58)^2$$
$$= 992$$

If there is considerable variation among the treatment means, it is logical that this term will be large. If the treatment means are similar, this term will be a small value. The smallest possible value would be zero. This would occur when all the treatment means are the same.

The other source of variation is referred to as the **random** component, or the error component.

> **RANDOM VARIATION** The sum of the squared differences between each observation and its treatment mean.

In the example this term is the sum of the squared differences between each value and the mean for that particular employee. The error variation is 90.

$$(55 - 56)^2 + (54 - 56)^2 + \cdots + (48 - 48)^2 = 90$$

LO4 Conduct a test of hypothesis among three or more treatment means.

We determine the test statistic, which is the ratio of the two estimates of the population variance, from the following equation.

$$F = \frac{\text{Estimate of the population variance based on the differences among the sample means}}{\text{Estimate of the population variance based on the variation within the sample}}$$

Our first estimate of the population variance is based on the treatments, that is, the difference *between* the means. It is 992/2. Why did we divide by 2? Recall from Chapter 3, to find a sample variance [see formula (3–9)], we divide by the number of observations minus one. In this case there are three treatments, so we divide by 2. Our first estimate of the population variance is 992/2.

The variance estimate *within* the treatments is the random variation divided by the total number of observations less the number of treatments. That is $90/(12 - 3)$. Hence, our second estimate of the population variance is 90/9. This is actually a generalization of formula (11–5), where we pooled the sample variances from two populations.

The last step is to take the ratio of these two estimates.

$$F = \frac{992/2}{90/9} = 49.6$$

Because this ratio is quite different from 1, we can conclude that the treatment means are not the same. There is a difference in the mean number of customers served by the three employees.

Here's another example, which deals with samples of different sizes.

Example

Recently airlines have cut services, such as meals and snacks during flights, and started charging for checking baggage. A group of four carriers (we have used historical names for confidentiality) hired Brunner Marketing Research, Inc., to survey recent passengers regarding their level of satisfaction with a recent flight. The survey included questions on ticketing, boarding, in-flight service, baggage handling, pilot communication, and so forth. Twenty-five questions offered a range of possible answers: excellent, good, fair, or poor. A response of excellent was given a score of 4, good a 3, fair a 2, and poor a 1. These responses were then totaled, so the total score was an indication of the satisfaction with the flight. The greater the score, the higher the level of satisfaction with the service. The highest possible score was 100.

Brunner randomly selected and surveyed passengers from the four airlines. Below is the sample information. Is there a difference in the mean satisfaction level among the four airlines? Use the .01 significance level.

Eastern	TWA	Allegheny	Ozark
94	75	70	68
90	68	73	70
85	77	76	72
80	83	78	65
	88	80	74
		68	65
		65	

Solution

We will use the five-step hypothesis testing procedure.

Step 1: State the null hypothesis and the alternate hypothesis. The null hypothesis is that the mean scores are the same for the four airlines.

$$H_0: \mu_1 = \mu_2 = \mu_3 = \mu_4$$

The alternate hypothesis is that the mean scores are not all the same for the four airlines.

H_1: The mean scores are not all equal.

We can also think of the alternate hypothesis as "at least two mean scores are not equal."

If the null hypothesis is not rejected, we conclude that there is no difference in the mean scores for the four airlines. If H_0 is rejected, we conclude that there is a difference in at least one pair of mean scores, but at this point we do not know which pair or how many pairs differ.

Step 2: Select the level of significance. We selected the .01 significance level.

Step 3: Determine the test statistic. The test statistic follows the F distribution.

Step 4: Formulate the decision rule. To determine the decision rule, we need the critical value. The critical value for the F statistic is found in Appendix B.4. The critical values for the .05 significance level are found on the first page and the .01 significance level on the second page. To use this table we need to know the degrees of freedom in the numerator and the denominator. The degrees of freedom in the numerator equals the number of treatments, designated as k, minus 1. The degrees of freedom in the denominator is the total number of observations, n, minus the number of treatments. For this problem there are four treatments and a total of 22 observations.

Degrees of freedom in the numerator = $k - 1 = 4 - 1 = 3$

Degrees of freedom in the denominator = $n - k = 22 - 4 = 18$

Refer to Appendix B.4 and the .01 significance level. Move horizontally across the top of the page to 3 degrees of freedom in the numerator. Then move down that column to the row with 18 degrees of freedom. The value at this intersection is 5.09. So the decision rule is to reject H_0 if the computed value of F exceeds 5.09.

Step 5: Select the sample, perform the calculations, and make a decision. It is convenient to summarize the calculations of the F statistic in an **ANOVA table.** The format for an ANOVA table is as follows. Statistical software packages also use this format.

LO5 Organize data into a *one-way ANOVA table*.

ANOVA Table				
Source of Variation	**Sum of Squares**	**Degrees of Freedom**	**Mean Square**	***F***
Treatments	SST	$k-1$	$SST/(k-1) = MST$	MST/MSE
Error	SSE	$n-k$	$SSE/(n-k) = MSE$	
Total	SS total	$n-1$		

There are three values, or sum of squares, used to compute the test statistic F. You can determine these values by obtaining SS total and SSE, then finding SST by subtraction. The SS total term is the total variation, SST is the variation due to the treatments, and SSE is the variation within the treatments or the random error.

We usually start the process by finding SS total. This is the sum of the squared differences between each observation and the overall mean. The formula for finding SS total is:

$$SS\ total = \Sigma(X - \overline{X}_G)^2 \qquad \textbf{[12–2]}$$

where:

X is each sample observation.
$\overline{X}_G$ is the overall or grand mean.

Next determine SSE or the sum of the squared errors. This is the sum of the squared differences between each observation and its respective treatment mean. The formula for finding SSE is:

$$SSE = \Sigma(X - \overline{X}_c)^2 \qquad \textbf{[12–3]}$$

where:

$\overline{X}_c$ is the sample mean for treatment c.

The detailed calculations of SS total and SSE for this example follow. To determine the values of SS total and SSE we start by calculating the overall or grand mean. There are 22 observations and the total is 1,664, so the grand mean is 75.64.

$$\overline{X}_G = \frac{1,664}{22} = 75.64$$

	Eastern	**TWA**	**Allegheny**	**Ozark**	**Total**
	94	75	70	68	
	90	68	73	70	
	85	77	76	72	
	80	83	78	65	
		88	80	74	
			68	65	
			65		
Column total	349	391	510	414	1,664
n	4	5	7	6	22
Mean	87.25	78.20	72.86	69.00	75.64

Next we find the deviation of each observation from the grand mean, square those deviations, and sum this result for all 22 observations. For example, the first sampled passenger had a score of 94 and the overall or grand mean is 75.64. So $(X - \overline{X}_G) = 94 - 75.64 = 18.36$. For the last passenger $(X - \overline{X}_G) = 65 - 75.64 = -10.64$. The calculations for all other passengers follow.

Eastern	TWA	Allegheny	Ozark
18.36	−0.64	−5.64	−7.64
14.36	−7.64	−2.64	−5.64
9.36	1.36	0.36	−3.64
4.36	7.36	2.36	−10.64
	12.36	4.36	−1.64
		−7.64	−10.64
		−10.64	

Then square each of these differences and sum all the values. Thus for the first passenger:

$$(X - \overline{X}_G)^2 = (94 - 75.64)^2 = (18.36)^2 = 337.09.$$

Finally, sum all the squared differences as formula (12–2) directs. Our SS total value is 1,485.10.

	Eastern	TWA	Allegheny	Ozark	Total
	337.09	0.41	31.81	58.37	
	206.21	58.37	6.97	31.81	
	87.61	1.85	0.13	13.25	
	19.01	54.17	5.57	113.21	
		152.77	19.01	2.69	
			58.37	113.21	
			113.21		
Total	649.92	267.57	235.07	332.54	1,485.10

To compute the term SSE find the deviation between each observation and its treatment mean. In the example the mean of the first treatment (that is, the passengers on Eastern Airlines) is 87.25, found by $\overline{X}_E = 349/4$. The subscript E refers to Eastern Airlines.

The first passenger rated Eastern a 94, so $(X - \overline{X}_E) = (94 - 87.25) = 6.75$. The first passenger in the TWA group responded with a total score of 75, so $(X - \overline{X}_{TWA}) = (75 - 78.20) = -3.2$. The detail for all the passengers follows.

Eastern	TWA	Allegheny	Ozark
6.75	−3.2	−2.86	−1
2.75	−10.2	0.14	1
−2.25	−1.2	3.14	3
−7.25	4.8	5.14	−4
	9.8	7.14	5
		−4.86	−4
		−7.86	

Each of these values is squared and then summed for all 22 observations. The values are shown in the following table.

	Eastern	TWA	Allegheny	Ozark	Total
	45.5625	10.24	8.18	1	
	7.5625	104.04	0.02	1	
	5.0625	1.44	9.86	9	
	52.5625	23.04	26.42	16	
		96.04	50.98	25	
			23.62	16	
			61.78		
Total	110.7500	234.80	180.86	68	594.41

So the SSE value is 594.41. That is $\Sigma(X - \bar{X}_c)^2 = 594.41$.

Finally we determine SST, the sum of the squares due to the treatments, by subtraction.

$$SST = SS\text{ total} - SSE \qquad\qquad \textbf{[12–4]}$$

For this example:

$$SST = SS\text{ total} - SSE = 1,485.10 - 594.41 = 890.69.$$

To find the computed value of F, work your way across the ANOVA table. The degrees of freedom for the numerator and the denominator are the same as in step 4 on page 364 when we were finding the critical value of F. The term **mean square** is another expression for an estimate of the variance. The mean square for treatments is SST divided by its degrees of freedom. The result is the **mean square for treatments** and is written MST. Compute the **mean square error** in a similar fashion. To be precise, divide SSE by its degrees of freedom. To complete the process and find F, divide MST by MSE.

Insert the particular values of F into an ANOVA table and compute the value of F as follows.

Source of Variation	Sum of Squares	Degrees of Freedom	Mean Square	F
Treatments	890.69	3	296.90	8.99
Error	594.41	18	33.02	
Total	1,485.10	21		

The computed value of F is 8.99, which is greater than the critical value of 5.09, so the null hypothesis is rejected. We conclude the population means are not all equal. The mean scores are not the same for the four airlines. It is likely that the passenger scores are related to the particular airline. At this point we can only conclude there is a difference in the treatment means. We cannot determine which treatment groups differ or how many treatment groups differ.

As noted in the previous example, the calculations are tedious if the number of observations in each treatment is large. There are many software packages that will perform the calculations and output the results. Following is the Excel output in the form of an ANOVA table for the previous example involving airlines and passenger ratings. There are some slight differences between the software output and the previous calculations. These differences are due to rounding.

Notice Excel uses the term "Between Groups" for treatments and "Within Groups" for error. However, they have the same meanings. The *p*-value is .0007. This is the probability of finding a value of the test statistic this large or larger when the null hypothesis is true. To put it another way, it is the likelihood of calculating an *F* value larger than 8.99 with 3 degrees of freedom in the numerator and 18 degrees of freedom in the denominator. So when we reject the null hypothesis in this instance there is a very small likelihood of committing a Type I error!

Following is the MINITAB output from the airline passenger ratings example, which is similar to the Excel output. The output is also in the form of an ANOVA table. In addition, MINITAB provides information about the differences between means. This is discussed in the next section.

The MINITAB system uses the term "Factor" instead of *treatment,* with the same intended meaning.

Self-Review 12–2 Citrus Clean is a new all-purpose cleaner being test-marketed by placing displays in three different locations within various supermarkets. The number of 12-ounce bottles sold from each location within the supermarket is reported below.

Near bread	18	14	19	17
Near beer	12	18	10	16
Other cleaners	26	28	30	32

At the .05 significance level, is there a difference in the mean number of bottles sold at the three locations?
(a) State the null hypothesis and the alternate hypothesis.
(b) What is the decision rule?
(c) Compute the values of SS total, SST, and SSE.
(d) Develop an ANOVA table.
(e) What is your decision regarding the null hypothesis?

Exercises

7. The following is sample information. Test the hypothesis that the treatment means are equal. Use the .05 significance level.

Treatment 1	Treatment 2	Treatment 3
8	3	3
6	2	4
10	4	5
9	3	4

a. State the null hypothesis and the alternate hypotheses.
b. What is the decision rule?
c. Compute SST, SSE, and SS total.
d. Complete an ANOVA table.
e. State your decision regarding the null hypothesis.

8. The following is sample information. Test the hypothesis at the .05 significance level that the treatment means are equal.

Treatment 1	Treatment 2	Treatment 3
9	13	10
7	20	9
11	14	15
9	13	14
12		15
10		

a. State the null hypothesis and the alternate hypotheses.
b. What is the decision rule?
c. Compute SST, SSE, and SS total.
d. Complete an ANOVA table.
e. State your decision regarding the null hypothesis.

9. A real estate developer is considering investing in a shopping mall on the outskirts of Atlanta, Georgia. Three parcels of land are being evaluated. Of particular importance is the income in the area surrounding the proposed mall. A random sample of four families is selected near each proposed mall. Following are the sample results. At the .05 significance level, can the developer conclude there is a difference in the mean income? Use the usual five-step hypothesis testing procedure.

Southwyck Area ($000)	Franklin Park ($000)	Old Orchard ($000)
64	74	75
68	71	80
70	69	76
60	70	78

10. The manager of a computer software company wishes to study the number of hours senior executives by type of industry spend at their desktop computers. The manager selected a sample of five executives from each of three industries. At the .05 significance level, can she conclude there is a difference in the mean number of hours spent per week by industry?

Banking	Retail	Insurance
12	8	10
10	8	8
10	6	6
12	8	8
10	10	10

Inferences about Pairs of Treatment Means

Suppose we carry out the ANOVA procedure and make the decision to reject the null hypothesis. This allows us to conclude that all the treatment means are not the same. Sometimes we may be satisfied with this conclusion, but in other instances we may want to know which treatment means differ. This section provides the details for such a test.

Recall that in the Brunner Research example regarding airline passenger ratings there was a difference in the treatment means. That is, the null hypothesis was rejected and the alternate hypothesis accepted. If the passenger ratings do differ, the question is: Between which groups do the treatment means differ?

Several procedures are available to answer this question. The simplest is through the use of confidence intervals, that is, formula (9–2). From the computer output of the previous example (see page 368), note that the sample mean score for those passengers rating Eastern's service is 87.25, and for those rating Ozark's service the sample mean score is 69.00. Is there enough disparity to justify the conclusion that there is a significant difference in the mean satisfaction scores of the two airlines?

The t distribution, described in Chapters 10 and 11, is used as the basis for this test. Recall that one of the assumptions of ANOVA is that the population variances are the same for all treatments. This common population value is the mean square error, or MSE, and is determined by $SSE/(n - k)$. A confidence interval for the difference between two populations is found by:

LO6 Develop
confidence intervals
for the difference in
treatment means.

| CONFIDENCE INTERVAL FOR THE DIFFERENCE IN TREATMENT MEANS | $(\bar{X}_1 - \bar{X}_2) \pm t\sqrt{MSE\left(\dfrac{1}{n_1} + \dfrac{1}{n_2}\right)}$ | [12–5] |

where
$\bar{X}_1$ is the mean of the first sample.
$\bar{X}_2$ is the mean of the second sample.
t is obtained from Appendix B.2. The degrees of freedom is equal to $n - k$.
MSE is the mean square error term obtained from the ANOVA table $[SSE/(n - k)]$.
n_1 is the number of observations in the first sample.
n_2 is the number of observations in the second sample.

How do we decide whether there is a difference in the treatment means? If the confidence interval includes zero, there is *not* a difference between the treatment means. For example, if the left endpoint of the confidence interval has a negative sign and the right endpoint has a positive sign, the interval includes zero and the two means do not differ. So if we develop a confidence interval from formula (12–5) and find the difference in the sample means was 5.00, that is, if $\bar{X}_1 - \bar{X}_2 = 5$ and $t\sqrt{MSE\left(\dfrac{1}{n_1} + \dfrac{1}{n_2}\right)} = 12$, the confidence interval would range from -7.00 up to 17.00. To put it in symbols:

$$(\bar{X}_1 - \bar{X}_2) \pm t\sqrt{MSE\left(\dfrac{1}{n_1} + \dfrac{1}{n_2}\right)} = 5.00 \pm 12.00 = -7.00 \text{ up to } 17.00$$

Note that zero is included in this interval. Therefore, we conclude that there is no significant difference in the selected treatment means.

On the other hand, if the endpoints of the confidence interval have the same sign, this indicates that the treatment means differ. For example, if $\bar{X}_1 - \bar{X}_2 = -0.35$ and $t\sqrt{MSE\left(\dfrac{1}{n_1} + \dfrac{1}{n_2}\right)} = 0.25$, the confidence interval would range from -0.60 up to -0.10. Because -0.60 and -0.10 have the same sign, both negative, zero is not in the interval and we conclude that these treatment means differ.

Using the previous airline example let us compute the confidence interval for the difference between the mean scores of passengers on Eastern and Ozark Airlines. With a 95 percent level of confidence, the endpoints of the confidence interval are 10.46 and 26.04.

$$(\bar{X}_E - \bar{X}_O) \pm t\sqrt{MSE\left(\dfrac{1}{n_E} + \dfrac{1}{n_O}\right)} = (87.25 - 69.00) \pm 2.101\sqrt{33.0\left(\dfrac{1}{4} + \dfrac{1}{6}\right)}$$
$$= 18.25 \pm 7.79$$

where
$\bar{X}_E$ is 87.25.
$\bar{X}_O$ is 69.00.
t is 2.101: from Appendix B.2 with $(n - k) = 22 - 4 = 18$ degrees of freedom.
MSE is 33.0: from the ANOVA table with $SSE/(n - k) = 594.4/18$.
n_E is 4.
n_O is 6.

The 95 percent confidence interval ranges from 10.46 up to 26.04. Both endpoints are positive; hence, we can conclude these treatment means differ significantly.

372   Chapter 12

That is, passengers on Eastern rated service significantly different from those on Ozark.

Approximate results can also be obtained directly from the MINITAB output. Following is the lower portion of the output from page 368. On the left side is the number of observations, the mean, and the standard deviation for each treatment. Seven passengers on Allegheny rated the service as 72.857 with a standard deviation of 5.490.

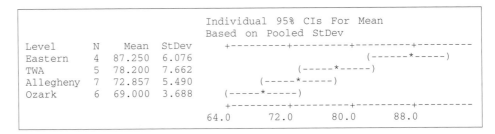

```
                                   Individual 95% CIs For Mean
                                   Based on Pooled StDev
Level       N   Mean   StDev       +---------+---------+---------+---------
Eastern     4  87.250  6.076                                 (------*-----)
TWA         5  78.200  7.662                   (-----*-----)
Allegheny   7  72.857  5.490             (-----*-----)
Ozark       6  69.000  3.688       (-----*-----)
                                   +---------+---------+---------+---------
                                  64.0      72.0      80.0      88.0
```

On the right side of the printout is a confidence interval for each treatment mean. The asterisk (*) indicates the location of the treatment mean and the open parenthesis and close parenthesis, the endpoints of the confidence interval. In those instances where the intervals overlap, the treatment means may not differ. If there is no common area in the confidence intervals, that pair of means differ.

The endpoints of a 95 percent confidence interval for mean passenger scores for Allegheny are about 69 and 77. For Ozark the endpoints of the 95 percent confidence interval for the mean passenger score are about 64 and 73. There is common area between these points, so we conclude this pair of means does not differ. In other words, there is no significant difference between the mean passenger ratings for Allegheny and Ozark. The difference in the mean scores is due to chance.

There are two pairs of means that differ. The mean scores of passengers on Eastern Airlines are significantly different from the mean ratings of passengers on Allegheny and on Ozark. There is no common area between these two pairs of confidence intervals.

We should emphasize that this investigation is a step-by-step process. The initial step is to conduct the ANOVA test. Only if the null hypothesis that the treatment means are equal is rejected should any analysis of the individual treatment means be attempted.

Self-Review 12–3

The following data are the semester tuition charges ($000) for a sample of private colleges in various regions of the United States. At the .05 significance level, can we conclude there is a difference in the mean tuition rates for the various regions?

Northeast ($000)	Southeast ($000)	West ($000)
10	8	7
11	9	8
12	10	6
10	8	7
12		6

(a) State the null and the alternate hypotheses.
(b) What is the decision rule?
(c) Develop an ANOVA table. What is the value of the test statistic?
(d) What is your decision regarding the null hypothesis?
(e) Could there be a significant difference between the mean tuition in the Northeast and that of the West? If so, develop a 95 percent confidence interval for that difference.

Exercises

connect™

11. Given the following sample information, test the hypothesis that the treatment means are equal at the .05 significance level.

Treatment 1	Treatment 2	Treatment 3
8	3	3
11	2	4
10	1	5
	3	4
	2	

a. State the null hypothesis and the alternate hypothesis.
b. What is the decision rule?
c. Compute SST, SSE, and SS total.
d. Complete an ANOVA table.
e. State your decision regarding the null hypothesis.
f. If H_0 is rejected, can we conclude that treatment 1 and treatment 2 differ? Use the 95 percent level of confidence.

12. Given the following sample information, test the hypothesis that the treatment means are equal at the .05 significance level.

Treatment 1	Treatment 2	Treatment 3
3	9	6
2	6	3
5	5	5
1	6	5
3	8	5
1	5	4
	4	1
	7	5
	6	
	4	

a. State the null hypothesis and the alternate hypothesis.
b. What is the decision rule?
c. Compute SST, SSE, and SS total.
d. Complete an ANOVA table.
e. State your decision regarding the null hypothesis.
f. If H_0 is rejected, can we conclude that treatment 2 and treatment 3 differ? Use the 95 percent level of confidence.

13. A senior accounting major at Midsouth State University has job offers from four CPA firms. To explore the offers further, she asked a sample of recent trainees how many months each worked for the firm before receiving a raise in salary. The sample information is submitted to MINITAB with the following results:

```
Analysis of Variance
Source    DF      SS      MS      F       P
Factor     3   32.33   10.78   2.36   0.133
Error     10   45.67    4.57
Total     13   78.00
```

At the .05 level of significance, is there a difference in the mean number of months before a raise was granted among the four CPA firms?

14. A stock analyst wants to determine whether there is a difference in the mean rate of return for three types of stock: utility, retail, and banking stocks. The following output is obtained:

```
Analysis of Variance
Source      DF         SS        MS         F         P
Factor       2      86.49     43.25     13.09     0.001
Error       13      42.95      3.30
Total       15     129.44
                                     Individual 95% CIs For Mean
                                     Based on Pooled StDev
Level        N       Mean     StDev   ----------+---------+---------+------
Utility      5     17.400     1.916                       (------*------)
Retail       5     11.620     0.356   (------*------)
Banking      6     15.400     2.356                (------*------)
                                     ----------+---------+---------+------
Pooled StDev = 1.818                    12.0      15.0      18.0
```

a. Using the .05 level of significance, is there a difference in the mean rate of return among the three types of stock?

b. Suppose the null hypothesis is rejected. Can the analyst conclude there is a difference between the mean rates of return for the utility and the retail stocks? Explain.

Chapter Summary

I. The characteristics of the F distribution are:
   A. It is continuous.
   B. Its values cannot be negative.
   C. It is positively skewed.
   D. There is a family of F distributions. Each time the degrees of freedom in either the numerator or the denominator changes, a new distribution is created.

II. The F distribution is used to test whether two population variances are the same.
   A. The sampled populations must follow the normal distribution.
   B. The larger of the two sample variances is placed in the numerator, forcing the ratio to be at least 1.00.
   C. The value of F is computed using the following equation:

$$F = \frac{s_1^2}{s_2^2}$$

[12–1]

III. A one-way ANOVA is used to compare several treatment means.
   A. A treatment is a source of variation.
   B. The assumptions underlying ANOVA are:
      1. The samples are from populations that follow the normal distribution.
      2. The populations have equal standard deviations.
      3. The samples are independent.
   C. The information for finding the value of F is summarized in an ANOVA table.
      1. The formula for SS total, the sum of squares total, is:

$$\text{SS total} = \Sigma(X - \bar{X}_G)^2$$

[12–2]

      2. The formula for SSE, the sum of squares error, is:

$$\text{SSE} = \Sigma(X - \bar{X}_c)^2$$

[12–3]

      3. The formula for the SST, the sum of squares treatment, is found by subtraction.

$$\text{SST} = \text{SS total} - \text{SSE}$$

[12–4]

4. This information is summarized in the following table and the value of F determined.

Source of Variation	Sum of Squares	Degrees of Freedom	Mean Square	F
Treatments	SST	$k - 1$	$SST/(k - 1) = MST$	MST/MSE
Error	SSE	$n - k$	$SSE/(n - k) = MSE$	
Total	SS total	$n - 1$		

IV. If a null hypothesis of equal treatment means is rejected, we can identify the pairs of means that differ from the following confidence interval.

$$(\bar{X}_1 - \bar{X}_2) \pm t\sqrt{MSE\left(\frac{1}{n_1} + \frac{1}{n_2}\right)} \qquad \text{[12–5]}$$

Pronunciation Key

SYMBOL	MEANING	PRONUNCIATION
SS total	Sum of squares total	S S total
SST	Sum of squares treatment	S S T
SSE	Sum of squares error	S S E
MSE	Mean square error	M S E

Chapter Exercises

connect™

15. A real estate agent in the coastal area of Georgia wants to compare the variation in the selling price of homes on the oceanfront with those one to three blocks from the ocean. A sample of 21 oceanfront homes sold within the last year revealed the standard deviation of the selling prices was $45,600. A sample of 18 homes, also sold within the last year, that were one to three blocks from the ocean revealed that the standard deviation was $21,330. At the .01 significance level, can we conclude that there is more variation in the selling prices of the oceanfront homes?

16. A new computer is sold with innovative flash memory. When compared to computers with conventional memory, the new machine is clearly faster, but initial tests indicate there is more variation in processing time. A sample of 16 computer runs showed that the standard deviation of the processing time was 22 hundredths of a second for the new machine and 12 hundredths of a second for the current machine. At the .05 significance level, can we conclude that there is more variation in the processing time of the new machine?

17. There are two Chevrolet dealers in Jamestown, New York. The mean monthly sales at Sharkey Chevy and Dave White Chevrolet are about the same. However, Tom Sharkey, the owner of Sharkey Chevy, believes his sales are more consistent. Below is the number of new cars sold at Sharkey in the last seven months and for the last eight months at Dave White. Do you agree with Mr. Sharkey? Use the .01 significance level.

Sharkey	98	78	54	57	68	64	70	
Dave White	75	81	81	30	82	46	58	101

18. Random samples of five were selected from each of three populations. The sum of squares total was 100. The sum of squares due to the treatments was 40.
a. Set up the null hypothesis and the alternate hypothesis.
b. What is the decision rule? Use the .05 significance level.

   c. Complete the ANOVA table. What is the value of F?
   d. What is your decision regarding the null hypothesis?

19. In an ANOVA table MSE was equal to 10. Random samples of six were selected from each of four populations, where the sum of squares total was 250.
   a. Set up the null hypothesis and the alternate hypothesis.
   b. What is the decision rule? Use the .05 significance level.
   c. Complete the ANOVA table. What is the value of F?
   d. What is your decision regarding the null hypothesis?

20. The following is a partial ANOVA table.

Source	Sum of Squares	df	Mean Square	F
Treatment		2		
Error			20	
Total	500	11		

Complete the table and answer the following questions. Use the .05 significance level.
   a. How many treatments are there?
   b. What is the total sample size?
   c. What is the critical value of F?
   d. Write out the null and alternate hypotheses.
   e. What is your conclusion regarding the null hypothesis?

21. A consumer organization wants to know whether there is a difference in the price of a particular toy at three different types of stores. The price of the toy was checked in a sample of five discount stores, five variety stores, and five department stores. The results are shown below. Use the .05 significance level.

Discount	Variety	Department
$12	$15	$19
13	17	17
14	14	16
12	18	20
15	17	19

22. A physician who specializes in weight control has three different diets she recommends. As an experiment, she randomly selected 15 patients and then assigned 5 to each diet. After three weeks the following weight losses, in pounds, were noted. At the .05 significance level, can she conclude that there is a difference in the mean amount of weight loss among the three diets?

Plan A	Plan B	Plan C
5	6	7
7	7	8
4	7	9
5	5	8
4	6	9

23. The City of Maumee comprises four districts. Chief of Police Andy North wants to determine whether there is a difference in the mean number of crimes committed among the four districts. He recorded the number of crimes reported in each district for a sample of six days. At the .05 significance level, can the chief of police conclude there is a difference in the mean number of crimes?

Number of Crimes			
Rec Center	Key Street	Monclova	Whitehouse
13	21	12	16
15	13	14	17
14	18	15	18
15	19	13	15
14	18	12	20
15	19	15	18

24. A study of the effect of television commercials on 12-year-old children measured their attention span, in seconds. The commercials were for clothes, food, and toys. At the .05 significance level is there a difference in the mean attention span of the children for the various commercials? Are there significant differences between pairs of means? Would you recommend dropping one of the three commercial types?

Clothes	Food	Toys
26	45	60
21	48	51
43	43	43
35	53	54
28	47	63
31	42	53
17	34	48
31	43	58
20	57	47
	47	51
	44	51
	54	

25. When only two treatments are involved, ANOVA and the Student t test (Chapter 11) result in the same conclusions. Also, $t^2 = F$. As an example, suppose that 14 randomly selected students were divided into two groups, one consisting of 6 students and the other of 8. One group was taught using a combination of lecture and programmed instruction, the other using a combination of lecture and television. At the end of the course, each group was given a 50-item test. The following is a list of the number correct for each of the two groups.

Lecture and Programmed Instruction	Lecture and Television
19	32
17	28
23	31
22	26
17	23
16	24
	27
	25

a. Using analysis of variance techniques, test H_0 that the two mean test scores are equal; $\alpha = .05$.

b. Using the t test from Chapter 11, compute t.

c. Interpret the results.

26. There are four auto body shops in Bangor, Maine, and all claim to promptly serve customers. To check if there is any difference in service, customers are randomly selected from each repair shop and their waiting times in days are recorded. The output from a statistical software package is:

Summary				
Groups	**Count**	**Sum**	**Average**	**Variance**
Body Shop A	3	15.4	5.133333	0.323333
Body Shop B	4	32	8	1.433333
Body Shop C	5	25.2	5.04	0.748
Body Shop D	4	25.9	6.475	0.595833

ANOVA					
Source of Variation	**SS**	**df**	**MS**	**F**	**p-value**
Between Groups	23.37321	3	7.791069	9.612506	0.001632
Within Groups	9.726167	12	0.810514		
Total	33.09938	15			

Is there evidence to suggest a difference in the mean waiting times at the four body shops? Use the .05 significance level.

27. The fuel efficiencies for a sample of 27 compact, midsize, and large cars are entered into a statistical software package. Analysis of variance is used to investigate if there is a difference in the mean mileage of the three cars. What do you conclude? Use the .01 significance level.

Summary				
Groups	**Count**	**Sum**	**Average**	**Variance**
Compact	12	268.3	22.35833	9.388106
Midsize	9	172.4	19.15556	7.315278
Large	6	100.5	16.75	7.303

Additional results are shown below.

ANOVA					
Source of Variation	**SS**	**df**	**MS**	**F**	**p-value**
Between Groups	136.4803	2	68.24014	8.258752	0.001866
Within Groups	198.3064	24	8.262766		
Total	334.7867	26			

28. Three assembly lines are used to produce a certain component for an airliner. To examine the production rate, a random sample of six hourly periods is chosen for each assembly line and the number of components produced during these periods for each line is recorded. The output from a statistical software package is:

Summary				
Groups	**Count**	**Sum**	**Average**	**Variance**
Line A	6	250	41.66667	0.266667
Line B	6	260	43.33333	0.666667
Line C	6	249	41.5	0.7

ANOVA					
Source of Variation	SS	df	MS	F	p-value
Between Groups	12.33333	2	6.166667	11.32653	0.001005
Within Groups	8.166667	15	0.544444		
Total	20.5	17			

    a. Use a .01 level of significance to test if there is a difference in the mean production of the three assembly lines.

    b. Develop a 99 percent confidence interval for the difference in the means between Line B and Line C.

29. The postal service groups first-class mail as letters, cards, flats, or parcels. Over a period of three weeks, one item of each kind was sent from a particular postal administrative center. The total time in transit was recorded. A statistical software package was then used to perform the analysis. The results follow.

```
Source    DF         SS       MS       F        P
Factor     3      13.82     4.61     2.72    0.051
Error     68     115.17     1.69
Total     71     128.99

S = 1.301      R-Sq = 10.71%      R-Sq(adj) = 6.77%

                                Individual 95% CIs for Mean Based on
                                Pooled StDev
Level      N    Mean   StDev   -----+---------+---------+---------+---
Letters   18   1.444   1.097   (---------*---------)
Cards     18   1.667   1.455     (---------*---------)
Flats     18   2.444   1.617                   (---------*---------)
Parcels   18   2.389   0.916                  (---------*---------)
                                -----+---------+---------+---------+---
                                   1.20      1.80      2.40      3.00
```

Use the .05 significance level to test if this evidence suggests a difference in the means for the different types of first-class mail.

30. For your email you use a filter to block spam from your inbox. The number of items blocked by day of week is recorded and a statistical software system is used to perform the analysis that follows. Here are the results:

```
Source    DF         SS       MS       F        P
Factor     6     1367.8    228.0     5.72    0.000
Error     48     1913.2     39.9
Total     54     3281.0

S = 6.313      R-Sq = 41.69%      R-Sq(adj) = 34.40%
```

```
                                Individual 95% CIs for Mean Based on
                                Pooled StDev
Level       N     Mean   StDev   ----+---------+---------+---------+-----
Monday     10   74.000   6.164                     (-----*------)
Tuesday     9   66.111   7.288           (------*------)
Wednesday   7   74.143   2.268                    (-------*-------)
Thursday    8   62.375   5.041   (-------*------)
Friday      8   75.125   4.454                      (------*-------)
Saturday    5   63.200   7.259   (--------*---------)
Sunday      8   72.375   9.164               (-------*------)
                                 ----+---------+---------+---------+-----
                                   60.0      66.0      72.0      78.0
```

Use the .05 significance level to test if this evidence suggests a difference in the means for the different days of the week.

Data Set Exercises

31. Refer to the Real Estate data, which report information on the homes sold in the Phoenix, Arizona, area last year.
   a. At the .02 significance level, is there a difference in the variability of the selling prices of the homes that have a pool versus those that do not have a pool?
   b. At the .02 significance level, is there a difference in the variability of the selling prices of the homes with an attached garage versus those that do not have an attached garage?
   c. At the .05 significance level, is there a difference in the mean selling price of the homes among the five townships?

32. Refer to the Baseball 2008 data, which report information on the 30 Major League Baseball teams for the 2008 season.
   a. At the .10 significance level, is there a difference in the variation in team salary among the American and National league teams?
   b. Create a variable that classifies a team's total attendance into three groups: less than 2.0 (million), 2.0 up to 3.0, and 3.0 or more. At the .05 significance level, is there a difference in the mean number of games won among the three groups? Use the .01 significance level.
   c. Using the same attendance variable developed in part (b), is there a difference in the mean team batting average? Use the .01 significance level.
   d. Using the same attendance variable developed in part (b), is there a difference in the mean salary of the three groups? Use the .01 significance level.

33. Refer to the Wage data, which report information on annual wages for a sample of 100 workers. Also included are variables relating to industry, years of education, and gender for each worker.
   a. Conduct a test of hypothesis to determine if there is a difference in the mean annual wages for workers in the three industries. If there is a difference in the means, which pair or pairs of means differ? Use the .05 significance level.
   b. Conduct a test of hypothesis to determine if there is a difference in the mean annual wages for workers in the six different occupations. If there is a difference in the means, which pair or pairs of means differ? Use the .05 significance level.

Practice Test

Part I Objective

1. The test statistic for comparing two population variances is the _____.
2. The shape of the F distribution is _____. (symmetrical, positively skewed, negatively skewed, uniform)
3. The F statistic is computed as the ratio of two _____.
4. Analysis of Variance (ANOVA) is used to compare two or more _____. (means, proportions, samples sizes, z-values)
5. The ANOVA test assumes equal _____. (population means, population standard deviations, sample sizes, z-values)
6. One-way ANOVA partitions Total Variation into two parts. One is called the treatment variation, and the other is the _____.
7. In one-way ANOVA, the null hypothesis is that the population means are _____.
8. A mean square is computed as a sum of squares divided by the _____.
9. In one-way ANOVA, treatment means are compared by developing _____. (confidence intervals, z-values, significance levels, variances)
10. For a one-way ANOVA, the treatments must be _____.

Part II Problems

1. Is there a difference in the variance of the distance traveled per week by each of the two taxi cab companies operating in the Grand Strand area? The *Sun News,* the local

newspaper, is investigating and obtained the following sample information. At the .10 significance level, is there a difference in the variance of the miles traveled?

Variable	Yellow Cab	Horse and Buggy Cab
Mean miles	837	797
Standard deviation	30	40
Sample size	14	12

2. The results of a one-way ANOVA are reported below.

ANOVA				
Source of Variation	**SS**	**df**	**MS**	**F**
Between Groups	6.90	2	3.45	5.15
Within Groups	12.04	18	0.67	
Total	19.34	20		

  a. How many treatments are in the study?
  b. What is the total sample size?
  c. What is the critical value of F?
  d. Write out the null hypothesis and the alternate hypothesis.
  e. What is your decision regarding the null hypothesis?
  f. Can we conclude any of the treatment means differ?

Software Commands

1. The Excel commands for the test of variances on page 359 are:
   a. Enter the data for U.S. 25 in column A and for I-75 in column B. Label the two columns.
   b. Select the **Data** tab on the top menu. Then, on the far right, select **Data Analysis.** Select

   F-Test: Two-Sample for Variances, then click **OK.**
   c. The range of the first variable is *A1:A8,* and *B1:B9* for the second. Click on **Labels,** enter *0.05* for **Alpha,** select *D1* for the **Output Range,** and click **OK.**

2. The Excel commands for the one-way ANOVA on page 368 are:

a. Key in data into four columns labeled: *Eastern, TWA, Allegheny,* and *Ozark.*

b. Select the **Data** tab on the top menu. Then, on the far right, select **Data Analysis.** Select **ANOVA: Single Factor,** then click **OK.**

c. In the subsequent dialog box make the input range *A1:D8,* click on **Grouped by Columns,** click on **Labels in first row,** the **Alpha** text box is *.05,* and finally select **Output Range** as *F1* and click **OK.**

3. The MINITAB commands for the one-way ANOVA on page 368 are:

a. Input the data into four columns and identify the columns as *Eastern, TWA, Allegheny,* and *Ozark.*

b. Select **Stat, ANOVA,** and **One-way (Unstacked),** select the data in columns C1 to C4, check on **Select** in the lower left, and then click **OK.**

Chapter 12   Answers to Self-Review

12–1 Let Mark's assemblies be population 1, then
$H_0: \sigma_1^2 \le \sigma_2^2; H_1: \sigma_1^2 > \sigma_2^2; df_1 = 10 - 1 = 9$; and df_2 also equals 9. H_0 is rejected if $F > 3.18$.

$$F = \frac{(2.0)^2}{(1.5)^2} = 1.78$$

H_0 is not rejected. The variation is the same for both employees.

12–2 a. $H_0: \mu_1 = \mu_2 = \mu_3$
H_1: At least one treatment mean is different.

b. Reject H_0 if $F > 4.26$

c. $\bar{X} = \frac{240}{12} = 20$

SS total $= (18 - 20)^2 + \cdots + (32 - 20)^2$
          $= 578$

SSE $= (18 - 17)^2 + (14 - 17)^2 + \cdots + (32 - 29)^2$
          $= 74$

SST $= 578 - 74 = 504$

d.

Source	Sum of Squares	Degrees of Freedom	Mean Square	F
Treatment	504	2	252	30.65
Error	74	9	8.22	
Total	578	11		

Source	Sum of Squares	df	Mean Square	F
Treatment	44.16	2	22.08	25.43
Error	9.55	11	0.8682	
Total	53.71	13		

e. H_0 is rejected. There is difference in the mean number of bottles sold at the various locations.

12–3 a. H_0: $\mu_1 = \mu_2 = \mu_3$
H_1: Not all means are equal.
b. H_0 is rejected if $F > 3.98$.
c. $\overline{X}_G = 8.86$, $\overline{X}_1 = 11$, $\overline{X}_2 = 8.75$, $\overline{X}_3 = 6.8$
SS total = 53.71
SST = 44.16
SSE = 9.55

d. H_0 is rejected. The treatment means differ.
e. $(11.0 - 6.8) \pm 2.201 \sqrt{0.8682(\frac{1}{5} + \frac{1}{5})} =$
$4.2 \pm 1.30 = 2.90$ and 5.50
These treatment means differ because both endpoints of the confidence interval are of the same sign—positive in this problem.

13

Linear Regression and Correlation

Learning Objectives

When you have completed this chapter, you will be able to:

LO1 Understand and apply the terms *dependent* and *independent variable*.

LO2 Calculate and interpret the *coefficient of correlation,* the *coefficient of determination,* and the *standard error of estimate.*

LO3 Conduct a test of hypothesis to determine whether the coefficient of correlation in the population is zero.

LO4 Calculate the least squares regression line.

LO5 Construct and interpret confidence and prediction intervals for the dependent variable.

Exercise 61 lists the movies with the largest world box office sales and their world box office budget. Find the correlation between world box office budget and world box office sales. Comment on the association between the two variables. (See LO2.)

Introduction

Chapters 2 through 4 dealt with *descriptive statistics*. We organized raw data into a frequency distribution, and computed several measures of location and measures of dispersion to describe the major characteristics of the data. Chapter 5 started the study of *statistical inference*. The main emphasis was on inferring something about a population parameter, such as the population mean, on the basis of a sample. We tested for the reasonableness of a population mean or a population proportion, the difference between two population means, or whether several population means were equal. All of these tests involved just *one* interval- or ratio-level variable, such as the weight of a plastic soft drink bottle, the income of bank presidents, or the number of patients admitted to a particular hospital.

We shift the emphasis in this chapter to the study of two variables. Recall in Chapter 4 we introduced the idea of showing the relationship between *two* variables with a scatter diagram. We plotted the price of vehicles sold at Whitner Autoplex on the vertical axis and the age of the buyer on the horizontal axis. See the statistical software output on page 111. In that case we observed that, as the age of the buyer increased, the amount spent for the vehicle also increased. In this chapter we carry this idea further. That is, we develop numerical measures to express the relationship between two variables. Is the relationship strong or weak, is it direct or inverse? In addition, we develop an equation to express the relationship between variables. This will allow us to estimate one variable on the basis of another. Here are some examples.

- Is there a relationship between the amount Healthtex spends per month on advertising and its sales in the month?
- Can we base an estimate of the cost to heat a home in January on the number of square feet in the home?
- Is there a relationship between the miles per gallon achieved by large pickup trucks and the size of the engine?
- Is there a relationship between the number of hours that students studied for an exam and the score earned?

Note in each of these cases there are two variables observed for each sampled observation. For the last example, we find, for each student selected for the sample, the hours studied and the score earned.

We begin this chapter by examining the meaning and purpose of **correlation analysis.** We continue our study by developing a mathematical equation that will allow us to estimate the value of one variable based on the value of another. This is called **regression analysis.** We will (1) determine the equation of the line that best fits the data, (2) use the equation to estimate the value of one variable based on another, (3) measure the error in our estimate, and (4) establish confidence and prediction intervals for our estimate.

What Is Correlation Analysis?

Correlation analysis is the study of the relationship between variables. To explain, suppose the sales manager of Copier Sales of America, which has a large sales force throughout the United States and Canada, wants to determine whether there is a relationship between the number of sales calls made in a month and the number of copiers sold that month. The manager selects a random sample of 10 representatives and determines the number of sales calls each representative made last month and the number of copiers sold. The sample information is shown in Table 13–1.

TABLE 13–1 Number of Sales Calls and Copiers Sold for 10 Salespeople

Sales Representative	Number of Sales Calls	Number of Copiers Sold
Tom Keller	20	30
Jeff Hall	40	60
Brian Virost	20	40
Greg Fish	30	60
Susan Welch	10	30
Carlos Ramirez	10	40
Rich Niles	20	40
Mike Kiel	20	50
Mark Reynolds	20	30
Soni Jones	30	70

By reviewing the data we observe that there does seem to be some relationship between the number of sales calls and the number of units sold. That is, the salespeople who made the most sales calls sold the most units. However, the relationship is not "perfect" or exact. For example, Soni Jones made fewer sales calls than Jeff Hall, but she sold more units.

Instead of talking in generalities as we did in Chapter 4 and have so far in this chapter, we will develop some statistical measures to portray more precisely the relationship between the two variables, sales calls and copiers sold. This group of statistical techniques is called **correlation analysis.**

> **CORRELATION ANALYSIS** A group of techniques to measure the association between two variables.

The basic idea of correlation analysis is to report the association between two variables. The usual first step is to plot the data in a **scatter diagram.** An example will show how a scatter diagram is used.

Example

Copier Sales of America sells copiers to businesses of all sizes throughout the United States and Canada. Ms. Marcy Bancer was recently promoted to the position of national sales manager. At the upcoming sales meeting, the sales representatives from all over the country will be in attendance. She would like to impress upon them the importance of making that extra sales call each day. She decides to gather some information on the relationship between the number of sales calls and the number of copiers sold. She selects a random sample of 10 sales representatives and determines the number of sales calls they made last month and the number of copiers they sold. The sample information is reported in Table 13–1. What observations can you make about the relationship between the number of sales calls and the number of copiers sold? Develop a scatter diagram to display the information.

Solution

Based on the information in Table 13–1, Ms. Bancer suspects there is a relationship between the number of sales calls made in a month and the number of copiers sold. Soni Jones sold the most copiers last month, and she was one of three representatives making 30 or more sales calls. On the other hand, Susan Welch and

Carlos Ramirez made only 10 sales calls last month. Ms. Welch, along with two others, had the lowest number of copiers sold among the sampled representatives.

The implication is that the number of copiers sold is related to the number of sales calls made. As the number of sales calls increases, it appears the number of copiers sold also increases. We refer to number of sales calls as the **independent variable** and number of copiers sold as the **dependent variable.**

LO1 Understand and apply the terms *dependent* and *independent variable.*

> **DEPENDENT VARIABLE** The variable that is being predicted or estimated. It is scaled on the *Y*-axis.
>
> **INDEPENDENT VARIABLE** The variable that provides the basis for estimation. It is the predictor variable. It is scaled on the *X*-axis.

It is common practice to scale the dependent variable (copiers sold) on the vertical or *Y*-axis and the independent variable (number of sales calls) on the horizontal or *X*-axis. To develop the scatter diagram of the Copier Sales of America sales information, we begin with the first sales representative, Tom Keller. Tom made 20 sales calls last month and sold 30 copiers, so *X* = 20 and *Y* = 30. To plot this point, move along the horizontal axis to *X* = 20, then go vertically to *Y* = 30 and place a dot at the intersection. This process is continued until all the paired data are plotted, as shown in Chart 13–1.

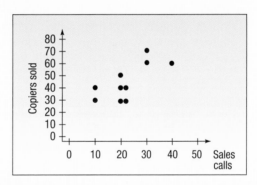

CHART 13–1 Scatter Diagram Showing Sales Calls and Copiers Sold

The scatter diagram shows graphically that the sales representatives who make more calls tend to sell more copiers. It is reasonable for Ms. Bancer, the national sales manager at Copier Sales of America, to tell her salespeople that, the more sales calls they make, the more copiers they can expect to sell. Note that, while there appears to be a positive relationship between the two variables, all the points do not fall on a line. In the following section you will measure the strength and direction of this relationship between two variables by determining the coefficient of correlation.

The Coefficient of Correlation

Interval- or ratio-level data are required.

Originated by Karl Pearson about 1900, the **coefficient of correlation** describes the strength of the relationship between two sets of interval-scaled or ratio-scaled variables. Designated *r,* it is often referred to as *Pearson's r* and as the *Pearson product-moment correlation coefficient*. It can assume any value from −1.00 to +1.00 inclusive. A correlation coefficient of −1.00 or +1.00 indicates *perfect correlation*. For example, a correlation coefficient for the preceding example computed to be +1.00 would indicate that the number of sales calls and the number of copiers sold are perfectly related in a positive linear sense. A computed value of −1.00 reveals that sales calls and the number of copiers sold are

Characteristics of *r*

LO2 Calculate and interpret the *coefficient of correlation,* the *coefficient of determination,* and the *standard error of estimate.*

perfectly related in an inverse linear sense. How the scatter diagram would appear if the relationship between the two sets of data were linear and perfect is shown in Chart 13–2.

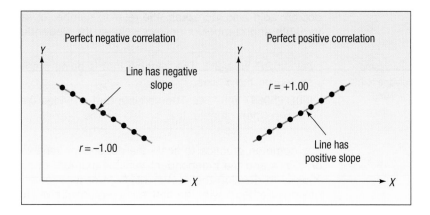

CHART 13–2 Scatter Diagrams Showing Perfect Negative Correlation and Perfect Positive Correlation

If there is absolutely no relationship between the two sets of variables, Pearson's *r* is zero. A coefficient of correlation *r* close to 0 (say, .08) shows that the linear relationship is quite weak. The same conclusion is drawn if $r = -.08$. Coefficients of $-.91$ and $+.91$ have equal strength; both indicate very strong correlation between the two variables. Thus, *the strength of the correlation does not depend on the direction (either − or +).*

Scatter diagrams for $r = 0$, a weak *r* (say, $-.23$), and a strong *r* (say, $+.87$) are shown in Chart 13–3. Note that, if the correlation is weak, there is considerable scatter about a line drawn through the center of the data. For the scatter diagram representing a strong relationship, there is very little scatter about the line. This indicates, in the example shown on the chart, that hours studied is a good predictor of exam score.

Examples of degrees of correlation

CHART 13–3 Scatter Diagrams Depicting Zero, Weak, and Strong Correlation

The following drawing summarizes the strength and direction of the coefficient of correlation.

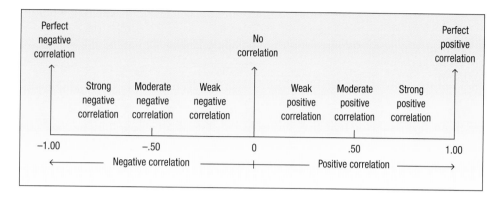

> **COEFFICIENT OF CORRELATION** A measure of the strength of the linear relationship between two variables.

The characteristics of the coefficient of correlation are summarized below.

> **CHARACTERISTICS OF THE COEFFICIENT OF CORRELATION**
> 1. The sample coefficient of correlation is identified by the lowercase letter *r*.
> 2. It shows the direction and strength of the linear (straight line) relationship between two interval- or ratio-scale variables.
> 3. It ranges from −1 up to and including +1.
> 4. A value near 0 indicates there is little association between the variables.
> 5. A value near 1 indicates a direct or positive association between the variables.
> 6. A value near −1 indicates inverse or negative association between the variables.

How is the value of the coefficient of correlation determined? We will use the Copier Sales of America data, which are reported in Table 13–2, as an example. We begin

TABLE 13–2 Sales Calls and Copiers Sold for 10 Salespeople

Sales Representative	Sales Calls, (X)	Copiers Sold, (Y)
Tom Keller	20	30
Jeff Hall	40	60
Brian Virost	20	40
Greg Fish	30	60
Susan Welch	10	30
Carlos Ramirez	10	40
Rich Niles	20	40
Mike Kiel	20	50
Mark Reynolds	20	30
Soni Jones	30	70
Total	220	450

with a scatter diagram, similar to Chart 13–2. Draw a vertical line through the data values at the mean of the X-values and a horizontal line at the mean of the Y-values. In Chart 13–4 we've added a vertical line at 22.0 calls ($\bar{X} = \Sigma X/n = 220/10 = 22$) and a horizontal line at 45.0 copiers ($\bar{Y} = \Sigma Y/n = 450/10 = 45.0$). These lines pass through the "center" of the data and divide the scatter diagram into four quadrants. Think of moving the origin from (0, 0) to (22, 45).

CHART 13–4 Computation of the Coefficient of Correlation

Two variables are positively related when the number of copiers sold is above the mean and the number of sales calls is also above the mean. These points appear in the upper-right quadrant (labeled Quadrant I) of Chart 13–4. Similarly, when the number of copiers sold is less than the mean, so is the number of sales calls. These points fall in the lower-left quadrant of Chart 13–4 (labeled Quadrant III). For example, the last person on the list in Table 13–2, Soni Jones, made 30 sales calls and sold 70 copiers. These values are above their respective means, so this point is located in Quadrant I which is in the upper-right quadrant. She made 8 ($X - \bar{X} = 30 - 22$) more sales calls than the mean and sold 25 ($Y - \bar{Y} = 70 - 45$) more copiers than the mean. Tom Keller, the first name on the list in Table 13–2, made 20 sales calls and sold 30 copiers. Both of these values are less than their respective mean; hence this point is in the lower-left quadrant. Tom made 2 less sales calls and sold 15 less copiers than the respective means. The deviations from the mean number of sales calls and for the mean number of copiers sold are summarized in Table 13–3 for the 10 sales representatives. The sum of the products of the deviations from the respective means is 900. That is, the term $\Sigma(X - \bar{X})(Y - \bar{Y}) = 900$.

In both the upper-right and the lower-left quadrants, the product of $(X - \bar{X})(Y - \bar{Y})$ is positive because both of the factors have the same sign. In our example this

TABLE 13–3 Deviations from the Mean and Their Products

Sales Representative	Calls, X	Sales, Y	X − X̄	Y − Ȳ	(X − X̄)(Y − Ȳ)
Tom Keller	20	30	−2	−15	30
Jeff Hall	40	60	18	15	270
Brian Virost	20	40	−2	−5	10
Greg Fish	30	60	8	15	120
Susan Welch	10	30	−12	−15	180
Carlos Ramirez	10	40	−12	−5	60
Rich Niles	20	40	−2	−5	10
Mike Kiel	20	50	−2	5	−10
Mark Reynolds	20	30	−2	−15	30
Soni Jones	30	70	8	25	200
					900

happens for all sales representatives except Mike Kiel. We can therefore expect the coefficient of correlation to have a positive value.

If the two variables are inversely related, one variable will be above the mean and the other below the mean. Most of the points in this case occur in the upper-left and lower-right quadrants, that is Quadrant II and IV. Now $(X - \bar{X})$ and $(Y - \bar{Y})$ will have opposite signs, so their product is negative. The resulting correlation coefficient is negative.

What happens if there is no linear relationship between the two variables? The points in the scatter diagram will appear in all four quadrants. The negative products of $(X - \bar{X})(Y - \bar{Y})$ offset the positive products, so the sum is near zero. This leads to a correlation coefficient near zero. So, the term $\Sigma(X - \bar{X})(Y - \bar{Y})$ drives the strength as well as the sign of the relationship between the two variables.

The correlation coefficient also needs to be unaffected by the units of the two variables. For example, if we had used hundreds of copiers sold instead of the number sold, the coefficient of correlation would be the same. The coefficient of correlation is independent of the scale used if we divide the term $\Sigma(X - \bar{X})(Y - \bar{Y})$ by the sample standard deviations. It is also made independent of the sample size and bounded by the values $+1.00$ and -1.00 if we divide by $(n - 1)$.

This reasoning leads to the following formula:

CORRELATION COEFFICIENT	$r = \dfrac{\Sigma(X - \bar{X})(Y - \bar{Y})}{(n - 1)s_x s_y}$	[13–1]

To compute the coefficient of correlation, we use the standard deviations of the sample of 10 sales calls and 10 copiers sold. We could use formula (3–12) to calculate the sample standard deviations or we could use a software package. For the specific Excel and MINITAB commands see the **Software Commands** section at the end of Chapter 3. The following is the Excel output. The standard deviation of the number of sales calls is 9.189 and of the number of copiers sold 14.337.

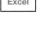
Excel

	A	B	C	D	E	F	G	H	I
1	Calls	Sales		Calls			Sales		
2	20	30		Mean	22.000		Mean	45.000	
3	40	60		Standard Error	2.906		Standard Error	4.534	
4	20	40		Median	20.000		Median	40.000	
5	30	60		Mode	20.000		Mode	30.000	
6	10	30		Standard Deviation	9.189		Standard Deviation	14.337	
7	10	40		Sample Variance	84.444		Sample Variance	205.556	
8	20	40		Kurtosis	0.396		Kurtosis	-1.001	
9	20	50		Skewness	0.601		Skewness	0.566	
10	20	30		Range	30.000		Range	40.000	
11	30	70		Minimum	10.000		Minimum	30.000	
12				Maximum	40.000		Maximum	70.000	
13				Sum	220.000		Sum	450.000	
14				Count	10.000		Count	10.000	
15									

num 1 dstats [Compatibility Mode]

We now insert these values into formula (13–1) to determine the coefficient of correlation:

$$r = \frac{\Sigma(X - \bar{X})(Y - \bar{Y})}{(n - 1)s_x s_y} = \frac{900}{(10 - 1)(9.189)(14.337)} = 0.759$$

How do we interpret a correlation of 0.759? First, it is positive, so we conclude there is a direct relationship between the number of sales calls and the number of copiers sold. This confirms our reasoning based on the scatter diagram,

Chart 13–4. The value of 0.759 is fairly close to 1.00, so we conclude that the association is strong.

We must be careful with the interpretation. The correlation of 0.759 indicates a strong positive association between the variables. Ms. Bancer would be correct to encourage the sales personnel to make that extra sales call, because the number of sales calls made is related to the number of copiers sold. However, does this mean that more sales calls *cause* more sales? No, we have not demonstrated cause and effect here, only that the two variables—sales calls and copiers sold—are related.

The Coefficient of Determination

In the previous example regarding the relationship between the number of sales calls and the units sold, the coefficient of correlation, 0.759, was interpreted as being "strong." Terms such as *weak, moderate,* and *strong,* however, do not have precise meaning. A measure that has a more easily interpreted meaning is the **coefficient of determination.** It is computed by squaring the coefficient of correlation. In the example, the coefficient of determination, r^2, is 0.576, found by $(0.759)^2$. This is a proportion or a percent; we can say that 57.6 percent of the variation in the number of copiers sold is explained, or accounted for, by the variation in the number of sales calls.

> **COEFFICIENT OF DETERMINATION** The proportion of the total variation in the dependent variable Y that is explained, or accounted for, by the variation in the independent variable X.

Further discussion of the coefficient of determination is found later in the chapter.

Correlation and Cause

If there is a strong relationship (say, .91) between two variables, we are tempted to assume that an increase or decrease in one variable *causes* a change in the other variable. For example, the consumption of Georgia peanuts and the consumption of aspirin have a strong correlation. However, this does not indicate that an increase in the consumption of peanuts *caused* the consumption of aspirin to increase. Likewise, the incomes of professors and the number of inmates in mental institutions have increased proportionately. Further, as the population of donkeys has decreased, there has been an increase in the number of doctoral degrees granted. Relationships such as these are called **spurious correlations.** What we can conclude when we find two variables with a strong correlation is that there is a relationship or association between the two variables, not that a change in one causes a change in the other.

Self-Review 13–1

Haverty's Furniture is a family business that has been selling to retail customers in the Chicago area for many years. The company advertises extensively on radio, TV, and the Internet, emphasizing low prices and easy credit terms. The owner would like to review the relationship between sales and the amount spent on advertising. Below is information on sales and advertising expense for the last four months.

Month	Advertising Expense ($ million)	Sales Revenue ($ million)
July	2	7
August	1	3
September	3	8
October	4	10

(a) The owner wants to forecast sales on the basis of advertising expense. Which variable is the dependent variable? Which variable is the independent variable?

(b) Draw a scatter diagram.
(c) Determine the coefficient of correlation.
(d) Interpret the strength of the correlation coefficient.
(e) Determine the coefficient of determination. Interpret.

Exercises

connect™

1. The following sample observations were randomly selected.

X:	4	5	3	6	10
Y:	4	6	5	7	7

Determine the coefficient of correlation and the coefficient of determination. Interpret.

2. The following sample observations were randomly selected.

X:	5	3	6	3	4	4	6	8
Y:	13	15	7	12	13	11	9	5

Determine the coefficient of correlation and the coefficient of determination. Interpret the association between X and Y.

3. Bi-lo Appliance Super-Store has outlets in several large metropolitan areas in New England. The general sales manager plans to air a commercial for a digital camera on selected local TV stations prior to a sale starting on Saturday and ending Sunday. She plans to get the information for Saturday–Sunday digital camera sales at the various outlets and pair them with the number of times the advertisement was shown on the local TV stations. The purpose is to find whether there is any relationship between the number of times the advertisement was aired and digital camera sales. The pairings are:

Location of TV Station	Number of Airings	Saturday–Sunday Sales ($ thousands)
Providence	4	15
Springfield	2	8
New Haven	5	21
Boston	6	24
Hartford	3	17

a. What is the dependent variable?
b. Draw a scatter diagram.
c. Determine the coefficient of correlation.
d. Determine the coefficient of determination.
e. Interpret these statistical measures.

4. The production department of Celltronics International wants to explore the relationship between the number of employees who assemble a subassembly and the number produced. As an experiment, two employees were assigned to assemble the subassemblies. They produced 15 during a one-hour period. Then four employees assembled them. They produced 25 during a one-hour period. The complete set of paired observations follows.

Number of Assemblers	One-Hour Production (units)
2	15
4	25
1	10
5	40
3	30

The dependent variable is production; that is, it is assumed that the level of production depends upon the number of employees.

a. Draw a scatter diagram.
b. Based on the scatter diagram, does there appear to be any relationship between the number of assemblers and production? Explain.
c. Compute the coefficient of correlation.
d. Evaluate the strength of the relationship by computing the coefficient of determination.

5. The city council of Pine Bluffs is considering increasing the number of police in an effort to reduce crime. Before making a final decision, the council asks the chief of police to survey other cities of similar size to determine the relationship between the number of police and the number of crimes reported. The chief gathered the following sample information.

City	Police	Number of Crimes	City	Police	Number of Crimes
Oxford	15	17	Holgate	17	7
Starksville	17	13	Carey	12	21
Danville	25	5	Whistler	11	19
Athens	27	7	Woodville	22	6

a. If we want to estimate crimes on the basis of the number of police, which variable is the dependent variable and which is the independent variable?
b. Draw a scatter diagram.
c. Determine the coefficient of correlation.
d. Determine the coefficient of determination.
e. Interpret these statistical measures. Does it surprise you that the relationship is inverse?

6. The owner of Maumee Ford-Mercury-Volvo wants to study the relationship between the age of a car and its selling price. Listed below is a random sample of 12 used cars sold at the dealership during the last year.

Car	Age (years)	Selling Price ($000)	Car	Age (years)	Selling Price ($000)
1	9	8.1	7	8	7.6
2	7	6.0	8	11	8.0
3	11	3.6	9	10	8.0
4	12	4.0	10	12	6.0
5	8	5.0	11	6	8.6
6	7	10.0	12	6	8.0

a. If we want to estimate selling price on the basis of the age of the car, which variable is the dependent variable and which is the independent variable?
b. Draw a scatter diagram.
c. Determine the coefficient of correlation.
d. Determine the coefficient of determination.
e. Interpret these statistical measures. Does it surprise you that the relationship is inverse?

Testing the Significance of the Correlation Coefficient

Recall that the sales manager of Copier Sales of America found the correlation between the number of sales calls and the number of copiers sold was 0.759. This indicated a strong association between the two variables. However, only 10 salespeople were sampled. Could it be that the correlation in the population is actually 0? This would mean the correlation of 0.759 was due to chance. The population in this example is all the salespeople employed by the firm.

Could the correlation in the population be zero?

Resolving this dilemma requires a test to answer the question: Could there be zero correlation in the population from which the sample was selected? To put it another way, did the computed r come from a population of paired observations with zero correlation? We continue the convention that Greek letters represent a population parameter, so ρ represents the correlation in the population. It is pronounced "row."

We employ the same hypothesis testing steps described in Chapter 10. The null hypothesis and the alternate hypothesis are:

H_0: ρ = 0   (The correlation in the population is zero.)
H_1: ρ ≠ 0   (The correlation in the population is different from zero.)

From the way H_1 is stated, we know that the test is two-tailed.
The formula for *t* is:

LO3 Conduct a test of hypothesis to determine whether the coefficient of correlation in the population is zero.

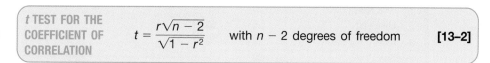

t TEST FOR THE COEFFICIENT OF CORRELATION
$$t = \frac{r\sqrt{n-2}}{\sqrt{1-r^2}} \quad \text{with } n-2 \text{ degrees of freedom} \qquad \textbf{[13–2]}$$

Using the .05 level of significance, the decision rule in this instance states that if the computed *t* falls in the area between plus 2.306 and minus 2.306, the null hypothesis is not rejected. To locate the critical value of 2.306, refer to Appendix B.2 for $df = n - 2 = 10 - 2 = 8$. See Chart 13–5.

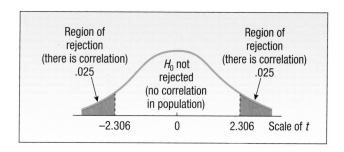

CHART 13–5 Decision Rule for Test of Hypothesis at .05 Significance Level and 8 *df*

Applying formula (13–2) to the example regarding the number of sales calls and units sold:

$$t = \frac{r\sqrt{n-2}}{\sqrt{1-r^2}} = \frac{.759\sqrt{10-2}}{\sqrt{1-.759^2}} = 3.297$$

The computed *t* is in the rejection region. Thus, H_0 is rejected at the .05 significance level. Hence we conclude the correlation in the population is not zero. From a practical standpoint, it indicates to the sales manager that there is correlation with respect to the number of sales calls made and the number of copiers sold in the population of salespeople.

We can also interpret the test of hypothesis in terms of *p*-values. A *p*-value is the likelihood of finding a value of the test statistic more extreme than the one computed, when H_0 is true. To determine the *p*-value, go to the *t* distribution in Appendix B.2 and find the row for 8 degrees of freedom. The value of the test statistic is 3.297, so in the row for 8 degrees of freedom and a two-tailed test, find the value closest to 3.297. For a two-tailed test at the .02 significance level, the critical value is 2.896, and the critical value at the .01 significance level is 3.355. Because 3.297 is between 2.896 and 3.355 we conclude that the *p*-value is between .01 and .02.

Both MINITAB and Excel will report the correlation between two variables. In addition to the correlation, MINITAB reports the *p*-value for the test of hypothesis that the correlation in the population between the two variables is 0. The MINITAB output is at the top of the following page.

Self-Review 13–2 A sample of 25 mayoral campaigns in medium-sized cities with populations between 50,000 and 250,000 showed that the correlation between the percent of the vote received and the amount spent on the campaign by the candidate was .43. At the .05 significance level, is there a positive association between the variables?

Exercises

connect

7. The following hypotheses are given.

   $H_0: \rho \le 0$
   $H_1: \rho > 0$

   A random sample of 12 paired observations indicated a correlation of .32. Can we conclude that the correlation in the population is greater than zero? Use the .05 significance level.

8. The following hypotheses are given.

   $H_0: \rho \ge 0$
   $H_1: \rho < 0$

   A random sample of 15 paired observations have a correlation of −.46. Can we conclude that the correlation in the population is less than zero? Use the .05 significance level.

9. Pennsylvania Refining Company is studying the relationship between the pump price of gasoline and the number of gallons sold. For a sample of 20 stations last Tuesday, the correlation was .78. At the .01 significance level, is the correlation in the population greater than zero?

10. A study of 20 worldwide financial institutions showed the correlation between their assets and pretax profit to be .86. At the .05 significance level, can we conclude that there is positive correlation in the population?

11. The Airline Passenger Association studied the relationship between the number of passengers on a particular flight and the cost of the flight. It seems logical that more passengers on the flight will result in more weight and more luggage, which in turn will result in higher fuel costs. For a sample of 15 flights, the correlation between the number of passengers and total fuel cost was .667. Is it reasonable to conclude that there is positive association in the population between the two variables? Use the .01 significance level.

12. The Student Government Association at Middle Carolina University wanted to demonstrate the relationship between the number of beers a student drinks and his or her blood alcohol content (BAC). A random sample of 18 students participated in a study in which each participating student was randomly assigned a number of 12-ounce cans of beer to drink. Thirty minutes after consuming their assigned number of beers a member of the local sheriff's office measured their blood alcohol content. The sample information is reported below.

Student	Beers	BAC	Student	Beers	BAC
1	6	0.10	10	3	0.07
2	7	0.09	11	3	0.05
3	7	0.09	12	7	0.08
4	4	0.10	13	1	0.04
5	5	0.10	14	4	0.07
6	3	0.07	15	2	0.06
7	3	0.10	16	7	0.12
8	6	0.12	17	2	0.05
9	6	0.09	18	1	0.02

Use a statistical software package to answer the following questions.
a. Develop a scatter diagram for the number of beers consumed and BAC. Comment on the relationship. Does it appear to be strong or weak? Does it appear to be direct or inverse?
b. Determine the coefficient of correlation.
c. Determine the coefficient of determination.
d. At the .01 significance level is it reasonable to conclude that there is a positive relationship in the population between the number of beers consumed and the BAC? What is the p-value?

Regression Analysis

In the previous section we developed measures to express the strength and the direction of the linear relationship between two variables. In this section we wish to develop an equation to express the *linear* (straight line) relationship between two variables. In addition we want to be able to estimate the value of the dependent variable Y based on a selected value of the independent variable X. The technique used to develop the equation and provide the estimates is called **regression analysis.**

In Table 13–1 we reported the number of sales calls and the number of units sold for a sample of 10 sales representatives employed by Copier Sales of America. Chart 13–1 portrayed this information in a scatter diagram. Now we want to develop a linear equation that expresses the relationship between the number of sales calls and the number of units sold. The equation for the line used to estimate Y on the basis of X is referred to as the **regression equation.**

> **REGRESSION EQUATION** An equation that expresses the linear relationship between two variables.

Least Squares Principle

The scatter diagram in Chart 13–1 is reproduced in Chart 13–6, with a line drawn with a ruler through the dots to illustrate that a straight line would probably fit the data. However, the line drawn using a straight edge has one disadvantage: Its position is based in part on the judgment of the person drawing the line. The hand-drawn lines in Chart 13–7 represent the judgments of four people. All the lines except line *A* seem to be reasonable. However, each would result in a different estimate of units sold for a particular number of sales calls.

CHART 13–6 Sales Calls and Copiers Sold for 10 Sales Representatives

CHART 13–7 Four Lines Superimposed on the Scatter Diagram

Least squares line gives "best" fit; subjective method is unreliable.

Judgment is eliminated by determining the regression line using a mathematical method called the **least squares principle.** This method gives what is commonly referred to as the "best-fitting" line.

> **LEAST SQUARES PRINCIPLE** Determining a regression equation by minimizing the sum of the squares of the vertical distances between the actual *Y* values and the predicted values of *Y*.

To illustrate this concept, the same data are plotted in the three charts that follow. The regression line in Chart 13–8 was determined using the least squares method. It is the best-fitting line because the sum of the squares of the vertical deviations about it is at a minimum. The first plot ($X = 3$, $Y = 8$) deviates by 2 from the line, found by $10 - 8$. The deviation squared is 4. The squared deviation for the plot $X = 4$, $Y = 18$ is 16. The squared deviation for the plot $X = 5$, $Y = 16$ is 4. The sum of the squared deviations is 24, found by $4 + 16 + 4$.

Assume that the lines in Charts 13–9 and 13–10 were drawn with a straight edge. The sum of the squared vertical deviations in Chart 13–9 is 44. For Chart 13–10

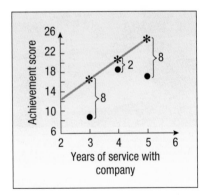

CHART 13–8 The Least Squares Line

CHART 13–9 Line Drawn with a Straight Edge

CHART 13–10 Different Line Drawn with a Straight Edge

it is 132. Both sums are greater than the sum for the line in Chart 13–8, found by using the least squares method.

The equation of a straight line has the form

LO4 Calculate the least squares regression line.

> **GENERAL FORM OF LINEAR REGRESSION EQUATION** $\hat{Y} = a + bX$ **[13–3]**

where

$\hat{Y}$, read Y hat, is the estimated value of the Y variable for a selected X value.

a is the Y-intercept. It is the estimated value of Y when $X = 0$. Another way to put it is: a is the estimated value of Y where the regression line crosses the Y-axis when X is zero.

b is the slope of the line, or the average change in $\hat{Y}$ for each change of one unit (either increase or decrease) in the independent variable X.

X is any value of the independent variable that is selected.

The formulas for a and b are:

> **SLOPE OF THE REGRESSION LINE** $b = r\dfrac{s_y}{s_x}$ **[13–4]**

where

r is the correlation coefficient.

s_y is the standard deviation of Y (the dependent variable).

s_x is the standard deviation of X (the independent variable).

> **Y-INTERCEPT** $a = \overline{Y} - b\overline{X}$ **[13–5]**

where

$\overline{Y}$ is the mean of Y (the dependent variable).

$\overline{X}$ is the mean of X (the independent variable).

Example

Recall the example involving Copier Sales of America. The sales manager gathered information on the number of sales calls made and the number of copiers sold for a random sample of 10 sales representatives. As a part of her presentation at the upcoming sales meeting, Ms. Bancer, the sales manager, would like to offer specific information about the relationship between the number of sales calls and the number of copiers sold. Use the least squares method to determine a linear equation to express the relationship between the two variables. What is the expected number of copiers sold by a representative who made 20 calls?

Solution

The first step in determining the regression equation is to find the slope of the least squares regression line. That is, we need the value of b. On page 391, we determined the correlation coefficient r (.759). In the Excel output on the same page, we determined the standard deviation of the independent variable X (9.189) and the standard deviation of the dependent variable Y (14.337). The values are inserted in formula (13–4).

$$b = r\left(\frac{s_y}{s_x}\right) = .759\left(\frac{14.337}{9.189}\right) = 1.1842$$

Next we need to find the value of a. To do this we use the value for b that we just calculated as well as the means for the number of sales calls and the number of copiers sold. These means are also available in the Excel printout on page 391. From formula (13–5):

$$a = \bar{Y} - b\bar{X} = 45 - 1.1842(22) = 18.9476$$

Thus, the regression equation is $\hat{Y} = 18.9476 + 1.1842X$. So if a salesperson makes 20 calls, he or she can expect to sell 42.6316 copiers, found by $\hat{Y} = 18.9476 + 1.1842X = 18.9476 + 1.1842(20)$. The b value of 1.1842 indicates that for each additional sales call made the sales representative can expect to increase the number of copiers sold by about 1.2. To put it another way, five additional sales calls in a month will result in about six more copiers being sold, found by 1.1842(5) = 5.921.

The a value of 18.9476 is the point where the equation crosses the Y-axis. A literal translation is that if no sales calls are made, that is, $X = 0$, 18.9476 copiers will be sold. Note that $X = 0$ is outside the range of values included in the sample and, therefore, should not be used to estimate the number of copiers sold. The sales calls ranged from 10 to 40, so estimates should be limited to that range.

Drawing the Regression Line

The least squares equation, $\hat{Y} = 18.9476 + 1.1842X$, can be drawn on the scatter diagram. The first sales representative in the sample is Tom Keller. He made 20 calls. His estimated number of copiers sold is $\hat{Y} = 18.9476 + 1.1842(20) = 42.6316$. The plot $X = 20$ and $Y = 42.6316$ is located by moving to 20 on the X-axis and then going vertically to 42.6316. The other points on the regression equation can be determined by substituting the particular value of X into the regression equation. All the points are connected to give the line. See Chart 13–11.

Statistics in Action

In finance, investors are interested in the trade-off between returns and risk. One technique to quantify risk is a regression analysis of a company's stock price (dependent variable) and an average measure of the stock market (independent variable). Often the Standard and Poor's (S&P) 500 Index is used to estimate the market. The regression coefficient, called beta in finance, shows the change in a company's stock price for a one-unit change in the S&P Index. For example, if a stock has a beta of 1.5, then when the S&P index *(continued)*

Sales Representative	Sales Calls (X)	Estimated Sales ($\hat{Y}$)	Sales Representative	Sales Calls (X)	Estimated Sales ($\hat{Y}$)
Tom Keller	20	42.6316	Carlos Ramirez	10	30.7896
Jeff Hall	40	66.3156	Rich Niles	20	42.6316
Brian Virost	20	42.6316	Mike Kiel	20	42.6316
Greg Fish	30	54.4736	Mark Reynolds	20	42.6316
Susan Welch	10	30.7896	Soni Jones	30	54.4736

CHART 13–11 The Line of Regression Drawn on the Scatter Diagram

The least squares regression line has some interesting and unique features. First, it will always pass through the point $(\overline{X}, \overline{Y})$. To show this is true, we can use the mean number of sales calls to predict the number of copiers sold. In this example the mean number of sales calls is 22.0, found by $\overline{X} = 220/10$. The mean number of copiers sold is 45.0, found by $\overline{Y} = 450/10 = 45$. If we let $X = 22$ and then use the regression equation to find the estimated value for $\hat{Y}$, the result is:

$$\hat{Y} = 18.9476 + 1.1842(22) = 45$$

The estimated number of copies sold is exactly equal to the mean number of copies sold. This simple example shows the regression line will pass through the point represented by the two means. In this case the regression equation will pass through the point $X = 22$ and $Y = 45$.

Second, as we discussed earlier in this section, there is no other line through the data where the sum of the squared deviations is smaller. To put it another way, the term $\Sigma(Y - \hat{Y})^2$ is smaller for the least squares regression equation than for any other equation. We use the Excel system to demonstrate this condition.

Regression Table 13.1 [Compatibility Mode]

	A	B	C	D	E	F	G	H	I	J	K
1	Sales	Calls	Sales	Estimates Sales							
2	Representative	(X)	(Y)	$\hat{Y}$	$(Y-\hat{Y})$	$(Y-\hat{Y})^2$	Y^*	$(Y-Y^*)^2$	Y^{**}	$(Y-Y^{**})^2$	
3	Tom Keller	20	30	42.6316	-12.6316	159.55731856	43	169	40	100	
4	Jeff Hall	40	60	66.3156	-6.3156	39.88680336	67	49	60	0	
5	Brian Virost	20	40	42.6316	-2.6316	6.92531856	43	9	40	0	
6	Greg Fish	30	60	54.4736	5.5264	30.54109696	55	25	50	100	
7	Susan Welch	10	30	30.7896	-0.7896	0.62346816	31	1	30	0	
8	Carlos Ramirez	10	40	30.7896	9.2104	84.83146816	31	81	30	100	
9	Rich Niles	20	40	42.6316	-2.6316	6.92531856	43	9	40	0	
10	Mike Kiel	20	50	42.6316	7.3684	54.29331856	43	49	40	100	
11	Mark Reynolds	20	30	42.6316	-12.6316	159.55731856	43	169	40	100	
12	Soni Jones	30	70	54.4736	15.5264	241.06909696	55	225	50	400	
13			Sum of		0.00	784.21052640		786		900	
14			Residuals								
15											
16				Least Squares							
17				Value							

In Columns A, B, and C in the Excel spreadsheet above we duplicated the sample information on sales and copiers sold from Table 13–1. In column D we provide the estimated sales values, the $\hat{Y}$ values, as calculated above.

In column E we calculate the **residuals,** or the error values. This is the difference between the actual values and the predicted values. That is, column E is $(Y - \hat{Y})$. For Soni Jones,

$$\hat{Y} = 18.9476 + 1.1842(30) = 54.4736$$

Her actual value is 70. So the residual, or error of estimate, is

$$(Y - \hat{Y}) = (70 - 54.4736) = 15.5264$$

This value reflects the amount the predicted value of sales is "off" from the actual sales value.

Next in Column F we square the residuals for each of the sales representatives and total the result. The total is 784.2105.

$$\Sigma(Y - \hat{Y})^2 = 159.5573 + 39.8868 + \cdots + 241.0691 = 784.2105$$

This is the sum of the squared differences or the least squares value. There is no other line through these 10 data points where the sum of the squared differences is smaller.

We can demonstrate the least squares criterion by choosing two arbitrary equations that are close to the least squares equation and determining the sum of the squared differences for these equations. In column G we use the equation $Y^* = 19 + 1.2X$ to find the predicted value. Notice this equation is very similar to the least squares equation. In Column H we determine the residuals and square these residuals. For the first sales representative, Tom Keller,

$$Y^* = 19 + 1.2(20) = 43$$

$$(Y - Y^*)^2 = (43 - 30)^2 = 169$$

This procedure is continued for the other nine sales representatives and the squared residuals totaled. The result is 786. This is a larger value (786 versus 784.2105) than the residuals for the least squares line.

In columns I and J on the output we repeat the above process for yet another equation $Y^{**} = 20 + X$. Again, this equation is similar to the least squares equation. The details for Tom Keller are:

$$Y^{**} = 20 + X = 20 + 20 = 40$$

$$(Y - Y^{**})^2 = (30 - 40)^2 = 100$$

This procedure is continued for the other nine sales representatives and the residuals totaled. The result is 900, which is also larger than the least squares values.

What have we shown with the example? The sum of the squared residuals $[\Sigma(Y - \hat{Y})^2]$ for the least squares equation is smaller than for other selected lines. The bottom line is you will not be able to find any line passing through these data points where the sum of the squared residuals is smaller.

Self-Review 13–3 Refer to Self-Review 13–1, where the owner of Haverty's Furniture Company was studying the relationship between sales and the amount spent on advertising. The sales information for the last four months is repeated below.

Month	Advertising Expense ($ million)	Sales Revenue ($ million)
July	2	7
August	1	3
September	3	8
October	4	10

(a) Determine the regression equation.
(b) Interpret the values of a and b.
(c) Estimate sales when $3 million is spent on advertising.

Exercises

connect

13. The following sample observations were randomly selected.

X:	4	5	3	6	10
Y:	4	6	5	7	7

a. Determine the regression equation.
b. Determine the value of $\hat{Y}$ when X is 7.

14. The following sample observations were randomly selected.

X:	5	3	6	3	4	4	6	8
Y:	13	15	7	12	13	11	9	5

a. Determine the regression equation.
b. Determine the value of $\hat{Y}$ when X is 7.
15. Bradford Electric Illuminating Company is studying the relationship between kilowatt-hours (thousands) used and the number of rooms in a private single-family residence. A random sample of 10 homes yielded the following.

Number of Rooms	Kilowatt-Hours (thousands)	Number of Rooms	Kilowatt-Hours (thousands)
12	9	8	6
9	7	10	8
14	10	10	10
6	5	5	4
10	8	7	7

a. Determine the regression equation.
b. Determine the number of kilowatt-hours, in thousands, for a six-room house.
16. Mr. James McWhinney, president of Daniel-James Financial Services, believes there is a relationship between the number of client contacts and the dollar amount of sales. To document this assertion, Mr. McWhinney gathered the following sample information. The X column indicates the number of client contacts last month, and the Y column shows the value of sales ($ thousands) last month for each client sampled.

Number of Contacts, X	Sales ($ thousands), Y	Number of Contacts, X	Sales ($ thousands), Y
14	24	23	30
12	14	48	90
20	28	50	85
16	30	55	120
46	80	50	110

a. Determine the regression equation.
b. Determine the estimated sales if 40 contacts are made.
17. A recent article in *BusinessWeek* listed the "Best Small Companies." We are interested in the current results of the companies' sales and earnings. A random sample of 12 companies was selected and the sales and earnings, in millions of dollars, are reported below.

Company	Sales ($ millions)	Earnings ($ millions)	Company	Sales ($ millions)	Earnings ($ millions)
Papa John's International	$89.2	$4.9	Checkmate Electronics	$17.5	$ 2.6
Applied Innovation	18.6	4.4	Royal Grip	11.9	1.7
Integracare	18.2	1.3	M-Wave	19.6	3.5
Wall Data	71.7	8.0	Serving-N-Slide	51.2	8.2
Davidson & Associates	58.6	6.6	Daig	28.6	6.0
Chico's FAS	46.8	4.1	Cobra Golf	69.2	12.8

Let sales be the independent variable and earnings be the dependent variable.
a. Draw a scatter diagram.
b. Compute the coefficient of correlation.
c. Compute the coefficient of determination.
d. Interpret your findings in parts (b) and (c).
e. Determine the regression equation.
f. For a small company with $50.0 million in sales, estimate the earnings.
18. We are studying mutual bond funds for the purpose of investing in several funds. For this particular study, we want to focus on the assets of a fund and its five-year performance. The question is: Can the five-year rate of return be estimated based on the assets of the

fund? Nine mutual funds were selected at random, and their assets and rates of return are shown below.

Fund	Assets ($ millions)	Return (%)	Fund	Assets ($ millions)	Return (%)
AARP High Quality Bond	$622.2	10.8	MFS Bond A	$494.5	11.6
Babson Bond L	160.4	11.3	Nichols Income	158.3	9.5
Compass Capital Fixed Income	275.7	11.4	T. Rowe Price Short-term	681.0	8.2
Galaxy Bond Retail	433.2	9.1	Thompson Income B	241.3	6.8
Keystone Custodian B-1	437.9	9.2			

    a. Draw a scatter diagram.
    b. Compute the coefficient of correlation.
    c. Compute the coefficient of determination.
    d. Write a brief report of your findings for parts (b) and (c).
    e. Determine the regression equation. Use assets as the independent variable.
    f. For a fund with $400.0 million in sales, determine the five-year rate of return (in percent).
19. Refer to Exercise 5.
    a. Determine the regression equation.
    b. Estimate the number of crimes for a city with 20 police.
    c. Interpret the regression equation.
20. Refer to Exercise 6.
    a. Determine the regression equation.
    b. Estimate the selling price of a 10-year-old car.
    c. Interpret the regression equation.

The Standard Error of Estimate

Note in the preceding scatter diagram (Chart 13–11) all of the points do not lie exactly on the regression line. If they all were on the line, there would be no error in estimating the number of units sold. To put it another way, if all the points were on the regression line, units sold could be predicted with 100 percent accuracy. Thus, there would be no error in predicting the Y variable based on an X variable. This is true in the following hypothetical case (see Chart 13–12). Theoretically, if $X = 4$, then an exact Y of 100 could be predicted with 100 percent confidence. Or if $X = 12$, then $Y = 300$. Because there is no difference between the observed values and the predicted values, there is no error in this estimate.

CHART 13–12 Example of Perfect Prediction: Horsepower and Cost of Electricity

Perfect prediction
unrealistic in business

    Perfect prediction in economics and business is practically impossible. For example, the revenue for the year from gasoline sales (Y) based on the number of automobile registrations (X) as of a certain date could no doubt be approximated fairly closely, but the prediction would not be exact to the nearest dollar, or probably even to the nearest thousand dollars. Even predictions of tensile strength of steel wires based on the outside diameters of the wires are not always exact due to slight differences in the composition of the steel.

What is needed, then, is a measure that describes how precise the prediction of Y is based on X or, conversely, how inaccurate the estimate might be. This measure is called the **standard error of estimate.** The standard error of estimate, symbolized by $s_{y \cdot x}$, is the same concept as the standard deviation discussed in Chapter 3. The standard deviation measures the dispersion around the mean. The standard error of estimate measures the dispersion about the regression line.

LO2 Calculate and interpret the *coefficient of correlation*, the *coefficient of determination,* and the *standard error of estimate.*

> **STANDARD ERROR OF ESTIMATE** A measure of the dispersion, or scatter, of the observed values around the line of regression.

The standard error of estimate is found using the following formula, (13–6). Note the following important features:

1. It is similar to the standard deviation in that it is based on squared deviations. The numerator of the standard deviation as we calculated in formula (3–9) on page 80 is based on squared deviations from the mean. The numerator of the standard error is based on squared deviations from the regression line.
2. The sum of the squared deviations is the least squares value used to find the best fitting regression line. Recall in the previous section we described how to find the least squares value (see Column F of the Excel spreadsheet on page 401). We compared the least squares value to values generated from other lines plotted through the data.
3. The denominator of the equation is $n - 2$. As usual, n is the number of observations. We lose two degrees of freedom because we are estimating two parameters. So the values of b, the slope of the line, and a, the Y-intercept, are sample values we use to estimate their corresponding population values. We are sampling from a population and are estimating the slope of the line and the intercept with the Y-axis. Hence the denominator is $n - 2$.

> **STANDARD ERROR OF ESTIMATE**
> $$s_{y \cdot x} = \sqrt{\frac{\Sigma(Y - \hat{Y})^2}{n - 2}}$$
> **[13–6]**

If $s_{y \cdot x}$ is small, this indicates that the data are relatively close to the regression line and the regression equation can be used to predict Y with little error. If $s_{y \cdot x}$ is large, this indicates that the data are widely scattered around the regression line and the regression equation will not provide a precise estimate Y.

Example

Recall the example involving Copier Sales of America. The sales manager determined the least squares regression equation to be $\hat{Y} = 18.9476 + 1.1842X$, where $\hat{Y}$ refers to the predicted number of copiers sold and X the number of sales calls made. Determine the standard error of estimate as a measure of how well the values fit the regression line.

Solution

To find the standard error, we begin by finding the difference between the value, Y, and the value estimated from the regression equation, $\hat{Y}$. Next we square this difference, that is, $(Y - \hat{Y})^2$. We do this for each of the n observations and sum the results. That is, we compute $\Sigma(Y - \hat{Y})^2$, which is the numerator of formula (13–6). Finally, we divide by the number of observations minus 2. The details of the calculations are summarized in Table 13–4.

TABLE 13–4 Computations Needed for the Standard Error of Estimate

Sales Representative	Actual Sales, (Y)	Estimated Sales, ($\hat{Y}$)	Deviation, ($Y - \hat{Y}$)	Deviation Squared, ($Y - \hat{Y})^2$
Tom Keller	30	42.6316	−12.6316	159.557
Jeff Hall	60	66.3156	−6.3156	39.887
Brian Virost	40	42.6316	−2.6316	6.925
Greg Fish	60	54.4736	5.5264	30.541
Susan Welch	30	30.7896	−0.7896	0.623
Carlos Ramirez	40	30.7896	9.2104	84.831
Rich Niles	40	42.6316	−2.6316	6.925
Mike Kiel	50	42.6316	7.3684	54.293
Mark Reynolds	30	42.6316	−12.6316	159.557
Soni Jones	70	54.4736	15.5264	241.069
			0.0000	784.211

The standard error of estimate is 9.901, found by using formula (13–6).

$$s_{y \cdot x} = \sqrt{\frac{\Sigma(Y - \hat{Y})^2}{n - 2}} = \sqrt{\frac{784.211}{10 - 2}} = 9.901$$

The deviations $(Y - \hat{Y})$ are the vertical deviations from the regression line. To illustrate, the 10 deviations from Table 13–4 are shown in Chart 13–13. Note in Table 13–4 that the sum of the signed deviations is zero. This indicates that the positive deviations (above the regression line) are offset by the negative deviations (below the regression line).

CHART 13–13 Sales Calls and Copiers Sold for 10 Salespeople

Statistical software eases computation when you are finding the least squares equation, the standard error of estimate, and the coefficient of correlation as well as other regression statistics. A portion of the Excel output for the Copier Sales of America example is included below. The intercept and slope values are cells F13 and F14, the standard error of estimate is in F8, and the coefficient of correlation (called Multiple R) is in cell F5.

	A	B	C	D	E	F	G
1	Sales Representative	Calls	Sales				
2	Tom Keller	20	30		SUMMARY OUTPUT		
3	Jeff Hall	40	60				
4	Brian Virost	20	40		*Regression Statistics*		
5	Greg Fish	30	60		Multiple R	0.759014109	
6	Susan Welch	10	30		R Square	0.576102418	
7	Carlos Ramirez	10	40		Adjusted R Square	0.52311522	
8	Rich Niles	20	40		Standard Error	9.900823995	
9	Mike Kiel	20	50		Observations	10	
10	Mark Reynolds	20	30				
11	Soni Jones	30	70				
12						*Coefficients*	
13					Intercept	18.94736842	
14					Calls	1.184210526	
15							

Regression analysis [Compatibility Mode]

Thus far we have presented linear regression only as a descriptive tool. In other words it is a simple summary ($\hat{Y} = a + bX$) of the relationship between the dependent Y variable and the independent X variable. When we make conclusions about a population based on sample data, we are doing inferential statistics. Then we need to recall the distinction between population parameters and sample statistics. In this case, we "model" the linear relationship in the population by the equation:

$$Y = \alpha + \beta X$$

where
  Y is any value of the dependent variable.
  α is the Y-intercept (the value of Y when $X = 0$) in the population.
  β is the slope (the amount by which Y changes when X increases by one unit) of the population line.
  X is any value of the independent variable.

Now α and β are population parameters and a and b, respectively, are estimates of those parameters. They are computed from a particular sample taken from the population. Fortunately, the formulas given earlier in the chapter for a and b do not change when we move from using regression as a descriptive tool to regression in statistical inference.

It should be noted that the linear regression equation for the sample of salespeople is only an estimate of the relationship between the two variables for the population. Thus, the values of a and b in the regression equation are usually referred to as the **estimated regression coefficients,** or simply the **regression coefficients.**

Assumptions Underlying Linear Regression

To properly apply linear regression, several assumptions are necessary. Chart 13–14 illustrates these assumptions.

1. For each value of X, there are corresponding Y values. These Y values follow the normal distribution.
2. The means of these normal distributions lie on the regression line.
3. The standard deviations of these normal distributions are all the same. The best estimate we have of this common standard deviation is the standard error of estimate ($s_{y \cdot x}$).

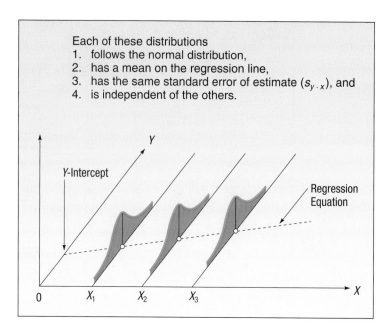

Each of these distributions
1. follows the normal distribution,
2. has a mean on the regression line,
3. has the same standard error of estimate ($s_{y \cdot x}$), and
4. is independent of the others.

CHART 13–14 Regression Assumptions Shown Graphically

4. The Y values are statistically independent. This means that in selecting a sample a particular X does not depend on any other value of X. This assumption is particularly important when data are collected over a period of time. In such situations, the errors for a particular time period are often correlated with those of other time periods.

Recall from Chapter 7 that if the values follow a normal distribution, then the mean plus or minus one standard deviation will encompass 68 percent of the observations, the mean plus or minus two standard deviations will encompass 95 percent of the observations, and the mean plus or minus three standard deviations will encompass virtually all of the observations. The same relationship exists between the predicted values $\hat{Y}$ and the standard error of estimate ($s_{y \cdot x}$).

1. $\hat{Y} \pm s_{y \cdot x}$ will include the middle 68 percent of the observations.
2. $\hat{Y} \pm 2s_{y \cdot x}$ will include the middle 95 percent of the observations.
3. $\hat{Y} \pm 3s_{y \cdot x}$ will include virtually all the observations.

We can now relate these assumptions to Copier Sales of America, where we studied the relationship between the number of sales calls and the number of copiers sold. Assume that we took a much larger sample than $n = 10$, but that the standard error of estimate was still 9.901. If we drew a parallel line 9.901 units above the regression line and another 9.901 units below the regression line, about 68 percent of the points would fall between the two lines. Similarly, a line 19.802 [$2s_{y \cdot x} = 2(9.901)$] units above the regression line and another 19.802 units below the regression line should include about 95 percent of the data values.

As a rough check, refer to the second column from the right in Table 13–4 on page 406, i.e., the column headed "Deviation." Three of the 10 deviations exceed one standard error of estimate. That is, the deviation of -12.6316 for Tom Keller, -12.6316 for Mark Reynolds, and $+15.5264$ for Soni Jones all exceed the value of 9.901, which is one standard error from the regression line. All of the values are within 19.802 units of the regression line. To put it another way, 7 of the 10 deviations in the sample are within one standard error of the regression line and all are within two—a good result for a relatively small sample.

Self-Review 13–4 Refer to Self-Reviews 13–1 and 13–3, where the owner of Haverty's Furniture was studying the relationship between sales and the amount spent on advertising. Determine the standard error of estimate.

Exercises

21. Refer to Exercise 13.
   a. Determine the standard error of estimate.
   b. Suppose a large sample is selected (instead of just five). About 68 percent of the predictions would be between what two values?

22. Refer to Exercise 14.
   a. Determine the standard error of estimate.
   b. Suppose a large sample is selected (instead of just eight). About 95 percent of the predictions would be between what two values?

23. Refer to Exercise 15.
   a. Determine the standard error of estimate.
   b. Suppose a large sample is selected (instead of just 10). About 95 percent of the predictions regarding kilowatt-hours would occur between what two values?

24. Refer to Exercise 16.
   a. Determine the standard error of estimate.
   b. Suppose a large sample is selected (instead of just 10). About 95 percent of the predictions regarding sales would occur between what two values?

25. Refer to Exercise 5. Determine the standard error of estimate.

26. Refer to Exercise 6. Determine the standard error of estimate.

Confidence and Prediction Intervals

LO5 Construct and interpret confidence and prediction intervals for the dependent variable.

The standard error of estimate is also used to establish confidence intervals when the sample size is large and the scatter around the regression line approximates the normal distribution. In our example involving the number of sales calls and the number of copiers sold, the sample size is small; hence, we need a correction factor to account for the size of the sample. In addition, when we move away from the mean of the independent variable, our estimates are subject to more variation, and we also need to adjust for this.

We are interested in providing interval estimates of two types. The first, which is called a **confidence interval,** reports the *mean* value of Y for a given X. The second type of estimate is called a **prediction interval,** and it reports the *range of values of Y* for a *particular* value of X. To explain further, suppose we estimate the salary of executives in the retail industry based on their years of experience. If we want an interval estimate of the mean salary of *all* retail executives with 20 years of experience, we calculate a confidence interval. If we want an estimate of the salary of Curtis Bender, a *particular* retail executive with 20 years of experience, we calculate a prediction interval.

To determine the confidence interval for the mean value of Y for a given X, the formula is:

CONFIDENCE INTERVAL FOR THE MEAN OF Y, GIVEN X	$$\hat{Y} \pm t(s_{y \cdot x})\sqrt{\dfrac{1}{n} + \dfrac{(X - \overline{X})^2}{\Sigma(X - \overline{X})^2}}$$	**[13–7]**

where

$\hat{Y}$ is the predicted value for any selected X value.

X is any selected value of X.

$\bar{X}$ is the mean of the Xs, found by $\Sigma X/n$.

n is the number of observations.

$s_{y \cdot x}$ is the standard error of estimate.

t is the value of t from Appendix B.2 with $n - 2$ degrees of freedom.

We first described the t distribution in Chapter 9. In review the concept of t was developed by William Gossett in the early 1900s. He noticed that $\bar{X} \pm zs_{\bar{x}}$ was not precisely correct for small samples. He observed, for example, for degrees of freedom of 120, that 95 percent of the items fell within $\bar{X} \pm 1.98s$ instead of $\bar{X} \pm 1.96s_{\bar{x}}$. This difference is not too critical, but note what happens as the sample size becomes smaller:

df	t
120	1.980
60	2.000
21	2.080
10	2.228
3	3.182

This is logical. The smaller the sample size, the larger the possible error. The increase in the t value compensates for this possibility.

Example

We return to the Copier Sales of America illustration. Determine a 95 percent confidence interval for all sales representatives who make 25 calls and a prediction interval for Sheila Baker, a West Coast sales representative who made 25 calls.

Solution

We use formula (13–7) to determine a confidence interval. Table 13–5 includes the necessary totals and a repeat of the information of Table 13–2 on page 389.

TABLE 13–5 Calculations Needed for Determining the Confidence Interval and Prediction Interval

Sales Representative	Sales Calls, (X)	Copier Sales, (Y)	(X − X̄)	(X − X̄)²
Tom Keller	20	30	−2	4
Jeff Hall	40	60	18	324
Brian Virost	20	40	−2	4
Greg Fish	30	60	8	64
Susan Welch	10	30	−12	144
Carlos Ramirez	10	40	−12	144
Rich Niles	20	40	−2	4
Mike Kiel	20	50	−2	4
Mark Reynolds	20	30	−2	4
Soni Jones	30	70	8	64
			0	760

The first step is to determine the number of copiers we expect a sales representative to sell if he or she makes 25 calls. It is 48.5526, found by $\hat{Y} = 18.9476 + 1.1842X = 18.9476 + 1.1842(25)$.

To find the t value, we need to first know the number of degrees of freedom. In this case the degrees of freedom is $n - 2 = 10 - 2 = 8$. We set the confidence level at 95 percent. To find the value of t, move down the left-hand column of Appendix B.2 to 8 degrees of freedom, then move across to the column with the 95 percent level of confidence. The value of t is 2.306.

In the previous section we calculated the standard error of estimate to be 9.901. We let $X = 25$, $\overline{X} = \Sigma X/n = 220/10 = 22$, and from Table 13–5 $\Sigma(X - \overline{X})^2 = 760$. Inserting these values in formula (13–7), we can determine the confidence interval.

$$\text{Confidence Interval} = \hat{Y} \pm ts_{y \cdot x} \sqrt{\frac{1}{n} + \frac{(X - \overline{X})^2}{\Sigma(X - \overline{X})^2}}$$

$$= 48.5526 \pm 2.306(9.901)\sqrt{\frac{1}{10} + \frac{(25 - 22)^2}{760}}$$

$$= 48.5526 \pm 7.6356$$

Thus, the 95 percent confidence interval for all sales representatives who make 25 calls is from 40.9170 up to 56.1882. To interpret, let's round the values. If a sales representative makes 25 calls, he or she can expect to sell 48.6 copiers. It is likely those sales will range from 40.9 to 56.2 copiers.

To determine the prediction interval for a particular value of Y for a given X, formula (13–7) is modified slightly: A 1 is added under the radical. The formula becomes:

PREDICTION INTERVAL FOR Y, GIVEN X
$$\hat{Y} \pm ts_{y \cdot x} \sqrt{1 + \frac{1}{n} + \frac{(X - \overline{X})^2}{\Sigma(X - \overline{X})^2}} \qquad \text{[13–8]}$$

Suppose we want to estimate the number of copiers sold by Sheila Baker, who made 25 sales calls. The 95 percent prediction interval is determined as follows:

$$\text{Prediction Interval} = \hat{Y} \pm ts_{y \cdot x} \sqrt{1 + \frac{1}{n} + \frac{(X - \overline{X})^2}{\Sigma(X - \overline{X})^2}}$$

$$= 48.5526 \pm 2.306(9.901)\sqrt{1 + \frac{1}{10} + \frac{(25 - 22)^2}{760}}$$

$$= 48.5526 \pm 24.0746$$

Thus, the interval is from 24.478 up to 72.627 copiers. We conclude that the number of copiers sold will be between about 24 and 73 for a particular sales representative who makes 25 calls. This interval is quite large. It is much larger than the confidence interval for all sales representatives who made 25 calls. It is logical, however, that there should be more variation in the sales estimate for an individual than for a group.

The following MINITAB graph shows the relationship between the regression line (in the center), the confidence interval (shown in crimson), and the prediction interval (shown in green). The bands for the prediction interval are always further from the regression line than those for the confidence interval. Also, as the values of X move away from the mean number of calls (22) in either the positive or the negative direction, the confidence interval and prediction interval bands widen. This is caused by the numerator of the right-hand term under the radical in formulas (13–7) and (13–8). That is, as the term $(X - \overline{X})^2$ increases, the widths of the confidence interval and the prediction interval also increase. To put it another way, there is less precision in our estimates as we move away, in either direction, from the mean of the independent variable.

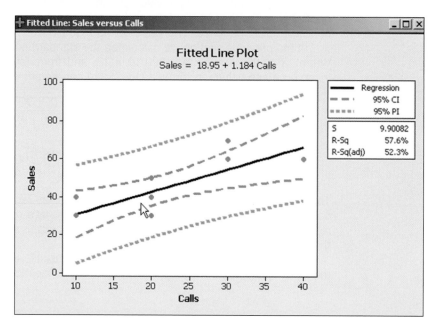

We wish to emphasize again the distinction between a confidence interval and a prediction interval. A confidence interval refers to all cases with a given value of X and is computed by formula (13–7). A prediction interval refers to a particular case for a given value of X and is computed using formula (13–8). The prediction interval will always be wider because of the extra 1 under the radical in the second equation.

Self-Review 13–5   Refer to the sample data in Self-Reviews 13–1, 13–3, and 13–4, where the owner of Haverty's Furniture was studying the relationship between sales and the amount spent on advertising. The sales information for the last four months is repeated below.

Month	Advertising Expense ($ million)	Sales Revenue ($ million)
July	2	7
August	1	3
September	3	8
October	4	10

The regression equation was computed to be $\hat{Y} = 1.5 + 2.2X$, and the standard error 0.9487. Both variables are reported in millions of dollars. Determine the 90 percent confidence interval for the typical month in which $3 million was spent on advertising.

Exercises

27. Refer to Exercise 13.
   a. Determine the .95 confidence interval for the mean predicted when $X = 7$.
   b. Determine the .95 prediction interval for an individual predicted when $X = 7$.
28. Refer to Exercise 14.
   a. Determine the .95 confidence interval for the mean predicted when $X = 7$.
   b. Determine the .95 prediction interval for an individual predicted when $X = 7$.

29. Refer to Exercise 15.
   a. Determine the .95 confidence interval, in thousands of kilowatt-hours, for the mean of all six-room homes.
   b. Determine the .95 prediction interval, in thousands of kilowatt-hours, for a particular six-room home.
30. Refer to Exercise 16.
   a. Determine the .95 confidence interval, in thousands of dollars, for the mean of all sales personnel who make 40 contacts.
   b. Determine the .95 prediction interval, in thousands of dollars, for a particular salesperson who makes 40 contacts.

More on the Coefficient of Determination

Earlier in the chapter, on page 392, we defined the coefficient of determination as the percent of the variation in the dependent variable that is accounted for by the independent variable. We indicated it is the square of the coefficient of correlation and that it is written r^2.

To further examine the basic concept of the coefficient of determination, suppose there is interest in the relationship between years on the job, X, and weekly production, Y. Sample data revealed:

Employee	Years on Job, X	Weekly Production, Y
Gordon	14	6
James	7	5
Ford	3	3
Salter	15	9
Artes	11	7

The sample data were plotted in a scatter diagram. Since the relationship between X and Y appeared to be linear, a line was drawn through the plots (see Chart 13–15). The equation is $\hat{Y} = 2 + 0.4X$.

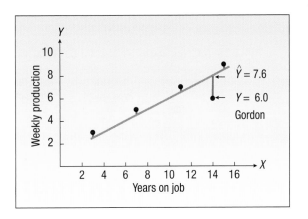

CHART 13–15 Observed Data and the Least Squares Line

Note in Chart 13–15 that, if we were to use that line to predict weekly production for an employee, in no case would our prediction be exact. That is, there would be some error in each of our predictions. As an example, for Gordon, who has been with the company 14 years, we would predict weekly production to be 7.6 units; however, he produces only 6 units.

To measure the overall error in our prediction, every deviation from the line is squared and the squares summed. The predicted point on the line is designated $\hat{Y}$, read Y hat, and the observed point is designated Y. For Gordon, $(Y - \hat{Y})^2 = (6 - 7.6)^2 = (-1.6)^2 = 2.56$. Logically, this variation cannot be explained by the independent variable, so it is referred to as the *unexplained variation*. Specifically, we cannot explain why Gordon's production of 6 units is 1.6 units below his predicted production of 7.6 units, based on the number of years he has been on the job.

The sum of the squared deviations, $\Sigma(Y - \hat{Y})^2$, is 4.00. (See Table 13–6.) The term $\Sigma(Y - \hat{Y})^2 = 4.00$ is the variation in Y (production) that cannot be predicted from X. It is the "unexplained" variation in Y.

TABLE 13–6 Computations Needed for the Unexplained Variation

	X	Y	$\hat{Y}$	$Y - \hat{Y}$	$(Y - \hat{Y})^2$
Gordon	14	6	7.6	−1.6	2.56
James	7	5	4.8	0.2	0.04
Ford	3	3	3.2	−0.2	0.04
Salter	15	9	8.0	1.0	1.00
Artes	11	7	6.4	0.6	0.36
Total	50	30		0.0*	4.00

*Must be 0.

Now suppose *only* the Y values (weekly production, in this problem) are known and we want to predict production for every employee. The actual production figures for the employees are 6, 5, 3, 9, and 7 (from Table 13–6). To make these predictions, we could assign the mean weekly production (6 units, found by $\Sigma Y/n = 30/5 = 6$) to each employee. This would keep the sum of the squared prediction errors at a minimum. (Recall from Chapter 3 that the sum of the squared deviations from the arithmetic mean for a set of numbers is smaller than the sum of the squared deviations from any other value, such as the median.) Table 13–7 shows the necessary calculations. The sum of the squared deviations is 20, as shown in Table 13–7. The value 20 is referred to as the *total variation in Y*.

TABLE 13–7 Calculations Needed for the Total Variation in Y

Name	Weekly Production, Y	Mean Weekly Production, $\bar{Y}$	$Y - \bar{Y}$	$(Y - \bar{Y})^2$
Gordon	6	6	0	0
James	5	6	−1	1
Ford	3	6	−3	9
Salter	9	6	3	9
Artes	7	6	1	1
Total			0*	20

*Must be 0.

What we did to arrive at the total variation in Y is shown diagrammatically in Chart 13–16.

Logically, the total variation in Y can be subdivided into unexplained variation and explained variation. To arrive at the explained variation, since we know the total variation and unexplained variation, we simply subtract: Explained variation = Total variation − Unexplained variation. Dividing the explained variation by the total

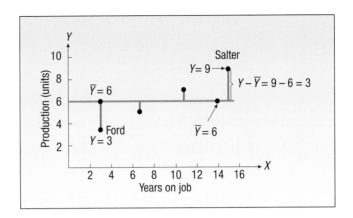

CHART 13–16 Plots Showing Deviations from the Mean of Y

variation gives the coefficient of determination, r^2, which is a proportion. In terms of a formula:

COEFFICIENT OF DETERMINATION	$$r^2 = \frac{\text{Total variation} - \text{Unexplained variation}}{\text{Total variation}}$$ $$= \frac{\Sigma(Y - \overline{Y})^2 - \Sigma(Y - \hat{Y})^2}{\Sigma(Y - \overline{Y})^2}$$ **[13–9]**

In this problem:

$$r^2 = \frac{20 - 4}{20} = \frac{16}{20}$$

Table 13–7

Table 13–6

Explained variation

Total variation

$$= .80$$

As mentioned, .80 is a proportion. We say that 80 percent of the variation in weekly production, Y, is determined, or accounted for, by its linear relationship with X (years on the job).

As a check, formula (13–1) for the coefficient of correlation could be used. Squaring r gives the coefficient of determination, r^2. Exercise 31 offers a check on the preceding problem.

Exercises

31. Using the preceding problem, involving years on the job and weekly production, verify that the coefficient of determination is in fact .80.

32. The number of shares of Icom, Inc., turned over during a month, and the price at the end of the month, are listed in the following table. Also given are the $\hat{Y}$ values.

Turnover (thousands of shares), X	Actual Price, Y	Estimated Price, $\hat{Y}$
4	$2	$2.7
1	1	0.6
5	4	3.4
3	2	2.0
2	1	1.3

a. Draw a scatter diagram. Plot a line through the dots.
b. Compute the coefficient of determination using formula (13–9).
c. Interpret the coefficient of determination.

The Relationships among the Coefficient of Correlation, the Coefficient of Determination, and the Standard Error of Estimate

In an earlier section, we discussed the standard error of estimate, which measures how close the actual values are to the regression line. When the standard error is small, it indicates that the two variables are closely related. In the calculation of the standard error, the key term is $\Sigma(Y - \hat{Y})^2$. If the value of this term is small, then the standard error will also be small.

The correlation coefficient measures the strength of the linear association between two variables. When the points on the scatter diagram appear close to the line, we note that the correlation coefficient tends to be large. Thus, the standard error of estimate and the coefficient of correlation relate the same information but use a different scale to report the strength of the association. However, both measures involve the term $\Sigma(Y - \hat{Y})^2$.

We also noted that the square of the correlation coefficient is the coefficient of determination. The coefficient of determination measures the percent of the variation in Y that is explained by the variation in X.

A convenient vehicle for showing the relationship among these three measures is an ANOVA table. This table is similar to the analysis of variance table developed in Chapter 12. In that chapter, the total variation was divided into two components: that due to the *treatments* and that due to *random error*. The concept is similar in regression analysis. The total variation, $\Sigma(Y - \overline{Y})^2$, is divided into two components: (1) that explained by the *regression* (explained by the independent variable) and (2) the *error,* or unexplained variation. These two categories are identified in the first column of the ANOVA table that follows. The column headed "*df*" refers to the degrees of freedom associated with each category. The total number of degrees of freedom is $n - 1$. The number of degrees of freedom in the regression is 1, since there is only one independent variable. The number of degrees of freedom associated with the error term is $n - 2$. The term "SS" located in the middle of the ANOVA table refers to the sum of squares—the variation. The terms are computed as follows:

$$\text{Regression} = \text{SSR} = \Sigma(\hat{Y} - \overline{Y})^2$$

$$\text{Error variation} = \text{SSE} = \Sigma(Y - \hat{Y})^2$$

$$\text{Total variation} = \text{SS total} = \Sigma(Y - \overline{Y})^2$$

The format for the ANOVA table is:

Source	df	SS	MS
Regression	1	SSR	SSR/1
Error	$n - 2$	SSE	SSE/$(n - 2)$
Total	$n - 1$	SS total*	

*SS total = SSR + SSE.

The coefficient of determination, r^2, can be obtained directly from the ANOVA table by:

COEFFICIENT OF DETERMINATION

$$r^2 = \frac{SSR}{SS\ total} = 1 - \frac{SSE}{SS\ total}$$

[13–10]

The term "SSR/SS total" is the proportion of the variation in Y *explained* by the independent variable, X. Note the effect of the SSE term on r^2. As SSE decreases, r^2 will increase. To put it another way, as the standard error decreases, the r^2 term increases.

The standard error of estimate can also be obtained from the ANOVA table using the following equation:

STANDARD ERROR OF ESTIMATE

$$s_{y \cdot x} = \sqrt{\frac{SSE}{n - 2}}$$

[13–11]

The Copier Sales of America example is used to illustrate the computations of the coefficient of determination and the standard error of estimate from an ANOVA table.

Example

In the Copier Sales of America example we studied the relationship between the number of sales calls made and the number of copiers sold. Use a computer software package to determine the least squares regression equation and the ANOVA table. Identify the regression equation, the standard error of estimate, and the coefficient of determination on the computer output. From the ANOVA table on the computer output, determine the coefficient of determination and the standard error of estimate using formulas (13–10) and (13–11).

Solution

The output from Excel follows.

Regression analysis

	A	B	C	D	E	F	G	H	I	J
1	Sales Representative	Calls	Sales							
2	Tom Keller	20	30		ANOVA					
3	Jeff Hall	40	60			df	SS	MS	F	
4	Brian Virost	20	40		Regression	1	1065.8	1065.79	10.87	
5	Greg Fish	30	60		Residual	8	784.2	98.03		
6	Susan Welch	10	30		Total	9	1850.0			
7	Carlos Ramirez	10	40							
8	Rich Niles	20	40							
9	Mike Kiel	20	50							
10	Mark Reynolds	20	30							
11	Soni Jones	30	70							

From formula (13–10) the coefficient of determination is .576, found by

$$r^2 = \frac{SSR}{SS\ total} = \frac{1,065.8}{1,850} = .576$$

This is the same value we computed earlier in the chapter, when we found the coefficient of determination by squaring the coefficient of correlation. Again, the interpretation is that the independent variable, Calls, explains 57.6 percent of the variation in the number of copiers sold. If we needed the coefficient of correlation, we could find it by taking the square root of the coefficient of determination:

$$r = \sqrt{r^2} = \sqrt{.576} = .759$$

A problem does remain, and that involves the sign for the coefficient of correlation. Recall that the square root of a value could have either a positive or a negative sign. The sign of the coefficient of correlation will always be the same as that of the slope. That is, b and r will always have the same sign. In this case the sign of the regression coefficient (b) is positive, so the coefficient of correlation is .759.

To find the standard error of estimate, we use formula (13–11):

$$s_{y \cdot x} = \sqrt{\frac{SSE}{n-2}} = \sqrt{\frac{784.2}{10-2}} = 9.901$$

Again, this is the same value calculated earlier in the chapter. These values are identified on the Excel computer output.

Transforming Data

The coefficient of correlation describes the strength of the *linear* relationship between two variables. It could be that two variables are closely related, but their relationship is not linear. Be cautious when you are interpreting the coefficient of correlation. A value of r may indicate there is no linear relationship, but it could be there is a relationship of some other nonlinear or curvilinear form.

To explain, below is a listing of 22 professional golfers, the number of events in which they participated, the amount of their winnings, and their mean score. In golf, the objective is to play 18 holes in the least number of strokes. So, we would expect that those golfers with the lower mean scores would have the larger winnings. In other words, score and winnings should be inversely related.

Tiger Woods played in a total of 19 events, earned $5,365,472, and had a mean score per round of 69.04. Fred Couples played in 16 events, earned $1,396,109, and had a mean score per round of 70.92. The data for the 22 golfers follows.

Player	Events	Winnings	Score
Vijay Singh	29	$10,905,166	68.84
Ernie Els	16	5,787,225	68.98
Phil Mickelson	22	5,784,823	69.16
Tiger Woods	19	5,365,472	69.04
Davis Love III	24	3,075,092	70.13
Chris DiMarco	27	2,971,842	70.28
John Daly	22	2,359,507	70.82
Charles Howell III	30	1,703,485	70.77
Kirk Triplett	24	1,566,426	70.31
Fred Couples	16	1,396,109	70.92
Tim Petrovic	32	1,193,354	70.91
Briny Baird	30	1,156,517	70.79
Hank Kuehne	30	816,889	71.36

continued

Player	Events	Winnings	Score
J. L. Lewis	32	807,345	71.21
Aaron Baddeley	27	632,876	71.61
Craig Perks	27	423,748	71.75
David Frost	26	402,589	71.75
Rich Beem	28	230,499	71.76
Dicky Pride	23	230,329	72.91
Len Mattiace	25	213,707	72.03
Esteban Toledo	36	115,185	72.36
David Gossett	25	21,250	75.01

The correlation between the variables Winnings and Score is -0.782. This is a fairly strong inverse relationship. However, when we plot the data on a scatter diagram the relationship does not appear to be linear; it does not seem to follow a straight line. See the scatter diagram on the right-hand side of the following MINITAB output. The data points for the lowest score and the highest score seem to be well away from the regression line. In addition, for the scores between 70 and 72, the winnings are below the regression line. If the relationship were linear, we would expect these points to be both above and below the line.

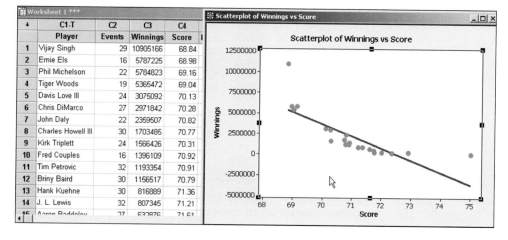

What can we do to explore other (nonlinear) relationships? One possibility is to transform one of the variables. For example, instead of using Y as the dependent variable, we might use its log, reciprocal, square, or square root. Another possibility is to transform the independent variable in the same way. There are other transformations, but these are the most common.

In the golf winnings example, changing the scale of the dependent variable is effective. We determine the log of each golfer's winnings and then find the correlation between the log of winnings and score. That is, we find the log to the base 10 of Tiger Woods' earnings of $5,365,472, which is 6.72961. Next we find the log to the base 10 of each golfer's winnings and then determine the correlation between log of winnings and the score. The correlation coefficient increases from -0.782 to -0.969. This means that the coefficient of determination is .939 $[r^2 = (-0.969)^2 = .939]$. That is, 93.9 percent of the variation in the log of winnings is accounted for by the independent variable score.

We have determined an equation that fits the data more closely than the straight line did. Clearly, as the mean score for a golfer increases, he can expect his winnings to decrease. It no longer appears that some of the data points are different from the regression line, as we found when using winnings instead of the log of winnings as the dependent variable. Also note the points between 70 and 72 in particular are now randomly distributed above and below the regression line.

We can also estimate the amount of winnings based on the score. Following is the MINITAB regression output using score as the independent variable and the log of winnings as the dependent variable.

To compute the earnings for a golfer with a mean score of 70, we first use the regression equation to compute the log of earnings.

$$\hat{Y} = 37.198 - .43944X = 37.198 - .43944(70) = 6.4372$$

The value 6.4372 is the log to the base 10 of winnings. The antilog of 6.4372 is 2,736,528. So a golfer that had a mean score of 70 could expect to earn $2,736,528. We can also evaluate the change in scores. The above golfer had a mean score of 70 and estimated earnings of $2,736,528. How much less would a golfer expect to win if his mean score was 71? Again solving the regression equation:

$$\hat{Y} = 37.198 - .43944X = 37.198 - .43944(71) = 5.99776$$

The antilog of this value is $994,855. So based on the regression analysis, there is a large financial incentive for a professional golfer to reduce his mean score by even one stroke. Those of you that play golf or know a golfer understand how difficult that change would be! That one stroke is worth over $1,700,000.

Exercises

33. Given the following ANOVA table:

SOURCE	DF	SS	MS	F
Regression	1	1000.0	1000.00	26.00
Error	13	500.0	38.46	
Total	14	1500.0		

a. Determine the coefficient of determination.
b. Assuming a direct relationship between the variables, what is the coefficient of correlation?
c. Determine the standard error of estimate.

34. On the first statistics exam the coefficient of determination between the hours studied and the grade earned was 80 percent. The standard error of estimate was 10. There were 20 students in the class. Develop an ANOVA table.

35. Given the following sample observations, develop a scatter diagram. Compute the coefficient of correlation. Does the relationship between the variables appear to be linear? Try squaring the X-variable and then determine the correlation coefficient.

X	-8	-16	12	2	18
Y	58	247	153	3	341

36. According to basic economics, as the demand for a product increases, the price will decrease. Listed below is the number of units demanded and the price.

Demand	Price
2	$120.0
5	90.0
8	80.0
12	70.0
16	50.0
21	45.0
27	31.0
35	30.0
45	25.0
60	21.0

a. Determine the correlation between price and demand. Plot the data in a scatter diagram. Does the relationship seem to be linear?
b. Transform the price to a log to the base 10. Plot the log of the price and the demand. Determine the correlation coefficient. Does this seem to improve the relationship between the variables?

Chapter Summary

I. A scatter diagram is a graphic tool to portray the relationship between two variables.
   A. The dependent variable is scaled on the Y-axis and is the variable being estimated.
   B. The independent variable is scaled on the X-axis and is the variable used as the estimator.
II. The coefficient of correlation measures the strength of the linear association between two variables.
   A. Both variables must be at least the interval scale of measurement.
   B. The coefficient of correlation can range from -1.00 up to 1.00.
   C. If the correlation between two variables is 0, there is no association between them.
   D. A value of 1.00 indicates perfect positive correlation, and -1.00 perfect negative correlation.
   E. A positive sign means there is a direct relationship between the variables, and a negative sign means there is an inverse relationship.
   F. It is designated by the letter r and found by the following equation:

$$r = \frac{\Sigma(X - \bar{X})(Y - \bar{Y})}{(n - 1)s_x s_y}$$ [13–1]

   G. The following equation is used to determine whether the correlation in the population is different from 0.

$$t = \frac{r\sqrt{n - 2}}{\sqrt{1 - r^2}} \quad \text{with } n - 2 \text{ degrees of freedom}$$ [13–2]

III. The coefficient of determination is the fraction of the variation in one variable that is explained by the variation in the other variable.

    A. It ranges from 0 to 1.0.
    B. It is the square of the coefficient of correlation.
  IV. In regression analysis we estimate one variable based on another variable.
    A. The variable being estimated is the dependent variable.
    B. The variable used to make the estimate is the independent variable.
      1. The relationship between the variables must be linear.
      2. Both the independent and the dependent variables must be interval or ratio scale.
      3. The least squares criterion is used to determine the regression equation.
  V. The least squares regression line is of the form $\hat{Y} = a + bX$.
    A. $\hat{y}$ is the estimated value of Y for a selected value of X.
    B. a is the constant or intercept.
      1. It is the value of $\hat{Y}$ when $X = 0$.
      2. a is computed using the following equation.

$$a = \overline{Y} - b\overline{X} \qquad \text{[13–5]}$$

    C. b is the slope of the fitted line.
      1. It shows the amount of change in $\hat{Y}$ for a change of one unit in X.
      2. A positive value for b indicates a direct relationship between the two variables, and a negative value an inverse relationship.
      3. The sign of b and the sign of r, the coefficient of correlation, are always the same.
      4. b is computed using the following equation.

$$b = r\left(\frac{s_y}{s_x}\right) \qquad \text{[13–4]}$$

    D. X is the value of the independent variable.
  VI. The standard error of estimate measures the variation around the regression line.
    A. It is in the same units as the dependent variable.
    B. It is based on squared deviations from the regression line.
    C. Small values indicate that the points cluster closely about the regression line.
    D. It is computed using the following formula.

$$s_{y \cdot x} = \sqrt{\frac{\Sigma(Y - \hat{Y})^2}{n - 2}} \qquad \text{[13–6]}$$

  VII. Inference about linear regression is based on the following assumptions.
    A. For a given value of X, the values of Y are normally distributed about the line of regression.
    B. The standard deviation of each of the normal distributions is the same for all values of X and is estimated by the standard error of estimate.
    C. The deviations from the regression line are independent, with no pattern to the size or direction.
  VIII. There are two types of interval estimates.
    A. In a confidence interval the mean value of Y is estimated for a given value of X.
      1. It is computed from the following formula.

$$\hat{Y} \pm t(s_{y \cdot x}) \sqrt{\frac{1}{n} + \frac{(X - \overline{X})^2}{\Sigma(X - \overline{X})^2}} \qquad \text{[13–7]}$$

      2. The width of the interval is affected by the level of confidence, the size of the standard error of estimate, and the size of the sample, as well as the value of the independent variable.
    B. In a prediction interval the individual value of Y is estimated for a given value of X.
      1. It is computed from the following formula.

$$\hat{Y} \pm ts_{y \cdot x} \sqrt{1 + \frac{1}{n} + \frac{(X - \overline{X})^2}{\Sigma(X - \overline{X})^2}} \qquad \text{[13–8]}$$

      2. The difference between formulas (13–7) and (13–8) is the 1 under the radical.
        a. The prediction interval will be wider than the confidence interval.
        b. The prediction interval is also based on the level of confidence, the size of the standard error of estimate, the size of the sample, and the value of the independent variable.

Pronunciation Key

SYMBOL	MEANING	PRONUNCIATION
ΣXY	Sum of the products of X and Y	Sum X Y
ρ	Coefficient of correlation in the population	Row
$\hat{Y}$	Estimated value of Y	Y hat
$s_{y \cdot x}$	Standard error of estimate	s sub y dot x
r^2	Coefficient of determination	r square

Chapter Exercises

37. A regional commuter airline selected a random sample of 25 flights and found that the correlation between the number of passengers and the total weight, in pounds, of luggage stored in the luggage compartment is 0.94. Using the .05 significance level, can we conclude that there is a positive association between the two variables?

38. A sociologist claims that the success of students in college (measured by their GPA) is related to their family's income. For a sample of 20 students, the coefficient of correlation is 0.40. Using the 0.01 significance level, can we conclude that there is a positive correlation between the variables?

39. An Environmental Protection Agency study of 12 automobiles revealed a correlation of 0.47 between engine size and emissions. At the .01 significance level, can we conclude that there is a positive association between these variables? What is the *p*-value? Interpret.

40. A suburban hotel derives its gross income from its hotel and restaurant operations. The owners are interested in the relationship between the number of rooms occupied on a nightly basis and the revenue per day in the restaurant. Below is a sample of 25 days (Monday through Thursday) from last year showing the restaurant income and number of rooms occupied.

Day	Income	Occupied	Day	Income	Occupied
1	$1,452	23	14	$1,425	27
2	1,361	47	15	1,445	34
3	1,426	21	16	1,439	15
4	1,470	39	17	1,348	19
5	1,456	37	18	1,450	38
6	1,430	29	19	1,431	44
7	1,354	23	20	1,446	47
8	1,442	44	21	1,485	43
9	1,394	45	22	1,405	38
10	1,459	16	23	1,461	51
11	1,399	30	24	1,490	61
12	1,458	42	25	1,426	39
13	1,537	54			

Use a statistical software package to answer the following questions.

a. Does the breakfast revenue seem to increase as the number of occupied rooms increases? Draw a scatter diagram to support your conclusion.

b. Determine the coefficient of correlation between the two variables. Interpret the value.

c. Is it reasonable to conclude that there is a positive relationship between revenue and occupied rooms? Use the .10 significance level.

d. What percent of the variation in revenue in the restaurant is accounted for by the number of rooms occupied?

41. The table below shows the number of cars (in millions) sold in the United States for various years and the percent of those cars manufactured by GM.

Year	Cars Sold (millions)	Percent GM	Year	Cars Sold (millions)	Percent GM
1950	6.0	50.2	1980	11.5	44.0
1955	7.8	50.4	1985	15.4	40.1
1960	7.3	44.0	1990	13.5	36.0
1965	10.3	49.9	1995	15.5	31.7
1970	10.1	39.5	2000	17.4	28.6
1975	10.8	43.1	2005	16.9	26.9

Use a statistical software package to answer the following questions.
  a. Is the number of cars sold directly or indirectly related to GM's percent of the market? Draw a scatter diagram to show your conclusion.
  b. Determine the coefficient of correlation between the two variables. Interpret the value.
  c. Is it reasonable to conclude that there is a negative association between the two variables? Use the .01 significance level.
  d. How much of the variation in GM's market share is accounted for by the variation in cars sold?

42. For a sample of 32 large U.S. cities, the correlation between the mean number of square feet per office worker and the mean monthly rental rate in the central business district is −.363. At the .05 significance level, can we conclude that there is a negative association in the population between the two variables?

43. What is the relationship between the amount spent per week on recreation and the size of the family? Do larger families spend more on recreation? A sample of 10 families in the Chicago area revealed the following figures for family size and the amount spent on recreation per week.

Family Size	Amount Spent on Recreation	Family Size	Amount Spent on Recreation
3	$ 99	3	$111
6	104	4	74
5	151	4	91
6	129	5	119
6	142	3	91

  a. Compute the coefficient of correlation.
  b. Determine the coefficient of determination.
  c. Can we conclude that there is a positive association between the amount spent on recreation and family size? Use the .05 significance level.

44. A sample of 12 homes sold last week in St. Paul, Minnesota, is selected. Can we conclude that, as the size of the home (reported below in thousands of square feet) increases, the selling price (reported in $ thousands) also increases?

Home Size (thousands of square feet)	Selling Price ($ thousands)	Home Size (thousands of square feet)	Selling Price ($ thousands)
1.4	100	1.3	110
1.3	110	0.8	85
1.2	105	1.2	105
1.1	120	0.9	75
1.4	80	1.1	70
1.0	105	1.1	95

  a. Compute the coefficient of correlation.
  b. Determine the coefficient of determination.
  c. Can we conclude that there is a positive association between the size of the home and the selling price? Use the .05 significance level.

45. The manufacturer of Cardio Glide exercise equipment wants to study the relationship between the number of months since the glide was purchased and the length of time the equipment was used last week.

Person	Months Owned	Hours Exercised	Person	Months Owned	Hours Exercised
Rupple	12	4	Massa	2	8
Hall	2	10	Sass	8	3
Bennett	6	8	Karl	4	8
Longnecker	9	5	Malrooney	10	2
Phillips	7	5	Veights	5	5

    a. Plot the information on a scatter diagram. Let hours of exercise be the dependent variable. Comment on the graph.
    b. Determine the coefficient of correlation. Interpret.
    c. At the .01 significance level, can we conclude that there is a negative association between the variables?

46. The following regression equation was computed from a sample of 20 observations:

$$\hat{Y} = 15 - 5X$$

SSE was found to be 100 and SS total 400.
    a. Determine the standard error of estimate.
    b. Determine the coefficient of determination.
    c. Determine the coefficient of correlation. (Caution: Watch the sign!)

47. City planners believe that larger cities are populated by older residents. To investigate the relationship, data on population and median age in ten large cities were collected.

City	Population (in millions)	Median age
Chicago, IL	2.833	31.5
Dallas, TX	1.233	30.5
Houston, TX	2.144	30.9
Los Angeles, CA	3.849	31.6
New York, NY	8.214	34.2
Philadelphia, PA	1.448	34.2
Phoenix, AZ	1.513	30.7
San Antonio, TX	1.297	31.7
San Diego, CA	1.257	32.5
San Jose, CA	0.930	32.6

    a. Plot this data on a scatter diagram with median age as the dependent variable.
    b. Find the correlation coefficient.
    c. A regression analysis was performed and the resulting regression equation is Median age = 31.4 + 0.272 population. Interpret the meaning of the slope.
    d. Estimate the median age for a city of 2.5 million people.
    e. Here is a portion of the regression software output. What does it tell you?

```
Predictor      Coef     SE Coef        T       P
Constant    31.3672      0.6158    50.94   0.000
Population   0.2722      0.1901     1.43   0.190
```

    f. Test at the .10 significance level whether there is a significant relationship between these two variables.

48. Emily Smith decides to buy a fuel-efficient used car. Here are several vehicles she is considering with the estimated cost to purchase and the age of the vehicle.

Vehicle	Estimated Cost	Age
Honda Insight	$5,555	8
Toyota Prius	$17,888	3
Toyota Prius	$9,963	6
Toyota Echo	$6,793	5
Honda Civic Hybrid	$10,774	5
Honda Civic Hybrid	$16,310	2
Chevrolet Prizm	$2,475	8
Mazda Protege	$2,808	10
Toyota Corolla	$7,073	9
Acura Integra	$8,978	8
Scion xB	$11,213	2
Scion xA	$9,463	3
Mazda3	$15,055	2
Mini Cooper	$20,705	2

a. Plot this data on a scatter diagram with estimated cost as the dependent variable.
b. Find the correlation coefficient.
c. A regression analysis was performed and the resulting regression equation is Estimated Cost = 18358 − 1534 age. Interpret the meaning of the slope.
d. Estimate the cost of a five-year-old car.
e. Here is a portion of the regression software output. What does it tell you?

```
Predictor       Coef    SE Coef        T        P
Constant       18358       1817    10.10    0.000
Age          -1533.6      306.3    -5.01    0.000
```

f. Test at the .10 significance level whether there is a significant relationship between these two variables.

49. The National Highway Association is studying the relationship between the number of bidders on a highway project and the winning (lowest) bid for the project. Of particular interest is whether the number of bidders increases or decreases the amount of the winning bid.

Project	Number of Bidders, X	Winning Bid ($ millions), Y	Project	Number of Bidders, X	Winning Bid ($ millions), Y
1	9	5.1	9	6	10.3
2	9	8.0	10	6	8.0
3	3	9.7	11	4	8.8
4	10	7.8	12	7	9.4
5	5	7.7	13	7	8.6
6	10	5.5	14	7	8.1
7	7	8.3	15	6	7.8
8	11	5.5			

a. Determine the regression equation. Interpret the equation. Do more bidders tend to increase or decrease the amount of the winning bid?
b. Estimate the amount of the winning bid if there were seven bidders.
c. A new entrance is to be constructed on the Ohio Turnpike. There are seven bidders on the project. Develop a 95 percent prediction interval for the winning bid.
d. Determine the coefficient of determination. Interpret its value.

50. Mr. William Profit is studying companies going public for the first time. He is particularly interested in the relationship between the size of the offering and the price per share. A sample of 15 companies that recently went public revealed the following information.

Company	Size ($ millions), X	Price per Share, Y	Company	Size ($ millions), X	Price per Share, Y
1	9.0	10.8	9	160.7	11.3
2	94.4	11.3	10	96.5	10.6
3	27.3	11.2	11	83.0	10.5
4	179.2	11.1	12	23.5	10.3
5	71.9	11.1	13	58.7	10.7
6	97.9	11.2	14	93.8	11.0
7	93.5	11.0	15	34.4	10.8
8	70.0	10.7			

a. Determine the regression equation.
b. Determine the coefficient of determination. Do you think Mr. Profit should be satisfied with using the size of the offering as the independent variable?

51. Bardi Trucking Co., located in Cleveland, Ohio, makes deliveries in the Great Lakes region, the Southeast, and the Northeast. Jim Bardi, the president, is studying the relationship between the distance a shipment must travel and the length of time, in days, it takes the shipment to arrive at its destination. To investigate, Mr. Bardi selected a random sample of 20 shipments made last month. Shipping distance is the independent variable, and shipping time is the dependent variable. The results are as follows:

Shipment	Distance (miles)	Shipping Time (days)	Shipment	Distance (miles)	Shipping Time (days)
1	656	5	11	862	7
2	853	14	12	679	5
3	646	6	13	835	13
4	783	11	14	607	3
5	610	8	15	665	8
6	841	10	16	647	7
7	785	9	17	685	10
8	639	9	18	720	8
9	762	10	19	652	6
10	762	9	20	828	10

a. Draw a scatter diagram. Based on these data, does it appear that there is a relationship between how many miles a shipment has to go and the time it takes to arrive at its destination?
b. Determine the coefficient of correlation. Can we conclude that there is a positive correlation between distance and time? Use the .05 significance level.
c. Determine and interpret the coefficient of determination.
d. Determine the standard error of estimate.

52. Super Markets, Inc., is considering expanding into the Scottsdale, Arizona, area. You as director of planning, must present an analysis of the proposed expansion to the operating committee of the board of directors. As a part of your proposal, you need to include information on the amount people in the region spend per month for grocery items. You would also like to include information on the relationship between the amount spent for grocery items and income. Your assistant gathered the following sample information. The data are available on the data disk supplied with the text.

Household	Amount Spent	Monthly Income
1	$ 555	$4,388
2	489	4,558
⋮	⋮	⋮
39	1,206	9,862
40	1,145	9,883

  a. Let the amount spent be the dependent variable and monthly income the independent variable. Create a scatter diagram, using a software package.
  b. Determine the regression equation. Interpret the slope value.
  c. Determine the coefficient of correlation. Can you conclude that it is greater than 0?

53. Below is information on the price per share and the dividend for a sample of 30 companies. The sample data are available on the data disk supplied with the text.

Company	Price per Share	Dividend
1	$20.00	$ 3.14
2	22.01	3.36
⋮	⋮	⋮
29	77.91	17.65
30	80.00	17.36

  a. Calculate the regression equation using selling price based on the annual dividend. Interpret the slope value.
  b. Determine the coefficient of determination. Interpret its value.
  c. Determine the coefficient of correlation. Can you conclude that it is greater than 0 using the .05 significance level?

54. A highway employee performed a regression analysis of the relationship between the number of construction work-zone fatalities and the number of unemployed people in a state. The regression equation is Fatalities = 12.7 + 0.000114 (Unemp). Some additional output is:

```
Predictor          Coef         SE Coef        T        P
Constant         12.726           8.115     1.57    0.134
Unemp        0.00011386      0.00002896     3.93    0.001

Analysis of Variance
Source            DF        SS         MS        F        P
Regression         1     10354      10354    15.46    0.001
Residual Error    18     12054        670
Total             19     22408
```

  a. How many states were in the sample?
  b. Determine the standard error of estimate.
  c. Determine the coefficient of determination.
  d. Determine the coefficient of correlation.
  e. At the .05 significance level does the evidence suggest there is a positive association between fatalities and the number unemployed?

55. A regression analysis relating the current market value in dollars to the size in square feet of homes in Greene County, Tennessee, follows. The regression equation is: Value = −37,186 + 65.0 Size.

```
Predictor      Coef     SE Coef        T         P
Constant     -37186        4629     -8.03     0.000
Size         64.993       3.047     21.33     0.000

Analysis of Variance
Source            DF             SS               MS         F        P
Regression         1    13548662082      13548662082    454.98    0.000
Residual Error    33      982687392         29778406
Total             34    14531349474
```

  a. How many homes were in the sample?
  b. Compute the standard error of estimate.
  c. Compute the coefficient of determination.
  d. Compute the coefficient of correlation.
  e. At the .05 significance level does the evidence suggest a positive association between the market value of homes and the size of the home in square feet?

56. The following table shows the mean annual percent return on capital (profitability) and the mean annual percentage sales growth for eight aerospace and defense companies.

Company	Profitability	Growth
Alliant Techsystems	23.1	8.0
Boeing	13.2	15.6
General Dynamics	24.2	31.2
Honeywell	11.1	2.5
L-3 Communications	10.1	35.4
Northrop Grunmman	10.8	6.0
Rockwell Collins	27.3	8.7
United Technologies	20.1	3.2

  a. Compute the coefficient of correlation. Conduct a test of hypothesis to determine if it is reasonable to conclude that the population correlation is greater than zero. Use the .05 significance level.
  b. Develop the regression equation for profitability based on growth. Comment on the slope value.
  c. Use a software package to determine the residual for each observation. Which company has the largest residual?

57. The following data show the retail price for 12 randomly selected laptop computers along with their corresponding processor speeds in gigahertz.

Computers	Speed	Price	Computers	Speed	Price
1	2.0	$2,017	7	2.0	$2,197
2	1.6	922	8	1.6	1,387
3	1.6	1,064	9	2.0	2,114
4	1.8	1,942	10	1.6	2,002
5	2.0	2,137	11	1.0	937
6	1.2	1,012	12	1.4	869

  a. Develop a linear equation that can be used to describe how the price depends on the processor speed.
  b. Based on your regression equation, is there one machine that seems particularly over- or underpriced?
  c. Compute the correlation coefficient between the two variables. At the .05 significance level conduct a test of hypothesis to determine if the population correlation could be greater than zero.

58. A consumer buying cooperative tested the effective heating area of 20 different electric space heaters with different wattages. Here are the results.

Heater	Wattage	Area	Heater	Wattage	Area
1	1,500	205	11	1,250	116
2	750	70	12	500	72
3	1,500	199	13	500	82
4	1,250	151	14	1,500	206
5	1,250	181	15	2,000	245
6	1,250	217	16	1,500	219
7	1,000	94	17	750	63
8	2,000	298	18	1,500	200
9	1,000	135	19	1,250	151
10	1,500	211	20	500	44

a. Compute the correlation between the wattage and heating area. Is there a direct or an indirect relationship?
b. Conduct a test of hypothesis to determine if it is reasonable that the coefficient is greater than zero. Use the .05 significance level.
c. Develop the regression equation for effective heating based on wattage.
d. Which heater looks like the "best buy" based on the size of the residual?

59. A dog trainer is exploring the relationship between the size of the dog (weight in pounds) and its daily food consumption (measured in standard cups). Below is the result of a sample of 18 observations.

Dog	Weight	Consumption	Dog	Weight	Consumption
1	41	3	10	91	5
2	148	8	11	109	6
3	79	5	12	207	10
4	41	4	13	49	3
5	85	5	14	113	6
6	111	6	15	84	5
7	37	3	16	95	5
8	111	6	17	57	4
9	41	3	18	168	9

a. Compute the correlation coefficient. Is it reasonable to conclude that the correlation in the population is greater than zero? Use the .05 significance level.
b. How much does each additional ten pounds of weight change the estimated number of cups of dog food consumed?
c. Is one of the dogs a big undereater or overeater?

60. Waterbury Insurance Company wants to study the relationship between the amount of fire damage and the distance between the burning house and the nearest fire station. This information will be used in setting rates for insurance coverage. For a sample of 30 claims for the last year, the director of the actuarial department determined the distance from the fire station (X) and the amount of fire damage, in thousands of dollars (Y). The MegaStat output is reported below. (You can find the actual data in the data set on the CD as prb13-60.)

```
ANOVA table
Source                    SS   df            MS          F
Regression       1,864.5782    1    1,864.5782      38.83
Residual         1,344.4934   28      48.0176
Total            3,209.0716   29


Regression output
Variables      Coefficients      Std. Error      t(df = 28)
Intercept          12.3601          3.2915           3.755
Distance-X          4.7956          0.7696           6.231
```

Answer the following questions.
a. Write out the regression equation. Is there a direct or indirect relationship between the distance from the fire station and the amount of fire damage?
b. How much damage would you estimate for a fire 5 miles from the nearest fire station?
c. Determine and interpret the coefficient of determination.
d. Determine the coefficient of correlation. Interpret its value. How did you determine the sign of the correlation coefficient?
e. Conduct a test of hypothesis to determine if there is a significant relationship between the distance from the fire station and the amount of damage. Use the .01 significance level and a two-tailed test.

61. Listed below are the movies with the largest world box office sales and their world box office budget (total amount available to spend making the picture).

Rank	Movie	Year	World Box Office ($ million)	Adjusted Budget ($ million)
1	Titanic	1997	$1,835.0	$789.3
2	LOTR: The Return of the King	2003	1,129.2	377
3	Pirates of the Caribbean: Dead Man's Chest	2006	1,060.6	321.4
4	Harry Potter and the Sorcerer's Stone	2001	968.7	338.3
5	Pirates of the Caribbean: At World's End	2007	958.4	308.9
6	Harry Potter and the Order of the Phoenix	2007	937.0	306.3
7	Star Wars: Episode I—The Phantom Menace	1999	925.5	511.7
8	The Lord of the Rings: The Two Towers	2002	920.5	354
9	Jurassic Park	1993	920	513.8
10	Shrek 2	2004	912	436.5
11	Harry Potter and the Goblet of Fire	2005	892.2	300.8
12	Spider-Man 3	2007	885.4	354
13	Harry Potter and the Chamber of Secrets	2002	866.4	272.4
14	The Lord of the Rings: The Fellowship of the Ring	2001	860.7	334.3
15	Finding Nemo	2003	853.2	339.7
16	Star Wars: Episode III—Revenge of the Sith	2005	848.5	278
17	Independence Day	1996	813.1	417.5
18	Spider-Man	2002	806.7	419.7
19	Star Wars	1977	797.9	1,084.3
20	Harry Potter and the Prisoner of Azkaban	2004	789.8	249.4
21	Spider-Man 2	2004	784.0	373.4
22	The Lion King	1994	771.9	446.2
23	E.T.	1982	757	860.6
24	The Matrix: Reloaded	2003	735.7	281.5
25	Forrest Gump	1994	680	470.2
26	The Sixth Sense	1999	661.5	348.4
27	Pirates of the Caribbean	2003	653.2	305.4
28	Star Wars: Episode II—Attack of the Clones	2002	648.3	323
29	The Incredibles	2004	631.2	261.4
30	The Lost World	1997	614.4	301
31	The Passion of the Christ	2004	611.8	370.3
32	Men In Black	1997	587.2	328.6
33	Return of the Jedi	1983	573	563.1
34	Mission: Impossible 2	2000	545.4	241
35	The Empire Strikes Back	1980	533.9	586.8
36	Home Alone	1990	533.8	401.6
37	Monsters, Inc.	2001	524.2	272.6
38	Ghost	1990	517.6	306.6
39	Meet the Fockers	2004	511.9	279.2
40	Aladdin	1992	502.4	311.7
41	Twister	1996	495	329.7
42	Toy Story 2	1999	485.7	291.8
43	Saving Private Ryan	1998	479.3	278.1
44	Jaws	1975	471	782.7
45	Shrek	2001	469.7	285.1
46	Bruce Almighty	2003	459	242.6
47	Cast Away	2000	424.3	261.4
48	Mrs. Doubtfire	1993	423.2	315.6
49	Batman	1989	413	375.2
50	Signs	2002	408	237
51	Raiders of the Lost Ark	1981	384	519.7
52	My Big Fat Greek Wedding	2002	356.5	251
53	Dr. Seuss' How the Grinch Stole Christmas	2000	340	290.9
54	Rush Hour 2	2001	329.1	240.9
55	Beverly Hills Cop	1984	316.4	416.4
56	Ghostbusters	1984	291.6	391.7

Find the correlation between the world box office budget and world box office sales. Comment on the association between the two variables. Does it appear that the movies with large budgets result in large box office revenues?

Data Set Exercises

62. Refer to the Real Estate data, which report information on homes sold in Phoenix, Arizona, last year.

    a. Let selling price be the dependent variable and size of the home the independent variable. Determine the regression equation. Estimate the selling price for a home with an area of 2,200 square feet. Determine the 95 percent confidence interval and the 95 percent prediction interval for the selling price of a home with 2,200 square feet.

    b. Let selling price be the dependent variable and distance from the center of the city the independent variable. Determine the regression equation. Estimate the selling price of a home 20 miles from the center of the city. Determine the 95 percent confidence interval and the 95 percent prediction interval for homes 20 miles from the center of the city.

    c. Can you conclude that the independent variables "distance from the center of the city" and "selling price" are negatively correlated and that the area of the home and the selling price are positively correlated? Use the .05 significance level. Report the *p*-value of the test.

63. Refer to the Baseball 2008 data, which report information on the 2008 Major League Baseball season.

    a. Let the games won be the dependent variable and total team salary, in millions of dollars, be the independent variable. Can you conclude that there is a positive association between the two variables? Determine the regression equation. Interpret the slope, that is, the value of *b*. How many additional wins will an additional $5 million in salary bring?

    b. Determine the correlation between games won and ERA and between games won and team batting average. Which has the stronger correlation? Can we conclude that there is a positive correlation between wins and team batting and a negative correlation between wins and ERA? Use the .05 significance level.

    c. Assume the number of games won is the dependent variable and attendance the independent variable. Can we conclude that the correlation between these two variables is greater than 0? Use the .05 significance level.

64. Refer to the Wage data, which report information on annual wages for a sample of 100 workers. Also included are variables relating to industry, years of education, and gender for each worker.

    a. Determine the correlation between the annual wage and the years of education. At the .05 significance level can we conclude there is a positive correlation between the two variables?

    b. Determine the correlation between the annual wage and the years of work experience. At the .05 significance level can we conclude there is a positive correlation between the two variables?

Practice Test

Part I Objective

1. The first step in correlation analysis is to plot the data in a _____ .
2. The range of the coefficient of correlation is between _____ .
3. In studying the relationship between two variables, if the value of one variable decreases with increases in the other variable, the coefficient of correlation is _____ . (less than zero, zero, greater than zero)
4. The proportion of total variation in the dependent variable that is explained by the variation in the independent variable is measured by the _____ .
5. To test the hypothesis that the coefficient of correlation is zero, the test statistic is the _____ distribution.
6. The least squares regression line minimizes the sum of the squared differences between the actual value of the dependent variable and the _____ value.
7. When studying the relationship between two variables, the coefficient of correlation and the slope of the regression line have the same _____ .

8. For a regression analysis, a small standard error of the estimate indicates that the coefficient of determination will be _____ . (large, small, always 0)

9. In regression analysis, confidence and prediction intervals calculate _____ associated with an estimated value of the dependent variable. (error, association, convergence, sample size)

10. A prediction interval is based on an individual value of the _____ variable. (dependent, independent, correlated, estimated)

Part II Problems

1. Quick-print firms in center city Philadelphia spend most of their advertising dollars on displays on bus benches. A research project involves predicting monthly sales based on the annual amount spent on placing ads on bus benches. A sample of quick-print firms revealed the following information:

Company	Annual Bus Bench Advertising ($000)	Monthly Sales ($000)
A	2	10
B	4	40
C	5	30
D	7	50
E	3	20

a. Draw a scatter diagram.

b. Compute the coefficient of correlation.

c. Compute the coefficient of determination.

d. Compute the regression equation.

e. Based on the regression equation, will an increase in advertising result in an increase or decrease in monthly sales?

f. How much will an additional $1,000 in annual bus bench advertising increase/decrease monthly sales?

g. Estimate the monthly sales of a quick-print firm that spends nothing on bus bench advertising.

h. Estimate the monthly sales of a quick-print firm that spends $4,500 on bus bench advertising.

Software Commands

1. The MINITAB commands for the output showing the coefficient of correlation on page 396 are:
   a. Enter the sales representative's name in *C1*, the number of calls in *C2*, and the sales in *C3*.
   b. Select **Stat, Basic Statistics,** and **Correlation.**
   c. Select *Calls* and *Units Sold* as the variables, click on **Display p-values,** and then click **OK.**

2. The computer commands for the Excel output on page 407 are:
   a. Enter the variable names in row 1 of columns A, B, and C. Enter the data in rows 2 through 11 in the same columns.
   b. Select the **Data** tab on the top of the menu. Then, on the far right, select **Data Analysis.** Select **Regression,** then click **OK.**

Regression   ? ✕

Input
Input Y Range: $C$1:$C$11   [≣]   OK
Input X Range: $B$1:$B$11   [≣]   Cancel
☑ Labels   ☐ Constant is Zero   Help
☐ Confidence Level: 95   %

Output options
◉ Output Range: $E$2   [≣]
○ New Worksheet Ply:
○ New Workbook
Residuals
☐ Residuals   ☐ Residual Plots
☐ Standardized Residuals   ☐ Line Fit Plots
Normal Probability
☐ Normal Probability Plots

c. For our spreadsheet we have *Calls* in column B and *Sales* in column C. The **Input Y-Range** is *C1:C11* and the **Input X-Range** is *B1:B11*. Click on **Labels,** select *E1* as the **Output Range,** and click **OK.**

3. The MINITAB commands to the confidence intervals and prediction intervals on page 412 are:
   a. Select **Stat, Regression,** and **Fitted line plot.**
   b. In the next dialog box the **Response (Y)** is Sales and **Predictor (X)** is Calls. Select **Linear** for the type of regression model and then click on **Options.**
   c. In the **Options** dialog box click on **Display confidence and prediction bands,** use the **95.0 for confidence level,** type an appropriate heading in the **Title** box, then click **OK** and then **OK** again.

Fitted Line Plot   ✕

C2   Calls   Response (Y):   [Sales]
C3   Sales   Predictor (X):   Calls

Type of Regression Model
◉ Linear   ○ Quadratic   ○ Cubic

Select   Graphs...   Options...   Storage...
Help   OK   Cancel

Chapter 13   Answers to Self-Review

13–1 a. Advertising expense is the independent variable, and sales revenue is the dependent variable.

b.

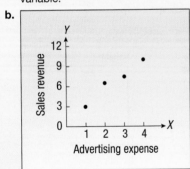

c.

X	Y	$(X - \bar{X})$	$(X - \bar{X})^2$	$(Y - \bar{Y})$	$(Y - \bar{Y})^2$	$(X - \bar{X})(Y - \bar{Y})$
2	7	−0.5	.25	0	0	0
1	3	−1.5	2.25	−4	16	6
3	8	0.5	.25	1	1	0.5
4	10	1.5	2.25	3	9	4.5
$\overline{10}$	$\overline{28}$		$\overline{5.00}$		$\overline{26}$	$\overline{11}$

$$\bar{X} = \frac{10}{4} = 2.5 \qquad \bar{Y} = \frac{28}{4} = 7$$

$$s_x = \sqrt{\frac{5}{3}} = 1.2909944$$

$$s_y = \sqrt{\frac{26}{3}} = 2.9439203$$

$$r = \frac{\Sigma(X - \bar{X})(Y - \bar{Y})}{(n - 1)s_x s_y} = \frac{11}{(4 - 1)(1.2909944)(2.9439203)}$$

$$= 0.9648$$

d. There is a strong correlation between the advertising expense and sales.

e. $r^2 = .93$, 93% of the variation in sales is "explained" by variation in advertising.

13–2 $H_0: \rho \le 0, H_1: \rho > 0$. H_0 is rejected if $t > 1.714$.

$$t = \frac{.43\sqrt{25 - 2}}{\sqrt{1 - (.43)^2}} = 2.284$$

H_0 is rejected. There is a positive correlation between the percent of the vote received and the amount spent on the campaign.

13–3 a. See the calculations in Self-Review 13–1, part (c).

$$b = \frac{rs_y}{s_x} = \frac{(0.9648)(2.9439)}{1.2910} = 2.2$$

$$a = \frac{28}{4} - 2.2\left(\frac{10}{4}\right) = 7 - 5.5 = 1.5$$

b. The slope is 2.2. This indicates that an increase of \$1 million in advertising will result in an increase of \$2.2 million in sales. The intercept is 1.5. If there was no expenditure for advertising, sales would be \$1.5 million.

c. $\hat{Y} = 1.5 + 2.2(3) = 8.1$

13–4 0.9487, found by:

Y	$\hat{Y}$	$(Y - \hat{Y})$	$(Y - \hat{Y})^2$
7	5.9	1.1	1.21
3	3.7	−0.7	.49
8	8.1	−0.1	.01
10	10.3	−0.3	.09
			$\overline{1.80}$

$$s_{y \cdot x} = \sqrt{\frac{\Sigma(Y - \hat{Y})^2}{n - 2}}$$

$$= \sqrt{\frac{1.80}{4 - 2}} = .9487$$

13–5 6.58 and 9.62, since $\hat{Y}$ for an X of 3 is 8.1, found by $\hat{Y} = 1.5 + 2.2(3) = 8.1$, then $\overline{X} = 2.5$ and $\Sigma(X - \overline{X})^2 = 5$.

t from Appendix B.2 for $4 - 2 = 2$ degrees of freedom at the .10 level is 2.920.

$$\hat{Y} \pm t(s_{y \cdot x})\sqrt{\frac{1}{n} + \frac{(X - \overline{X})^2}{\Sigma(X - \overline{X})^2}}$$

$$= 8.1 \pm 2.920(0.9487)\sqrt{\frac{1}{4} + \frac{(3 - 2.5)^2}{5}}$$

$$= 8.1 \pm 2.920(0.9487)(0.5477)$$

$$= 6.58 \text{ and } 9.62 \text{ (in \$ millions)}$$

14

Learning Objectives

When you have completed this chapter you will be able to:

LO1 Describe the relationship between several independent variables and a dependent variable using *multiple regression analysis.*

LO2 Set up, interpret, and apply an ANOVA table.

LO3 Compute and interpret the *multiple standard error of estimate,* the *coefficient of multiple determination,* and the *adjusted coefficient of multiple determination.*

LO4 Conduct a test of hypothesis to determine whether a set of regression coefficients differ from zero.

LO5 Conduct a test of hypothesis on each of the regression coefficients.

LO6 Use residual analysis to evaluate the assumptions of multiple regression analysis.

LO7 Evaluate the effects of correlated independent variables.

LO8 Use and understand qualitative independent variables.

Multiple Regression and Correlation Analysis

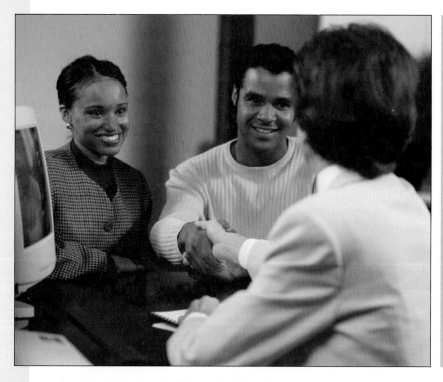

A mortgage department of a large bank is studying its recent loans. A random sample of 25 recent loans is obtained and searched for factors such as the value of the home, education level of borrower, age, monthly mortgage payment and gender relate to the family income. Are these variables effective predictors of the income of the household? (See Exercise 22 and LO1.)

Introduction

In Chapter 13 we described the relationship between a pair of interval- or ratio-scaled variables. We began the chapter by studying the coefficient of correlation, which measures the strength of the relationship. A coefficient near plus or minus 1.00 ($-.88$ or .78, for example) indicates a very strong linear relationship, whereas a value near 0 ($-.12$ or .18, for example) means that the relationship is weak. Next we developed a procedure to determine a linear equation to express the relationship between the two variables. We referred to this as a *regression line*. This line describes the relationship between the variables. It also describes the overall pattern of a dependent variable (Y) to a single independent or explanatory variable (X).

In multiple linear correlation and regression we use additional independent variables (denoted $X_1, X_2, \ldots$, and so on) that help us better explain or predict the dependent variable (Y). Almost all of the ideas we saw in simple linear correlation and regression extend to this more general situation. However, the additional independent variables do lead to some new considerations. Multiple regression analysis can be used either as a descriptive or as an inferential technique.

Multiple Regression Analysis

The general descriptive form of a multiple linear equation is shown in formula (14–1). We use k to represent the number of independent variables. So k can be any positive integer.

LO1 Describe the relationship between several independent variables and a dependent variable using *multiple regression analysis.*

| GENERAL MULTIPLE REGRESSION EQUATION | $\hat{Y} = a + b_1X_1 + b_2X_2 + b_3X_3 + \cdots + b_kX_k$ | **[14–1]** |

where

a is the intercept, the value of Y when all the X's are zero.

b_j is the amount by which Y changes when that particular X_j increases by one unit, with the values of all other independent variables held constant. The subscript j is simply a label that helps to identify each independent variable; it is not used in any calculations. Usually the subscript is an integer value between 1 and k, which is the number of independent variables. However, the subscript can also be a short or abbreviated label. For example, age could be used as a subscript.

In Chapter 13, the regression analysis described and tested the relationship between a dependent variable, $\hat{Y}$, and a single independent variable, X. The relationship between $\hat{Y}$ and X was graphically portrayed by a line. When there are two independent variables, the regression equation is

$$\hat{Y} = a + b_1X_1 + b_2X_2$$

Because there are two independent variables, this relationship is graphically portrayed as a plane and is shown in Chart 14–1. The chart shows the residuals as the difference between the actual Y and the fitted $\hat{Y}$ on the plane. If a multiple regression analysis includes more than two independent variables, we cannot use a graph to illustrate the analysis since graphs are limited to three dimensions.

To illustrate the interpretation of the intercept and the two regression coefficients, suppose a vehicle's mileage per gallon of gasoline is directly related to the octane rating of the gasoline being used (X_1) and inversely related to the weight of the automobile (X_2). Assume that the regression equation, calculated using statistical software, is:

$$\hat{Y} = 6.3 + 0.2X_1 - 0.001X_2$$

CHART 14–1 Regression Plane with 10 Sample Points

The intercept value of 6.3 indicates the regression equation intersects the Y-axis at 6.3 when both X_1 and X_2 are zero. Of course, this does not make any physical sense to own an automobile that has no (zero) weight and to use gasoline with no octane. It is important to keep in mind that a regression equation is not generally used outside the range of the sample values.

The b_1 of 0.2 indicates that for each increase of 1 in the octane rating of the gasoline, the automobile would travel 2/10 of a mile more per gallon, *regardless of the weight of the vehicle*. The b_2 value of −0.001 reveals that for each increase of one pound in the vehicle's weight, the number of miles traveled per gallon decreases by 0.001, *regardless of the octane of the gasoline being used*.

As an example, an automobile with 92-octane gasoline in the tank and weighing 2,000 pounds would travel an average 22.7 miles per gallon, found by:

$$\hat{Y} = a + b_1 X_1 + b_2 X_2 = 6.3 + 0.2(92) - 0.001(2{,}000) = 22.7$$

The values for the coefficients in the multiple linear equation are found by using the method of least squares. Recall from the previous chapter that the least squares method makes the sum of the squared differences between the fitted and actual values of Y as small as possible, that is, the term $\Sigma(Y - \hat{Y})^2$ is minimized. The calculations are very tedious, so they are usually performed by a statistical software package, such as Excel or MINITAB.

In the following example, we show a multiple regression analysis using three independent variables using Excel and MINITAB. Both packages report a standard set of statistics and reports. However, MINITAB also provides advanced regression analysis techniques that we will use later in the chapter.

Example

Salsberry Realty sells homes along the east coast of the United States. One of the questions most frequently asked by prospective buyers is: If we purchase this home, how much can we expect to pay to heat it during the winter? The research department at Salsberry has been asked to develop some guidelines regarding heating costs for single-family homes. Three variables are thought to relate to the heating costs: (1) the mean daily outside temperature, (2) the number of inches of insulation in the attic, and (3) the age in years of the furnace. To investigate, Salsberry's research department selected a random sample of 20 recently sold homes. It determined the cost to heat each home last January, as well as the January outside temperature in the region, the number of inches of insulation in the attic, and the age of the furnace. The sample information is reported in Table 14–1.

TABLE 14–1 Factors in January Heating Cost for a Sample of 20 Homes

Home	Heating Cost ($)	Mean Outside Temperature (°F)	Attic Insulation (inches)	Age of Furnace (years)
1	$250	35	3	6
2	360	29	4	10
3	165	36	7	3
4	43	60	6	9
5	92	65	5	6
6	200	30	5	5
7	355	10	6	7
8	290	7	10	10
9	230	21	9	11
10	120	55	2	5
11	73	54	12	4
12	205	48	5	1
13	400	20	5	15
14	320	39	4	7
15	72	60	8	6
16	272	20	5	8
17	94	58	7	3
18	190	40	8	11
19	235	27	9	8
20	139	30	7	5

The data in Table 14–1 is available in both Excel and MINITAB formats on the student CD. The basic instructions for using Excel and MINITAB for this data are in the Software Commands section at the end of this chapter.

Determine the multiple regression equation. Which variables are the independent variables? Which variable is the dependent variable? Discuss the regression coefficients. What does it indicate if some coefficients are positive and some coefficients are negative? What is the intercept value? What is the estimated heating cost for a home if the mean outside temperature is 30 degrees, there are 5 inches of insulation in the attic, and the furnace is 10 years old?

Solution

We begin the analysis by defining the dependent and independent variables. The dependent variable is the January heating cost. It is represented by Y. There are three independent variables:

- The mean outside temperature in January, represented by X_1.
- The number of inches of insulation in the attic, represented by X_2.
- The age in years of the furnace, represented by X_3.

Given these definitions, the general form of the multiple regression equation follows. The value $\hat{Y}$ is used to estimate the value of Y.

$$\hat{Y} = a + b_1X_1 + b_2X_2 + b_3X_3.$$

Now that we have defined the regression equation, we are ready to use either Excel or MINITAB to compute all the statistics needed for the analysis. The outputs from the two software systems are shown below.

To use the regression equation to predict the January heating cost, we need to know the values of the regression coefficients, b_j. These are highlighted in the software reports. Note that the software used the variable names or labels associated with each independent variable. The regression equation intercept, a, is labeled as "constant" in the MINITAB output and "intercept" in the Excel output.

Tbl14-1.mtw ***

↓	C1	C2	C3	C4
	Cost	Temp	Insul	Age
4	43	60	6	9
5	92	65	5	6
6	200	30	5	5
7	355	10	6	7
8	290	7	10	10
9	230	21	9	11
10	120	55	2	5
11	73	54	12	4
12	205	48	5	1
13	400	20	5	15
14	320	39	4	7
15	72	60	8	6
16	272	20	5	8
17	94	58	7	3
18	190	40	8	11
19	235	27	9	8
20	139	30	7	5
21				
22				
23				
24				

Session

———— 6/14/2008 10:31:38 AM ————

Welcome to Minitab, press F1 for help.

Results for: Tbl14-1.mtw

Regression Analysis: Cost versus Temp, Insul, Age

The regression equation is
Cost = 427 - 4.58 Temp - 14.8 Insul + 6.10 Age

```
Predictor      Coef    SE Coef      T      P
Constant     427.19      59.60   7.17  0.000
Temp         -4.5827     0.7723  -5.93  0.000
Insul       -14.831       4.754  -3.12  0.007
Age           6.101       4.012   1.52  0.148
```

S = 51.0486   R-Sq = 80.4%   R-Sq(adj) = 76.7%

Analysis of Variance

```
Source           DF      SS      MS      F      P
Regression        3  171220   57073  21.90  0.000
Residual Error   16   41695    2606
Total            19  212916
```

regression [Compatibility Mode]

	A	B	C	D	F	G	H	I	J	K	L
1	Cost	Temp	Insul	Age		SUMMARY OUTPUT					
2	250	35	3	6							
3	360	29	4	10		*Regression Statistics*					
4	165	36	7	3		Multiple R	0.897				
5	43	60	6	9		R Square	0.804				
6	92	65	5	6		Adjusted R Square	0.767				
7	200	30	5	5		Standard Error	51.049				
8	355	10	6	7		Observations	20				
9	290	7	10	10							
10	230	21	9	11		ANOVA					
11	120	55	2	5			*df*	*SS*	*MS*	*F*	*Significance F*
12	73	54	12	4		Regression	3	171220.473	57073.491	21.901	0.000
13	205	48	5	1		Residual	16	41695.277	2605.955		
14	400	20	5	15		Total	19	212915.750			
15	320	39	4	7							
16	72	60	8	6			*Coefficients*	*Standard Error*	*t Stat*	*P-value*	
17	272	20	5	8		Intercept	427.194	59.601	7.168	0.000	
18	94	58	7	3		Temp	-4.583	0.772	-5.934	0.000	
19	190	40	8	11		Insul	-14.831	4.754	-3.119	0.007	
20	235	27	9	8		Age	6.101	4.012	1.521	0.148	
21	139	30	7	5							

In this case the estimated regression equation is:

$$\hat{Y} = 427.194 - 4.583X_1 - 14.831X_2 + 6.101X_3$$

We can now estimate or predict the January heating cost for a home if we know the mean outside temperature, the inches of insulation, and the age of the furnace. For an example home, the mean outside temperature for the month is 30 degrees (X_1), there are 5 inches of insulation in the attic (X_2), and the furnace is 10 years old (X_3). By substituting the values for the independent variables:

$$\hat{Y} = 427.194 - 4.583(30) - 14.831(5) + 6.101(10) = 276.56$$

The estimated January heating cost is $276.56.

The regression coefficients, and their algebraic signs, also provide information about their individual relationships with the January heating cost. The regression coefficient for mean outside temperature is −4.583. The coefficient is negative and shows an inverse relationship between heating cost and temperature. This is not surprising. As the outside temperature increases, the cost to heat the home decreases. The numeric value of the regression coefficient provides more information. If we increase temperature by 1 degree and hold the other two independent variables constant, we can estimate a decrease of $4.583 in monthly heating cost. So if the mean temperature in Boston is 25 degrees and it is 35 degrees in Philadelphia, all other things being the same (insulation and age of furnace), we expect the heating cost would be $45.83 less in Philadelphia.

The attic insulation variable also shows an inverse relationship: the more insulation in the attic, the less the cost to heat the home. So the negative sign for this coefficient is logical. For each additional inch of insulation, we expect the cost to heat the home to decline $14.83 per month, holding the outside temperature and the age of the furnace constant.

The age of the furnace variable shows a direct relationship. With an older furnace, the cost to heat the home increases. Specifically, for each additional year older the furnace is, we expect the cost to increase $6.10 per month.

Self-Review 14–1

There are many restaurants in northeastern South Carolina. They serve beach vacationers in the summer, golfers in the fall and spring, and snowbirds in the winter. Bill and Joyce Tuneall manage several restaurants in the North Jersey area and are considering moving to Myrtle Beach, SC, to open a new restaurant. Before making a final decision they wish to investigate existing restaurants and what variables seem to be related to profitability. They gather sample information where profit (reported in $000) is the dependent variable and the independent variables are:

X_1 the number of parking spaces near the restaurant.
X_2 the number of hours the restaurant is open per week.
X_3 the distance from Broadway at the Beach, a landmark in Myrtle Beach.
X_4 the number of servers employed.
X_5 the number of years the current owner has owned the restaurant.

The following is part of the output obtained using statistical software.

Predictor	Coef	SE Coef	T
Constant	2.50	1.50	1.667
X_1	3.00	1.500	2.000
X_2	4.00	3.000	1.333
X_3	−3.00	0.20	−15.00
X_4	0.20	.05	4.00
X_5	1.00	1.50	0.667

(a) What is the amount of profit for a restaurant with 40 parking spaces and that is open 72 hours per week, is 10 miles from Broadway at the Beach, has 20 servers, and has been open 5 years?
(b) Interpret the values of b_2 and b_3 in the multiple regression equation.

Exercises

connect

1. The director of marketing at Reeves Wholesale Products is studying monthly sales. Three independent variables were selected as estimators of sales: regional population, per capita income, and regional unemployment rate. The regression equation was computed to be (in dollars):

$$\hat{Y} = 64{,}100 + 0.394X_1 + 9.6X_2 - 11{,}600X_3$$

a. What is the full name of the equation?
b. Interpret the number 64,100.
c. What are the estimated monthly sales for a particular region with a population of 796,000, per capita income of $6,940, and an unemployment rate of 6.0 percent?

2. Thompson Photo Works purchased several new, highly sophisticated processing machines. The production department needed some guidance with respect to qualifications needed by an operator. Is age a factor? Is the length of service as an operator (in years) important? In order to explore further the factors needed to estimate performance on the new processing machines, four variables were listed:

$$X_1 = \text{Length of time an employee was in the industry.}$$
$$X_2 = \text{Mechanical aptitude test score.}$$
$$X_3 = \text{Prior on-the-job rating.}$$
$$X_4 = \text{Age}$$

Performance on the new machine is designated Y.

Thirty employees were selected at random. Data were collected for each, and their performances on the new machines were recorded. A few results are:

Name	Performance on New Machine, Y	Length of Time in Industry, X_1	Mechanical Aptitude Score, X_2	Prior On-the-Job Performance, X_3	Age, X_4
Mike Miraglia	112	12	312	121	52
Sue Trythall	113	2	380	123	27

The equation is:

$$\hat{Y} = 11.6 + 0.4X_1 + 0.286X_2 + 0.112X_3 + 0.002X_4$$

a. What is this equation called?
b. How many dependent variables are there? Independent variables?
c. What is the number 0.286 called?
d. As age increases by one year, how much does estimated performance on the new machine increase?
e. Carl Knox applied for a job at Photo Works. He has been in the business for six years, and scored 280 on the mechanical aptitude test. Carl's prior on-the-job performance rating is 97, and he is 35 years old. Estimate Carl's performance on the new machine.

3. A sample of General Mills employees was studied to determine their degree of satisfaction with their present life. A special index, called the index of satisfaction, was used to measure satisfaction. Six factors were studied, namely, age at the time of first marriage (X_1), annual income (X_2), number of children living (X_3), value of all assets (X_4), status of health in the form of an index (X_5), and the average number of social activities per week—such as bowling and dancing (X_6). Suppose the multiple regression equation is:

$$\hat{Y} = 16.24 + 0.017X_1 + 0.0028X_2 + 42X_3 + 0.0012X_4 + 0.19X_5 + 26.8X_6$$

a. What is the estimated index of satisfaction for a person who first married at 18, has an annual income of $26,500, has three children living, has assets of $156,000, has an index of health status of 141, and has 2.5 social activities a week on the average?
b. Which would add more to satisfaction, an additional income of $10,000 a year or two more social activities a week?

4. Cellulon, a manufacturer of home insulation, wants to develop guidelines for builders and consumers on how the thickness of the insulation in the attic of a home and the outdoor

temperature affect natural gas consumption. In the laboratory it varied the insulation thickness and temperature. A few of the findings are:

Monthly Natural Gas Consumption (cubic feet), Y	Thickness of Insulation (inches), X_1	Outdoor Temperature (°F), X_2
30.3	6	40
26.9	12	40
22.1	8	49

On the basis of the sample results, the regression equation is:

$$\hat{Y} = 62.65 - 1.86X_1 - 0.52X_2$$

a. How much natural gas can homeowners expect to use per month if they install 6 inches of insulation and the outdoor temperature is 40 degrees F?

b. What effect would installing 7 inches of insulation instead of 6 have on the monthly natural gas consumption (assuming the outdoor temperature remains at 40 degrees F)?

c. Why are the regression coefficients b_1 and b_2 negative? Is this logical?

How Well Does the Equation Fit the Data?

Once you have the multiple regression equation, it is natural to ask "how well does the equation fit the data?" In linear regression, discussed in the previous chapter, you used summary statistics such as the standard error of estimate and the coefficient of determination to describe how effectively a single independent variable explained the variation of the dependent variable. The same procedures, broadened to additional independent variables, are used in multiple regression.

Multiple Standard Error of Estimate

LO3 Compute and interpret the *multiple standard error of estimate,* the *coefficient of multiple determination,* and the *adjusted coefficient of multiple determination.*

We begin with the **multiple standard error of estimate.** Recall that the standard error of estimate is comparable to the standard deviation. The standard deviation uses squared deviations from the mean, $(Y - \overline{Y})^2$, whereas the standard error of estimate utilizes squared deviations from the regression line, $(Y - \hat{Y})^2$. To explain the details of the standard error of estimate, refer to the first sampled home in Table 14–1 in the previous example on page 439. The actual heating cost for the first observation, Y, is $250, the outside temperature, X_1, is 35 degrees, the depth of insulation, X_2, is 3 inches, and the age of the furnace, X_3, is 6 years. Using the regression equation developed in the previous section, the estimated heating cost for this home is:

$$\hat{Y} = 427.194 - 4.583X_1 - 14.831X_2 + 6.101X_3$$

$$= 427.194 - 4.583(35) - 14.831(3) + 6.101(6)$$

$$= 258.90$$

So we would estimate that a home with a mean January outside temperature of 35 degrees, 3 inches of insulation, and a 6-year-old furnace would cost $258.90 to heat. The actual heating cost was $250, so the residual—which is the difference between the actual value and the estimated value—is $Y - \hat{Y} = 250 - 258.90 = -8.90$. This difference of $8.90 is the random or unexplained error for the first home sampled. Our next step is to square this difference, that is find $(Y - \hat{Y})^2 = (250 - 258.90)^2 = (-8.90)^2 = 79.21$. We repeat these operations for the other 19 observations and total these squared values. This value is the numerator of the multiple standard error of estimate. The denominator is the degrees of free-dom, that is $n - (k + 1)$. The formula for the standard error is:

MULTIPLE STANDARD ERROR OF ESTIMATE	$$s_{Y.123...k} = \sqrt{\frac{\Sigma(Y - \hat{Y})^2}{n - (k + 1)}}$$	[14–2]

where
    Y is the actual observation.
    $\hat{Y}$ is the estimated value computed from the regression equation.
    n is the number of observations in the sample.
    k is the number of independent variables.

In this example $n = 20$ and $k = 3$ (three independent variables) and we use the Excel software system to find the term $\Sigma(Y - \hat{Y})^2$. Note: There are small discrepancies due to rounding.

reg with predition and residuals [Compatibility Mode]

	A Cost	B Temp	C Insul	D Age	F $\hat{Y}$	G $Y - \hat{Y}$	H $(Y-\hat{Y})^2$	I	J
1	Cost	Temp	Insul	Age	$\hat{Y}$	$Y-\hat{Y}$	$(Y-\hat{Y})^2$		
2	250	35	3	6	258.91	-8.91	79.46		
3	360	29	4	10	295.98	64.02	4098.12		
4	165	36	7	3	176.71	-11.71	137.01		
5	43	60	6	5	118.16	-75.16	5648.75		
6	92	65	5	6	91.77	0.23	0.05		
7	200	30	5	5	246.06	-46.06	2121.96		
8	355	10	6	7	335.09	19.91	396.44		
9	290	7	10	10	307.82	-17.82	317.44		
10	230	21	9	11	264.59	-34.59	1196.57		
11	120	55	2	5	175.99	-55.99	3134.97		
12	73	54	12	4	26.16	46.84	2193.63		
13	205	48	5	1	139.17	65.83	4333.23		
14	400	20	5	15	352.90	47.10	2218.25		
15	320	39	4	7	231.85	88.15	7769.76		
16	72	60	8	6	70.19	1.81	3.26		
17	272	20	5	8	310.19	-38.19	1458.82		
18	94	58	7	3	75.89	18.11	328.10		
19	190	40	8	11	192.35	-2.35	5.53		
20	235	27	9	8	218.79	16.21	262.69		$\Sigma(Y-\hat{Y})^2$
21	139	30	7	5	216.40	-77.40	5991.23		
22							41695.28		

Since we have 3 independent variables, we identify the multiple standard error as $s_{Y.123}$. The subscripts indicate that three independent variables are being used to estimate Y.

$$s_{Y.123} = \sqrt{\frac{\Sigma(Y - \hat{Y})^2}{n - (k + 1)}} = \sqrt{\frac{41{,}695.28}{20 - (3 + 1)}} = 51.05$$

How do we interpret the standard error of estimate of 51.05? It is the typical "error" when we use this equation to predict the cost. First, the units are the same as the dependent variable, so the standard error is in dollars, $51.05. Second, we expect the residuals to be approximately normally distributed, so about 68 per-cent of the residuals will be within ±$51.05 and about 95 percent within ±2(51.05) = ±$102.10. Refer to column G of the Excel output, headed $Y - \hat{Y}$. Of the 20 values in this column, 14 (or 70 percent) are less than ±$51.05 and all are within ±$102.10, which is very close to the guidelines of 68 percent and 95 percent.

The ANOVA Table

As we said before, the multiple regression computations are long. Luckily, many statistical software systems are available to perform the detailed calculations. Most of them report the results in a standard format. The outputs from Excel and MINITAB on page 440 are typical. In particular, they include an analysis of variance (ANOVA) table. The output from MINITAB is repeated here.

	C1	C2	C3	C4
	Cost	Temp	Insul	Age
4	43	60	6	9
5	92	65	5	6
6	200	30	5	5
7	355	10	6	7
8	290	7	10	10
9	230	21	9	11
10	120	55	2	5
11	73	54	12	4
12	205	48	5	1
13	400	20	5	15
14	320	39	4	7
15	72	60	8	6
16	272	20	5	8
17	94	58	7	3
18	190	40	8	11
19	235	27	9	8
20	139	30	7	5
21				
22				
23				
24				

Regression Analysis: Cost versus Temp, Insul, Age

```
The regression equation is
Cost = 427 - 4.58 Temp - 14.8 Insul + 6.10 Age


Predictor    Coef  SE Coef       T      P
Constant   427.19    59.60    7.17  0.000
Temp      -4.5827   0.7723   -5.93  0.000
Insul     -14.831    4.754   -3.12  0.007
Age         6.101    4.012    1.52  0.148


S = 51.0486    R-Sq = 80.4%    R-Sq(adj) = 76.7%


Analysis of Variance

Source           DF      SS     MS      F      P
Regression        3  171220  57073  21.90  0.000
Residual Error   16   41695   2606
Total            19  212916


Source  DF  Seq SS
Temp     1  140215
Insul    1   24980
Age      1    6026
```

Focus on the analysis of variance table. It is similar to the ANOVA table used in Chapter 12. In that chapter the variation was divided into two components: variation due to the *treatments* and variation due to *random error*. Here total variation is also separated into two components:

- Variation in the dependent variable explained by the *regression* model (the independent variables).
- The *residual or error* variation. This is the random error due to sampling.

Incidentally, the term *residual error* will sometimes be called *random error* or just *error*.

There are three categories identified in the first or Source column in the ANOVA table; namely, the regression or explained variation, the residual or unexplained variation, and the total variation.

The second column is labeled *df* in the ANOVA table. It is the degrees of freedom. The degrees of freedom in the "Regression" row is the number of independent variables. We let k represent the number of independent variables, so $k = 3$. The degrees of freedom in the "Error" is $n - (k + 1) = 20 - (3 + 1) = 16$. In this example, there are 20 observations so $n = 20$. The total degrees of freedom is $n - 1 = 20 - 1 = 19$.

The heading SS in the third column of the ANOVA table is the sum of squares or the variation.

$$\text{Total variation} = \text{SS total} = \Sigma(Y - \overline{Y})^2 = 212{,}916$$

$$\text{Residual error or error variance} = \text{SSE} = \Sigma(Y - \hat{Y})^2 = 41{,}695$$

$$\text{Regression variation} = \text{SSR} = \Sigma(\hat{Y} - \bar{Y})^2 = \text{SS total} - \text{SSE}$$

$$= 212{,}916 - 41{,}695 = 171{,}220$$

(There is a small "round off" difference of one unit, which will have no effect on later calculations.)

The fourth column heading, MS or mean square, is obtained by dividing the SS quantity by the matching *df*. Thus MSR, the mean square regression, is equal to SSR/*k*. Similarly, MSE, the mean square error, is SSE/$(n - (k + 1))$.

The following ANOVA table summarizes the process.

LO2 Set up, interpret, and apply an ANOVA table.

Source	*df*	SS	MS	*F*
Regression	k	SSR	MSR = SSR/k	MSR/MSE
Residual or error	$n - (k + 1)$	SSE	MSE = SSE/$(n - (k + 1))$	
Total	$n - 1$	SS total		

Each value in the ANOVA table plays an important role in the evaluation and interpretation of a multiple regression equation. Notice, for example, that the standard error of estimate can very easily be computed from the ANOVA table.

$$s_{Y.123} = \sqrt{\text{MSE}} = \sqrt{2{,}606} = 51.05$$

Coefficient of Multiple Determination

Next, let's look at the coefficient of multiple determination. Recall from the previous chapter the coefficient of determination is defined as the percent of variation in the dependent variable explained, or accounted for, by the independent variable. In the multiple regression case we extend this definition as follows.

> **COEFFICIENT OF MULTIPLE DETERMINATION** The percent of variation in the dependent variable, *Y*, explained by the set of independent variables, X_1, X_2, X_3, ... X_k.

LO3 Compute and interpret the *multiple standard error of estimate,* the *coefficient of multiple determination,* and the *adjusted coefficient of multiple determination.*

The characteristics of the coefficient of multiple determination are:

1. **It is symbolized by a capital *R* squared.** In other words, it is written as R^2 because it behaves like the square of a correlation coefficient.
2. **It can range form 0 to 1.** A value near 0 indicates little association between the set of independent variables and the dependent variable. A value near 1 means a strong association.
3. **It cannot assume negative values.** Any number that is squared or raised to the second power cannot be negative.
4. **It is easy to interpret.** Because R^2 is a value between 0 and 1 it is easy to interpret, compare, and understand.

We can calculate the coefficient of determination from the information found in the ANOVA table. We look in the sum of squares column, which is labeled SS in the MINITAB output, and use the regression sum of squares, SSR, then divide by the total sum of squares, SS total.

COEFFICIENT OF MULTIPLE DETERMINATION	$R^2 = \dfrac{\text{SSR}}{\text{SS total}}$	**[14–3]**

The ANOVA portion of the MINITAB output in the heating cost example is repeated below.

```
Analysis of Variance
Source           DF      SS      MS      F       P
Regression        3   171220   57073   21.90   0.000
Residual Error   16    41695    2606
Total            19   212916
```

Use formula (14–3) to calculate the coefficient of multiple determination.

$$R^2 = \frac{SSR}{SS\ total} = \frac{171{,}220}{212{,}916} = .804$$

How do we interpret this value? We conclude that the independent variables (outside temperature, amount of insulation, and age of furnace) explain, or account for, 80.4 percent of the variation in heating cost. To put it another way, 19.6 percent of the variation is due to other sources, such as random error or variables not included in the analysis. Using the ANOVA table, 19.6 percent is the error sum of squares divided by the total sum of squares. Knowing that the SSR + SSE = SS total, the following relationship is true.

$$1 - R^2 = 1 - \frac{SSR}{SS\ total} = \frac{SSE}{SS\ total} = \frac{41{,}695}{212{,}916} = .196$$

Adjusted Coefficient of Determination

The number of independent variables in a multiple regression equation makes the coefficient of determination larger. Each new independent variable causes the predictions to be more accurate. That, in turn, makes SSE smaller and SSR larger. Hence, R^2 increases only because of the total number of independent variables and not because the added independent variable is a good predictor of the dependent variable. In fact, if the number of variables, k, and the sample size, n, are equal, the coefficient of determination is 1.0. In practice, this situation is rare and would also be ethically questionable. To balance the effect that the number of independent variables has on the coefficient of multiple determination, statistical software packages use an *adjusted* coefficient of multiple determination.

LO3 Compute and interpret the *multiple standard error of estimate,* the *coefficient of multiple determination,* and the *adjusted coefficient of multiple determination.*

> **ADJUSTED COEFFICIENT OF DETERMINATION**
> $$R^2_{adj} = 1 - \frac{\dfrac{SSE}{n - (k + 1)}}{\dfrac{SS\ total}{n - 1}}$$
> **[14–4]**

The error and total sum of squares are divided by their degrees of freedom. Notice especially the degrees of freedom for the error sum of squares includes k, the number of independent variables. For the cost of heating example, the adjusted coefficient of determination is:

$$R^2_{adj} = 1 - \frac{\dfrac{41{,}695}{20 - (3 + 1)}}{\dfrac{212{,}916}{20 - 1}} = 1 - \frac{2{,}606}{11{,}206.0} = 1 - .23 = .77$$

If we compare the R^2 (0.80) to the adjusted R^2 (0.77), the difference in this case is small.

Self-Review 14–2

Refer to Self-Review 14–1 on the subject of restaurants in Myrtle Beach. The ANOVA portion of the regression output is presented below.

```
Analysis of Variance
Source           DF    SS    MS
Regression        5   100    20
Residual Error   20    40     2
Total            25   140
```

(a) How large was the sample?
(b) How many independent variables are there?
(c) How many dependent variables are there?
(d) Compute the standard error of estimate. About 95 percent of the residuals will be between what two values?
(e) Determine the coefficient of multiple determination. Interpret this value.
(f) Find the coefficient of multiple determination, adjusted for the degrees of freedom.

Exercises

connect

5. Consider the ANOVA table that follows.

```
Analysis of Variance
Source           DF        SS        MS        F        P
Regression        2    77.907    38.954     4.14    0.021
Residual Error   62   583.693     9.414
Total            64   661.600
```

a. Determine the standard error of estimate. About 95 percent of the residuals will be between what two values?
b. Determine the coefficient of multiple determination. Interpret this value.
c. Determine the coefficient of multiple determination, adjusted for the degrees of freedom.

6. Consider the ANOVA table that follows.

```
Analysis of Variance
Source           DF        SS        MS        F
Regression        5   3710.00    742.00    12.89
Residual Error   46   2647.38     57.55
Total            51   6357.38
```

a. Determine the standard error of estimate. About 95 percent of the residuals will be between what two values?
b. Determine the coefficient of multiple determination. Interpret this value.
c. Determine the coefficient of multiple determination, adjusted for the degrees of freedom.

Inferences in Multiple Linear Regression

Thus far, multiple regression analysis has been viewed only as a way to describe the relationship between a dependent variable and several independent variables. However, the least squares method also has the ability to draw inferences or generalizations about the relationship for an entire population. Recall that when you create confidence intervals or perform hypothesis tests as a part of inferential statistics, you view the data as a random sample taken from some population.

In the multiple regression setting, we assume there is an unknown population regression equation that relates the dependent variable to the k independent variables. This is sometimes called a **model** of the relationship. In symbols we write:

$$\hat{Y} = \alpha + \beta_1 X_1 + \beta_2 X_2 + \cdots + \beta_k X_k$$

This equation is analogous to formula (14–1) except the coefficients are now reported as Greek letters. We use the Greek letters to denote *population parameters*. Then under a certain set of assumptions, which will be discussed shortly, the computed values of a and b_j are sample statistics. These sample statistics are point estimates of the corresponding population parameters α and β_j. For example, the sample regression coefficient b_2 is a point estimate of the population parameter β_2. The sampling distribution of these point estimates follows the normal probability distribution. These sampling distributions are each centered at their respective parameter values. To put it another way, the means of the sampling distributions are equal to the parameter values to be estimated. Thus, by using the properties of the sampling distributions of these statistics, inferences about the population parameters are possible.

Global Test: Testing the Multiple Regression Model

We can test the ability of the independent variables $X_1, X_2, \ldots, X_k$ to explain the behavior of the dependent variable Y. To put this in question form: Can the dependent variable be estimated without relying on the independent variables? The test used is referred to as the **global test.** Basically, it investigates whether it is possible all the independent variables have zero regression coefficients.

To relate this question to the heating cost example, we will test whether the independent variables (amount of insulation in the attic, mean daily outside temperature, and age of furnace) effectively estimate home heating costs. In testing a hypothesis, we first state the null hypothesis and the alternate hypothesis. In the heating cost example, there are three independent variables. Recall that b_1, b_2, and b_3 are sample regression coefficients. The corresponding coefficients in the population are given the symbols β_1, β_2, and β_3. We now test whether the regression coefficients in the population are all zero. The null hypothesis is:

$$H_0: \beta_1 = \beta_2 = \beta_3 = 0$$

The alternate hypothesis is:

$$H_1: \text{Not all the } \beta_i\text{'s are 0.}$$

If the null hypothesis is true, it implies the regression coefficients are all zero and, logically, are of no use in estimating the dependent variable (heating cost). Should that be the case, we would have to search for some other independent variables— or take a different approach—to predict home heating costs.

To test the null hypothesis that the multiple regression coefficients are all zero, we employ the F distribution introduced in Chapter 12. We will use the .05 level of significance. Recall these characteristics of the F distribution:

1. **There is a family of F distributions.** Each time the degrees of freedom in either the numerator or the denominator changes a new F distribution is created.
2. **The F distribution cannot be negative.** The smallest possible value is 0.
3. **It is a continuous distribution.** The distribution can assume an infinite number of values between 0 and positive infinity.
4. **It is positively skewed.** The long tail of the distribution is to the right-hand side. As the number of degrees of freedom increases in both the numerator and the denominator, the distribution approaches the normal probability distribution. That is, the distribution will move toward a symmetric distribution.
5. **It is asymptotic.** As the values of X increase, the F curve will approach the horizontal axis, but will never touch it.

The degrees of freedom for the numerator and the denominator may be found in the Excel ANOVA table that follows. The ANOVA output is highlighted in light green. The top number in the column marked "df" is 3, indicating there are 3 degrees of freedom in the numerator. This value corresponds to the number of independent variables. The middle number in the "df" column (16) indicated there are 16 degrees of freedom in the denominator. The number 16 is found by $(n - (k + 1)) = 20 - (3 + 1) = 16$.

Excel

	A	B	C	D	F	G	H	I	J	K	L
						regression [Compatibility Mode]					
1	Cost	Temp	Insul	Age		SUMMARY OUTPUT					
2	250	35	3	6							
3	360	29	4	10		*Regression Statistics*					
4	165	36	7	3		Multiple R	0.897				
5	43	60	6	9		R Square	0.804				
6	92	65	5	6		Adjusted R Square	0.767				
7	200	30	5	5		Standard Error	51.049				
8	355	10	6	7		Observations	20				
9	290	7	10	10							
10	230	21	9	11		ANOVA					
11	120	55	2	5			*df*	*SS*	*MS*	*F*	*Significance F*
12	73	54	12	4		Regression	3	171220.473	57073.491	21.901	0.000
13	205	48	5	1		Residual	16	41695.277	2605.955		
14	400	20	5	15		Total	19	212915.750			
15	320	39	4	7							
16	72	60	8	6			*Coefficients*	*Standard Error*	*t Stat*	*P-value*	
17	272	20	5	8		Intercept	427.194	59.601	7.168	0.000	
18	94	58	7	3		Temp	-4.583	0.772	-5.934	0.000	
19	190	40	8	11		Insul	-14.831	4.754	-3.119	0.007	
20	235	27	9	8		Age	6.101	4.012	1.521	0.148	
21	139	30	7	5							

The critical value of F is found in Appendix B.4. Using the table for the .05 significance level, move horizontally to 3 degrees of freedom in the numerator, then down to 16 degrees of freedom in the denominator, and read the critical value. It is 3.24. The region where H_0 is not rejected and the region where H_0 is rejected are shown in the following diagram.

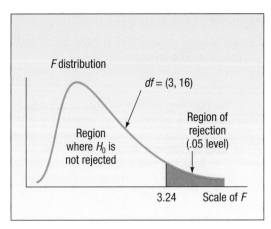

Continuing with the global test, the decision rule is: Do not reject the null hypothesis that all the regression coefficients are 0 if the computed value of F is less than or equal to 3.24. If the computed F is greater than 3.24, reject H_0 and accept the alternate hypothesis, H_1.

The value of F is found from the following equation.

LO4 Conduct a test of hypothesis to determine whether a set of regression coefficients differ from zero.

GLOBAL TEST
$$F = \frac{SSR/k}{SSE/[n - (k + 1)]}$$
[14–5]

SSR is the sum of the squares regression, SSE the sum of squares error, n the number of observations, and k the number of independent variables. Inserting the heating cost example values in formula (14–5) gives:

$$F = \frac{SSR/k}{SSE/[n - (k + 1)]} = \frac{171,220/3}{41,695/[20 - (3 + 1)]} = 21.90$$

The computed value of F is 21.90, which is in the rejection region. The null hypothesis that all the multiple regression coefficients are zero is therefore rejected. This means that some of the independent variables (amount of insulation, etc.) do have the ability to explain the variation in the dependent variable (heating cost). We expected this decision. Logically, the outside temperature, the amount of insulation, and age of the furnace have a great bearing on heating costs. The global test assures us that they do.

Evaluating Individual Regression Coefficients

So far we have shown that at least one, but not necessarily all, of the regression coefficients are not equal to zero and thus useful for predictions. The next step is to test the independent variables *individually* to determine which regression coefficients may be 0 and which are not.

Why is it important to know if any of the β_i's equal 0? If a β could equal 0, it implies that this particular independent variable is of no value in explaining any variation in the dependent value. If there are coefficients for which H_0 cannot be rejected, we may want to eliminate them from the regression equation.

We will now conduct three separate tests of hypothesis—for temperature, for insulation, and for the age of the furnace.

For temperature:	For insulation:	For furnace age:
$H_0: \beta_1 = 0$	$H_0: \beta_2 = 0$	$H_0: \beta_3 = 0$
$H_1: \beta_1 \neq 0$	$H_1: \beta_2 \neq 0$	$H_1: \beta_3 \neq 0$

We will test the hypotheses at the .05 level. The way the alternate hypothesis is stated indicates that the test is two-tailed.

The test statistic follows Student's t distribution with $n - (k + 1)$ degrees of freedom. The number of sample observations is n. There are 20 homes in the study, so $n = 20$. The number of independent variables is k, which is 3. Thus, there are $n - (k + 1) = 20 - (3 + 1) = 16$ degrees of freedom.

The critical value for t is in Appendix B.2. For a two-tailed test with 16 degrees of freedom using the .05 significance level, H_0 is rejected if t is less than -2.120 or greater than 2.120.

Refer to the Excel output in the previous section. (See page 450.) The column highlighted in yellow, headed Coefficients, shows the values for the multiple regression equation:

$$\hat{Y} = 427.194 - 4.583X_1 - 14.831X_2 + 6.101X_3$$

Interpreting the term $-4.583X_1$ in the equation: For each degree the temperature increases, it is expected that the heating cost will decrease about \$4.58, holding the two other variables constant.

The column on the Excel output labeled Standard Error indicates the standard error of the sample regression coefficient. Recall that Salsberry Realty selected a sample of 20 homes along the east coast of the United States. If it was to select a second random sample and compute the regression coefficients of that sample, the values would not be exactly the same. If it repeated the sampling process many times, however, we could design a sampling distribution of these regression coefficients. The column labeled Standard Error estimates the variability of these regression coefficients. The sampling distribution of Coefficients/Standard Error follows the t distribution with $n - (k + 1)$ degrees of freedom. Hence, we are able to test the independent variables individually to determine whether the net regression coefficients differ from zero. The computed t ratio is -5.934 for temperature and -3.119 for insulation. Both of these t values are in the rejection region to the left of -2.120. Thus, we conclude that the regression coefficients for the temperature and insulation variables are *not* zero. The computed t for the age of the furnace is 1.521, so we conclude that b_3 could equal 0. The independent variable age of the furnace is not a significant predictor of heating cost. It can be dropped from the analysis. We can test individual regression coefficients using the t distribution. The formula is:

LO5 Conduct a test of hypothesis on each of the regression coefficients.

| TESTING INDIVIDUAL REGRESSION COEFFICIENTS | $t = \dfrac{b_i - 0}{s_{b_i}}$ | [14–6] |

The b_i refers to any one of the regression coefficients and s_{b_i} refers to standard deviation of that distribution of the regression coefficient. We include 0 in the equation because the null hypothesis is $\beta_i = 0$.

To illustrate this formula, refer to the test of the regression coefficient for the independent variable temperature. We let b_1 refer to the regression coefficient. From the computer output on page 450 it is -4.583. s_{b_i} is the standard deviation of the sampling distribution of the regression coefficient for the independent variable temperature. Again, from the same computer output, it is 0.772. Inserting these values in formula (14–6):

$$t = \frac{b_1 - 0}{s_{b_1}} = \frac{-4.583 - 0}{0.772} = -5.936$$

This is the value found in the t Stat column of the Excel output. [There is a slight difference due to rounding.]

At this point we need to develop a strategy for deleting independent variables. In the Salsberry Realty case there were three independent variables, and one (the age of the furnace) had a regression coefficient that did not differ from 0. It is clear that we should drop that variable and rerun the regression equation. Below is the MINITAB output where heating cost is the dependent variable and outside temperature and amount of insulation are the independent variables.

↓	C1	C2	C3
	Cost	Temp	Insul
1	250	35	3
2	360	29	4
3	165	36	7
4	43	60	6
5	92	65	5
6	200	30	5
7	355	10	6
8	290	7	10
9	230	21	9
10	120	55	2
11	73	54	12
12	205	48	5
13	400	20	5
14	320	39	4
15	72	60	8
16	272	20	5
17	94	58	7
18	190	40	8
19	235	27	9

Session

Regression Analysis: Cost versus Temp, Insul

```
The regression equation is
Cost = 490 - 5.15 Temp - 14.7 Insul


Predictor      Coef   SE Coef       T      P
Constant     490.29     44.41   11.04  0.000
Temp        -5.1499    0.7019   -7.34  0.000
Insul       -14.718     4.934   -2.98  0.008


S = 52.9824   R-Sq = 77.6%   R-Sq(adj) = 74.9%


Analysis of Variance

Source          DF      SS      MS      F      P
Regression       2  165195   82597  29.42  0.000
Residual Error  17   47721    2807
Total           19  212916


Source  DF  Seq SS
Temp     1  140215
Insul    1   24980
```

Summarizing the results from this new MINITAB output:

1. The new regression equation is:

$$\hat{Y} = 490.29 - 5.1499X_1 - 14.718X_2$$

Notice that the regression coefficients for outside temperature (X_1) and amount of insulation (X_2) are similar to but not exactly the same as when we included the independent variable age of the furnace. Compare the above equation to that in the Excel output on page 450. Both of the regression coefficients are negative as in the earlier equation.

2. The details of the global test are as follows:

$$H_0: \beta_1 = \beta_2 = 0$$
$$H_1: \text{Not all of the } \beta_i\text{'s} = 0$$

The F distribution is the test statistic and there are $k = 2$ degrees of freedom in the numerator and $n - (k + 1) = 20 - (2 + 1) = 17$ degrees of freedom in the denominator. Using the .05 significance level and Appendix B.4, the decision rule is to reject H_0 if F is greater than 3.59. We compute the value of F as follows:

$$F = \frac{SSR/k}{SSE/(n - (k + 1))} = \frac{165,195/2}{47,721/(20 - (2 + 1))} = 29.42$$

Because the computed value of F (29.42) is greater than the critical value (3.59), the null hypothesis is rejected and the alternate accepted. We conclude that at least one of the regression coefficients is different from 0.

3. The next step is to conduct a test of the regression coefficients individually. We want to find out if one or both of the regression coefficients are different from 0. The null and alternate hypotheses for each of the independent variables are:

Outside Temperature   Insulation
$$H_0: \beta_1 = 0 \qquad\qquad H_0: \beta_2 = 0$$
$$H_1: \beta_1 \neq 0 \qquad\qquad H_1: \beta_2 \neq 0$$

The test statistic is the t distribution with $n - (k + 1) = 20 - (2 + 1) = 17$ degrees of freedom. Using the .05 significance level and Appendix B.2, the decision rule is to reject H_0 if the computed value of t is less than -2.110 or greater than 2.110.

Outside Temperature   Insulation

$$t = \frac{b_1 - 0}{s_{b_1}} = \frac{-5.1499 - 0}{0.7019} = -7.34 \quad t = \frac{b_2 - 0}{s_{b_2}} = \frac{-14.718 - 0}{4.934} = -2.98$$

In both tests we reject H_0 and accept H_1. We conclude that each of the regression coefficients is different from 0. Both outside temperature and amount of insulation are useful variables in explaining the variation in heating costs.

In the heating cost example, it was clear which independent variable to delete. However, in some instances which variable to delete may not be as clear-cut. To explain, suppose we develop a multiple regression equation based on five independent variables. We conduct the global test and find that some of the regression coefficients are different from zero. Next, we test the regression coefficients individually and find that three are significant and two are not. The preferred procedure is to drop the single independent variable with the *smallest absolute* t *value* or *largest* p-*value* and rerun the regression equation with the four remaining variables, then, on the new regression equation with four independent variables, conduct the individual tests. If there are still regression coefficients that are not significant, again drop the variable with the smallest absolute *t* value. To describe the process in another way, we should delete only one variable at a time. Each time we delete a variable, we need to rerun the regression equation and check the remaining variables.

This process of selecting variables to include in a regression model can be automated, using Excel, MINITAB, MegaStat, or other statistical software. Most of the software systems include methods to sequentially remove and/or add independent variables and at the same time provide estimates of the percentage of variation explained (the *R*-square term). Two of the common methods are **stepwise regression** and **best subset regression.** It may take a long time, but in the extreme we could compute every regression between the dependent variable and any possible subset of the independent variables.

Unfortunately, on occasion, the software may work "too hard" to find an equation that fits all the quirks of your particular data set. The suggested equation may not represent the relationship in the population. A judgment is needed to choose among the equations presented. Consider whether the results are logical. They should have a simple interpretation and be consistent with your knowledge of the application under study.

Self-Review 14–3

The regression output about eating places in Myrtle Beach is repeated below (see earlier self-reviews).

```
Predictor       Coef    SE Coef          T
Constant        2.50    1.50         1.667
X₁              3.00    1.500        2.000
X₂              4.00    3.000        1.333
X₃             -3.00    0.20       -15.00
X₄              0.20     .05         4.00
X₅              1.00    1.50         0.667


Analysis of Variance
Source           DF     SS    MS
Regression        5    100    20
Residual Error   20     40     2
Total            25    140
```

(a) Perform a global test of hypothesis to check if any of the regression coefficients are different from 0. What do you decide? Use the .05 significance level.
(b) Do an individual test of each independent variable. Which variables would you consider eliminating? Use the .05 significance level.
(c) Outline a plan for possibly removing independent variables.

Exercises

connect™

7. Given the following regression output,

```
Predictor       Coef    SE Coef        T        P
Constant      84.998    1.863       45.61    0.000
X₁             2.391    1.200        1.99    0.051
X₂            -0.4086   0.1717      -2.38    0.020


Analysis of Variance
Source          DF        SS       MS       F       P
Regression       2    77.907   38.954    4.14   0.021
Residual Error  62   583.693    9.414
Total           64   661.600
```

answer the following questions:
a. Write the regression equation.
b. If X_1 is 4 and X_2 is 11, what is the value of the dependent variable?
c. How large is the sample? How many independent variables are there?
d. Conduct a global test of hypothesis to see if any of the set of regression coefficients could be different from 0. Use the .05 significance level. What is your conclusion?

    e. Conduct a test of hypothesis for each independent variable. Use the .05 significance level. Which variable would you consider eliminating?

    f. Outline a strategy for deleting independent variables in this case.

8. The following regression output was obtained from a study of architectural firms. The dependent variable is the total amount of fees in millions of dollars.

```
Predictor          Coef      SE Coef        T
Constant          7.987        2.967      2.69
X₁               0.12242      0.03121      3.92
X₂              -0.12166      0.05353     -2.27
X₃              -0.06281      0.03901     -1.61
X₄               0.5235       0.1420       3.69
X₅              -0.06472      0.03999     -1.62

Analysis of Variance
Source            DF          SS          MS        F
Regression         5      3710.00      742.00    12.89
Residual Error    46      2647.38       57.55
Total             51      6357.38
```

    X_1 is the number of architects employed by the company.
    X_2 is the number of engineers employed by the company.
    X_3 is the number of years involved with health care projects.
    X_4 is the number of states in which the firm operates.
    X_5 is the percent of the firm's work that is health care–related.

    a. Write out the regression equation.

    b. How large is the sample? How many independent variables are there?

    c. Conduct a global test of hypothesis to see if any of the set of regression coefficients could be different from 0. Use the .05 significance level. What is your conclusion?

    d. Conduct a test of hypothesis for each independent variable. Use the .05 significance level. Which variable would you consider eliminating?

    e. Outline a strategy for deleting independent variables in this case.

Evaluating the Assumptions
of Multiple Regression

In the previous section, we described the methods to statistically evaluate the multiple regression equation. The results of the test let us know if at least one of the coefficients was not equal to zero and we described a procedure of evaluating each regression coefficient. We also discussed the decision-making process for including and excluding independent variables in the multiple regression equation.

It is important to know that the validity of the statistical global and individual tests rely on several assumptions. That is, if the assumptions are not true, the results might be biased or misleading. It should be mentioned, however, that in practice strict adherence to the following assumptions is not always possible. Fortunately the statistical techniques discussed in this chapter appear to work well even when one or more of the assumptions are violated. Even if the values in the multiple regression equation are "off" slightly, our estimates using a multiple regression equation will be closer than any that could be made otherwise. Usually the statistical procedures are robust enough to overcome violations of some assumptions.

In Chapter 13 we listed the necessary assumptions for regression when we considered only a single independent variable. (See page 407.) The assumptions for multiple regression are similar.

1. **There is a linear relationship.** That is, there is a straight-line relationship between the dependent variable and the set of independent variables.

2. **The variation in the residuals is the same for both large and small values of $\hat{Y}$.** The put it another way, $(Y - \hat{Y})$ is unrelated to whether $\hat{Y}$ is large or small.

3. **The residuals follow the normal probability distribution.** Recall the residual is the difference between the actual value of Y and the estimated value $\hat{Y}$. So the term $(Y - \hat{Y})$ is computed for every observation in the data set. These residuals should approximately follow a normal probability distribution. In addition, the mean of the residuals should be 0.

4. **The independent variables should not be correlated.** That is, we would like to select a set of independent variables that are not themselves correlated.

5. **The residuals are independent.** This means that successive observations of the dependent variable are not correlated. This assumption is often violated when time is involved with the sampled observations.

In this section we present a brief discussion of each of these assumptions. In addition, we provide methods to validate these assumptions and indicate the consequences if these assumptions cannot be met. For those interested in additional discussion, Kutner, Nachtscheim, and Neter, *Applied Linear Regression Models*, 4th ed. (McGraw-Hill: 2004), is an excellent reference.

Linear Relationship

Let's begin with the linearity assumption. The idea is that the relationship between the set of independent variables and the dependent variable is linear. If we are considering two independent variables, we can visualize this assumption. The two independent variables and the dependent variable would form a three-dimensional space. The regression equation would then form a plane as shown on page 438. We can evaluate this assumption with scatter diagrams and residual plots.

Using Scatter Diagrams The evaluation of a multiple regression equation should always include a scatter diagram that plots the dependent variable against each independent variable. These graphs help us to visualize the relationships and provide some initial information about the direction (positive or negative), linearity, and strength of the relationship. For example, the scatter diagrams for the home heating example follow. The plots suggest a fairly strong negative, linear relationship between heating cost and temperature, and a negative relationship between heating cost and insulation.

LO6 Use residual analysis to evaluate the assumptions of multiple regression analysis.

Using Residual Plots Recall that a residual $(Y - \hat{Y})$ can be computed using the multiple regression equation for each observation in a data set. In Chapter 13, we

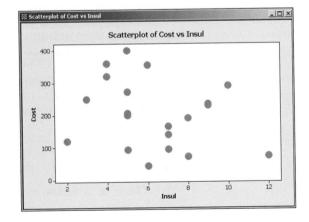

discussed the idea that the best regression line passed through the center of the data in a scatter plot. In this case, you would find a good number of the observations above the regression line (these residuals would have a positive sign), and a good number of the observations below the line (these residuals would have a negative sign). Further, the observations would be scattered above and below the line over the entire range of the independent variable.

The same concept is true for multiple regression, but we cannot graphically portray the multiple regression. However, plots of the residuals can help us evaluate the linearity of the multiple regression equation. To investigate, the residuals are plotted on the vertical axis against the predictor variable, $\hat{Y}$. The graph on the left below show the residual plots for the home heating cost example. Notice the following:

- The residuals are plotted on the vertical axis and are centered around zero. There are both positive and negative residuals.
- The residual plots show a random distribution of positive and negative values across the entire range of the variable plotted on the horizontal axis.
- The points are scattered and there is no obvious pattern, so there is no reason to doubt the linearity assumption.

This plot supports the assumption of linearity.

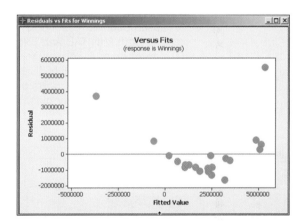

If there is a pattern to the points in the scatter plot, further investigation is necessary. The points in the graph on the right above show nonrandom residuals. See that the residual plot does *not* show a random distribution of positive and negative values across the entire range of the variable plotted on the horizontal axis. In fact, the graph shows a curvature to the residual plots. This indicates the relationship may not be linear. In this case perhaps the equation is quadratic, indicating that the square of one of the variables is needed. We discussed this possibility in Chapter 13.

Variation in Residuals Same for Large and Small $\hat{Y}$ Values

This requirement indicates that the variation about the predicted values is constant, regardless of whether the predicted values are large or small. To cite a specific example, which may violate the assumption, suppose we use the single independent variable age to explain the variation in income. We suspect that as age increases so does salary, but it also seems reasonable that as age increases there may be more variation around the regression line. That is, there will likely be more variation in income for a 50-year-old person than for a 35-year-old person. The requirement for constant variation around the regression line is called **homoscedasticity.**

> **HOMOSCEDASTICITY** The variation around the regression equation is the same for all of the values of the independent variables.

To check for homoscedasticity the residuals are plotted against the fitted values of Y. This is the same graph that we used to evaluate the assumption of linearity. (See page 457.) Based on the scatter diagram in that software output, it is reasonable to conclude that this assumption has not been violated.

Distribution of Residuals

To be sure that the inferences that we make in the global and individual hypotheses tests are valid, we evaluate the distribution of residuals. Ideally, the residuals should follow a normal probability distribution.

To evaluate this assumption, we can organize the residuals into a frequency distribution. The MINITAB histogram of the residuals is shown following on the left for the home heating cost example. Although it is difficult to show that the residuals follow a normal distribution with only 20 observations, it does appear the normality assumption is reasonable.

Both MINITAB and Excel offer another graph that helps to evaluate the assumption of normally distributed residuals. It is a called a **normal probability plot** and is shown to the right of the histogram. Without detailing the calculations, the normal probability plot supports the assumption of normally distributed residuals if the plotted points are fairly close to a straight line drawn from the lower left to the upper right of the graph.

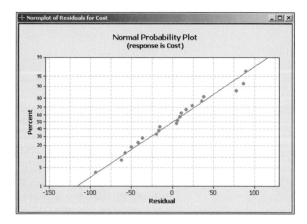

In this case, both graphs support the assumption that the residuals follow the normal probability distribution. Therefore, the inferences that we made based on the global and individual hypothesis tests are supported with the results of this evaluation.

Multicollinearity

Multicollinearity exists when independent variables are correlated. Correlated independent variables make it difficult to make inferences about the individual regression coefficients and their individual effects on the dependent variable. In practice, it is nearly impossible to select variables that are completely unrelated. To put it another way, it is nearly impossible to create a set of independent variables that are not correlated to some degree. However, a general understanding of the issue of multicollinearity is important.

LO7 Evaluate the effects of correlated independent variables.

First, we should point out that multicollinearity does not affect a multiple regression equation's ability to predict the dependent variable. However, when we are interested in evaluating the relationship between each independent variable and the dependent variable, multicollinearity may show unexpected results.

For example, if we use two highly multicollinear variables, high school GPA and high school class rank, to predict the GPA of incoming college freshmen (dependent variable), we would expect that both independent variables would be positively related to the dependent variable. However, because the independent variables are highly correlated, one of the independent variables may have an unexpected and inexplicable negative sign. In essence, these two independent variables are redundant in that they explain the same variation in the dependent variable.

A second reason for avoiding correlated independent variables is they may lead to erroneous results in the hypothesis tests for the individual independent variables. This is due to the instability of the standard error of estimate. Several clues that indicate problems with multicollinearity include the following:

1. An independent variable known to be an important predictor ends up having a regression coefficient that is not significant.
2. A regression coefficient that should have a positive sign turns out to be negative, or vice versa.
3. When an independent variable is added or removed, there is a drastic change in the values of the remaining regression coefficients.

In our evaluation of a multiple regression equation, an approach to reducing the effects of multicollinearity is to carefully select the independent variables that are included in the regression equation. A general rule is if the correlation between two independent variables is between -0.70 and 0.70 there likely is not a problem using both of the independent variables. A more precise test is to use the **variance inflation factor.** It is usually written *VIF*. The value of *VIF* is found as follows:

VARIANCE INFLATION FACTOR	$VIF = \dfrac{1}{1 - R_j^2}$	[14–7]

The term R_j^2 refers to the coefficient of determination, where the selected *independent variable* is used as a dependent variable and the remaining independent variables are used as independent variables. A *VIF* greater than 10 is considered unsatisfactory, indicating that the independent variable should be removed from the analysis. The following example will explain the details of finding the *VIF*.

Example

Refer to the data in Table 14–1, which relates the heating cost to the independent variables outside temperature, amount of insulation, and age of furnace. Develop a correlation matrix for all the independent variables. Does it appear there is a problem with multicollinearity? Find and interpret the variance inflation factor for each of the independent variables.

Solution

We begin by using the MINITAB system to find the correlation matrix for the dependent variable and the three independent variables. A portion of that output follows:

```
              Cost       Temp     Insul
Temp       -0.812
Insul      -0.257     -0.103
Age         0.537     -0.486     0.064

Cell Contents: Pearson correlation
```

The highlighted area indicates the correlation among the independent variables. None of the correlations among the independent variables exceed $-.70$ or $.70$, so we do not suspect problems with multicollinearity. The largest correlation among the independent variables is -0.486 between age and temperature.

To confirm this conclusion we compute the *VIF* for each of the three independent variables. We will consider the independent variable temperature first. We use MINITAB to find the multiple coefficient of determination with temperature as the *dependent variable* and amount of insulation and age of the furnace as independent variables. The relevant MINITAB output follows.

```
Regression Analysis: Temp versus Insul, Age

The regression equation is
Temp = 58.0 - 0.51 Insul - 2.51 Age

Predictor      Coef    SE Coef        T        P     VIF
Constant      57.99      12.35     4.70    0.000
Insul        -0.509      1.488    -0.34    0.737     1.0
Age          -2.509      1.103    -2.27    0.036     1.0

S = 16.0311   R-Sq = 24.1%   R-Sq(adj) = 15.2%

Analysis of Variance
Source              DF        SS        MS        F        P
Regression           2    1390.3     695.1     2.70    0.096
Residual Error      17    4368.9     257.0
Total               19    5759.2
```

The coefficient of determination is .241, so inserting this value into the *VIF* formula:

$$VIF = \frac{1}{1 - R_1^2} = \frac{1}{1 - .241} = 1.32$$

The *VIF* value of 1.32 is less than the upper limit of 10. This indicates that the independent variable temperature is not strongly correlated with the other independent variables.

Again, to find the *VIF* for insulation we would develop a regression equation with insulation as the *dependent variable* and temperature and age of furnace as independent variables. For this equation we would determine the coefficient of determination. This would be the value for R_2^2. We would substitute this value in equation 14–7, and solve for *VIF*.

Fortunately, MINITAB will generate the *VIF* values for each of the independent variables. These values are reported in the right-hand column under the heading *VIF* of the MINITAB output. Both of these values are 1.0, hence we conclude there is not a problem with multicollinearity in this example.

Independent Observations

The fifth assumption about regression and correlation analysis is that successive residuals should be independent. This means that there is not a pattern to the residuals, the residuals are not highly correlated, and there are not long runs of positive or negative residuals. When successive residuals are correlated we refer to this condition as **autocorrelation.**

Autocorrelation frequently occurs when the data are collected over a period of time. For example, we wish to predict yearly sales of Ages Software, Inc., based on the time and the amount spent on advertising. The dependent variable is yearly sales and the independent variables are time and amount spent on advertising. It is likely that for a period of time the actual points will be above the regression plane (remember there are two independent variables) and then for a period of time the points will be below the regression plane. The graph below shows the residuals plotted on the vertical axis and the fitted values $\hat{Y}$ on the horizontal axis. Note the run of residuals above the mean of the residuals, followed by a run below the mean. A scatter plot such as this would indicate possible autocorrelation.

There is a test for detecting autocorrelation, which is called the Durbin-Watson statistic. Check a more advanced statistics text for the details of this test.

Qualitative Independent Variables

In the previous example regarding heating cost, the two independent variables outside temperature and insulation were quantitative; that is, numerical in nature. Frequently we wish to use nominal-scale variables—such as gender, whether the home has a swimming pool, or whether the sports team was the home or the visiting team—in our analysis. These are called **qualitative variables** because they describe a particular quality, such as male or female. To use a qualitative variable in regression analysis, we use a scheme of **dummy variables** in which one of the two possible conditions is coded 0 and the other 1.

> **DUMMY VARIABLE** A variable in which there are only two possible outcomes. For analysis, one of the outcomes is coded a 1 and the other a 0.

LO8 Use and understand qualitative independent variables.

For example, we might be interested in estimating an executive's salary on the basis of years of job experience and whether he or she graduated from college. "Graduation from college" can take on only one of two conditions: yes or no. Thus, it is considered a qualitative variable.

Suppose in the Salsberry Realty example that the independent variable "garage" is added. For those homes without an attached garage, 0 is used; for homes with an attached garage, a 1 is used. We will refer to the "garage" variable as X_4. The data from Table 14–2 are entered into the MINITAB system.

TABLE 14–2 Home Heating Costs, Temperature, Insulation, and Presence of a Garage for a Sample of 20 Homes

Cost, Y	Temperature, X_1	Insulation, X_2	Garage, X_4
$250	35	3	0
360	29	4	1
165	36	7	0
43	60	6	0
92	65	5	0
200	30	5	0
355	10	6	1
290	7	10	1
230	21	9	0
120	55	2	0
73	54	12	0
205	48	5	1
400	20	5	1
320	39	4	1
72	60	8	0
272	20	5	1
94	58	7	0
190	40	8	1
235	27	9	0
139	30	7	0

The output from MINITAB is:

What is the effect of the garage variable? Should it be included in the analysis? To show the effect of the variable, suppose we have two houses exactly alike next to each other in Buffalo, New York; one has an attached garage, and the other does not. Both homes have 3 inches of insulation, and the mean January temperature in Buffalo is 20 degrees. For the house without an attached garage, a 0 is substituted for X_4 in the regression equation. The estimated heating cost is $280.90, found by:

$$\hat{Y} = 394 - 3.96X_1 - 11.3X_2 + 77.4X_4$$

$$= 394 - 3.96(20) - 11.3(3) + 77.4(0) = 280.90$$

For the house with an attached garage, a 1 is substituted for X_4 in the regression equation. The estimated heating cost is $358.30, found by:

$$\hat{Y} = 394 - 3.96X_1 - 11.3X_2 + 77.4X_4$$

$$= 394 - 3.96(20) - 11.3(3) + 77.4(1) = 358.30$$

The difference between the estimated heating costs is $77.40 ($358.30 − $280.90). Hence, we can expect the cost to heat a house with an attached garage to be $77.40 more than the cost for an equivalent house without a garage.

We have shown the difference between the two types of homes to be $77.40, but is the difference significant? We conduct the following test of hypothesis.

$$H_0: \beta_4 = 0$$

$$H_1: \beta_4 \neq 0$$

The information necessary to answer this question is on the MINITAB output above. The net regression coefficient for the independent variable garage is 77.43, and the standard deviation of the sampling distribution is 22.78. We identify this as the fourth independent variable, so we use a subscript of 4. Finally, we insert these values in formula (14–6).

$$t = \frac{b_4 - 0}{s_{b_4}} = \frac{77.43 - 0}{22.78} = 3.40$$

There are three independent variables in the analysis, so there are $n - (k + 1) = 20 - (3 + 1) = 16$ degrees of freedom. The critical value from Appendix B.2 is 2.120. The decision rule, using a two-tailed test and the .05 significance level, is to reject H_0 if the computed t is to the left of −2.120 or to the right of 2.120. Since the computed value of 3.40 is to the right of 2.120, the null hypothesis is rejected. It is concluded that the regression coefficient is not zero. The independent variable garage should be included in the analysis.

Is it possible to use a qualitative variable with more than two possible outcomes? Yes, but the coding scheme becomes more complex and will require a series of dummy variables. To explain, suppose a company is studying its sales as they relate to advertising expense by quarter for the last 5 years. Let sales be the dependent variable and advertising expense be the first independent variable, X_1. To include the qualitative information regarding the quarter, we use three additional independent variables. For the variable X_2, the five observations referring to the first quarter of each of the 5 years are coded 1 and the other quarters 0. Similarly, for X_3 the five observations referring to the second quarter are coded 1 and the other quarters 0. For X_4 the five observations referring to the third quarter are coded 1 and the other quarters 0. An observation that does not refer to any of the first three quarters must refer to the fourth quarter, so a distinct independent variable referring to this quarter is not necessary.

Self-Review 14–4 A study by the American Realtors Association investigated the relationship between the commissions earned by sales associates last year and the number of months since the associates earned their real estate licenses. Also of interest in the study is the gender of the sales associate. Below is a portion of the regression output. The dependent variable is commissions, which is reported in $000, and the independent variables are months since the license was earned and gender (female = 1 and male = 0).

```
Regression Analysis
         R²  0.642
Adjusted R²  0.600                  n    20
         R   0.801                  k    2
Std. Error   3.219      Dep. Var.   Commissions

ANOVA table
Source            SS     df         MS        F      p-value
Regression   315.9291     2    157.9645    15.25    .0002
Residual     176.1284    17     10.3605
Total        492.0575    19

Regression output
Variables    coefficients   std. error   t (df = 17)   p-value   95% lower   95% upper
Intercept        15.7625       3.0782         5.121      .0001      9.2680     22.2570
   Months         0.4415       0.0839         5.263      .0001      0.2645      0.6186
   Gender         3.8598       1.4724         2.621      .0179      0.7533      6.9663
```

(a) Write out the regression equation. How much commission would you expect a female agent to make who earned her license 30 months ago?

(b) Do the female agents on the average make more or less than the male agents? How much more?

(c) Conduct a test of hypothesis to determine if the independent variable gender should be included in the analysis. Use the 0.05 significance level. What is your conclusion?

Chapter Summary

I. The general form of a multiple regression equation is:

$$\hat{Y} = a + b_1X_1 + b_2X_2 + \cdots + b_kX_k \qquad \text{[14–1]}$$

where a is the Y-intercept when all X's are zero, b_j refers to the sample regression coefficients, and X_j refers to the value of the various independent variables.

A. There can be any number of independent variables.

B. The least squares criterion is used to develop the regression equation.

C. A statistical software package is needed to perform the calculations.

II. There are two measures of the effectiveness of the regression equation.

A. The multiple standard error of estimate is similar to the standard deviation.

  1. It is measured in the same units as the dependent variable.

  2. It is based on squared deviations from the regression equation.

  3. It ranges from 0 to plus infinity.

  4. It is calculated from the following equation.

$$s_{Y.123\ldots k} = \sqrt{\frac{\Sigma(Y - \hat{Y})^2}{n - (k + 1)}} \qquad \text{[14–2]}$$

B. The coefficient of multiple determination reports the percent of the variation in the dependent variable explained by the set of independent variables.

  1. It may range from 0 to 1.

  2. It is also based on squared deviations from the regression equation.

  3. It is found by the following equation.

$$R^2 = \frac{\text{SSR}}{\text{SS total}} \qquad \text{[14–3]}$$

4. When the number of independent variables is large, we adjust the coefficient of determination for the degrees of freedom as follows.

$$R_{adj}^2 = 1 - \frac{\dfrac{SSE}{n - (k + 1)}}{\dfrac{SS\ total}{n - 1}}$$ [14–4]

III. An ANOVA table summarizes the multiple regression analysis.
A. It reports the total amount of the variation in the dependent variable and divides this variation into that explained by the set of independent variables and that not explained.
B. It reports the degrees of freedom associated with the independent variables, the error variation, and the total variation.
IV. A correlation matrix shows all possible simple correlation coefficients between pairs of variables.
A. It shows the correlation between each independent variable and the dependent variable.
B. It shows the correlation between each pair of independent variables.
V. A global test is used to investigate whether any of the independent variables have significant regression coefficients.
A. The null hypothesis is: All the regression coefficients are zero.
B. The alternate hypothesis is: At least one regression coefficient is not zero.
C. The test statistic is the F distribution with k (the number of independent variables) degrees of freedom in the numerator and $n - (k + 1)$ degrees of freedom in the denominator, where n is the sample size.
D. The formula to calculate the value of the test statistic for the global test is:

$$F = \frac{SSR/k}{SSE/[n - (k + 1)]}$$ [14–5]

VI. The test for individual variables determines which independent variables have nonzero regression coefficients.
A. The variables that have zero regression coefficients are usually dropped from the analysis.
B. The test statistic is the t distribution with $n - (k + 1)$ degrees of freedom.
C. The formula to calculate the value of the test statistic for the individual test is:

$$t = \frac{b_i - 0}{s_{b_i}}$$ [14–6]

VII. Dummy variables are used to represent qualitative variables and can assume only one of two possible outcomes.
VIII. There are five assumptions to use multiple regression analysis.
A. The relationship between the dependent variable and the set of independent variables must be linear.
1. To verify this assumption develop a scatter diagram and plot the residuals on the vertical axis and the fitted values on the horizontal axis.
2. If the plots appear random, we conclude the relationship is linear.
B. The variation is the same for both large and small values of $\hat{Y}$.
1. Homoscedasticity means the variation is the same for all fitted values of the dependent variable.
2. This condition is checked by developing a scatter diagram with the residuals on the vertical axis and the fitted values on the horizontal axis.
3. If there is no pattern to the plots—that is, they appear random—the residuals meet the homoscedasticity requirement.
C. The residuals follow the normal probability distribution.
1. This condition is checked by developing a histogram of the residuals to see if they follow a normal distribution.
2. The mean of the distribution of the residuals is 0.
D. The independent variables are not correlated.
1. A correlation matrix will show all possible correlations among independent variables. Signs of trouble are correlations larger than 0.70 or less than -0.70.

2. Signs of correlated independent variables include when an important predictor variable is found insignificant, when an obvious reversal occurs in signs in one or more of the independent variables, or when a variable is removed from the solution, there is a large change in the regression coefficients.
3. The variance inflation factor is used to identify correlated independent variables.

$$VIF = \frac{1}{1 - R_j^2}$$ [14–7]

E. Each residual is independent of other residuals.
   1. Autocorrelation occurs when successive residuals are correlated.
   2. When autocorrelation exists, the value of the standard error will be biased and will return poor results for tests of hypothesis regarding the regression coefficients.

Pronunciation Key

SYMBOL	MEANING	PRONUNCIATION
b_1	Regression coefficient for the first independent variable	b sub 1
b_k	Regression coefficient for any independent variable	b sub k
$s_{Y.123...k}$	Multiple standard error of estimate	s sub Y dot 1, 2, 3 . . . k

Chapter Exercises

connect

9. A multiple regression equation yields the following partial results.

Source	Sum of Squares	df
Regression	750	4
Error	500	35

   a. What is the total sample size?
   b. How many independent variables are being considered?
   c. Compute the coefficient of determination.
   d. Compute the standard error of estimate.
   e. Test the hypothesis that none of the regression coefficients is equal to zero. Let $\alpha = .05$.

10. In a multiple regression equation two independent variables are considered, and the sample size is 25. The regression coefficients and the standard errors are as follows.

$$b_1 = 2.676 \qquad s_{b_1} = 0.56$$

$$b_2 = -0.880 \qquad s_{b_2} = 0.71$$

Conduct a test of hypothesis to determine whether either independent variable has a coefficient equal to zero. Would you consider deleting either variable from the regression equation? Use the .05 significance level.

11. The following output was obtained.

```
Analysis of variance

SOURCE          DF          SS          MS
Regression       5         100          20
Error           20          40           2
Total           25         140

Predictor      Coef       StDev     t-ratio
Constant       3.00        1.50        2.00
    X₁         4.00        3.00        1.33
    X₂         3.00        0.20       15.00
    X₃         0.20        0.05        4.00
    X₄        -2.50        1.00       -2.50
    X₅         3.00        4.00        0.75
```

   a. What is the sample size?
   b. Compute the value of R^2.
   c. Compute the multiple standard error of estimate.
   d. Conduct a global test of hypothesis to determine whether any of the regression coefficients are significant. Use the .05 significance level.
   e. Test the regression coefficients individually. Would you consider omitting any variable(s)? If so, which one(s)? Use the .05 significance level.
12. In a multiple regression equation $k = 5$ and $n = 20$, the MSE value is 5.10, and SS total is 519.68. At the .05 significance level, can we conclude that any of the regression coefficients are not equal to 0?
13. The district manager of Jasons, a large discount electronics chain, is investigating why certain stores in her region are performing better than others. She believes that three factors are related to total sales: the number of competitors in the region, the population in the surrounding area, and the amount spent on advertising. From her district, consisting of several hundred stores, she selects a random sample of 30 stores. For each store she gathered the following information.

   Y = total sales last year (in $ thousands)
   X_1 = number of competitors in the region
   X_2 = population of the region (in millions)
   X_3 = advertising expense (in $ thousands)

The sample data were run on MINITAB, with the following results.

```
Analysis of variance

SOURCE          DF          SS          MS
Regression       3     3050.00     1016.67
Error           26     2200.00       84.62
Total           29     5250.00

Predictor      Coef       StDev     t-ratio
Constant      14.00        7.00        2.00
    X₁        -1.00        0.70       -1.43
    X₂        30.00        5.20        5.77
    X₃         0.20        0.08        2.50
```

   a. What are the estimated sales for the Bryne store, which has four competitors, a regional population of 0.4 (400,000), and advertising expense of 30 ($30,000)?
   b. Compute the R^2 value.
   c. Compute the multiple standard error of estimate.
   d. Conduct a global test of hypothesis to determine whether any of the regression coefficients are not equal to zero. Use the .05 level of significance.
   e. Conduct tests of hypotheses to determine which of the independent variables have significant regression coefficients. Which variables would you consider eliminating? Use the .05 significance level.
14. Suppose that the sales manager of a large automotive parts distributor wants to estimate as early as April the total annual sales of a region. On the basis of regional sales, the total sales for the company can also be estimated. If, based on past experience, it is found that the April estimates of annual sales are reasonably accurate, then in future years the April forecast could be used to revise production schedules and maintain the correct inventory at the retail outlets.
   Several factors appear to be related to sales, including the number of retail outlets in the region stocking the company's parts, the number of automobiles in the region registered as of April 1, and the total personal income for the first quarter of the year. Five independent variables were finally selected as being the most important (according to the sales manager). Then the data were gathered for a recent year. The total annual sales for that year for each region were also recorded. Note in the following table that for region 1 there were 1,739 retail outlets stocking the company's automotive parts, there were

9,270,000 registered automobiles in the region as of April 1 and so on. The sales for that year were $37,702,000.

Annual Sales ($ millions), Y	Number of Retail Outlets, X_1	Number of Automobiles Registered (millions), X_2	Personal Income ($ billions), X_3	Average Age of Automobiles (years), X_4	Number of Supervisors, X_5
37.702	1,739	9.27	85.4	3.5	9.0
24.196	1,221	5.86	60.7	5.0	5.0
32.055	1,846	8.81	68.1	4.4	7.0
3.611	120	3.81	20.2	4.0	5.0
17.625	1,096	10.31	33.8	3.5	7.0
45.919	2,290	11.62	95.1	4.1	13.0
29.600	1,687	8.96	69.3	4.1	15.0
8.114	241	6.28	16.3	5.9	11.0
20.116	649	7.77	34.9	5.5	16.0
12.994	1,427	10.92	15.1	4.1	10.0

a. Consider the following correlation matrix. Which single variable has the strongest correlation with the dependent variable? The correlations between the independent variables outlets and income and between cars and outlets are fairly strong. Could this be a problem? What is this condition called?

```
          sales      outlets       cars     income        age
outlets   0.899
cars      0.605       0.775
income    0.964       0.825      0.409
age      -0.323      -0.489     -0.447     -0.349
bosses    0.286       0.183      0.395      0.155      0.291
```

b. The output for all five variables is below. What percent of the variation is explained by the regression equation?

```
The regression equation is
sales = -19.7 - 0.00063 outlets + 1.74 cars + 0.410 income
        + 2.04 age - 0.034 bosses

          Predictor        Coef        StDev      t-ratio
          Constant       -19.672        5.422       -3.63
          outlets      -0.000629     0.002638       -0.24
          cars           1.7399       0.5530        3.15
          income        0.40994      0.04385        9.35
          age            2.0357       0.8779        2.32
          bosses        -0.0344       0.1880       -0.18

Analysis of Variance
          SOURCE        DF           SS           MS
          Regression     5      1593.81       318.76
          Error          4         9.08         2.27
          Total          9      1602.89
```

c. Conduct a global test of hypothesis to determine whether any of the regression coefficients are not zero. Use the .05 significance level.
d. Conduct a test of hypothesis on each of the independent variables. Would you consider eliminating "outlets" and "bosses"? Use the .05 significance level.

e. The regression has been rerun below with "outlets" and "bosses" eliminated. Compute the coefficient of determination. How much has R^2 changed from the previous analysis?

```
The regression equation is
sales = -18.9 + 1.61 cars + 0.400 income + 1.96 age

          Predictor          Coef         StDev       t-ratio
          Constant         -18.924        3.636        -5.20
          cars               1.6129       0.1979        8.15
          income             0.40031      0.01569      25.52
          age                1.9637       0.5846        3.36

Analysis of Variance
          SOURCE        DF           SS          MS
          Regression     3       1593.66      531.22
          Error          6          9.23        1.54
          Total          9       1602.89
```

f. Following is a histogram and a stem-and-leaf chart of the residuals. Does the normality assumption appear reasonable?

```
Histogram of residual N = 10        Stem-and-leaf of residual N = 10
                                     Leaf Unit = 0.10
Midpoint  Count
   -1.5     1    *                   1   -1   7
   -1.0     1    *                   2   -1   2
   -0.5     2    **                  2   -0
   -0.0     2    **                  5   -0   440
    0.5     2    **                  5    0   24
    1.0     1    *                   3    0   68
    1.5     1    *                   1    1
                                     1    1   7
```

g. Following is a plot of the fitted values of Y (i.e., $\hat{Y}$) and the residuals. Do you see any violations of the assumptions?

15. The administrator of a new paralegal program at Seagate Technical College wants to estimate the grade point average in the new program. He thought that high school GPA, the verbal score on the Scholastic Aptitude Test (SAT), and the mathematics score on the SAT would be good predictors of paralegal GPA. The data on nine students are:

Student	High School GPA	SAT Verbal	SAT Math	Paralegal GPA
1	3.25	480	410	3.21
2	1.80	290	270	1.68
3	2.89	420	410	3.58

continued

Student	High School GPA	SAT Verbal	SAT Math	Paralegal GPA
4	3.81	500	600	3.92
5	3.13	500	490	3.00
6	2.81	430	460	2.82
7	2.20	320	490	1.65
8	2.14	530	480	2.30
9	2.63	469	440	2.33

a. Consider the following correlation matrix. Which variable has the strongest correlation with the dependent variable? Some of the correlations among the independent variables are strong. Does this appear to be a problem?

```
                  legal           gpa           verbal
gpa              0.911
verbal           0.616          0.609
math             0.487          0.636          0.599
```

b. Consider the following output. Compute the coefficient of multiple determination.

```
The regression equation is
legal = -0.411 + 1.20 gpa + 0.00163 verbal - 0.00194 math

Predictor              Coef              StDev            t-ratio
Constant            -0.4111            0.7823             -0.53
gpa                  1.2014            0.2955              4.07
verbal               0.001629          0.002147            0.76
math                -0.001939          0.002074           -0.94

Analysis of Variance
SOURCE          DF              SS                MS
Regression       3           4.3595            1.4532
Error            5           0.7036            0.1407
Total            8           5.0631
```

c. Conduct a global test of hypothesis from the preceding output. Does it appear that any of the regression coefficients are not equal to zero?

d. Conduct a test of hypothesis on each independent variable. Would you consider eliminating the variables "verbal" and "math"? Let $\alpha = .05$.

e. The analysis has been rerun without "verbal" and "math." See the following output. Compute the coefficient of determination. How much has R^2 changed from the previous analysis?

```
The regression equation is
legal = -0.454 + 1.16 gpa

 Predictor             Coef              StDev            t-ratio
 Constant           -0.4542            0.5542             -0.82
 gpa                 1.1589            0.1977              5.86

Analysis of Variance
SOURCE          DF              SS                MS
Regression       1           4.2061            4.2061
Error            7           0.8570            0.1224
Total            8           5.0631
```

f. Following are a histogram and a stem-and-leaf diagram of the residuals. Does the normality assumption for the residuals seem reasonable?

```
Histogram of residual N = 9

Midpoint             Count
    -0.4               1   *
    -0.2               3   ***
     0.0               3   ***
     0.2               1   *
     0.4               0
     0.6               1   *

Stem-and-leaf of residual N = 9
Leaf unit = 0.10
    1    -0   4
    2    -0   2
   (3)   -0   110
    4     0   00
    2     0
    1     0
    1     0   6
```

g. Following is a plot of the residuals and the $\hat{Y}$ values. Do you see any violation of the assumptions?

16. Mike Wilde is president of the teachers' union for Otsego School District. In preparing for upcoming negotiations, he would like to investigate the salary structure of classroom teachers in the district. He believes there are three factors that affect a teacher's salary: years of experience, a rating of teaching effectiveness given by the principal, and whether the teacher has a master's degree. A random sample of 20 teachers resulted in the following data.

Salary ($ thousands), Y	Years of Experience, X_1	Principal's Rating, X_2	Master's Degree,* X_3
31.1	8	35	0
33.6	5	43	0
29.3	2	51	1
43.0	15	60	1
38.6	11	73	0
45.0	14	80	1
42.0	9	76	0
36.8	7	54	1
48.6	22	55	1
31.7	3	90	1
25.7	1	30	0
30.6	5	44	0
51.8	23	84	1
46.7	17	76	0

continued

Salary ($ thousands), Y	Years of Experience, X_1	Principal's Rating, X_2	Master's Degree,* X_3
38.4	12	68	1
33.6	14	25	0
41.8	8	90	1
30.7	4	62	0
32.8	2	80	1
42.8	8	72	0

*1 = yes, 0 = no.

    a. Develop a correlation matrix. Which independent variable has the strongest correlation with the dependent variable? Does it appear there will be any problems with multicollinearity?

    b. Determine the regression equation. What salary would you estimate for a teacher with five years' experience, a rating by the principal of 60, and no master's degree?

    c. Conduct a global test of hypothesis to determine whether any of the regression coefficients differ from zero. Use the .05 significance level.

    d. Conduct a test of hypothesis for the individual regression coefficients. Would you consider deleting any of the independent variables? Use the .05 significance level.

    e. If your conclusion in part (d) was to delete one or more independent variables, run the analysis again without those variables.

    f. Determine the residuals for the equation of part (e). Use a stem-and-leaf chart or a histogram to verify that the distribution of the residuals is approximately normal.

    g. Plot the residuals computed in part (f) in a scatter diagram with the residuals on the Y-axis and the $\hat{Y}$ values on the X-axis. Does the plot reveal any violations of the assumptions of regression?

17. A consumer analyst collected the following data on the screen sizes of popular LCD televisions sold recently at a large retailer:

Manufacturer	Screen	Price	Manufacturer	Screen	Price
Sharp	46	$1473.00	Sharp	37	$1314.50
Samsung	52	2300.00	Sharp	32	853.50
Samsung	46	1790.00	Sharp	52	2778.00
Sony	40	1250.00	Samsung	40	1749.50
Sharp	42	1546.50	Sharp	32	1035.00
Samsung	46	1922.50	Samsung	52	2950.00
Samsung	40	1372.00	Sony	40	1908.50
Sharp	37	1149.50	Sony	52	3103.00
Sharp	46	2000.00	Sony	46	2606.00
Sony	40	1444.50	Sony	46	2861.00
Sony	52	2615.00	Sony	52	3434.00
Samsung	32	747.50			

    a. Does there appear to be a linear relationship between the screen size and the price?

    b. Which variable is the "dependent" variable?

    c. Using statistical software determine the regression equation. Interpret the value of the slope in the regression equation.

    d. Include the manufacturer in a multiple linear regression analysis using a "dummy" variable. Does it appear that some manufacturers can command a premium price? *Hint:* You will need to use a set of indicator variables.

    e. Test each of the individual coefficients to see if they are significant.

    f. Make a plot of the residuals and comment on whether they appear to follow a normal distribution.

    g. Plot the residuals versus the fitted values. Do they seem to have the same amount of variation?

18. A regional planner is studying the demographics in a region of a particular state. She has gathered the following data on nine counties.

County	Median Income	Median Age	Coastal
A	$48,157	57.7	1
B	48,568	60.7	1
C	46,816	47.9	1
D	34,876	38.4	0
E	35,478	42.8	0
F	34,465	35.4	0
G	35,026	39.5	0
H	38,599	65.6	0
J	33,315	27.0	0

a. Is there a linear relationship between the median income and median age?
b. Which variable is the "dependent" variable?
c. Use statistical software to determine the regression equation. Interpret the value of the slope in a simple regression equation.
d. Include the aspect that the county is "coastal" or not in a multiple linear regression analysis using a "dummy" variable. Does it appear to be a significant influence on incomes?
e. Test each of the individual coefficients to see if they are significant.
f. Make a plot of the residuals and comment on whether they appear to follow a normal distribution.
g. Plot the residuals versus the fitted values. Do they seem to have the same amount of variation?

19. Great Plains Roofing and Siding Company, Inc., sells roofing and siding products to home repair retailers, such as Lowe's and Home Depot, and commercial contractors. The owner is interested in studying the effects of several variables on the value of shingles sold ($000). The marketing manager is arguing that the company should spend more money on advertising, while a market researcher suggests it should focus more on making its brand and product more distinct from its competitors.

The company has divided the United States into 26 marketing districts. In each district it collected information on the following variables: volume of sales (in thousands of dollars), advertising dollars (in thousands), number of active accounts, number of competing brands, and a rating of district potential.

Sales (000s)	Advertising Dollars (000s)	Number of Accounts	Number of Competitors	Market Potential
79.3	5.5	31	10	8
200.1	2.5	55	8	6
163.2	8.0	67	12	9
200.1	3.0	50	7	16
146.0	3.0	38	8	15
177.7	2.9	71	12	17
30.9	8.0	30	12	8
291.9	9.0	56	5	10
160.0	4.0	42	8	4
339.4	6.5	73	5	16
159.6	5.5	60	11	7
86.3	5.0	44	12	12
237.5	6.0	50	6	6
107.2	5.0	39	10	4
155.0	3.5	55	10	4

continued

Sales (000s)	Advertising Dollars (000s)	Number of Accounts	Number of Competitors	Market Potential
291.4	8.0	70	6	14
100.2	6.0	40	11	6
135.8	4.0	50	11	8
223.3	7.5	62	9	13
195.0	7.0	59	9	11
73.4	6.7	53	13	5
47.7	6.1	38	13	10
140.7	3.6	43	9	17
93.5	4.2	26	8	3
259.0	4.5	75	8	19
331.2	5.6	71	4	9

Conduct a multiple regression analysis to find the best predictors of sales.

a. Draw a scatter diagram comparing sales volume with each of the independent variables. Comment on the results.

b. Develop a correlation matrix. Do you see any problems? Does it appear there are any redundant independent variables?

c. Develop a regression equation. Conduct the global test. Can we conclude that some of the independent variables are useful in explaining the variation in the dependent variable?

d. Conduct a test of each of the independent variables. Are there any that should be dropped?

e. Refine the regression equation so the remaining variables are all significant.

f. Develop a histogram of the residuals and a normal probability plot. Are there any problems?

g. Determine the variance inflation factor for each of the independent variables. Are there any problems?

20. The *Times-Observer* is a daily newspaper in Metro City. Like many city newspapers, the *Times-Observer* is suffering through difficult financial times. The circulation manager is studying other papers in similar cities in the United States and Canada. She is particularly interested in what variables relate to the number of subscriptions to the paper. She is able to obtain the following sample information on 25 newspapers in similar cities. The following notation is used:

$$Sub = \text{Number of subscriptions (in thousands)}$$
$$Popul = \text{The metropolitan population (in thousands)}$$
$$Adv = \text{The advertising budget of the paper (in \$ hundreds)}$$
$$Income = \text{The median family income in the metropolitan area (in \$ thousands)}$$

Paper	Sub	Popul	Adv	Income	Paper	Sub	Popul	Adv	Income
1	37.95	588.9	13.2	35.1	14	38.39	586.5	15.4	35.5
2	37.66	585.3	13.2	34.7	15	37.29	544.0	11.0	34.9
3	37.55	566.3	19.8	34.8	16	39.15	611.1	24.2	35.0
4	38.78	642.9	17.6	35.1	17	38.29	643.3	17.6	35.3
5	37.67	624.2	17.6	34.6	18	38.09	635.6	19.8	34.8
6	38.23	603.9	15.4	34.8	19	37.83	598.9	15.4	35.1
7	36.90	571.9	11.0	34.7	20	39.37	657.0	22.0	35.3
8	38.28	584.3	28.6	35.3	21	37.81	595.2	15.4	35.1
9	38.95	605.0	28.6	35.1	22	37.42	520.0	19.8	35.1
10	39.27	676.3	17.6	35.6	23	38.83	629.6	22.0	35.3
11	38.30	587.4	17.6	34.9	24	38.33	680.0	24.2	34.7
12	38.84	576.4	22.0	35.4	25	40.24	651.2	33.0	35.8
13	38.14	570.8	17.6	35.0					

a. Determine the regression equation.
b. Conduct a global test of hypothesis to determine whether any of the regression coefficients are not equal to zero.
c. Conduct a test for the individual coefficients. Would you consider deleting any coefficients?
d. Determine the residuals and plot them against the fitted values. Do you see any problems?
e. Develop a histogram of the residuals. Do you see any problems with the normality assumption?

21. How important is GPA in determining the starting salary of recent business school graduates? Does graduating from a business school increase the starting salary? The director of undergraduate studies at a major university wanted to study these questions. She gathered the following sample information on 15 graduates last spring to investigate these questions.

Student	Salary	GPA	Business	Student	Salary	GPA	Business
1	$31.5	3.245	0	9	$34.7	3.355	1
2	33.0	3.278	0	10	32.5	3.080	0
3	34.1	3.520	1	11	31.5	3.025	0
4	35.4	3.740	1	12	32.2	3.146	0
5	34.2	3.520	1	13	34.0	3.465	1
6	34.0	3.421	1	14	32.8	3.245	0
7	34.5	3.410	1	15	31.8	3.025	0
8	35.0	3.630	1				

The salary is reported in $000, GPA on the traditional 4-point scale. A 1 indicates the student graduated from a school of business; a 0 indicates that the student graduated from one of the other schools.
a. Develop a correlation matrix. Do you see any problems with multicollinearity?
b. Determine the regression equation. Discuss the regression equation. How much does graduating from a college of business add to a starting salary? What starting salary would you estimate for a student with a GPA of 3.00 who graduated from a college of business?
c. What is the value of R^2? Can we conclude that this value is greater than 0?
d. Would you consider deleting either of the independent variables?
e. Plot the residuals in a histogram. Is there any problem with the normality assumption?
f. Plot the fitted values against the residuals. Does this plot indicate any problems with homoscedasticity?

22. A mortgage department of a large bank is studying its recent loans. Of particular interest is how such factors as the value of the home (in thousands of dollars), education level of the head of the household, age of the head of the household, current monthly mortgage payment (in dollars), and gender of the head of the household (male = 1, female = 0) relate to the family income. Are these variables effective predictors of the income of the household? A random sample of 25 recent loans is obtained.

Income ($ thousands)	Value ($ thousands)	Years of Education	Age	Mortgage Payment	Gender
$40.3	$190	14	53	$230	1
39.6	121	15	49	370	1
40.8	161	14	44	397	1
40.3	161	14	39	181	1
40.0	179	14	53	378	0
38.1	99	14	46	304	0
40.4	114	15	42	285	1
40.7	202	14	49	551	0
40.8	184	13	37	370	0
37.1	90	14	43	135	0
39.9	181	14	48	332	1

continued

Income ($ thousands)	Value ($ thousands)	Years of Education	Age	Mortgage Payment	Gender
40.4	143	15	54	217	1
38.0	132	14	44	490	0
39.0	127	14	37	220	0
39.5	153	14	50	270	1
40.6	145	14	50	279	1
40.3	174	15	52	329	1
40.1	177	15	47	274	0
41.7	188	15	49	433	1
40.1	153	15	53	333	1
40.6	150	16	58	148	0
40.4	173	13	42	390	1
40.9	163	14	46	142	1
40.1	150	15	50	343	0
38.5	139	14	45	373	0

a. Determine the regression equation.
b. What is the value of R^2? Comment on the value.
c. Conduct a global hypothesis test to determine whether any of the independent variables are different from zero.
d. Conduct individual hypothesis tests to determine whether any of the independent variables can be dropped.
e. If variables are dropped, recompute the regression equation and R^2.

Data Set Exercises

23. Refer to the Real Estate data, which report information on homes sold in the Phoenix, Arizona, area during the last year. Use the selling price of the home as the dependent variable and determine the regression equation with number of bedrooms, size of the house, whether there is a pool, whether there is an attached garage, distance from the center of the city, and number of bathrooms as independent variables.
   a. Write out the regression equation. Discuss each of the variables. For example, are you surprised that the regression coefficient for distance from the center of the city is negative? How much does a garage or a swimming pool add to the selling price of a home?
   b. Determine the value of R^2. Interpret.
   c. Develop a correlation matrix. Which independent variables have strong or weak correlations with the dependent variable? Do you see any problems with multicollinearity?
   d. Conduct the global test on the set of independent variables. Interpret.
   e. Conduct a test of hypothesis on each of the independent variables. Would you consider deleting any of the variables? If so, which ones?
   f. Rerun the analysis until only significant regression coefficients remain in the analysis. Identify these variables.
   g. Develop a histogram or a stem-and-leaf display of the residuals from the final regression equation developed in part (f). Is it reasonable to conclude that the normality assumption has been met?
   h. Plot the residuals against the fitted values from the final regression equation developed in part (f) against the fitted values of Y. Plot the residuals on the vertical axis and the fitted values on the horizontal axis.
24. Refer to the Baseball 2008 data, which report information on the 30 Major League Baseball teams for the 2008 season. Let the number of games won be the dependent variable and the following variables be independent variables: team batting average, number of stolen bases, number of errors committed, team ERA, number of home runs, and whether the team's home field is natural grass or artificial turf.

a. Write out the regression equation. Discuss each of the variables. For example, are you surprised that the regression coefficient for ERA is negative? How many wins does playing on natural grass for a home field add to or subtract from the total wins for the season?
b. Determine the value of R^2. Interpret.
c. Develop a correlation matrix. Which independent variables have strong or weak correlations with the dependent variable? Do you see any problems with multicollinearity?
d. Conduct a global test on the set of independent variables. Interpret.
e. Conduct a test of hypothesis on each of the independent variables. Would you consider deleting any of the variables? If so, which ones?
f. Rerun the analysis until only significant net regression coefficients remain in the analysis. Identify these variables.
g. Develop a histogram of the residuals from the final regression equation developed in part (f). Is it reasonable to conclude that the normality assumption has been met?
h. Plot the residuals against the fitted values from the final regression equation developed in part (f) against the fitted values of Y. Plot the residuals on the vertical axis and the fitted values on the horizontal axis.

25. Refer to the Wage data, which report information on annual wages for a sample of 100 workers. Also included are variables relating to industry, years of education, and gender for each worker. Determine the regression equation using annual wage as the dependent variable and years of education, gender, years of work experience, age in years, and whether or not the worker is a union member.
a. Write out the regression equation. Discuss each variable.
b. Determine and interpret the R^2 value.
c. Develop a correlation matrix. Which independent variables have strong or weak correlations with the dependent variable? Do you see any problems with multicollinearity?
d. Conduct a global test of hypothesis on the set of independent variables. Interpret your findings. Is it reasonable to continue with the analysis or should you stop here?
e. Conduct a test of hypothesis on each of the independent variables. Would you consider deleting any of these variables? If so, which ones?
f. Rerun the analysis deleting any of the independent variables that are not significant. Delete the variables one at a time.
g. Develop a histogram or a stem-and-leaf chart of the residuals from the final regression equation. Is it reasonable to conclude that the normality assumption has been met?
h. Plot the residuals against the fitted values from the final regression equation. Plot the residuals on the vertical axis and the fitted values on the horizontal axis.

Practice Test

Part I Objective

1. Multiple regression analysis describes the relationship between one dependent variable and two or more _____ .
2. In multiple regression analysis, the regression coefficients are computed using the method of _____ . (residuals, normality, least squares, standardized)
3. In multiple regression, the multiple standard error of the estimate is the square root of the _____ . (mean square error, residual, residual squared, explained variation)
4. The coefficient of multiple determination is the percent of variation in the dependent variable that is explained by the set of _____ .
5. The adjusted coefficient of determination compensates for the number of _____ . (dependent variables, errors, independent variables, explained variation)
6. In the Global Test of the regression coefficients, when the hypothesis is rejected, at least one coefficient is _____ .
7. The test statistic for the Global Test of regression coefficients is the _____ .
8. The test statistic for testing individual regression coefficients is the _____ .
9. In a plot of residuals, a random distribution of the residuals supports the assumption of _____ .
10. Multicollinearity exists when independent variables are _____ .
11. The variance inflation factor is used to detect _____ .
12. Another term for a qualitative variable is a _____ .

Part II Problems

1. Given the following ANOVA output:

Source	Sum of Squares	DF	MS
Regression	1050.8	4	262.70
Error	83.8	20	4.19
Total	1134.6	24	

Predictor	Coefficient	St. Dev	t-ratio
Constant	70.06	2.13	32.89
X_1	0.42	0.17	2.47
X_2	0.27	0.21	1.29
X_3	0.75	0.30	2.50
X_4	0.42	0.07	6.00

a. How many independent variables are there in the regression equation?
b. Write out the regression equation.
c. Compute the coefficient of multiple determination.
d. Compute the multiple standard error of estimate.
e. Conduct a test of hypothesis to determine if any of the regression coefficients are different from zero.
f. Conduct a test of hypothesis on each of the regression coefficients. Can any of them be deleted?

Software Commands

Note: We do not show steps for all the statistical software used in this chapter. Below are the first two, which show the basic steps.

1. The MINITAB commands for the multiple regression output on page 440 are:
  a. Import the data from the CD. The file name is **Tbl14–1.**
  b. Select **Stat, Regression,** and then click on **Regression.**
  c. Select *Cost* as the **Response** variable, and *Temp, Insul,* and *Age* as the **Predictors,** then click on **OK.**

2. The Excel commands to produce the multiple regression output on page 440 are:
  a. Import the data from the CD. The file name is **Tbl14.**
  b. Select the **Data** tab on the top menu. Then on the far right, select **Data analysis.** Select **Regression** and click **OK.**
  c. Make the **Input Y Range** *A1:A21,* the **Input X Range** *B1:D21,* check the **Labels** box, the **Output Range** is *G1,* then click **OK.**

Chapter 14   Answers to Self-Review

14–1 a. $389,500 or 389.5 (in \$000); found by

$$2.5 + 3(40) + 4(72) - 3(10) + .2(20) + 1(5)$$
$$= 3895$$

b. The b_2 of 4 shows profit will go up \$4,000 for each extra hour the restaurant is open (if none of the other variables change). The b_3 of -3 implies profit will fall \$3,000 for each added mile away from the central area (if none of the other variables change).

14–2 a. The total degrees of freedom $(n - 1)$ is 25. So the sample size is 26.

b. There are 5 independent variables.

c. There is only 1 dependent variable (profit).

d. $S_{Y.12345} = 1.414$, found by $\sqrt{2}$ Ninety-five percent of the residuals will be between -2.828 and 2.828, found by $\pm 2(1.414)$.

e. $R^2 = .714$, found by 100/140. 71.4% of the deviation in profit is accounted for by these five variables.

f. $R^2_{adj} = .643$, found by

$$1 - \left[\frac{40}{(26 - (5 + 1))} \right] \Big/ \left[\frac{140}{(26 - 1)} \right]$$

14–3 a. $H_0: \beta_1 = \beta_2 = \beta_3 = \beta_4 = \beta_5 = 0$

H_1: Not all of the β's are 0.

The decision rule is to reject H_0 if $F > 2.71$. The computed value of F is 10, found by 20/2. So, you reject H_0, which indicates at least one of the regression coefficients is different from zero.

b. For variable 1: $H_0: \beta_1 = 0$ and $H_1: \beta_1 \neq 0$
The decision rule is: Reject H_0 if $t < -2.086$ or $t > 2.086$. Since 2.000 does not go beyond either of those limits. We fail to reject the null hypothesis. This regression coefficient could be zero. We can consider dropping this variable. By parallel logic the null hypothesis is rejected for variables 3 and 4.

c. We should consider dropping variables 1, 2 and 5. Variable 5 has the smallest absolute value of t. So delete it first and refigure the regression analysis.

14–4 a. $\hat{Y} = 15.7625 + 0.4415X_1 + 3.8598X_2$
$\hat{Y} = 15.7625 + 0.4415(30) + 3.8598(1)$
$= 32.87$

b. Female agents make \$3,860 more than male agents.

c. $H_0: \beta_3 = 0$
$H_1: \beta_3 \neq 0$
$df = 17$, reject H_0 if $t < -2.110$ or $t > 2.110$

$$t = \frac{3.8598 - 0}{1.4724} = 2.621$$

Reject H_0. Gender should be included in the regression equation.

15

Learning Objectives

When you have completed this chapter, you will be able to:

LO1 List and understand the characteristics of the *chi-square distribution.*

LO2 Conduct a test of hypothesis comparing an observed set of frequencies to an expected distribution.

LO3 Conduct a test of hypothesis to determine whether two classification criteria are related.

Chi-Square Applications

Many years, TV executives used the guideline that 30 percent of the audience were watching each of the traditional big three prime-time networks and 10 percent were watching cable stations on a weekday night. A random sample of 500 viewers in the Tampa–St. Petersburg, Florida, area last Monday night showed that 165 homes were tuned in to the ABC affiliate, 140 to the CBS affiliate, 125 to the NBC affiliate, and the remainder were viewing a cable station. At the .05 significance level, can we conclude that the guideline is still reasonable? (Exercise 12, LO2)

Introduction

Chapters 9 through 12 discuss data of interval or ratio scale, such as weights of steel ingots, incomes of minorities, and years of employment. We conducted hypothesis tests about a single population mean, two population means, and three or more population means. For these tests we assume the populations follow the normal probability distribution. However, there are tests available in which no assumption regarding the shape of the population is necessary. This means the assumption of a normal population is not necessary.

There are also tests exclusively for data of nominal scale of measurement. Recall from Chapter 1 that nominal data is the "lowest" or most primitive. For this type of measurement, data are classified into categories where there is no natural order. Examples include gender of congressional representatives, state of birth of students, or brand of peanut butter purchased. In this chapter we introduce a new test statistic, the chi-square statistic. We use it for data measured with a nominal scale.

Goodness-of-Fit Test: Equal Expected Frequencies

LO2 Conduct a test of hypothesis comparing an observed set of frequencies to an expected distribution.

The goodness-of-fit test is one of the most commonly used statistical tests. The first illustration of this test involves the case in which the expected cell frequencies are equal.

As the full name implies, the purpose of the goodness-of-fit test is to compare an observed distribution to an expected distribution. An example will describe the hypothesis-testing situation.

Example

Ms. Jan Kilpatrick is the marketing manager for a manufacturer of sports cards. She plans to begin selling a series of cards with pictures and playing statistics of former Major League Baseball players. One of the problems is the selection of the former players. At a baseball card show at Southwyck Mall last weekend, she set up a booth and offered cards of the following six Hall of Fame baseball players: Tom Seaver, Nolan Ryan, Ty Cobb, George Brett, Hank Aaron, and Johnny Bench. At the end of the day she sold a total of 120 cards. The number of cards sold for each old-time player is shown in Table 15–1. Can she conclude the sales are not the same for each player?

TABLE 15–1 Number of Cards Sold for Each Player

Player	Cards Sold
Tom Seaver	13
Nolan Ryan	33
Ty Cobb	14
George Brett	7
Hank Aaron	36
Johnny Bench	17
Total	120

If there is no significant difference in the popularity of the players, we would expect that the observed frequencies (f_o) would be equal—or nearly equal. That is, we would expect to sell as many cards for Tom Seaver as for Nolan Ryan. Thus, any discrepancy in the observed and expected frequencies could be attributed to sampling (chance).

What about the level of measurement in this problem? Notice when a card is sold, the "measurement" of the card is based on the player's name. There is no natural order to the players. No one player is assumed better than another. Therefore, a nominal scale is used to evaluate each observation.

Because there are 120 cards in the sample, we expect that 20 (f_e) cards, i.e., the expected frequency f_e, will fall in each of the six categories (Table 15–2). These categories are called **cells**. An examination of the set of observed frequencies in Table 15–1 indicates that the card for George Brett is sold rather infrequently, whereas the cards for Hank Aaron and Nolan Ryan are sold more often. Is the difference in sales due to chance, or can we conclude that there is a preference for the cards of certain players?

TABLE 15–2 Observed and Expected Frequencies for the 120 Cards Sold

Player	Cards Sold, f_o	Expected Number Sold, f_e
Tom Seaver	13	20
Nolan Ryan	33	20
Ty Cobb	14	20
George Brett	7	20
Hank Aaron	36	20
Johnny Bench	17	20
Total	120	120

Solution

We will use the five-step, hypothesis-testing procedure followed in previous chapters.

Step 1: State the null hypothesis and the alternate hypothesis. The null hypothesis, H_0, is that there is no difference between the set of observed frequencies and the set of expected frequencies; that is, any difference between the two sets of frequencies is attributed to sampling (chance). The alternate hypothesis, H_1, is that there is a difference between the observed and expected sets of frequencies. If H_0 is rejected and H_1 is accepted, we conclude sales are not equally distributed among the six categories (cells).

Step 2: Select the level of significance. We selected the .05 significance level. The probability is .05 that a true null hypothesis will be rejected.

Step 3: Select the test statistic. The test statistic follows the chi-square distribution, designated as χ^2:

CHI-SQUARE TEST STATISTIC
$$\chi^2 = \Sigma \left[\frac{(f_o - f_e)^2}{f_e} \right]$$
[15–1]

with $k - 1$ degrees of freedom, where:

k is the number of categories.
f_o is an observed frequency in a particular category.
f_e is an expected frequency in a particular category.

We will examine the characteristics of the chi-square distribution in more detail shortly.

Step 4: Formulate the decision rule. Recall that the decision rule in hypothesis testing requires finding a number that separates the region where we do not reject H_0 from the region of rejection. This number is called the *critical value.* As we will soon see, the chi-square distribution is really a family of distributions. Each distribution has a slightly different shape, depending on the number of degrees of freedom. The number of degrees of freedom in this type of problem is found by $k - 1$, where k is the number of categories. In this particular problem there are six. Since there are six categories, there are $k - 1 = 6 - 1 = 5$ degrees of freedom. As noted, a category is called a *cell,* so there are six cells. The critical value for 5 degrees of freedom and the .05 level of significance is found in Appendix B.3. A portion of that table is shown in Table 15–3. The critical value is 11.070, found by locating 5 degrees of freedom in the left margin and then moving horizontally (to the right) and reading the critical value in the .05 column.

TABLE 15–3 A Portion of the Chi-Square Table

Degrees of Freedom df	Right-Tail Area			
	.10	.05	.02	.01
1	2.706	3.841	5.412	6.635
2	4.605	5.991	7.824	9.210
3	6.251	7.815	9.837	11.345
4	7.779	9.488	11.668	13.277
5	9.236	11.070	13.388	15.086

The decision rule is to reject H_0 if the computed value of chi-square is greater than 11.070. If it is less than or equal to 11.070, do not reject H_0. Chart 15–1 shows the decision rule.

CHART 15–1 Chi-Square Probability Distribution for 5 Degrees of Freedom, Showing the Region of Rejection, .05 Level of Significance

The decision rule indicates that if there are large differences between the observed and expected frequencies, resulting in a computed χ^2 of more than 11.070, the null hypothesis should be rejected. However, if the differences between f_o and f_e are small, the computed χ^2 value will be 11.070 or less, and the null hypothesis should not be rejected. The reasoning is that such small differences between the observed and expected frequencies are probably due to chance. Remember, the 120 observations are a sample of the population.

Step 5: Compute the value of chi-square and make a decision. Of the 120 cards sold in the sample, we counted the number of times Tom Seaver and Nolan Ryan and each of the others were sold. The counts are reported in Table 15–1. The calculations for chi-square follow. (Note again that the expected frequencies are the same for each cell.)

Column 1:   Determine the differences between each f_o and f_e. That is, $(f_o - f_e)$. The sum of these differences is zero.

Column 2:   Square the difference between each observed and expected frequency, that is, $(f_o - f_e)^2$.

Column 3:   Divide the result for each observation by the expected frequency. That is, $\dfrac{(f_o - f_e)^2}{f_e}$. Finally, sum these values.

The result is the value of χ^2, which is 34.40.

Baseball Player	f_o	f_e	(1) $(f_o - f_e)$	(2) $(f_o - f_e)^2$	(3) $\dfrac{(f_o - f_e)^2}{f_e}$
Tom Seaver	13	20	−7	49	49/20 = 2.45
Nolan Ryan	33	20	13	169	169/20 = 8.45
Ty Cobb	14	20	−6	36	36/20 = 1.80
George Brett	7	20	−13	169	169/20 = 8.45
Hank Aaron	36	20	16	256	256/20 = 12.80
Johnny Bench	17	20	−3	9	9/20 = 0.45
			0		34.40

Must be ↗ χ^2 ↗

The computed χ^2 of 34.40 is in the rejection region beyond the critical value of 11.070. The decision, therefore, is to reject H_0 at the .05 level and to accept H_1. The difference between the observed and the expected frequencies is not due to chance. Rather, the differences between f_o and f_e are large enough to be considered significant. The chance these differences are due to sampling error is very small. So we conclude that it is unlikely that card sales are the same among the six players.

We can use software to compute the value of chi-square. The output of MegaStat follows. The steps are shown in the **Software Commands** section at the end of the chapter. The computed value of chi-square is 34.40, the same value obtained in our earlier calculations. Also note the p-value is much less than .05 (.00000198).

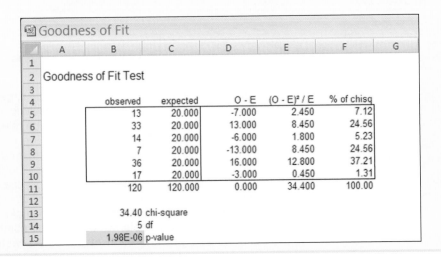

The chi-square distribution, which is used as the test statistic in this chapter, has the following characteristics.

1. **Chi-square values are never negative.** This is because the difference between f_o and f_e is squared, that is, $(f_o - f_e)^2$.
2. **There is a family of chi-square distributions.** There is a chi-square distribution for 1 degree of freedom, another for 2 degrees of freedom, another for 3 degrees of freedom, and so on. In this type of problem the number of degrees of freedom is determined by $k - 1$, where k is the number of categories. Therefore, the shape of the chi-square distribution does *not* depend on the size of the sample, but on the number of categories used. For example, if 200 employees of an airline were classified into one of three categories—flight personnel, ground support, and administrative personnel—there would be $k - 1 = 3 - 1 = 2$ degrees of freedom.
3. **The chi-square distribution is positively skewed.** However, as the number of degrees of freedom increases, the distribution begins to approximate the normal probability distribution. Chart 15–2 shows the distributions for selected degrees of freedom. Notice that for 10 degrees of freedom the curve is approaching a normal distribution.

Shape of χ^2 distribution approaches normal distribution as *df* becomes larger

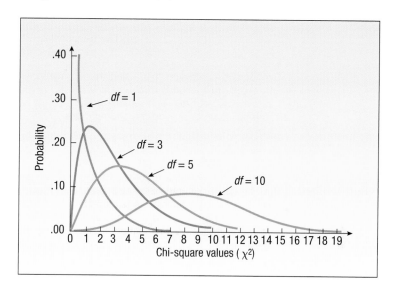

CHART 15–2 Chi-Square Distributions for Selected Degrees of Freedom

---

Self-Review 15–1

The human resources director at Georgetown Paper, Inc., is concerned about absenteeism among hourly workers. She decides to sample the company records to determine whether absenteeism is distributed evenly throughout the six-day workweek. The hypotheses are:

H_0: Absenteeism is evenly distributed throughout the workweek.
H_1: Absenteeism is *not* evenly distributed throughout the workweek.

The sample results are:

	Number Absent		Number Absent
Monday	12	Thursday	10
Tuesday	9	Friday	9
Wednesday	11	Saturday	9

(a) What are the numbers 12, 9, 11, 10, 9, and 9 called?
(b) How many categories (cells) are there?
(c) What is the *expected* frequency for each day?
(d) How many degrees of freedom are there?
(e) What is the chi-square critical value at the 1 percent significance level?
(f) Compute the χ^2 test statistic.
(g) What is the decision regarding the null hypothesis?
(h) Specifically, what does this indicate to the human resources director?

Exercises

connect

1. In a particular chi-square goodness-of-fit test there are four categories and 200 observations. Use the .05 significance level.
   a. How many degrees of freedom are there?
   b. What is the critical value of chi-square?
2. In a particular chi-square goodness-of-fit test there are six categories and 500 observations. Use the .01 significance level.
   a. How many degrees of freedom are there?
   b. What is the critical value of chi-square?
3. The null hypothesis and the alternate are:

H_0: The frequencies are equal.
H_1: The frequencies are not equal.

Category	f_o
A	10
B	20
C	30

   a. State the decision rule, using the .05 significance level.
   b. Compute the value of chi-square.
   c. What is your decision regarding H_0?
4. The null hypothesis and the alternate are:

H_0: The frequencies are equal.
H_1: The frequencies are not equal.

Category	f_o
A	10
B	20
C	30
D	20

   a. State the decision rule, using the .05 significance level.
   b. Compute the value of chi-square.
   c. What is your decision regarding H_0?
5. A six-sided die is rolled 30 times and the numbers 1 through 6 appear as shown in the following frequency distribution. At the .10 significance level, can we conclude that the die is fair?

Outcome	Frequency	Outcome	Frequency
1	3	4	3
2	6	5	9
3	2	6	7

6. Classic Golf, Inc., manages five courses in the Jacksonville, Florida, area. The director of golf wishes to study the number of rounds of golf played per weekday at the five courses. He gathered the following sample information shown to the left. At the .05 significance level, is there a difference in the number of rounds played by day of the week?

Day	Rounds
Monday	124
Tuesday	74
Wednesday	104
Thursday	98
Friday	120

7. A group of department store buyers viewed a new line of dresses and gave their opinions of them. The results were:

Opinion	Number of Buyers	Opinion	Number of Buyers
Outstanding	47	Good	39
Excellent	45	Fair	35
Very good	40	Undesirable	34

Because the largest number (47) indicated the new line is outstanding, the head designer thinks that this is a mandate to go into mass production of the dresses. The head sweeper (who somehow became involved in this) believes that there is not a clear mandate and claims that the opinions are evenly distributed among the six categories. He further states that the slight differences among the various counts are probably due to chance. Test the null hypothesis that there is no significant difference among the opinions of the buyers. Test at the .01 level of risk. Follow a formal approach; that is, state the null hypothesis, the alternate hypothesis, and so on.

8. The safety director of Honda USA took samples at random from company records of minor work-related accidents and classified them according to the time the accident took place.

Time	Number of Accidents	Time	Number of Accidents
8 up to 9 A.M.	6	1 up to 2 P.M.	7
9 up to 10 A.M.	6	2 up to 3 P.M.	8
10 up to 11 A.M.	20	3 up to 4 P.M.	19
11 up to 12 P.M.	8	4 up to 5 P.M.	6

Using the goodness-of-fit test and the .01 level of significance, determine whether the accidents are evenly distributed throughout the day. Write a brief explanation of your conclusion.

Goodness-of-Fit Test: Unequal Expected Frequencies

The expected frequencies (f_e) in the previous distribution involving baseball cards were all equal (20). According to the null hypothesis, it was expected that a card of Tom Seaver would sell 20 times at random, a card of Johnny Bench would sell 20 times out of 120 trials, and so on. The chi-square distribution can also be used if the expected frequencies are not equal.

Expected frequencies not equal in this problem

The following example illustrates the case of unequal frequencies and also gives a practical use of the chi-square goodness-of-fit test—namely, to find whether a local experience differs from the national experience.

Example

The American Hospital Administrators Association (AHAA) reports the following information concerning the number of times senior citizens are admitted to a hospital during a one-year period. Forty percent are not admitted; 30 percent are admitted once; 20 percent are admitted twice, and the remaining 10 percent are admitted three or more times.

A survey of 150 residents of Bartow Estates, a community devoted to active seniors located in central Florida, revealed 55 residents were not admitted during the last year, 50 were admitted to a hospital once, 32 were admitted twice, and the rest of those in the survey were admitted three or more times. Can we conclude the survey at Bartow Estates is consistent with the information suggested by the AHAA? Use the .05 significance level.

Solution

We begin by organizing the above information into Table 15–4. Clearly, we cannot compare percentages given in the study by the Hospital Administrators to the frequencies reported for the Bartow Estates. However, these percentages can be converted to expected frequencies, f_e. According to the Hospital Administrators, 40 percent of the Bartow residents in the survey did not require hospitalization. Thus, if there is no difference between the national experience and those of Bartow Estates, then 40 percent of the 150 seniors surveyed (60 residents) would not have been hospitalized. Further, 30 percent of those surveyed were admitted once (45 residents), and so on. The observed frequencies for Bartow residents and the expected frequencies based on the percents in the national study are given in Table 15–4.

TABLE 15–4 Summary of Study by AHAA and a Survey of Bartow Estates Residents

Number of Times Admitted	AHAA Percent of Total	Number of Bartow Residents (f_o)	Expected Number of Residents (f_e)
0	40	55	60
1	30	50	45
2	20	32	30
3 or more	10	13	15
Total	100	150	150

The null hypothesis and the alternate hypothesis are:

H_0: There is no difference between local and national experience for hospital admissions.

H_1: There is a difference between local and national experience for hospital admissions.

To find the decision rule we use Appendix B.3 and the .05 significance level. There are four admitting categories, so the degrees of freedom are $df = 4 - 1 = 3$. The critical value is 7.815. Therefore, the decision rule is to reject the null hypothesis if $\chi^2 > 7.815$. The decision rule is portrayed in Chart 15–3.

Now to compute the chi-square test statistic:

Number of Times Admitted	(f_o)	(f_e)	$f_o - f_e$	$(f_o - f_e)^2/f_e$
0	55	60	−5	0.4167
1	50	45	5	0.5556
2	32	30	2	0.1333
3 or more	13	15	−2	0.2667
Total	150	150	0	1.3723

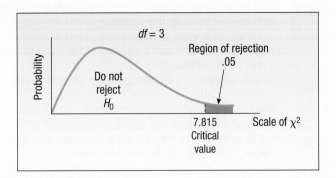

CHART 15–3 Decision Criteria for the Bartow Estates Research Study

The computed value of χ^2 (1.3723) lies to the left of 7.815. Thus, we cannot reject the null hypothesis. We conclude that there is no evidence of a difference between the local and national experience for hospital admissions.

Limitations of Chi-Square

Be careful in applying χ^2 to some problems.

If there is an unusually small expected frequency in a cell, chi-square (if applied) might result in an erroneous conclusion. This can happen because f_e appears in the denominator, and dividing by a very small number makes the quotient quite large! Two generally accepted policies regarding small cell frequencies are:

1. If there are only two cells, the *expected* frequency in each cell should be at least 5. The computation of chi-square would be permissible in the following problem, involving a minimum f_e of 6.

Individual	f_o	f_e
Literate	643	642
Illiterate	7	6

2. For more than two cells, chi-square should *not* be used if more than 20 percent of the f_e cells have expected frequencies less than 5. According to this policy, it would not be appropriate to use the goodness-of-fit test on the following data. Three of the seven cells, or 43 percent, have expected frequencies (f_e) of less than 5.

Level of Management	f_o	f_e
Foreman	30	32
Supervisor	110	113
Manager	86	87
Middle management	23	24
Assistant vice president	5	2
Vice president	5	4
Senior vice president	4	1
Total	263	263

To show the reason for the 20 percent policy, we conducted the goodness-of-fit test on the above data on the levels of management. The MegaStat output follows.

Goodness of Fit 2

	A	B	C	D	E	F	G
16							
17	Goodness of Fit Test						
18							
19		observed	expected	O - E	(O - E)² / E	% of chisq	
20		30	32.000	-2.000	0.125	0.89	
21		110	113.000	-3.000	0.080	0.57	
22		86	87.000	-1.000	0.011	0.08	
23		23	24.000	-1.000	0.042	0.30	
24		5	2.000	3.000	4.500	32.12	
25		5	4.000	1.000	0.250	1.78	
26		4	1.000	3.000	9.000	64.25	
27		263	263.000	0.000	14.008	100.00	
28							
29		14.01 chi-square					
30		6 df					
31		.0295 p-value					

For this test at the .05 significance level, H_0 is rejected if the computed value of chi-square is greater than 12.592. The computed value is 14.01, so we reject the null hypothesis that the observed frequencies represent a random sample from the population of the expected values. Examine the MegaStat output. More than 98 percent of the computed chi-square value is accounted for by the three vice president categories ([4.500 + .250 + 9.000]/14.008 = 0.9815). Logically, too much weight is being given to these categories.

The dilemma can be resolved by combining categories if it is logical to do so. In the above example we combine the three vice presidential categories, which satisfies the 20 percent policy.

Level of Management	f_o	f_e
Foreman	30	32
Supervisor	110	113
Manager	86	87
Middle management	23	24
Vice president	14	7
Total	263	263

The computed value of chi-square with the revised categories is 7.26. See the following MegaStat output. This value is less than the critical value of 9.488 for the .05 significance level. The null hypothesis is, therefore, not rejected at the .05 significance level. This indicates there is not a significant difference between the observed distribution and the expected distribution.

Goodness of Fit 3

	A	B	C	D	E	F	G
32							
33	Goodness of Fit Test						
34							
35		observed	expected	O - E	(O - E)² / E	% of chisq	
36		30	32.000	-2.000	0.125	1.72	
37		110	113.000	-3.000	0.080	1.10	
38		86	87.000	-1.000	0.011	0.16	
39		23	24.000	-1.000	0.042	0.57	
40		14	7.000	7.000	7.000	96.45	
41		263	263.000	0.000	7.258	100.00	
42							
43		7.26 chi-square					
44		4 df					
45		.1229 p-value					

Self-Review 15–2   The American Accounting Association classifies accounts receivable as "current," "late," and "not collectible." Industry figures show that 60 percent of accounts receivable are current, 30 percent are late, and 10 percent are not collectible. Massa and Barr, a law firm in Greenville, Ohio, has 500 accounts receivable: 320 are current, 120 are late, and 60 are not collectible. Are these numbers in agreement with the industry distribution? Use the .05 significance level.

Exercises

connect™

Category	f_o
A	30
B	20
C	10

9. The following hypotheses are given:

   H_0: Forty percent of the observations are in category A, 40 percent are in B, and 20 percent are in C.
   H_1: The distribution of the observations is not as described in H_0.

   We took a sample of 60, with the results to the left.
   a. State the decision rule using the .01 significance level.
   b. Compute the value of chi-square.
   c. What is your decision regarding H_0?

10. The chief of security for Mall of the Dakotas conducted a study of missing goods. He selected a sample of 100 boxes that had been tampered with and ascertained that, for 60 of the boxes, the missing pants, shoes, and so on were attributed to shoplifting. For 30 other boxes employees had stolen the goods, and for the remaining 10 boxes he blamed poor inventory control. In his report to the mall management, can he say that shoplifting is *twice* as likely to be the cause of the loss as compared with either employee theft or poor inventory control and that employee theft and poor inventory control are equally likely? Use the .02 significance level.

11. The bank credit card department of Carolina Bank knows from experience that 5 percent of its card holders have had some high school, 15 percent have completed high school, 25 percent have had some college, and 55 percent have completed college. Of the 500 card holders whose cards have been called in for failure to pay their charges this month, 50 had some high school, 100 had completed high school, 190 had some college, and 160 had completed college. Can we conclude that the distribution of card holders who do not pay their charges is different from all others? Use the .01 significance level.

12. For many years TV executives used the guideline that 30 percent of the audience were watching each of the traditional big three prime-time networks and 10 percent were watching cable stations on a weekday night. A random sample of 500 viewers in the Tampa–St. Petersburg, Florida, area last Monday night showed that 165 homes were tuned in to the ABC affiliate, 140 to the CBS affiliate, 125 to the NBC affiliate, and the remainder were viewing a cable station. At the .05 significance level, can we conclude that the guideline is still reasonable?

Contingency Table Analysis

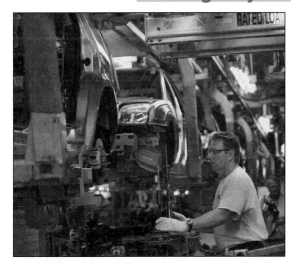

LO3 Conduct a test of hypothesis to determine whether two classification criteria are related.

In Chapter 4 we discussed bivariate data, where we studied the relationship between two variables. We described a contingency table, which simultaneously summarizes two nominal-scale variables of interest. For example, a sample of students enrolled in the School of Business is classified by gender (male or female) and major (accounting, management, finance, marketing, or quantitative methods). This classification is based on the nominal scale, because there is no natural order to the classifications.

We discussed contingency tables in Chapter 5. On page 143, we illustrated the relationship between loyalty to a company and the length of employment and explored whether older employees were likely to be more loyal to the company.

We can use the chi-square statistic to formally test for a relationship between two nominal-scaled variables. To put it another way, Is one variable *independent* of the other? Here are some examples where we are interested in testing whether two variables are related.

- Ford Motor Company operates an assembly plant in Dearborn, Michigan. The plant operates three shifts per day, 5 days a week. The quality control manager wishes to compare the quality level on the three shifts. Vehicles are classified by quality level (acceptable, unacceptable) and shift (day, afternoon, night). Is there a difference in the quality level on the three shifts? That is, is the quality of the product related to the shift when it was manufactured? Or is the quality of the product independent of the shift on which it was manufactured?

- A sample of 100 drivers who were stopped for speeding violations was classified by gender and whether or not they were wearing a seat belt. For this sample, is wearing a seatbelt related to gender?
- Does a male released from federal prison make a different adjustment to civilian life if he returns to his hometown or if he goes elsewhere to live? The two variables are adjustment to civilian life and place of residence. Note that both variables are measured on the nominal scale.

The following example illustrates the study of the relationship between two nominal-scale variables using the chi-square distribution.

Example	The Federal Correction Agency is investigating the last question cited above: Does a male released from federal prison make a different adjustment to civilian life if he returns to his hometown or if he goes elsewhere to live? To put it another way, is there a relationship between adjustment to civilian life and place of residence after release from prison? Use the .01 significance level.
Solution	As before, the first step in hypothesis testing is to state the null and alternate hypotheses.

H_0: There is no relationship between adjustment to civilian life and where the individual lives after being released from prison.

H_1: There is a relationship between adjustment to civilian life and where the individual lives after being released from prison.

The agency's psychologists interviewed 200 randomly selected former prisoners. Using a series of questions, the psychologists classified the adjustment of each individual to civilian life as outstanding, good, fair, or unsatisfactory. The classifications for the 200 former prisoners were tallied as follows. Joseph Camden, for example, returned to his hometown and has shown outstanding adjustment to civilian life. His case is one of the 27 tallies in the upper left box.

Residence after Release from Prison	Adjustment to Civilian Life			
	Outstanding	**Good**	**Fair**	**Unsatisfactory**
Hometown	*IHT IHT IHT IHT IHT II*	*IHT IHT IHT IHT IHT IHT IHT*	*IHT IHT IHT IHT IHT IHT III*	*IHT IHT IHT IHT IHT*
Not hometown	*IHT IHT III*	*IHT IHT IHT*	*IHT IHT IHT IHT IHT II*	*IHT IHT IHT IHT IHT*

The tallies in each box, or *cell,* were counted. The counts are given in the following **contingency table.** (See Table 15–5.) In this case, the Federal Correction Agency wondered whether adjustment to civilian life is *contingent on* where the prisoner goes after release from prison.

Contingency table consists of count data.

TABLE 15–5 Adjustment to Civilian Life and Place of Residence

Residence after Release from Prison	Adjustment to Civilian Life				Total
	Outstanding	Good	Fair	Unsatisfactory	
Hometown	27	35	33	25	120
Not hometown	13	15	27	25	80
Total	40	50	60	50	200

Once we know how many rows (2) and columns (4) there are in the contingency table, we can determine the critical value and the decision rule. For a chi-square test of significance where two traits are classified in a contingency table, the degrees of freedom are found by:

$$df = (\text{number of rows} - 1)(\text{number of columns} - 1) = (r - 1)(c - 1)$$

In this problem:

$$df = (r - 1)(c - 1) = (2 - 1)(4 - 1) = 3$$

To find the critical value for 3 degrees of freedom and the .01 level (selected earlier), refer to Appendix B.3. It is 11.345. The decision rule is to reject the null hypothesis if the computed value of χ^2 is greater than 11.345. The decision rule is portrayed graphically in Chart 15–4.

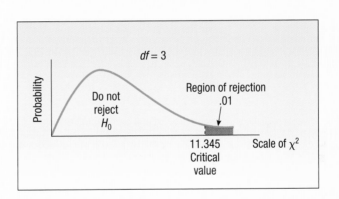

CHART 15–4 Chi-Square Distribution for 3 Degrees of Freedom

Next we find the computed value of χ^2. The observed frequencies, f_o, are shown in Table 15–5. How are the corresponding expected frequencies, f_e, determined? Note in the "Total" column of Table 15–5 that 120 of the 200 former prisoners (60 percent) returned to their hometowns. *If there were no relationship* between adjustment and residency after release from prison, we would expect 60 percent of the 40 ex-prisoners who made outstanding adjustment to civilian life to reside in their hometowns. Thus, the expected frequency f_e for the upper left cell is .60 × 40 = 24. Likewise, if there were no relationship between adjustment and present residence, we would expect 60 percent of the 50 ex-prisoners (30) who had "good" adjustment to civilian life to reside in their hometowns.

Further, notice that 80 of the 200 ex-prisoners studied (40 percent) did not return to their hometowns to live. Thus, of the 60 considered by the psychologists to have

Statistics in Action

A study of 1,000 Americans over the age of 24 showed that 28 percent never married. Of those, 22 percent completed college. Twenty-three percent of the 1,000 married and completed college. Can we conclude for the information given that being married is related to completing college? The study indicated that the two variables were related, that the computed value of the chi-square statistic was 9.368, and the *p*-value was .002. Can you duplicate these results?

made "fair" adjustment to civilian life, .40 × 60, or 24, would be expected not to return to their hometowns.

The expected frequency for any cell can be determined by

EXPECTED FREQUENCY	$f_e = \dfrac{\text{(Row total)(Column total)}}{\text{Grand total}}$	[15–2]

From this formula, the expected frequency for the upper left cell in Table 15–5 is:

$$\text{Expected frequency} = \frac{\text{(Row total)(Column total)}}{\text{Grand total}} = \frac{(120)(40)}{200} = 24$$

The observed frequencies, f_o, and the expected frequencies, f_e, for all of the cells in the contingency table are listed in Table 15–6.

TABLE 15–6 Observed and Expected Frequencies

Residence after Release from Prison	Adjustment to Civilian Life								Total	
	Outstanding		Good		Fair		Unsatisfactory		Total	
	f_o	f_e	f_o	f_e	f_o	f_e	f_o	f_e	f_o	f_e
Hometown	27	24	35	30	33	36	25	30	120	120
Not hometown	13	16	15	20	27	24	25	20	80	80
Total	40	40	50	50	60	60	50	50	200	200

Must be equal

$\dfrac{(80)(50)}{200}$

Must be equal

Recall that the computed value of chi-square using formula (15–1) is found by:

$$\chi^2 = \Sigma\left[\frac{(f_o - f_e)^2}{f_e}\right]$$

Starting with the upper left cell:

$$\chi^2 = \frac{(27 - 24)^2}{24} + \frac{(35 - 30)^2}{30} + \frac{(33 - 36)^2}{36} + \frac{(25 - 30)^2}{30}$$

$$+ \frac{(13 - 16)^2}{16} + \frac{(15 - 20)^2}{20} + \frac{(27 - 24)^2}{24} + \frac{(25 - 20)^2}{20}$$

$$= 0.375 + 0.833 + 0.250 + 0.833 + 0.563 + 1.250 + 0.375 + 1.250$$

$$= 5.729$$

Because the computed value of chi-square (5.729) lies in the region to the left of 11.345, the null hypothesis is not rejected at the .01 significance level. We conclude there is no evidence of a relationship between adjustment to civilian life and where the prisoner resides after being released from prison. For the Federal Correction Agency's advisement program, adjustment to civilian life is not related to where the ex-prisoner lives.

The following output is from the MINITAB system.

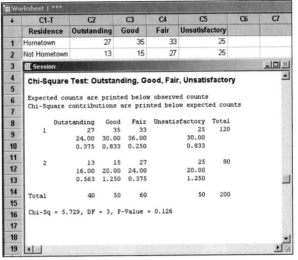

Observe that the value of chi-square is the same as that computed earlier. In addition, the *p*-value is reported, .126. So the probability of finding a value of the test statistic as large or larger is .126 when the null hypothesis is true. The *p*-value also results in the same decision, do not reject the null hypothesis.

Self-Review 15–3   A social scientist sampled 140 people and classified them according to income level and whether or not they played a state lottery in the last month. The sample information is reported below. Is it reasonable to conclude that playing the lottery is related to income level? Use the .05 significance level.

		Income		
	Low	Middle	High	Total
Played	46	28	21	95
Did not play	14	12	19	45
Total	60	40	40	140

(a) What is this table called?
(b) State the null hypothesis and the alternate hypothesis.
(c) What is the decision rule?
(d) Determine the value of chi-square.
(e) Make a decision on the null hypothesis. Interpret the result.

Exercises

connect

13. The director of advertising for the *Carolina Sun Times,* the largest newspaper in the Carolinas, is studying the relationship between the type of community in which a subscriber resides and the section of the newspaper he or she reads first. For a sample of readers, she collected the sample information at the top of the next page.

	National News	Sports	Comics
City	170	124	90
Suburb	120	112	100
Rural	130	90	88

At the .05 significance level, can we conclude there is a relationship between the type of community where the person resides and the section of the paper read first?

14. Four brands of lightbulbs are being considered for use in the final assembly area. The director of purchasing asked for samples of 100 from each manufacturer. The numbers of acceptable and unacceptable bulbs from each manufacturer are shown below. At the .05 significance level, is there a difference in the quality of the bulbs?

	Manufacturer			
	A	B	C	D
Unacceptable	12	8	5	11
Acceptable	88	92	95	89
Total	100	100	100	100

15. The quality control department at Food Town, Inc., a grocery chain in upstate New York, conducts a monthly check on the comparison of scanned prices to posted prices. The chart below summarizes the results of a sample of 500 items last month. Company management would like to know whether there is any relationship between error rates on regularly priced items and specially priced items. Use the .01 significance level.

	Regular Price	Advertised Special Price
Undercharge	20	10
Overcharge	15	30
Correct price	200	225

16. The use of cellular phones in automobiles has increased dramatically in the last few years. Of concern to traffic experts, as well as manufacturers of cellular phones, is the effect on accident rates. Is someone who is using a cellular phone more likely to be involved in a traffic accident? What is your conclusion from the following sample information? Use the .05 significance level.

	Had Accident in the Last Year	Did Not Have an Accident in the Last Year
Uses a cell phone	25	300
Does not use a cell phone	50	400

Chapter Summary

I. The characteristics of the chi-square distribution are:
  A. The value of chi-square is never negative.
  B. The chi-square distribution is positively skewed.
  C. There is a family of chi-square distributions.
    1. Each time the degrees of freedom change, a new distribution is formed.
    2. As the degrees of freedom increase, the distribution approaches a normal distribution.

II. A goodness-of-fit test will show whether an observed set of frequencies could have come from a hypothesized population distribution.

  A. The degrees of freedom are $k - 1$, where k is the number of categories.

  B. The formula for computing the value of chi-square is

$$\chi^2 = \Sigma \left[\frac{(f_o - f_e)^2}{f_e} \right]$$ **[15–1]**

III. A contingency table is used to test whether two traits or characteristics are related.

  A. Each observation is classified according to two traits.

  B. The expected frequency is determined as follows:

$$f_e = \frac{(\text{Row total})(\text{Column total})}{\text{Grand total}}$$ **[15–2]**

  C. The degrees of freedom are found by:

$$df = (\text{Rows} - 1)(\text{Columns} - 1)$$

  D. The usual hypothesis testing procedure is used.

Pronunciation Key

SYMBOL	MEANING	PRONUNCIATION
χ^2	Probability distribution	*ki square*
f_o	Observed frequency	*f sub oh*
f_e	Expected frequency	*f sub e*

Chapter Exercises

17. Vehicles heading west on Front Street may turn right, left, or go straight ahead at Elm Street. The city traffic engineer believes that half of the vehicles will continue straight through the intersection. Of the remaining half, equal proportions will turn right and left. Two hundred vehicles were observed, with the following results. Can we conclude that the traffic engineer is correct? Use the .10 significance level.

	Straight	**Right Turn**	**Left Turn**
Frequency	112	48	40

18. The publisher of a sports magazine plans to offer new subscribers one of three gifts: a sweatshirt with the logo of their favorite team, a coffee cup with the logo of their favorite team, or a pair of earrings also with the logo of their favorite team. In a sample of 500 new subscribers, the number selecting each gift is reported below. At the .05 significance level, is there a preference for the gifts or should we conclude that the gifts are equally well liked?

Gift	Frequency
Sweatshirt	183
Coffee cup	175
Earrings	142

19. In a particular market there are three commercial television stations, each with its own evening news program from 6:00 to 6:30 P.M. According to a report in this morning's local newspaper, a random sample of 150 viewers last night revealed 53 watched the news on WNAE (channel 5), 64 watched on WRRN (channel 11), and 33 on WSPD (channel 13). At the .05 significance level, is there a difference in the proportion of viewers watching the three channels?

20. There are four entrances to the Government Center Building in downtown Philadelphia. The building maintenance supervisor would like to know if the entrances are equally utilized. To investigate, 400 people were observed entering the building. The number using each entrance is reported below. At the .01 significance level, is there a difference in the use of the four entrances?

Entrance	Frequency
Main Street	140
Broad Street	120
Cherry Street	90
Walnut Street	50
Total	400

21. The owner of a mail-order catalog would like to compare her sales with the geographic distribution of the population. According to the United States Bureau of the Census, 21 percent of the population lives in the Northeast, 24 percent in the Midwest, 35 percent in the South, and 20 percent in the West. Listed below is a breakdown of a sample of 400 orders randomly selected from those shipped last month. At the .01 significance level, does the distribution of the orders reflect the population?

Region	Frequency
Northeast	68
Midwest	104
South	155
West	73
Total	400

22. Banner Mattress and Furniture Company wishes to study the number of credit applications received per day for the last 300 days. The sample information is reported below.

Number of Credit Applications	Frequency (Number of Days)
0	50
1	77
2	81
3	48
4	31
5 or more	13

To interpret, there were 50 days on which no credit applications were received, 77 days on which only one application was received, and so on. Would it be reasonable to conclude that the population distribution is Poisson with a mean of 2.0? Use the .05 significance level. *Hint:* To find the expected frequencies use the Poisson distribution with a mean of 2.0. Find the probability of exactly one success given a Poisson distribution with a mean of 2.0. Multiply this probability by 300 to find the expected frequency for the number of days in which there was exactly one application. Determine the expected frequency for the other days in a similar manner.

23. Each of the digits in a raffle is thought to have the same chance of occurrence. The table shows the frequency of each digit for consecutive drawings in a California lottery. Perform the chi-square test to see if you reject the hypothesis at the .05 significance level that the digits are from a uniform population.

Digit	Frequency	Digit	Frequency
0	44	5	24
1	32	6	31
2	23	7	27
3	27	8	28
4	23	9	21

24. John Isaac, Inc., a designer and installer of industrial signs, employs 60 people. The company recorded the type of the most recent visit to a doctor by each employee. A national assessment conducted in 2008 found that 53 percent of all physician visits were to primary care physicians, 19 percent to medical specialists, 17 percent to surgical specialists and 11 percent to emergency departments. Test at the 0.01 significance level if Isaac employees differ significantly from the survey distribution. Here are their results:

Visit Type	Number of Visits
Primary care	29
Medical specialist	11
Surgical specialist	16
Emergency	4

25. A survey by *USA Today* investigated the public's attitude toward the federal deficit. Each sampled citizen was classified as to whether they felt the government should reduce the deficit, increase the deficit, or if they had no opinion. The sample results of the study by gender are reported below.

Gender	Reduce the Deficit	Increase the Deficit	No Opinion
Female	244	194	68
Male	305	114	25

At the .05 significance level, is it reasonable to conclude that gender is independent of a person's position on the deficit?

26. A study regarding the relationship between age and the amount of pressure sales personnel feel in relation to their jobs revealed the following sample information. At the .01 significance level, is there a relationship between job pressure and age?

Age (years)	Degree of Job Pressure		
	Low	Medium	High
Less than 25	20	18	22
25 up to 40	50	46	44
40 up to 60	58	63	59
60 and older	34	43	43

27. The claims department at Wise Insurance Company believes that younger drivers have more accidents and, therefore, should be charged higher insurance rates. Investigating a sample of 1,200 Wise policyholders revealed the following breakdown on whether a claim had been filed in the last three years and the age of the policyholder. Is it reasonable to conclude that there is a relationship between the age of the policyholder and whether or not the person filed a claim? Use the .05 significance level.

Age Group	No Claim	Claim
16 up to 25	170	74
25 up to 40	240	58
40 up to 55	400	44
55 or older	190	24
Total	1,000	200

28. A sample of employees at a large chemical plant was asked to indicate a preference for one of three pension plans. The results are given in the following table. Does it seem that there is a relationship between the pension plan selected and the job classification of the employees? Use the .01 significance level.

| | Pension Plan | | |
Job Class	Plan A	Plan B	Plan C
Supervisor	10	13	29
Clerical	19	80	19
Labor	81	57	22

29. Did you ever purchase a bag of M&M's candies and wonder about the distribution of colors? You can go to the website www.baking.m-ms.com and click the United States on the map, then click **About M&M's,** then **Products** and **Peanut** and find the percentage breakdown according to the manufacturer, as well as a brief history of the product. Did you know in the beginning they were all brown? For peanut M&M's 12 percent are brown, 15 percent yellow, 12 percent red, 23 percent blue, 23 percent orange, and 15 percent green. A 6-oz. bag purchased at the Book Store at Coastal Carolina University on November 1, 2008, had 12 blue, 14 brown, 13 yellow, 14 red, 7 orange, and 12 green. Is it reasonable to conclude that the actual distribution agrees with the expected distribution? Use the .05 significance level. Conduct your own trial. Be sure to share with your instructor.

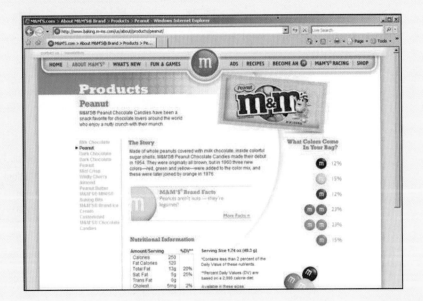

Data Set Exercises

30. Refer to the Real Estate data, which report information on homes sold in the Phoenix, Arizona, area last year.
    a. Develop a contingency table that shows whether a home has a pool and the township in which the house is located. Is there an association between the variables pool and township? Use the .05 significance level.
    b. Develop a contingency table that shows whether a home has an attached garage and the township in which the home is located. Is there an association between the variables attached garage and township? Use the .05 significance level.
31. Refer to the Baseball 2008 data, which report information on the 30 Major League Baseball teams for the 2008 season. Set up a variable that divides the teams into two groups, those that had a winning season and those that did not. There are 162 games in the

season, so define a winning season as having won 81 or more games. Next, divide the teams into two salary groups. Let the 15 teams with the largest salaries be in one group and the 15 teams with the smallest salaries in the other. At the .05 significance level is there a relationship between salaries and winning?

32. Refer to the Wage data, which report information on annual wages for a sample of 100 workers. Also included are variables relating to industry, years of education, and gender for each worker. Develop a table showing the industry of employment by gender. At the .05 significance level is it reasonable to conclude that industry of employment and gender are related?

Practice Test

Part I Objective

1. The _____ level of measurement is required for the chi-square goodness-of-fit test.
2. To use the chi-square distribution as the test statistic, we assume the population _____. (follows the normal distribution, meets the binomial conditions, or no assumption is necessary about the population shape)
3. Which of the following is *not* a characteristic of the chi-square distribution? (positively skewed, based on degrees of freedom, cannot be negative, at least 30 observations)
4. In a contingency table, _____ identifiable characteristics are considered for each variable? (two, fifty, only ratio)
5. In a contingency table, there are 4 columns and 3 rows; hence, there are _____ degrees of freedom.
6. In a contingency table, we test the null hypothesis that the two variables are _____. (independent, dependent, mutually exclusive, normally distributed)
7. A sample of 100 undergraduate business students is classified by major (five groups); hence, there are _____ degrees of freedom.
8. The sum of the observed and expected frequencies _____. (are the same, must be more than 30, can assume negative values, must be at least 5 percent.)
9. In a goodness-of-fit test with 200 observations and 4 degrees of freedom, the critical value of chi-square is _____ assuming the .05 significance level.
10. The shape of the chi-square distribution is based on _____. (shape of the population, degrees of freedom, level of significance, level of measurement)

Part II Problems

1. A recent census report indicated 65 percent of families have two parents, 20 percent have a mother only present, 10 percent have a father only present, and 5 percent have no parent present. A random sample of 200 children from a rural school district revealed the following:

Two Parents	Mother Only	Father Only	No Parent	Total
120	40	30	10	200

Is there sufficient evidence to conclude that the proportion of families by type of parent present in the particular rural school district differs from that reported in the recent census? Use the .05 significance level.

2. A book publisher wants to investigate the type of books selected for recreational reading by adult men and women. A random sample provided the following information. At the .05 significance level, should we conclude that gender is related or unrelated to the type of book selected?

Gender	Mystery	Romance	Self-Help	Total
Men	250	100	190	540
Women	130	170	200	500

Software Commands

1. The MegaStat commands to create the chi-square goodness-of-fit test on page 484 are:
   a. Enter the information from Table 15–2 into a worksheet as shown.
   b. Select **MegaStat, Chi-Square/Crosstabs,** and **Goodness of Fit Test** and hit **Enter.**
   c. In the dialog box select *B2:B7* as the **Observed values,** *C2:C7* as the **Expected values,** and enter *0* as the **Number of parameters estimated from the data.** Click on **OK.**

2. The MegaStat commands to create the chi-square goodness-of-fit tests on pages 489 and 490 are the same except for the number of items in the observed and expected frequency columns. Only one dialog box is shown.
   a. Enter the Levels of Management information shown on page 489.
   b. Select **MegaStat, Chi-Square/Crosstabs,** and **Goodness of Fit Test** and hit **Enter.**
   c. In the dialog box select *B2:B8* as the **Observed values,** *C2:C8* as the **Expected values,** and enter *0* as the **Number of parameters estimated from the data.** Click on **OK.**

3. The MINITAB commands for the chi-square analysis on page 495 are:
   a. Enter the names of the variables in the first row and the data in the next two rows.
   b. Select **Stat, Table,** and then click on **Chi-Square Test** and hit **Enter.**
   c. In the dialog box select the columns labeled *Outstanding* to *Unsatisfactory* and click **OK.**

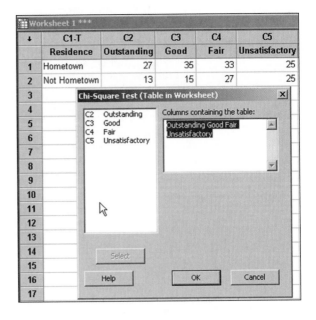

Chapter 15 Answers to Self-Review

15–1 a. Observed frequencies.
    b. Six (six days of the week).
    c. 10. Total observed frequencies $\div$ 6 = 60/6 = 10.
    d. 5; $k - 1 = 6 - 1 = 5$.
    e. 15.086 (from the chi-square table in Appendix B.3).
    f.

$$\chi^2 = \Sigma\left[\frac{(f_o - f_e)^2}{f_e}\right] = \frac{(12 - 10)^2}{10} + \cdots + \frac{(9 - 10)^2}{10} = 0.8$$

    g. Do not reject H_0.
    h. Absenteeism is distributed evenly throughout the week. The observed differences are due to sampling variation.

15–2 H_0: $P_C = .60$, $P_L = .30$, and $P_U = .10$.
H_1: Distribution is not as above.
Reject H_0 if $\chi^2 > 5.991$.

Category	f_o	f_e	$\dfrac{(f_o - f_e)^2}{f_e}$
Current	320	300	1.33
Late	120	150	6.00
Uncollectible	60	50	2.00
	500	500	9.33

Reject H_0. The accounts receivable data does not reflect the national average.

15–3 a. Contingency table
    b. H_0: There is no relationship between income and whether the person played the lottery.
    H_1: There is a relationship between income and whether the person played the lottery.
    c. Reject H_0 if χ^2 is greater than 5.991.
    d.

$$\chi^2 = \frac{(46 - 40.71)^2}{40.71} + \frac{(28 - 27.14)^2}{27.14} + \frac{(21 - 27.14)^2}{27.14}$$
$$+ \frac{(14 - 19.29)^2}{19.29} + \frac{(12 - 12.86)^2}{12.86} + \frac{(19 - 12.86)^2}{12.86}$$
$$= 6.544$$

    e. Reject H_0. There is a relationship between income level and playing the lottery.

Appendixes

Appendix A: Data Sets

A.1 Data Set 1—Real Estate

Variables

x_1 = Selling price in $000
x_2 = Number of bedrooms
x_3 = Size of the home in square feet
x_4 = Pool (1 = yes, 0 = no)
x_5 = Distance from the center of the city in miles
x_6 = Township
x_7 = Garage attached (1 = yes, 0 = no)
x_8 = Number of bathrooms
105 homes sold

Price, x_1	Bedrooms, x_2	Size, x_3	Pool, x_4	Distance, x_5	Township, x_6	Garage, x_7	Baths, x_8
263.1	4	2,300	0	17	5	1	2.0
182.4	4	2,100	1	19	4	0	2.0
242.1	3	2,300	1	12	3	0	2.0
213.6	2	2,200	1	16	2	0	2.5
139.9	2	2,100	1	28	1	0	1.5
245.4	2	2,100	0	12	1	1	2.0
327.2	6	2,500	1	15	3	1	2.0
271.8	2	2,100	1	9	2	1	2.5
221.1	3	2,300	0	18	1	0	1.5
266.6	4	2,400	1	13	4	1	2.0
292.4	4	2,100	1	14	3	1	2.0
209.0	2	1,700	1	8	4	1	1.5
270.8	6	2,500	1	7	4	1	2.0
246.1	4	2,100	1	18	3	1	2.0
194.4	2	2,300	1	11	3	0	2.0
281.3	3	2,100	1	16	2	1	2.0
172.7	4	2,200	0	16	3	0	2.0
207.5	5	2,300	0	21	4	0	2.5
198.9	3	2,200	0	10	4	1	2.0
209.3	6	1,900	0	15	4	1	2.0
252.3	4	2,600	1	8	4	1	2.0
192.9	4	1,900	0	14	2	1	2.5
209.3	5	2,100	1	20	5	0	1.5
345.3	8	2,600	1	9	4	1	2.0
326.3	6	2,100	1	11	5	1	3.0
173.1	2	2,200	0	21	5	1	1.5
187.0	2	1,900	1	26	4	0	2.0
257.2	2	2,100	1	9	4	1	2.0
233.0	3	2,200	1	14	3	1	1.5
180.4	2	2,000	1	11	5	0	2.0

(*continued*)

Appendix A

A.1 Data Set 1—Real Estate (*continued*)

Price, x_1	Bedrooms, x_2	Size, x_3	Pool, x_4	Distance, x_5	Township, x_6	Garage, x_7	Baths, x_8
234.0	2	1,700	1	19	3	1	2.0
207.1	2	2,000	1	11	5	1	2.0
247.7	5	2,400	1	16	2	1	2.0
166.2	3	2,000	0	16	2	1	2.0
177.1	2	1,900	1	10	5	1	2.0
182.7	4	2,000	0	14	4	0	2.5
216.0	4	2,300	1	19	2	0	2.0
312.1	6	2,600	1	7	5	1	2.5
199.8	3	2,100	1	19	3	1	2.0
273.2	5	2,200	1	16	2	1	3.0
206.0	3	2,100	0	9	3	0	1.5
232.2	3	1,900	0	16	1	1	1.5
198.3	4	2,100	0	19	1	1	1.5
205.1	3	2,000	0	20	4	0	2.0
175.6	4	2,300	0	24	4	1	2.0
307.8	3	2,400	0	21	2	1	3.0
269.2	5	2,200	1	8	5	1	3.0
224.8	3	2,200	1	17	1	1	2.5
171.6	3	2,000	0	16	4	0	2.0
216.8	3	2,200	1	15	1	1	2.0
192.6	6	2,200	0	14	1	0	2.0
236.4	5	2,200	1	20	3	1	2.0
172.4	3	2,200	1	23	3	0	2.0
251.4	3	1,900	1	12	2	1	2.0
246.0	6	2,300	1	7	3	1	3.0
147.4	6	1,700	0	12	1	0	2.0
176.0	4	2,200	1	15	1	1	2.0
228.4	3	2,300	1	17	5	1	1.5
166.5	3	1,600	0	19	3	0	2.5
189.4	4	2,200	1	24	1	1	2.0
312.1	7	2,400	1	13	3	1	3.0
289.8	6	2,000	1	21	3	1	3.0
269.9	5	2,200	0	11	4	1	2.5
154.3	2	2,000	1	13	2	0	2.0
222.1	2	2,100	1	9	5	1	2.0
209.7	5	2,200	0	13	2	1	2.0
190.9	3	2,200	0	18	3	1	2.0
254.3	4	2,500	0	15	3	1	2.0
207.5	3	2,100	0	10	2	0	2.0
209.7	4	2,200	0	19	2	1	2.0
294.0	2	2,100	1	13	2	1	2.5
176.3	2	2,000	0	17	3	0	2.0
294.3	7	2,400	1	8	4	1	2.0
224.0	3	1,900	0	6	1	1	2.0
125.0	2	1,900	1	18	4	0	1.5

Appendix A

A.1 Data Set 1—Real Estate (*concluded*)

Price, x_1	Bedrooms, x_2	Size, x_3	Pool, x_4	Distance, x_5	Township, x_6	Garage, x_7	Baths, x_8
236.8	4	2,600	0	17	5	1	2.0
164.1	4	2,300	1	19	4	0	2.0
217.8	3	2,500	1	12	3	0	2.0
192.2	2	2,400	1	16	2	0	2.5
125.9	2	2,400	1	28	1	0	1.5
220.9	2	2,300	0	12	1	1	2.0
294.5	6	2,700	1	15	3	1	2.0
244.6	2	2,300	1	9	2	1	2.5
199.0	3	2,500	0	18	1	0	1.5
240.0	4	2,600	1	13	4	1	2.0
263.2	4	2,300	1	14	3	1	2.0
188.1	2	1,900	1	8	4	1	1.5
243.7	6	2,700	1	7	4	1	2.0
221.5	4	2,300	1	18	3	1	2.0
175.0	2	2,500	1	11	3	0	2.0
253.2	3	2,300	1	16	2	1	2.0
155.4	4	2,400	0	16	3	0	2.0
186.7	5	2,500	0	21	4	0	2.5
179.0	3	2,400	0	10	4	1	2.0
188.3	6	2,100	0	15	4	1	2.0
227.1	4	2,900	1	8	4	1	2.0
173.6	4	2,100	0	14	2	1	2.5
188.3	5	2,300	1	20	5	0	1.5
310.8	8	2,900	1	9	4	1	2.0
293.7	6	2,400	1	11	5	1	3.0
179.0	3	2,400	1	8	4	1	2.0
188.3	6	2,100	0	14	2	1	2.5
227.1	4	2,900	1	20	5	0	1.5
173.6	4	2,100	1	9	4	1	2.0
188.3	5	2,300	1	11	5	1	3.0

Appendix A

A.2 Data Set 2—Major League Baseball (2008)

Variables
x_1 = Team
x_2 = League (American = 1, National = 0)
x_3 = Built (year stadium was built)
x_4 = Size (stadium capacity)
x_5 = Surface (natural = 0, artificial = 1)
x_6 = Salary (total 2008 team salary $ Mil)
x_7 = Wins
x_8 = Attendance (total for team in Mil)
x_9 = Batting
x_{10} = ERA (earned run average)
x_{11} = HR (home runs)
x_{12} = Errors
x_{13} = SB (stolen bases)
x_{14} = Year
x_{15} = Average player salary ($)

Team, x_1	League, x_2	Built, x_3	Size, x_4	Surface, x_5	Total Salary, x_6	Wins, x_7	Attendance, x_8	Batting, x_9	ERA, x_{10}	HR, x_{11}	Errors, x_{12}	SB, x_{13}	Year, x_{14}	Average Salary, x_{15}
Arizona Diamondbacks	0	1998	49,033	0	66.2	82	2.51	0.251	3.98	159	113	58	1989	$ 512,930
Atlanta Braves	0	1996	50,091	0	102.4	72	2.53	0.270	4.46	130	107	58	1990	578,930
Baltimore Orioles	1	1992	48,876	0	67.2	68	1.95	0.267	5.13	172	100	81	1991	891,188
Boston Red Sox	1	1912	39,928	0	133.4	95	3.05	0.280	4.01	173	85	120	1992	1,084,408
Chicago Cubs	0	1914	41,118	0	118.6	89	3.30	0.278	3.87	184	99	87	1993	1,120,254
Chicago White Sox	1	1991	40,615	0	121.2	97	2.50	0.263	4.06	235	108	67	1994	1,188,679
Cincinnati Reds	0	2003	42,059	0	74.3	74	2.06	0.247	4.55	187	114	85	1995	1,071,029
Cleveland Indians	1	1994	43,345	0	79.0	81	2.17	0.262	4.45	171	94	77	1996	1,176,967
Colorado Rockies	0	1995	50,445	0	68.7	74	2.65	0.263	4.77	160	96	141	1997	1,383,578
Detroit Tigers	1	2000	41,782	0	138.7	74	3.20	0.271	4.90	200	113	63	1998	1,441,406
Florida Marlins	0	1987	36,331	0	21.8	84	1.34	0.254	4.43	208	117	76	1999	1,720,050
Houston Astros	0	2000	40,950	0	88.9	86	2.78	0.263	4.36	167	67	114	2000	1,988,034
Kansas City Royals	1	1973	40,793	0	58.2	75	1.58	0.269	4.48	120	96	79	2001	2,264,403
Los Angeles Angels	1	1966	45,050	0	119.2	100	3.34	0.268	3.99	159	91	129	2002	2,383,235
Los Angeles Dodgers	0	1962	56,000	0	118.5	84	3.73	0.264	3.68	137	101	126	2003	2,555,476
Milwaukee Brewers	0	2001	42,200	0	81.0	90	3.07	0.253	3.85	198	101	108	2004	2,486,609
Minnesota Twins	1	1982	46,564	1	62.2	88	2.30	0.279	4.16	111	108	102	2005	2,632,655
New York Mets	0	2009	45,000	0	138.3	89	4.04	0.266	4.07	172	83	138	2006	2,866,544
New York Yankees	1	2009	52,325	0	209.1	89	4.30	0.271	4.28	180	83	118	2007	2,944,556
Oakland Athletics	1	1966	34,077	0	48.0	75	1.67	0.242	4.01	125	98	88	2008	3,154,845
Philadelphia Phillies	0	2004	43,647	0	98.3	92	3.42	0.255	3.88	214	90	136		
Pittsburgh Pirates	0	2001	38,496	0	49.4	67	1.61	0.258	5.08	153	107	57		
San Diego Padres	0	2004	42,445	0	73.7	63	2.43	0.250	4.41	154	85	36		
San Francisco Giants	0	2000	41,503	0	76.9	72	2.86	0.262	4.38	94	96	108		
Seattle Mariners	1	1999	47,116	0	118.0	61	2.33	0.265	4.73	124	99	90		
St. Louis Cardinals	0	2006	49,660	0	100.6	86	3.43	0.281	4.19	174	85	73		
Tampa Bay Rays	1	1990	36,048	1	43.8	97	1.78	0.260	3.82	180	90	142		
Texas Rangers	1	1994	49,115	0	68.2	79	1.95	0.283	5.37	194	132	81		
Toronto Blue Jays	1	1989	50,516	1	98.6	86	2.40	0.264	3.49	126	84	80		
Washington Nationals	0	2008	41,888	0	55.0	59	2.32	0.251	4.66	117	123	81		

Appendix A

A.3 Data Set 3—Wages and Wage Earners

Variables

x_1 = Annual wage in dollars
x_2 = Industry (1 = manufacturing, 2 = construction, 0 = other)
x_3 = Occupation (1 = management, 2 = sales, 3 = clerical, 4 = service, 5 = professional, 0 = other)
x_4 = Years of education
x_5 = Southern resident (1 = yes, 0 = no)
x_6 = Nonwhite (1 = yes, 0 = no)
x_7 = Hispanic (1 = yes, 0 = no)
x_8 = Female (1 = yes, 0 = no)
x_9 = Years of work experience
x_{10} = Married (1 = yes, 0 = no)
x_{11} = Age in years
x_{12} = Union member (1 = yes, 0 = no)
100 observations

Row	Wage, x_1	Industry, x_2	Occupation, x_3	Education, x_4	South, x_5	Nonwhite, x_6	Hispanic, x_7	Female, x_8	Experience, x_9	Married, x_{10}	Age, x_{11}	Union, x_{12}
1	19,388	1	0	6	1	0	0	0	45	1	57	0
2	49,898	2	0	12	0	0	0	0	33	1	51	1
3	28,219	0	3	12	1	0	0	0	12	1	30	0
4	83,601	0	5	17	0	0	1	0	18	1	41	0
5	29,736	0	4	8	0	0	1	0	47	1	61	1
6	50,235	1	0	16	0	0	0	0	12	1	34	0
7	45,976	0	2	12	0	0	0	0	43	1	61	1
8	33,411	1	2	12	1	0	0	0	20	1	38	0
9	21,716	0	5	12	0	0	0	1	11	0	29	0
10	37,664	0	5	18	0	0	0	0	19	1	43	0
11	26,820	0	5	18	0	0	0	0	33	0	57	1
12	29,977	0	4	16	0	1	0	1	6	1	28	0
13	33,959	0	5	17	0	0	0	1	26	1	49	1
14	11,780	0	2	11	0	0	0	1	33	1	50	0
15	10,997	0	4	14	0	1	0	0	0	0	20	0
16	17,626	0	3	12	0	0	0	1	45	1	63	0
17	22,133	0	5	16	0	0	0	1	10	0	32	1
18	21,994	0	1	12	0	0	0	1	24	1	42	0
19	29,390	0	0	13	0	0	0	0	18	1	37	0
20	32,138	0	4	14	0	0	0	0	22	1	42	1
21	30,006	1	3	16	0	0	0	1	27	1	49	0
22	68,573	0	5	16	1	0	0	0	14	1	36	1
23	17,694	0	4	8	0	0	0	1	38	1	52	0
24	26,795	0	0	7	1	0	0	0	44	1	57	0
25	19,981	0	4	4	0	0	0	0	54	1	64	0
26	14,476	0	5	12	0	0	0	1	3	1	21	0
27	19,452	0	4	13	0	1	0	0	3	0	22	0
28	28,168	1	0	13	0	0	0	0	17	0	36	0
29	19,306	0	5	9	1	1	0	1	34	1	49	1
30	13,318	1	0	11	1	0	0	1	25	1	42	1

510

A.3 Data Set 3—Wages and Wage Earners (*continued*)

Row	Wage, x_1	Industry, x_2	Occupation, x_3	Education, x_4	South, x_5	Nonwhite, x_6	Hispanic, x_7	Female, x_8	Experience, x_9	Married, x_{10}	Age, x_{11}	Union, x_{12}
31	25,166	0	4	12	0	0	0	1	10	0	28	0
32	18,121	1	3	12	0	0	0	1	18	1	36	0
33	13,162	1	0	12	0	1	0	0	6	0	24	1
34	32,094	0	3	12	1	0	0	1	14	1	32	0
35	16,667	0	3	12	1	0	0	0	4	0	22	0
36	50,171	0	5	12	0	0	0	0	39	1	57	1
37	31,691	1	0	12	0	0	0	0	13	0	31	0
38	36,178	0	3	12	0	0	0	1	40	1	58	0
39	15,234	0	1	12	1	0	1	1	4	0	22	0
40	16,817	0	3	12	1	0	0	1	26	0	44	0
41	22,485	0	3	12	0	0	0	0	22	0	40	0
42	30,308	0	4	12	0	0	0	0	10	1	28	0
43	11,702	0	2	14	1	0	0	1	6	1	26	0
44	11,186	0	0	12	0	0	0	0	0	0	18	0
45	12,285	0	1	12	0	0	0	1	42	1	60	0
46	19,284	1	4	16	0	0	0	0	3	0	25	0
47	11,451	1	0	12	0	0	0	1	8	1	26	0
48	57,623	0	1	15	0	0	0	0	31	1	52	0
49	25,670	0	3	13	0	0	0	1	8	0	27	1
50	83,443	0	5	17	0	0	0	1	5	0	28	0
51	49,974	1	1	16	0	1	0	0	26	1	48	1
52	46,646	2	0	5	1	0	0	0	44	1	55	0
53	31,702	0	3	12	1	0	0	1	39	1	57	0
54	13,312	0	4	12	1	0	0	1	9	1	27	0
55	44,543	0	2	18	0	0	0	0	10	1	34	0
56	15,013	0	4	16	0	0	0	0	21	1	43	0
57	33,389	0	1	14	0	1	0	0	22	0	42	0
58	60,626	0	5	18	0	0	0	0	7	1	31	0
59	24,509	0	5	14	0	0	1	1	15	0	35	0
60	20,852	1	0	12	0	0	0	1	38	1	56	0
61	30,133	2	0	10	0	0	0	0	27	1	43	0
62	31,799	0	3	12	0	0	0	1	25	0	43	0
63	16,796	0	4	12	0	0	0	1	14	1	32	0
64	20,793	0	0	12	1	0	0	1	6	0	24	0
65	29,407	0	4	10	1	0	0	0	19	0	35	0
66	29,191	0	0	12	0	0	0	0	9	0	27	0
67	15,957	0	2	12	1	0	0	1	10	0	28	0
68	34,484	0	3	13	1	0	0	1	28	0	47	0
69	35,185	1	3	14	0	0	0	1	12	1	32	0
70	26,614	1	0	12	0	0	0	1	19	1	37	0
71	41,780	0	0	12	1	0	0	0	9	1	27	0
72	55,777	0	1	14	1	0	0	0	21	1	41	0
73	15,160	0	4	8	1	0	0	1	45	0	59	0
74	66,738	0	0	9	1	0	0	0	29	1	44	0
75	33,351	0	5	16	1	0	0	1	4	1	26	0

(*continued*)

Appendix A

A.3 Data Set 3—Wages and Wage Earners (*concluded*)

Row	Wage, x_1	Industry, x_2	Occupation, x_3	Education, x_4	South, x_5	Nonwhite, x_6	Hispanic, x_7	Female, x_8	Experience, x_9	Married, x_{10}	Age, x_{11}	Union, x_{12}
76	33,498	0	1	10	0	0	0	0	20	1	36	0
77	29,809	0	4	8	0	1	0	1	29	0	43	0
78	15,193	1	0	12	0	0	0	1	15	0	33	0
79	23,027	0	4	14	0	1	0	0	34	1	54	1
80	75,165	0	1	15	0	0	0	0	12	1	33	0
81	18,752	0	4	11	0	0	0	1	45	0	62	1
82	83,569	0	1	18	0	0	0	0	29	1	53	0
83	32,235	0	3	12	0	0	0	1	38	1	56	0
84	20,852	0	0	12	1	0	0	0	1	0	19	0
85	13,787	0	4	11	0	0	0	0	4	1	21	0
86	34,746	0	3	14	1	0	0	1	15	1	35	0
87	17,690	0	1	12	1	1	0	0	14	1	32	0
88	52,762	0	5	18	0	0	0	0	7	1	31	0
89	60,152	0	5	16	1	0	0	0	38	1	60	0
90	33,461	0	1	16	0	0	1	0	7	1	29	1
91	13,481	0	4	12	1	0	1	0	7	0	25	0
92	9,879	0	3	12	1	0	0	1	28	1	46	0
93	16,789	0	3	13	1	0	0	1	6	1	25	0
94	31,304	0	1	16	0	0	0	1	26	1	48	0
95	37,771	0	5	15	0	0	0	0	5	0	26	0
96	50,187	0	3	12	0	0	0	1	24	1	42	0
97	39,888	0	3	12	1	0	0	0	5	0	23	0
98	19,227	0	3	12	0	0	0	1	15	1	33	0
99	32,786	1	0	11	1	0	0	0	37	1	54	1
100	28,440	0	4	12	0	0	0	1	24	1	42	0

Appendix A

A.4 Data Set 4—Whitner Autoplex

x_1 = Selling price in $
x_2 = Selling price in $000
x_3 = Age of buyer
x_4 = Domestic (0), Imported (1)
80 observations (Autos Sold)

Price, x_1	Price ($000), x_2	Age, x_3	Type, x_4	Price, x_1	Price ($000), x_2	Age, x_3	Type, x_4
23,197	23.197	46	0	20,642	20.642	39	1
23,372	23.372	48	0	21,981	21.981	43	1
20,454	20.454	40	1	24,052	24.052	56	0
23,591	23.591	40	0	25,799	25.799	44	0
26,651	26.651	46	1	15,794	15.794	30	1
27,453	27.453	37	1	18,263	18.263	39	1
17,266	17.266	32	1	35,925	35.925	53	0
18,021	18.021	29	1	17,399	17.399	29	1
28,683	28.683	38	1	17,968	17.968	30	1
30,872	30.872	43	0	20,356	20.356	44	0
19,587	19.587	32	0	21,442	21.442	41	1
23,169	23.169	47	0	21,722	21.722	41	0
35,851	35.851	56	0	19,331	19.331	35	1
19,251	19.251	42	1	22,817	22.817	51	1
20,047	20.047	28	1	19,766	19.766	44	1
24,285	24.285	56	0	20,633	20.633	51	1
24,324	24.324	50	1	20,962	20.962	49	1
24,609	24.609	31	1	22,845	22.845	41	1
28,670	28.670	51	1	26,285	26.285	44	0
15,546	15.546	26	1	27,896	27.896	37	0
15,935	15.935	25	1	29,076	29.076	42	1
19,873	19.873	45	1	32,492	32.492	51	0
25,251	25.251	56	1	18,890	18.890	31	1
25,277	25.277	47	0	21,740	21.740	39	0
28,034	28.034	38	1	22,374	22.374	53	0
24,533	24.533	51	0	24,571	24.571	55	1
27,443	27.443	39	0	25,449	25.449	40	0
19,889	19.889	44	1	28,337	28.337	46	0
20,004	20.004	46	1	20,642	20.642	35	1
17,357	17.357	28	1	23,613	23.613	47	1
20,155	20.155	33	1	24,220	24.220	58	1
19,688	19.688	35	1	30,655	30.655	51	0
23,657	23.657	35	0	22,442	22.442	41	1
26,613	26.613	42	1	17,891	17.891	33	1
20,895	20.895	35	0	20,818	20.818	46	1
20,203	20.203	36	1	26,237	26.237	47	0
23,765	23.765	48	0	20,445	20.445	34	1
25,783	25.783	53	1	21,556	21.556	43	1
26,661	26.661	46	1	21,639	21.639	37	1
32,277	32.277	55	0	24,296	24.296	47	0

Appendix B: Tables

B.1 Areas under the Normal Curve

Example:
If $z = 1.96$, then
$P(0$ to $z) = 0.4750$.

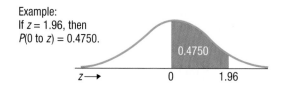

z	0.00	0.01	0.02	0.03	0.04	0.05	0.06	0.07	0.08	0.09
0.0	0.0000	0.0040	0.0080	0.0120	0.0160	0.0199	0.0239	0.0279	0.0319	0.0359
0.1	0.0398	0.0438	0.0478	0.0517	0.0557	0.0596	0.0636	0.0675	0.0714	0.0753
0.2	0.0793	0.0832	0.0871	0.0910	0.0948	0.0987	0.1026	0.1064	0.1103	0.1141
0.3	0.1179	0.1217	0.1255	0.1293	0.1331	0.1368	0.1406	0.1443	0.1480	0.1517
0.4	0.1554	0.1591	0.1628	0.1664	0.1700	0.1736	0.1772	0.1808	0.1844	0.1879
0.5	0.1915	0.1950	0.1985	0.2019	0.2054	0.2088	0.2123	0.2157	0.2190	0.2224
0.6	0.2257	0.2291	0.2324	0.2357	0.2389	0.2422	0.2454	0.2486	0.2517	0.2549
0.7	0.2580	0.2611	0.2642	0.2673	0.2704	0.2734	0.2764	0.2794	0.2823	0.2852
0.8	0.2881	0.2910	0.2939	0.2967	0.2995	0.3023	0.3051	0.3078	0.3106	0.3133
0.9	0.3159	0.3186	0.3212	0.3238	0.3264	0.3289	0.3315	0.3340	0.3365	0.3389
1.0	0.3413	0.3438	0.3461	0.3485	0.3508	0.3531	0.3554	0.3577	0.3599	0.3621
1.1	0.3643	0.3665	0.3686	0.3708	0.3729	0.3749	0.3770	0.3790	0.3810	0.3830
1.2	0.3849	0.3869	0.3888	0.3907	0.3925	0.3944	0.3962	0.3980	0.3997	0.4015
1.3	0.4032	0.4049	0.4066	0.4082	0.4099	0.4115	0.4131	0.4147	0.4162	0.4177
1.4	0.4192	0.4207	0.4222	0.4236	0.4251	0.4265	0.4279	0.4292	0.4306	0.4319
1.5	0.4332	0.4345	0.4357	0.4370	0.4382	0.4394	0.4406	0.4418	0.4429	0.4441
1.6	0.4452	0.4463	0.4474	0.4484	0.4495	0.4505	0.4515	0.4525	0.4535	0.4545
1.7	0.4554	0.4564	0.4573	0.4582	0.4591	0.4599	0.4608	0.4616	0.4625	0.4633
1.8	0.4641	0.4649	0.4656	0.4664	0.4671	0.4678	0.4686	0.4693	0.4699	0.4706
1.9	0.4713	0.4719	0.4726	0.4732	0.4738	0.4744	0.4750	0.4756	0.4761	0.4767
2.0	0.4772	0.4778	0.4783	0.4788	0.4793	0.4798	0.4803	0.4808	0.4812	0.4817
2.1	0.4821	0.4826	0.4830	0.4834	0.4838	0.4842	0.4846	0.4850	0.4854	0.4857
2.2	0.4861	0.4864	0.4868	0.4871	0.4875	0.4878	0.4881	0.4884	0.4887	0.4890
2.3	0.4893	0.4896	0.4898	0.4901	0.4904	0.4906	0.4909	0.4911	0.4913	0.4916
2.4	0.4918	0.4920	0.4922	0.4925	0.4927	0.4929	0.4931	0.4932	0.4934	0.4936
2.5	0.4938	0.4940	0.4941	0.4943	0.4945	0.4946	0.4948	0.4949	0.4951	0.4952
2.6	0.4953	0.4955	0.4956	0.4957	0.4959	0.4960	0.4961	0.4962	0.4963	0.4964
2.7	0.4965	0.4966	0.4967	0.4968	0.4969	0.4970	0.4971	0.4972	0.4973	0.4974
2.8	0.4974	0.4975	0.4976	0.4977	0.4977	0.4978	0.4979	0.4979	0.4980	0.4981
2.9	0.4981	0.4982	0.4982	0.4983	0.4984	0.4984	0.4985	0.4985	0.4986	0.4986
3.0	0.4987	0.4987	0.4987	0.4988	0.4988	0.4989	0.4989	0.4989	0.4990	0.4990

B.2 Student's *t* Distribution

Confidence interval

Left-tailed test

Right-tailed test

Two-tailed test

	Confidence Intervals, *c*								Confidence Intervals, *c*					
	80%	90%	95%	98%	99%	99.9%		80%	90%	95%	98%	99%	99.9%
	Level of Significance for One-Tailed Test, α							Level of Significance for One-Tailed Test, α					
df	0.10	0.05	0.025	0.01	0.005	0.0005	*df*	0.10	0.05	0.025	0.01	0.005	0.0005
	Level of Significance for Two-Tailed Test, α							Level of Significance for Two-Tailed Test, α					
	0.20	0.10	0.05	0.02	0.01	0.001		0.20	0.10	0.05	0.02	0.01	0.001
1	3.078	6.314	12.706	31.821	63.657	636.619	36	1.306	1.688	2.028	2.434	2.719	3.582
2	1.886	2.920	4.303	6.965	9.925	31.599	37	1.305	1.687	2.026	2.431	2.715	3.574
3	1.638	2.353	3.182	4.541	5.841	12.924	38	1.304	1.686	2.024	2.429	2.712	3.566
4	1.533	2.132	2.776	3.747	4.604	8.610	39	1.304	1.685	2.023	2.426	2.708	3.558
5	1.476	2.015	2.571	3.365	4.032	6.869	40	1.303	1.684	2.021	2.423	2.704	3.551
6	1.440	1.943	2.447	3.143	3.707	5.959	41	1.303	1.683	2.020	2.421	2.701	3.544
7	1.415	1.895	2.365	2.998	3.499	5.408	42	1.302	1.682	2.018	2.418	2.698	3.538
8	1.397	1.860	2.306	2.896	3.355	5.041	43	1.302	1.681	2.017	2.416	2.695	3.532
9	1.383	1.833	2.262	2.821	3.250	4.781	44	1.301	1.680	2.015	2.414	2.692	3.526
10	1.372	1.812	2.228	2.764	3.169	4.587	45	1.301	1.679	2.014	2.412	2.690	3.520
11	1.363	1.796	2.201	2.718	3.106	4.437	46	1.300	1.679	2.013	2.410	2.687	3.515
12	1.356	1.782	2.179	2.681	3.055	4.318	47	1.300	1.678	2.012	2.408	2.685	3.510
13	1.350	1.771	2.160	2.650	3.012	4.221	48	1.299	1.677	2.011	2.407	2.682	3.505
14	1.345	1.761	2.145	2.624	2.977	4.140	49	1.299	1.677	2.010	2.405	2.680	3.500
15	1.341	1.753	2.131	2.602	2.947	4.073	50	1.299	1.676	2.009	2.403	2.678	3.496
16	1.337	1.746	2.120	2.583	2.921	4.015	51	1.298	1.675	2.008	2.402	2.676	3.492
17	1.333	1.740	2.110	2.567	2.898	3.965	52	1.298	1.675	2.007	2.400	2.674	3.488
18	1.330	1.734	2.101	2.552	2.878	3.922	53	1.298	1.674	2.006	2.399	2.672	3.484
19	1.328	1.729	2.093	2.539	2.861	3.883	54	1.297	1.674	2.005	2.397	2.670	3.480
20	1.325	1.725	2.086	2.528	2.845	3.850	55	1.297	1.673	2.004	2.396	2.668	3.476
21	1.323	1.721	2.080	2.518	2.831	3.819	56	1.297	1.673	2.003	2.395	2.667	3.473
22	1.321	1.717	2.074	2.508	2.819	3.792	57	1.297	1.672	2.002	2.394	2.665	3.470
23	1.319	1.714	2.069	2.500	2.807	3.768	58	1.296	1.672	2.002	2.392	2.663	3.466
24	1.318	1.711	2.064	2.492	2.797	3.745	59	1.296	1.671	2.001	2.391	2.662	3.463
25	1.316	1.708	2.060	2.485	2.787	3.725	60	1.296	1.671	2.000	2.390	2.660	3.460
26	1.315	1.706	2.056	2.479	2.779	3.707	61	1.296	1.670	2.000	2.389	2.659	3.457
27	1.314	1.703	2.052	2.473	2.771	3.690	62	1.295	1.670	1.999	2.388	2.657	3.454
28	1.313	1.701	2.048	2.467	2.763	3.674	63	1.295	1.669	1.998	2.387	2.656	3.452
29	1.311	1.699	2.045	2.462	2.756	3.659	64	1.295	1.669	1.998	2.386	2.655	3.449
30	1.310	1.697	2.042	2.457	2.750	3.646	65	1.295	1.669	1.997	2.385	2.654	3.447
31	1.309	1.696	2.040	2.453	2.744	3.633	66	1.295	1.668	1.997	2.384	2.652	3.444
32	1.309	1.694	2.037	2.449	2.738	3.622	67	1.294	1.668	1.996	2.383	2.651	3.442
33	1.308	1.692	2.035	2.445	2.733	3.611	68	1.294	1.668	1.995	2.382	2.650	3.439
34	1.307	1.691	2.032	2.441	2.728	3.601	69	1.294	1.667	1.995	2.382	2.649	3.437
35	1.306	1.690	2.030	2.438	2.724	3.591	70	1.294	1.667	1.994	2.381	2.648	3.435

(*continued*)

Appendix B

B.2 Student's *t* Distribution (*concluded*)

	Confidence Intervals, *c*					
	80%	**90%**	**95%**	**98%**	**99%**	**99.9%**
	Level of Significance for One-Tailed Test, α					
df	**0.10**	**0.05**	**0.025**	**0.01**	**0.005**	**0.0005**
	Level of Significance for Two-Tailed Test, α					
	0.20	**0.10**	**0.05**	**0.02**	**0.01**	**0.001**
71	1.294	1.667	1.994	2.380	2.647	3.433
72	1.293	1.666	1.993	2.379	2.646	3.431
73	1.293	1.666	1.993	2.379	2.645	3.429
74	1.293	1.666	1.993	2.378	2.644	3.427
75	1.293	1.665	1.992	2.377	2.643	3.425
76	1.293	1.665	1.992	2.376	2.642	3.423
77	1.293	1.665	1.991	2.376	2.641	3.421
78	1.292	1.665	1.991	2.375	2.640	3.420
79	1.292	1.664	1.990	2.374	2.640	3.418
80	1.292	1.664	1.990	2.374	2.639	3.416
81	1.292	1.664	1.990	2.373	2.638	3.415
82	1.292	1.664	1.989	2.373	2.637	3.413
83	1.292	1.663	1.989	2.372	2.636	3.412
84	1.292	1.663	1.989	2.372	2.636	3.410
85	1.292	1.663	1.988	2.371	2.635	3.409
86	1.291	1.663	1.988	2.370	2.634	3.407
87	1.291	1.663	1.988	2.370	2.634	3.406
88	1.291	1.662	1.987	2.369	2.633	3.405

	Confidence Intervals, *c*					
	80%	**90%**	**95%**	**98%**	**99%**	**99.9%**
	Level of Significance for One-Tailed Test, α					
df	**0.10**	**0.05**	**0.025**	**0.01**	**0.005**	**0.0005**
	Level of Significance for Two-Tailed Test, α					
	0.20	**0.10**	**0.05**	**0.02**	**0.01**	**0.001**
89	1.291	1.662	1.987	2.369	2.632	3.403
90	1.291	1.662	1.987	2.368	2.632	3.402
91	1.291	1.662	1.986	2.368	2.631	3.401
92	1.291	1.662	1.986	2.368	2.630	3.399
93	1.291	1.661	1.986	2.367	2.630	3.398
94	1.291	1.661	1.986	2.367	2.629	3.397
95	1.291	1.661	1.985	2.366	2.629	3.396
96	1.290	1.661	1.985	2.366	2.628	3.395
97	1.290	1.661	1.985	2.365	2.627	3.394
98	1.290	1.661	1.984	2.365	2.627	3.393
99	1.290	1.660	1.984	2.365	2.626	3.392
100	1.290	1.660	1.984	2.364	2.626	3.390
120	1.289	1.658	1.980	2.358	2.617	3.373
140	1.288	1.656	1.977	2.353	2.611	3.361
160	1.287	1.654	1.975	2.350	2.607	3.352
180	1.286	1.653	1.973	2.347	2.603	3.345
200	1.286	1.653	1.972	2.345	2.601	3.340
∞	1.282	1.645	1.960	2.326	2.576	3.291

Appendix B

B.3 Critical Values of Chi-Square

This table contains the values of χ^2 that correspond to a specific right-tail area and specific number of degrees of freedom.

Example: With 17 *df* and a .02 area in the upper tail, $\chi^2 = 30.995$

Degrees of Freedom, *df*	Right-Tail Area			
	0.10	0.05	0.02	0.01
1	2.706	3.841	5.412	6.635
2	4.605	5.991	7.824	9.210
3	6.251	7.815	9.837	11.345
4	7.779	9.488	11.668	13.277
5	9.236	11.070	13.388	15.086
6	10.645	12.592	15.033	16.812
7	12.017	14.067	16.622	18.475
8	13.362	15.507	18.168	20.090
9	14.684	16.919	19.679	21.666
10	15.987	18.307	21.161	23.209
11	17.275	19.675	22.618	24.725
12	18.549	21.026	24.054	26.217
13	19.812	22.362	25.472	27.688
14	21.064	23.685	26.873	29.141
15	22.307	24.996	28.259	30.578
16	23.542	26.296	29.633	32.000
17	24.769	27.587	30.995	33.409
18	25.989	28.869	32.346	34.805
19	27.204	30.144	33.687	36.191
20	28.412	31.410	35.020	37.566
21	29.615	32.671	36.343	38.932
22	30.813	33.924	37.659	40.289
23	32.007	35.172	38.968	41.638
24	33.196	36.415	40.270	42.980
25	34.382	37.652	41.566	44.314
26	35.563	38.885	42.856	45.642
27	36.741	40.113	44.140	46.963
28	37.916	41.337	45.419	48.278
29	39.087	42.557	46.693	49.588
30	40.256	43.773	47.962	50.892

Appendix B

B.4 Critical Values of the *F* Distribution at a 5 Percent Level of Significance

		Degrees of Freedom for the Numerator														
	1	**2**	**3**	**4**	**5**	**6**	**7**	**8**	**9**	**10**	**12**	**15**	**20**	**24**	**30**	**40**
1	161	200	216	225	230	234	237	239	241	242	244	246	248	249	250	251
2	18.5	19.0	19.2	19.2	19.3	19.3	19.4	19.4	19.4	19.4	19.4	19.4	19.4	19.5	19.5	19.5
3	10.1	9.55	9.28	9.12	9.01	8.94	8.89	8.85	8.81	8.79	8.74	8.70	8.66	8.64	8.62	8.59
4	7.71	6.94	6.59	6.39	6.26	6.16	6.09	6.04	6.00	5.96	5.91	5.86	5.80	5.77	5.75	5.72
5	6.61	5.79	5.41	5.19	5.05	4.95	4.88	4.82	4.77	4.74	4.68	4.62	4.56	4.53	4.50	4.46
6	5.99	5.14	4.76	4.53	4.39	4.28	4.21	4.15	4.10	4.06	4.00	3.94	3.87	3.84	3.81	3.77
7	5.59	4.74	4.35	4.12	3.97	3.87	3.79	3.73	3.68	3.64	3.57	3.51	3.44	3.41	3.38	3.34
8	5.32	4.46	4.07	3.84	3.69	3.58	3.50	3.44	3.39	3.35	3.28	3.22	3.15	3.12	3.08	3.04
9	5.12	4.26	3.86	3.63	3.48	3.37	3.29	3.23	3.18	3.14	3.07	3.01	2.94	2.90	2.86	2.83
10	4.96	4.10	3.71	3.48	3.33	3.22	3.14	3.07	3.02	2.98	2.91	2.85	2.77	2.74	2.70	2.66
11	4.84	3.98	3.59	3.36	3.20	3.09	3.01	2.95	2.90	2.85	2.79	2.72	2.65	2.61	2.57	2.53
12	4.75	3.89	3.49	3.26	3.11	3.00	2.91	2.85	2.80	2.75	2.69	2.62	2.54	2.51	2.47	2.43
13	4.67	3.81	3.41	3.18	3.03	2.92	2.83	2.77	2.71	2.67	2.60	2.53	2.46	2.42	2.38	2.34
14	4.60	3.74	3.34	3.11	2.96	2.85	2.76	2.70	2.65	2.60	2.53	2.46	2.39	2.35	2.31	2.27
15	4.54	3.68	3.29	3.06	2.90	2.79	2.71	2.64	2.59	2.54	2.48	2.40	2.33	2.29	2.25	2.20
16	4.49	3.63	3.24	3.01	2.85	2.74	2.66	2.59	2.54	2.49	2.42	2.35	2.28	2.24	2.19	2.15
17	4.45	3.59	3.20	2.96	2.81	2.70	2.61	2.55	2.49	2.45	2.38	2.31	2.23	2.19	2.15	2.10
18	4.41	3.55	3.16	2.93	2.77	2.66	2.58	2.51	2.46	2.41	2.34	2.27	2.19	2.15	2.11	2.06
19	4.38	3.52	3.13	2.90	2.74	2.63	2.54	2.48	2.42	2.38	2.31	2.23	2.16	2.11	2.07	2.03
20	4.35	3.49	3.10	2.87	2.71	2.60	2.51	2.45	2.39	2.35	2.28	2.20	2.12	2.08	2.04	1.99
21	4.32	3.47	3.07	2.84	2.68	2.57	2.49	2.42	2.37	2.32	2.25	2.18	2.10	2.05	2.01	1.96
22	4.30	3.44	3.05	2.82	2.66	2.55	2.46	2.40	2.34	2.30	2.23	2.15	2.07	2.03	1.98	1.94
23	4.28	3.42	3.03	2.80	2.64	2.53	2.44	2.37	2.32	2.27	2.20	2.13	2.05	2.01	1.96	1.91
24	4.26	3.40	3.01	2.78	2.62	2.51	2.42	2.36	2.30	2.25	2.18	2.11	2.03	1.98	1.94	1.89
25	4.24	3.39	2.99	2.76	2.60	2.49	2.40	2.34	2.28	2.24	2.16	2.09	2.01	1.96	1.92	1.87
30	4.17	3.32	2.92	2.69	2.53	2.42	2.33	2.27	2.21	2.16	2.09	2.01	1.93	1.89	1.84	1.79
40	4.08	3.23	2.84	2.61	2.45	2.34	2.25	2.18	2.12	2.08	2.00	1.92	1.84	1.79	1.74	1.69
60	4.00	3.15	2.76	2.53	2.37	2.25	2.17	2.10	2.04	1.99	1.92	1.84	1.75	1.70	1.65	1.59
120	3.92	3.07	2.68	2.45	2.29	2.18	2.09	2.02	1.96	1.91	1.83	1.75	1.66	1.61	1.55	1.50
∞	3.84	3.00	2.60	2.37	2.21	2.10	2.01	1.94	1.88	1.83	1.75	1.67	1.57	1.52	1.46	1.39

Degrees of Freedom for the Denominator (row label at left)

B.4 Critical Values of the *F* Distribution at a 1 Percent Level of Significance (*concluded*)

		Degrees of Freedom for the Numerator														
		1	**2**	**3**	**4**	**5**	**6**	**7**	**8**	**9**	**10**	**12**	**15**	**20**	**24**	**30**	**40**
	1	4052	5000	5403	5625	5764	5859	5928	5981	6022	6056	6106	6157	6209	6235	6261	6287
	2	98.5	99.0	99.2	99.2	99.3	99.3	99.4	99.4	99.4	99.4	99.4	99.4	99.4	99.5	99.5	99.5
	3	34.1	30.8	29.5	28.7	28.2	27.9	27.7	27.5	27.3	27.2	27.1	26.9	26.7	26.6	26.5	26.4
	4	21.2	18.0	16.7	16.0	15.5	15.2	15.0	14.8	14.7	14.5	14.4	14.2	14.0	13.9	13.8	13.7
	5	16.3	13.3	12.1	11.4	11.0	10.7	10.5	10.3	10.2	10.1	9.89	9.72	9.55	9.47	9.38	9.29
	6	13.7	10.9	9.78	9.15	8.75	8.47	8.26	8.10	7.98	7.87	7.72	7.56	7.40	7.31	7.23	7.14
	7	12.2	9.55	8.45	7.85	7.46	7.19	6.99	6.84	6.72	6.62	6.47	6.31	6.16	6.07	5.99	5.91
	8	11.3	8.65	7.59	7.01	6.63	6.37	6.18	6.03	5.91	5.81	5.67	5.52	5.36	5.28	5.20	5.12
	9	10.6	8.02	6.99	6.42	6.06	5.80	5.61	5.47	5.35	5.26	5.11	4.96	4.81	4.73	4.65	4.57
	10	10.0	7.56	6.55	5.99	5.64	5.39	5.20	5.06	4.94	4.85	4.71	4.56	4.41	4.33	4.25	4.17
Degrees of Freedom for the Denominator	11	9.65	7.21	6.22	5.67	5.32	5.07	4.89	4.74	4.63	4.54	4.40	4.25	4.10	4.02	3.94	3.86
	12	9.33	6.93	5.95	5.41	5.06	4.82	4.64	4.50	4.39	4.30	4.16	4.01	3.86	3.78	3.70	3.62
	13	9.07	6.70	5.74	5.21	4.86	4.62	4.44	4.30	4.19	4.10	3.96	3.82	3.66	3.59	3.51	3.43
	14	8.86	6.51	5.56	5.04	4.69	4.46	4.28	4.14	4.03	3.94	3.80	3.66	3.51	3.43	3.35	3.27
	15	8.68	6.36	5.42	4.89	4.56	4.32	4.14	4.00	3.89	3.80	3.67	3.52	3.37	3.29	3.21	3.13
	16	8.53	6.23	5.29	4.77	4.44	4.20	4.03	3.89	3.78	3.69	3.55	3.41	3.26	3.18	3.10	3.02
	17	8.40	6.11	5.18	4.67	4.34	4.10	3.93	3.79	3.68	3.59	3.46	3.31	3.16	3.08	3.00	2.92
	18	8.29	6.01	5.09	4.58	4.25	4.01	3.84	3.71	3.60	3.51	3.37	3.23	3.08	3.00	2.92	2.84
	19	8.18	5.93	5.01	4.50	4.17	3.94	3.77	3.63	3.52	3.43	3.30	3.15	3.00	2.92	2.84	2.76
	20	8.10	5.85	4.94	4.43	4.10	3.87	3.70	3.56	3.46	3.37	3.23	3.09	2.94	2.86	2.78	2.69
	21	8.02	5.78	4.87	4.37	4.04	3.81	3.64	3.51	3.40	3.31	3.17	3.03	2.88	2.80	2.72	2.64
	22	7.95	5.72	4.82	4.31	3.99	3.76	3.59	3.45	3.35	3.26	3.12	2.98	2.83	2.75	2.67	2.58
	23	7.88	5.66	4.76	4.26	3.94	3.71	3.54	3.41	3.30	3.21	3.07	2.93	2.78	2.70	2.62	2.54
	24	7.82	5.61	4.72	4.22	3.90	3.67	3.50	3.36	3.26	3.17	3.03	2.89	2.74	2.66	2.58	2.49
	25	7.77	5.57	4.68	4.18	3.85	3.63	3.46	3.32	3.22	3.13	2.99	2.85	2.70	2.62	2.54	2.45
	30	7.56	5.39	4.51	4.02	3.70	3.47	3.30	3.17	3.07	2.98	2.84	2.70	2.55	2.47	2.39	2.30
	40	7.31	5.18	4.31	3.83	3.51	3.29	3.12	2.99	2.89	2.80	2.66	2.52	2.37	2.29	2.20	2.11
	60	7.08	4.98	4.13	3.65	3.34	3.12	2.95	2.82	2.72	2.63	2.50	2.35	2.20	2.12	2.03	1.94
	120	6.85	4.79	3.95	3.48	3.17	2.96	2.79	2.66	2.56	2.47	2.34	2.19	2.03	1.95	1.86	1.76
	∞	6.63	4.61	3.78	3.32	3.02	2.80	2.64	2.51	2.41	2.32	2.18	2.04	1.88	1.79	1.70	1.59

Appendix B

B.5 Poisson Distribution

	μ								
x	0.1	0.2	0.3	0.4	0.5	0.6	0.7	0.8	0.9
0	0.9048	0.8187	0.7408	0.6703	0.6065	0.5488	0.4966	0.4493	0.4066
1	0.0905	0.1637	0.2222	0.2681	0.3033	0.3293	0.3476	0.3595	0.3659
2	0.0045	0.0164	0.0333	0.0536	0.0758	0.0988	0.1217	0.1438	0.1647
3	0.0002	0.0011	0.0033	0.0072	0.0126	0.0198	0.0284	0.0383	0.0494
4	0.0000	0.0001	0.0003	0.0007	0.0016	0.0030	0.0050	0.0077	0.0111
5	0.0000	0.0000	0.0000	0.0001	0.0002	0.0004	0.0007	0.0012	0.0020
6	0.0000	0.0000	0.0000	0.0000	0.0000	0.0000	0.0001	0.0002	0.0003
7	0.0000	0.0000	0.0000	0.0000	0.0000	0.0000	0.0000	0.0000	0.0000

	μ								
x	1.0	2.0	3.0	4.0	5.0	6.0	7.0	8.0	9.0
0	0.3679	0.1353	0.0498	0.0183	0.0067	0.0025	0.0009	0.0003	0.0001
1	0.3679	0.2707	0.1494	0.0733	0.0337	0.0149	0.0064	0.0027	0.0011
2	0.1839	0.2707	0.2240	0.1465	0.0842	0.0446	0.0223	0.0107	0.0050
3	0.0613	0.1804	0.2240	0.1954	0.1404	0.0892	0.0521	0.0286	0.0150
4	0.0153	0.0902	0.1680	0.1954	0.1755	0.1339	0.0912	0.0573	0.0337
5	0.0031	0.0361	0.1008	0.1563	0.1755	0.1606	0.1277	0.0916	0.0607
6	0.0005	0.0120	0.0504	0.1042	0.1462	0.1606	0.1490	0.1221	0.0911
7	0.0001	0.0034	0.0216	0.0595	0.1044	0.1377	0.1490	0.1396	0.1171
8	0.0000	0.0009	0.0081	0.0298	0.0653	0.1033	0.1304	0.1396	0.1318
9	0.0000	0.0002	0.0027	0.0132	0.0363	0.0688	0.1014	0.1241	0.1318
10	0.0000	0.0000	0.0008	0.0053	0.0181	0.0413	0.0710	0.0993	0.1186
11	0.0000	0.0000	0.0002	0.0019	0.0082	0.0225	0.0452	0.0722	0.0970
12	0.0000	0.0000	0.0001	0.0006	0.0034	0.0113	0.0263	0.0481	0.0728
13	0.0000	0.0000	0.0000	0.0002	0.0013	0.0052	0.0142	0.0296	0.0504
14	0.0000	0.0000	0.0000	0.0001	0.0005	0.0022	0.0071	0.0169	0.0324
15	0.0000	0.0000	0.0000	0.0000	0.0002	0.0009	0.0033	0.0090	0.0194
16	0.0000	0.0000	0.0000	0.0000	0.0000	0.0003	0.0014	0.0045	0.0109
17	0.0000	0.0000	0.0000	0.0000	0.0000	0.0001	0.0006	0.0021	0.0058
18	0.0000	0.0000	0.0000	0.0000	0.0000	0.0000	0.0002	0.0009	0.0029
19	0.0000	0.0000	0.0000	0.0000	0.0000	0.0000	0.0001	0.0004	0.0014
20	0.0000	0.0000	0.0000	0.0000	0.0000	0.0000	0.0000	0.0002	0.0006
21	0.0000	0.0000	0.0000	0.0000	0.0000	0.0000	0.0000	0.0001	0.0003
22	0.0000	0.0000	0.0000	0.0000	0.0000	0.0000	0.0000	0.0000	0.0001

02711	08182	75997	79866	58095	83319	80295	79741	74599	84379
94873	90935	31684	63952	09865	14491	99518	93394	34691	14985
54921	78680	06635	98689	17306	25170	65928	87709	30533	89736
77640	97636	37397	93379	56454	59818	45827	74164	71666	46977
61545	00835	93251	87203	36759	49197	85967	01704	19634	21898
17147	19519	22497	16857	42426	84822	92598	49186	88247	39967
13748	04742	92460	85801	53444	65626	58710	55406	17173	69776
87455	14813	50373	28037	91182	32786	65261	11173	34376	36408
08999	57409	91185	10200	61411	23392	47797	56377	71635	08601
78804	81333	53809	32471	46034	36306	22498	19239	85428	55721
82173	26921	28472	98958	07960	66124	89731	95069	18625	92405
97594	25168	89178	68190	05043	17407	48201	83917	11413	72920
73881	67176	93504	42636	38233	16154	96451	57925	29667	30859
46071	22912	90326	42453	88108	72064	58601	32357	90610	32921
44492	19686	12495	93135	95185	77799	52441	88272	22024	80631
31864	72170	37722	55794	14636	05148	54505	50113	21119	25228
51574	90692	43339	65689	76539	27909	05467	21727	51141	72949
35350	76132	92925	92124	92634	35681	43690	89136	35599	84138
46943	36502	01172	46045	46991	33804	80006	35542	61056	75666
22665	87226	33304	57975	03985	21566	65796	72915	81466	89205
39437	97957	11838	10433	21564	51570	73558	27495	34533	57808
77082	47784	40098	97962	89845	28392	78187	06112	08169	11261
24544	25649	43370	28007	06779	72402	62632	53956	24709	06978
27503	15558	37738	24849	70722	71859	83736	06016	94397	12529
24590	24545	06435	52758	45685	90151	46516	49644	92686	84870
48155	86226	40359	28723	15364	69125	12609	57171	86857	31702
20226	53752	90648	24362	83314	00014	19207	69413	97016	86290
70178	73444	38790	53626	93780	18629	68766	24371	74639	30782
10169	41465	51935	05711	09799	79077	88159	33437	68519	03040
81084	03701	28598	70013	63794	53169	97054	60303	23259	96196
69202	20777	21727	81511	51887	16175	53746	46516	70339	62727
80561	95787	89426	93325	86412	57479	54194	52153	19197	81877
08199	26703	95128	48599	09333	12584	24374	31232	61782	44032
98883	28220	39358	53720	80161	83371	15181	11131	12219	55920
84568	69286	76054	21615	80883	36797	82845	39139	90900	18172
04269	35173	95745	53893	86022	77722	52498	84193	22448	22571
10538	13124	36099	13140	37706	44562	57179	44693	67877	01549
77843	24955	25900	63843	95029	93859	93634	20205	66294	41218
12034	94636	49455	76362	83532	31062	69903	91186	65768	55949
10524	72829	47641	93315	80875	28090	97728	52560	34937	79548
68935	76632	46984	61772	92786	22651	07086	89754	44143	97687
89450	65665	29190	43709	11172	34481	95977	47535	25658	73898
90696	20451	24211	97310	60446	73530	62865	96574	13829	72226
49006	32047	93086	00112	20470	17136	28255	86328	07293	38809
74591	87025	52368	59416	34417	70557	86746	55809	53628	12000
06315	17012	77103	00968	07235	10728	42189	33292	51487	64443
62386	09184	62092	46617	99419	64230	95034	85481	07857	42510
86848	82122	04028	36959	87827	12813	08627	80699	13345	51695
65643	69480	46598	04501	40403	91408	32343	48130	49303	90689
11084	46534	78957	77353	39578	77868	22970	84349	09184	70603

Appendix B

B.7 Wilcoxon *T* Values

			2α				
	.15	.10	.05	.04	.03	.02	.01
				α			
n	.075	.050	.025	.020	.015	.010	.005
4	0						
5	1	0					
6	2	2	0	0			
7	4	3	2	1	0	0	
8	7	5	3	3	2	1	0
9	9	8	5	5	4	3	1
10	12	10	8	7	6	5	3
11	16	13	10	9	8	7	5
12	19	17	13	12	11	9	7
13	24	21	17	16	14	12	9
14	28	25	21	19	18	15	12
15	33	30	25	23	21	19	15
16	39	35	29	28	26	23	19
17	45	41	34	33	30	27	23
18	51	47	40	38	35	32	27
19	58	53	46	43	41	37	32
20	65	60	52	50	47	43	37
21	73	67	58	56	53	49	42
22	81	75	65	63	59	55	48
23	89	83	73	70	66	62	54
24	98	91	81	78	74	69	61
25	108	100	89	86	82	76	68
26	118	110	98	94	90	84	75
27	128	119	107	103	99	92	83
28	138	130	116	112	108	101	91
29	150	140	126	122	117	110	100
30	161	151	137	132	127	120	109
31	173	163	147	143	137	130	118
32	186	175	159	154	148	140	128
33	199	187	170	165	159	151	138
34	212	200	182	177	171	162	148
35	226	213	195	189	182	173	159
40	302	286	264	257	249	238	220
50	487	466	434	425	413	397	373
60	718	690	648	636	620	600	567
70	995	960	907	891	872	846	805
80	1,318	1,276	1,211	1,192	1,168	1,136	1,086
90	1,688	1,638	1,560	1,537	1,509	1,471	1,410
100	2,105	2,045	1,955	1,928	1,894	1,850	1,779

B.8 Factors for Control Charts

Number of Items in Sample, n	Chart for Averages	Chart for Ranges		
	Factors for Control Limits	Factors for Central Line	Factors for Control Limits	
	A_2	d_2	D_3	D_4
2	1.880	1.128	0	3.267
3	1.023	1.693	0	2.575
4	.729	2.059	0	2.282
5	.577	2.326	0	2.115
6	.483	2.534	0	2.004
7	.419	2.704	.076	1.924
8	.373	2.847	.136	1.864
9	.337	2.970	.184	1.816
10	.308	3.078	.223	1.777
11	.285	3.173	.256	1.744
12	.266	3.258	.284	1.716
13	.249	3.336	.308	1.692
14	.235	3.407	.329	1.671
15	.223	3.472	.348	1.652

SOURCE: Adapted from American Society for Testing and Materials, *Manual on Quality Control of Materials,* 1951, Table B2, p. 115. For a more detailed table and explanation, see J. Duncan Acheson, *Quality Control and Industrial Statistics,* 3d ed. (Homewood, Ill.: Richard D. Irwin, 1974), Table M, p. 927.

Appendix B

B.9 Binomial Probability Distribution

n = 1

Probability

x	0.05	0.10	0.20	0.30	0.40	0.50	0.60	0.70	0.80	0.90	0.95
0	0.950	0.900	0.800	0.700	0.600	0.500	0.400	0.300	0.200	0.100	0.050
1	0.050	0.100	0.200	0.300	0.400	0.500	0.600	0.700	0.800	0.900	0.950

n = 2

Probability

x	0.05	0.10	0.20	0.30	0.40	0.50	0.60	0.70	0.80	0.90	0.95
0	0.903	0.810	0.640	0.490	0.360	0.250	0.160	0.090	0.040	0.010	0.003
1	0.095	0.180	0.320	0.420	0.480	0.500	0.480	0.420	0.320	0.180	0.095
2	0.003	0.010	0.040	0.090	0.160	0.250	0.360	0.490	0.640	0.810	0.903

n = 3

Probability

x	0.05	0.10	0.20	0.30	0.40	0.50	0.60	0.70	0.80	0.90	0.95
0	0.857	0.729	0.512	0.343	0.216	0.125	0.064	0.027	0.008	0.001	0.000
1	0.135	0.243	0.384	0.441	0.432	0.375	0.288	0.189	0.096	0.027	0.007
2	0.007	0.027	0.096	0.189	0.288	0.375	0.432	0.441	0.384	0.243	0.135
3	0.000	0.001	0.008	0.027	0.064	0.125	0.216	0.343	0.512	0.729	0.857

n = 4

Probability

x	0.05	0.10	0.20	0.30	0.40	0.50	0.60	0.70	0.80	0.90	0.95
0	0.815	0.656	0.410	0.240	0.130	0.063	0.026	0.008	0.002	0.000	0.000
1	0.171	0.292	0.410	0.412	0.346	0.250	0.154	0.076	0.026	0.004	0.000
2	0.014	0.049	0.154	0.265	0.346	0.375	0.346	0.265	0.154	0.049	0.014
3	0.000	0.004	0.026	0.076	0.154	0.250	0.346	0.412	0.410	0.292	0.171
4	0.000	0.000	0.002	0.008	0.026	0.063	0.130	0.240	0.410	0.656	0.815

n = 5

Probability

x	0.05	0.10	0.20	0.30	0.40	0.50	0.60	0.70	0.80	0.90	0.95
0	0.774	0.590	0.328	0.168	0.078	0.031	0.010	0.002	0.000	0.000	0.000
1	0.204	0.328	0.410	0.360	0.259	0.156	0.077	0.028	0.006	0.000	0.000
2	0.021	0.073	0.205	0.309	0.346	0.313	0.230	0.132	0.051	0.008	0.001
3	0.001	0.008	0.051	0.132	0.230	0.313	0.346	0.309	0.205	0.073	0.021
4	0.000	0.000	0.006	0.028	0.077	0.156	0.259	0.360	0.410	0.328	0.204
5	0.000	0.000	0.000	0.002	0.010	0.031	0.078	0.168	0.328	0.590	0.774

B.9 Binomial Probability Distribution (*continued*)

n = 6

					Probability						
x	0.05	0.10	0.20	0.30	0.40	0.50	0.60	0.70	0.80	0.90	0.95
0	0.735	0.531	0.262	0.118	0.047	0.016	0.004	0.001	0.000	0.000	0.000
1	0.232	0.354	0.393	0.303	0.187	0.094	0.037	0.010	0.002	0.000	0.000
2	0.031	0.098	0.246	0.324	0.311	0.234	0.138	0.060	0.015	0.001	0.000
3	0.002	0.015	0.082	0.185	0.276	0.313	0.276	0.185	0.082	0.015	0.002
4	0.000	0.001	0.015	0.060	0.138	0.234	0.311	0.324	0.246	0.098	0.031
5	0.000	0.000	0.002	0.010	0.037	0.094	0.187	0.303	0.393	0.354	0.232
6	0.000	0.000	0.000	0.001	0.004	0.016	0.047	0.118	0.262	0.531	0.735

n = 7

					Probability						
x	0.05	0.10	0.20	0.30	0.40	0.50	0.60	0.70	0.80	0.90	0.95
0	0.698	0.478	0.210	0.082	0.028	0.008	0.002	0.000	0.000	0.000	0.000
1	0.257	0.372	0.367	0.247	0.131	0.055	0.017	0.004	0.000	0.000	0.000
2	0.041	0.124	0.275	0.318	0.261	0.164	0.077	0.025	0.004	0.000	0.000
3	0.004	0.023	0.115	0.227	0.290	0.273	0.194	0.097	0.029	0.003	0.000
4	0.000	0.003	0.029	0.097	0.194	0.273	0.290	0.227	0.115	0.023	0.004
5	0.000	0.000	0.004	0.025	0.077	0.164	0.261	0.318	0.275	0.124	0.041
6	0.000	0.000	0.000	0.004	0.017	0.055	0.131	0.247	0.367	0.372	0.257
7	0.000	0.000	0.000	0.000	0.002	0.008	0.028	0.082	0.210	0.478	0.698

n = 8

					Probability						
x	0.05	0.10	0.20	0.30	0.40	0.50	0.60	0.70	0.80	0.90	0.95
0	0.663	0.430	0.168	0.058	0.017	0.004	0.001	0.000	0.000	0.000	0.000
1	0.279	0.383	0.336	0.198	0.090	0.031	0.008	0.001	0.000	0.000	0.000
2	0.051	0.149	0.294	0.296	0.209	0.109	0.041	0.010	0.001	0.000	0.000
3	0.005	0.033	0.147	0.254	0.279	0.219	0.124	0.047	0.009	0.000	0.000
4	0.000	0.005	0.046	0.136	0.232	0.273	0.232	0.136	0.046	0.005	0.000
5	0.000	0.000	0.009	0.047	0.124	0.219	0.279	0.254	0.147	0.033	0.005
6	0.000	0.000	0.001	0.010	0.041	0.109	0.209	0.296	0.294	0.149	0.051
7	0.000	0.000	0.000	0.001	0.008	0.031	0.090	0.198	0.336	0.383	0.279
8	0.000	0.000	0.000	0.000	0.001	0.004	0.017	0.058	0.168	0.430	0.663

(continued)

B.9 Binomial Probability Distribution (*continued*)

n = 9

Probability

x	0.05	0.10	0.20	0.30	0.40	0.50	0.60	0.70	0.80	0.90	0.95
0	0.630	0.387	0.134	0.040	0.010	0.002	0.000	0.000	0.000	0.000	0.000
1	0.299	0.387	0.302	0.156	0.060	0.018	0.004	0.000	0.000	0.000	0.000
2	0.063	0.172	0.302	0.267	0.161	0.070	0.021	0.004	0.000	0.000	0.000
3	0.008	0.045	0.176	0.267	0.251	0.164	0.074	0.021	0.003	0.000	0.000
4	0.001	0.007	0.066	0.172	0.251	0.246	0.167	0.074	0.017	0.001	0.000
5	0.000	0.001	0.017	0.074	0.167	0.246	0.251	0.172	0.066	0.007	0.001
6	0.000	0.000	0.003	0.021	0.074	0.164	0.251	0.267	0.176	0.045	0.008
7	0.000	0.000	0.000	0.004	0.021	0.070	0.161	0.267	0.302	0.172	0.063
8	0.000	0.000	0.000	0.000	0.004	0.018	0.060	0.156	0.302	0.387	0.299
9	0.000	0.000	0.000	0.000	0.000	0.002	0.010	0.040	0.134	0.387	0.630

n = 10

Probability

x	0.05	0.10	0.20	0.30	0.40	0.50	0.60	0.70	0.80	0.90	0.95
0	0.599	0.349	0.107	0.028	0.006	0.001	0.000	0.000	0.000	0.000	0.000
1	0.315	0.387	0.268	0.121	0.040	0.010	0.002	0.000	0.000	0.000	0.000
2	0.075	0.194	0.302	0.233	0.121	0.044	0.011	0.001	0.000	0.000	0.000
3	0.010	0.057	0.201	0.267	0.215	0.117	0.042	0.009	0.001	0.000	0.000
4	0.001	0.011	0.088	0.200	0.251	0.205	0.111	0.037	0.006	0.000	0.000
5	0.000	0.001	0.026	0.103	0.201	0.246	0.201	0.103	0.026	0.001	0.000
6	0.000	0.000	0.006	0.037	0.111	0.205	0.251	0.200	0.088	0.011	0.001
7	0.000	0.000	0.001	0.009	0.042	0.117	0.215	0.267	0.201	0.057	0.010
8	0.000	0.000	0.000	0.001	0.011	0.044	0.121	0.233	0.302	0.194	0.075
9	0.000	0.000	0.000	0.000	0.002	0.010	0.040	0.121	0.268	0.387	0.315
10	0.000	0.000	0.000	0.000	0.000	0.001	0.006	0.028	0.107	0.349	0.599

n = 11

Probability

x	0.05	0.10	0.20	0.30	0.40	0.50	0.60	0.70	0.80	0.90	0.95
0	0.569	0.314	0.086	0.020	0.004	0.000	0.000	0.000	0.000	0.000	0.000
1	0.329	0.384	0.236	0.093	0.027	0.005	0.001	0.000	0.000	0.000	0.000
2	0.087	0.213	0.295	0.200	0.089	0.027	0.005	0.001	0.000	0.000	0.000
3	0.014	0.071	0.221	0.257	0.177	0.081	0.023	0.004	0.000	0.000	0.000
4	0.001	0.016	0.111	0.220	0.236	0.161	0.070	0.017	0.002	0.000	0.000
5	0.000	0.002	0.039	0.132	0.221	0.226	0.147	0.057	0.010	0.000	0.000
6	0.000	0.000	0.010	0.057	0.147	0.226	0.221	0.132	0.039	0.002	0.000
7	0.000	0.000	0.002	0.017	0.070	0.161	0.236	0.220	0.111	0.016	0.001
8	0.000	0.000	0.000	0.004	0.023	0.081	0.177	0.257	0.221	0.071	0.014
9	0.000	0.000	0.000	0.001	0.005	0.027	0.089	0.200	0.295	0.213	0.087
10	0.000	0.000	0.000	0.000	0.001	0.005	0.027	0.093	0.236	0.384	0.329
11	0.000	0.000	0.000	0.000	0.000	0.000	0.004	0.020	0.086	0.314	0.569

B.9 Binomial Probability Distribution (*continued*)

n = 12
Probability

x	0.05	0.10	0.20	0.30	0.40	0.50	0.60	0.70	0.80	0.90	0.95
0	0.540	0.282	0.069	0.014	0.002	0.000	0.000	0.000	0.000	0.000	0.000
1	0.341	0.377	0.206	0.071	0.017	0.003	0.000	0.000	0.000	0.000	0.000
2	0.099	0.230	0.283	0.168	0.064	0.016	0.002	0.000	0.000	0.000	0.000
3	0.017	0.085	0.236	0.240	0.142	0.054	0.012	0.001	0.000	0.000	0.000
4	0.002	0.021	0.133	0.231	0.213	0.121	0.042	0.008	0.001	0.000	0.000
5	0.000	0.004	0.053	0.158	0.227	0.193	0.101	0.029	0.003	0.000	0.000
6	0.000	0.000	0.016	0.079	0.177	0.226	0.177	0.079	0.016	0.000	0.000
7	0.000	0.000	0.003	0.029	0.101	0.193	0.227	0.158	0.053	0.004	0.000
8	0.000	0.000	0.001	0.008	0.042	0.121	0.213	0.231	0.133	0.021	0.002
9	0.000	0.000	0.000	0.001	0.012	0.054	0.142	0.240	0.236	0.085	0.017
10	0.000	0.000	0.000	0.000	0.002	0.016	0.064	0.168	0.283	0.230	0.099
11	0.000	0.000	0.000	0.000	0.000	0.003	0.017	0.071	0.206	0.377	0.341
12	0.000	0.000	0.000	0.000	0.000	0.000	0.002	0.014	0.069	0.282	0.540

n = 13
Probability

x	0.05	0.10	0.20	0.30	0.40	0.50	0.60	0.70	0.80	0.90	0.95
0	0.513	0.254	0.055	0.010	0.001	0.000	0.000	0.000	0.000	0.000	0.000
1	0.351	0.367	0.179	0.054	0.011	0.002	0.000	0.000	0.000	0.000	0.000
2	0.111	0.245	0.268	0.139	0.045	0.010	0.001	0.000	0.000	0.000	0.000
3	0.021	0.100	0.246	0.218	0.111	0.035	0.006	0.001	0.000	0.000	0.000
4	0.003	0.028	0.154	0.234	0.184	0.087	0.024	0.003	0.000	0.000	0.000
5	0.000	0.006	0.069	0.180	0.221	0.157	0.066	0.014	0.001	0.000	0.000
6	0.000	0.001	0.023	0.103	0.197	0.209	0.131	0.044	0.006	0.000	0.000
7	0.000	0.000	0.006	0.044	0.131	0.209	0.197	0.103	0.023	0.001	0.000
8	0.000	0.000	0.001	0.014	0.066	0.157	0.221	0.180	0.069	0.006	0.000
9	0.000	0.000	0.000	0.003	0.024	0.087	0.184	0.234	0.154	0.028	0.003
10	0.000	0.000	0.000	0.001	0.006	0.035	0.111	0.218	0.246	0.100	0.021
11	0.000	0.000	0.000	0.000	0.001	0.010	0.045	0.139	0.268	0.245	0.111
12	0.000	0.000	0.000	0.000	0.000	0.002	0.011	0.054	0.179	0.367	0.351
13	0.000	0.000	0.000	0.000	0.000	0.000	0.001	0.010	0.055	0.254	0.513

(*continued*)

Appendix B

B.9 Binomial Probability Distribution (*concluded*)

n = 14

Probability

x	0.05	0.10	0.20	0.30	0.40	0.50	0.60	0.70	0.80	0.90	0.95
0	0.488	0.229	0.044	0.007	0.001	0.000	0.000	0.000	0.000	0.000	0.000
1	0.359	0.356	0.154	0.041	0.007	0.001	0.000	0.000	0.000	0.000	0.000
2	0.123	0.257	0.250	0.113	0.032	0.006	0.001	0.000	0.000	0.000	0.000
3	0.026	0.114	0.250	0.194	0.085	0.022	0.003	0.000	0.000	0.000	0.000
4	0.004	0.035	0.172	0.229	0.155	0.061	0.014	0.001	0.000	0.000	0.000
5	0.000	0.008	0.086	0.196	0.207	0.122	0.041	0.007	0.000	0.000	0.000
6	0.000	0.001	0.032	0.126	0.207	0.183	0.092	0.023	0.002	0.000	0.000
7	0.000	0.000	0.009	0.062	0.157	0.209	0.157	0.062	0.009	0.000	0.000
8	0.000	0.000	0.002	0.023	0.092	0.183	0.207	0.126	0.032	0.001	0.000
9	0.000	0.000	0.000	0.007	0.041	0.122	0.207	0.196	0.086	0.008	0.000
10	0.000	0.000	0.000	0.001	0.014	0.061	0.155	0.229	0.172	0.035	0.004
11	0.000	0.000	0.000	0.000	0.003	0.022	0.085	0.194	0.250	0.114	0.026
12	0.000	0.000	0.000	0.000	0.001	0.006	0.032	0.113	0.250	0.257	0.123
13	0.000	0.000	0.000	0.000	0.000	0.001	0.007	0.041	0.154	0.356	0.359
14	0.000	0.000	0.000	0.000	0.000	0.000	0.001	0.007	0.044	0.229	0.488

n = 15

Probability

x	0.05	0.10	0.20	0.30	0.40	0.50	0.60	0.70	0.80	0.90	0.95
0	0.463	0.206	0.035	0.005	0.000	0.000	0.000	0.000	0.000	0.000	0.000
1	0.366	0.343	0.132	0.031	0.005	0.000	0.000	0.000	0.000	0.000	0.000
2	0.135	0.267	0.231	0.092	0.022	0.003	0.000	0.000	0.000	0.000	0.000
3	0.031	0.129	0.250	0.170	0.063	0.014	0.002	0.000	0.000	0.000	0.000
4	0.005	0.043	0.188	0.219	0.127	0.042	0.007	0.001	0.000	0.000	0.000
5	0.001	0.010	0.103	0.206	0.186	0.092	0.024	0.003	0.000	0.000	0.000
6	0.000	0.002	0.043	0.147	0.207	0.153	0.061	0.012	0.001	0.000	0.000
7	0.000	0.000	0.014	0.081	0.177	0.196	0.118	0.035	0.003	0.000	0.000
8	0.000	0.000	0.003	0.035	0.118	0.196	0.177	0.081	0.014	0.000	0.000
9	0.000	0.000	0.001	0.012	0.061	0.153	0.207	0.147	0.043	0.002	0.000
10	0.000	0.000	0.000	0.003	0.024	0.092	0.186	0.206	0.103	0.010	0.001
11	0.000	0.000	0.000	0.001	0.007	0.042	0.127	0.219	0.188	0.043	0.005
12	0.000	0.000	0.000	0.000	0.002	0.014	0.063	0.170	0.250	0.129	0.031
13	0.000	0.000	0.000	0.000	0.000	0.003	0.022	0.092	0.231	0.267	0.135
14	0.000	0.000	0.000	0.000	0.000	0.000	0.005	0.031	0.132	0.343	0.366
15	0.000	0.000	0.000	0.000	0.000	0.000	0.000	0.005	0.035	0.206	0.463

Appendix C: Answers

Answers to Odd-Numbered Chapter Exercises

CHAPTER 1
1. a. Interval
   b. Ratio
   c. Nominal
   d. Nominal
   e. Ordinal
   f. Ratio
3. Answers will vary.
5. Qualitative data is not numerical, whereas quantitative data is numerical. Examples will vary by student.
7. A discrete variable may assume only certain values. A continuous variable may assume an infinite number of values within a given range. The number of traffic citations issued each day during February in Garden City Beach, South Carolina, is a discrete variable. The weight of commercial trucks passing the weigh station at milepost 195 on Interstate 95 in North Carolina is a continuous variable.
9. a. Ordinal
   b. Ratio
   c. The newer system provides information on the distance between exits.
11. If you were using the Ridgedale Mall store as typical of all Gap stores, then it would be sample data. However, if you were considering it as the only store of interest, then the data would be population data.
13.

	Discrete Variable	Continuous Variable
Qualitative	b. Gender d. Soft drink preference	
Quantitative	f. SAT scores g. Student rank in class h. Rating of a finance professor i. Number of home computers	a. Salary c. Sales volume of MP3 players e. Temperature

	Discrete	Continuous
Nominal	b. Gender	
Ordinal	d. Soft drink preference g. Student rank in class h. Rating of a finance professor	
Interval	f. SAT scores	e. Temperature
Ratio	i. Number of home computers	a. Salary c. Sales volume of MP3 players

15. According to the sample information, 120/300 or 40% would accept a job transfer.
17. a. Sales declined by 57,799 units or 5.8 percent.
    b. GM declined by 16.6 percent and Ford by 19.0 percent. Toyota increased by 9.5 percent and Nissan by 8.9 percent.
19. Earnings have increased every year over all previous years.
21. a. Grass or artificial turf field is a qualitative variable, the others are quantitative.
    b. Grass or artificial turf field is a nominal-level variable, the others are ratio-level variables.

CHAPTER 2
1. Answers will vary.
3.

Season	Frequency	Relative Frequency
Winter	100	.10
Spring	300	.30
Summer	400	.40
Fall	200	.20
	1,000	1.00

5. a. Frequency table
   b.

   c.

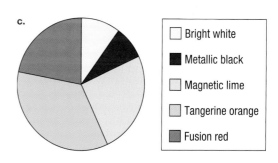

   - Bright white
   - Metallic black
   - Magnetic lime
   - Tangerine orange
   - Fusion red

   d.

Color	Frequency	Relative Frequency	Production
Bright white	130	0.10	100,000
Metallic black	104	0.08	80,000
Magnetic lime	325	0.25	250,000
Tangerine orange	455	0.35	350,000
Fusion red	286	0.22	220,000
	1,300	1.00	1,000,000

Note: Production estimates are found by multiplying the relative frequency by the total production of 1,000,000 units.

7. $2^5 = 32$, $2^6 = 64$, therefore, 6 classes

9. $2^7 = 128$, $2^8 = 256$, suggests 8 classes

$i \geq \dfrac{567 - 235}{8} = 41$ Class intervals of 40, 45, or 50 all would be acceptable.

11. a. $2^4 = 16$ Suggests 5 classes.

b. $i \geq \dfrac{31 - 25}{5} = 1.2$ Use interval of 1.5.

c. 24

d.

Patients	f	Relative Frequency
24.0 up to 25.5	2	0.125
25.5 up to 27.0	4	0.250
27.0 up to 28.5	8	0.500
28.5 up to 30.0	0	0.000
30.0 up to 31.5	2	0.125
Total	16	1.000

e. The largest concentration is in the 27.0 up to 28.5 class (8).

13. a.

Number of Visits	f
0 up to 3	9
3 up to 6	21
6 up to 9	13
9 up to 12	4
12 up to 15	3
15 up to 18	1
Total	51

b. The largest group of shoppers (21) shop at the BiLo Supermarket 3, 4, or 5 times during a month period. Some customers visit the store only 1 time during the month, but others shop as many as 15 times.

c.

Number of Visits	Percent of Total
0 up to 3	17.65
3 up to 6	41.18
6 up to 9	25.49
9 up to 12	7.84
12 up to 15	5.88
15 up to 18	1.96
Total	100.00

15. a. Histogram

b. 100

c. 5

d. 28

e. 0.28

f. 12.5

g. 13

17. a. 50

b. 1.5 thousand miles, or 1,500 miles.

c.

d. $X = 1.5$, $Y = 5$

e.

f. For the 50 employees about half traveled between 6,000 and 9,000 miles. Five employees traveled less than 3,000 miles, and 2 traveled more than 12,000 miles.

19. a. 40

b. 5

c. 11 or 12

d. About \$18/hr

e. About \$9/hr

f. About 75%

21. a. 5

b.

Frequent Flier Miles	f	CF
0 up to 3	5	5
3 up to 6	12	17
6 up to 9	23	40
9 up to 12	8	48
12 up to 15	2	50

c.

d. About 8.7 thousand miles

23. a. A qualitative variable uses either the nominal or ordinal scale of measurement. It is usually the result of counts. Quantitative variables are either discrete or continuous. There is a natural order to the results for a quantitative variable. Quantitative variables can use the either the interval or ratio scale of measurement.

b. Both types of variables can be used for samples and populations.

25. a. Frequency table

b.

c.

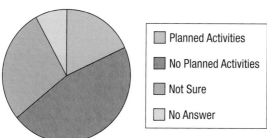

Legend
■ Planned Activities
■ No Planned Activities
■ Not Sure
□ No Answer

d. A pie chart would be better because it clearly shows that nearly half of the customers prefer no planned activities.

27. $2^6 = 64$ and $2^7 = 128$, suggest 7 classes

29. **a.** 5, because $2^4 = 16 < 25$ and $2^5 = 32 > 25$

b. $i \geq \dfrac{48 - 16}{5} = 6.4$ Use interval of 7.

c. 15

d.

Class	Frequency	
15 up to 22	III	3
22 up to 29	JHf III	8
29 up to 36	JHf II	7
36 up to 43	JHf	5
43 up to 50	II	2
		25

e. It is fairly symmetric, with most of the values between 22 and 36.

31. **a.** $2^5 = 32$, $2^6 = 64$, 6 classes recommended.

b. $i = \dfrac{10 - 1}{6} = 1.5$, use an interval of 2.

c. 0

d.

Class	Frequency
0 up to 2	1
2 up to 4	5
4 up to 6	12
6 up to 8	17
8 up to 10	8
10 up to 12	2

e. The distribution is fairly symmetric or bell-shaped with a large peak in the middle of the two classes of 4 up to 8.

33.

Class	Frequency
0 up to 200	19
200 up to 400	1
400 up to 600	4
600 up to 800	1
800 up to 1000	2

This distribution is positively skewed with a large "tail" to the right or positive values. Notice that the top 7 tunes account for 4,342 plays out of a total of 5,968 or about 73 percent of all plays.

35. **a.** 56
b. 10 (found by $60 - 50$)
c. 55
d. 17

37. **a.** $30.50, found by ($265 − $82)/6.
b. $35

c.

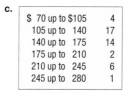

$ 70 up to $105	4
105 up to 140	17
140 up to 175	14
175 up to 210	2
210 up to 245	6
245 up to 280	1

d. The purchases range from a low of about $70 to a high of about $280. The concentration is in the $105 up to $140 and $140 up to $175 classes.

39.

41.

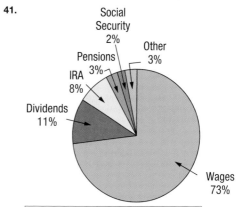

SC Income	Percent	Cumulative
Wages	73	73
Dividends	11	84
IRA	8	92
Pensions	3	95
Social Security	2	97
Other	3	100

By far the largest part of income in South Carolina is earned income. Almost three-fourths of the adjusted gross income comes from wages and salaries. Dividends and IRAs each contribute roughly another 10%.

43. **a.** Since $2^6 = 64 < 70 < 128 = 2^7$, 7 classes are recommended. The interval should be at least $(1,002.2 − 3.3)/7 = 142.7$. Use 150 as a convenient value.

b.

45.

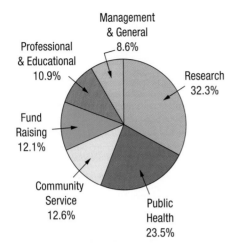

More than half of the expenses are concentrated in the categories Research and Public Health Education.

47.

Partner	Imports	Relative Frequency
Japan	9,550	0.52
United Kingdom	4,556	0.25
South Korea	2,441	0.13
China	1,182	0.06
Australia	618	0.03
	18,347	

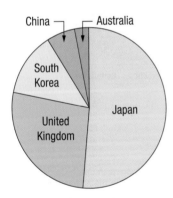

More than half of Canadian imports are from Japan. Japan and the United Kingdom make up more than 75 percent of Canadian imports.

49.

Color	Frequency
Brown	130
Yellow	98
Red	96
Blue	52
Orange	35
Green	33
	444

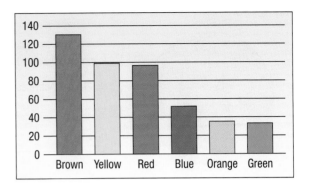

51. 25% market share

53. a.

Bedrooms	Frequency
2	24
3	26
4	26
5	11
6	14
7	2
8	2

1. A typical home had either 3 or 4 bedrooms. Seventy-two percent of the homes had 2, 3, or 4 bedrooms.
2. The fewest bedrooms was 2 and the most 8.

b. $i \geq \dfrac{345.3 - 125.0}{7} = 31.47$. Use interval of 35.

Selling Price ($000)	F	CF
110 up to 145	3	3
145 up to 180	19	22
180 up to 215	31	53
215 up to 250	25	78
250 up to 285	14	92
285 up to 320	10	102
320 up to 355	3	105

1. Most homes (53%) are in the 180 up to 250 range.
2. The largest value is near 355, the smallest near 110.

c.

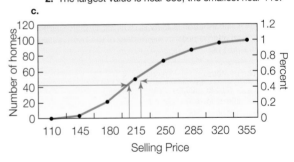

1. About 42 homes sold for less than 200.
2. About 55 percent of the homes sold for less than 220, so 45% sold for more.
3. Less than 1% of the homes sold for less than 125.
d. The selling price ranges from about $120,000 up to about $360,000. A typical home sold for about $210,000.

55.

Occupational category 2 has the fewest members and most of the others are around 19.

CHAPTER 3

1. $\mu = 5.4$, found by $27/5$

3. **a.** $\overline{X} = 7.0$, found by $28/4$

b. $(5 - 7) + (9 - 7) + (4 - 7) + (10 - 7) = 0$

5. $\overline{X} = 14.58$, found by $43.74/3$.

7. **a.** 15.4, found by $154/10$

b. Population parameter, since it includes all the sales at Midtown Ford

9. **a.** $54.55, found by $1,091/20

b. A sample statistic—assuming that the power company serves more than 20 customers

11. $\overline{X} = \dfrac{\Sigma X}{n}$ so

$\Sigma X = \overline{X} \cdot n = (\$5430)(30) = \$162,900$

13. $22.91, found by $\dfrac{300(\$20) + 400(\$25) + 400(\$23)}{300 + 400 + 400}$

15. $17.75, found by ($400 + $750 + $2,400)/200

17. **a.** No mode

b. The given value would be the mode.

c. 3 and 4 bimodal

19. **a.** Mean = 3.25

b. Median = 5,

c. Mode = 5

21. **a.** Median = 2.9

b. Mode = 2.9

23. $\overline{X} = \dfrac{647}{11} = 58.82$

Median = 58, Mode = 58

Any of the three measures would be satisfactory.

25. **a.** $\overline{X} = \dfrac{90.4}{12} = 7.53$

b. Median = 7.45. There are several modes: 6.5, 7.3, 7.8, and 8.7

c. $\overline{X} = \dfrac{33.8}{4} = 8.45$,

Median = 8.7

About 1 percentage point higher in Winter

27. **a.** 6, found by $30/5$.

b. 7, found by $10 - 3$.

c. 2.4, found by $12/5$.

29. **a.** 38, found by $380/10$.

b. 30, found by $54 - 24$.

c. 7.2, found by $72/10$.

31.

State	Mean	Median	Range
California	33.10	34.0	32
Iowa	24.50	25.0	19

The mean and median ratings were higher, but there was also more variation in California.

33. **a.** 5

b. 4.4, found by

$$\dfrac{(8 - 5)^2 + (3 - 5)^2 + (7 - 5)^2 + (3 - 5)^2 + (4 - 5)^2}{5}$$

35. **a.** $2.77

b. 1.26, found by

$$\dfrac{\substack{(2.68 - 2.77)^2 + (1.03 - 2.77)^2 + (2.26 - 2.77)^2 \\ + (4.30 - 2.77)^2 + (3.58 - 2.77)^2}}{5}$$

37. **a.** Range: 7.3, found by $11.6 - 4.3$. Arithmetic mean: 6.94, found by $34.7/5$. Variance: 6.5944, found by $32.972/5$. Standard deviation: 2.568, found by $\sqrt{6.5944}$.

b. Dennis has a higher mean return ($11.76 > 6.94$). However, Dennis has greater spread in its returns on equity ($16.89 > 6.59$).

39. **a.** $\overline{X} = 4$

$s^2 = \dfrac{(7 - 4)^2 + \cdots + (3 - 4)^2}{5 - 1} = 5.5$

$s^2 = \dfrac{22}{5 - 1} = 5.50$

b. $s = 2.3452$

41. **a.** $\overline{X} = 38$

$s^2 = \dfrac{(28 - 38)^2 + \cdots + (42 - 38)^2}{10 - 1} = 82.667$

$s^2 = \dfrac{744}{10 - 1} = 82.667$

b. $s = 9.0921$

43. **a.** $\overline{X} = \dfrac{951}{10} = 95.1$

$s^2 = \dfrac{(101 - 95.1)^2 + \cdots + (88 - 95.1)^2}{10 - 1}$

$= \dfrac{1,112.9}{9} = 123.66$

b. $s = \sqrt{123.66} = 11.12$

45. About 69%, found by $1 - 1/(1.8)^2$

47. **a.** About 95%

b. 47.5%, 2.5%

49. **a.** Mean = 5, found by $(6 + 4 + 3 + 7 + 5)/5$. Median is 5, found by rearranging the values and selecting the middle value.

b. Population, because all partners were included

c. $\Sigma(X - \mu) = (6 - 5) + (4 - 5) + (3 - 5) + (7 - 5) + (5 - 5) = 0$.

51. $\overline{X} = \dfrac{545}{16} = 34.06$

Median = 37.50

53. The data indicates that the communication industry favors older workers, the retail trade favors younger workers. The production workers showed the greatest difference in age. For communication, the distribution is skewed toward older workers. For retail trade, the ages are skewed toward younger workers.

55. $\overline{X}_w = \dfrac{\$5.00(270) + \$6.50(300) + \$8.00(100)}{270 + 300 + 100} = \$6.12$

57. $\overline{X}_w = \dfrac{[15,300(4.5) + 10,400(3.0) + 150,600(10.2)]}{176,300} = 9.28$

59. a. 55, found by $72 - 17$
b. 14.4, found by $144/10$, where $\bar{X} = 43.2$
c. 17.6245

61. a. There were 13 flights, so all items are considered.
b. $\mu = \dfrac{2{,}259}{13} = 173.77$
Median = 195
c. Range = $301 - 7 = 294$
$s = \sqrt{\dfrac{133{,}846}{13}} = 101.47$

63. a. The mean is $717.20, found by $17,930/25. The median is $717.00 and there are two modes, $710 and $722.
b. The range is $90, found by $771 − $681, and the standard deviation is $24.87, found by the square root of 14,850/24.
c. From $667.46 up to $766.94, found by $717.20 ± 2($24.87).

65. a. The mean 0.8654, found by 17.309/20. The median is 0.86 and the mode is 0.792.
b. The range is 0.269, found by $1.025 - 0.756$ and the standard deviation is 0.0853, found by the square root of 0.138167/19.
c. From 0.6948 up to 1.036, found by $0.8654 \pm 2(0.0853)$.

67. a. $\bar{X} = \dfrac{\Sigma X}{n} = \dfrac{273}{30} = 9.1$, Median = 9.0
b. Range = $18 - 4 = 14$
$s = \sqrt{\dfrac{368.7}{30 - 1}} = 3.57$

69. a. $\bar{X} = 89.91$, median = 79.99, $s = 37.84$
b. Using 2009 as the current year:
$\bar{X} = 20.83$, median = 13.50, $s = 24.0$
c. $\bar{X} = 44{,}234$, median = 42,895, $s = 5222$

CHAPTER 4

1. a. Dot plot **b.** 15
c. 1, 7 **d.** 2 and 3

3. Median = 53, found by $(11 + 1)(\frac{1}{2}) \therefore$ 6th value in from lowest
$Q_1 = 49$, found by $(11 + 1)(\frac{1}{4}) \therefore$ 3rd value in from lowest
$Q_3 = 55$, found by $(11 + 1)(\frac{3}{4}) \therefore$ 9th value in from lowest

5. a. $Q_1 = 33.25$, $Q_3 = 50.25$
b. $D_2 = 27.8$, $D_8 = 52.6$
c. $P_{67} = 47$

7. a. 350
b. $Q_1 = 175$, $Q_3 = 930$
c. $930 - 175 = 755$
d. Less than 0, or more than about 2,060
e. There are no outliers.
f. The distribution is positively skewed.

9.

The distribution is somewhat positively skewed. Note that the dashed line above 35 is longer than below 18.

11. a. The mean is 30.8, found by 154/5. The median is 31.0, and the standard deviation is 3.96, found by
$$\sqrt{\dfrac{62.8}{4}}$$
b. -0.15, found by $\dfrac{3(30.8 - 31.0)}{3.96}$

c.

Salary	$\left(\dfrac{(X - \bar{X})}{s}\right)$	$\left(\dfrac{(X - \bar{X})}{s}\right)^3$
36	1.313131	2.264250504
26	−1.212121	−1.780894343
33	0.555556	0.171467764
28	−0.707071	−0.353499282
31	0.050505	0.000128826
		0.301453469

0.125, found by $[5/(4 \times 3)] \times 0.301$

13. a. The mean is 21.93, found by 328.9/15. The median is 15.8, and the standard deviation is 21.18, found by
$$\sqrt{\dfrac{6283}{14}}$$
b. 0.868, found by $[3(21.93 - 15.8)]/21.18$
c. 2.444, found by $[15/(14 \times 13)] \times 29.658$

15.

Scatter Diagram of Y versus X

There is a positive relationship between the variables.

17. a. Both variables are nominal scale.
b. Contingency table
c. Men are about twice as likely to order a dessert. From the table 32 percent of the men ordered dessert, but only 15 percent of the women.

19. a. Dot plot
b. 15
c. 5

21. a. $L_{50} = (20 + 1)\frac{50}{100} = 10.50$
Median = $\dfrac{83.7 + 85.6}{2} = 84.65$
$L_{25} = (21)(.25) = 5.25$
$Q_1 = 66.6 + .25(72.9 - 66.6) = 68.175$
$L_{75} = 21(.75) = 15.75$
$Q_3 = 87.1 + .75(90.2 - 87.1) = 89.425$
b. $L_{26} = 21(.26) = 5.46$
$P_{26} = 66.6 + .46(72.9 - 66.6) = 69.498$
$L_{83} = 21(.83) = 17.43$
$P_{83} = 93.3 + .43(98.6 - 93.3)$
$= 95.579$

c.

23. a. $Q_1 = 26.25$, $Q_3 = 35.75$, Median $= 31.50$

b. $Q_1 = 33.25$, $Q_3 = 38.75$, Median $= 37.50$

c. The median time for public transportation is about 6 minutes less. There is more variation in public transportation. The difference between Q_1 and Q_3 is 9.5 minutes for public transportation and 5.5 minutes for private transportation.

25. The distribution is positively skewed. The first quartile is approx. $20 and the third quartile is approx. $90. There is one outlier located at $255. The median is about $50.

27. a.

Median is 3373. First quartile is 1478. Third quartile is 6141. So prices over 13,135.5, found by 6141 + 1.5 (6141 − 1478), are outliers. There are three (13,925; 20,413 and 44,312).

b.

Median is 0.84. First quartile is 0.515. Third quartile is 1.12. So sizes over 2.0275, found by 1.12 + 1.5 (1.12 − 0.515), are outliers. There are three (2.03, 2.35, and 5.03).

c.

There is a direct association between them. The first observation is larger on both scales.

d.

Shape\ Cut	Average	Good	Ideal	Premium	Ultra Ideal	All
Emerald	0	0	1	0	0	1
Marquise	0	2	0	1	0	3
Oval	0	0	0	1	0	1
Princess	1	0	2	2	0	5
Round	1	3	3	13	3	23
Total	2	5	6	17	3	33

The majority of the diamonds are round (23). Premium cut is most common (17). The Round Premium combination occurs most often (13).

29. $sk = 0.065$ or $sk = \dfrac{3(7.7143 - 8.0)}{3.9036} = -0.22$

31.

As age increases, the number of accidents decreases.

33. a. 139,340,000
  b. 5.4% unemployed, found by (7523/139,340)100
  c. Men $= 5.64\%$
  Women $= 5.12\%$

35. a. There are three outliers, Wrigley Field in Chicago and Fenway Park in Boston. Both of these stadiums are more than 90 years old. Dodger Stadium in Los Angeles is also an outlier. It was 47 years old in 2009.
  b. $Q_1 = \$65.20$ million and $Q_3 = \$118.6$ million. The distribution is positively skewed, with the New York Yankees an outlier.
  c. Higher salaries lead to more wins; lower salaries, fewer wins.
  d. There is little pattern to the distribution of wins. Eleven of the 30 teams have between 84 and 90 wins. Seven teams have between 72 and 75 wins.

CHAPTER 5

1.

	Person	
Outcome	1	2
1	A	A
2	A	F
3	F	A
4	F	F

3. a. .176, found by $\dfrac{6}{34}$
  b. Empirical
5. a. Empirical
  b. Classical
  c. Classical
  d. Empirical, based on seismological data

7. a. The survey of 40 people about environmental issues
   b. 26 or more respond yes, for example
   c. 10/40 = .25
   d. Empirical
   e. The events are not equally likely, but they are mutually exclusive.

9. a. Answers will vary. Here are some possibilities: 123, 124, 125, 999
   b. $(1/10)^3$
   c. Classical

11. $P(A \text{ or } B) = P(A) + P(B) = .30 + .20 = .50$
   $P(\text{neither}) = 1 - .50 = .50$.

13. a. 102/200 = .51
   b. .49, found by 61/200 + 37/200 = .305 + .185. Special rule of addition.

15. $P(\text{above } C) = .25 + .50 = .75$

17. $P(A \text{ or } B) = P(A) + P(B) - P(A \text{ and } B)$
   $= .20 + .30 - .15 = .35$

19. When two events are mutually exclusive, it means that if one occurs the other event cannot occur. Therefore, the probability of their joint occurrence is zero.

21. a. $P(P \text{ and } F) = 0.20$
   b. $P(P \text{ and } D) = 0.30$
   c. No
   d. Joint probability
   e. $P(P \text{ or } D \text{ or } F) = 1 - P(P \text{ and } D \text{ and } F)$
   $= 1 - .10 = .90$

23. $P(A \text{ and } B) = P(A) \times P(B|A) = .40 \times .30 = .12$

25. .90, found by (.80 + .60) − .5.
   .10, found by (1 − .90).

27. a. $P(A_1) = 3/10 = .30$
   b. $P(B_1|A_2) = 1/3 = .33$
   c. $P(B_2 \text{ and } A_3) = 1/10 = .10$

29. a. A contingency table
   b. .27, found by $300/500 \times 135/300$
   c. The tree diagram would appear as:

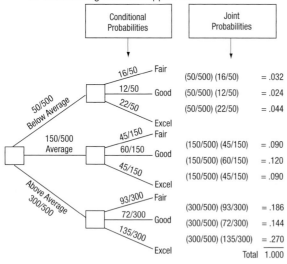

31. Probability the first presentation wins = 3/5 = .60
   Probability the second presentation wins = (2/5)(3/4) = .30
   Probability the third presentation wins = (2/5)(1/4)(3/3) = .10

33. a. 78,960,960
   b. 840, found by (7)(6)(5)(4). That is 7!/3!
   c. 10, found by 5!/3!2!

35. 210, found by (10)(9)(8)(7)/(4)(3)(2)

37. 120, found by 5!

39. 10,897,286,400, found by
   $_{15}P_{10} = (15)(14)(13)(12)(11)(10)(9)(8)(7)(6)$

41. a. Asking teenagers to compare their reactions to a newly developed soft drink.
   b. Answers will vary. One possibility is more than half of the respondents like it.

43. Subjective

45. a. 4/9, found by (2/3) · (2/3).
   b. 3/4, because (3/4) · (2/3) = 0.5.

47. a. .8145, found by $(.95)^4$
   b. Special rule of multiplication
   c. $P(A \text{ and } B \text{ and } C \text{ and } D) = P(A) \times P(B) \times P(C) \times P(D)$

49. a. .08, found by .80 × .10
   b. No; 90% of females attended college, 78% of males
   c.

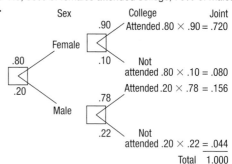

   d. Yes, because all the possible outcomes are shown on the tree diagram.

51. a. 0.57, found by 57/100
   b. 0.97, found by (57/100) + (40/100)
   c. Yes, because an employee cannot be both.
   d. 0.03, found by 1 − 0.97

53. a. 0.5
   b. $\dfrac{1}{12}$
   c. $\dfrac{11}{12}$

55. a. 0.9039, found by $(0.98)^5$
   b. 0.0961, found by 1 − 0.9039

57. a. 0.0333, found by (4/10)(3/9)(2/8)
   b. 0.1667, found by (6/10)(5/9)(4/8)
   c. 0.8333, found by 1 − 0.1667
   d. Dependent

59. a. 0.3818, found by (9/12)(8/11)(7/10)
   b. 0.6182, found by 1 − 0.3818

61. a. $P(S) \cdot P(R|S) = .60(.85) = 0.51$
   b. $P(S) \cdot P(PR|S) = .60(1 - .85) = 0.09$

63. a. $P(\text{not perfect}) = P(\text{bad sector}) + P(\text{defective})$
   $= \dfrac{112}{1,000} + \dfrac{31}{1,000} = .143$
   b. $P(\text{defective/not perfect}) = \dfrac{.031}{.143} = .217$

65. a. $P(P \text{ or } D) = (1/50)(9/10) + (49/50)(1/10) = 0.116$
   b. $P(\text{No}) = (49/50)(9/10) = 0.882$
   c. $P(\text{No on 3}) = (0.882)^3 = 0.686$
   d. $P(\text{at least one prize}) = 1 - 0.686 = 0.314$

67. Yes, 256 is found by 2^8

69. .9744, found by $1 - (.40)^4$

71. a. .185, found by (.15)(.95) + (.05)(.85)
   b. .0075, found by (.15)(.05)

73. a. $P(F \text{ and } {>}60) = .25$, found by solving with the general rule of multiplication:
   $P(F) \cdot P({>}60|F) = (.5)(.5)$
   b. 0
   c. .3333, found by 1/3

75. $26^4 = 456,976$

77. 1/3, 628,800

79. 0.512, found by $(0.8)^3$

81. .525, found by $1 - (.78)^3$

83. **a.**

Winning Season	Attendance			
	Low	Medium	High	Total
No	5	7	1	13
Yes	2	6	9	17
Total	7	13	10	30

  1. $P(\text{win}) = .5667$
  2. $P(\text{win or high}) = .60$
  3. $P(\text{win}|\text{high}) = .90$
  4. $P(\text{lose and low}) = .1667$

b.

Winning Season	Grass	Artificial	Total
No	13	0	13
Yes	14	3	17
Total	27	3	30

  1. $P(\text{grass}) = \dfrac{27}{30} = 0.90$
  2. $P(\text{win}|\text{grass}) = 0.5185$
    $P(\text{win}|\text{art}) = \dfrac{3}{3} = 1.00$
    Teams playing on artificial surface have higher winning percentage.
  3. $P(\text{win or artificial}) = P(\text{win}) + P(\text{artificial})$
        $- P(\text{win and artificial})$
        $= \dfrac{17}{30} + \dfrac{3}{30} - \dfrac{3}{30} = .5667$

CHAPTER 6

1. Mean = 1.3, variance = .81, found by:
$$\mu = 0(.20) + 1(.40) + 2(.30) + 3(.10) = 1.3$$
$$\sigma^2 = (0 - 1.3)^2(.2) + (1 - 1.3)^2(.4)$$
$$+ (2 - 1.3)^2(.3) + (3 - 1.3)^2(.1)$$
$$= .81$$

3. **a.** The second, or middle, one
  b. **1.** .2
      2. .4
      3. .9
  c. $\mu = 14.5$, variance = 27.25, found by:
  $$\mu = 5(.1) + 10(.3) + 15(.2) + 20(.4) = 14.5$$
  $$\sigma^2 = (5 - 14.5)^2(.1) + (10 - 14.5)^2(.3)$$
  $$+ (15 - 14.5)^2(.2) + (20 - 14.5)^2(.4)$$
  $$= 27.25$$
  $$\sigma = 5.22, \text{ found by } \sqrt{27.25}$$

5. **a.**

Calls, x	Frequency	$P(x)$	$xP(x)$	$(x - \mu)^2 P(x)$
0	8	.16	0	.4624
1	10	.20	.20	.0980
2	22	.44	.88	.0396
3	9	.18	.54	.3042
4	1	.02	.08	.1058
	50		1.70	1.0100

  b. Discrete distribution, because only certain outcomes are possible.
  c. $\mu = \Sigma x \cdot P(x) = 1.70$
  d. $\sigma = \sqrt{1.01} = 1.005$

7.

Amount	$P(x)$	$xP(x)$	$(x - \mu)^2 P(x)$
10	.50	5	60.50
25	.40	10	6.40
50	.08	4	67.28
100	.02	2	124.82
		21	259.00

  a. $\mu = \Sigma xP(x) = 21$
  b. $\sigma^2 = \Sigma(x - \mu)^2 P(x) = 259$
    $\sigma = \sqrt{259} = 16.093$

9. **a.** $P(2) = \dfrac{4!}{2!(4 - 2)!}(.25)^2(.75)^{4-2} = .2109$
  b. $P(3) = \dfrac{4!}{3!(4 - 3)!}(.25)^3(.75)^{4-3} = .0469$

11. **a.**

X	$P(X)$
0	.064
1	.288
2	.432
3	.216

  b. $\mu = 1.8$
    $\sigma^2 = 0.72$
    $\sigma = \sqrt{0.72} = .8485$

13. **a.** .2668, found by $P(2) = \dfrac{9!}{(9 - 2)!2!}(.3)^2(.7)^7$
  b. .1715, found by $P(4) = \dfrac{9!}{(9 - 4)!4!}(.3)^4(.7)^5$
  c. .0404, found by $P(0) = \dfrac{9!}{(9 - 0)!0!}(.3)^0(.7)^9$

15. **a.** .2824, found by $P(0) = \dfrac{12!}{(12 - 0)!0!}(.10)^0(.9)^{12}$
  b. .3765, found by $P(1) = \dfrac{12!}{(12 - 1)!1!}(.10)^1(.9)^{11}$
  c. .2301, found by $P(2) = \dfrac{12!}{(12 - 2)!2!}(.10)^2(.9)^{10}$
  d. $\mu = 1.2$, found by 12(.10)
    $\sigma = 1.0392$, found by $\sqrt{1.08}$

17. **a.** 0.1858, found by $\dfrac{15!}{2!13!}(0.23)^2(0.77)^{13}$
  b. 0.1416, found by $\dfrac{15!}{5!10!}(0.23)^5(0.77)^{10}$
  c. 3.45, found by (0.23)(15)

19. **a.** 0.296, found by using Appendix B.9 with n of 8, π of 0.30, and x of 2
  b. $P(x \leq 2) = 0.058 + 0.198 + 0.296 = 0.552$
  c. 0.448, found by $P(x \geq 3) = 1 - P(x \leq 2) = 1 - 0.552$

21. **a.** 0.387, found from Appendix B.9 with n of 9, π of 0.90, and x of 9
  b. $P(X < 5) = 0.001$
  c. 0.992, found by $1 - 0.008$
  d. 0.947, found by $1 - 0.053$

23. **a.** $\mu = 10.5$, found by 15(0.7) and $\sigma = \sqrt{15(0.7)(0.3)} = 1.7748$
  b. 0.2061, found by $\dfrac{15!}{10!5!}(0.7)^{10}(0.3)^5$
  c. 0.4247, found by $0.2061 + 0.2186$
  d. 0.5154, found by
    $0.2186 + 0.1700 + 0.0916 + 0.0305 + 0.0047$

25. **a.** .6703
  b. .3297

27. **a.** .0613
  b. .0803

537

29. $\mu = 6$
$P(X \geq 5) = .7149$
$= 1 - (.0025 + .0149 + .0446 + .0892 + .1339)$

31. A random variable is a quantitative or qualitative outcome that results from a chance experiment. A probability distribution also includes the likelihood of each possible outcome.

33. $\mu = \$1,000(.25) + \$2,000(.60) + \$5,000(.15) = \$2,200$
$\sigma^2 = (1,000 - 2,200)^2 .25 + (\$2,000 - \$2,200)^2 .60 +$
$\quad (5,000 - 2,200)^2 .15$
$= 1,560,000$

35. $\mu = 12(.25) + \cdots + 15(.1) = 13.2$
$\sigma^2 = (12 - 13.2)^2 .25 + \cdots + (15 - 13.2)^2 .10 = 0.86$
$\sigma = \sqrt{0.86} = .927$

37. **a.** $\mu = 10(.35) = 3.5$
  b. $P(X = 4) = {}_{10}C_4 (.35)^4 (.65)^6 = 210(.0150)(.0754) = .2375$
  c. $P(X \geq 4) = {}_{10}C_x (.35)^X (.65)^{10-X}$
$\quad = .2375 + .1536 + \cdots + .0000 = .4862$

39. **a.** 6, found by 0.4×15
  b. 0.0245, found by $\dfrac{15!}{10!5!} (0.4)^{10}(0.6)^5$
  c. 0.0338, found by
$\quad 0.0245 + 0.0074 + 0.0016 + 0.0003 + 0.0000$
  d. 0.0093, found by $0.0338 - 0.0245$

41. **a.** $\mu = 20(0.075) = 1.5$
$\quad \sigma = \sqrt{20(0.075)(0.925)} = 1.1779$
  b. 0.2103, found by $\dfrac{20!}{0!20!} (0.075)^0(0.925)^{20}$
  c. 0.7897, found by $1 - 0.2103$

43. **a.** 0.1311, found by $\dfrac{16!}{4!12!} (0.15)^4(0.85)^{12}$
  b. 2.4, found by $(0.15)(16)$
  c. 0.2100, found by
$\quad 1 - 0.0743 - 0.2097 - 0.2775 - 0.2285$

45. $P(2) = \dfrac{[{}_6C_2][{}_4C_2]}{[{}_{10}C_4]} = \dfrac{(15)(6)}{210} = 0.4286$

47. **a.**

0	0.0002	7	0.2075
1	0.0019	8	0.1405
2	0.0116	9	0.0676
3	0.0418	10	0.0220
4	0.1020	11	0.0043
5	0.1768	12	0.0004
6	0.2234		

  b. $\mu = 12(0.52) = 6.24$
$\quad \sigma = \sqrt{12(0.52)(0.48)} = 1.7307$
  c. 0.1768
  d. 0.3343, found by $0.0002 + 0.0019$
$\quad + 0.0116 + 0.0418 + 0.1020 + 0.1768$

49. **a.** .0498
  b. .7746, found by $(1 - .0498)^5$

51. $\mu = 4.0$, from Appendix B.5
  a. .0183
  b. .1954
  c. .6289
  d. .5665

53. **a.** 0.1733, found by $\dfrac{(3.1)^4 e^{-3.1}}{4!}$
  b. 0.0450, found by $\dfrac{(3.1)^0 e^{-3.1}}{0!}$
  c. 0.9550, found by $1 - 0.0450$

55. $\mu = n\pi = 23\left(\dfrac{2}{123}\right) = .374$

$P(2) = \dfrac{(.407)^2 e^{-.407}}{2!} = 0.0551$

$P(0) = \dfrac{(.407)^0 e^{-.407}}{0!} = 0.6656$

57. Let $\mu = n\pi = 155(1/3,709) = 0.042$
$P(5) = \dfrac{0.042^5 e^{-0.042}}{5!} = 0.000000001$
Very unlikely!

59. **a.** $\mu = n\pi = 15(.67) = 10.05$
$\quad \sigma = \sqrt{n\pi(1 - \pi)} = \sqrt{15(.67)(.33)} = 1.8211$
  b. $P(8) = {}_{15}C_8(.67)^8(.33)^7 = 6435(.0406)(.000426) = .1114$
  c. $P(x \geq 8) = .1114 + .1759 + \cdots + .0025 = .9163$

CHAPTER 7

1. **a.** $b = 10, a = 6$
  b. $\mu = \dfrac{6 + 10}{2} = 8$
  c. $\sigma = \sqrt{\dfrac{(10 - 6)^2}{12}} = 1.1547$
  d. Area $= \dfrac{1}{(10 - 6)} \cdot \dfrac{(10 - 6)}{1} = 1$
  e. $P(X > 7) = \dfrac{1}{(10 - 6)} \cdot \dfrac{10 - 7}{1} = \dfrac{3}{4} = .75$
  f. $P(7 \leq x \leq 9) = \dfrac{1}{(10 - 6)} \cdot \dfrac{(9 - 7)}{1} = \dfrac{2}{4} = .50$

3. **a.** 0.30, found by $(30 - 27)/(30 - 20)$
  b. 0.40, found by $(24 - 20)/(30 - 20)$

5. **a.** $a = 0.5, b = 3.00$
  b. $\mu = \dfrac{0.5 + 3.00}{2} = 1.75$
$\quad \sigma = \sqrt{\dfrac{(3.00 - .50)^2}{12}} = .72$
  c. $P(x < 1) = \dfrac{1}{(3.0 - 0.5)} \cdot \dfrac{1 - .5}{1} = \dfrac{.5}{2.5} = 0.2$
  d. 0, found by $\dfrac{1}{(3.0 - 0.5)} \cdot \dfrac{(1.0 - 1.0)}{1}$
  e. $P(x > 1.5) = \dfrac{1}{(3.0 - 0.5)} \cdot \dfrac{3.0 - 1.5}{1} = \dfrac{1.5}{2.5} = 0.6$

7. The actual shape of a normal distribution depends on its mean and standard deviation. Thus, there is a normal distribution, and an accompanying normal curve, for a mean of 7 and a standard deviation of 2. There is another normal curve for a mean of $25,000 and a standard deviation of $1,742, and so on.

9. **a.** 490 and 510, found by $500 \pm 1(10)$
  b. 480 and 520, found by $500 \pm 2(10)$
  c. 470 and 530, found by $500 \pm 3(10)$

11. $Z_{Rob} = \dfrac{\$50,000 - \$60,000}{\$5,000} = -2$
$Z_{Rachel} = \dfrac{\$50,000 - \$35,000}{\$8,000} = 1.875$
Adjusting for their industries, Rob is well below average and Rachel well above.

13. **a.** 1.25, found by $z = \dfrac{25 - 20}{4.0} = 1.25$
  b. 0.3944, found in Appendix B.1
  c. 0.3085, found by $z = \dfrac{18 - 20}{2.5} = -0.5$
$\quad$ Find 0.1915 in Appendix B.1 for $z = -0.5$,
$\quad$ then $0.5000 - 0.1915 = 0.3085$

15. **a.** 0.3413, found by $z = \dfrac{\$24 - \$20.50}{\$3.50} = 1.00$,

then find 0.3413 in Appendix B.1 for $z = 1$

b. 0.1587, found by $0.5000 - 0.3413 = 0.1587$

c. 0.3336, found by $z = \dfrac{\$19.00 - \$20.50}{\$3.50} = -0.43$

Find 0.1664 in Appendix B.1, for $z = -0.43$,
then $0.5000 - 0.1664 = 0.3336$

17. **a.** 0.8276: First find $z = -1.5$, found by $(44 - 50)/4$ and
$z = 1.25 = (55 - 50)/4$. The area between -1.5 and 0 is
0.4332 and the area between 0 and 1.25 is 0.3944, both
from Appendix B.1. Then adding the two areas we find
that $0.4332 + 0.3944 = 0.8276$.

b. 0.1056, found by $0.5000 - .3944$, where $z = 1.25$

c. 0.2029: Recall that the area for $z = 1.25$ is 0.3944, and
the area for $z = 0.5$, found by $(52 - 50)/4$, is 0.1915.
Then subtract $0.3944 - 0.1915$ and find 0.2029.

19. **a.** 0.3264, found by $0.5000 - 0.1736$, where $z = 0.45$,
found by $((3000 - 2708)/650)$.

b. 0.2152; the z-value for \$3,500 is 1.22, found by
$((3500 - 2708)/650)$, and the corresponding area is
0.3888, which leads to $0.3888 - 0.1736 = 0.2152$.

c. 0.5143; the z-value for \$2,500 is -0.32, found by
$((2,500 - 2708)/650)$, and the corresponding area is
0.1255, which leads to $0.1255 + 0.3888 = 0.5143$.

21. **a.** 0.0764, found by $z = (20 - 15)/3.5 = 1.43$,
then $0.5000 - 0.4236 = 0.0764$

b. 0.9236, found by $0.5000 + 0.4236$, where $z = 1.43$

c. 0.1185, found by $z = (12 - 15)/3.5 = -0.86$.
The area under the curve is 0.3051, then
$z = (10 - 15)/3.5 = -1.43$. The area is 0.4236.
Finally, $0.4236 - 0.3051 = 0.1185$.

23. $X = 56.60$, found by adding 0.5000 (the area left of
the mean) and then finding a z value that forces
45 percent of the data to fall inside the curve. Solving for
X: $1.65 = (X - 50)/4 = 56.60$.

25. \$1,630, found by $\$2,100 - 1.88(\$250)$

27. **a.** 214.8 hours: Find a z value where 0.4900 of area is
between 0 and z. That value is $z = 2.33$. Then solve
for X: $2.33 = (X - 195)/8.5$, so $X = 214.8$ hours.

b. 270.2 hours: Find a z value where 0.4900 of area is
between 0 and $(-z)$. That value is $z = -2.33$. Then solve
for X: $-2.33 = (X - 290)/8.5$, so $X = 270.2$ hours.

29. 214 copies: Find a z value where $0.3000(0.50 - 0.20)$ of
area is between 0 and z. That value is 0.84. Then solve for
X: $0.84 = (X - 200)/17$, so $X = 214$ copies.

31. **a.** $\mu = \dfrac{11.96 + 12.05}{2} = 12.005$

b. $\sigma = \sqrt{\dfrac{(12.05 - 11.96)^2}{12}} = .0260$

c. $P(X < 12) = \dfrac{1}{(12.05 - 11.96)} \dfrac{12.00 - 11.96}{1} = \dfrac{.04}{.09} = .44$

d. $P(X > 11.98) = \dfrac{1}{(12.05 - 11.96)} \left(\dfrac{12.05 - 11.98}{1} \right)$

$= \dfrac{.07}{.09} = .78$

e. All cans have more than 11.00 ounces, so the
probability is 100%.

33. **a.** $\mu = \dfrac{4 + 10}{2} = 7$

b. $\sigma = \sqrt{\dfrac{(10 - 4)^2}{12}} = 1.732$

c. $P(X < 6) = \dfrac{1}{(10 - 4)} \cdot \left(\dfrac{6 - 4}{1} \right) = \dfrac{2}{6} = .33$

d. $P(X > 5) = \dfrac{1}{(10 - 4)} \cdot \left(\dfrac{10 - 5}{1} \right) = \dfrac{5}{6} = .83$

35. **a.** -0.4 for net sales, found by $(170 - 180)/25$.
2.92 for employees, found by $(1,850 - 1,500)/120$.

b. Net sales are 0.4 standard deviations below the mean.
Employees is 2.92 standard deviations above the mean.

c. 65.54 percent of the aluminum fabricators have greater
net sales compared with Clarion, found by $0.1554 +
0.5000$. Only 0.18 percent have more employees than
Clarion, found by $0.5000 - 0.4982$.

37. **a.** 0.5000, because $z = \dfrac{30 - 490}{90} = -5.11$

b. 0.2514, found by $0.5000 - 0.2486$

c. 0.6374, found by $0.2486 + 0.3888$

d. 0.3450, found by $0.3888 - 0.0438$

39. **a.** 0.3015, found by $0.5000 - 0.1985$

b. 0.2579, found by $0.4564 - 0.1985$

c. 0.0011, found by $0.5000 - 0.4989$

d. 1,818, found by $1,280 + 1.28(420)$

41. **a.** 90.82%: First find $z = 1.33$ found by $(40 - 34)/4.5$. The
area between 0 and 1.33 is 0.4082. Then add 0.5000
and 0.4082 and find 0.9082 or 90.82%.

b. 78.23%: First find $z = -0.78$ found by $(25 - 29)/5.1$.
The area between 0 and (-0.78) is 0.2823. Then add
0.5000 and 0.2823 and find 0.7823 or 78.23%.

c. 44.5 hours/week for women: Find a z value where
0.4900 of the area is between 0 and z. That value
is 2.33. Then solve for X: $2.33 = (X - 34)/4.5$, so
$X = 44.5$ hours/week. 40.9 hours/week for men:
$2.33 = (X - 29)/5.1$, so $X = 40.9$ hours/week.

43. About 4,099 units, found by solving for X.
$1.65 = (X - 4,000)/60$

45. **a.** 15.39%, found by $(8 - 10.3)/2.25 = -1.02$,
then $0.5000 - 0.3461 = 0.1539$.

b. 17.31%, found by:
$z = (12 - 10.3)/2.25 = 0.76$. Area is 0.2764.
$z = (14 - 10.3)/2.25 = 1.64$. Area is 0.4495.
The area between 12 and 14 is 0.1731,
found by $0.4495 - 0.2764$.

c. Yes, but it is rather remote. Reasoning:
On 99.73% of the days, returns are between 3.55 and
17.05, found by $10.3 \pm 3(2.25)$. Thus, the chance of less
than 3.55 returns is rather remote.

47. **a.** 21.19 percent found by $z = (9.00 - 9.20)/0.25 = -0.80$,
so $0.5000 - 0.2881 = 0.2119$

b. Increase the mean. $z = (9.00 - 9.25)/0.25 = -1.00$,
$P = 0.5000 - 0.3413 = 0.1587$.
Reduce the standard deviation. $\sigma = (9.00 - 9.20)/
0.15 = -1.33$; $P = 0.5000 - 0.4082 = 0.0918$.
Reducing the standard deviation is better because a
smaller percent of the hams will be below the limit.

49. **a.** $z = (52 - 60)/5 = 1.60$, so $0.5000 - 0.4452 = 0.0548$

b. Let $z = 0.67$, so $0.67 = (X - 52)/5$ and $X = 55.35$, set
mileage at 55,350

c. $z = (45 - 52)/5 = -1.40$, so $0.5000 - 0.4192 = 0.0808$

51. $\dfrac{470 - \mu}{\sigma} = 0.25$ $\quad$ $\dfrac{500 - \mu}{\sigma} = 1.28$ $\quad$ $\sigma = 29,126$ and

$\mu = 462,718$

53. **a.** .2946, found by $.5000 - .2054$

$z = \dfrac{100 - 83.9}{30} = 0.54$

b. Very little chance, $z = 3.87$

$z = \dfrac{200 - 83.9}{30} = 3.87$

c. 140.3, found by $X = 83.9 + 30.9(1.88) = 140.3$

55. **a.** 0.1210, found by $0.5000 - 0.3790$ with $z =
(3500 - 2620)/751 = 1.17$; leads to 3.6 teams,
found by $30(0.1210)$. Three teams actually had
attendance of more than 3.5 million, so the estimate is
fairly accurate.

b. 0.8531, found by 0.5000 + 0.3531 with $z = (50 - 89.91)/37.84 = -1.05$; leads to 25.6 teams, found by 30(0.8531). Twenty-six teams actually had salaries of more than $50 million, so the estimate is accurate.

CHAPTER 8

1. a. 303 Louisiana, 5155 S. Main, 3501 Monroe, 2652 W. Central
   b. Answers will vary.
   c. 630 Dixie Hwy, 835 S. McCord Rd, 4624 Woodville Rd, and 2607 Starr Ave. (Cycle back to start to obtain 4th member of sample.)
   d. Answers will vary.
3. a. Bob Schmidt Chevrolet
   Great Lakes Ford Nissan
   Grogan Towne Chrysler
   Southside Lincoln Mercury
   Rouen Chrysler Jeep Eagle
   b. Answers will vary.
   c. Yark Automotive
   Thayer Chevrolet Toyota
   Franklin Park Lincoln Mercury
   Mathews Ford Oregon, Inc.
   Valiton Chrysler
5. a.

Sample	Values	Sum	Mean
1	12, 12	24	12
2	12, 14	26	13
3	12, 16	28	14
4	12, 14	26	13
5	12, 16	28	14
6	14, 16	30	15

   b. $\mu_{\bar{x}} = (12 + 13 + 14 + 13 + 14 + 15)/6 = 13.5$
   $\mu = (12 + 12 + 14 + 16)/4 = 13.5$
   c. More dispersion with population data compared to the sample means. The sample means vary from 12 to 15, whereas the population varies from 12 to 16.
7. a.

Sample	Values	Sum	Mean
1	12, 12, 14	38	12.66
2	12, 12, 15	39	13.00
3	12, 12, 20	44	14.66
4	14, 15, 20	49	16.33
5	12, 14, 15	41	13.66
6	12, 14, 15	41	13.66
7	12, 15, 20	47	15.66
8	12, 15, 20	47	15.66
9	12, 14, 20	46	15.33
10	12, 14, 20	46	15.33

   b. $\mu_{\bar{x}} = \dfrac{(12.66 + \cdots + 15.33 + 15.33)}{10} = 14.6$
   $\mu = (12 + 12 + 14 + 15 + 20)/5 = 14.6$
   c. The dispersion of the population is greater than that of the sample means. The sample means vary from 12.66 to 16.33, whereas the population varies from 12 to 20.
9. a. 20, found by $_6C_3$
   b.

Sample	Cases	Sum	Mean
Ruud, Wu, Sass	3, 6, 3	12	4.00
Ruud, Sass, Flores	3, 3, 3	9	3.00
⋮	⋮	⋮	⋮
Sass, Flores, Schueller	3, 3, 1	7	2.33

   c. $\mu_{\bar{x}} = 2.67$, found by $\dfrac{53.33}{20}$.
   $\mu = 2.67$, found by $(3 + 6 + 3 + 3 + 0 + 1)/6$.
   They are equal.

d.

Sample Mean	Number of Means	Probability
1.33	3	.1500
2.00	3	.1500
2.33	4	.2000
3.00	4	.2000
3.33	3	.1500
4.00	3	.1500
	20	1.0000

The population has more dispersion than the sample means. The sample means vary from 1.33 to 4.0. The population varies from 0 to 6.

11. a.

$\mu = \dfrac{0 + 1 + \cdots + 9}{10} = 4.5$

b.

Sample	Sum	$\overline{X}$
1	11	2.2
2	31	6.2
3	21	4.2
4	24	4.8
5	21	4.2
6	20	4.0
7	23	4.6
8	29	5.8
9	35	7.0
10	27	5.4

The mean of the 10 sample means is 4.84, which is close to the population mean of 4.5. The sample means range from 2.2 to 7.0, whereas the population values range from 0 to 9. From the above graph, the sample means tend to cluster between 4 and 5.

13. a.–c. Answers will vary depending on the coins in your possession.

15. a. $z = \dfrac{63 - 60}{12/\sqrt{9}} = 0.75$

$P = .2266$, found by $.5000 - .2734$

b. $z = \dfrac{56 - 60}{12/\sqrt{9}} = -1.00$

$P = .1587$, found by $.5000 - .3413$

c. $P = .6147$, found by $0.3413 + 0.2734$

17. $z = \dfrac{1,950 - 2,200}{250/\sqrt{50}} = -7.07$ $P = 1$, or virtually certain

19. a. Formal Man, Summit Stationers, Bootleggers, Leather Ltd, Petries

b. Answers may vary.

c. Elder-Beerman, Frederick's of Hollywood, Summit Stationers, Lion Store, Leather Ltd., Things Remembered, County Seat, Coach House Gifts, Regis Hairstylists

21. a.

Samples	Mean	Deviation from Mean	Square of Deviation
1, 1	1.0	−1.0	1.0
1, 2	1.5	−0.5	0.25
1, 3	2.0	0.0	0.0
2, 1	1.5	−0.5	0.25
2, 2	2.0	0.0	0.0
2, 3	2.5	0.5	0.25
3, 1	2.0	0.0	0.0
3, 2	2.5	0.5	0.25
3, 3	3.0	1.0	1.0

b. Mean of sample means is $(1.0 + 1.5 + 2.0 + \cdots + 3.0)/9 = 18/9 = 2.0$. The population mean is $(1 + 2 + 3)/3 = 6/3 = 2$. They are the same value.

c. Variance of sample means is $(1.0 + 0.25 + 0.0 + \cdots + 3.0)/9 = 3/9 = 1/3$. The population mean is $(1 + 1.0)/9 = 1/3$. Variance of the population values is $(1 + 0 + 1)/3 = 2/3$. The variance of the population is twice as large as that of the sample means.

d. Sample means follow a triangular shape peaking at 2. The population is uniform between 1 and 3.

23. Larger samples provide narrower estimates of a population mean. So the company with 200 sampled customers can provide more precise estimates. In addition, they are selected consumers who are familiar with laptop computers and may be better able to evaluate the new computer.

25. a. We selected 60, 104, 75, 72, and 48. Answers will vary.

b. We selected the third observation. So the sample consists of 75, 72, 68, 82, 48. Answers will vary.

c. Number the first 20 motels from 00 to 19. Randomly select three numbers. Then number the last five numbers 20 to 24. Randomly select two numbers from that group.

27. a. 15, found by $_6C_2$

b.

Sample	Value	Sum	Mean
1	79, 64	143	71.5
2	79, 84	163	81.5
⋮	⋮	⋮	⋮
15	92, 77	169	84.5
			1,195.0

c. $\mu_{\overline{x}} = 79.67$, found by $1,195/15$.

$\mu = 79.67$, found by $478/6$.

They are equal.

d. No. The student is not graded on all available information. He/she is as likely to get a lower grade based on the sample as a higher grade.

29. a. 10, found by $_5C_2$

b.

Number of Shutdowns	Mean	Number of Shutdowns	Mean
4, 3	3.5	3, 3	3.0
4, 5	4.5	3, 2	2.5
4, 3	3.5	5, 3	4.0
4, 2	3.0	5, 2	3.5
3, 5	4.0	3, 2	2.5

Sample Mean	Frequency	Probability
2.5	2	.20
3.0	2	.20
3.5	3	.30
4.0	2	.20
4.5	1	.10
	10	1.00

c. $\mu_{\overline{x}} = (3.5 + 4.5 + \cdots + 2.5)/10 = 3.4$

$\mu = (4 + 3 + 5 + 3 + 2)/5 = 3.4$

The two means are equal.

d. The population values are relatively uniform in shape. The distribution of sample means tends toward normality.

31. a. The distribution will be normal.

b. $\sigma_{\overline{x}} = \dfrac{5.5}{\sqrt{25}} = 1.1$

c. $z = \dfrac{36 - 35}{5.5/\sqrt{25}} = 0.91$

$P = 0.1814$, found by $0.5000 - 0.3186$

d. $z = \dfrac{34.5 - 35}{5.5/\sqrt{25}} = -0.45$

$P = 0.6736$, found by $0.5000 + 0.1736$

e. 0.4922, found by $0.3186 + 0.1736$

33. $z = \dfrac{\$335 - \$350}{\$45/\sqrt{40}} = -2.11$

$P = 0.9826$, found by $0.5000 + 0.4826$

35. $z = \dfrac{25.1 - 24.8}{2.5/\sqrt{60}} = 0.93$

$P = 0.8238$, found by $0.5000 + 0.3238$

37. Between 5,954 and 6,046, found by
$6,000 \pm 1.96\,(150/\sqrt{40})$

39. $z = \dfrac{900 - 947}{205/\sqrt{60}} = -1.78$

$P = 0.0375$, found by $0.5000 - 0.4625$

41. a. $z = \dfrac{600 - 510}{14.28/\sqrt{10}} = 19.9$, $P = 0.00$,

    or virtually never

  b. $z = \dfrac{500 - 510}{14.28/\sqrt{10}} = -2.21$,

    $P = 0.4864 + 0.5000 = 0.9864$

  c. $z = \dfrac{500 - 510}{14.28/\sqrt{10}} = -2.21$,

    $P = 0.5000 - 0.4864 = 0.0136$

43. a. $\sigma_{\bar{X}} = \dfrac{2.1}{\sqrt{81}} = 0.23$

  b. $z = \dfrac{7.0 - 6.5}{2.1/\sqrt{81}} = 2.14$, $z = \dfrac{6.0 - 6.5}{2.1/\sqrt{81}} = -2.14$,

    $P = .4838 + .4838 = .9676$

  c. $z = \dfrac{6.75 - 6.5}{2.1/\sqrt{81}} = 1.07$, $z = \dfrac{6.25 - 6.5}{2.1/\sqrt{81}} = -1.07$,

    $P = .3577 + .3577 = .7154$

  d. .0162 found by $.5000 - .4838$.

CHAPTER 9

1. 51.314 and 58.686, found by $55 \pm 2.58(10/\sqrt{49})$

3. a. 1.581, found by $\sigma_{\bar{X}} = 5/\sqrt{10}$

  b. The population is normally distributed and the population variance is known.

  c. 16.901 and 23.099, found by 20 ± 3.099

5. a. \$20. It is our best estimate of the population mean.

  b. \$18.60 and \$21.40, found by $20 \pm 1.96(\$5/\sqrt{49})$. About 95 percent of the intervals similarly constructed will include the population mean.

7. a. 8.60 gallons.

  b. 7.83 and 9.37, found by $8.60 \pm 2.58(2.30/\sqrt{60})$

  c. If 100 such intervals were determined, the population mean would be included in about 99 intervals.

9. a. 2.201

  b. 1.729

  c. 3.499

11. a. The population mean is unknown, but the best estimate is 20, the sample mean.

  b. Use the t distribution as the standard deviation is unknown. However, assume the population is normally distributed.

  c. 2.093

  d. Between 19.06 and 20.94, found by $20 \pm 2.093(2/\sqrt{20})$

  e. Neither value is reasonable, because they are not inside the interval.

13. Between 95.39 and 101.81, found by
$98.6 \pm 1.833(5.54/\sqrt{10})$

15. a. 0.8, found by 80/100

  b. Between 0.72 and 0.88, found by

    $0.8 \pm 1.96\left(\sqrt{\dfrac{0.8(1 - 0.8)}{100}}\right)$

  c. We are reasonably sure the population proportion is between 72 and 88 percent.

17. a. 0.625, found by 250/400

  b. Between 0.563 and 0.687, found by

    $0.625 \pm 2.58\left(\sqrt{\dfrac{0.625(1 - 0.625)}{400}}\right)$

  c. We are reasonably sure the population proportion is between 56 and 69 percent.

19. 33.41 and 36.59, found by

$35 \pm 2.030\left(\dfrac{5}{\sqrt{36}}\right)\sqrt{\dfrac{300 - 36}{300 - 1}}$

21. 1.683 and 2.037, found by

$1.86 \pm 2.680\left(\dfrac{0.5}{\sqrt{50}}\right)\sqrt{\dfrac{400 - 50}{400 - 1}}$

23. 97, found by $n = \left(\dfrac{1.96 \times 10}{2}\right)^2 = 96.04$

25. 196, found by $n = 0.15(0.85)\left(\dfrac{1.96}{0.05}\right)^2 = 195.9216$

27. 554, found by $n = \left(\dfrac{1.96 \times 3}{0.25}\right)^2 = 553.19$

29. a. 577, found by $n = 0.60(0.40)\left(\dfrac{1.96}{0.04}\right)^2 = 576.24$

  b. 601, found by $n = 0.50(0.50)\left(\dfrac{1.96}{0.04}\right)^2 = 600.25$

31. 6.13 years to 6.87 years, found by $6.5 \pm 1.989(1.7/\sqrt{85})$

33. a. Between 2.018 and 2.040, found by

    $2.029 \pm 2.680\left(\dfrac{0.03}{\sqrt{50}}\right)$

  b. \$1.50 is not reasonable, because it is outside the confidence interval.

35. a. The population mean is unknown.

  b. Between 7.50 and 9.14, found by
$8.32 \pm 1.685(3.07/\sqrt{40})$

  c. 10 is not reasonable because it is not in the interval.

37. a. 65.49 up to 71.71 hours, found by $68.6 \pm 2.680(8.2/\sqrt{50})$

  b. The value suggested by the NCAA is included in the confidence interval. Therefore, it is reasonable.

  c. Changing the confidence interval to 95 would reduce the width of the interval. The value of 2.680 would change to 2.010.

39. 61, found by $1.96(16/\sqrt{n}) = 4$

41. Between \$13,734 up to \$15,028, found by
$14,381 \pm 1.711(1,892/\sqrt{25})$. 15,000 is reasonable because it is inside the confidence interval.

43. a. \$62.583, found by \$751/12

  b. Between \$60.54 and \$64.63, found by
$62.583 \pm 1.796(3.94/\sqrt{12})$

  c. \$60 is not reasonable, because it is outside the confidence interval.

45. a. 89.4667, found by 1,342/15

  b. Between 84.99 and 93.94, found by
$89.4667 \pm 2.145(8.08/\sqrt{15})$

  c. Yes, because even the lower limit of the confidence interval is above 80.

47. Between 0.648 and 0.752, found by

$.7 \pm 2.58\left(\sqrt{\dfrac{0.7(1 - 0.7)}{500}}\right)\left(\sqrt{\dfrac{20,000 - 500}{20,000 - 1}}\right)$

Yes, because even the lower limit of the confidence interval is above 0.500.

49. \$52.51 and \$55.49, found by

$\$54.00 \pm 2.032\dfrac{\$4.50}{\sqrt{35}}\sqrt{\dfrac{(500 - 35)}{500 - 1}}$

51. 369, found by $n = 0.60(1 - 0.60)(1.96/0.05)^2$

53. 97, found by $[(1.96 \times 500)/100]^2$

55. a. Between 7,849 and 8,151, found by
$8,000 \pm 2.756(300/\sqrt{30})$

  b. 554, found by $n = \left(\dfrac{(1.96)(300)}{25}\right)^2$

57. a. Between 75.44 and 80.56, found by $78 \pm 2.010(9/\sqrt{50})$

b. 221, found by $n = \left(\dfrac{(1.65)(9)}{1.0}\right)^2$

59. a. 30, found by $180/\sqrt{36}$

b. \$355.10 and \$476.90, found by $416 \pm 2.030\left(\dfrac{\$180}{\sqrt{36}}\right)$

c. About 1245, found by $\left(\dfrac{2.030(180)}{10}\right)^2$

61. a. 708.13, rounded up to 709, found by $0.21(1 - 0.21)(1.96/0.03)^2$

b. 1,068, found by $0.50(0.50)(1.96/0.03)^2$

63. Between 0.573 and 0.653, found by

$.613 \pm 2.58\left(\sqrt{\dfrac{0.613(1 - 0.613)}{1,000}}\right)$. Yes, because even the

lower limit of the confidence interval is above 0.500.

65. a. Between 0.156 and 0.184, found by

$0.17 \pm 1.96\sqrt{\dfrac{(0.17)(1 - 0.17)}{2700}}$

b. Yes, because 18 percent is inside the confidence interval.

c. 21,682; found by $0.17(1 - 0.17)[1.96/0.005]^2$

67. Between 12.69 and 14.11, found by $13.4 \pm 1.96 \, (6.8/\sqrt{352})$

69. a. For selling price: 211.99 up to 230.22, found by $221.1 \pm (1.983)(47.11/\sqrt{105}) = 221.1 \pm 9.12$

b. For distance: 13.685 up to 15.572, found by $14.629 \pm (1.983)(4.874/\sqrt{105}) = 14.629 \pm 0.943$

c. For garage: 0.5867 up to 0.7657, found by $0.6762 \pm$

$(1.96)\sqrt{\dfrac{0.6762(1 - 0.6762)}{105}} = 0.6762 \pm 0.0895$

71. a. $\$30,833 \pm 1.984 \dfrac{\$16,947}{\sqrt{100}} = \$30,833 \pm 3362$, so the

limits are \$27,471 and \$34,196. It is not reasonable that the population mean is \$35,000.

b. $12.73 \pm 1.984 \dfrac{\$2.792}{\sqrt{100}} = \$12.73 \pm 0.55$, so the limits

are 12.18 and 13.28. The population mean could be 13 years.

c. $39.11 \pm 1.984 \dfrac{12.57}{\sqrt{100}} = 39.11 \pm 2.49$, so the limits are

36.62 and 41.60. The mean age of the worker could be 40 years.

CHAPTER 10

1. a. Two-tailed

b. Reject H_0 when z does not fall in the region between -1.96 and 1.96.

c. -1.2, found by $z = (49 - 50)/(5/\sqrt{36}) = -1.2$

d. Fail to reject H_0

e. $p = .2302$, found by $2(.5000 - .3849)$. A 23.02% chance of finding a z value this large when H_0 is true.

3. a. One-tailed

b. Reject H_0 when $z > 1.65$.

c. 1.2, found by $z = (21 - 20)/(5/\sqrt{36}) = 1.2$

d. Fail to reject H_0 at the .05 significance level

e. $p = .1151$, found by $.5000 - .3849$. An 11.51 percent chance of finding a z value this large or larger.

5. a. $H_0: \mu = 60,000 \qquad H_1: \mu \neq 60,000$

b. Reject H_0 if $z < -1.96$ or $z > 1.96$.

c. -0.69, found by:

$$z = \dfrac{59,500 - 60,000}{(5,000/\sqrt{48})} = -0.69$$

d. Do not reject H_0

e. $p = .4902$, found by $2(.5000 - .2549)$. Crosset's experience is not different from that claimed by the manufacturer. If H_0 is true, the probability of finding a value more extreme than this is .4902.

7. a. $H_0: \mu \geq 6.8 \qquad H_1: \mu < 6.8$

b. Reject H_0 if $z < -1.65$

c. $z = \dfrac{6.2 - 6.8}{0.5/\sqrt{36}} = -7.2$

d. H_0 is rejected.

e. $p = 0$. The mean number of DVDs watched is less than 6.8 per month. If H_0 is true, there is virtually no chance of getting a statistic this small.

9. a. Reject H_0 when $t > 1.833$

b. $t = \dfrac{12 - 10}{(3/\sqrt{10})} = 2.108$

c. Reject H_0. The mean is greater than 10.

11. $H_0: \mu \leq 40 \qquad H_1: \mu > 40$

Reject H_0 if $t > 1.703$.

$$t = \dfrac{42 - 40}{(2.1/\sqrt{28})} = 5.040$$

Reject H_0 and conclude that the mean number of calls is greater than 40 per week.

13. $H_0: \mu \leq 22,100 \qquad H_1: \mu > 22,100$

Reject H_0 if $t > 1.740$

$$t = \dfrac{23,400 - 22,100}{(1,500/\sqrt{18})} = 3.680$$

Reject H_0 and conclude that the mean life of the spark plugs is greater than 22,100 miles.

15. a. Reject H_0 if $t < -3.747$

b. $\overline{X} = 17$ and $s = \sqrt{\dfrac{50}{5 - 1}} = 3.536$

$$t = \dfrac{17 - 20}{(3.536/\sqrt{5})} = -1.90$$

c. Do not reject H_0. We cannot conclude the population mean is less than 20.

d. Between .05 and .10, about .065

17. $H_0: \mu \leq 4.35 \qquad H_1: \mu > 4.35$

Reject H_0 if $t > 2.821$

$$t = \dfrac{4.368 - 4.35}{(0.0339/\sqrt{10})} = 1.68$$

Do not reject H_0. The additive did not increase the mean weight of the chickens. The p-value is between 0.10 and 0.05.

19. $H_0: \mu \leq 4.0 \qquad H_1: \mu > 4.0$

Reject H_0 if $t > 1.796$

$$t = \dfrac{4.50 - 4.0}{(2.68/\sqrt{12})} = 0.65$$

Do not reject H_0. The mean number of fish caught has not been shown to be greater than 4.0. The p-value is greater than 0.10.

21. a. H_0 is rejected if $z > 1.65$

b. 1.09, found by $z = (0.75 - 0.70)/\sqrt{(0.70 \times 0.30)/100}$

c. H_0 is not rejected

23. a. $H_0: \pi \leq 0.52 \qquad H_1: \pi > 0.52$

b. H_0 is rejected if $z > 2.33$

c. 1.62, found by $z = (.5667 - .52)/\sqrt{(0.52 \times 0.48)/300}$

d. H_0 is not rejected. We cannot conclude that the proportion of men driving on the Ohio Turnpike is larger than 0.52.

25. a. $H_0: \pi \geq 0.90 \qquad H_1: \pi < 0.90$

b. H_0 is rejected if $z < -1.28$

c. -2.67, found by $z = (0.82 - 0.90)/\sqrt{(0.90 \times 0.10)/100}$

d. H_0 is rejected. Fewer than 90 percent of the customers receive their orders in less than 10 minutes.

27. $H_0: \mu = \$45,000 \qquad H_1: \mu \neq \$45,000$

Reject H_0 if $z < -1.65$ or $z > 1.65$

$$z = \dfrac{45,500 - 45,000}{\$3,000/\sqrt{120}} = 1.83$$

Reject H_0. We can conclude that the mean salary is not \$45,000. p-value 0.0672, found by $2(0.5000 - 0.4664)$.

29. $H_0: \mu \geq 10$ $H_1: \mu < 10$

Reject H_0 if $z < -1.65$

$$z = \frac{9.0 - 10.0}{2.8/\sqrt{50}} = -2.53$$

Reject H_0. The mean weight loss is less than 10 pounds. p-value $= 0.5000 - 0.4943 = 0.0057$

31. $H_0: \mu \geq 7.0$ $H_1: \mu < 7.0$

Assuming a 5% significance level, reject H_0 if $t < -1.677$.

$$t = \frac{6.8 - 7.0}{0.9/\sqrt{50}} = -1.57$$

Do not reject H_0. West Virginia students are not sleeping less than 6 hours. p-value is between .05 and .10.

33. $H_0: \mu \leq \$3.75$ $H_1: \mu > \$3.75$

Reject H_0 if $t > 1.691$

$$t = \frac{\$3.77 - \$3.75}{\$0.05/\sqrt{35}} = 2.37$$

Reject H_0. The mean price of gasoline is greater than $3.75 in Milwaukee. p-value: $(.025 > p\text{-value} > .01)$

35. $H_0: \mu \leq 14$ $H_1: \mu > 14$

Reject H_0 if $t > 2.821$

$\overline{X} = 15.66$ $s = 1.544$

$$t = \frac{15.66 - 14.00}{1.544/\sqrt{10}} = 3.400$$

Reject H_0. The average rate is greater than 14 percent.

37. $H_0: \mu = 3.1$ $H_1: \mu \neq 3.1$ Assume a normal population.

Reject H_0 if $t < -2.201$ or $t > 2.201$

$$\overline{X} = \frac{41.1}{12} = 3.425$$

$$s = \sqrt{\frac{4.0625}{12 - 1}} = .6077$$

$$t = \frac{3.425 - 3.1}{.6077/\sqrt{12}} = 1.853$$

Do not reject H_0. Cannot show a difference between senior citizens and the national average. p-value is about 0.09.

39. $H_0: \mu \geq 6.5$ $H_1: \mu < 6.5$ Assume a normal population.

Reject H_0 if $t < -2.718$

$\overline{X} = 5.1667$ $s = 3.1575$

$$t = \frac{5.1667 - 6.5}{3.1575/\sqrt{12}} = -1.463$$

Do not reject H_0. The p-value is greater than 0.05.

41. $H_0: \mu = 0$ $H_1: \mu \neq 0$

Reject H_0 if $t < -2.110$ or $t > 2.110$

$\overline{X} = -0.2322$ $s = 0.3120$

$$t = \frac{-0.2322 - 0}{0.3120/\sqrt{18}} = -3.158$$

Reject H_0. The mean gain or loss does not equal 0. The p-value is less than 0.01, but greater than 0.001.

43. $H_0: \mu \leq 100$ $H_1: \mu > 100$ Assume a normal population.

Reject H_0 if $t > 1.761$

$$\overline{X} = \frac{1,641}{15} = 109.4$$

$$s = \sqrt{\frac{1,389.6}{15 - 1}} = 9.9628$$

$$t = \frac{109.4 - 100}{9.9628/\sqrt{15}} = 3.654$$

Reject H_0. The mean number with the scanner is greater than 100. p-value is 0.001.

45. $H_0: \mu = 1.5$ $H_1: \mu \neq 1.5$

Reject H_0 if $t > 3.250$ or $t < -3.250$

$$t = \frac{1.3 - 1.5}{0.9/\sqrt{10}} = -0.703$$

Fail to reject H_0

47. $H_0: \pi \leq 0.02$ $H_1: \pi > 0.02$

Reject H_0 if $z > 1.65$

$$z = \frac{0.03 - 0.02}{\sqrt{(0.02 \times 0.98)/400}} = 1.43$$

Fail to reject H_0

49. $H_0: \pi \leq 0.60$ $H_1: \pi > 0.60$

H_0 is rejected if $z > 2.33$

$$z = \frac{.70 - .60}{\sqrt{\dfrac{.60(.40)}{200}}} = 2.89$$

H_0 is rejected. Ms. Dennis is correct. More than 60 percent of the accounts are more than three months old.

51. $H_0: \pi \leq 0.44$ $H_1: \pi > 0.44$

H_0 is rejected if $z > 1.65$

$$z = \frac{0.480 - 0.44}{\sqrt{(0.44 \times 0.56)/1.000}} = 2.55$$

H_0 is rejected. We conclude that there has been an increase in the proportion of people wanting to go to Europe.

53. $H_0: \pi \leq 0.20$ $H_1: \pi > 0.20$

H_0 is rejected if $z > 2.33$

$$z = \frac{(56/200) - 0.20}{\sqrt{(0.20 \times 0.80)/200}} = 2.83$$

H_0 is rejected. More than 20 percent of the owners move during a particular year. p-value $= 0.5000 - 0.4977 = 0.0023$.

55. $H_0: \pi = 0.50$ $H_1: \pi \neq 0.50$

Reject H_0 if z is not between -1.96 and 1.96

$$z = \frac{0.482 - 0.500}{\sqrt{(0.5)(0.5)/1,002}} = -1.14$$

Do not reject the null. The nation may be evenly divided.

57. $H_0: \pi \geq 0.0008$ $H_1: \pi < 0.0008$

H_0 is rejected if $z < -1.645$

$$z = \frac{0.0006 - 0.0008}{\sqrt{\dfrac{0.0008\,(0.9992)}{10,000}}} = -0.707 \ H_0 \text{ is not rejected.}$$

This data does not prove there is a reduced fatality rate.

59. **a.** $H_0: \mu = 80$ $H_1: \mu \neq 80$

Reject H_0 if $t < -2.045$ or $t > 2.045$

$$t = \frac{89.91 - 80.0}{37.84/\sqrt{30}} = 1.434$$

Do not reject H_0. The mean salary could be $80.0 million.

b. $H_0: \mu < 2.0$ $H_1: \mu > 2.0$

Reject H_0 if $t > 1.699$

$$t = \frac{2.62 - 2.0}{0.751/\sqrt{30}} = 4.522$$

Reject H_0. The mean attendance is greater than 2.0 million.

CHAPTER 11

1. a. Two-tailed test

b. Reject H_0 if $z < -2.05$ or $z > 2.05$

c. $z = \dfrac{102 - 99}{\sqrt{\dfrac{5^2}{40} + \dfrac{6^2}{50}}} = 2.59$

d. Reject H_0

e. p-value $= .0096$, found by $2(.5000 - .4952)$

3. **Step 1** $H_0: \mu_1 \geq \mu_2 \qquad H_1: \mu_1 < \mu_2$
   Step 2 The .05 significance level was chosen.
   Step 3 Reject H_0 if $z < -1.65$.
   Step 4 -0.94, found by:

   $$z = \frac{7.6 - 8.1}{\sqrt{\frac{(2.3)^2}{40} + \frac{(2.9)^2}{55}}} = -0.94$$

   Step 5 Fail to reject H_0. Babies using the Gibbs brand did not gain less weight. p-value = .1736, found by .5000 − .3264.

5. Two-tailed test, because we are trying to show that a difference exists between the two means.
   Reject H_0 if $z < -2.58$ or $z > 2.58$.

   $$z = \frac{31.4 - 34.9}{\sqrt{\frac{(5.1)^2}{32} + \frac{(6.7)^2}{49}}} = -2.66$$

   Reject H_0 at the .01 level. There is a difference in the mean turnover rate. p-value = 2(.5000 − .4961) = .0078

7. **a.** H_0 is rejected if $z > 1.65$
   b. 0.64, found by $p_c = \dfrac{70 + 90}{100 + 150}$
   c. 1.61, found by

   $$z = \frac{0.70 - 0.60}{\sqrt{(0.64 \times 0.36)/100 + (0.64 \times 0.36)/150}}$$

   d. H_0 is not rejected

9. **a.** $H_0: \pi_1 = \pi_2 \qquad H_1: \pi_1 \neq \pi_2$
   b. H_0 is rejected if $z < -1.96$ or $z > 1.96$
   c. $p_c = \dfrac{24 + 40}{400 + 400} = 0.08$
   d. -2.09, found by

   $$z = \frac{0.06 - 0.10}{\sqrt{(0.08 \times 0.92)/400 + (0.08 \times 0.92)/400}}$$

   e. H_0 is rejected. The proportion infested is not the same in the two fields.

11. $H_0: \pi_d \leq \pi_r \qquad H_1: \pi_d > \pi_r$
    H_0 is rejected if $z > 2.05$

    $$p_c = \frac{168 + 200}{800 + 1{,}000} = 0.2044$$

    $$z = \frac{0.21 - 0.20}{\sqrt{\frac{(0.2044)(0.7956)}{800} + \frac{(0.2044)(0.7956)}{1{,}000}}} = 0.52$$

    H_0 is not rejected. We cannot conclude that a larger proportion of Democrats favor lowering the standards. p-value = 0.3015.

13. **a.** Reject H_0 if $t > 2.120$ or $t < -2.120$
    $df = 10 + 8 - 2 = 16$
    b. $s_p^2 = \dfrac{(10 - 1)(4)^2 + (8 - 1)(5)^2}{10 + 8 - 2} = 19.9375$
    c. $t = \dfrac{23 - 26}{\sqrt{19.9375\left(\frac{1}{10} + \frac{1}{8}\right)}} = -1.416$
    d. Do not reject H_0
    e. p-value is greater than 0.10 and less than 0.20

15. $H_0: \mu_f \leq \mu_m \qquad H_1: \mu_f > \mu_m$
    $df = 9 + 7 - 2 = 14$
    Reject H_0 if $t > 2.624$

    $$s_p^2 = \frac{(7 - 1)(6.88)^2 + (9 - 1)(9.49)^2}{7 + 9 - 2} = 71.749$$

    $$t = \frac{79 - 78}{\sqrt{71.749\left(\frac{1}{7} + \frac{1}{9}\right)}} = 0.234$$

    Do not reject H_0. There is no difference in the mean grades.

17. $H_0: \mu_s \leq \mu_a \qquad H_1: \mu_s > \mu_a$
    $df = 6 + 7 - 2 = 11$
    Reject H_0 if $t > 1.363$

    $$s_p^2 = \frac{(6 - 1)(12.2)^2 + (7 - 1)(15.8)^2}{6 + 7 - 2} = 203.82$$

    $$t = \frac{142.5 - 130.3}{\sqrt{203.82\left(\frac{1}{6} + \frac{1}{7}\right)}} = 1.536$$

    Reject H_0. The mean daily expenses are greater for the sales staff. The p-value is between 0.05 and 0.10.

19. **a.** Reject H_0 if $t > 2.353$
    b. $\overline{d} = \dfrac{12}{4} = 3.00 \qquad s_d = \sqrt{\dfrac{2}{3}} = 0.816$
    c. $t = \dfrac{3.00}{0.816/\sqrt{4}} = 7.35$
    d. Reject H_0. There are more defective parts produced on the day shift.
    e. p-value is less than 0.005, but greater than 0.0005

21. $H_0: \mu_d \leq 0 \qquad H_1: \mu_d > 0$
    $\overline{d} = 25.917$
    $s_d = 40.791$
    Reject H_0 if $t > 1.796$

    $$t = \frac{25.917}{40.791/\sqrt{12}} = 2.20$$

    Reject H_0. The incentive plan resulted in an increase in daily income. The p-value is about .025.

23. $H_0: \mu_M = \mu_W \qquad H_1: \mu_M \neq \mu_W$
    Reject H_0 if $z < -2.58$ or $z > 2.58$.

    $$z = \frac{24.51 - 22.69}{\sqrt{\frac{4.48^2}{35} + \frac{3.86^2}{40}}} = 1.87$$

    Do not reject the null hypothesis. There is no difference in the means. The p-value is .0614, found by 2(.5000 − .4693).

25. $H_0: \mu_1 = \mu_2 \qquad H_1: \mu_1 \neq \mu_2$
    Reject H_0 if $z < -1.96$ or $z > 1.96$

    $$z = \frac{4.77 - 5.02}{\sqrt{\frac{(1.05)^2}{40} + \frac{(1.23)^2}{50}}} = -1.04$$

    H_0. is not rejected. There is no difference in the mean number of calls. p-value = 2(0.5000 − 0.3508) = 0.2984.

27. $H_0: \mu_A \geq \mu_B \qquad H_1: \mu_A > \mu_B$
    $df = 40 + 30 - 2 = 68$. Reject the null hypothesis if $t < -1.668$

    $$s_p^2 = \frac{(40 - 1)(9200)^2 + (30 - 1)(7100)^2}{40 + 30 - 2} = 70{,}042{,}000$$

    Reject H_0 if $t < -1.668$

    $$t = \frac{57000 - 61000}{\sqrt{70{,}042{,}000\left(\frac{1}{40} + \frac{1}{30}\right)}} = -1.979$$

    Reject H_0. The mean income of those selecting Plan B is larger. The p-value is between 0.025 and 0.01. The coefficients of skewness do not affect the results. The sample sizes are both at least 30. So the Central Limit Theorem ensures the sample means follow a normal distribution.

29. $H_0: \pi_1 \leq \pi_2 \qquad H_1: \pi_1 > \pi_2$
    Reject H_0 if $z > 1.65$

    $$p_c = \frac{180 + 261}{200 + 300} = 0.882$$

    $$z = \frac{0.90 - 0.87}{\sqrt{\frac{0.882(0.118)}{200} + \frac{0.882(0.118)}{300}}} = 1.019$$

    H_0 is not rejected. There is no difference in the proportions that found relief with the new and the old drugs.

31. $H_0: \pi_1 \le \pi_2$ $H_1: \pi_1 > \pi_2$
If $z > 2.33$, reject H_0.

$$p_c = \frac{990 + 970}{1{,}500 + 1{,}600} = 0.63$$

$$z = \frac{.6600 - .60625}{\sqrt{\dfrac{.63(.37)}{1{,}500} + \dfrac{.63(.37)}{1{,}600}}} = 3.10$$

Reject the null hypothesis. We can conclude the proportion of men who believe the division is fair is greater.

33. $H_0: \pi_m = \pi_f$ $H_1: \pi_m \ne \pi_f$
Reject H_0 if $z > 1.96$ or $z < -1.96$

$$p_c = \frac{68 + 45}{98 + 85} = 0.6175$$

$$z = \frac{0.6939 - 0.5294}{\sqrt{\dfrac{(0.6175)(0.3825)}{98} + \dfrac{(0.6175)(0.3875)}{85}}} = 2.28$$

Reject the null hypothesis. There is a difference of opinion.

35. $H_0: \pi_1 \ge \pi_2$ $H_1: \pi_1 < \pi_2$ If $z < -1.65$, reject H_0.

$$p_c = \frac{13 + 7}{180 + 67} = 0.081$$

$$z = \frac{0.07222 - 0.10448}{\sqrt{\dfrac{(0.081)(0.919)}{180} + \dfrac{(0.081)(0.919)}{67}}} = -0.826$$

Do not reject the null. We cannot determine the 32-bit machines are inferior to the 8-bit ones.

37. Assume equal population standard deviations.
$H_0: \mu_n = \mu_s$ $H_1: \mu_n \ne \mu_s$
Reject H_0 if $t < -2.086$ or $t > 2.086$

$$s_p^2 = \frac{(10 - 1)(10.5)^2 + (12 - 1)(14.25)^2}{10 + 12 - 2} = 161.2969$$

$$t = \frac{83.55 - 78.8}{\sqrt{161.2969\left(\dfrac{1}{10} + \dfrac{1}{12}\right)}} = 0.874$$

p-value > 0.10. Do not reject H_0. There is no difference in the mean number of hamburgers sold at the two locations.

39. Assume equal population standard deviations.
$H_0: \mu_1 \le \mu_2$ $H_1: \mu_1 > \mu_2$ Reject H_0 if $t > 2.567$

$$s_p^2 = \frac{(8 - 1)(2.2638)^2 + (11 - 1)(2.4606)^2}{8 + 11 - 2} = 5.672$$

$$t = \frac{10.375 - 5.636}{\sqrt{5.672\left(\dfrac{1}{8} + \dfrac{1}{11}\right)}} = 4.28$$

Reject H_0. The mean number of transactions by the young adults is more than for the senior citizens.

41. $H_0: \mu_d \le 0$ $H_1: \mu_d > 0$ Reject H_0 if $t > 1.895$
$\bar{d} = 1.75$ $s_d = 2.9155$

$$t = \frac{1.75}{2.9155/\sqrt{8}} = 1.698$$

Do not reject H_0. There is no difference in the mean number of absences. The p-value is greater than 0.05 but less than .10.

43. $H_0: \mu_1 = \mu_2$ $H_1: \mu_1 \ne \mu_2$
Reject H_0 if $t < -2.024$ or $t > 2.204$.

$$s_p^2 = \frac{(15 - 1)(40)^2 + (25 - 1)(30)^2}{15 + 25 - 2} = 1157.89$$

$$t = \frac{150 - 180}{\sqrt{1157.89\left(\dfrac{1}{15} + \dfrac{1}{25}\right)}} = -2.699$$

Reject the null hypothesis. The population means are different.

45. $H_0: \mu_d \le 0$ $H_1: \mu_d > 0$
Reject H_0 if $t > 1.895$
$\bar{d} = 3.11$ $s_d = 2.91$

$$t = \frac{3.11}{2.91/\sqrt{8}} = 3.02$$

Reject H_0. The mean is lower.

47. $H_0: \mu_O = \mu_R$, $H_1: \mu_O \ne \mu_R$
$df = 25 + 28 - 2 = 51$
Reject H_0 if t is less than -2.008 or t is greater than 2.008
$\bar{X}_O = 86.24$, $s_O = 23.43$
$\bar{X}_R = 92.04$, $s_R = 24.12$

$$s_p^2 = \frac{(25 - 1)(23.43)^2 + (28 - 1)(24.12)^2}{25 + 28 - 2} = 566.335$$

$$t = \frac{86.24 - 92.04}{\sqrt{566.335\left(\dfrac{1}{25} + \dfrac{1}{28}\right)}} = -0.886$$

Do not reject H_0. There is no difference in the mean number of cars in the two lots.

49. $H_0: \mu_F \ge \mu_B$ $H_1: \mu_F < \mu_B$
$df = 15 + 12 - 2 = 25$, reject H_0 if $t < -2.485$

$$s_p^2 = \frac{(15 - 1)(53.2)^2 + (12 - 1)(48.3)^2}{15 + 12 - 2} = 2611.41$$

$$t = \frac{39.4 - 187.5}{\sqrt{2611.41\left(\dfrac{1}{15} + \dfrac{1}{12}\right)}} = \frac{-148.1}{19.79} = -7.484$$

Reject H_0. Starting in the first five rows (in contrast to the last four) lowers the odds.

51. a. $\mu_1 =$ without pool $\mu_2 =$ with pool
$H_0: \mu_1 = \mu_2$ $H_1: \mu_1 \ne \mu_2$
Reject H_0 if $t < -2.000$ or $t > 2.000$

$$s_p^2 = \frac{(38 - 1)(33.7)^2 + (67 - 1)(50.6)^2}{38 + 67 - 2} = 2048.59$$

$$t = \frac{202.8 - 231.5}{\sqrt{2048.59\left(\dfrac{1}{38} + \dfrac{1}{67}\right)}} = -3.122$$

Reject H_0. There is a difference in the mean selling price of homes with a pool and without a pool.

b. $\mu_1 =$ without attached garage $\mu_2 =$ with garage
$H_0: \mu_1 = \mu_2$ $H_1: \mu_1 \ne \mu_2$
Reject H_0 if $t > 2.000$ or $t < -2.000$
$\alpha = 0.05$ $df = 34 + 71 - 2 = 103$
$\bar{X}_1 = 185.45$ $s_1 = 28.00$
$\bar{X}_2 = 238.18$ $s_2 = 44.88$

$$s_p^2 = \frac{(34 - 1)(28.00)^2 + (71 - 1)(44.88)^2}{103} = 1{,}620.07$$

$$t = \frac{185.45 - 238.18}{\sqrt{1{,}620.07\left(\dfrac{1}{34} + \dfrac{1}{71}\right)}} = -6.28$$

Reject H_0. There is a difference in mean selling price for homes with and without an attached garage.

c. $H_0: \mu_1 = \mu_2$ $H_1: \mu_1 \ne \mu_2$
Reject H_0 if $t > 2.036$ or $t < -2.036$
$\bar{X}_1 = 196.91$ $s_1 = 35.78$ $n_1 = 15$
$\bar{X}_2 = 227.45$ $s_2 = 44.19$ $n_2 = 20$

$$s_p^2 = \frac{(15 - 1)(35.78)^2 + (20 - 1)(44.19)^2}{15 + 20 - 2} = 1{,}667.43$$

$$t = \frac{196.91 - 227.45}{\sqrt{1{,}667.43\left(\dfrac{1}{15} + \dfrac{1}{20}\right)}} = -2.19$$

Reject H_0. There is a difference in mean selling price for homes in Township 1 and Township 2.

d. $H_0: \pi_1 = \pi_2 \quad H_1: \pi_1 \neq \pi_2$

If z is not between -1.96 and 1.96, reject H_0

$$p_c = \frac{24 + 43}{52 + 53} = 0.64$$

$$z = \frac{0.462 - 0.811}{\sqrt{0.64 \times 0.36/52 + 0.64 \times 0.36/53}} = -3.73$$

Reject the null hypothesis. There is a difference.

53. a. $H_0: \mu_s = \mu_{ns} \quad H_1: \mu_s \neq \mu_{ns}$

Reject H_0 if $t < -1.984$ or $t > 1.984$.

Answer worked in thousands.

$$s_p^2 = \frac{(67 - 1)(17.403)^2 + (33 - 1)(16.062)^2}{67 + 33 - 2} = 288.21$$

$$t = \frac{31.798 - 28.876}{\sqrt{288.21\left(\frac{1}{67} + \frac{1}{33}\right)}} = \frac{2.922}{3.610} = 0.803$$

Do not reject H_0. No difference in the mean wages.

b. $H_0: \mu_w = \mu_{nw} \quad H_1: \mu_w \neq \mu_{nw}$

Note, because one sample is less than 30, use t and pool variances. Also answer reported in \$000.

Reject H_0 if $t < -1.984$ or $t > 1.984$.

$$s_p^2 = \frac{(90 - 1)(17.358)^2 + (10 - 1)(11.536)^2}{90 + 10 - 2} = 285.85$$

$$t = \frac{31.517 - 24.678}{\sqrt{285.85\left(\frac{1}{90} + \frac{1}{10}\right)}} = 1.214$$

Do not reject H_0. No difference in the mean wages.

c. $H_0: \mu_h = \mu_{nh} \quad H_1: \mu_h \neq \mu_{nh}$

Reject H_0 if $t < -1.984$ or $t > 1.984$.

Because one sample is less than 30, use t. Answer reported in \$000.

$$s_p^2 = \frac{(94 - 1)(16.413)^2 + (6 - 1)(25.843)^2}{94 + 6 - 2} = 289.72$$

$$t = \frac{30.674 - 33.337}{\sqrt{289.72\left(\frac{1}{94} + \frac{1}{6}\right)}} = -0.37$$

Do not reject H_0. No difference in the mean wages.

d. $H_0: \mu_m = \mu_f \quad H_1: \mu_m \neq \mu_f$

Reject H_0 if $t < -1.984$ or $t > 1.984$

$$t = \frac{\$36{,}493 - \$24{,}452}{\sqrt{(15914.75)^2\left(\frac{1}{53} + \frac{1}{47}\right)}} = 3.776$$

Reject H_0. There is a difference in the mean wages for men and women.

e. $H_0: \mu_m = \mu_{nm} \quad H_1: \mu_m \neq \mu_{nm}$

Reject H_0 if $t < -1.984$ or $t > 1.984$.

$$t = \frac{24{,}864 - 33{,}773}{\sqrt{(16499.33)^2\left(\frac{1}{33} + \frac{1}{67}\right)}} = -2.539$$

Reject H_0. There is a difference in the mean wages of the two groups.

CHAPTER 12

1. 9.01, from Appendix B.4

3. Reject H_0 if $F > 10.5$, where degrees of freedom in the numerator are 7 and 5 in the denominator. Computed $F = 2.04$, found by:

$$F = \frac{s_1^2}{s_2^2} = \frac{(10)^2}{(7)^2} = 2.04$$

Do not reject H_0. There is no difference in the variations of the two populations.

5. $H_0: \sigma_1^2 = \sigma_2^2 \quad H_1: \sigma_1^2 \neq \sigma_2^2$

Reject H_0 where $F > 3.10$. (3.10 is about halfway between 3.14 and 3.07.) Computed $F = 1.44$, found by:

$$F = \frac{(12)^2}{(10)^2} = 1.44$$

Do not reject H_0. There is no difference in the variations of the two populations.

7. a. $H_0: \mu_1 = \mu_2 = \mu_3; H_1:$ Treatment means are not all the same.

b. Reject H_0 if $F > 4.26$

c & d.

Source	SS	df	MS	F
Treatment	62.17	2	31.08	21.94
Error	12.75	9	1.42	
Total	74.92	11		

e. Reject H_0. The treatment means are not all the same.

9. $H_0: \mu_1 = \mu_2 = \mu_3; H_1:$ Treatment means are not all the same. Reject H_0 if $F > 4.26$.

Source	SS	df	MS	F
Treatment	276.50	2	138.25	14.18
Error	87.75	9	9.75	

Reject H_0. The treatment means are not all the same.

11. a. $H_0: \mu_1 = \mu_2 = \mu_3; H_1:$ Not all means are the same.

b. Reject H_0 if $F > 4.26$

c. SST = 107.20, SSE = 9.47, SS total = 116.67.

d.

Source	SS	df	MS	F
Treatment	107.20	2	53.600	50.96
Error	9.47	9	1.052	
Total	116.67	11		

e. Since $50.96 > 4.26$. H_0 is rejected. At least one of the means differs.

f. $(\overline{X}_1 - \overline{X}_2) \pm t\sqrt{MSE(1/n_1 + 1/n_2)}$
$= (9.667 - 2.20) \pm 2.262 \sqrt{1.052(1/3 + 1/5)}$
$= 7.467 \pm 1.69$
$= [5.777, 9.157]$
Yes, we can conclude that treatments 1 and 2 have different means.

13. $H_0: \mu_1 = \mu_2 = \mu_3 = \mu_4; H_1:$ Not all means are equal. H_0 is rejected if $F > 3.71$.

Source	SS	df	MS	F
Treatment	32.33	3	10.77	2.36
Error	45.67	10	4.567	
Total	78.00	13		

Because 2.36 is less than 3.71, H_0 is not rejected. There is no difference in the mean number of weeks.

15. $H_0: \sigma_1^2 \leq \sigma_2^2; H_1: \sigma_1^2 > \sigma_2^2$. $df_1 = 21 - 1 = 20$; $df_2 = 18 - 1 = 17$. H_0 is rejected if $F > 3.16$.

$$F = \frac{(45{,}600)^2}{(21{,}330)^2} = 4.57$$

Reject H_0. There is more variation in the selling price of oceanfront homes.

17. Sharkey: $n = 7$ $s_s = 14.79$
White: $n = 8$ $s_w = 22.95$
$H_0: \sigma_w^2 \le \sigma_s^2; H_1: \sigma_w^2 > \sigma_s^2. \; df_s = 7 - 1 = 6;$
$df_w = 8 - 1 = 7.$ Reject H_0 if $F > 8.26.$

$$F = \frac{(22.95)^2}{(14.79)^2} = 2.41$$

Cannot reject H_0. There is no difference in the variation of the monthly sales.

19. a. $H_0: \mu_1 = \mu_2 = \mu_3 = \mu_4$
H_1: Treatment means are not all equal.
b. $\alpha = .05$ Reject H_0 if $F > 3.10.$
c.

Source	SS	df	MS	F
Treatment	50	$4 - 1 = 3$	50/3	1.67
Error	200	$24 - 4 = 20$	10	
Total	250	$24 - 1 = 23$		

d. Do not reject H_0

21. $H_0: \mu_1 = \mu_2 = \mu_3; H_1$: Not all treatment means are equal.
H_0 is rejected if $F > 3.89.$

Source	SS	df	MS	F
Treatment	63.33	2	31.667	13.38
Error	28.40	12	2.367	
Total	91.73	14		

H_0 is rejected. There is a difference in the treatment means.

23. $H_0: \mu_1 = \mu_2 = \mu_3 = \mu_4; H_1$: Not all means are equal.
H_0 is rejected if $F > 3.10.$

Source	SS	df	MS	F
Factor	87.79	3	29.26	9.12
Error	64.17	20	3.21	
Total	151.96	23		

Because computed F of $9.12 > 3.10$, the null hypothesis of no difference is rejected at the .05 level.

25. a. $H_0: \mu_1 = \mu_2; H_1: \mu_1 \ne \mu_2$. Critical value of $F = 4.75.$

Source	SS	df	MS	F
Treatment	219.43	1	219.43	23.10
Error	114.00	12	9.5	
Total	333.43	13		

b. $t = \dfrac{19 - 27}{\sqrt{9.5\left(\dfrac{1}{6} + \dfrac{1}{8}\right)}} = -4.806$

Then $t^2 = F$. That is $(-4.806)^2 = 23.10.$
c. H_0 is rejected. There is a difference in the mean scores.

27. The null hypothesis is rejected because the F statistic (8.26) is greater than the critical value (5.61) at the .01 significance level. The p-value (.0019) is also less than the significance level. The mean gasoline mileages are not the same.

29. $H_0: \mu_1 = \mu_2 = \mu_3 = \mu_4.$ H_1: At least one mean is different.
Reject H_0 if $F > 2.7395$. Since 2.72 is less than 2.7395, H_0 is not rejected. You can also see this conclusion from the p-value of 0.051, which is greater than 0.05. There is no difference in the means for the different types of first-class mail.

31. a. $H_0: \sigma_{np}^2 = \sigma_p^2$ $H_1: \sigma_{np}^2 \ne \sigma_p^2.$

Reject H_0 if $F > 2.05$ (estimated).
$df_1 = 67 - 1 = 66; df_2 = 38 - 1 = 37.$

$$F = \frac{(50.57)^2}{(33.71)^2} = 2.25$$

Reject H_0. There is a difference in the variance of the two selling prices.

b. $H_0: \sigma_g^2 = \sigma_{ng}^2; H_1: \sigma_g^2 \ne \sigma_{ng}^2.$
Reject H_0 if $F > 2.21$ (estimated).

$$F = \frac{(44.88)^2}{(28.00)^2} = 2.57$$

Reject H_0. There is a difference in the variance of the two selling prices.
c.

Source	SS	df	MS	F
Township	13,263	4	3,316	1.52
Error	217,505	100	2,175	
Total	230,768	104		

$H_0: \mu_1 = \mu_2 = \mu_3 = \mu_4 = \mu_5; H_1$: Not all treatment means are equal. Reject H_0 if $F > 2.46.$
Do not reject H_0. There is no difference in the mean selling prices in the five townships.

33. a. $H_0: \mu_1 = \mu_2 = \mu_3; H_1$: Treatment means are not equal.
Reject H_0 if $F > 3.09$. The computed value of F is 1.30. We conclude there is no difference among the industries.

b. $H_0: \mu_1 = \mu_2 = \mu_3 = \mu_4 = \mu_5; H_1$: Treatment means are not equal.
Reject H_0 if $F > 2.31$. The computed value of F is 4.85. The treatment means differ. The MINITAB output follows.

```
Level    N      Mean      StDev
0       22     28921      14517
1       13     40074      22733
2        6     27228      16101
3       21     27619       9821
4       21     21510       6946
5       17     43002      22062

Pooled St Dev = 15507
```

From this graph the following means differ: 0 and 5, 1 and 4, 3 and 5, and 4 and 5.
c. $H_0: \sigma_u^2 = \sigma_{nu}^2; H_1: \sigma_u^2 \ne \sigma_{nu}^2$; reject H_0 if $F > 1.99.$
Computed F is 1.36, found by $(17,413)^2/(14,940)^2.$ There is no difference in the variation of union and nonunion members.

CHAPTER 13
1. $\Sigma(X - \bar{X})(Y - \bar{Y}) = 10.6, s_x = 2.7019, s_y = 1.3038$

$$r = \frac{10.6}{(5 - 1)(2.7019)(1.3038)} = 0.7522$$

The 0.7522 coefficient indicates a rather strong positive correlation between X and Y. The coefficient of determination is 0.5658, found by $(0.7522)^2$. More than 56 percent of the variation in Y is accounted for by X.

3. a. Sales.

b.

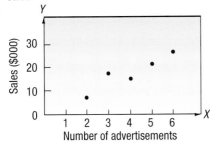

c. $\Sigma(X - \bar{X})(Y - \bar{Y}) = 36$, $n = 5$, $s_x = 1.5811$, $s_y = 6.1237$

$$r = \frac{36}{(5 - 1)(1.5811)(6.1237)} = 0.9295$$

d. The coefficient of determination is 0.8640, found by $(0.9295)^2$.

e. There is a strong positive association between the variables. About 86 percent of the variation in sales is explained by the number of airings.

5. a. Police is the independent variable, and crime is the dependent variable.

b.

c. $n = 8$, $\Sigma(X - \bar{X})(Y - \bar{Y}) = -231.75$, $s_x = 5.8737$, $s_y = 6.4462$

$$r = \frac{-231.75}{(8 - 1)(5.8737)(6.4462)} = -0.8744$$

d. 0.7646, found by $(-0.8744)^2$

e. Strong inverse relationship. As the number of police increases, the crime decreases.

7. Reject H_0 if $t > 1.812$

$$t = \frac{.32\sqrt{12 - 2}}{\sqrt{1 - (.32)^2}} = 1.068$$

Do not reject H_0

9. $H_0: \rho \le 0$; $H_1: \rho > 0$. Reject H_0 if $t > 2.552$. $df = 18$.

$$t = \frac{.78\sqrt{20 - 2}}{\sqrt{1 - (.78)^2}} = 5.288$$

Reject H_0. There is a positive correlation between gallons sold and the pump price.

11. $H_0: \rho \le 0$ $H_1: \rho > 0$
Reject H_0 if $t > 2.650$

$$t = \frac{0.667\sqrt{15 - 2}}{\sqrt{1 - 0.667^2}} = 3.228$$

Reject H_0. There is a positive correlation between the number of passengers and plane weight.

13. a. $\hat{Y} = 3.7671 + 0.3630X$

$$b = 0.7522\left(\frac{1.3038}{2.7019}\right) = 0.3630$$

$$a = 5.8 - 0.3630(5.6) = 3.7671$$

b. 6.3081, found by $\hat{Y} = 3.7671 + 0.3630(7)$

15. a. $\Sigma(X - \bar{X})(Y - \bar{Y}) = 44.6$, $s_x = 2.726$, $s_y = 2.011$

$$r = \frac{44.6}{(10 - 1)(2.726)(2.011)} = .904$$

$$b = .904\left(\frac{2.011}{2.726}\right) = 0.667$$

$$a = 7.4 - .677(9.1) = 1.333$$

b. $\hat{Y} = 1.333 + .667(6) = 5.335$

17. a.

b. $\Sigma(X - \bar{X})(Y - \bar{Y}) = 629.64$, $s_x = 26.17$, $s_y = 3.248$

$$r = \frac{629.64}{(12 - 1)(26.17)(3.248)} = .6734$$

c. $r^2 = (0.673)^2 = 0.4529$

d. A strong positive association between the variables. About 45 percent of the variation in earnings is accounted for by sales.

e. $b = .6734\left(\frac{3.248}{26.170}\right) = 0.0836$

$$a = \frac{64.1}{12} - 0.0836\left(\frac{501.10}{12}\right) = 1.8507$$

f. $\hat{Y} = 1.8507 + 0.0836(50.0) = 6.0307$ ($ millions)

19. a. $b = -.8744\left(\frac{6.4462}{5.8737}\right) = -0.9596$

$$a = \frac{95}{8} - (-0.9596)\left(\frac{146}{8}\right) = 29.3877$$

b. 10.1957, found by $29.3877 - 0.9596(20)$

c. For each policeman added, crime goes down by almost one.

21. a. $\sqrt{\dfrac{2.958}{5 - 2}} = .993$

b. $\hat{Y} \pm .993$

23. a. $\sqrt{\dfrac{6.667}{10 - 2}} = 0.913$

b. $\hat{Y} \pm 1.826$

25. $\sqrt{\dfrac{68.4877}{8 - 2}} = 3.379$

27. a. $6.308 \pm (3.182)(.993)\sqrt{.2 + \dfrac{(7 - 5.6)^2}{29.2}}$

$$= 6.308 \pm 1.633$$
$$= [4.675, 7.941]$$

b. $6.308 \pm (3.182)(.993)\sqrt{1 + 1/5 + .0671}$

$$= [2.751, 9.865]$$

29. a. 4.2939, 6.3721
b. 2.9854, 7.6806

31. $\bar{X} = 10$, $\bar{Y} = 6$, $\Sigma(X - \bar{X})(Y - \bar{Y}) = 40$, $s_y = 2.2361$,
$s_x = 5.0$

$$r = \frac{40}{(5 - 1)(2.2361)(5.0)} = .8944$$

Then, $(.8944)^2 = .80$, the coefficient of determination.

33. a. $r^2 = 1{,}000/1{,}500 = .667$
b. .82, found by $\sqrt{.667}$

c. 6.20, found by $s_{y \cdot x} = \sqrt{\dfrac{500}{15 - 2}}$

35. The correlation between the two variables is 0.298. By squaring X, the correlation increases to .998.

37. H_0: $\rho \leq 0$; H_1: $\rho > 0$. Reject H_0 if $t > 1.714$.

$$t = \frac{.94 \sqrt{25 - 2}}{\sqrt{1 - (.94)^2}} = 13.213$$

Reject H_0. There is a positive correlation between passengers and weight of luggage.

39. H_0: $\rho \leq 0$; H_1: $\rho > 0$. Reject H_0 if $t > 2.764$.

$$t = \frac{.47 \sqrt{12 - 2}}{\sqrt{1 - (.47)^2}} = 1.684$$

Do not reject H_0. There is not a positive correlation between engine size and performance. p-value is greater than .05, but less than .10.

41. a. The total number of cars sold decreases as the percent market share increases. The relationship is inverse so as one increases, the other decreases.

b. $r = \dfrac{-305.19}{(12 - 1)(3.849)(8.185)} = -0.881$

The value of r indicates a fairly strong negative association between the variables.

c. H_0: $\rho \geq 0$ H_1: $\rho < 0$
Reject H_0 if $t < -2.764$

$$t = \frac{-0.881 \sqrt{12 - 2}}{\sqrt{1 - (-0.881)^2}} = -5.89$$

Reject H_0. There is a negative correlation.

d. 77.6 percent, found by $(-0.881)^2$, of the variation in market share is accounted for by variation in cars sold.

43. a. $r = 0.589$
b. $r^2 = (0.589)^2 = 0.3469$
c. H_0: $\rho \leq 0$; H_1: $\rho > 0$. Reject H_0 if $t > 1.860$.

$$t = \frac{0.589 \sqrt{10 - 2}}{\sqrt{1 - (.589)^2}} = 2.062$$

H_0 is rejected. There is a positive association between family size and the amount spent on food.

45. a.

Months

There is an inverse relationship between the variables. As the months owned increase, the number of hours exercised decreases.

b. $r = -0.827$

c. H_0: $\rho \geq 0$; H_1: $\rho < 0$. Reject H_0 if $t < -2.896$.

$$t = \frac{-0.827 \sqrt{10 - 2}}{\sqrt{1 - (-0.827)^2}} = -4.16$$

Reject H_0. There is a negative association between months owned and hours exercised.

47. a. Median age and population are directly related.

b. $r = \dfrac{11.93418}{(10 - 1)(2.207)(1.330)} = 0.452$

c. The slope of 0.272 indicates that for each increase of 1 million in the population, the median age increases on average by 0.272 years.

d. The median age is 32.08 years, found by $31.4 + 0.272(2.5)$.

e. The p-value (0.190) for the population variable is greater than, say 0.05. A test for significance of that coefficient would fail to be rejected. In other words, it is possible the population coefficient is zero.

f. H_0: $\rho = 0$ H_1: $\rho \neq 0$ Reject H_0 if t is not between -2.306 and 2.306.

$$\text{df} = 8 \qquad t = \frac{0.452 \sqrt{10 - 2}}{\sqrt{1 - (0.452)^2}} = 1.433 \text{ Do not reject } H_0.$$

There may be no relationship between age and population.

49. a. $b = -0.4667$, $a = 11.2358$
b. $\hat{Y} = 11.2358 - 0.4667(7.0) = 7.9689$

c. $7.9689 \pm (2.160)(1.114)\sqrt{1 + \dfrac{1}{15} + \dfrac{(7 - 7.1333)^2}{73.7333}}$
$= 7.9689 \pm 2.4854$
$= [5.4835, 10.4543]$

d. $r^2 = 0.499$. Nearly 50 percent of the variation in the amount of the bid is explained by the number of bidders.

51. a.

Distance

There appears to be a relationship between the two variables. As the distance increases, so does the shipping time.

b. $r = 0.692$
H_0: $\rho \leq 0$; H_1: $\rho > 0$. Reject H_0 if $t > 1.734$.

$$t = \frac{0.692 \sqrt{20 - 2}}{\sqrt{1 - (0.692)^2}} = 4.067$$

H_0 is rejected. There is a positive association between shipping distance and shipping time.

c. $r^2 = 0.479$. Nearly half of the variation in shipping time is explained by shipping distance.

d. $s_{y \cdot x} = 1.987$

53. a. $b = 2.41$
$a = 26.8$
The regression equation is: Price $= 26.8 + 2.41 \times$ Dividend. For each additional dollar of dividend, the price increases by $2.41.

b. $r^2 = \dfrac{5,057.6}{7,682.7} = 0.658$ Thus, 65.8 percent of the

variation in price is explained by the dividend.

c. $r = \sqrt{.658} = 0.811$ $H_0: \rho \le 0$ $H_1: \rho > 0$
At the 5 percent level, reject H_0 when $t > 1.701$.

$$t = \dfrac{0.811\sqrt{30 - 2}}{\sqrt{1 - (0.811)^2}} = 7.34$$

Thus H_0 is rejected. The population correlation is positive.

55. a. 35

b. $s_{y \cdot x} = \sqrt{29,778,406} = 5,456.96$

c. $r^2 = \dfrac{13,548,662,082}{14,531,349,474} = 0.932$

d. $r = \sqrt{0.932} = 0.966$

e. $H_0: \rho \le 0$, $H_1: \rho > 0$; reject H_0 if $t > 1.692$

$$t = \dfrac{.966\sqrt{35 - 2}}{\sqrt{1 - (.966)^2}} = 21.46$$

Reject H_0. There is a direct relationship between size of the house and its market value.

57. a. The regression equation is Price $= -773 + 1,408$ Speed.

b. The second laptop (1.6, 922) with a residual of -557.60, is priced $557.60 below the predicted price. That is a noticeable "bargain."

c. The correlation of Speed and Price is 0.835.
$H_0: \rho \le 0$ $H_1: \rho > 0$ Reject H_0 if $t > 1.8125$

$$t = \dfrac{0.835\sqrt{12 - 2}}{\sqrt{1 - (0.835)^2}} = 4.799$$

Reject H_0. It is reasonable to say the population correlation is positive.

59. a. $r = .987$, $H_0: \rho \le 0$, $H_1: \rho > 0$. Reject H_0 if $t > 1.746$.

$$t = \dfrac{.987\sqrt{18 - 2}}{\sqrt{1 - (.987)^2}} = 24.564$$

b. The regression equation is
Consumption $= 1.398 + 0.0425 \times$ Weight.
Ten more pounds of weight would add 0.425, found by 0.0425(10), cups to the dog's consumption.

c. Dog number 4 is an overeater. He eats 0.86, found by $4 - 3.14$, cups more than predicted.

61. $r = 0.297$
$H_0: \rho \le 0$ $H_1: \rho > 0$
Level of significance $= 0.05$
Reject H_0 if $t > 1.674$

$$t = \dfrac{0.297\sqrt{56 - 2}}{\sqrt{(1 - 0.297)^2}} = 2.292$$

Reject H_0. There is a positive correlation between movie sales and budget. "Big budget" movies do lead to large box office.

63. a. The correlation between wins and salary is 0.332.
$H_0: \rho \le 0$, $H_1: \rho > 0$. Reject H_0 if $t > 1.701$.

$$t = \dfrac{0.332\sqrt{30 - 2}}{\sqrt{1 - (0.332)^2}} = 1.862$$

Reject H_0. There is a positive association between wins and salary.
The regression equation is:
wins $= 72.2 + 0.097$(salary)
An additional $5 million would increases wins by 0.5, found by 0.097(5).

b. The correlation between games won and ERA is -0.663; and between games won and batting average is 0.301. ERA has the stronger correlation,

• Wins: ERA   critical value is -1.701.

$$t = \dfrac{-0.663\sqrt{30 - 2}}{\sqrt{1 - (-0.663)^2}} = -4.686$$

Conclude there is a negative association between wins and ERA.

• Wins: Batting critical value is 1.701.

$$t = \dfrac{.301\sqrt{30 - 2}}{\sqrt{1 - (.301)^2}} = 1.67$$

Cannot conclude there is a positive association between wins and batting.

c. The correlation between wins and attendance is .408.
$H_0: \rho \le 0$ $H_1: \rho > 0$. At the 5 percent level, reject H_0 if $t > 1.701$.

$$t = \dfrac{.408\sqrt{30 - 2}}{\sqrt{1 - (.408)^2}} = 2.365$$

Reject H_0. The population correlation is positive.

CHAPTER 14

1. a. Multiple regression equation

b. The Y-intercept

c. $\hat{Y} = 64,100 + 0.394(796,000) + 9.6(6,940)$
$- 11,600(6.0) = \$374,748$

3. a. 497.736, found by
$\hat{Y} = 16.24 + 0.017(18)$
$+ 0.0028(26,500) + 42(3)$
$+ 0.0012(156,000)$
$+ 0.19(141) + 26.8(2.5)$

b. Two more social activities. Income added only 28 to the index; social activities added 53.6.

5. a. $s_{Y \cdot 12} = \sqrt{\dfrac{\text{SSE}}{n - (k + 1)}} = \sqrt{\dfrac{583.693}{65 - (2 + 1)}}$
$= \sqrt{9.414} = 3.068$
95% of the residuals will be between ± 6.136, found by
2(3.068)

b. $R^2 = \dfrac{\text{SSR}}{\text{SS total}} = \dfrac{77.907}{661.6} = .118$
The independent variables explain 11.8% of the variation.

c. $R^2_{adj} = 1 - \dfrac{\dfrac{\text{SSE}}{n - (k + 1)}}{\dfrac{\text{SS total}}{n - 1}} = 1 - \dfrac{\dfrac{583.693}{65 - (2 + 1)}}{\dfrac{661.6}{65 - 1}}$

$= 1 - \dfrac{9.414}{10.3375} = 1 - .911 = .089$

7. a. $\hat{Y} = 84.998 + 2.391X_1 - 0.4086X_2$

b. 90.0674, found by $\hat{Y} = 84.998 + 2.391(4) - 0.4086(11)$

c. $n = 65$ and $k = 2$

d. $H_0: \beta_1 = \beta_2 = 0$ $H_1:$ Not all β's are 0
Reject H_0 if $F > 3.15$
$F = 4.14$, reject H_0. Not all net regression coefficients equal zero.

e. For X_1 For X_2
$H_0: \beta_1 = 0$ $H_0: \beta_2 = 0$
$H_1: \beta_1 \ne 0$ $H_1: \beta_2 \ne 0$
$t = 1.99$ $t = -2.38$
Reject H_0 if $t > 2.0$ or $t < -2.0$.
Delete variable 1 and keep 2.

f. The regression analysis should be repeated with only X_2 as the independent variable.

9. a. $n = 40$

b. 4

c. $R^2 = \dfrac{750}{1250} = .60$

d. $s_{y \cdot 1234} = \sqrt{500/35} = 3.7796$

e. $H_0: \beta_1 = \beta_2 = \beta_3 = \beta_4 = 0$
$H_1:$ Not all the βs equal zero.
H_0 is rejected if $F > 2.65$.

$$F = \dfrac{750/4}{500/35} = 13.125$$

H_0 is rejected. At least one β_i does not equal zero.

11. **a.** $n = 26$
b. $R^2 = 100/140 = .7143$
c. 1.4142, found by $\sqrt{2}$
d. H_0: $\beta_1 = \beta_2 = \beta_3 = \beta_4 = \beta_5 = 0$
H_1: Not all the βs are 0.
H_0 is rejected if $F > 2.71$.
Computed $F = 10.0$. Reject H_0. At least one regression coefficient is not zero.
e. H_0 is rejected in each case if $t < -2.086$ or $t > 2.086$.
X_1 and X_5 should be dropped.

13. **a.** $28,000
b. $R^2 = \dfrac{\text{SSR}}{\text{SS total}} = \dfrac{3{,}050}{5{,}250} = .5809$
c. 9.199, found by $\sqrt{84.62}$
d. H_0 is rejected if $F > 2.97$ (approximately)
$$\text{Computed } F = \frac{1{,}016.67}{84.62} = 12.01$$
H_0 is rejected. At least one regression coefficient is not zero.
e. If computed t is to the left of -2.056 or to the right of 2.056, the null hypothesis in each of these cases is rejected. Computed t for X_2 and X_3 exceed the critical value. Thus, "population" and "advertising expenses" should be retained and "number of competitors," X_1, dropped.

15. **a.** The strongest correlation is between GPA and legal. No problem with multicollinearity.
b. $R^2 = \dfrac{4.3595}{5.0631} = .8610$
c. H_0 is rejected if $F > 5.41$
$$F = \frac{1.4532}{0.1407} = 10.328$$
At least one coefficient is not zero.
d. Any H_0 is rejected if $t < -2.571$ or $t > 2.571$. It appears that only GPA is significant. Verbal and math could be eliminated.
e. $R^2 = \dfrac{4.2061}{5.0631} = .8307$
R^2 has only been reduced .0303.
f. The residuals appear slightly skewed (positive), but acceptable.
g. There does not seem to be a problem with the plot.

17. **a.** The correlation of Screen and Price is 0.893. So there does appear to be a linear relationship between the two.
b. Price is the "dependent" variable.
c. The regression equation is Price $= -2484 + 101$ Screen. For each inch increase in screen size, the price increases $101 on average.
d. Using "dummy" indicator variables for Sharp and Sony, the regression equation is Price $= -2308 + 94.1$ Screen $+ 15$ Manufacturer Sharp $+ 381$ Manufacturer Sony. Sharp can obtain on average $15 more than Samsung and Sony can collect an additional benefit of $381 more than Samsung.
e. Here is some of the output.

Predictor	Coef	SE Coef	T	P
Constant	-2308.2	492.0	-4.69	0.000
Screen	94.12	10.83	8.69	0.000
Manufacturer_Sharp	15.1	171.6	0.09	0.931
Manufacturer_Sony	381.4	168.8	2.26	0.036

The p-value for Sharp is relatively large. A test of their coefficient would not be rejected. That means they may not have any real advantage over Samsung. On the other hand, the p-value for the Sony coefficient is quite small. That indicates that it did not happen by chance and there is some real advantage to Sony over Samsung.

f. A histogram of the residuals indicates they follow a normal distribution.
g. The residual variation may be increasing for larger fitted values.

19. **a.**

Scatter Diagram of Sales vs Advertising, Accounts, Competitors, Potential

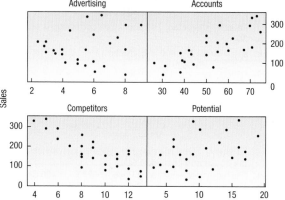

Sales seem to fall with the number of competitors and rise with the number of accounts and potential.

b. Pearson correlations

	Sales	Advertising	Accounts	Competitors
Advertising	0.159			
Accounts	0.783	0.173		
Competitors	-0.833	-0.038	-0.324	
Potential	0.407	-0.071	0.468	-0.202

The number of accounts and the market potential are moderately correlated.

c. The regression equation is:
Sales $= 178 + 1.81$ Advertising $+ 3.32$ Accounts $- 21.2$ Competitors $+ 0.325$ Potential

Predictor	Coef	SE Coef	T	P
Constant	178.32	12.96	13.76	0.000
Advertising	1.807	1.081	1.67	0.109
Accounts	3.3178	0.1629	20.37	0.000
Competitors	-21.1850	0.7879	-26.89	0.000
Potential	0.3245	0.4678	0.69	0.495

$S = 9.60441$ R-Sq $= 98.9\%$ R-Sq(adj) $= 98.7\%$

Analysis of Variance

Source	DF	SS	MS	F	P
Regression	4	176777	44194	479.10	0.000
Residual Error	21	1937	92		
Total	25	178714			

The computed F value is quite large. So we can reject the null hypothesis that all of the regression coefficients are zero. We conclude that some of the independent variables are effective in explaining sales.

d. Market potential and advertising have large p-values (0.495 and 0.109, respectively). You would probably drop them.

e. If you omit potential, the regression equation is:
Sales $= 180 + 1.68$ Advertising $+ 3.37$ Accounts $- 21.2$ Competitors

Predictor	Coef	SE Coef	T	P
Constant	179.84	12.62	14.25	0.000
Advertising	1.677	1.052	1.59	0.125
Accounts	3.3694	0.1432	23.52	0.000
Competitors	-21.2165	0.7773	-27.30	0.000

Now advertising is not significant. That would also lead you to cut out the advertising variable and report that the polished regression equation is:
Sales = 187 + 3.41 Accounts − 21.2 Competitors

```
Predictor      Coef SE Coef       T      P
Constant     186.69   12.26   15.23  0.000
Accounts     3.4081  0.1458   23.37  0.000
Competitors -21.1930  0.8028  -26.40  0.000
```

f.

Histogram of the Residuals
(response is Sales)

The histogram looks to be normal. There are no problems shown in this plot.

g. The variance inflation factor for both variables is 1.1. They are less than 10. There are no troubles as this value indicates the independent variables are not strongly correlated with each other.

21. a. The correlation matrix is:

	Salary	GPA
GPA	0.902	
Business	0.911	0.851

The two independent variables are related. There may be multicollinearity.

b. The regression equation is: Salary = 23.447 + 2.775 GPA + 1.307 Business. As GPA increases by one point, salary increases by $2,775. The average business school graduate makes $1,307 more than a corresponding nonbusiness graduate. Estimated salary is $33,079, found by $23,447 + 2,775(3.00) + 1,307(1).

c. $R^2 = \dfrac{21.182}{23.857} = 0.888$

To conduct the global test: $H_0: = \beta_1 = \beta_2 = 0$;
H_1: Not all β_i's = 0
At the 0.05 significance level, H_0 is rejected if $F > 3.89$.

Source	SS	df	MS	F	p
Regression	21.182	2	10.591	47.50	0.000
Error	2.676	12	0.223		
Total	23.857	14			

The computed value of F is 47.50, so H_0 is rejected. Some of the regression coefficients are not zero.

d. Since the p-values are less than 0.05, there is no need to delete variables.

Predictor	Coef	SE Coef	T	P
Constant	23.447	3.490	6.72	0.000
GPA	2.775	1.107	2.51	0.028
Business	1.3071	0.4660	2.80	0.016

e. The residuals appear normally distributed.

Histogram of the Residuals
(Response Is Salary)

f. The variance is the same as we move from small values to large. So there is no homoscedasticity problem.

23. The computer output is as follows:

```
Predictor      Coef   SE Coef        T      P
Constant      38.71     39.02     0.99  0.324
Bedrooms       7.118    2.551     2.79  0.006
Size         0.03800  0.01468     2.59  0.011
Pool          18.321    6.999     2.62  0.010
Distance     -0.9295   0.7279    -1.28  0.205
Garage        35.810    7.638     4.69  0.000
Baths         23.315    9.025     2.58  0.011

s = 33.2111   R-Sq = 53.2%   R-Sq(adj) = 50.3%

Analysis of Variance
SOURCE            DF      SS     MS      F      P
Regression         6  122676  20446  18.54  0.000
Residual Error    98  108092   1103
Total            104  230768
```

a. Each additional bedroom adds $7,100 to the selling price, each additional square foot adds $38, a pool adds $18,300, an attached garage adds $35,800, each mile the home is from the center of the city reduces the selling price by $900, and a bathroom adds $23,300.

b. The R-square value is 0.532.

c. The correlation matrix is as follows:

	Price	Bedrooms	Size	Pool	Distance	Garage
Bedrooms	0.467					
Size	0.371	0.383				
Pool	0.294	0.005	0.201			
Distance	−0.347	−0.153	−0.117	−0.139		
Garage	0.526	0.234	0.083	0.114	−0.359	
Baths	0.382	0.329	0.024	0.055	−0.195	0.221

The independent variable *garage* has the strongest correlation with *price*. *Distance* is inversely related to *price,* as expected. There does not seem to be a problem with correlation among the independent variables.

   d. The results of the global test suggest that some of the regression coefficients are different from zero.

   e. We can delete the independent variable *distance*.

   f. The new regression output follows.

```
Predictor       Coef   SE Coef       T       P
Constant       17.01     35.24    0.48   0.630
Bedrooms        7.169     2.559    2.80   0.006
Size            0.03919   0.01470  2.67   0.009
Pool           19.110     6.994    2.73   0.007
Garage         38.847     7.281    5.34   0.000
Baths          24.624     8.995    2.74   0.007

S = 33.3167  R-Sq = 52.4%  R-Sq(adj) = 50.0%

Analysis of Variance
SOURCE           DF       SS     MS      F       P
Regression        5   120877  24175  21.78   0.000
Residual Error   99   109890   1110
Total           104   230768
```

    In reviewing the *p*-values for the regression coefficients, all are less than .05. We leave all the independent variables in the equation.

   g. & h. Analysis of the residuals, not shown, indicates the normality assumption is reasonable. In addition, there is no pattern to the plot of the fitted values and the residuals.

25. a. $\hat{Y} = -14{,}174 + 3{,}325X_1 - 11{,}675X_2 + 448X_3 - 5{,}355X_4$ Note age is dropped because of association with other variables. Women earn \$11,675 less than men, and union members \$5,355 less than nonunion workers. Wages increase \$3,325 for each year of education and \$448 for each year of experience.

   b. $R^2 = .366$, which is rather low.

   c. Education and gender have the strongest association with wages; age and experience have a nearly perfect association. Drop age.

   d. The computed value of *F* is 13.69, so we conclude some of the regression coefficients are not equal to zero.

   e. Drop the union variable, $t = -1.40$

   f. Deleting union decreases R^2 to .352

   g. & h. Analysis of the residuals, not shown, indicates the normality assumption is reasonable. In addition, there is no pattern to the plots of the residuals and the fitted values of *Y*.

CHAPTER 15

1. a. 3

   b. 7.815

3. a. Reject H_0 if $\chi^2 > 5.991$

   b. $\chi^2 = \dfrac{(10 - 20)^2}{20} + \dfrac{(20 - 20)^2}{20} + \dfrac{(30 - 20)^2}{20} = 10.0$

   c. Reject H_0. The proportions are not equal.

5. H_0: The outcomes are the same; H_1: The outcomes are not the same. Reject H_0 if $\chi^2 > 9.236$.

$$\chi^2 = \frac{(3 - 5)^2}{5} + \cdots + \frac{(7 - 5)^2}{5} = 7.60$$

Do not reject H_0. Cannot reject H_0 that outcomes are the same.

7. H_0: There is no difference in the proportions. H_1: There is a difference in the proportions. Reject H_0 if $\chi^2 > 15.086$.

$$\chi^2 = \frac{(47 - 40)^2}{40} + \cdots + \frac{(34 - 40)^2}{40} = 3.400$$

Do not reject H_0. There is no difference in the proportions.

9. a. Reject H_0 if $\chi^2 > 9.210$

   b. $\chi^2 = \dfrac{(30 - 24)^2}{24} + \dfrac{(20 - 24)^2}{24} + \dfrac{(10 - 12)^2}{12} = 2.50$

   c. Do not reject H_0

11. H_0: Proportions are as stated; H_1: Proportions are not as stated. Reject H_0 if $\chi^2 > 11.345$.

$$\chi^2 = \frac{(50 - 25)^2}{25} + \cdots + \frac{(160 - 275)^2}{275} = 115.22$$

Reject H_0. The proportions are not as stated.

13. H_0: There is no relationship between community size and section read. H_1: There is a relationship. Reject H_0 if $\chi^2 > 9.488$.

$$\chi^2 = \frac{(170 - 157.50)^2}{157.50} + \cdots + \frac{(88 - 83.62)^2}{83.62} = 7.340$$

Do not reject H_0. There is no relationship between community size and section read.

15. H_0: No relationship between error rates and item type. H_1: There is a relationship between error rates and item type. Reject H_0 if $\chi^2 > 9.21$.

$$\chi^2 = \frac{(20 - 14.1)^2}{14.1} + \cdots + \frac{(225 - 225.25)^2}{225.25} = 8.033$$

Do not reject H_0. There is not a relationship between error rates and item type.

17. H_0: $\pi_s = 0.50$, $\pi_r = \pi_e = 0.25$
H_1: Distribution is not as given above.
$df = 2$. Reject H_0 if $\chi^2 > 4.605$.

Turn	f_o	f_e	$f_o - f_e$	$(f_o - f_e)^2/f_e$
Straight	112	100	12	1.44
Right	48	50	−2	0.08
Left	40	50	−10	2.00
Total	200	200		3.52

H_0 is not rejected. The proportions are as given in the null hypothesis.

19. H_0: There is no preference with respect to TV stations. H_1: There is a preference with respect to TV stations. $df = 3 - 1 = 2$. H_0 is rejected if $\chi^2 > 5.991$.

TV Station	f_o	f_e	$f_o - f_e$	$(f_o - f_e)^2$	$(f_o - f_e)^2/f_e$
WNAE	53	50	3	9	0.18
WRRN	64	50	14	196	3.92
WSPD	33	50	−17	289	5.78
	150	150	0		9.88

H_0 is rejected. There is a preference for TV stations.

21. H_0: $\pi_n = 0.21$, $\pi_m = 0.24$, $\pi_s = 0.35$, $\pi_w = 0.20$.
H_1: The distribution is not as given.
Reject H_0 if $\chi^2 > 11.345$.

Region	f_o	f_e	$f_o - f_e$	$(f_o - f_e)^2/f_e$
Northeast	68	84	−16	3.0476
Midwest	104	96	8	0.6667
South	155	140	15	1.6071
West	73	80	−7	0.6125
Total	400	400	0	5.9339

H_0 is not rejected. The distribution of order destinations reflects the population.

23. H_0: The proportions are the same.
H_1: The proportions are not the same.
Reject H_0 if $\chi^2 > 16.919$.

f_o	f_e	$f_o - f_e$	$(f_o - f_e)^2$	$(f_o - f_e)^2/f_e$
44	28	16	256	9.143
32	28	4	16	0.571
23	28	−5	25	0.893
27	28	−1	1	0.036
23	28	−5	25	0.893
24	28	−4	16	0.571
31	28	3	9	0.321
27	28	−1	1	0.036
28	28	0	0	0.000
21	28	−7	49	1.750
				14.214

Do not reject H_0. The digits are evenly distributed.

25. H_0: Gender and attitude toward the deficit are not related.
H_1: Gender and attitude toward the deficit are related.
Reject H_0 if $\chi^2 > 5.991$.

$$\chi^2 = \frac{(244 - 292.41)^2}{292.41} + \frac{(194 - 164.05)^2}{164.05}$$
$$+ \frac{(68 - 49.53)^2}{49.53} + \frac{(305 - 256.59)^2}{256.59}$$
$$+ \frac{(114 - 143.95)^2}{143.95} + \frac{(25 - 43.47)^2}{43.47} = 43.578$$

Because 43.578 is greater than the critical value of 5.991 the null hypothesis is rejected. A person's position on the deficit is related to gender.

27. H_0: Whether a claim is filed and age are not related.
H_1: Whether a claim is filed and age are related.
Reject H_0 if $\chi^2 > 7.815$.

$$\chi^2 = \frac{(170 - 203.33)^2}{203.33} + \cdots + \frac{(24 - 35.67)^2}{35.67} = 53.639$$

Reject H_0. Age is related to whether a claim is filed.

29. H_0: $\pi_{BL} = \pi_O = .23$, $\pi_Y = \pi_G = .15$, $\pi_{BR} = \pi_R = .12$. H_1: The proportions are not as given. Reject H_0 if $\chi^2 > 15.086$.

Color	f_o	f_e	$(f_o - f_e)^2/f_e$
Blue	12	16.56	1.256
Brown	14	8.64	3.325
Yellow	13	10.80	0.448
Red	14	8.64	3.325
Orange	7	16.56	5.519
Green	12	10.80	0.133
Total	72		14.006

Do not reject H_0. The color distribution agrees with the manufacturer's information.

31. H_0: Salary and winning are not related.
H_1: Salary and winning are related.
Reject H_0 if $\chi^2 > 3.84$.

	Salary		
Winning	Lower Half	Top Half	Total
No	10	3	13
Yes	5	12	17
Total	15	15	

$$\chi^2 = \frac{(10 - 6.5)^2}{6.5} + \frac{(3 - 6.5)^2}{6.5} + \frac{(5 - 8.5)^2}{8.5} + \frac{(12 - 8.5)^2}{8.5} = 6.652$$

Reject H_0. Conclude that salary and winning are related.

Appendix C

Solutions to Practice Tests

PRACTICE TEST—CHAPTER 1
Part I
1. Statistics
2. Descriptive statistics
3. Statistical inference
4. Sample
5. Population
6. Nominal
7. Ratio
8. Ordinal
9. Interval
10. Discrete
11. Nominal
12. Nominal

Part II
1. a. Pie Chart
   b. 11.1
   c. Three times
   d. 65%
2.

Students by class Rank

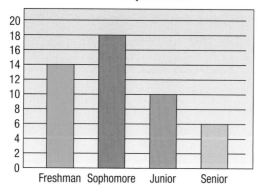

PRACTICE TEST—CHAPTER 2
Part I
1. Frequency table
2. Frequency distribution
3. Bar chart
4. Pie chart
5. Histogram or frequency polygon
6. 7
7. Class interval
8. Midpoint
9. Total number of observations
10. Upper class limits

Part II
1. a. $30
   b. 105
   c. 52
   d. .19
   e. $165
   f. $120, $330

g.

Selling Price of Homes Warren, PA

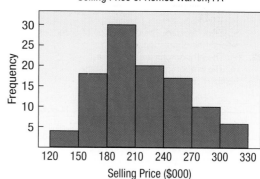

Selling Price ($000)

Selling Price of Homes Warren, PA

Selling Price ($000)

PRACTICE TEST—CHAPTER 3
Part I
1. Parameter
2. Statistic
3. Zero
4. Median
5. 50%
6. Mode
7. Range
8. Variance
9. Variance
10. Never
11. Median
12. Normal rule or empirical rule

Part II
1. a. $\bar{X} = \dfrac{560}{8} = 70$
   b. Median = 71.5
   c. Range = $80 - 52 = 28$
   d. $s = \sqrt{\dfrac{610.0}{8 - 1}} = 9.335$

2. $\bar{X}_w = \dfrac{200(\$36) + 300(\$40) + 500(\$50)}{200 + 300 + 500} = \$44.20$

3. $-0.88 \pm 2(1.41)$
-0.88 ± 2.82
$-3.70, 1.94$

PRACTICE TEST—CHAPTER 4
Part I
1. Dot plot
2. Box plot
3. Scatter diagram
4. Contingency table
5. Quartile
6. Percentile
7. Skewness
8. First quartile
9. Inter quartile range

Part II
1. a.

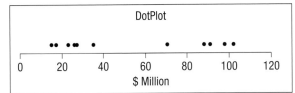

DotPlot

$ Million

b. $L_{50} = (11 + 1)\dfrac{50}{100} = 6$
median $= 35$

c. $L_{25} = (11 + 1)\dfrac{25}{100} = 3$
$Q_1 = 23$

d. $L_{75} = (11 + 1)\dfrac{75}{100} = 9$
$Q_3 = 91$

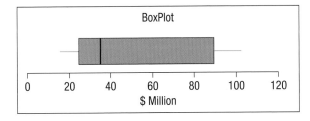

BoxPlot

$ Million

2. a. $P(H) = \dfrac{144}{449} = 0.32$

b. $P(H < 30) = \dfrac{21}{89} = 0.24$

c. $P(H > 60) = \dfrac{75}{203} = 0.37$. Age is related to high blood pressure, because $P(H > 60)$ is greater than $P(H < 30)$.

PRACTICE TEST—CHAPTER 5
Part I
1. Probability
2. Experiment
3. Event
4. Relative frequency
5. Subjective
6. Classical
7. Mutually exclusive
8. Exhaustive
9. Mutually exclusive
10. Complement rule
11. Joint probability
12. Independent

Part II
1. a. $P(\text{Both}) = P(B_1) \cdot P(B_2|B_1)$
$= \left(\dfrac{5}{20}\right)\left(\dfrac{4}{19}\right) = .0526$

b. $P(\text{at least 1}) = 1 - P(\text{neither})$
$= 1 - \left(\dfrac{15}{20}\right)\left(\dfrac{14}{19}\right) = 1 - .5526 = .4474$

2. $P(\text{At least 1}) = P(\text{Jogs}) + P(\text{Bike}) - P(\text{Both})$
$= .30 + .20 - 12 = .38.$

3. $X = 5! = 120$

PRACTICE TEST—CHAPTER 6
Part I
1. Probability distribution
2. Probability
3. One
4. Mean
5. Two
6. Never
7. Equal
8. Binomial
9. .075
10. .183

Part II
1. a. Binomial
b. $P(x = 1) = {}_{16}C_1(.15)^1(.85)^{15} = (16)(.15)(.0874) = .210$
c. $P(x \geq 1) = 1 - P(x = 0) = 1 - {}_{16}C_0(.15)^0(.85)^{16} = .9257$
2. a. Poisson
b. $P(x = 3) = \dfrac{3^3 e^{-3}}{3!} = \dfrac{9}{(6)(20.0855)} = .224$
c. $P(x = 0) = \dfrac{3^0 e^{-3}}{0!} = .050$
d. $P(x \geq 1) = 1 - P(x = 0) = 1 - .050 = .950$

3.

Exemptions x	Probability P(x)	X · P(x)	$(x-2.2)^2 \cdot P(x)$
1	0.2	0.2	0.288
2	0.5	1	0.02
3	0.2	0.6	0.128
4	0.1	0.4	0.324
		2.2	0.76

a. $\mu = 1(.2) + 2(.5) + 3(.2) + 4(.1) = 2.2$
b. $\sigma^2 = (1 - 2.2)^2(.2) + \cdots + (4 - 2.2)^2(.4) = 0.76$

PRACTICE TEST—CHAPTER 7
Part I
1. One
2. Infinite
3. Discrete
4. Always equal
5. Infinite
6. One
7. All of them
8. .2764
9. .9396
10. .0450

Part II

1. **a.** $z = \dfrac{2000 - 1600}{850} = .47$

   $P(0 \leq z < .47) = .1808.$

   b. $z = \dfrac{900 - 1600}{850} = -0.82$

   $P(-0.82 \leq z \leq .47) = .2939 + .1808 = .4747$

   c. $z = \dfrac{1800 - 1600}{850} = 0.24$

   $P(0.24 \leq z \leq .47) = .1808 - .0948 = -.0860$

   d. $1.65 = \dfrac{X - 1600}{850}$

   $X = 1600 + 1.65(850) = 3002.5$

PRACTICE TEST—CHAPTER 8
Part I

1. Random sample
2. No size restriction
3. Strata
4. Sampling error
5. Sampling distribution of sample means
6. 120
7. Standard error of the mean
8. Always equal
9. Decrease
10. Normal distribution

Part II

1. $z = \dfrac{11 - 12.2}{2.3/\sqrt{12}} = -1.81$

   $P(z < -1.81) = .5000 - .4649 = .0351$

PRACTICE TEST—CHAPTER 9
Part I

1. Point estimate
2. Confidence interval
3. Wider
4. Proportion
5. 95
6. Standard deviation
7. Binomial
8. Five
9. Size of the population
10. Population mean

Part II

1. **a.** Unknown

   b. 9.3 years

   c. $s_{\bar{x}} = \dfrac{2.0}{\sqrt{26}} = 0.392$

   d. $9.3 \pm (1.708)\dfrac{2.0}{\sqrt{26}}$

   9.3 ± 0.67

   $(8.63, 9.97)$

2. $n = (.27)(.73)\left(\dfrac{2.33}{.02}\right)^2 = 2676$

3. $.64 \pm 1.96\sqrt{\dfrac{.64(.36)}{100}}$

   $.64 \pm .094$

   $[.546, .734]$

PRACTICE TEST—CHAPTER 10
Part I

1. Null hypothesis
2. Accept
3. Significant level
4. Test statistic

5. Critical value
6. Two
7. Standard deviation (or variance)
8. *p*-value
9. Binomial
10. Five

Part II

1. $H_0{:}\mu \leq 90,\ H_1{:}\mu > 90$

   $df = 18 - 1 = 17$

   Reject H_0 if $t > 2.567$

   $t = \dfrac{96 - 90}{12/\sqrt{18}} = 2.121$

   Do not reject H_0. We cannot conclude that the mean time in the park is more than 90 minutes.

2. $H_0{:}\mu \leq 9.75 \qquad H_1{:}\mu \leq 9.75$

   Reject H_0 if $z > 1.65$

   note σ is known, so z is used and we assume a .05 significance level.

   $z = \dfrac{9.85 - 9.75}{0.27/\sqrt{25}} = 1.852.$

   Reject H_0. The mean weight is more than 9.75 ounces.

3. $H_0{:}\pi \geq 0.67,\ H_1{:}\pi < 0.67$

   Reject H_0 if $z < -1.65$

   $z = \dfrac{\dfrac{180}{300} - 0.67}{\sqrt{\dfrac{0.67(1 - 0.67)}{300}}} = -2.578$

   Reject H_0. Less than .67 of the couples seek their mate's approval.

PRACTICE TEST—CHAPTER 11
Part I

1. Zero
2. *z*
3. Proportion
4. Population standard deviation
5. Difference
6. *t* distribution
7. Samples or parameters estimated
8. Paired
9. Independent
10. Dependent sample

Part II

1. $H_0{:}\mu_y = \mu_h;\ H_1{:}\mu_y \neq \mu_h$

   $df = 14 + 12 - 2 = 24$

   Reject H_0 if $t < -2.064$ or $t > 2.064$

   $s_p^2 = \dfrac{(14 - 1)30^2 + (12 - 1)(40)^2}{14 + 12 - 2} = 1220.83$

   $t = \dfrac{837 - 797}{\sqrt{1220.83\left(\dfrac{1}{14} + \dfrac{1}{12}\right)}} = \dfrac{40.0}{13.7455} = 2.910$

   Reject H_0. There is a difference in the mean miles traveled.

2. $H_0{:}\pi_E = \pi_T \qquad H_1{:}\pi_E \neq \pi_T$

   Reject H_0 if $z < -1.96$ or $z > 1.96$

   $P_c = \dfrac{128 + 149}{300 + 400} = \dfrac{277}{700} = .396$

   $z = \dfrac{\dfrac{128}{300} - \dfrac{149}{400}}{\sqrt{\dfrac{.396(1 - .396)}{300} + \dfrac{.396(1 - .396)}{400}}} = \dfrac{.054}{.037} = 1.459$

   Do not reject H_0. There is no difference on the proportion that liked the soap in the two cities.

PRACTICE TEST—CHAPTER 12
Part I
1. F distribution
2. Positively skewed
3. Variances
4. Means
5. Population standard deviations
6. Error or Residual
7. Equal
8. Degrees of freedom
9. Variances
10. Independent

Part II
1. $H_0: \sigma_h^2 = \sigma_y^2$; $H_1: \sigma_h^2 \neq \sigma_y^2$

   $df_y = 12 - 1 = 11 \qquad df_h = 14 - 1 = 13$

   Reject H_0 if $F > 2.635$

   $F = \dfrac{(40)^2}{(30)^2} = 1.78$

   Do not reject H_0. Cannot conclude there is a difference in the variation of the miles traveled.
2. a. 3
   b. 21
   c. 3.55
   d. $H_0: \mu_1 = \mu_2 = \mu_3$
      H_1: not all treatment means are the same
   e. Reject H_0
   f. The treatment means are not the same.

PRACTICE TEST—CHAPTER 13
Part I
1. Scatter diagram
2. -1 and 1
3. Less than zero
4. Coefficient of determination
5. t
6. Predicted or fitted
7. Sign
8. Larger
9. Error
10. Independent

Part II
1. a.

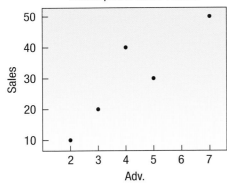

Scatterplot of Sales vs Adv.

   b. 0.904
   c. 0.818
   d. $\hat{Y} = 1.216 + 7.432\ \text{Adv}$
   e. An increase
   f. Increase of $7,432

g. Negative $1,216
h. $33.443, found by $\hat{Y} = 1.216 + 7.432(4.5)$

PRACTICE TEST—CHAPTER 14
Part I
1. Independent variables
2. Least squares
3. Mean square error
4. Independent variable
5. Independent variable
6. Different from zero
7. F distribution
8. t distribution
9. Linearity
10. Correlated
11. Multicollinearity
12. Dummy variable

Part II
1. a. Four
   b. $\hat{Y} = 70.06 + 0.42x_1 + 0.27x_2 + 0.75x_3 + 0.42x_4$
   c. $R^2 = \dfrac{1050.8}{1134.6} = 0.926$
   d. $s_{y.1234} = \sqrt{4.19} = 2.05$
   e. $H_0: \beta_1 = \beta_2 = \beta_3 = \beta_4 = 0$
      H_1: not all $\beta_i = 0$
      Reject H_0 if $F > 2.87$
      $F = \dfrac{262.70}{4.19} = 62.70$
      Reject H_0. Not all the regression coefficients equal zero.
   d. $H_0: \beta_i = 0$, $H_1: \beta_i \neq 0$
      Reject H_0 if $t < -2.086$ or $t > 2.086$

$\beta_1 = 0$	$\beta_2 = 0$	$\beta_3 = 0$	$\beta_4 = 0$
$\beta_1 \neq 0$	$\beta_2 \neq 0$	$\beta_3 \neq 0$	$\beta_4 \neq 0$
$t = 2.47$	$t = 1.29$	$t = 2.50$	$t = 6.00$
Reject H_0	Do not reject H_0	Reject H_0	Reject H_0

Conclusion. Drop variable 2 and retain the others.

PRACTICE TEST—CHAPTER 15
Part I
1. Nominal
2. No assumption
3. At least 30 observations
4. Contingency Table
5. 6
6. Independent
7. 4
8. The same
9. 9.488
10. Degrees of freedom

Part II
1. H_0: There is no difference between the school district and census data.
   H_1: There is a difference between the school district and census data.
   Reject H_0 if $\chi^2 > 7.815$

   $\chi^2 = \dfrac{(120-130)^2}{130} + \dfrac{(40-40)^2}{40} + \dfrac{(30-20)^2}{20} + \dfrac{(10-10)^2}{10} = 5.76$

   Do not reject H_0. There is no difference between the census and school district data.
2. H_0: Gender and book type are independent.
   H_1: Gender and book type are related.
   Reject H_0 if $\chi^2 > 5.991$

   $\chi^2 = \dfrac{(250-197.31)^2}{197.31} + \cdots + \dfrac{(200-187.5)^2}{187.5} = 54.842$

   Reject H_0. Men and women read different types of books.

Photo Credits

Index